Lecture Notes in Computer Science 534

H. Ehrig K. P. Jantke
F. Orejas H. Reichel (Eds.)

Recent Trends in Data Type Specification

7th Workshop on Specification of Abstact Data Types
Wusterhausen/Dosse, Germany, April 17-20, 1990
Proceedings

Springer-Verlag
Berlin Heidelberg New York
London Paris Tokyo
Hong Kong Barcelona
Budapest

Series Editors

Gerhard Goos
GMD Forschungsstelle
Universität Karlsruhe
Vincenz-Priessnitz-Straße 1
W-7500 Karlsruhe, FRG

Juris Hartmanis
Department of Computer Science
Cornell University
Upson Hall
Ithaca, NY 14853, USA

Volume Editors

Hartmut Ehrig
Technische Universität Berlin, Fachbereich Informatik
Franklinstraße 28/29, W-1000 Berlin 10, FRG

Klaus P. Jantke
Technische Hochschule Leipzig, FB Mathematik und Informatik
Postfach 66, O-7300 Leipzig, FRG

Fernando Orejas
Universitat Politècnica de Catalunya, Facultat d'Informatica
Pau Gargallo 5, 08028 Barcelona, Spain

Horst Reichel
Technische Universität Dresden, Fakultät Informatik
Institut für Theoretische Informatik
Mommsenstraße 13, O-8027 Dresden, FRG

CR Subject Classification (1991): D.3.1-3, F.3.1-2, D.2.1-2, D.2.4

ISBN 3-540-54496-8 Springer-Verlag Berlin Heidelberg New York
ISBN 0-387-54496-8 Springer-Verlag New York Berlin Heidelberg

Typesetting: Camera ready by author
Printing and binding: Druckhaus Beltz, Hemsbach/Bergstr.
2145/3140-543210 - Printed on acid-free paper

Preface

Since 1974 the algebraic specification of abstract data types has been a well established research topic in computer science. This area influences both applications and theoretical foundations of methodologies which support the design and formal development of reliable software. The main topics covered by the Seventh Workshop on Specification of Abstract Data Types are:

- Modularization
- Object orientation
- Higher-order types and dependent types
- Inductive completion
- Algebraic high-level nets.

The Seventh Workshop on Specification of Abstract Data Types took place in the small town of Wusterhausen/Dosse, April 17–20, 1990, and was organized by Klaus P. Jantke and Horst Reichel in cooperation with the ESPRIT Basic Research Working Group COMPASS represented by Hartmut Ehrig and Fernando Orejas

Stimulated by the high scientific level of many contributions, we followed the example of Hans-Jörg Kreowski (3rd Workshop) and Don Sannella and Andrzej Tarlecki (5th Workshop) and selected 19 talks, from 31 contributions, which in the view of the editors represent the most interesting ideas and reflect the main trends in current research.

The present volume contains the final versions of the selected papers. All of them underwent a careful refereeing process, and we extend our special thanks to the following people who agreed to referee the selected papers:

E. Astesiano, J. Bergstra, C. Dimitrovici, H.-D. Ehrich, W. Fey, H. Ganzinger, R. Harper, M. Große-Rhode, R. Hennicker, H. Hussmann, H.-J. Kreowski, J. Loeckx, M. Löwe, B. Möller, T. Nipkow, P. Padawitz, F. Parisi-Presicce, O. Schoett, D. Sannella, T. Streicher, M. Thomas, R. Wiehagen, M. Wirsing, T. Zeugmann.

Last but not least, we are grateful to Springer-Verlag for quick publication.

Berlin	Hartmut Ehrig
Leipzig	Klaus P. Jantke
Barcelona	Fernando Orejas
Dresden	Horst Reichel

July 1991

Contents

ADT IMPLEMENTATION AND COMPLETION BY INDUCTION FROM EXAMPLES

Guntis Barzdins *

Institute of Mathematics and Computer Science
University of Latvia, Rainis blvd. 29, Riga 226250, Latvia
gbarzdin@nmsu.edu

Abstract. There exists a fast algorithm [2] for inductive synthesis of terminating and ground confluent term rewriting systems from samples. The principles of this algorithm and the methodology of its use for implementation and completion of abstract data types are described.

1 INTRODUCTION

Automatic implementation of Abstract Data Types (ADT) is of interest because of at least two reasons - first, to get an executable prototype and, second, to verify the correctness and completeness of the ADT definition. The standard input for the procedures implementing ADT by means of Knuth-Bendix algorithm [4] is the triplet:

- signature *C*,
- set of equations (axioms) over terms of signature *C*,
- partial simplification ordering >> on the terms of signature *C*.

Equations are oriented as term rewriting rules by means of the term ordering >> and then completed by the Knuth-Bendix algorithm. Obtained in this way a confluent and terminating rewrite system is an implementation of the ADT.

The above mentioned Knuth-Bendix method has two shortcomings which can be avoided by the inductive synthesis method described in this paper:

1) Knuth-Bendix method does not work for every ADT - it may fail or not stop in some cases. This happens partially because Knuth-Bendix algorithm is trying to find a completely confluent rewrite system, whereas for implementation it is sufficient to have a ground confluent rewrite system.

---

* Current Address: Department of Computer Science, New Mexico State University.

2) The Knuth-Bendix method cannot detect the incompleteness of the given set of axioms. This is the most common error in the ADT definitions and we would like to check it. Some additional input information is necessary to do such checking.

There is an inductive inference method described in [7] which sometimes allows to overcome the first problem by means of generalizing the critical pairs generated by the Knuth-Bendix algorithm. This method is good in the sense that it does not requires any additional input information, but its weakness is that it is not general. We are going to overcome booth mentioned shortcomings of the Knuth-Bendix method for the general case by considering additional input information, called sample.

The *sample* of the ADT is a finite set of ground term equalities which should hold in ADT to be specified. In other words, sample is a finite set of ground terms divided into the equivalence classes.

If the ADT *nat* (natural numbers) with operations *o* (zero), *s* (successor) and + (plus) is specified, the input quadruplet could be the following:

- the signature *C=*

  { o: ->nat;

  s: nat->nat;

  _+_: nat,nat->nat }

- the set of equations (axioms); there is "forgotten" an axiom *X+o==o*:

  s(X)+Y == s(X+Y); (A1)

  X+Y == Y+X (A2)

- the sample:

  o = o+o

  s(o) = o+s(o) = s(o)+o

  s(s(o)) = s(o)+s(o) = o+s(s(o)) =s(s(o))+o

  s(s(s(o))) = s(o)+s(s(o)) = s(s(o))+s(o) =

  = o+s(s(s(o))) = s(s(s(o)))+o

- the ordering >> of the terms of signature *C*: ordering >> is defined as *recursive path ordering* [5] induced by the following ordering > of signature *C*:

  +> s> o

Frequently it is more convenient to describe the sample by means of the graph (Fig.1), where square nodes stand for the equivalence classes and round nodes for the application of operations to them.

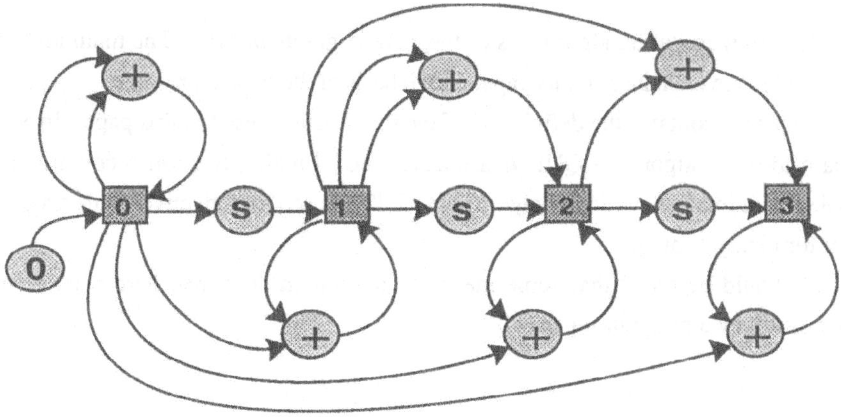

Fig.1. Sample graph of ADT *nat*.

If such quadruplet of input information is given, then:

1) It is always possible to verify local consistency of axioms and the sample, i.e. whether booth sides of axioms match only equal ground terms of the sample. In this way inconsistent axioms can be found.

2) If Knuth-Bendix method succeeds for the given set of axioms and ordering >>, then it is possible to verify the total consistency of the given axiom system and the sample.

3) It is always possible to verify whether the given axiom system, oriented as rewrite system by ordering >> (and probably completed by Knuth-Bendix algorithm), is sufficient for deriving all ground term equalities of the sample. If it is not sufficient, then sometimes it is possible to find additional rewrite rules inductively from the sample.

This paper is devoted to Point 3 - inductive synthesis of rewrite rules from the sample. In the worst case we assume that the set of given axioms is empty and we have to synthesize all rules inductively. In the first moment it could seem that this is the traditional task of function synthesis from the input/output samples, which is known to be solvable for non restricted classes of functions only by exhaustive search [1]. Recent research [2,8] shows that rewrite systems oriented by simplification orderings is a sufficiently restricted class which can be synthesized inductively without great search. In this paper we describe such a fast synthesis algorithm, called QUITA [2], which synthesizes inductively ground confluent and terminating rewrite systems from the samples and incomplete sets of axioms. In this sense QUITA can be considered as a completion tool not using Knuth-Bendix algorithm. QUITA is based on the special properties of the simplification orderings >> and on the fluid flow imitating algorithms of the sample graph analysis. The main ideas of this new algorithm are explained in this paper on the basis of the typical example.

Section 2 contains the definitions of the main notions used in this paper. In Section 3 the main ideas of algorithm QUITA are described. Finally, Section 4 contains the real example where implementation of algorithm QUITA is used for inductive synthesis of rewrite system for binary adding.

It should be noted that some ideas of the method described here were developed independently by a group in Japan [8].

2 PRELIMINARIES

More information about the notions described in this section can be found in [1,4,5].

Let *T(C)* be the set of all ground terms in the signature *C* and let *R* be a rewrite system of the signature *C*. A ground term *t* from *T(C)* is said to be a *normal form* term in *R* if it cannot be rewritten by *R*. If *R* is ground confluent and terminating, then in a finite number of steps any ground term *t* can be rewritten to the normal form term *t'* and *t'* is the same for any strategy of applying rewrite rules. Two ground terms are said to be *equal* according the ground confluent and terminating rewrite system if this system rewrites both terms to the same normal form term. It is said that a ground confluent and terminating rewrite system *R* of signature *C implements* ADT *A* of the same signature *C*, if the equivalence relation on ground terms defined by *R* is the same specified by *A*.

Let >> be the partial ordering of the terms of signature C. If *v>>t* for some terms *t,v* then we say that *t* is *lighter* than *v* in ordering >>. The rewrite system *R* is said to be *>>-oriented* if *l>>r* for any rewrite rule *l->r* in *R*. Ordering >> is said to be *simplification ordering* [5] if:

1) >> is *well-founded*, i.e. there are no infinite sequences t_0>>t_1>>t_2>>...

2) >> is *stable*, i.e. *u>>v* implies *t[u]>>t[v]* and *u'>>v'*, for every term *u,v*, a context term *t[]*, and a substitution of variables *u',v'*.

If >> is simplification ordering then any >>-oriented rewrite system is terminating. The *recursive path ordering* [5] is one of the most popular simplification orderings used for orientation of rewrite systems. Given an ordering > of the signature *C*, recursive path ordering induces a partial simplification ordering >> of the terms of signature *C*. For example, if ordering > of signature is defined as:

*>+>*o*

then induced recursive path ordering >> orders the terms as follows:

$A*(B+C) >> A*B+A*C$

$A*o >> A$

etc.

The following are notions related to inductive synthesis. The *sample* of the ADT A of signature C is a finite set of ground terms of signature C divided into equivalence classes. The *inductive synthesis machine* is an algorithm $M(Ex,>>)$ which given a sample Ex and a constructive description >> of the term ordering, outputs some >>-oriented rewrite system $R=M(Ex,>>)$.

The sequence $Ex_1, Ex_2,...$ of the samples of ADT A of signature C is said to be *complete* if for any term t from $T(C)$ there exists a natural n such that t belongs to all samples Ex_i where $i>n$. We say that inductive synthesis machine M *synthesizes in limit* an implementation for ADT A by ordering >>, if for any complete sequence $Ex_1, Ex_2,...$ of samples of A, the sequence of rewrite systems $R_1, R_2,...$ obtained by M ($Ri=M(Exi,>>)$) has the property: there exists a natural n such that for any $i>n$ rewrite system R_i is ground confluent, terminating and implements ADT A.

The next theorem shows the principal possibility to synthesize inductively the implementations of ADT.

Theorem 1 [2,8].

There exists an inductive synthesis machine *M* such that, given a simplification ordering >>, *M* in limit synthesizes the implementation of any ADT *A*, which can be implemented by the >>-oriented rewrite system.

This theorem is proved by constructing an exhaustive search based algorithm in [8]. In the next Section the main ideas of the non exhaustive search algorithm, called QUITA [2], are described.

3 INDUCTIVE SYNTHESIS ALGORITHM QUITA

There are several sources of efficiency for algorithm QUITA:

1) Algorithm QUITA can use partial specifications of the rewrite systems to be synthesized, i.e. it can accept axioms given by the user and to synthesize inductively only insufficient rewrite rules.

2) In each step algorithm QUITA synthesizes one rewrite rule and no backtracking is necessary.

3) In each step a rule not derivable from the previous rules is synthesized, i.e in this sense algorithm QUITA synthesizes the minimal rewrite system.

4) The new fluid flow imitating polynomial time algorithm [3] is used for enumeration of the shortest paths in the graphic sample, what significantly reduces the search in every step.

To give the idea of algorithm QUITA [2] (not formal description or proof!) we will consider the quadruplet from Introduction, specifying functions *o,s,+*. The synthesis method by QUITA consists of four steps (see Fig.2). Instead of algorithm *M* mentioned in the previous section, QUITA has one extra parameter *Axioms*, which allows to input known axioms of the ADT to be implemented; QUITA works, of course, also if this extra parameter is empty.

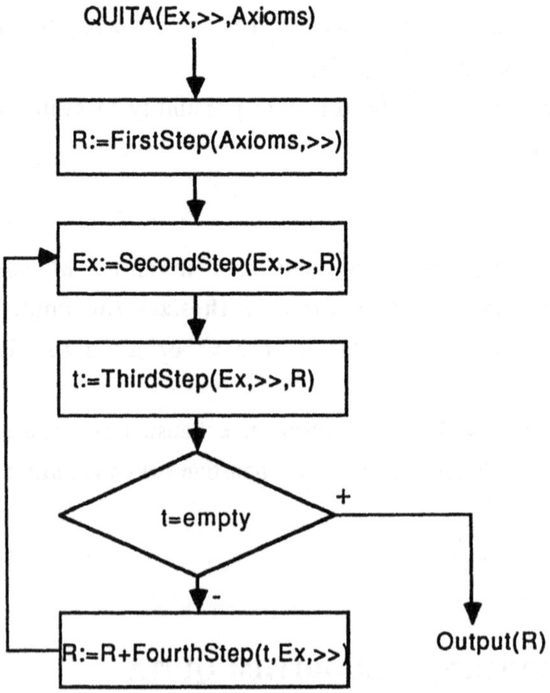

Fig.2. Control and data flow diagram of QUITA algorithm

First step is to orient given axioms as rewrite rules by means of the given partial ordering >> of terms. We can orient, of course, only those axioms for which the ordering >> is defined. So, from axioms A1, A2 only the first one can be oriented as a rewrite rule:

$$s(X)+Y \text{ -> } s(X+Y) \qquad \text{(R1)}$$

This only rule becomes the *current rewrite system R*.

Second step is updating the sample. First we delete from the sample all terms which contain subterms not belonging to the sample. Then in each equivalence class of the sample we find the lightest in ordering >> term, which we call the ***main*** term of the equivalence class. Some main terms are the normal form terms with respect to the current rewrite system *R* and them we call *good main* terms. All terms belonging to the equivalence classes whose main terms are not good we delete from sample (idea here is that in any >>-oriented rewrite system the normal form term of each equivalence class is the lightest term of this class; thus we actually delete from the sample the equivalence classes whose main terms surely are not normal form terms in *R*). After this step all main terms are good and subterms of all sample's terms belong to the sample, too.

Third step. From some terms of the sample the main term of the same equivalence class can be derived by the current system *R*. If the main terms can be derived from all terms of the sample, algorithm QUITA terminates and the current rewrite system *R* is the output. Otherwise the lightest term of the sample, from which the main term cannot be derived by *R*, is chosen to be the *pattern term t*. In the case of our example pattern term *t* is *o+o*. Evidently all subterms of the pattern term *t* are the main terms, therefore to find pattern term *t* we actually have to test only those terms for which all subterms are main terms. This significantly reduces search in this step.

Fourth step. Existence of pattern term *t* means that some additional rewrite rule is needed to rewrite *t* to the corresponding main term. It is sufficient that the new rule had the following properties:

1) In ordering >> the right hand side of the new rule should be lighter than left hand side.

2) Left hand side of the new rule should match term *t* in the root level (because all subterms of *t* are main terms).

3) The new rule applied to term *t* should rewrite it to term *t'* of the same equivalence class of the sample; *t'* in ordering >> should be lighter than *t* (in this case *t'* can be rewritten to the corresponding main term by the current rewrite system *R*).

4) The new rewrite rule should be locally consistent with the sample, i.e. left- and right- hand sides of the new rule should match only equal ground terms of the sample.

Since all these properties can be tested efficiently for the certain rule and all rewrite rules of the given signature can be efficiently enumerated, we can use exhaustive search to find the rule satisfying all these properties. But in this case QUITA algorithm would be inapplicable due to exhaustive search. The point is that the rule satisfying these properties can be found using very restricted search. First of all, due to property 2, the left hand side of the new rule has the pattern *t* and therefore only terms matching *t* should be considered as the left hand sides. In our case for pattern term $t=o+o$ possible left hand sides are:

$X+Y$ -> ?

$X+o$ -> ?

$o+X$ -> ?

$o+o$ -> ?

For each of these left hand sides *l* we can find in sample all terms which *l* match - to those the new rule would be applicable. Because of properties 3,4 new rule should rewrite matched terms only to the equal terms of sample and of weight in >> lighter than *l*. Finding all such terms in the sample we have a set of patterns for the right hand side of the new rule. Thus no exhaustive search is necessary in this step. The complete description of this fast method is given in [3]. It uses the fluid flow imitating sample graph analysis method which is the generalization of the method for finding shortest paths between two nodes in the directed graph [6].

In our case the new rule found by step four is the following:

$X+o$ -> o (R2)

After these four steps we already have a current rewrite system R consisting of two rules R1 and R2. We repeat steps two, three and four until algorithm stops in step three. Rules which we find this way are:

$o+X$ -> o (R3)

$X+s(Y)$ -> $s(X+Y)$ (R4)

The synthesized rewrite system R1-R4 is ground confluent and terminating and it implements the specified ADT of natural numbers with the operations $o,s,+$. It takes 10 seconds to perform the described synthesis process by QUITA algorithm on the IBM/AT.

The non trivial thing that needs to be proved is that algorithm QUITA founds in limit ground confluent and terminating implementation of any ADT which can be implemented by the given ordering >> (Theorem 1). Once this is proved [2], the only question is how efficient algorithm QUITA is for non trivial applications (precise mathematical speed estimations are not obtained yet).

4 A MORE COMPLICATED EXAMPLE

Here we consider the application of the QUITA algorithm to a more complicated example, where the synthesized rewrite system implements binary adding algorithm. New operations $d(X)=2*X$ and $t(X)=2*X+1$ are added to signature $o,s,+$ and ordering >> is defined as recursive path ordering induced by the following ordering > of signature:

$$+ > s > t > d > o$$

Axioms are not given at all, but a sample up to 6 is given:

$o = o+o = d(o)$

$s(o) = o+s(o) = s(o)+o = t(o)$

$s(s(o)) = s(o)+s(o) = o+s(s(o)) = s(s(o))+o = d(s(o))$

. . . .

$s(s(s(s(s(s(o))))))=d(t(t(o)))=...$

The following rewrite system is synthesized by QUITA algorithm in 2 minutes on the IBM/AT (here an advanced QUITA algorithm [2] which can synthesize quasi-terminating rewrite systems with equations is used):

$d(o) \to o$

$s(o) \to t(o)$

$s(d(X)) \to t(X)$

$s(t(X)) \to d(s(X))$

$X+o \to X$

$X+Y \leftrightarrow Y+X$

$t(X)+d(Y) \to t(X+Y)$

$d(X)+d(Y) \to d(X+Y)$

$t(X)+t(Y) \to d(s(X+Y))$

It is easy to see that this is a complete (quasi-terminating and ground confluent) rewrite system implementing all specified operations. The normal forms of ground terms in this rewrite system are strings of operations o,d,t and they represent inverted binary codes of natural numbers where t stands for "1" and d for "0"

o	0
$t(o)$	1
$d(t(o))$	10
$t(t(o))$	11
$d(d(t(o)))$	100
. . .	. . .

It means that the binary counting and binary adding algorithm, what was a great success in the history of mathematics, can be synthesized by this method in 2 minutes!

Algorithm QUITA has been tested for some other data types specifying different arithmetic, string and set operations. Most of them were synthesized in a few minutes on the IBM/AT from reasonably small samples.

CONCLUSIONS

This paper presents an efficient approach to synthesis of computational algorithms (implementations of ADT) by means of partial specifications (axioms) and sets of samples. Theorem 1 characterizes the class of algorithms which can be synthesized this way.

The further development of the method could relate the "learning" of the implemented functions and their use in the synthesis of implementations of the more complicated functions. The other thing, which could significantly increase the area of QUITA's use, would be development of methods for treating conditional rewrite rules.

References.

[1] D.Angluin and C.H.Smith, Inductive Inference: Theory and Methods, Computing Surveys 15, 237-264, 1983.

[2] G.Barzdins, Inductive synthesis of term rewriting systems, In: Baltic Computer Science, Lecture Notes in Computer Science; Springer Verlag 1991 (to appear).

[3] J.M.Barzdin and G.J.Barzdin, Rapid construction of algebraic axioms from samples, In: Images of Programming; North-Holland 1991 (to appear).

[4] G.Huet and D.C.Oppen, Equations and Rewrite Rules: A Survey. In (Book, R., ed.) Formal Language theory: Perspectives and Open Problems, 349-405, 1980.

[5] N.Dershowitz, Termination of Rewriting, Symbolic Computation 3, 69-116, 1987.

[6] E.W.Dijkstra, A note on two problems in connection with graphs, Numerische Math 1, 269-271, 1959.

[7] M.Thomas and K.P.Jantke, Inductive inference for solving divergence in Knuth-Bendix completion, Lecture Notes in Artificial Intelligence 397, 288-303, 1989.

[8] A.Togashi and S.Noguchi, Inductive inference of term rewriting systems realizing algebras, Proceedings of the Workshop on Algorithmic Learning Theory (North-Holland), 411-423, 1 90.

An Association of Algebraic Term Nets and Abstract Data Types for Specifying Real Communication Protocols

Mohamed Bettaz
Institut d'Informatique - Universite de Constantine
Constantine 25 000 - Algeria

Abstract

This paper presents a method for specifying real communication protocols within the frame of the Open System Interconnection Model. A protocol specification is achieved in two steps:

First, we use a constructive approach based on Algebraic Term Nets to build a compact model of the given protocol. Algebraic Term Nets are a form of high-level Petri nets, using terms of a given signature as tokens. This allows to build sufficiently refined models without using implementation details.

Second, we use the algebraic approach to specify the abstract data types related to the tokens, and a transformation technique to get an algebraic specification of the protocol from its model.

The method is illustrated by an application to a real-world protocol: The Ethernet data link layer protocol.

The style of the paper is kept intentionally informal in order to emphasize the practical aspect of the work rather than its theoretical one.

Related Works

To our knowledge, the concept of Algebraic Term Net is introduced for the first time in this work. However our specification approach is partly similar to that used by the research groups at Telecom Australia Research Laboratories, the LAAS Toulouse, the University of Southern California, the University of Montreal, the University of Liege, the University of Paris-Sud and the Technical University of Berlin.

1. Introduction

The communication protocols studied in the literature are often small and the formalisms used for their specification are relatively

---

This work is supported by a grant from the Algerian Ministry of Higher Education under research-contract number B2501/01/01187. However, points of view or opinions stated herein are those of the author.

trivial. Real protocols are large and rather complex. To overcome this complexity ISO suggests, through its standard for Open Systems Interconnection (OSI), a layered model based on the "divide and conquer" strategy [ISO78, ISO82]. In terms of protocol specification, this strategy allows to replace a protocol specification by the specifications of each of its layers [Hal88, Tan88]. A layer specification has then to be expressed in terms of its related protocols and services. We follow the idea in [Lam83] distinguishing between two main approaches: the constructive approach which consists in building an abstract model and then describing it, and the axiomatic approach which consists in stating directly the properties of the objects. In the case of communication protocols' modeling the constructive approach is often suffering from the adequacy of the used formalism which in many cases fits only for some aspects of the protocol at the expense of many others. Today, we admit easily the necessity of combining two or more formalisms [Ber86, Bil86, Bil88,Ehr89a, Hal88,Sun82, Sym78, Sym80, Vau86, Wil87]. In this paper we present a specification method based on two formalisms: Algebraic Term Nets (ATNets) and abstract data types (ADTs). Perhaps the main difference between our approach and the one in [Ber86] is that Ber's approach generalizes the Predicate Transition Nets while our's generalizes Numerical Petri Nets (defined for the first time in [Sym78]).

In our method a protocol specification is achieved in two steps:

First, we use a constructive approach based on ATNets to build a compact model of the given protocol. ATNets use terms of a given signature as tokens. This allows to build sufficiently refined models without using implementation details.

Second, we use the algebraic approach to specify the abstract data types related to the tokens and a transformation technique to get an algebraic specification of the protocol from its model.

The combination of these two formalisms is motivated by several facts:

(1) From the theoretical point of view, ADTs are known for their solid mathematical foundation and for the tools being developped for their transformation and proving.

(2) From the practical point of view:

*** Nets allow to express in a natural way the control flow while ADTs are suitable for describing the data flow in communication protocols,**

*** ADTs are suitable for implementing the "divide and conquer" strategy retained by the OSI model.**

Contents

In section 2, we introduce ATNets.

In section 3, we present a transformation technique allowing to convert ATNets in algebraic specifications.

In section 4.1, we informally introduce the Ethernet data link layer main functions. This introduction (taken mainly from [DEC80])is intended for a reader not familiarized with the CSMA/CD transmission discipline.

In section 4.2, ATNets are used to construct a model for the protocol and its service.

Section 4.3 is devoted to the algebraic specification of the model. The specification is written in a version of the Clear language [Bur80,Bur81], allowing however a certain syntactic flexibility and a simplification of the text. The reader not introduced to this language may consult section 3 for a short introduction of Clear notions. In section 5, we give some concluding remarks and outline some perspectives.

2. ATNets

In this section we introduce ATNets, a formalism derived from Numerical Petri Nets [Sym78,Wil87], which seems to be very promising for industrial applications [Bil86, Bil88]. There are however some aspects which have to be improved from the abstraction level point of view. This led to the ideas behind ATNets, in which tokens are generalized to algebraic terms (defined on a given signature), instead of tuples of attributes. This allows to build sufficiently refined models without being forced to use implementation details. The definition is based on an algebraic structure specified by the following (Clear) theories:

```
const Bag % is a theory on a basic bag structure %  = theory
  sorts name % is a set of place names %,
        nat % is the set of natural numbers %,
        term % is a set of terms of a given signature % ,token, bag
  opns <_>:term --> token
```

```
      emptybag:bag
      _#_#:nat,name --> bag
      _,_#:nat --> bag
      __:nat,token -->bag
      _(_+_),_(_-_):nat,bag,bag --> bag
  eropns errorbag:bag
  ereqns % a set of equations denoting error bag elements % endth
const Input_Condition %is a theory on the Input Condition% =theory
  let Ic = derive % renaming some sorts and opns from bag %
    sorts ic,term,name,nat,token
    opns emptyic,_#_#,_,_#,<_>,__,_(_+_),_(_-_)  eropns erroric
    from Bag by ic is bag emptyic is emptybag erroric is errorbag
  in  enrich Ic by sorts pure
    opns (_):token --> pure
         _-_:pure,pure --> pure
         ^_(_):nat,pure --> ic
         zero:ic
         o=_:token --> ic
         ~_:ic --> ic
         _&_,_|_,=_+_,=_-_:ic,ic --> ic
ereqns %a set of equations denoting the error elements of ic% enden
const Destroyed_tokens % is a theory on Destroyed Tokens% = theory
  let Dt = derive sorts dt,term,name,nat,token
    opns emptydt,_#_#,_,_#,<_>,__,_(_+_),_(_-_)  eropns errordt
    from Bag by dt is bag  emptydt is emptybag  errordt is errorbag
  in enrich Dt by  sorts pure
    opns (_):token --> pure
         _-_:pure,pure --> pure
         ^_(_):nat,pure --> dt
         zero:dt
         o:_:token --> dt
ereqns %a set of equations denoting the error elements of dt% enden
const Created_Tokens %is a theory on Created Tokens % = theory
  let Ct = derive sorts ct,term,name,nat,token
    opns emptyct,_#_#,_,_#,<_>,__,_(_+_),_(_-_)
    eropns errorct
    from Bag by ct is bag  emptyct is emptybag
                           errorct is errorbag
          in enrich Ct by opns _/nat --> ct
                     _/_/:nat,name --> ct enden
```

Definition 2.1

1.Let IC, DT and CT be the signatures of the theories Input_Condition, Destroyed_Tokens and Created_Tokens respectively and let SIG be a given signature. Let X_{IC}, X_{DT}, X_{CT} and X be sets of variables associated with IC, DT, CT and SIG respectively. Let G be a set of (global) variables. $T_{IC,ic}(X_{IC} \cup G)$ is the set of terms (defined on IC) of sort ic. $T_{DT,dt}(X_{DT} \cup G)$, is the set of terms (defined on DT) of sort dt. $T_{CT,ct}(X_{CT} \cup G)$ is the set of terms (defined on Ct) of sort ct. $T_{SIG}(X \cup G)$ is the set of terms defined on SIG.

2.Let N be the set of natural numbers. $[T_{SIG}(X \cup G)]$ is the set of applications from $T_{SIG}(X \cup G)$ into N.

3.$\{T_{SIG}(X \cup G)\}$ is the set of relations on $T_{SIG}(X \cup G)$

Definition 2.2

An ATNet is a 6_tuple ATN = (P,T,Pre,Post,In,Cap) where:

* P is a set of places and T is a set of transitions
* Pre is an application
  from (P x T) into $(T_{IC,ic}(X_{IC} \cup G) \times T_{DT,dt}(X_{DT} \cup G))$
* Post is an application from (P x T) into $T_{CT,ct}(X_{CT} \cup G)$
* In is an application from T into $(T_{SIG}(X \cup G) \cup \{T_{SIG}(X \cup G)\})$
* Cap is an application from P into $((k,k^*)/k \in (2,3,4,\ldots),$
  $k^* \in (2,3,4,\ldots)$ with $k \le k^*) \cup (2,3,4,\ldots))$

remark 2.1: Pre defines the Input Condition and the Destroyed Tokens inscriptions associated with a transition input arc. Post defines the Created Tokens inscription associated with a transition output arc. In defines the Transition Condition and the Transition Operation. Cap defines two sorts of capacities: k sets a bound on the number of tokens of a particular value that can be resident in a place, while k^* sets a bound on the total number of tokens allowed in a place (see [Bil88] or [Wil87]).

Definition 2.3

A marked ATNet is a pair (ATN,M) where ATN is an ATNet and M an application from P into $([T_{SIG}(X \cup G)] \cup N)$. M(p) is the marking of the place p.

remark 2.2: The operation of an ATNet is similar to that of a Numerical Petri Net and is briefly summarized below [Wil87]:

A transition is enabled when various conditions are simultaneously true. The first condition is that every arc's Input Condition must be true. An Input Condition is a condition on the tokens in an input place. The second condition is that the Transition Condition must be true. Finally the addition of Created Tokens to the output places must not result in any place exceeding its capacity. If a transition is enabled then that transition may fire. When a transition is fired several events occur simultaneously: the Destroyed Tokens are removed from every input place of the transition; the transition operation is executed and the Created Tokens are deposited into every output place of the transition. All this is one indivisible event.

Notations

In the remaining part of this paper, we will use a subset of notations taken from [Bil88]. The elements (t,n) of an application belonging to $[T_{SIG}(X \cup G)]$ are denoted by n<t>.

* **tokens:** tokens are enclosed in angular brackets, ie.,they are denoted as bag elements of the form 1<t> where 1 is omitted.

* **Input Condition:** an Input Condition is written to the left of a transition input arc, as seen by an observer at the transition.

Notation	Condition on Input Place Marking M(p)
t	$t \in M(p)$
0 (zero)	$M(p) = \emptyset$
# (1#)	$M(p) = M(p)$
o=t	"oldest" token in input place is t
~t	$t \notin M(p)$

* **Destroyed Tokens:** the Destroyed Tokens are written to the right of each input arc, as seen by our observer.

Notation	Destroyed Tokens Bag D(p)
t	{t}
0 (zero)	$\emptyset$
# (1#)	M(p)
: (1:)	The "enabling" tokens
o:	"oldest" token singleton set

* **Created Tokens:** The Created Tokens are written next to each output arc of a transition.

Notation	Created Tokens Bag C(p)
t	{t}

* **Transition Condition:** a Transition Condition is delimited by square brackets, and written inside the associated transition.

* **Transition Operation:** a Transition Operation is also written inside the associated transition, but, without any particular delimitation.

3.Converting ATNets in Algebraic Specifications

Because our specifications are denoted in a version of the Clear language, it may be useful to give a short introduction of Clear notions taken mainly from [Bur81] and [San84]. Clear was invented by Burstall and Goguen for writing structured algebraic specifications; ie., the language provides facilities (specification-building operations) for combining small specifications in various ways to make large specifications. With a tool such this, the specification of a large real-world system could be built from small, easy to understand, and (in many cases) reusable bits. Burstall and Goguen have given in [Bur80] a denotational semantics for Clear, relying heavily on a number of concepts from category theory to give the meaning of Clear specification-building operations. A different semantics for Clear is presented in [Sun84]. This uses straithforward set-theoretic constructs to define the semantics of the specification-building operations. Perhaps the most important building operation is the application of a parameterized specification to a suitable argument. other operations will permit specifications to be enriched (by using an operation called enrich), or to leave some of the other parts hidden (by using an operation called derive), or to be additively combined (by using an operation called +). The main purpose of a Clear specification is to provide a theory of what some piece of software (or hardware) is supposed to do. Thus the Clear specification-building operations are in fact upon theories. Some theories specify particular data structures (canonical theories), while others assert some axioms which may be satisfied by a variety of structures (loose theories). A more complex situation is when we wish to specify some particular structure as canonical only once some other structure, satisfying a loose specification, has been fixed. For example the parameterized specification Sequence(El) specifies the data structure of sequences of El elements, once El has been given; but any interpretation of El is permitted. All this is formalized with the notion of a data constraint which is an assertion that one theory shall be interpreted canonically relative to another (possibly empty) theory. Theories not so constrained are interpreted loosely. Canonical interpretations are defined mathematically by use of initial algebra semantics. When combining theories sharing the same subtheory the result will contain just one *copy* of this subtheory.

An ATNet coupled with a set of algebraic specifications is sufficient to describe the operation of a complex protocol. It may however be helpful to transform the ATNet component itself in an

algebraic specification in order to take benefit from the suitability of the algebraic approach for the verification and proof purposes. The proposed transformation technique is based on a method working in terms of states rather than operations [Lam83]. The first problem to solve is then to search for a suitable representation of ATNets' states. A first solution may be given by considering a net state as a set of pairs (global variable,value) and (place,marking), where (in the simple case) value is a term. This solution may however be improved by considering net states as sets of pairs (var, a_val) where var is either a global variable or a place, and a_val is itself a pair (type,value) where type is its type and value its value. This improvement leads to a substantial simplification in the syntactical as well as in the semantical part of the ATNet state specification:

```
const Atn-state = theory  sorts var,type,val,a_val
  opns cons:type,val --> a_val % is the actual value of var %
       type-of:a_val --> type
       val-of:a_val --> val
       init:state
       gen:var,a_val,state --> state
       take :var,state --> a_val
       ini:var --> a_val
  eropns ertype:type  erval:val  era_val:a_val  erstate:state
  eqns all v:var..init = gen(v,ini(v),init)
       all var1,var2:var,i1,i2:item,s:state..
           gen(var1,i1,gen(var2,i2,s)) = gen(var1,i1,s)
             if var1==var2 and type-of(i1)==type-of(i2)
       all var1,var2:var,i1,i2:item,s:state..
           gen(var1,i1,gen(var2,i2,s))=gen(var2,i2,gen(var1,i1,s))
                                                      if var1≠var2
       all var1,var2:var,i:item,s:state..take(var1,gen(var2,i,s))=
                             if var1==var2 then i else take(var1,s)
  ereqns all var1:var,i1,i2:item,s:state..
    gen(var1,i1,gen(var1,i2,s)=erstate iftype-of(i1)≠type-of(i2) endth
```

The defined states are *total* ones [Sim80], i.e., each global variable is assigned an initial value and each place is assigned an initial marking. Defining *partial* states is however possible [Bet84]. Once the ATNet state representation problem is solved, the ATNet specification may be achieved by specifying, for each transition, the state in which this transition is enabled and the state resulting from its firing. An ATNet specification may have the following form:

```
const Atn-spec = enrich Atn-state by sorts event %is the set transit.%
  opns efct %is the effect of a transition % :event,state -->state
  eqns %the firing of each transition is specified by a set of
                                    conditional equations% enden
```

Thus concurrent firing of two or more net transitions is not described explicitly by the used approach, but is rather implicitly coded in the ATNet transformation technique: two or more transitions are fired concurrently if their corresponding sets of conditional equations denote the same *enabling* states.

4. Example:The Ethernet Data Link Layer Protocol

4.1. Informal Introduction [DEC80]

The Ethernet data link layer defines a medium independent link level communication facility, built on the physical channel provided by the Physical Layer. It is applicable to a general class of a local area broadcast media suitable for use with the channel access discipline known as CSMA/CD (Carrier Sense Multiple-Access with Collision Detection). The notion of a data link between two entities does not correspond directly to a distinct physical connection. Nevertheless, the two main functions generally associated with a data link control procedure are present: Data Framing (Encapsulation, Decapsulation) and Link Management. Data Encapsulation and Transmit Link Management form the Transmit Data Link Control Procedure which is implemented in the transmitting station. Data Decapsulation and Receice Link Management form the Receive Data Link Control Procedure which is implemented in the receiving station. These two procedures together with the channel form the Ethernet data link layer protocol. In the remaining part of this paper we will not distinguish neither between the Data Link Control Procedure and the station implementing it,nor between the Ethernet data link layer and the protocol related to it.

4.1.1. Frame Transmission

When the User Layer requests the transmission of a frame, the Transmit Data Encapsulation component constructs the frame from the user-supplied data and appends a frame check sequence for error detection. The frame is then handed to the Transmit Link Management component for transmission. Transmit Link Mangement tries to avoid collision with other traffic on the channel by monitoring the carrier sense signal (CS) and deferring to passing traffic. When the channel is clear, frame transmission is initiated (after a brief interframe delay called interframe spacing). Then the Data Link Layer provides a serial stream of bits to the Physical Layer for transmission. While transmitting the Physical Layer simultaneously monitors the channel in order to generate the collision detect signal (CD). In a collision-free situation, the CD remains off for the duration of the frame. If the transmission is completed without collision, the Data Link Layer informs the User Layer and waits for the next request for frame transmission. In the case of a collision, the Physical Layer first detects the interference on the channel and then turns on the collision detect signal. This is detected in turn by the Transmit Link Management component and collision handling begins. In the beginning, Transmit Link Management strengthens the collision by transmitting a bit sequence called jam. This ensures, that the duration of the collision is sufficient enough to be noticed by the other transmitting stations concerned by the collision. After the jam is sent, Transmit Link Management terminates the transmission and schedules a retransmission attempt for a randomly selected time in the near future. Retransmission is attempted repeatedly in the face of repeated collisions. Eventually, either the transmission succeeds, or the attempt is abandoned on the assumption that the channel has failed. In this case, the User Layer is also informed.

4.1.2. Frame Reception

At the receiving station, the arrival of a frame is first detected by the Physical Layer which turns on the carrier sense signal. Meanwhile, the Receive Link Management component having seen the carrier sense going on, has been waiting for the incoming bits to be delivered. Receive Link Management collects bits from the Physical Layer as long as the carrier sense signal remains on. When the carrier sense signal goes off, the frame is passed to the Receive Data Decapsulation for processing. Receive Data Decapsulation checks the frame destination address field to decide whether the frame should be received by this station. If so, it passes the contents of the frame to the User Layer along with an appropriate status code. The status code is generated by inspecting the frame check sequence and by checking for proper octet boundary alignment of the end of the frame. The bits resulting from a collision are received and decoded by the Physical Layer in the same way as for the bits of a valid frame. The fragmentary frames received during collisions are distinguished from valid frames by the Receive Link Management component, by noting that a collision fragment is always smaller than the shortest valid frame. Such fragments are discarded by Receive Link Management.

4.2. Modeling with ATNets

In this section, we use the narrative description given in section 4.1, to build an ATNet model. We start with the description of the interfaces between the architectural layers represented.

4.2.1. Inter-Layer Interfaces

Each interface is described as a bag of tokens and shared places, which collectively provide the only valid interactions between layers. In this context a shared place may be considered as an access point to a service. A service is then requested (or provided) by putting a token in a shared place.

4.2.1.1. User Layer to Data Link Layer

At the sending end, the User and the Data Link Layer are sharing the places FROM-USER1 and TO-USER1 (Fig.1). The USER Layer requests a frame transmission by putting the token trans(d,s,data) into FROM-USER1, where data is the amount of information to be transmitted and, d and s are respectively the receiver and sender addresses. The Data Link Layer informs the USER LAYER of the transmission result by putting trans-ok, eventually col-er into TO-USER1. At the receiving end, the User and the Data Link Layer are sharing the places FROM-USER2 and TO-USER2 (Fig.2). The User Layer requests a frame reception by putting receive into FROM-USER2. The Data Link Layer informs the User Layer of the reception result by putting receive-ok(d,s,data), eventually f-error or a-error, into TO-USER2.

4.2.1.2. Data Link Layer to Physical Layer

The Data Link and Physical Layers are sharing the places CHAN, CS and CD. CHAN and CS are common to the sending and receiving end; CD is particular to sending end. Tokens passed by the Physical Layer to the Data Link Layer are either bit or boolean values. A t (true) value in CS allows the sending station to ovoid collision by deferring to passing traffic. A t value in CD allows the sending station to detect a collision on the channel. The sending station requests the physical transmission of a frame bit by putting head(fr) into CHAN. At the receiving end, the condition o=b means receiving bits b from CHAN in their incomoing order.

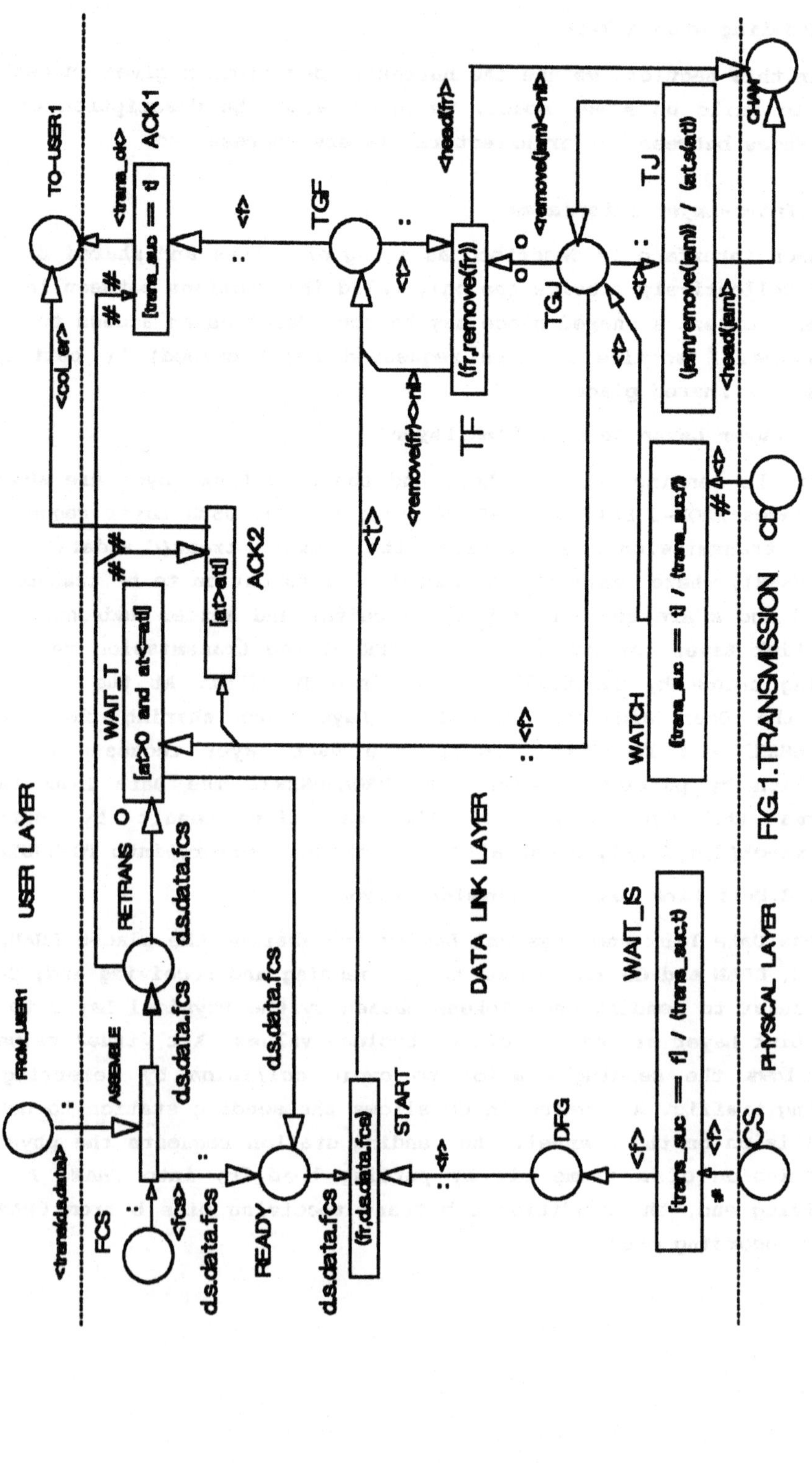

FIG.1.TRANSMISSION

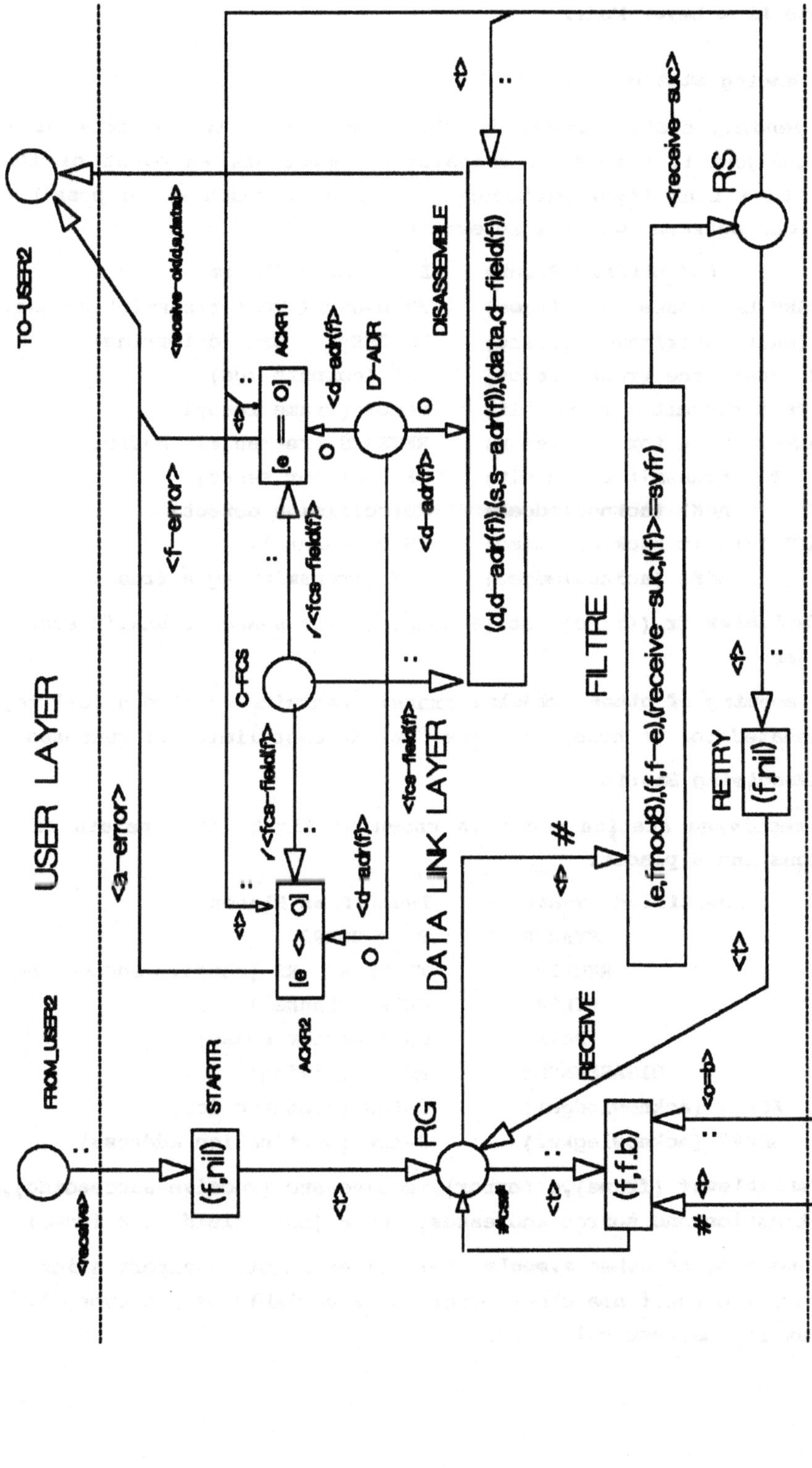

FIG.2.RECEPTION

4.2.2. Data Link Layer Model

4.2.2.1. Sending Station

The sending station model is shown on Fig.1. It consists of 9 transitions and 11 places. A transition represents an event of the Transmit Data Link Layer Procedure. A Place represents the possible interactions between two or more events.

Indentified Events	Identified Places
ASSEMBLE (assemble a frame)	FROM-USER1 TGJ(transmitting jam)
WAIT-IS (wait interframe spacing)	TO-USER1 DFG (deferring)
START (start the transmission)	FCS (compute fcs)
TF (transmit a frame bit)	READY (frame ready)
WATCH (wath for collision)	RETRANS (retransmit buffer)
TJ (transmit a jam bit)	CS (carrier sense)
ACK1 (acknowledge1)	CD(collision detect)
WAIT-T (wait back-off-time)	CHAN (channel)
ACK2 (acknowledge2)	TGF (transmitting a frame)

Global Variables: fr (frame), at (attempts), trans-suc (transmit succeeding), jam

Informal meaning of other symbols: trans: transmit, == : identical to, .:concatenated to, t: true, f: false, atl:attempt limit, s: successor

4.2.2.2. Receiving Station

The receiving station model is shown on Fig.2. it consists of 7 transitions and 8 places.

Identified Events	Identified Places
STARTR	FROM-USER2
RECEIVE	TO-USER2 RS (receive succeeding)
FILTRE	CHAN (channel)
RETRY	CS (carrier sense)
DISASSEMBLE	RG (receiving)
ACKR1 (acknowledge1)	C-FCS (computed fcs)
ACKR2 (acknowlegke2)	D-ADR (destination address)

Global variables: f (frame), e (error), receive-suc (receive-succeeding), d,s (destination and source addresses), data (data field of a frame)

Informal meaning of other symbols: <>: different of, a-error: alignment error, f-error:frame check error, b: a variable of bit type, l: length, svfr: smallest valid frame.

4.3. Algebraic Specification

In this section we show how to get a *complete* algebraic specification of the protocol represented by the ATNets represented in Fig.1 and Fig.2. This specification is obtained by giving a set of algebraic specifications related to the inscriptions used in the net (see section 2), but also by considering the ATNets themselves as abstract data types. Our work consists then in writing specifications denoting different abstract data types. These specifications will be structured in order to relate the protocol to the requested service. For the sending end, the final step is to find a relation between the operations trans, trans-ok and col-er, expressing the behavior of the Transmit Data Link Management Procedure. To find such a relation, we will consider the Transmit Data Link Control Procedure as an exhaustive set of states and its behavior as a set of series of observable states generated by concurrent and indivisible events. We assume the existence of a specification library containing the usual theories' declarations like Nat, Bool, etc...and the procedure schemes Sequence(El:Element),Set(El:Element), Set-with-order (El: Element), where El is a formal parameter and Element is its metatype. Element is a trivial theory declaration containing just one sort named element and one error element named erelement.The following declarations are closely related to Fig.1 and Fig.2. The same identifiers (when used in these figures and in the following theories' declarations) denote the same objects. The variables *d* and *s* take their values from the set address declared in the following Address theory:

```
const Address = enrich Bitseq+Nat+Bool by data sorts address
  opns seq-as-adr: bitseq --> address
       adr-as-seq: address --> bitseq
       adr_length: nat
  eropns eraddress: address
  eqns all s:bitseq..adr-as-seq(seq-as-adr(s)) = s
       all..adr-length = ...%length of the address field%
        ereqns all s:bitseq..seq-as-adr(s) = eraddress if
                                  length(s)≠adr_length enden
```

Bitseq is Sequence(Bit[element is bit]), length returns the length of a given sequence s.The global variables fr, f and jam take their values in a set called info defined in a theory Info. The variable fcs takes its values in a set called erctrl defined in a theory Errorctrl. The declarations of Info and Errorctrl are similar to that of Address and are omitted for lack of space. The following theory Frame specifies the operation of frame construction from the previous theories.

```
const Frame=enrich Info+Address+Errorctrl by data sorts frame
  opns _._._._ : address,address,info,erctrl --> frame
       nil: frame
       head: frame --> bit %is declared in a theory Bit on bits%
       remove: frame --> frame
       seq-as-fr :bitseq --> frame
       fr-as-seq :frame --> bitseq
       jval % is jam value % : frame
  eropns erframe: frame
  eqns all d,s:address,data:info,fcs:erctrl..d.s.data.fcs =
             seq-as-fr(conc(adr-as-seq(d),conc(adr-as-seq(s),
                   conc(info-as-seq(data),fcs-as-seq(fcs)))))
       all s:sequence..fr-as-seq(seq-as-fr(s)) = s
       all f:frame..head(f) = first(fr-as-seq(f))
       all f:frame..remove(f)=seq-as-fr(rest(fr-as-seq(f)))
       all..nil=seq-as-fr(nils) % nils is the empty sequence %
       all ..jval=...% a given natural number %
   ereqns all s:sequence..seq-as-fr(s)=erframe if
          length(s) > 2*adr_length+info_length+fcs_length enden
```

The following theory specifies the service requested by the User Layer at the sending end, and the response returned by the Data Link Layer.

```
const Status=enrich Address+Info by data sorts  status
  opns trans:address,address,info --> status
       trans-ok,col-er:status
  eropns erstatus:status enden
```

The following theory specifies the net places and global variables (see Fig.1) as *state* variables:

```
const Var = theory  data sorts var
  opns trans-suc,at,fr,jam,TGF,DFG,TGJ,CD,CS,RETRANS,READY,FROM-
           USER1,TO-USER1,FCS,CHAN:var   eropns ervar:var endth
```

The following theory defines the types of the different *state* variables.

```
const  Type=theory  data sorts type
  opns bool,nat,frame,bit,status,s-of-bool(declared in S-of-bool),
s-of-frame (declared in S-of-frame), s-of-status (declared in
S-of-status), s-of-erctrl (declared in S-of-errorctrl), so-of-bit
(declared in So-of-bit):type
  eropns ertype:type endth
```

The following theory Value defines the different values which might be taken by the *state* variables

```
const Value = enrich Bool+Nat+Frame+Bit+S-of-bool+S-of-frame+
     S-of-status+S-of-errorctrl+So-of-bit By data sorts value
  opns fr-asv:frame --> value
  % the other values are defined in a similar way %
  eropns ervalue:value endth
```

S-of-bool is Set(Bool[element is bool]), etc...
The following theory A_val states that the actual state variables'values are type-value pairs naimed a_val:

```
const  A_val=enrich Type + Value by  data sorts a_val
  opns cons:type,value --> a_val
       type-of:a_val --> type
       b-val:a_val --> bool
       fr-val:a_val --> frame
       ...% The other values are returned by similar opns %
  eropns era_val:a_val
  eqns all t:type,v:value..type-of(cons(t,v))=t
       all b:bool..b-val(cons(bool,bool-asv(b)))=b
       ...
  ereqns all t:type,b:bool..b-val(cons(t,bool-asv(b))) =
                                        erbool if t≠bool enden
```

The following theory State shows how the states of the sending station are generated:

```
const State = enrich Var+A_val by data sorts state
  opns init:state
       gen:var,a_val,state --> state
       take:var,state --> a_val
       ini:var --> a_val
  eropns erstate:state
  eqns all ini(fr) = cons(frame,fr-asv(nil))
   % the other variables are assigned initial values in a similar way;
     see the Atn-state for cons and take %
  ereqns all v1,v2:var,t1,t2:type,vl1,vl2:value..
    gen(v1,cons(t1,vl1),gen(v2,cons(t2,vl2),s))=erstate if t1≠t2 enden
```

The following theory Event defines the net transitions (see Fig.1) as events leading to the observable states of the sending station.

```
const Event = theory data sorts event
  opns ASSEMBLE,WAIT-IS,START,TF,TJ,ACK1,WATCH,WAIT-T,ACK2 :event
  eropns erevent:event endth
```

The theory Transmitter defines the operation of the sending station:

```
const Transmitter = enrich  Event+State by
  opns efct %is the effect of a transition% :event,state --> state
  eqns % eqns that leave a variable unchanged are not explicitly
        specified; we begin by giving the eqns specifying the
        Transmit Data Encapsulation component,ie.,the effect of
        the transition ASSEMBLE %
        all d,s:address,data:info,s:state..sfr-val(take(READY,
              efct(ASSEMBLE,s))) =ins(sfr-val(take(READY,s))),
                                          d.s.data.fcs) if cndl
            %The effect of ASSEMBLE on the other variables is
                                     described  in  a similar way%
                          cndl is in(sstatus-val(take(FROM-USER1,s)),
         trans(d,s,data)) and in(ser-val(take(comp-fcs,s)),fcs)
      %Specification of the Transmit Link Management component%
      % Effect of WAIT-IS%
  all s:state..bval(take(trans-suc,efct(WAIT-IS,s)))=t if cnd2
  %The effect on the other vars is  described in a similar way%
cnd2 is in(sb-val(take(CS,s)),f) and bval(take(trans-suc,s))==f
%The effect of the other transit. is described in a similar way%enden
```

The following theory Trans-behavior relates the protocol specification to the specification of its service at the sending end. The specification of the protocol in relation with its service at the receiving end may be specified by a similar theory Receive-behavior; The whole protocol is then specified by a combination of the two theories.

```
const Trans-behavior=enrich Transmitter+Eventseq by
  opns eval:eventseq --> state
  eqns all..eval(nile)=init % nile is the empty event sequence %
       all e:event,es:eventseq..eval(seq(e,es))=efct(e,eval(es))
       all d,s:address,data:info,es:eventseq..  trans(d,s,data)=
           if in(sstatus-val(take(TO-USER1,eval(es))),trans-ok)
             then trans-ok else if in(sstatus-val(take(TO-USER1,
             eval(es))),col-er) then col-er else erstatus enden
Eventseq is Sequence(Event[element is event])
```

5.Some Concluding Remarks and Future Work

The proposed method has several advantages from the specification as well as the proving point of view. In this paper, emphasis was put on the specification rather than on the proving capabilities. The size of the treated example shows the ability of ATNets to specify real-world computer communication protocols with respect to their services.

The graphical representation allows to obtain a good understanding of the dynamics of the protocol by using interactive simulation [Bil88]. A whole environment for ATNets,including a graphical editor-simulator and a semigraphical language, is being implemented on a Sun Workstation in our laboratory.

Moreover, converting ATNets in algebraic specification yields to direct and easy proofs [Cho86] without having to build the marking graph or to search for net invariants. Particularly the theory Trans-behavior allows to conclude that the computation flow graph (CFG) [Bil86], used with graphical representaions of Petri nets, may be replaced by equation solving. Another advantage of ATNets' conversion is the possiblity of relating the protocol specification to the specification of its service, and to make safety verifications, ie., to check, if the designed protocol implements correctly the requested service. It is worthwhile to indicate that in many studies, the verification problem is tackled through an artificial extending of the service specification.

We project further to investigate the verification and proving techniques and mainly those related to protocol aspects, for which classical Petri net representations have shown their limitations.

Acknowledgements

I wish to thank C. Choppy and M. Bidoit from the University of Paris-Sud for their precious and kind support. I want also to express my gratitude to H. Ehrig, W. Fey, M. Lowe and C. Dimitrovici from the Technical University of Berlin, G. Scollo from the University of Twente, D. Sannella from the University of Edinburgh (actually at the Univ. of Bremen), L. Mackenzie from the University of Glasgow for providing me some documentation. Finally I want to thank my colleagues M. Maouche and Z. Sahnoun for their helpful comments on an earlier draft of this paper.

6. References

[Ber86] B. Berthomieu & al.,"Abstract Data Nets, Combining Petri Nets and Abstract Data Types for High-Level Specifications of Dis. Systems", 7th Europ. Work on Petri Nets, Oxford, 6/1986

[Bet84] M. Bettaz, "Specif. algeb. des protoc. de com.et preuve de leur correction", These de Doctorat d'Etat, Universite Technique de Prague, 1/1984

[Bet88] M.Bettaz, "Implement. of Tools for the Specif. and Validation of ADTs: Application to com. protoc., 6th ADT Workshop, Berlin 8/1988

[Bil86] J.Billington et al.,"Automated Protoc. Verification", In: Protoc. Specif.,Testing and Verif., (ed. M. Diaz), Elsevier Science

Publishers B.V. (North-Holland) C IFIP, 1986

[Bil88] J. Billington et al.,"PROTEAN:A High-Level Petri Net Tool for the Specif.and Verif.of Com. Protoc.",IEEE Transactions on Software Engin., Vol.14, № 3, 3/1988

[Bur80] R.M. Burstall, J.A. Goguen, "The Semantics of Clear, a Specif. Language",In:Abstract Software Specif., LNCS 86, 292-332, 1980

[Bur81] R.M. Burstall, J.A. Goguen, "An Informal Introduction to Specifications Using Clear", In: The Correctness Problem in Computer Science (eds. Boyer & Moore), Academic Press, 1981

[Cho86] C. Choppy, C. Johnen, "Petrireve, Petri Net Transformations and Proofs with Rewriting Systems", Proc. 6th Europ. Workshop on Applications and Theory of Petri Nets, Helsinki 6/1985

[DEC80] DEC, INTEL, XEROX, "The Ethernet, a Local Area Network, Data Link and Physical Layer Specifications", 9/1980

[Ehr85] H. Ehrig, B. Mahr, "Fundamentals of Algebraic Specifications 1", Springer EATCS Monographs on Theor. Comp. Sci., 1985

[Ehr89a] H. Ehrig et al. "Algebraic High Level Nets with Capacities", Institut fur Software und Theoretische Informatik, T.U Berlin, 1/1989

[Ehr89b] H. Ehrig et al. "Algebraic Concepts for Software Development in Act One, Act Two and Lotos", Institut fur Software und Theoretische Informatik, T.U Berlin, 3/1989

[Ehr90] H. Ehrig, B. Mahr, "Fundamentals of Algebraic Specifications 2", Springer EATCS Monographs on Theor. Comp. Sci., 1990

[Gog81] J.A. Goguen, J. Meseguer, "OBJ-1, a Study in Executable Algeb. Formal Specif.", T.R.,SRI International,Comp. Sci. Lab.,7/1981

[Hal88] F. Halsall, "Data Communications, Computer Networks and OSI", Addison-Wesley P.C., 1988

[ISO78] ISO:Ref. Model of Open Systems Architec.ISO/TC97/SC16N,11/1978

[ISO82] ISO/TC97, "Information Processing Systems - Open Systems Interconnection - Basic Reference Model", ISO/DIS 7498, 4/1982

[Lam83] L. Lamport, "What Good is Temporal Logic?", In: Inf. Processing 83, R.E.A. Mason (ed.), Elsevier Science Publishers B.V. (North-Holland), C IFIP, 1983

[San84] D.T. Sannella, "A Set-Theoretic Semantics for Clear", Acta Informatica 21, 443-472, 1984

[Sun82] C.A. Sunshine et al. "Specif. and Verif. of Com. Protoc in Affirm using State Transition Models", IEEE Transactions on Software Engin., Vol.8, №5, 9/1982

[Sim80] S. Sima, "Algebraic Specification of a Computer with a Multilayered Architecture",Ph.D Thesis,Dpt of Comp.Sci. T.U. Prag,1981

[Sym78] F.J.W. Symons, "Protocols Using Numerical Petri Nets", Ph.D. Dissertation, Dpt Elec. Eng. Sci., Univ. Essex, 1978

[Sym80] F.J.W. Symons, "Introduction to Numerical Petri Nets, a General Graphical Model of Concurrent Processing Systems", Australian Telecom. Research, Vol. 14, №1, 28-32, 1980

[Tan88] A. Tanenbaum, "Computer Networks", Prentice Hall, 1988

[Vau86] J. Vautherin, Parallel Sys. Specif. with Colored Petri Nets and Algeb. Abstract Data Types, 7th Europ. Workshop on Applic. and Theory of Petri Nets, Oxford, 1986

[Wil87] M. Wilbur-Ham, "Numerical Petri Nets a Guide", version 2, Telecom Australia, Research Lab., 1987

The Specification Language GSBL

S. Clerici, F. Orejas
Dept. de Llenguatges i Sistemes Informàtics
Univ. Polit. de Catalunya
Barcelona, Spain

The specification language GSBL, introduced in this paper, has been designed following the ideas developed formally in [OSC 89]. It is intended to serve as support for the incremental development of specifications from informal requirements. The full semantic definition of the language may be found in [Cle 89].

A very preliminary version of GSBL was presented in [CO 88]. From that paper up to now the language has considerably changed, although the underlying methodological ideas are the same. In particular, these changes are especially related with a) the instantiation mechanism which was almost completely redefined and b) the correctness conditions associated to the language constructs. Also, the full semantic definition obtained later than [CO 88] has caused a number of other minor changes.

The main principles followed on the design of the language are the following:

1. The possibility of dealing with incomplete specifications. We believe that any language aiming at providing support to the specification process in realistic cases must be able to deal with specifications which are incomplete. The reason is that, in general, informal requirements are incomplete. As a consequence, the specifier, with the help of the customer, may have to take "design" decisions in order to finally produce a complete specification. Now, if the language would only allow the writing of complete specifications these decisions may have to be taken too early. In GSBL all specifications are considered incomplete, although some parts of them may be considered complete. Formally, complete subparts of a specification denote free generating constraints [BG 80, Rei 80, OSC 89]. Then, the semantics of a specification in GSBL is the class of all its models satisfying those constraints.

2. Genericity. Another critical aspect for the development of specifications is genericity, i.e. a specification language must promote the writing of highly generic specifications. Genericity is important to facilitate the reusability of specifications. Again, it is not realistic to think that every time we have to write a specification we can start from scratch. The more generic a specification is the more likely we would reuse it. In GSBL genericity goes together with incompleteness. Every incomplete specification is, implicitly, generic. Conversely, what in other languages would be considered generic (or parameterized) here is just an incomplete specification. Additionally, in GSBL, the way of handling genericity has the advantage (with respect to ease of writing) that formal parameters do not have to be

explicitly declared, since every specification is considered implicitly parameterized by its incomplete parts.

3. Inheritance. Another aspect which is crucial for supporting the incremental development of specifications is having adequate inheritance mechanisms [Mey 87]. In GSBL the *subclass* construction provides a specialization relation very similar, in many senses, to the subclass relation in object oriented programming languages. In particular, as in [Mey 86], in GSBL inheritance is a generalization of genericity.

4. Powerful binding mechanisms. One of the problems that can be found in many specification languages is that the systematic use of generic specifications is hampered by the verbose binding mechanisms that have to be used for instantiation. In this sense, one of the aims of GSBL was to design powerful and concise binding mechanisms. The solution found takes into account specification structure in order to provide a powerful mechanism for implicit binding.

Some of the methodological ideas underlying GSBL may be found in the languages Larch [GH 86] and Look [ETLZ 82]. However, in our opinion, GSBL goes beyond these languages in various aspects: a) in Larch, the constructs for dealing with generic specifications are slightly more complicated and less powerful than in GSBL. b) GSBL has a precise semantic definition [Cle 89] but, to our knowledge, no formal semantics of Larch exist. c) The semantics of GSBL has been defined at the specification level and at the model level in a compatible way. This was possible because of solving some semantic problems underlying Look. d) Finally, the instantiation and implicit binding mechanisms are more powerful in GSBL than in the other two languages.

The current situation of GSBL is the following one. After [Cle 89] the design was considered finished. Since then, some effort has been put in building tools, although no coherent set of tools have been produced yet. On the other hand, GSBL has greatly influenced the design of the specification language GLIDER, designed within the Esprit project ICARUS. As a consequence, a number of case studies designed within Glider have served as a test bed of some GSBL constructs. These case studies were unfortunately not very large but they have showed the good behaviour of these constructs.

The paper is organized as follows. In the first section we give an overview of the main constructions of the language and a simplified semantics for them. In the second section we study the structuring relations underlying the specifications in GSBL. In the third section we describe, in some detail, the instantiation and binding mechanisms. Finally, in section 4, we show a small example of specification design in GSBL. The presentation will be largely informal. For a detailed view on the semantic ideas underlying the language the reader is addressed to [OSC 89]. For the detailed semantic definition [Cle 89] may be consulted.

1. Introduction to the language

The only kind of specification unit in GSBL is the *class* which denotes an incomplete specification. There are two different ways of defining a new class from an existing one. The first one is by extension of a given specification; in this case we say that the new class has been defined *over* the previously existing one. The second way is by redefining consistently some incompletely defined parts of a given specification. In this case, the resulting class refines or specializes the previously existing one. In this sense, we say that the former is a *subclass* of the latter. This construction can be seen as a multiple inheritance mechanism similar to the one found in object oriented programming languages.

A class may introduce any number of new sorts; if one of them has the same name as the class, this sort is considered the *sort of interest* of the class. The mechanism of the language that creates the new specification is the *class definition*:

```
CLASS Class name
    OVER  < overlist >                               →  over clause
    SUBCLASS-OF  < subclasslist >                    →  subclass clause
    WITH
            SORTS  < sortlist >                      →  with clause
            OPS  < opslist >
            EQS  < varlist >  < equationlist >
    DEFINE                                                →  define clause
            SORTS  < sortlist >
            OPS  < opslist >
            EQS  < varlist >  < equationlist >
END-CLASS
```

The first two clauses declare the imported and inherited subspecifications, respectively, and the last two ones either add new sorts, operations or equations, or complete the definition of some inherited sort or operation. All the clauses are optional.

At a very low level, we can consider that a class in GSBL denotes a specification in the sense of [OSC 89], i.e. a pair (P,ζ), where P is the *presentation* of the specification (its sorts, operations and equations) and ζ is the set of *constraints* associated to the completely defined parts of the specification. However, this approach is too flat to be satisfactory. Indeed, in GSBL, specifications are considered structured objects. This structure is based on two relations associated to the two specification building mechanisms. The *over relation* defines which specifications are considered *components* of a given specification. Similarly, the *subclass relation* defines which specifications must be considered *subclasses* or *superclasses* of a given specification. In section 2 we will study how these relations are defined. Nevertheless, in order to provide a first intuitive idea of the meaning of the main GSBL constructs, in the rest of the section we will present them in terms of the flat semantics sketched above.

1.1 The *with* clause

With this clause new sorts, operations or equations are added. It is assumed that this enrichment is incomplete, i.e. there are not enough equations to specify the new operations or there are not enough operations to "generate" all values of a given sort. The following example gives the definition of the class *ANY*. This class is predefined in the language and is considered to be an implicit superclass of any class having a sort of interest. The specification denoted by *ANY* consists of a presentation P, formed by solely a sort of interest, and an empty family ζ.

```
CLASS  ANY
        WITH  SORTS  ANY
END CLASS
```

In general, the flat semantics of a class A will be:

$$\text{Flatsem}[\textit{CLASS}\ \ A\ \ \alpha\ \textit{WITH}\ (S,\Sigma,E)\ ] = (P_\alpha \cup (S,\Sigma,E),\ \zeta_\alpha)$$

where α denotes the rest of the class clauses and (P_α, ζ_α) is the specification is denoted by α.

1.2 The *define* clause

The *define* clause either declares new sorts, operations or equations, that are *completely defined*, or completes the definition of some sort or operation, belonging to some superclass, that was not completely defined. This clause adds a new constraint C to the meaning of the class. This constraint consists of a pair of presentations, $C=(P_1,P_2)$, where P_1 is the smallest presentation containing all sorts and operations which either are not defined in the clause but that are part of the arity of the defined operations or appear in the equations, and P_2 is P_1 enriched by all the sorts operations and equations of the clause. Please, note that P_1 contains no equations. In some situations, this definition does not depend on any other one, as, for instance, in the following definition of the booleans in which the operations and equations do not involve any sort or operation outside the clause. In these cases we have an *initial constraint* of the form $(\emptyset, P)$.

```
CLASS Boolean
    DEFINE  SORTS    Boolean
            OPS      true, false : → Boolean
                     ¬ : Boolean → Boolean
                     _∧_, _∨_, _⇒_ : Boolean × Boolean → Boolean
            EQS      {p, q : Boolean}
                     ¬(true) = false
                     ...
END CLASS
```

The flat semantics of this clause is:

$$\text{Flatsem}\ [\textit{CLASS}\ \ A\ \ \alpha\ \textit{DEFINE}\ (S,\Sigma,E)\ ] = (P_\alpha \cup (S,\Sigma,E),\ \zeta_\alpha \cup C)$$

where C is defined as sketched above.

1.3 The over clause

The *over clause* corresponds to an enrichment construction. The specification denoted by a class extends all the *component* specifications declared in the *<overlist>*. Let us consider, for example, the following generic specification of a traversable data structure:

CLASS Traversable
OVER Boolean, ANY
WITH SORTS Traversable
OPS first : Traversable → ANY
rest : Traversable → Traversable
end? : Traversable → Boolean
END-CLASS

Using the *over* clause, the new class is built by putting together the *Boolean* and *ANY* specifications. Next, the *WITH* clause adds the *own* sorts and operations of *Traversable.*

The flat semantics of this clause is the following:

$$\text{Flatsem } [\mathit{CLASS}\ \ A\ \mathit{OVER}\ \ C_1,.., C_n\ ] = (P_1 \cup ... \cup P_n,\ \zeta_1 \cup ... \cup \zeta_n)$$

We should notice that when performing the components' union and, in general, in any moment of the construction of a class, it is possible for a pair of sorts or operations with the same arity to have the same name; when this happens they are identified. If this is not the intended effect, it would be necessary to rename one of them. We have adopted this criteria since what is intended, according to the design philosophy of GSBL, is building a problem's specification by "melting" classes that represent partial aspects of the problem. If we had adopted the opposite criteria it would have been necessary to declare explicitly all the identifications, and the writing would have been extremely tedious. Obviously, we are aware of the danger of this policy that may cause undesired identifications, especially when writing large specifications. However we think that this danger can be limited by having adequate tools in the environment.

1.4 The subclass clause

The *subclass* clause builds a new specification from the classes' specifications that appear in the list *<subclasslist>*. Then, the specifications of the list will be considered as superclasses of the defined class. If a superclass has a sort of interest, it is implicitly renamed in the resulting specification with the name of the class being defined.

For instance, let us suppose that we want to specify a type having an equivalent relation defined over it. Let us also suppose that we have already defined three classes, called *With-reflexiv*, *With-symmetry* and *With-transit*, each of them being the specification of a type having, respectively, a reflexive, symmetric and transitive relation defined over it. Moreover, let us assume that the name of this relation is always the same, e.g. ρ. For instance, the class *With-reflexive* may be the following one:

CLASS With-reflexiv
OVER Boolean
WITH SORTS With-reflexiv
OPS $\_\rho\_$ *: With-reflexiv × With-reflexiv → Boolean*
EQS { a : With-reflexiv }
$a \rho a = true$
END CLASS

Then, the class *With-equiv* can be defined as follows:

CLASS With-equiv
SUBCLASS OF With-reflexiv, With-symmetry, With-transit
END CLASS

The specification denoted by *With-equiv* has, apart from the booleans, an unique sort derived from the implicit renaming of the sorts *With-reflexiv, With-symmetry* and *With-transit* by *With-equiv*, an unique operation *_ρ_ : With-equiv × With-equiv → Boolean*, and the union of all the equations. On the contrary, if the name of the operation in the three superclasses would have been different, *With-equiv* wold have included three different operations satisfying each of them a different property. In the following paragraph, we will see how this situation can be coped with.

The previous example shows, for a very simple case, the underlying philosophy of GSBL, i.e. that specifications should be built by putting together other (previously existing) specifications describing partially what we want to specify.

The flat semantics of the *subclass* clause is defined as follows:

Flatsem [*CLASS* A α *SUBCLASS OF* $C_1,.., C_n$] = $(P_\alpha \cup P_1 \cup ... \cup P_n,\ \zeta_\alpha \cup \zeta_1 \cup ... \cup \zeta_n)$

where (P_i, ζ_i) are the specifications denoted by the superclasses.

1.5 Local instances and renaming

As we have already seen, there are two different ways of reusing a class when building the specification of a new problem: adding it as a component or using it as a superclass. In both cases it may happen that the pre-existing class is not exactly the class that we need, the simplest case being that the needed specification may be obtained by renaming some sort or operation. The language mechanism to do this consists in creating an instance of the class to be locally used in the class being defined. As we will see later, local class creation can be much more powerful but, for the moment, we will only use it as a renaming mechanism. The syntax for defining a local instance of a class, say A, in which every sort s_i and every operation o_i are renamed as s'_i and o'_i, respectively, is A[$s'_1 : s_1$, ..., $o'_1 : o_1$...].

For instance, let us suppose that in the last example the name of the relations in the superclasses *With-reflexiv, With-symmetry* and *With-transit* would have been ρ, σ, and τ, respectively. If we want to call ε the resulting equivalence operation, we may use the following clause:

SUBCLASS OF With-reflexiv[ε: ρ], With-symmetry [ε: σ], With-transit [ε: τ]

Local instances may also be defined in the over clause with the following syntax:

CLASS C
OVER C1: A[$s'_1 : s_1$, ..., $o'_1 : o_1$...]
. . .

This declaration has the following effects: a) a class C1 is locally created within the scope of C; b) C1 is defined by renaming, according to the declaration, the sorts and operations in A. This renaming also includes, implicitly, the sort of interest of A, if it has one; and c) C1 becomes a *local component* of C.

For instance, the class *Traversable* (cf. 1.3) could have been defined as follows:

CLASS Traversable
OVER Boolean, Element: ANY
WITH SORTS Traversable
OPS first : Traversable → Element
...

1.6 Flat semantics of classes and internal correctness

In order to have a first global idea of how specifications are defined in GSBL, let us present a simple example. Suppose that we want to specify a type of values over which a total order ≤ is defined together with the induced relational operations ==, ≥, < and >

CLASS With-order
SUBCLASS OF With-equiv [==: ε], With-reflexiv[≤: ρ],With-transit [≤: τ]
WITH EQS { a, b, c: With-order }
$(a \le b) \vee (b \le a) = true$
DEFINE OPS
$==, \_\ge\_, \_<\_, \_>\_$ *: With-order × With-order → Boolean*
EQS { a, b : With-order }
$(a == b) = (a \le b) \wedge (b \le a)$
$a \ge b = b \le a$
$a > b = \neg(a \le b)$
$a < b = b > a$
END-CLASS

The *subclass* clause states that *With-order* includes, at least, an equivalence relation, called ==, and reflexive and transitive relation, called ≤. Indirectly, the *subclass* clause also states the inclusion of the Boolean specification in *With-order*.

The *with* clause simply expresses the totality condition for ≤. Finally, the *define clause* presents the complete definitions of the inherited operation == and of the new operations ≥, < *and* >. Please, notice that the definition of these operations depends on the precise definition of ≤.

More formally, the presentation denoted by *With-order* consists of a) the sorts *Boolean* and *With-order*, b) the boolean operations plus ≤, == and ≥, < *and* > and c) all the equations that can be found in the classes *Boolean, With-equiv, With-reflexiv* and *With-transit* (translated by the renaming morphism), plus the equations from the *with* and the *define* clauses. The family of constraints denoted by *With-order* includes the *initial* constraint (∅,*Boolean*) defining the booleans, which is inherited, plus a new constraint according to which the operations ==, ≥, < and > are completely defined.

In this sense, the flat semantics of a class definition is:

$$\text{Flatsem}\ [\mathit{CLASS}\ \ A\ \mathit{OVER}\ \ C_1,..,\ C_n\ \mathit{SUBCLASS\ OF}\ \ S_1,..,\ S_n\ \mathit{WITH}\ (S,\Sigma,E)\ \mathit{DEFINE}\ (S',\Sigma',E')\ ] =$$

$$(\ P_{C_1}\cup...\cup P_{C_n}\cup P_{S_1}\cup...\cup P_{S_n}\cup(S,\Sigma,E\ )\cup(S',\Sigma',E'),\ \zeta_{C_1}\cup...\cup\zeta_{C_n}\cup\zeta_{S_1}\cup...\cup\zeta_{S_n}\cup C')$$

where (P_{C_i}, ζ_{C_i}) are the specifications denoted by the components C_i, (P_{S_i}, ζ_{S_i}) are the specifications denoted by the instances of the superclasses S_i and C' is the constraint established in the *define* clause.

In GSBL not every class definition is considered (internally) correct. The correctness conditions that specifications must satisfy may be, on the one hand, justified from a methodological point of view. This justification may be found in [OSC 89]. But, on the other hand, these conditions guarantee the compatibility of the two levels of semantics used to define GSBL [Cle 89].

Being specific, a specification must satisfy the following conditions to be considered correct:

1. A correct specification must be *consistent*, i.e. it must have a non empty set of models. It must be noted that in this approach a specification may have no models. For instance, this happens in the following example:

```
CLASS Inconsistent
    OVER  Boolean
    WITH  EQS
    true=false
END-CLASS
```

the reason is that no model can satisfy, at the same time, the equation *true = false* and the constraint defining the booleans.

2. A correct specification must be a *loose* (or *conservative*) *extension* [OSC 89] of its components. This means that if SP is defined over SP' then the class of models SP, when restricted to the signature of SP', must coincide with the class of models of SP'.

3. Superclasses and subclass must be bound by a *refinement morphism* [OSC 89]. A refinement morphism is a special kind of specification morphism that "preserves" the constraints in a strong sense. In particular, the morphism must be injective on constrained sorts and operations.

2. Specifications as structured objects: structuring relations

As said before, in GSBL specifications are not flat but structured objects. This structure is based on the *over* and the *subclass* relations. In this section we will study in some detail the *internal structure* of GSBL specifications and the way of establishing these relations.

2.1 Internal structure of specifications

The specification SP denoted by a class is considered to be divided into two parts: a sub-specification SP_{over}, which we will call the *over part* of SP, formed by the union of the specifications denoted by its components, and the *own part*, say SP_{own}, formed by the remaining sorts, operations and equations, i.e. SP_{own}=SP - SP_{over}. Note that SP_{own} is not necessarily a specification.

Given a class A, its *own part* consists of all the sorts operations and equations declared in the *with* and *define* clauses together with the union of the *own parts*, adequately renamed, of its superclasses. Its *over part* consists of the rest of the specification, i.e. the sorts, operations and equations imported with the *over clause* or inherited from the *over parts* of its superclasses. However, when defining a class, if there is an identification of an element (sort or operation) of the *own* part of a superclass with some element of the *over* part of the class being defined (we will see later how this identifications are done), then this element will belong to the *over* part of the new class.

For instance, given the class *With-order*, its *over part* coincides with the *Boolean* specification (inherited from *With-equiv*, *With-reflexiv* and *With-transit*). Its *own part* consists of the sort *With-order*, the operations $\leq$, $==$, $\geq$, $<$, and $>$, and of all the equations used to define them.

2.2 The over and subclass relations

The semantics of GSBL texts is defined in terms of a *specification environment*. This environment, on the one hand, associates its meaning to every class identifier and, on the other, it includes the two structuring relations among specifications. In this sense, the effect of a class definition may be seen as the construction of a new specification which is added to the specification environment together with the relationships stated by the *over* and *subclass* clauses.

A specification in whose class definition neither the *over* nor the subclass clauses exist is considered as solely composed by its *own part* (i.e. SP_{over}=Ø and SP_{own}=SP). Therefore, it has not an *over* relationship with any class of the environment; nor can we consider it as a subclass of any class, with the exception of the implicit relationship with the class *ANY* if SP has a sort of interest.

A class A has an *over relationship* r_{over} with all of the components declared in the *over* clause and, by transitivity, with all the components of its components, and so on. Also, A is in *over relationship* with all the components of its superclasses that have not been modified through the instantiation (more details will be given later).

A class A in whose definition there is a *SUBCLASS OF* S_1,..., S_n clause, has a subclass relationship with any of the classes S_i and, due to transitivity, with all their superclasses.

Note that a class A may have an *over relationship* with another class B and, at the same time, have a *subclass relationship* also with B. Let us consider, for instance, the following specification for inducing an order relation over some set, through a function from this set onto another one previously ordered.

CLASS Orderable
  OVER Inductor : With-order
  SUBCLASS-OF With-order
  WITH *OPS* f *: Orderable* $\rightarrow$ *Inductor*
  DEFINE *OPS* $\leq$*: Orderable* $\times$ *Orderable* $\rightarrow$ *Boolean*
  EQS $\{ a, b :$ *Orderable* $\}$
  $a \leq b = f(a) \leq f(b)$
END-CLASS

In this case *Orderable* has, at the same time, a *subclass relationship* with *With-order* and an *over relationship* with *Inductor* which is a renaming of *With-order*. It should be noticed that there is some overloading in the names of the operations $==, \leq, \geq, <$ and $>$, since they have not been renamed in any of the two instances, but this does not cause any implicit identification since their arity is different.

2.3 The subclass declaration

As we have already seen, the use of the *subclass* clause has two effects. On the one hand, it has a constructive effect: the subclass clause helps in building another class. On the other hand, it has a declarative effect, since it adds to the environment the *subclass* relationship with each of them.

Now, as it will be presented below, in the instantiation mechanism it is only possible to substitute a class A by another B if, according to the environment, B is *subclass* of A. In this sense, it is important to have an "a posteriori" construction that allows to declare that, for two classes already defined, one is *subclass* of the other. This construction is the *subclass declaration.* whose syntax is

A IS SUBCLASS OF B [b].

For example, the stacks of elements could be considered as instances of *Traversable* using the following declaration:

Stack IS SUBCLASS-OF Traversable [top: first; pop: rest; emptystack?: end?]

Similarly, sequences, lists, queues, etc. can also be declared as subclasses of *Traversable* by defining the appropriate renaming for their access and is_empty test operations. The subclass declaration is in some sense similar to the declaration of *view* of OBJ, in which we declare that an *object* fulfills a certain *theory.* In our approach, this distinction between object and theory is not necessary, since the concept of class includes both aspects.

3. The instantiation mechanism

In this section we will present the instantiation mechanism of GSBL. This mechanism may be used in two different forms. The first one is to define a new class D in the environment. In this case the instantiation occurs in the subclass clause:

CLASS D ... ***SUBCLASS-OF*** A *[< binding-list >] ...*

The second one is to define a local component D of a new class E. In this case the instantiation occurs in the over clause:

CLASS E ***OVER*** D : A *[<binding-list>] ...*

In GSBL genericity is a consequence of combining the *subclass* and *over* relations. In this sense, parameterization can be seen as a special case of such combination, with parameter passing being just a special case of our instantiation mechanism. Indeed, when dealing with incomplete specifications, the *over relation* is used simultaneously for defining a new specification as an enrichment of another one, and for defining the "parameters" of the new specification. That is, if a class A is defined over a class B then B is implicitly converted into a formal parameter of A. Then, if C is a subclass of B, the instantiation mechanism allows to define a class D obtained by substituting, in the subspecification of A, B by C. This result will be considered as a *subclass* of A and *over* C.

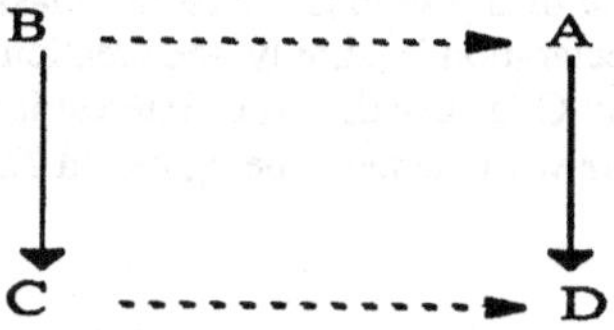

In this sense, it is interesting to point out that the difference between *imported subspecifications* and *theories that must be fulfilled by the parameters*, which is present in nearly all specification languages, is not necessary in GSBL. In particular, the *over clause* is equivalent, for instance, to the *imports* and *assumes* clauses of LARCH.

Nevertheless, the instantiation mechanism in GSBL is more powerful than standard parameter passing. The reason is that in other specification languages formal parameters are (almost) flat specifications, while in GSBL the components of a specification may have subcomponents, acting as parameters of the component, and so on. In this sense, the instantiation mechanism in GSBL may bound, simultaneously, actual parameters for all the formal parameters of a class, including the parameters' parameters, and so on.

In the rest of the section we will study, first, how explicit bindings are declared; second, how implicit bindings are established; third, the model of "semantic environment" used in the formal definition of GSBL in order to describe the binding mechanisms; then, we will present the structure of specifications obtained by instantiation, i.e. its structuring relationships; and, finally, we will discuss some of the ideas presented providing some comparison with other specification languages.

3.1 Explicit binding declaration

Explicit bindings are established with the same syntax as the renaming mechanism that we have introduced in the previous section. Indeed, renaming in GSBL is a form of binding because of the names identification policy followed. That is, in the example above, the class D would be defined as the instance A *[* C : B *]*. Hence, the syntax of a class instantiation is *Class-name [<binding-list >]*, where the ordered elements of the list *<binding-list >* can be pairs of class names C1: C2, being C2 a component of *Class-name*, pairs of sorts s1: s2, and/or pairs of operations o1: o2 with s2 and o2 belonging to the own part of *Class-name* .

The different kind of bindings that we can have in a binding list are the following:

1. A *[*C: B*]*, where C is a class already existing in the environment and B is a component of A. The effect of this declaration is the creation of an instance of A in which the component B is substituted by C. For instance, if we had the instance *Traversable[Natural: Element]* we would have obtained a traversable structure of naturals. In order to consider this kind of instantiation correct C must be a subclass of B. In particular, if B is a global component, there must already exist in the environment a subclass relationship between C and B. If B is a local renaming of a class F, there must already exist in the environment a subclass relationship between C and F. In the previous example, the binding would be correct since Element is a local renaming of ANY, which is considered as implicit superclass of any class having a sort of interest (and therefore of the naturals).

2. A *[*C: B*]*, where C is not the name of a previously existing class in the environment and B is a component of A. The effect of this declaration is, simply, the creation of an instance of A in which the name of a component B is changed by C (as usual, sort of interest is also renamed). For example, we could build an instance of *Traversable* with elements being called *Thing* instead of *Element* by doing *Traversable[Thing: Element]*.

3. A *[*s1: s2*]* or A *[*o1: o2*]* in which a sort or operation from A is renamed. As a result of this renaming it could happen that some other sort or operation from a component of A, or even from its own part, could be identified with the renamed sort or operation.

1.2 Implicit bindings

Implicit bindings in GSBL are a consequence of the name policy followed. As said before, when two sorts or operations have the same name (and, in the case of operations, the same arity) they are implicitly identified. This policy, in the context of parameter passing, implies that whenever an actual and a formal sort or operation have the same name (and arity) they will be implicitly bound.

Nevertheless, implicit bindings do not only occur among sorts and operations but also among classes. Being specific, components from the specification being defined and from the specification being instantiated may be implicitly bound. This may happen a) when the two components bound are the same one (according to the current environment) or b) when one may be considered as a subclass of the other. An example of the first situation can be the definition of B as subclass of A, when both B and A have been declared to be over the booleans. In this case, the two boolean subspecifications would be identified. This kind of implicit identification of subspecifications can be found in many specification languages. For instance, Clear [BG 80] used the same policy by means of their notion of *environment*.

The second kind of implicit binding is more interesting and, to our knowledge, not considered in previous specification languages. The following example will provide intuition about how it works. Let us consider the following definition for the classical problem of finding the maximum element of a structure. Obviously, the elements are an ordered type. As this may be seen as a special case of traversing a structure, its specification is built as a subclass of *Traversable*, where the elements must be an ordered set, i.e. they need being a subclass of *With-order*.

```
CLASS Maximizable
    OVER Element: With-order
    SUBCLASS OF Traversable
    DEFINE  OPS
            maxim : Maximizable → Element
            update: Maximizable × Element → Element
            EQS {m: Element; x: Maximizable}
            maxim(x) = update(rest(x), first(x))
            update( x, m ) =        CASE
end?( x ) : m
                                    m < first(x): update(rest(x), first(x))
                                    m ≥ first(x): update(rest(x), m)
                                END CASE
END-CLASS
```

This specification is equivalent to the following one:

```
CLASS Maximizable
        OVER  Element1: With-order
        SUBCLASS OF Traversable [Element1: Element]
        DEFINE    OPS maxim : Maximizable → Element1
```

but in the former an implicit binding has occurred that is explicit in the latter. In particular, in the second specification *Maximizable* is defined as a subclass of *Traversable* substituting *Element* (which is a renaming of *ANY*) by *Element1* which is a renaming of *With-order*. In short, *Maximizable* is a traversable structure over an ordered set of elements. This is also obtained with the first specification, but in that case there is an implicit instantiation. There, the *Element* (local) class declared in the over clause as a renaming of *With-order* is implicitly bound to the *Element* (local) class declared within *Traversable* as a renaming of *ANY*. This binding causes the implicit instantiation of *Traversable* in the subclass clause. The reason why this binding has taken place is because: a) the two (local) classes have the same name and b) because one can be considered subclass of the other, since one is a renaming of *With-order* and the other is a renaming of *ANY*.

3.3 The environment model

To have a clear idea of how bindings work, we must now study how is the environment in which these bindings are evaluated and how this evaluation takes place. In order to do that, we will, first, informally describe the structure of the specification environment and, then, how bindings are evaluated.

The specification environment is organized into two levels: there is a global environment and, for each class, there is a local one. In the first level, we will have the global specifications, i.e. those that have been built by a *global class* definition. As seen, two global classes can be related between them by either the *over* or *subclass* relationships, stated during its definition, or by a subclass relationship, stated "a posteriori" with a *subclass declaration.* As also seen, the information of *A* having a *subclass relationship* with *B*, will be used when instantiating another class *D*, having *B* or an instance of *B* as component, for stating that *A* might be a valid substitution of that component. On the other hand, *A* having an *over relationship* with *B* means that, when instantiating the class *A*, the only valid substitutions of *B* will be those classes that, according to the information of the environment, can be considered as subclasses of B.

The second level corresponds to the local environments for each class, formed by the local *components.* Each local component is related to the global class, of which it is an instance, by means of a subclass relationship. In particular, this relation may be just a renaming. A local component is also related to each of its components, that in turn might be global classes or local components, by means of an over relationship.

When evaluating an instantiation *A[B: C]* in the context of the definition of a global class *X*, the class identifier *B* is, first, evaluated in the local environment of the class *X*. If such a local class *B* does not exist, the identifier is evaluated in the global environment if it exists there. Otherwise, the binding is just a component renaming. On the other hand, the identifier *C* must be the name of a component of *A* and, therefore, it is evaluated in the environment of the class *A*.

3.4 Structure of the result

With respect to the components' structure of *A[b]*, all the components of *A* that have not been modified during the instantiation process will be considered as components of the instantiated class. Also, if *A[b]* occurs in the context of the definition of a class called X then all components of X which are is used as actual parameters in the instantiation become components of *A[b]*. A component of *A* is considered to be modified, not only if it has been explicitly or implicitly bound to a different specification, but also if it is contained, or has a part in common, with another one that has been modified.

For instance, *Traversable* has as components the booleans and *Element: Any* which is local. If we define the naturals' traversable structures as

CLASS Natraversable OVER Natural SUBCLASS OF Traversable [Natural : Element] ...

the components of the instance *Traversable [Natural : Element]* are, in this context, the class *Natural*, since it is a component of *Natraversable*, and the booleans, since they have not been modified in the instantiation (and, possibly, since it is a component of *Natural* as well). If, on the contrary, we had defined

CLASS Natraversable SUBCLASS OF Traversable [Natural : Element] ...

Natural would not be a component of the instance *Traversable [Natural : Element]* since it is not a component of the class under definition *Natraversable.*

3.5 A discussion on the instantiation and binding mechanisms

The methodology underlying GSBL is the incremental construction of specifications by combination of previously existing pieces that partially describe aspects of the problem to be solved. Being more specific, our approach is based on the following principles:

1. Reusability of specifications. We think that, in order to build reasonably large specifications, it is necessary to reuse pieces from other, previously existing, specifications. Now, we strongly believe (as [Mey 87]) that reusability can only be attained if specification components are systematically organized by means of adequate "object oriented" structuring relations. We think that our subclass and over relations provide such kind of notion at the specification level.

2. Genericity. As said in the introduction, genericity is also an important component of reusability. However it is our opinion that genericity, as found in most specification languages, is not enough. Two are the problems from our point of view. The first one is concerned with the flat structure of parameterized specifications. Specifically, in most languages parameterized specifications consist of only two levels of structuring: at the bottom level we have the formal parameter(s) and at the top level we have the body. There may be a third level, if the formal parameter is defined over some previously existing data types. We think that this is not sufficient. If we are dealing with large specifications then we may have to deal with large parameterized subcomponents of these specifications. In that case, two levels are not enough. The second problem is concerned with the explicit declaration of formal parameters. This implies that specifications can only be instantiated in only one way. We think that this is too rigid. For instance, if we have a specification SP with parameters SP1,...,SPn, we may want to instantiate just SP2 (passing as actual parameter SP2'). In most specification languages, to do this, we would be forced to create dummy arguments for all the other actual parameters. We think that our notion of incomplete specification provides the adequate concept to avoid this problem. In Look a similar approach was taken but they were unable to find the adequate correctness conditions to obtain "compatibility" results.

3. Building specifications by combination of "incomplete" specifications. In most languages it is only possible to combine "complete" specifications. That is, in these cases, if we combine two specifications, one describing n data types and the other one describing m data types, we would obtain a specification with n+m data types. Of course, some kind of sharing is often allowed but it would usually refer to complete subspecifications. As seen in some previous examples, our approach goes beyond this situation. We may combine m specifications describing (incompletely) one data type in order to obtain a specification of one data type. This approach is shared by the languages Look and Larch.

The instantiation mechanism of GSBL, in our opinion, gives uniform support to the needs expressed above.

One critical aspect of the proposed instantiation mechanism is the implicit binding discipline followed in the language. In our opinion, algebraic specification languages may be too verbose with respect to binding declaration. This kind of situation may occur when doing parameter passing (all the formal parameter sorts and operations have to be bound to the actual parameter ones) and when combining specifications (all the common subparts have to be identified). In a certain number of languages (Act One, Clear,...) this verbosity is limited by providing some naming conventions or implicit binding facilities that allow to avoid overdeclaration. In particular, there are two rules commonly followed:

1. Identification of sorts and operations with the same name and arity.

2. Identification of "shared" subspecifications by taking into account how specifications were built. This was first used in Clear by means of the notion of *environment*.

In GSBL we follow these two rules but additionally we have considered two more:

3. Implicit matching class-subclass when some "formal parameter" can be considered as a superclass of an "actual parameter" with the same name. We have seen an example of this in section 3.2.

4. Implicit renaming of its sort of interest when renaming a class. This facilitates the implicit matching of operations (according to rule 1) and of classes (according to rule 3.)

We are aware that implicit binding may favour unreliability, since undesired specifications may take place. However we think that our decisions were right based on the following considerations:

1. Undesired identifications can be detected with the use of the adequate tools in the specification "operating" environment.

2. Undesired identifications can be limited if using additional knowledge about the objects that may be identified. This is the case in GSBL with respect to classes. In particular, asking for a subclass relationship between classes may often prevent undesired identifications.

3. The kind of incremental construction that supports GSBL is based on frequent bindings among sorts, operations and classes. If all bindings would have to be explicit the language would become unacceptably verbose.

4. An example

Once we have seen the main issues of the language, we will present now the specification of a (not too small) example. The example is the specification of the solution to the linear knapsack problem by means of the greedy method. Some of the specifications used in the example have already been used as examples along the paper. In certain sense the example is not very adequate since it is the specification of the solution to a problem rather than the specification of the problem. However, it shows quite well the use of genericity and inheritance in GSBL.

The greedy method (see, for instance, [HS 76]) is an algorithmic method for solving optimization problems in which the solution to the problem is obtained by, starting with the empty solution, step by step enriching the current solution with a new "element" until no possible enrichment can occur without violating the constraints of the problem. Additionally, at every step the elements used for an enrichment are optimal in some well defined sense. The specification for this method is the following:

```
CLASS Greedy
    OVER      Data , Solution:  ANY
              Input : Traversable [ Data:  Element , select: first ]
    WITH      OPS  init: Input  →  Solution
              stop-cond: Input × Solution  →  Boolean
              feasible: Solution × Data  →  Boolean
              unite: Solution × Data  →  Solution
    DEFINE    OPS
              solve: Input  →  Solution
              apply: Input × Solution  →  Solution
EQS  { c: Input; s: Solution }
              solve( c ) = apply( c, init( c ) )
              apply( c, s ) =  IF stop-cond.( c, s ) THEN s
                               ELSE        IF feasible( s, select( c ) )
                                           THEN apply( rest( c ), unite( s, select( c ) ) )
                                           ELSE apply( rest( c ), s )
END-CLASS
```

The *solve* operation, when applied to *Input Data*, builds recursively, using the *apply* operation, a solution of sort *Solution*. Starting by the initial solution, given by the *init* operation, at each step a new data from the input is selected (*select* operation) with some criteria. If this new element provides a still feasible solution, it is added (*unite*). Otherwise, it is rejected and a new data from the remaining input (*rest*) is selected, until some termination condition (*stop-cond)* is attained.

Since there are no conditions on the input data type, of which we only require being "traversable", nor on the solution, the *Greedy* class has been defined *over* the renamings *Data* and *Solution* of *ANY*. Also, *Input* has been defined as an instance of *Traversable* in which *Element* is replaced by *Data* and the *first* operation is renamed by *select*. All the sorts and operations introduced by the *over* and *with* clauses, in terms of which *solve* and *apply* are now completely defined, are *partially defined*, forming what would be equivalent to an extended parameter. It should be noticed that this class does not have a sort of interest.

The knapsack problem consists in, given a set of objects, selecting a subset of them in order to fill a knapsack with some capacity restriction. Namely, the subset of the objects included in the knapsack cannot exceed a certain weight. Additionally, we want the best solution in the sense that the cost of all the objects in the knapsack is the highest possible one. The fact that the knapsack problem we are dealing with is linear means that we can put into the knapsack fractions of an object.

Let us suppose that we have already defined in the environment the sequence type, with constructor operations *emptysq* and *put*. The solution (the knapsack type) can be defined as a sequence of pairs of the form *<object, quantity>* with the following additional operations: a) a real constant *capacity* whose value may be not determined; b) an operation *put-object* such that it adds to the knapsack a complete given object, if its weight does not exceed the remaining capacity, or the exact fraction of the object that completes the capacity, otherwise; c) the operations *remaining-cap* and *performance* defined in the following way for a knapsack $k = < o_1, q_1 >, \ldots\ldots, < o_n, q_n >$.:

$$remaining\text{-}cap\,(k) = capacity - \sum_{i=1}^{n} q_i \qquad performance\,(k) = \sum_{i=1}^{n} profit\,(o_i) * q_i$$

The specification of this class is:

```
CLASS  Knapsack
       OVER  Real , Object: Tool
             Obj-quant : Pair [Object: Elem1; Real: Elem2; which: selec1;  quant:  selec2]
       SUBCLASS-OF                Sequence [ Obj-quant : Element ]
       WITH    OPS
               capacity: → Real
       DEFINE OPS  remaining-cap,  performance:   Knapsack  →  Real
                   put-object:   Knapsack  ×  Object  →  Knapsack
               EQS  { x: Object;   q: Real;   k:  Knapsack  }
                   remaining-cap( emptysq )= capacity
                   remaining-cap( put(k , < x,  q > ) )= remaining-cap( k )- weight(x) * q
                   performance ( emptysq )= 0
                   performance( put (k  , < x,  q > ) = performance( k ) +  profit (x)  *  q
                   put-object( k, x) = IF remaining-cap( k ) ≥ weight( x )
                                       THEN  put (k  , < x,  1 > )
                                       ELSE  put( k , < x, remaining-cap(k)/ weight(x) > )
     END-CLASS
```

Where *Tool* is the specification of a type whose elements have associated a profit and a weight

```
CLASS  Tool
  OVER      Real
  WITH    SORT  Tool
           OPS  profit:  Tool   → Real
                weight:  Tool  → Real
END-CLASS
```

It is known that the knapsack problem over the reals may be solved using the greedy method, using the quotient profit/weight as the criterium for deciding the optimality of the objects. Let *Useful-objects* be the following specification of a class describing how to find the most useful object of a set, assuming that the utility of an object is defined by the ratio profit/weight.

```
CLASS  Useful-objects
    OVER  Object:Tool
    SUBCLASS-OF  Maximizable[ Object: Element;  the-most-useful:  maxim ]
       WHERE    Object SUBCLASS-OF Orderable[ Real: Inductor ;  utility:  f ]
```

```
                              DEFINE OPS utility
                                     EQS  { a : Object }
                                          utility(a ) = profit(a) / weight(a)
      END-WHERE
   END-CLASS
```

Note that in this example the class *Object* is defined in a *where* clause. Such clauses are used for defining local classes that cannot be defined just by instantiation.

Now suppose that we have defined in the environment a subclass of *Traversable* called *Traverset* with, among others, the operation *remove* for eliminating an element. Then, a solution to the problem applying the greedy method is the following:

```
CLASS Greedy-knapsack
  OVER  Object: Tool,  Objects-set: Traverset [ Object: Element ] ,   Optim-knap:  Knapsack
  SUBCLASS-OF Greedy[ Objects-set: Input;  Optim-knap: Solution;  empty-knapsack: init
                      not-full: feasible ; put-object: unite;  fill-knapsack: solve ]
     WHERE  Objects-set
       SUBCLASS-OF   Useful-Objects ,
           Traversable [ Object: Element;  the-most-useful: first ;  remove-optim : rest  ]
       DEFINE   OPS     remove-optim
                EQS     { x: Object ;     s : Object-set  }
                        remove-optim( s ) = remove( s, the-most-useful( s ) )
     END-WHERE
  DEFINE    OPS   stop-cond;   empty-knapsack;    not-full
            EQS   {  s: Objects-set;  x: Object;    k: Optim-knap  }
                        stop-cond( s, k ) =  end?( s )  ∨ ( remaining-cap( k )  ≡  0 )
                        empty-knapsack( s ) =   emptysq
                        not-full( k, x ) =  remaining-cap( k )  >  0
END-CLASS
```

In the instance of Greedy defined in the subclass clause, *Solution* will be an optimal knapsack *Optim-knap*, that will be filled with objects coming from a set *Objects-set* of tools. The *init*, *feasible* and *solve* operations have simply been renamed with identifiers more adequate to the specific problem. On the contrary, the *unite* operation will be identified with the operation of putting a new object in the knapsack, which, in this context, means adding a new element which improves the solution. The *select* operation (that renamed the *first* operation) and the *rest* operation of the *Input* component, are respectively identified with the *the-most-useful* and *remove-optim* operations of *Objects-set*, according to the indicated instance in the *where* clause. In this clause, *Object-set* has locally incorporated the *the-most-useful* operation, coming from *Useful-Object*. This operation permits calculating the most useful object and incorporating, from *Traversable*, a new set of traversing operations, that allow to do the traversal by decreasing value of utility. Notice, that the termination condition *end?* still is the same that existed as instance of *Traverset*, since it has not been renamed in this instance. The definition of *remove-optim* is completed with the *remove* operation that already existed, since it was an instance of *Traverset*.

Finally, in the *define* clause, the definition of the own operations, inherited from *Greedy*, is completed. The termination condition is the knapsack being full or running out of objects. The initial solution does not depend on the set of objects and it is the empty knapsack. Therefore, it is always feasible adding a new element to the solution, as far as the knapsack capacity has not already been exceeded; actually, this condition will always be true when *stop-cond* is false).

It should be noticed that the obtained specification is a generic specification whose "parameters" are the concrete objects and data structure types selected for representing the set of feasible objects, as well as the knapsack capacity. The figure below represents graphically the environment used in this example. Global classes are represented by straight line boxes and local classes are represented by dotted line boxes. The over and subclass relationships are represented by horizontal and vertical arrows, respectively. Again, straight line arrows represent the global relationships and dotted arrows represent local relationships:

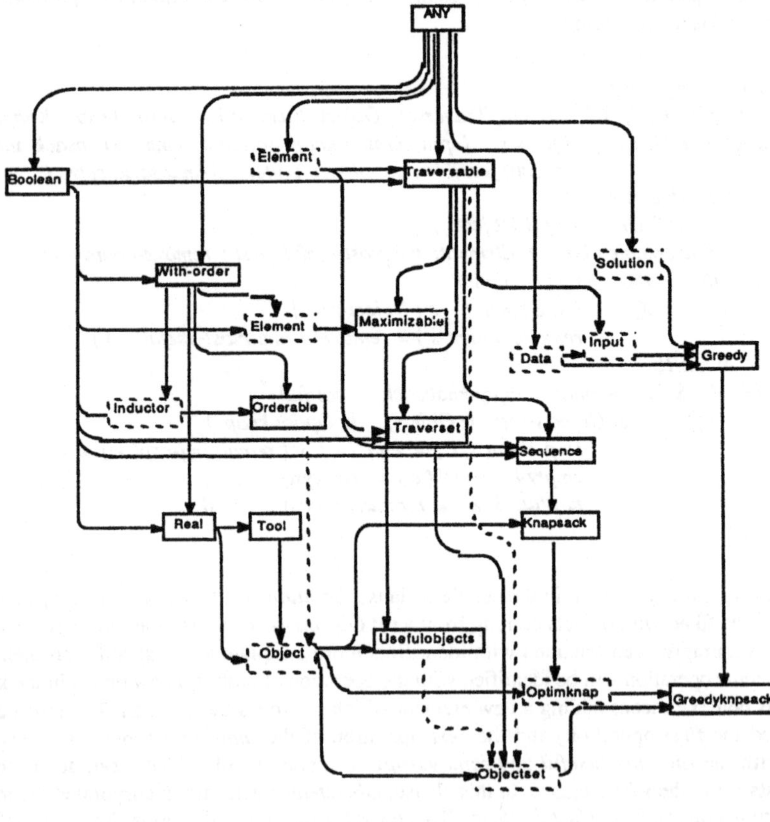

Acknowledgements

The authors would like to thank an unknown referee for his (or her) careful reading and for all his/her suggestions that have considerably improved the paper. This work has been partially supported by the C.E.C in the Esprit Basic Research Working Group COMPASS.

5. References

[BG 80] R.M. Burstall, ; J.A. Goguen, The semantics of Clear, a specification language, Proc. Copenhagen Winter School on Abstract Software Specification, Springer LNCS 86, pp. 292-332, 1980.

[Cle 89] S. Clerici, Un lenguaje para el diseño y validación de especificaciones algebraicas. Tesis doctoral. Depto. de Lenguajes y Sist. Informáticos. Univ. Polit. de Cataluña, 1989.

[CO 88] S. Clerici, ; F. Orejas, GSBL: an algebraic specification language based on inheritance, Proc. Europ. Conf. on Object Oriented Programming, (Oslo, 1988), Springer LNCS.

[Ehg 89] H. Ehrig, A categorical concept of constraints for algebraic specifications, Proc. International Workshop on Categorical Methods in Computer Science with Aspects from Topology, Berlin 1988, Springer LNCS 332, (1989).

[EM 85] H. Ehrig, B. Mahr, Fundamentals of algebraic specification 1, EATCS Monographs on Theor. Comp. Sc., Springer Verlag, 1985.

[ETLZ 82] H. Ehrig, H., J.W. Thatcher, P. Lucas, S.N. Zilles, Denotational and initial algebra semantics of the algebraic specification language LOOK, Draft Report, IBM Research, 1982.

[FGJM 85] K. Futatsugi, J.A. Goguen, J.P. Jouannaud, J. Meseguer, Principles of OBJ 2, Proc. POPL 85, ACM (1985) 221-231.

[GH 86] J. V. Guttag, J.J. Horning, Report on the Larch Shared Language, Science of Computer Programming 6, 2 (1986) 103-134.

[HS 76] E. Horowitz, S. Sahni, Fundamentals of computer algorithms, Pitman 1976.

[Mey 86] B. Meyer, Genericity versus Inheritance, Proc. ACM conf. Object-Oriented Programming Syst, Languages, and Applications, ACM, New York, 1986, pp. 391-405

[Mey 86] B. Meyer, Reusability: the case for object oriented design, IEEE Software, March 1987.

[OSC 89] F. Orejas, V. Sacristan, S. Clerici, Development of Algebraic Specifications with Constraints, Proc. International Workshop on Categorical Methods in Computer Science with Aspects from Topology, Berlin 1988, Springer LNCS 332, (1989)

[Rei 80] H. Reichel, Initially restricting algebraic theories, Proc. MFCS 80, Springer LNCS 88 (1980), pp. 504-514.

Composition of Algebraic High-Level Nets

Cristian Dimitrovici/Udo Hummert

Technische Universität Berlin
Institut für Software und Theoretische Informatik
Sekr. FR 6-1
Franklinstr. 28/29
1000 Berlin 12

Abstract

The aim of this paper is the study, formulated in categorical terms, of semantics and composition of algebraic high-level nets, which are couples between algebraic net scheme (as in /Va85/ or /RV87/) and algebra. We show that the algebraic high-level nets can be composed in a elegant manner using colimits and especially pushouts. We define the semantics for algebraic high-level nets as a functor into the category of coloured nets and prove that it is compositional, i.e. this functor commutes with colimits, especially pushouts. Based on these results we reduce the analysis of net invariants of larger nets to computation of net invariants of components.

1. Introduction

In the last years, research about high-level nets has been considerably developped: coloured nets (see /Je81/, /Je87/), algebraic net schemes (see /Re85a/, /Re85b/, Re90/) and algebraic high-level nets (see /Va85/, /Hu87/, /Hu89/). Algebraic net schemes are a variant of predicate/transition nets. An algebraic net scheme is a pair consisting of an algebraic specification as in /EM85/, /EM90/ and a net sorted places, with transitions which have predicates (each transition is associated with a set of equations) and with arcs marked with terms over the specification (see also /DiHu89a/, /DiHu89b/). Algebraic high-level nets are couples (algebraic net scheme, algebra) (see /Hu89/). Studying an algebraic high-level net consists iin analyzing the net properties of its interpretation , where this interpretation is defined as coloured net (see /Va85/, /Hu89/, /Re90/). The main interest of algebraic high-level nets is the possibility to describe compactly complex systems, using Petri nets to model synchronization constraints and abstract data types for specifying the data they use (see /BP89/). This approach is consistent with recent programming methods.

A difficult problem of net theory is to find compositions on nets, especially on high-level nets, compositions which are compatible with invariant calcul. The purpose of this paper is the study of semantics, formulated in categorical terms, of composition and net invariants of algebraic high-level nets. We study the following objects: coloured nets, algebraic net schemes and high-level nets. For all these objects we define suitable morphisms and categories, and based on them we show that these objects can be combined as colimits, especially as pushouts. For the category of coloured nets we show that the invariants functors preserve limits or colimits. After we have defined for algebraic high-level nets the semantics as a functor into the category of coloured nets (like /Va85/, /Hu89/), we prove that it is compatible with our composition, particullary pushouts, i.e. this functor preserves colimits. We prove how the P-invariants of semantics of a composition of high-level nets can be reduced to the composition of the corresponding P-invariants of the components semantics. this study is not new. Category theory was used for example in /Wi87/ or /MM88/ for study of place/transition nets. Different morphism notions are described in /Wi87/, with additional pre- and post conditions, which guarantees that the nets build a category. The view of /MM88/ is that the nets are transition systems with algebraic structure, such that hier, the morphisms capture the graph structure of place/transition nets. In both articles the considered categories have generally colimits.

In chapter 2, we define the coloured nets as in /Je83/ or /MM88/ using groups for describing the algebraic structure of markings and transitions, and we introduce two notions of morphisms, CN- and CNg-morphisms, leading two categories, called **CN** and **CNg**. As in /Wi87/ or /MM88/ our notions of morphisms preserve the net behaviour. We study categorical properties of both categories, we prove the existence of colimits in **CNg**, especially of pushouts, which permit the composition and decomposition of coloured nets. Using technique of /MM88/ we define the T- and P-invariants of coloured nets as functors from **CN** or **CNg** into the category of abelian groups and show that they preserve limits, respectively transform colimits into limits, i.e. these functors are compatible with composition of nets.

In chapter 3, we define the algebraic net schemes, high-level nets, their semantics as in /Va85/, /Hu87/, /DiHu89a/, /Hu89/ and morphisms. With these morphisms build the algebraic net schemes and high-level nets two categories, **ANS** and **AHL**. Our notion of morphism generalizes that of /Va85/, which is defined only on specification level. The morphisms for algebraic net schemes and high-level nets are defined on both levels, net schems and specifications, which we permet to show that the semantics can be extended to a functor from algebraic high-level nets into **CNg**. We prove that both categories **ANS** and **AHL** are cocomplete, which means that we can compose schemes or high-level nets in a elegent manner, and that the semantics functor preserves colimits, especially pushouts (namely the semantics of a pushout is the pushout of the corresponding semantics). We combine the results of chapter 2 and 3 and become method for the calcul of P-invariants of semantics of larger high-level nets using the P-invariants of the components semantics.

We do not study the relationship between semantics and syntactical invariants of schemes or net properties (like quasi-liveness, deadlocks, termination, boundedness of places, coveredness with T- or P-invariants). The syntactical invariants are defined and studied in /Re90/, in /Hu89/ is presented a generalization of P-invariants which includes the syntactical invariants of /Re90/. For the study of net properties of algebraic high-level nets (see /Va85/, /Hu87/) w.r.t. preservation by morphisms and compatibility with composition we indicate /DHP90/.

The results presented here will be a starting point for further works, and will certainly be useful to study many problems still considered as difficult (reductions, equivalences and others properties; see /Be86/, /DDPS85/).

2. Coloured nets

The coloured nets, introduced by Jensen (see /Je81/, /Je87/), give the possibility to describe compactly complex systems. In coloured nets, places become multisets of coloured tokens, and transitions multisets of firing modes. As in /Je87/, we consider the marking and firing vectors as abelian groups. The behaviour of a coloured net is modelled with two functions Pre and Post which are compatible with the algebraic structure of firing and marking vectors. We arrive to a notion of morphisms for coloured nets as in /Hu87/, /DiHua/, /DiHu89b/, /Hu89/. We also present the categorical properties of coloured nets (see also /Hu89/).

2.1 Definitions, morphisms

Let A be a set. A^{ab} denotes the free abelian group over the set A which can be constructed as the set of all functions from A into the integers **Z** with finite support.

Definition 2.1.1

A *coloured net* is a 6-tuple $N=(P,T,C_P,C_T,Pre,Post)$ where :

(i) P is a set of places and T a set of transitions

(ii) $C_P=(C_{Pp})_{p\in P}$ and $C_T=(C_{Tt})_{t\in T}$ are sets (of tokens and firing colours) families

(iii) Pre, Post$\in$ **Ab**(Tv(N),Pv(N))[1] with $Tv(N):=\oplus_{t\in T} C_{Tt}^{ab}$ and $Pv(N):=\oplus_{p\in P} C_{Pp}^{ab}$.

The elements of Tv(N) are *firing vectors*, and those of Pv(N) are *markings*. The firing vectors $Tv(N)\equiv\{x\in[T\rightarrow\cup_{t\in T} C_{Tt}^{ab}] \mid x(t)\in C_{Tt}^{ab}\ \&\ \{(t,b) \mid x(t)(b)\neq 0\}\text{ finite}\}$ and the markings $Pv(N)\equiv\{M\in[P\rightarrow\cup_{p\in P} C_{Pp}^{ab}] \mid M(p)\in C_{Pp}^{ab}\ \&\ \{(p,a) \mid M(p)(a)\neq 0\}\text{ finite}\}$ build free abelian groups with generating systems $\{1_{t,b} \mid t\in T, b\in C_{Tt}\}$ and $\{1_{p,a} \mid p\in P, a\in C_{Pp}\}$.

Definition 2.1.2

Let N be a net as in definition 2.1.1 and $M\in Pv(N)$, $x\in Tv(N)$ be a marking respectively a firing vector. x has *consesion* under M if it holds $Pre(x)\leq M$. In this case the following marking M′ is defined as follows: $M'=M-Pre(x)+Post(x)$. We denote this situation by M[x> M′ and with [M> the set of all following markings which are generated by M.

We consider only such coloured nets without initial markings, because we are interested only in such operations on nets which are compatible with invariants calcul.

Definition 2.1.3

Let $N_i=(P_i,T_i,C_{P_i},C_{T_i},Pre_i,Post_i)$, i=1,2, be coloured nets and let $f=(f_P,f_T):N_1\rightarrow N_2$ be a pair of functions.

(i) f is a *CN-morphism* if :

(a) $f_T\in$ **Ab**$(Tv(N_1),Tv(N_2))$, $f_P\in$ **Ab**$(Pv(N_1),Pv(N_2))$ and f_P is monotone[2]

(b) $Pre_2\circ f_T=f_P\circ Pre_1$ and $Post_2\circ f_T=f_P\circ Post_1$

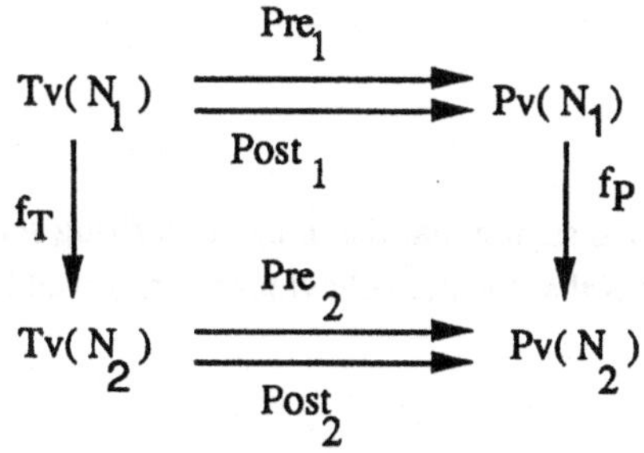

(ii) $f=(f_P,f_T,f_{C_P},f_{C_T})$ is a *CNg-morphism* if :

(a) $f_P:P_1\rightarrow P_2$, $f_T:T_1\rightarrow T_2$,

---

[1] **Ab** means the category of abelian groups and **Ab**(G,H) is the set of linear morphisms between the corresponding groups. ⊕ is the symbol for direct sum of groups.

[2] Pv(N) is an ordonable abelian group, i.e., the group operation is compatible with the order.

$f_{C_P}=(f_{C_{Pp}}:C_{P_{1p}}\rightarrow C_{P_{2f_P(p)}})_{p\in P}$, $f_{C_T}=(f_{C_{Tt}}:C_{T_{1t}}\rightarrow C_{T_{2f_T(t)}})_{t\in T}$,

(b) $Pre_2 \circ f_T^{\oplus}=f_P^{\oplus}\circ Pre_1$ and $Post_2 \circ f_T^{\oplus}=f_P^{\oplus}\circ Post_1$ with $f_P^{\oplus}\in$ **Ab**$(Pv(N_1),Pv(N_2))$,

$f_T^{\oplus}\in$ **Ab**$(Tv(N_1),Tv(N_2)$ and $f_P^{\oplus}(1_{p,a})=1_{(f_P(p),f_{C_{Pp}}(a))}$,

$f_T^{\oplus}(1_{t,b})=1_{(f_T(t),f_{C_{Tt}}(b))}$, $\forall p\in P_1, a\in C_{P_{1p}}, t\in T_1, b\in C_{T_{1t}}$.

The CNg-morphisms build the corresponding generators on generators (g states for generators).The applications $f_P^{\oplus}$ and $f_T^{\oplus}$ are extensions of (f_P,f_{C_P}) and (f_T,f_{C_T}) in the corresponding free abelian groups. It is clear that the class of coloured nets with CN-morphisms builds a category **CN**. The class of coloured nets with CNg-morphisms builds another category denoted **CNg**. Of course is each CNg-morphism a CN-morphism (see example below).

<u>Example 2.1.4</u>

Let $N_i=(P_i,T_i,C_{P_i},C_{T_i},Pre_i,Post_i)$ for i=1,2, be two nets such that the sets of colours contain only one element. N_1 and N_2 are places/transitions nets.

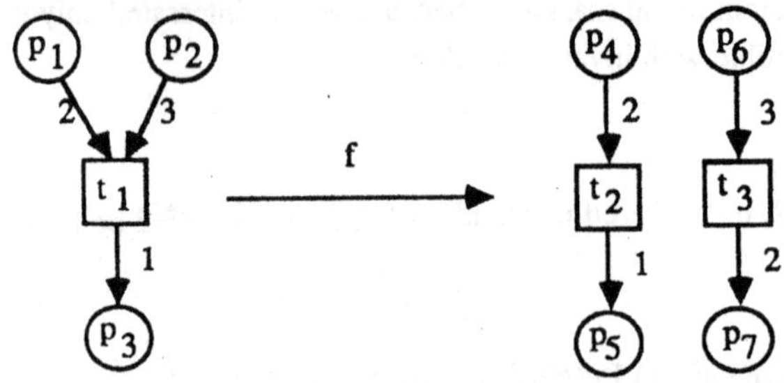

N_1 N_2

$f_P(1_{p_1})=1_{p_4}$ $\quad f_T(1_{t_1})=1_{t_2}+1_{t_3}$

$f_P(1_{p_2})=1_{p_6}$ $\quad f_P(1_{p_3})=1_{p_5}+2*1_{p_7}$

f is a CN-morphism, but not a CNg-morphism.

The following proposition is proved in /Hu89/. It is saying that the image of a firing sequence of transitions is also a firing sequence. This means that the net behaviour is preserved by CN-respectively CNg-morphisms.

<u>Proposition 2.1.5</u>

Let $f:N_1\rightarrow N_2$ be a CN-morphism (resp. a CNg-morphism). Suppose that $M_1[x>M_2$ in N_1. Then, in N_2, $f_P(M_1)[f_T(x)>f_P(M_2)$ (resp. $f_P^{\oplus}(M_1)[f_T^{\oplus}(x)>f_P^{\oplus}(M_2)$).

<u>Theorem 2.1.6</u>

The following statements are valid:

(i) The category **CN** is preadditive, has null objects, finite products, arbitrary coproducts and

equalizers[3].
(ii) The category **CNg** is cocomplete[4].

Proof:
(i) It is trivial to see that the set of CN-morphisms $CN(N_1,N_2)$ builds an abelian group and that the composition is bilinear with respect to addition. The null object is the net $(\emptyset,\emptyset,\emptyset,\emptyset,0,0)$. The existence of the arbitrary coproducts of nets follows from the fact that the free functor for abelian groups commutes with arbitrary coproducts of sets. It is easy to check that the finite products are finite coproducts.
Let $f=(f_P,f_T):N_1\to N_2$ be a CN-morphism. The subgroups $ker(f_P)<Pv(N_1)$ and $ker(f_T)<Tv(N_1)$ are free[5] with generating systems E_P, respectively E_T. We define $ker(N_1\to N_2)=(E_P,E_T,C_P,C_T,Pre,Post)$ with $Pre(1_e)=Pre_1(e)$ for each $e\in E_P$ (analog Post) and $C_{Pp}=\{1\}=C_{Tt}$ for each $p\in E_P$, $t\in E_T$. It can be proved that $ker(N_1\to N_2)$ is the equalizer of f.

(ii) It is sufficient to show the existence in **CNg** of (arbitrary) coproducts and coequalizers. The coproducts are constructed as in (i).
Let $f,g:N_1\to N_2$ be two CNg-morphisms with $N_i=(P_i,T_i,C_{P_i},C_{T_i},Pre_i,Post_i)$ for i=1,2. Let $N=(P,T,C_P,C_T,Pre,Post)$ be the net constructed as follows:
$P:=coeq(P_1 \rightrightarrows P_2)$ with $q_P:P_2\to P$ (the coequalizer in the category **Set**[6]),
$T:=coeq(T_1 \rightrightarrows T_2)$ with $q_T:T_2\to T$ (the coequalizer in the category **Set**),
$C_P:=coeq(C_{P_1} \rightrightarrows C_{P_2})$ with $q_{C_P}:C_{P_2}\to C_P$ (the coequalizer in the category $\mathbf{Set_I}$),
$C_T:=coeq(C_{T_1} \rightrightarrows C_{T_2})$ with $q_{C_T}:C_{T_2}\to C_T$ (the coequalizer in the category $\mathbf{Set_I}$),
$Pre(1_{[t],[b]})=q_P^{\oplus}(Pre_2(1_{t,b}))$ and $Post(1_{[t],[b]})=q_P^{\oplus}(Post_2(1_{t,b}))$ for all $t\in T_2$, $b\in C_{T_2t}$, where [t],[b] denote the corresponding equivalence classes. It is easy to prove that N is the coequalizer of f,g.

qed.

In the category **CN** the existence of coequalizer is not guaranteed because the factor group of an free abelian group is not always a free abelian group. The importance of this proposition relies in the possibility to use the pushout construction as a basic concept for parametrization of coloured nets as in the theory of algebraic data types (see /EM85/, /EM90/).

---

[3] For categorical notions, see the appendix or /ML72/.

[4] See def. 6.4 and theorem 6.5 in appendix.

[5] For each morphism of abelian groups $f:G\to H$, $ker(f)=\{x\in G \mid f(x)=0\}$ (see also the appendix def. 6.4). Subgroups of free abelian groups are free (s. /KM77/, Theorem 7.14).

[6] Set is tha category of sets and $\mathbf{Set_I}$ is the category of I-indexed sets.

2.2 Nets invariants

The invariants are useful to decide about some properties of a net such as the liveness, the boundedness of places, etc. The P-invariants can be interpreted as sums of tokens, which remain constant with the firing of transitions. The T-invariants are repetitive firing sequences. The same sort of invariants for coloured nets as for places/transitions nets is defined (see /MV86/, /Re85a/, /Wi87/ and /MM88/). For coloured nets also exist other special invariants (see /Re85a/, /Re85b/, /Re90/, /Je81/, /Je87/).

Definition 2.2.1

Let $N=(P,T,C_P,C_T,Pre,Post)$ be a coloured net.

(i) A *T-invariant* is an element of the set $TInv(N) = \ker(Post - Pre)$, i.e., TInv(N) is the equalizer of the pair (Pre,Post).

(ii) A *P-invariant* is an element of the set $PInv(N) = \ker((Post - Pre)^*)$ where $(\_)^*$ is the dual operator the corresponding abelian groups, i.e., PInv(N) is the equalizer of the pair $(Pre^*, Post^*)$[7].

The following proposition which is proved in /Hu89/ gives the interpretation of the net invariants; the T-invariants reproduce markings and the weighted summes of P-invariants are constant. In the next proposition we use the notation $M \cdot x = \Sigma\, M_i \cdot x_i$.where M_i and x_i are the non-zero components of M, respectively of x. Such summes are well-defined because the number of non-zero components of an element of Pv(N) or Tv(N) is finite.

Proposition 2.2.2

Let N be a coloured net.The following statements are valid :

(i) $\forall x \in TInv(N): \forall M,M' \in Pv(N): M[x>M' \Rightarrow M=M'$

(ii) $\forall x \in PInv(N): \forall M' \in [M>, M \cdot x = M' \cdot x$.

CN- and CNg-morphisms are compatible with the invariants. T-invariants are preserved by morphisms, while P-invariants are preserved from codomains to domains (see /Wi87/). We obtain two functors from the category **CN**, respectively **CNg** into the category of abelian groups which preserves the finite limits, respectively transforms finite colimits into limits (see /DiHu89b/, /MM88/). We have defined the PInv functor on the category **CNg** because in this category the existence of coequalizer is guaranteed.

Theorem 2.2.3

The following statements are valid:

(i) TInv: **CN**→**Ab** is a left exact covariant functor[8].

(ii) PInv: **CNg**→**Ab** is a right exact contravariant functor [9].

---

[7] The dual operator for a group G is defined as the set of all linear applications from G into **Z**, Hom(G,**Z**).

[8] The functor transforms finite limits into limits (see also the appendix def. 6.6 and theorem 6.7).

Proof:

(i) It is necessary to show the following relation: $f_T(TInv(N_1)) \subseteq TInv(N_2)$ for $f=(f_T,f_P):N_1 \to N_2$ a CN-morphism.

Let be $x \in TInv(N_1)$. Then it follows: $(Post_2\text{-}Pre_2)(f_T(x))=Post_2(f_T(x))\text{-}Pre_2(f_T(x))=$ $=f_P(Post_1(x))\text{-}f_P(Pre_1(x))=f_P(Post_1(x)\text{-}Pre_1(x))=f_P(0)=0$. This means $f_T(x) \in TInv(N_2)$.

We define $TInv(f)={f_T}/_{TInv(N_1)}$. Then TInv is a covariant functor.

For the left exactness of TInv it is suficiently to prove that TInv transforms products into products and equalizers into equalizers. The first statement follows because in **CN** the finite products coincide with coproducts (see theorem 2.1.6) and because in **Ab** the finite products of exact sequences are exact sequences. The second statement about equalizers results from the 9-lemmas for abelian groups.

(ii) We show the following relation: $f_P^*(PInv(N_2)) \subseteq PInv(N_1)$.

Let be $\lambda \in PInv(N_2)$. Then it follows: $(Post_1\text{-}Pre_1)^*(f_P^*(\lambda))=(Post_1^*\text{-}Pre_1^*)(f_P^*(\lambda))=$ $=(Post_1^*\text{-}Pre_1^*)(\lambda \circ f_P)=\lambda \circ f_P \circ Post_1\text{-}\lambda \circ f_P \circ Pre_1=\lambda \circ Post_2 \circ f_T\text{-}\lambda \circ Pre_2 \circ f_T =$ $=(Post_2 \circ f_T)^*(\lambda)\text{-}(Pre_2 \circ f_T)^*(\lambda)=f_T^*(Post_2^*(\lambda))\text{-}f_T^*(Pre_2^*(\lambda))=f_T^*(Post_2^*(\lambda)\text{-}Pre_2^*(\lambda))=$ $=f_T^*((Post_2^*\text{-}Pre_2^*)(\lambda))=f_T^*((Post_2\text{-}Pre_2)^*(\lambda))=f_T^*(0)=0$. This means $f_P^*(\lambda) \in PInv(N_1)$.

Let be $f=(f_T,f_P):N_1 \to N_2$ a CNg-morphism. We define $PInv(f)={f_P^*}/_{PInv(N_2)}$. Then PInv is a contravariant functor because $(\_)^*$ is a contravariant functor.

For the right exactness of Pinv we show that PInv transforms arbitrary coproducts into products, respectively coequalizers into equalizers.

Let N_i, $i \in I$, be CNg-nets, $N_i=(P_i,T_i,Cp_i,CT_i,Pre_i,Post_i)$. Let $(\amalg_i N_i, in_i:N_i \to \amalg_i N_i)$ be the corresponding coproduct. It is simple to check that $(PInv(\amalg_i N_i), PInv(in_i):PInv(\amalg_i N_i) \to PInv(N_i))$ is the product in **Ab** of the family of abelian groups $PInv(N_i)$.

Let $f,g:N_1 \to N_2$ be CNg-morphisms and $(N,q:N_2 \to N)$ be the coequalizer of (f,g). It is simple to check that $(PInv(N), PInv(q):PInv(N) \to PInv(N_2))$ is the equalizer of $(PInv(f),PInv(g))$ in **Ab**.

qed.

This theorem allows to compute the invariants of a net which can be composed/decomposed into nets (the net is a pullback or pushout) from the invariants of its components.

Example 2.2.4

In the below diagram the net N is the pullback of N_1 and N_2 over N_0 in the category CN

[9] The functor transforms finite colimits into finite limits (see also the appendix def. 6.6 and theorem 6.7).

where the arrows are inclusions, and we write $N=N_1\Pi_{N_0}N_2$[10]. The we can compute with the last theorem-(i) the T-invariants of N as it follows:

$TInv(N)\cong TInv(N_1\Pi_{N_0}N_2)\cong TInv(N_1)\Pi_{TInv(N_0)}TInv(N_2)\cong$

$\cong\langle 1_{t_2}+1_{t_3}\rangle\Pi_{\langle 1_{t_2}+1_{t_3},1_{t_1}+1_{t_4}\rangle}\langle 1_{t_2}+1_{t_3}\rangle\cong\langle 1_{t_2}+1_{t_3}\rangle$, where we have $TInv(N_1)=$ $=\langle 1_{t_2}+1_{t_3}\rangle=TInv(N_2)$ and $TInv(N)=\langle 1_{t_2}+1_{t_3},1_{t_1}+1_{t_4}\rangle$.

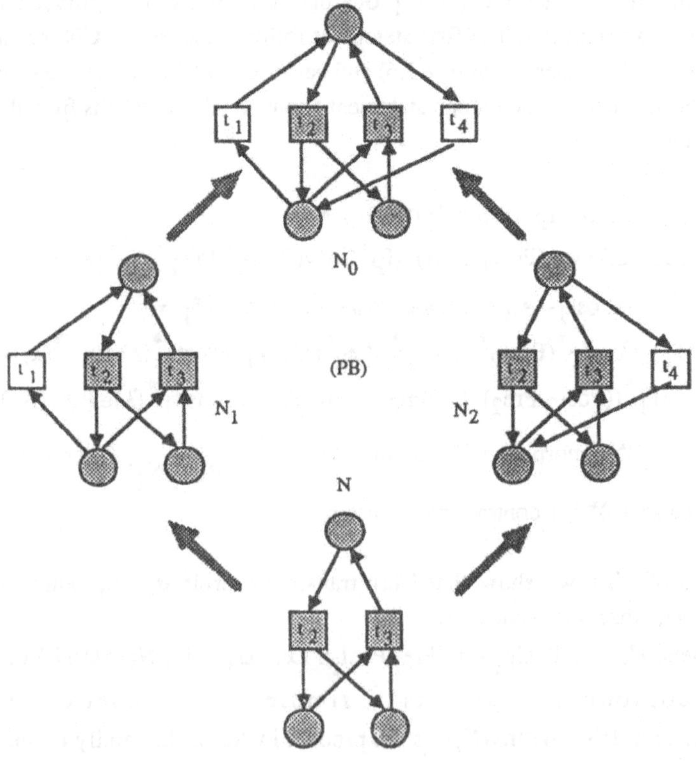

<u>Example 2.2.5</u>

In the below diagram the net N is the pushout of N_1 and N_2 over N_0 in the category CNg where the arrows are inclusions, and we write $N=N_1\sqcup_{N_0}N_2$[11]. Then we can compute with the last theorem-(ii) the P-invariants of N as it follows:

$PInv(N)\cong PInv(N_1\sqcup_{N_0}N_2)\cong PInv(N_1)\Pi_{SInv(N_0)}PInv(N_2)\cong\langle 2\cdot\lambda 1_{s_1}+\lambda 1_{s_2},\lambda 1_{s_3}\rangle\Pi_{\langle 2\cdot\lambda 1_{s_1}}$

[10] $A\Pi_C B$ denotes the pullback of A and B over C in every category (see also the appendix def. 6.4).

[11] $A\sqcup_C B$ denotes the pushout of A and B over C in every category (see also the appendix def. 6.4).

$+\lambda 1_{s_2}>^{<2\cdot\lambda 1_{s_1}+\lambda 1_{s_2}+2\cdot\lambda 1_{s_3}>}) \equiv <2\cdot\lambda 1_{s_1}+\lambda 1_{s_2}+2\cdot\lambda 1_{s_3}>$, where we have the linear function $\lambda 1_s:\{s_1,s_2,s_3\}^{ab}\rightarrow\mathbb{Z}$ defined: $\lambda 1_s(1_s)=1$ and $\lambda 1_s(1_{s'})=0$ for $s\neq s'$, and the P-invariants of the components are the following: $PInv(N_1)\equiv<2\cdot\lambda 1_{s_1}+\lambda 1_{s_2},\lambda 1_{s_3}>$, $PInv(N_0)\equiv<2\cdot\lambda 1_{s_1}+\lambda 1_{s_2}>$ and $PInv(N_2)\equiv<2\cdot\lambda 1_{s_1}+\lambda 1_{s_2}+2\cdot\lambda 1_{s_3}>$

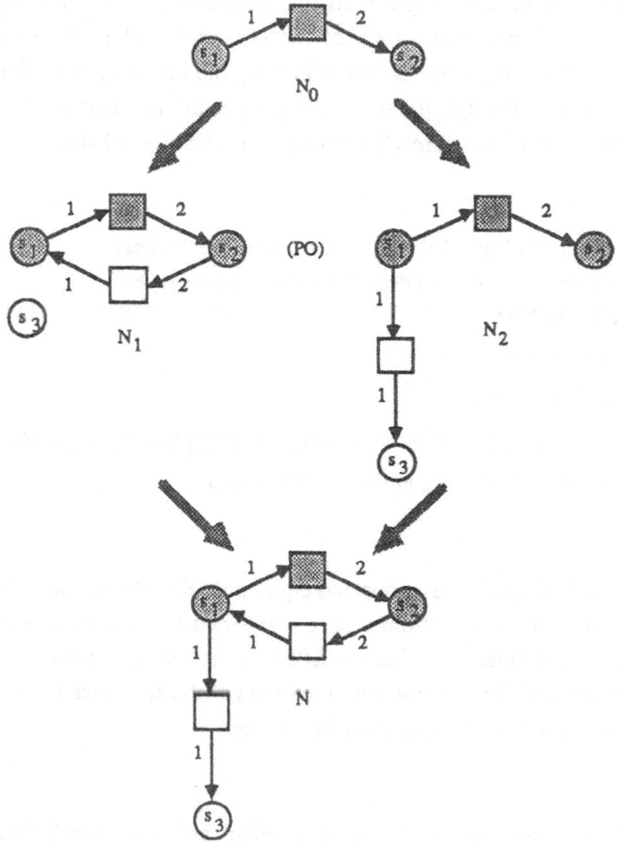

3. Algebraic net schemes and high-level nets

In this chapter, we present the algebraic net schemes and algebraic high-level nets based on the works /Va85/, /Va87/, /Re85b/, /Hu87/, /EHH89/, /Hu89/ and /Re85c/. Algebraic net schemes are a variant of predicate/transition nets, algebraic high-level nets are couples (algebraic net schemes, algebras). The semantics of algebraic high-level nets are defined in terms of coloured nets. Between algebraic net schemes or high-level nets we define the ANS-morphisms, respectively AHL-morphisms. In this paper we define these morphisms on the net level. In /Va85/ they are defined only on specification level and in /Hu89/ on both levels. Both classes of objects build with the corresponding morphisms categories (over a given specification and with a fixed set of variables), which are cocomplete, i.e. pushouts, coproducts and coequalizers exist. We show that the semantics preserves categorical constructions such as pushouts and coproducts (see also /Hu89/).

3.1 Definitions, semantics

An algebraic net scheme consists in a basic coloured net where colours and firing rules are represented by interpretations of terms over a given algebraic specification as in /EM85/ or /EM898/. The Pre and Post functions assign a set of terms with variables to each pair (place,transition). The firing of each transition is determined by the classical conditions for tokens, plus a set of equations over the specification (the predicates) associated with each transition. We consider schemes without initial markings 9see also /Wi87/ or /MM88/).

Definition 3.1.1

An *algebraic net scheme* is a tuple N=(SPEC,X,P,T,Pre,Post,eqns,sort) where :

(i) SPEC=(SO,OP,EQ) is an algebraic specification of an abstract data types,

(ii) X is a family of SO-sorted variables,

(iii) P and T are the sets of places and transitions,

(iv) $Pre, Post \in Ab(T^{ab}, \oplus_{p \in P} T_{OP}(X)_{sort(p)}{}^{ab})$,

(v) $eqns: T \rightarrow 2^{T_{OP}(X) \times T_{OP}(X)}$ with $eqns(t) \subseteq T_{OP}(Var(t)) \times T_{OP}(Var(t))\ \forall t \in T$, where $Var(t) \subseteq X$ represents the family of variables occurring in $Pre(1_t)$ or $Post(1_t)$

(vi) $sort: P \rightarrow SO$.

The specification SPEC consists of sorts, operations and equations. X is the set of SO-sorted variables. Pre and Post associate with each arc from a place p to a transition t, respectively from t to p, a finite set of terms over the given specification SPEC. Function eqns associates with each transition a set of equations and the function sort associates with each place a sort of the specification. The set of equations of each transition can be infinite.

Example 3.1.2

Senders (with action "send") and a receiver (with actions "receive" and "consume") share data through a canal, the capacity of which is n. Each of the senders sends a piece of information and only one. The specification for the canal is the following :

DTS=NAT+BOOL+

sorts: *data, queue*

opns: e: →*data*

nil: →*queue*

inqueue: *data queue*→*queue*

dequeue: *queue*→*queue*

first: *queue*→*data*

empty: *queue*→*bool*

length: *queue→nat*
eqns: dequeue(nil)=nil
dequeue(inqueue(x,nil))=nil
dequeue(inqueue(x,inqueue(y,q)))=inqueue(x,dequeue(y,q))
first(nil)=e
first(inqueue(x,nil))=x
first(inqueue(x,inqueue(y,q)))=first(inqueue(y,q))
empty(nil)=true
empty(inqueue(x,q))=false
length(nil)=0
length(inqueue(x,q))=lenth(q)+1

Constant e is an error element (first element of an empty queue). The communication medium is represented by place p. Transition se (with eqns(se)={(length(q)≤n-1,true)}) takes a data from place p1 and puts it into the queue q of place p, when this queue contains strictly less than n elements. Transition re takes data out of the queue, when not empty (eqns(re)={(empty(q),false)}). And transition co (with no equation) consumes data.

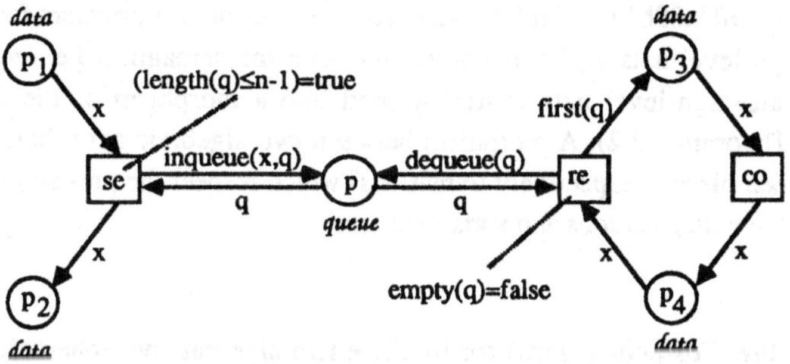

Algebraic net scheme SE

Definition 3.1.3
An *algebraic high-level net* (AHL-net) is a tuple (N,A) where N is an algebraic net scheme, and A∈**Alg(SPEC)** is a SPEC-algebra.

The semantics of an algebraic high-level net is the associated coloured net where the colours of places are the corresponding sets of the given algebra and the colours of transitions are the sets of all assignments for which all equations of the corresponding transitions are valid; the pre- and postconditions are defined as interpretations of Pre- and Postfunctions (see def 3.1.1) in the given algebra. The semantics of an algebraic high-level net consists of all possible place/transition nets in which the transitions can be fired by validation of pre- and postconditions interpreted in the given algebra. All these place/transition nets are captured in a coloured net.

Definition 3.1.4

Let AN=(N,A) be an AHL-net with N=(SPEC,X,P,T,Pre,Post,eqns,sort). Then the *semantics of AN* in terms of coloured nets is defined as follows :

$Sem(AN)=(P_{sem},T_{sem},Cp_{sem},CT_{sem},Pre_{sem},Post_{sem})$ with :

(i) $P_{sem}=P$ and $T_{sem}=T$

(ii) $Cp_{sem}p=A_{sort(p)}\ \forall p\in P$,

$CT_{sem}t=\{ass_A\in[Var(t),A] \mid \underline{ass}_A(L)=\underline{ass}_A(R)\ \forall(L,R)\in eqns(t)\}\ \forall t\in T$

(iii) $Pre_{sem}(1_{t,ass_A})=\underline{ass}_A{}^{\oplus}(Pre(1_t))$,

$Post_{sem}(1_{t,ass_A})=\underline{ass}_A{}^{\oplus}(Post(1_t))\ \forall t\in T, ass_A\in CT_{sem}t$, where $\underline{ass}_A{}^{\oplus}:T_{OP}(X)^{ab}\rightarrow A^{ab}$ represents the extension of $\underline{ass}_A:T_{OP}(X)\rightarrow A$ in free abelian groups with $\underline{ass}_A{}^{\oplus}(1_{\underline{t}})=1_{\underline{ass}_A(\underline{t})}$ $\forall \underline{t}\in T_{OP}(X)$. $\underline{ass}_A$ is the extension of ass_A, interpretation of terms with variables in the algebra A.

In all the next sections we consider the specification SPEC and the set of variables X as fixed.

As in /DiHu89a/, /DiHu89b/ and /Hu89/, we introduce a notion of morphism for algebraic net schemes and high-level nets which is compatible with the semantics, i.e. every morphism between algebraic high-level nets is transformed into a morphism of the corresponding semantics (see Theorem 3.2.2). A morphism between two algebraic net schemes is a pair of functions (between places, respectively transitions) which respect the pre- and postconditions and are compatible with equations and sorts functions.

Definition 3.1.5

Let $NS_i=(S_i,T_i,Pre_i,Post_i,eqns_i,sort_i)$ for i=1,2 be two algebraic net schemes. $f:NS_1\rightarrow NS_2$ with $f=(f_{SPEC},f_S,f_T)$ is a *ANS-morphism*, if

(i) $f_S:S_1\rightarrow S_2$ and $f_T:T_1\rightarrow T_2$,

(ii) $f_S{}^{\oplus}\circ Pre_1=Pre_2\circ f_T{}^{\oplus}$ and $f_S{}^{\oplus}\circ Post_1=Post_2\circ f_T{}^{\oplus}$, with $f_S{}^{\oplus}(1_{s,\underline{t}})=1_{f_S(s),\underline{t}}$ for all $s\in S_1$, $\underline{t}\in T_{OP}(X)$ and $f_T{}^{\oplus}(1_t)=1_{f_T(t)}$ for all $t\in T_1$,

(iii) $eqns_1=eqns_2\circ f_T$,

(iv) $Var(t))=Var(f_T(t))$ for all $t\in T_1$

(v) $sort_2\circ f_S=f_{SO}\circ sort_1$

With f_S and f_T we can variate the net structure. The condition (iv) assures that each variable assignment of each transition t can be mapped on a variable assignment of $f_T(t)$. The algebraic net schemes builds together with ANS-morphisms a category, denoted ANS. The third condition assures that the net behaviour of semantics is preserved by the corresponding interpretations of AHL-morphisms (see Theorem 3.2.2).

Definition 3.1.6
Let $AH_1=(N_1,A_1)$ and $AH_2=(N_2,A_2)$ be AHL-nets. An *AHL-morphism* is $f=(f_{ANS},f_A):AH_1 \to AH_2$ with: $f_{ANS}=(f_P,f_T)$ is an ANS-morphism and f_A is an SPEC-morphism between A_1 and A_2.

The AHL-nets builds with the AHL-morphisms a category **AHL**.

3.2 Categorical properties

We now present the properties of the categories we just introduced, i.e. we show how the algebraic net schemes or high-level nets can be composed. These properties make possible the composition algebraic net schemes or high-level nets on syntactical level, as graphs. They are the same as for category **CNg**. We show also that the semantics functor preserves pushouts and coproducts. This means that we can compose or decompose algebraic net schemes or high-level nets and all interpretetions of the result can be deduced from the interpretations of the components.

Theorem 3.2.1
The categories **ANS** and **AHL** are cocomplete.

Proof:
We prove that there are coproducts in **ANS**.
Let NS_i, $i \in I$, be algebraic net schemes with $NS_i=(P_i,T_i,Pre_i,Post_i,eqns_i,sort_i)$. It is easy to check that $\amalg_{i\in I}NS_i=(P,T,Pre,Post,eqns,sort)$ can be defined as disjoint reunion of specifications and net parts:
$P=\amalg_{i\in I}P_i$ with $in_{iP}:P_i \to P$ and $T=\amalg_{i\in I}T_i$ with $in_{iT}:T_i \to T$ in the category **Set**;
Pre, Post: $T^{ab} \to \oplus_{p\in P}\, T_{OP}(X)^{ab}$ are defined as the sum of the Pre_i, respectively $Post_i$ because the following relation holds: $T^{ab}=(\amalg_{i\in I}T_i)^{ab} \cong \oplus_{i\in I}(T_i^{ab})$ and sort and eqns are defined as disjoint sums. Let $in_i=(in_{iP},in_{iT})$ be the natural inclusions. It is trivial to check that in_i are ANS-morphisms.

We show that there are coequalizers in **ANS**.
Let NS_1 and NS_2 be two algebraic net schemes with $NS_i=(P_i,T_i,Pre_i,Post_i,eqns_i,sort_i)$ for $i=1,2$ and $f,g\in \mathbf{ANS}(NS_1,NS_2)$ be two ANS-morphisms.

We define (NS,q) of f and g with $NS=(P,T,Pre,Post,eqns,sort)$ as follows:
(P,q_P) with $q_P:P_2 \to P$ is the coequalizer of $f_P,g_P:P_1 \to P_2$ in **Set**;
(T,q_T) with $q_T:T_2 \to T$ is the coequalizer of $f_T,g_T:T_1 \to T_2$ in **Set**;
the definition of $Pre,Post:T^{ab} \to \oplus_{p\in P}\, T_{OP}(X)^{ab}$ follows from $q_P^{\oplus} \circ f_P^{\oplus}=q_P^{\oplus} \circ g_P^{\oplus}$ and from

the universal property of the coequalizer in **Ab** as in the below diagram

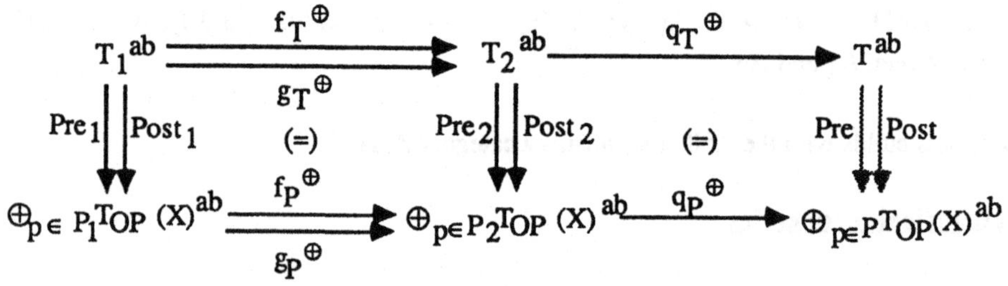

;

$eqns(q_T(t))=eqns_2(t))$ for all $t\in T_2$; $sort:P\to SO$ with $sort(q_P(p))=sort_2(p)$ for all $p\in P_2$ and $q:NS_2\to NS$ with $q=(q_P,q_T)$.

It is trivial to check that q is an ANS-moprhism and that (NS,q) is the coequalizer of f,g.

The category **AHL** is cocomplete because the categories of SPEC-algebras and **ANS** are cocomplete

qed.

<u>Theorem 3.2.2</u>

The association Sem: **AHL**$\to$**CNg** can be canonically extended to a functor, called semantics functor. The semantics functor Sem is right exact, i.e. transforms colimits into colimits.

<u>Proof:</u>

We show that Sem is a functor, i.e. we need only to define the mapping of morphisms.

Let $f=(f_P,f_T,f_A):AH_1\to AH_2$ be an AHL-morphism between the algebraic high-level nets $AH_i=(NS_i,A_i)$, with $NS_i=(P_i,T_i,Pre_i,Post_i,eqns_i,sort_i)$ for i=1,2. Then there is a CNg-morphism $Sem(f):Sem(AH_1)\to Sem(AH_2)$ (see definition 3.1.3; with $Sem(AH_i)=$ $=(P_i,T_i,CP_i,CT_i,Pre_{i_{sem}},Post_{i_{sem}})$ for i=1,2) which is defined as follows:

$Sem(f)_P:P_1\to P_2$ with $Sem(f)_P:=f_P$, $Sem(f)_T:T_1\to T_2$ with $Sem(f)_T:=f_T$,

$Sem(f)_{CP}:CP_1\to CP_2$ with $Sem(f)_{CP_p}:=(f_{A_{sort_1(p)}}:A1_{sort_1(p)}\to A2_{sort_1(p)})$ and

$Sem(f)_{CT}:CT_1\to CT_2$ with $Sem(f)_{CT_t}(ass_{A_1}):=f_A\bullet ass_{A_1}$ for all $t\in T_1$, $ass_{A_1}\in CT_{1t}$.

It is easy to prove that $Sem(f)_{CT}$ is welldefined CNg-morphism.

Now we prove that Sem is right exact functor, i.e. it transforms colimits into colimits.

We show that Sem preserves coequalizers.

Let $((NS=(P,T,Pre,Post,eqns,sort),A),q=(q_P,q_T,q_A))$ be the coequalizer of $f=(f_P,f_T,f_A),g=(g_P,g_T,g_A)\in$ **AHL**$((NS_1,A_1),(NS_2,A_2))$ with $q\in$ **AHL**$((NS_2,A_2),(NS,A))$

and $NS_i=(P_i,T_i,Pre_i,Post_i,eqns_i,sort_i)$ for i=1,2. We prove that (Sem(NS),Sem(q)) is the coequalizer of the pair (Sem(f),Sem(g)).

We show $Sem(q)\circ Sem(f)=Sem(q)\circ Sem(g)$.

(a) $Sem(q)_P\circ Sem(f)_P=q_P\circ f_P=q_P\circ g_P=Sem(q)_P\circ Sem(g)_P$

Analogous $Sem(q)_T\circ Sem(f)_T=Sem(q)_T\circ Sem(f)_T$.

(b) $Sem(q)_{C_P}\circ Sem(f)_{C_P}=q_A\circ f_A=q_A\circ g_A=Sem(q)_{C_P}\circ Sem(g)_{C_P}$

(c) Let be $t\in T_1$, $ass_{A_1}\in {C_{T1}}_{Sem}t\subseteq[Var(t),A_1]$. It results:

$Sem(q)_{C_{T}f_T(t)}(Sem(f)_{C_{Tt}}(ass_{A_1}))=q_A\circ f_A\circ ass_{A_1}=q_A\circ g_A\circ ass_{A_1}=$

$=Sem(q)_{C_{T}g_T(t)}(Sem(g)_{C_{Tt}}(ass_{A_1}))$

We show the universal property of (Sem(NS),Sem(q)).

Let be $h\in CNg(Sem(NS_2,A_2),N')$ with $N'=(P',T',C_P',C_T',Pre',Post')$, $h=(h_P,h_T,h_{C_P},h_{C_T})$ and $h\circ Sem(f)=h\circ Sem(g)$.

Let $Sem(NS,A)=(P,T,C_{P_{sem}},C_{T_{sem}},Pre_{sem},Post_{sem})$ be the semantics of (NS,A) with $P=coker(P_1 \rightrightarrows P_2)$, $T=coker(T_1\rightrightarrows T_2)$, $C_{P_{sem}}p=A_{sort(p)}$ $\forall p\in P$ and $C_{T_{sem}}t=\{ass_A\in[Var(t),A] \mid \underline{ass}_A(L)=\underline{ass}_A(R)\ \forall(L,R)\in eqns(t)\}$ $\forall t\in T$. We have the following commutative diagram where $\Psi:Sem(NS,A)\rightarrow N'$ is defined as follows:

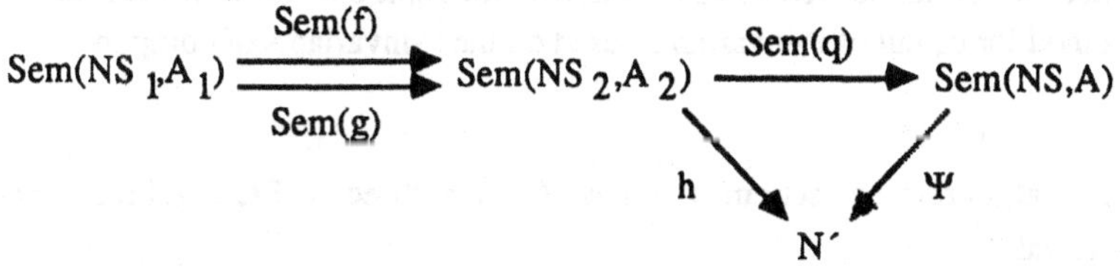

$\Psi_P(q_P(p))=h_P(p)$ $\forall p\in P_2$, $\Psi_T(q_T(t))=h_T(t)$ $\forall t\in T_2$,

$\Psi_{C_{P}q_P(p)}:A_{sort(p)}\rightarrow C_P'h_P(p)$ with $\Psi_{C_{P}q_P(p)}(q_A(a))=h_{C_{Pp}}(a)$ $\forall p\in P_2, a\in A_2$,

$\Psi_{C_{T}q_T(t)}:\{q_A\circ ass_{A_2}\in[Var(q_T(t)),A] \mid (q_A\circ\underline{ass}_{A_2})(L)=(q_A\circ\underline{ass}_{A_2})(R)\ \forall(L,R)\in eqns(q_T(t))\}$

$\rightarrow C_T'h_T(t)$ with $\Psi_{C_{T}q_T(t)}(q_A\circ ass_{A_2})=h_{C_{Tt}}(ass_{A_2})$ $\forall t\in T_2, ass_{A_2}\in C_{T2}t$.

The welldefinedness of Ψ is valid because it holds $h\circ Sem(f)=h\circ Sem(g)$.

Ψ is an CNg-morphism because we have:

$\Psi_P^{\oplus}(Pre_{sem}(1_{q_T(t)},q_A\circ ass_{A_2}))=$

$=\Psi_P^{\oplus}(Pre_{sem}(Sem(q)_T^{\oplus}(1_{t,ass_{A_2}})))=\Psi_P^{\oplus}(Sem(q)_P^{\oplus}(Pre_{2sem}(1_{t,ass_{A_2}})))=$

$=\Psi_P^{\oplus}(Sem(q)_P^{\oplus}(\underline{ass}_{A_2}{}^{\oplus}(Pre_2(1_t))))=$

$=\Psi_P^{\oplus}(Sem(q)_P^{\oplus}(\underline{ass}_{A_2}{}^{\oplus}(\Sigma_{p\in P_2}\Sigma_{\underline{t}\in T_{OP}(X)} Pre_2(1_t)(p)(\underline{t})\cdot 1_{p,\underline{t}})))=$

$=\Psi_P^{\oplus}(Sem(q)_P^{\oplus}(\Sigma_{p\in P_2}\Sigma_{\underline{t}\in T_{OP}(X)} Pre_2(1_t)(p)(\underline{t})\cdot 1_{p,\underline{ass}_{A_2}(\underline{t})}))$

$=\Psi_P^{\oplus}(\Sigma_{p\in P_2}\Sigma_{\underline{t}\in T_{OP}(X)} Pre_2(1_t)(p)(\underline{t})\cdot 1_{Sem(q)_P(p),Sem(q)_{C_P}(\underline{ass}_{A_2}(\underline{t}))})=$

$=\Psi_P^{\oplus}(\Sigma_{p\in P_2}\Sigma_{\underline{t}\in T_{OP}(X)} Pre_2(1_t)(p)(\underline{t})\cdot 1_{q_P(p),q_A(\underline{ass}_{A_2}(\underline{t}))})=$

$=\Sigma_{p\in P_2}\Sigma_{\underline{t}\in T_{OP}(X)} Pre_2(1_t)(p)(\underline{t})\cdot 1_{\Psi_P(q_P(p)),\Psi_{C_P}(q_A(\underline{ass}_{A_2}(\underline{t})))}=$

$=\Sigma_{p\in P_2}\Sigma_{\underline{t}\in T_{OP}(X)} Pre_2(1_t)(p)(\underline{t})\cdot (1_{h_P(p),h_{C_P}(\underline{ass}_{A_2}(\underline{t}))})=$

$=\Sigma_{p\in P_2}\Sigma_{\underline{t}\in T_{OP}(X)} Pre_2(1_t)(p)(\underline{t})\cdot h_P^{\oplus}(1_{p,\underline{ass}_{A_2}(\underline{t})})=$

$=h_P^{\oplus}(\Sigma_{p\in P_2}\Sigma_{\underline{t}\in T_{OP}(X)} Pre_2(1_t)(p)(\underline{t})\cdot (1_{p,\underline{ass}_{A_2}(\underline{t})}))=$

$=h_P^{\oplus}(\underline{ass}_{A_2}{}^{\oplus}(Pre_2(1_t)))=h_P^{\oplus}(Pre_{2sem}(1_{t,ass_{A_2}}))=Pre'(h_T^{\oplus}(1_{t,ass_{A_2}}))=$

$=Pre'(1_{h_T(t),h_{C_{Tt}}(ass_{A_2})})=Pre'(1_{\Psi_T(q_T(t)),\Psi_{C_{Tq_T(t)}}(q_A\circ ass_{A_2})})=$

$=Pre'(\Psi_T^{\oplus}(1_{q_T(t),q_A\circ ass_{A_2}}))$ for all $t\in T_2$, $ass_{A_2}\in C_{T_{2Sem}t}$.

It is trivial to see that $\Psi\circ q=h$ and that Ψ is unique.
It is easy to check that Sem preserves coproducts and the theorem is proved.

qed.

The next corollary gives results about the semantics of an algebraic high-level net interpreted in an algebra which is a pushout of algebras, and about the semantics of a pushout of schemes for a given algebra. In both cases, the semantics of the result is the composition of the corresponding semantics. We combine also these results with the right-exactness of the functor PInv and become a method for calcul of P-invariants based on the P-invariants of components.

<u>Corollary 3.2.3</u>
Let N, N_1, N_2 be three algebraic net schemes and A, A_1, A_2 three SPEC-algebras. The following statements are valid :

(i) $Sem(N,A_1 \sqcup_A A_2)=Sem(N,A_1)\sqcup_{Sem(N,A)} Sem(N,A_2)$.

(ii) $Sem(N_1 \sqcup_N N_2,A)=Sem(N_1,A)\sqcup_{Sem(N,A)} Sem(N_2,A)$.

(iii) $PInv(Sem(N,A_1 \sqcup_A A_2))=PInv(Sem(N,A_1))\sqcap_{PInv(Sem(N,A))} PInv\ (Sem(N,A_2))$.

(iv) $PInv(Sem(N_1 \sqcup_N N_2,A))=PInv(Sem(N_1,A))\sqcap_{PInv(Sem(N,A))} PInv\ (Sem(N_2,A))$.

<u>Proof</u>: The existence of pushouts is insured by 3.2.1 and 2.1.6. All equalities result of theorems 3.2.2 and 2.2.3 qed.

In the above corollary we have cosidered only the P-invariants of the semantics, but we did not compare the syntactical invariants of an algebraic net scheme. The syntactical invariants are defined in /Re90/ or /Hu89/. If we "interprete" the syntactical invariants into an arbitrary algebra, we do not become all P-invariants of the semantics, only if they are compatible with term equivalence relation induced by the specification (see /Re90/ or /Hu89/).

Example 3.2.4

We decompose the net modelling the producers/consumer problem in two nets. The first one represents the processes producers while the second one represents the process consummer. The previous net scheme is the pushout of these two nets having place p (communication medium) in common. This is shown on the following diagram :

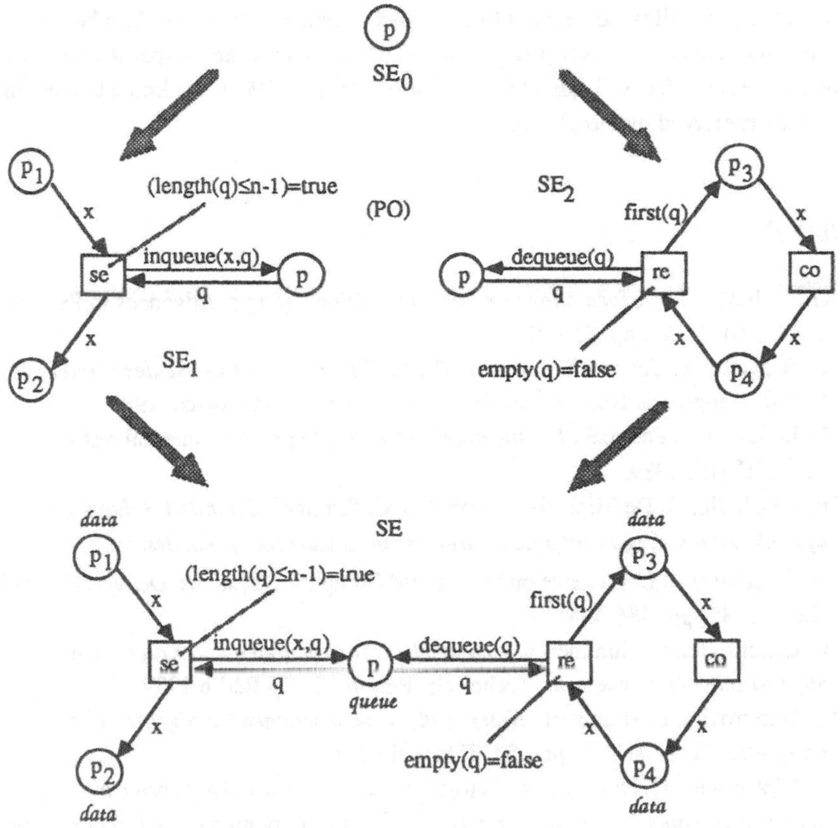

The algebraic net scheme SE is the pushout of SE_1 and SE_2 over SE_0.

4. Conclusions

In this paper, we defined several categories of coloured nets, algebraic net schemes and algebraic high-level nets. We proved that the composition/decomposition of algebraic net schemes and high-level nets using categorical constructions is compatible with semantics. We have defined for coloured nets the T- and P-invariants as functors and we have shown that the invariants functors preserve the composition/decomposition, such that the invariants can be calculated in a modular way. We have combined the results about invariants for coloured nets with those about compatibility of semantics with composition. We have shown that also for algebraic high-level nets the P-invariants of semantics can be caculated modulary.

We plan to give another semantics for algebraic high-level nets (see /BJP89/, /DHP90/), denoted normed semantics. We also foresee to study new semantics which would map an algebraic net scheme to the minimal covering graph of its skeleton and its normed scheme. This last idea, if fruitful, will allow to decide of the normed schemes properties. Another research direction is to study the relation between categorical properties and net properties (non quasi-livenes, boundedness of places, deadlocks, termination; see /DHP90/). We know that the most net properties are preserved by morphisms.

5. Bibliography

/Be86/ G.Berthelot : *Transformations and decompositions of nets*. Advances in Petri Nets 1986, LNCS 254, pp. 359-376.

/BJP89/ G. Berthelot, C. Johnen, L.Petrucci : *PAPETRI : Poste d'Analyse des réseaux de PETRI*. Rapport de Recherche LRI 527, Université de Paris-Sud, 1989.

/BP89/ G. Berthelot, L. Petrucci : *Putting algebraic nets into practice*. Internal report CEDRIC-IIE, 1989.

/DDPS85/ F. De Cindio, G. De Michelis, L. Pomello, C. Simone : *Exhibited-Behaviour equivalence and Organizational abstraction in concurrent system design.* 5th International Conference on Distributed Computing Systems, Denver, Colorado, IEEE, 1985, pp. 486-495.

/DiHu89a/ C. Dimitrovici, U. Hummert : *Semantische Konstruktionen und Kategorien algebraischer Netzschemata.* Technische Report 12, TU Berlin 1989.

/DiHu89b/ C. Dimitrovici, U. Hummert : *Kategorielle Konstruktionen für algebraische Petrinetze.* Technische Report 23, TU Berlin 1989.

/DHP90/ C. Dimitrovici, U. Hummert, L. Petrucci : *The Properties of Algebraic Net Schemes in Some Semantics*. Report of the 11th international conference on petri nets, France 1990).

/EHH89/ H. Ehrig, A. Heise, U. Hummert : *Algebraic High-Level Nets with Capacities*. Technische Report, TU Berlin 1989.

/EM85/ H. Ehrig, B. Mahr : *Fundamentals of Algebraic Specifications 1*. Springer Verlag 1985.

/EM90/ H. Ehrig, B. Mahr : *Fundamentals of Algebraic Specifications 2*. Springer Verlag 1990.

/Hu87/ U. Hummert : *High-Level-Netze*. Technische Report 10, TU Berlin 1987.

/Hu89/ U. Hummert : *Algebraische Theorie von High-Level-Netzen*. Doktorarbeit, TU Berlin 1989.

/Je81/ K. Jensen : *Colored Petri Nets and the Invariant Method*. TCS 14, 1981, pp. 317-336.

/Je87/ K. Jensen : *Colored Petri Nets*. Advances in Petri Nets 1986, LNCS 254, 1987, pp. 248-299.

/KM77/ M.I. Kargapolow, Ju.I. Merzljakow: *Fundamentals of the Theory of Groups*, Springer Verlag New York Heidelberg Berlin 1977.

/ML72/ S. MacLane : *Categories for the Working Mathematician*. Springer Verlag, 1971.

/MM88/ J. Meseguer, U. Montanari : *Petri Nets Are Monoids*. Stanford Research Institute, Report SRI-CSL-88-3, 1988.

/MV86/ G. Memmi, J. Vautherin : *Analysing Petri Nets by the Invariant Method*. Rapport de Recherche LRI 319, Université de Paris-Sud, 1986.

/Re85a/ W. Reisig : *Petri Nets*. Springer Verlag, 1985.

/Re85b/ W. Reisig : *Petri Nets with Individual Tokens*. TCS 41, 1985, pp. 185-213.

/Re90/ W. Reisig : *Petri Nets and Algebraic Specifications*. Tech. Rep. of Technische Universität München, 342/1/90.

/RV87/ W. Reisig, J. Vautherin : *An Algebraic Approach to High Level Petri Nets*. Proc. 8th Workshop on Applications and Theory of Petri nets, Zaragoza 1987, S. 51-72.

/Va85/ J. Vautherin : *Un modèle algébrique, basé sur les réseaux de Petri, pour l'étude des systèmes parallèles*. Thèse de doctorat d'ingénieur, Université de Paris-Sud, 1985.

/Va87/ J. Vautherin : *Parallel Systems Specifications with Colored Petri Nets and Algebraic Specifications*. Advances in Petri Nets 1987, LNCS 266, p. 293-308.

/Wi87/ G. Winskel : *Petri Nets, Algebras, Morphisms, and Compositionality*. Inf. and Comp. 72, 1987, pp. 197-238.

6. Appendix: categorical notions

In this appendix we reproduce like in /ML72/ the categorical notions which are used in this paper. We define only the notion of category without doing set theoretical considerations (see for discussion /ML72/ chapter 1).

Definition 6.1 (category)
A *category* **C** consists of a class *objects* C,D,E,..., a class of *arrows* f,g,h,..., two operations dom and codom, which associate with each arrow f an object of **C** (both operations on f are indicated by displaying f as an actual arrow f:C→D), an identity, which assigns to each object C an arrow 1_C :C→C, and a composition, denoted with o, which assigns to each pair (f,g) with dom(g)=codom(f) their composite gof. All these operations satisfy the following equations:

ho(gof)=(hog)of (associativity)

$1_D$of=f and fo1_C=f (unit laws).

The arrows are called *morphisms*. A category is called *small* if the classes of objects and morphisms are sets.

It is obviously that each small category can be represented as a graph, called also diagram. The identities are not represented.

Definition 6.2 (functor)
A *functor* T: $\mathbf{C}\to\mathbf{D}$ consists of two suitably related functions: the *object function*, which assigns to each object C of **C** an object T(C) of **D** and the *arrow function* which assigns to each arrow f:C→D of **C** an arrow T(f):T(C)→T(D) of **D**, in a such way that $T(1_C)=1_{T(C)}$ and T(gof)=T(g)oT(f). Such a functor is called *covariant* and if it changes the composition order of morphisms then it is called a contravariant.

Definition 6.3 (small-complete and -cocomplete categories)
Let **C** be a category.

(1) Let **I** be a small category and T:**I**→**C** be a covariant functor. A *limit* of T consists of an object C of **C** together with a family of morphisms $\{p_i:C\to T(i)\}_{i\in I}$ such that the following conditions are satisfied:
   a) for each f:i→j in **I** $T(f)op_i=p_j$ and
   b) for each D of **C** together with a family of morphisms $\{t_i:D\to T(i)\}_{i\in I}$ which satisfy the condition a), i.e., for each f:i→j in **I** $T(f)ot_i=t_j$, there is a unique morphism t:D→C in **C** such that $p_i ot=t_i$ for each i of **I**.

(2) The notion of colimit is defined dual, i.e., the arrows direction will be changed.

(3) **C** is called *small-complete* (*-cocomplete*) if every functor T:**I**→**C** to **C** from a small category **I** has a limit (colimit). We call shortly such categories as complete or cocomplete. **C** is called *finitely complete* (*cocomplete*) if every functor T:**I**→**C** to **C** from a finite category **I** has a limit (colimit).

Definition 6.4 (special limits and colimits) Let **C** be a category.

(1) A limit, respectively colimit of every functor to **C** defined on the (finite or infinite) diagram •• • is called (finite or infinite) *product*, respectively *coproduct*. For the denotation of products or coproducts, we use the symbols Π, respectively ∐. In the category **Ab** of abelian groups we denote the coproducts with the symbol ⊕.

(2) A limit of every functor to **C** defined on the below diagram is called *pullback*.

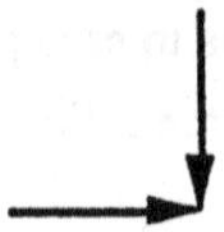

For a such diagram (A in the corner) we denote with $B\Pi_A C$ the pullback.

(3) A colimit of every functor to **C** defined on the below diagram is called *pushout*.

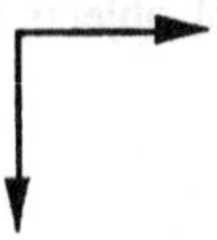

For a such diagram (A in the corner) we denote with $B \sqcup_A C$ the pushout.

(4) A limit, respectively colimit of every functor to **C** defined on the following diagram $\rightrightarrows$ is called *equalizer*, respectively *coequalizer* of the corresponding pair of morphisms of **C**. In the category **Ab** of abelian groups, the equalizer of a pair $(f,g:G \to H)$ coincides with the set $\ker(f-g)=\{x\in G \mid (f-g)(x)=0\}$.

Theorem 6.5 (about completness and cocompletness)

(i) A category is small-complete iff it has arbitrary products and equalizers for arbitrary pairs.

(ii) A category is small-cocomplete iff it has arbitrary coproducts and coequalizers.

Definitions 6.6 (left- and right-exactness)

A functor T: $\mathbf{C} \to \mathbf{D}$ is called left- (right-) exact if it transforms finite limits (colimits) of **C** into limits (colimits) of **D**.

Theorem 6.7 (about exact functors)

A functor is (right) left-exact iff it preserves finite (co-) products and (co-) equalizers.

A MATCH OPERATION
FOR RULE-BASED MODULAR SYSTEM DESIGN

Hartmut Ehrig
Technische Universitat Berlin
FB 20 Informatik
Franklinstr. 28/29
W - 1000 Berlin 10 Germany

Francesco Parisi-Presicce
Universita' degli Studi - L'Aquila
Dipartimento di Matematica
Via Vetoio - Loc. Coppito
I - 67100 L'Aquila Italy

ABSTRACT

The theory of algebraic module specifications treats the interconnection mechanisms for modular system design as operations on modules, the basic ones being composition, union and actualization. Here we introduce yet another operation on module specifications which, under suitable conditions, allows to "compose" two module specifications after specifying only a subpart common to the import of one and the export of the other one. This operation, which generalizes the basic ones, is used in the rule-based approach to the design of modular systems, recently introduced by the second author. In this approach, sequences of derivations which use the interfaces of a given set of modules can be realized by applying the match operation to the modules employed in the derivation.

1.INTRODUCTION

Algebraic methods for the specification of abstract data types have been proposed almost 20 years ago and have produced a number of similar approaches, distinguished by the choice of the semantics, and a number of extensions ([COMP89]). Some of the variations involved the form of the specifications (from equational to conditional, with or without logical constraints), others were aimed at developing structuring techniques (in particular the concepts of parameterization and parameter passing) to facilitate the gradual definition of complex specifications.

The algebraic approach has been adopted for the formal specification of complex software systems with generic reusable components. The "building blocks" of such systems are algebraic module specifications ([EW85], [BEPP87], [EM90]) which combine the notions of parameterization, implementation and information hiding. An algebraic module specification consists of four algebraic specifications (and four specification morphisms relating them) : the import interface, describing the data type needed by the module to operate, an export interface, describing the data type produced and made available to the outside (anything else is hidden), a parameter part shared by the interfaces which can be instantiated with a data type, and a body part which describes how the export interface is implemented using the import interface. The semantics of the module is a (functorial) transformation from models of the import interface to models of the export interface.

A system of interconnections allows the development of a large software system in a stepwise manner. The interconnections are viewed as operations on module specifications and the basic ones are union, composition and actualization ([BEPP87]). In each case, the resulting module is syntactically and semantically correct if the arguments of the operations are and the resulting semantics can be expressed explicitly in terms of those of the arguments ([EM90]).

The match operation introduced in this paper also guarantees the correctness of the result and the compositionality of its semantics. Furthermore, it can be taken as *the* basic interconnection of modules since, as it is shown in the next section, composition, actualization and a simplified kind of union can be seen as special cases of the match operation.

The problem of designing a modular system with given overall import and export interfaces using a set of predefined modules, has been tackled by the second author in [PP89] and [PP90b] where a rule-based approach is proposed. The approach is based on the fact that the only parts of a module specification which are visible to the system designer are the export and import interfaces and their shared parameter part, and that this triple of specifications can be seen as a production or a rewrite rule. If a set of predefined modules is represented by their interfaces, viewed as productions, then the existence of an interconnection of these modules with a given import INIT and a given export GOAL is reduced to the problem of transforming INIT into GOAL using the productions. The order and the way the productions are applied gives the needed interconnection. In previous papers ([PP89], [PP90a]) it has been shown how particular types of derivation sequences can be translated into a modular system obtained by using only composition, union with respect to a shared parameter part and actualization on the modules realizing the productions. The match operation introduced here provides the missing link which allows to translate ANY derivation sequence which transforms INIT into GOAL into a modular design.

2. THE MATCH OPERATION ON MODULES

In this section, we first review briefly the notions of algebraic specification and of module specification referring the reader to [EM85] and [EM90], respectively, for details and additional examples. After discussing a simple special case, we introduce the new operation and show that it leads to a syntactically and semantically correct new module. Furthermore we will show how its semantics can be expressed directly in terms of those of the argument modules. For simplicity of presentation, only the basic algebraic case is treated here. It can be extended to the case of modules with constraints ([EFPB86]) and over more general institutions ([EHKP90]).

2.1 Definition (Algebraic Specifications and Morphisms)

An *algebraic specification* SPEC is a triple (S, OP, E) where S is a set of sorts, OP a set of operator symbols and E a set of (universally quantified positive conditional) equations over the signature (S,OP)=Sig(SPEC).
The set of equations over a signature Σ=(S,OP) is denoted by Eqn(S,OP).

A *specification morphism* f : SPEC1$\rightarrow$ SPEC2 is a triple of functions (f_S, f_{OP}, f_E) where f_Σ=(f_S, f_{OP}) : $\Sigma1 \rightarrow \Sigma2$ is a signature morphism and f_E : E1 $\rightarrow$ E2 is the obvious restriction to the equations in E1 of the unique morphism $f_\Sigma{}^{\#} : T_{\Sigma1}(X) \rightarrow T_{\Sigma2}(X)$ induced by f_Σ.
Given a SPEC=(S,OP,E), a *SPEC-algebra* A consists of a collection of domains $\{A_s : s\in S\}$ and operations $\{N_A : A_{s1} \times ... \times A_{sn} \rightarrow A_s \mid N : s1 ... sn \rightarrow s \in OP\}$ satisfying the properties in E. A *SPEC-homomorphism* h : A $\rightarrow$ B is a family of functions $h_s : A_s \rightarrow B_s$ ($s\in S$) such that $h_s(N_A(a1, ..., an)) = N_B(h_{s1}(a1), ..., h_{sn}(an))$. The category of SPEC-algebras and SPEC-homomorphisms is Alg(SPEC). Each specification morphism f : SPEC1 $\rightarrow$ SPEC2 defines a *forgetful functor* V_f: Alg(SPEC2) $\rightarrow$ Alg(SPEC1) given by $V_f\,(A2)_s = A2_{\,f_s(s)}$ and $N_{V_f(A2)} = f_{OP}(N)_{A2}$ and its left adjoint, the *free functor* F_f : Alg(SPEC1) $\rightarrow$ Alg(SPEC2).

2.2 FACT (Pushouts in CATSPEC)

The category CATSPEC of algebraic specifications and specification morphisms (with the obvious composition and identity morphism)has pushouts ([EM85]) which can be constructed as follows. Given specification morphisms fj : SPEC0 $\rightarrow$ SPECj , j=1,2, the pushout object SPEC3 is constructed componentwise by defining

- S3 = S1 $+_{S0}$ S2 (pushout of $f1_S$ and $f2_S$ in the category SET of sets)
- OP3 = OP1 $+_{OP0}$ OP2 (pushout object of $f1_{OP}$ and $f2_{OP}$ in SET)
- E3 = E1 $+_{E0}$ E2 (pushout object of $f1_E$ and $f2_E$ in SET)

SPEC3 is denoted by SPEC1 $+_{SPEC0}$ SPEC2 and SPEC1 is the pushout complement of SPEC2 in SPEC3 with respect to SPEC0.

While given f1 and f2 as above, SPEC1 $+_{SPEC0}$ SPEC2 always exists, the pushout complement SPEC1 = SPEC3 $-_{SPEC0}$ SPEC2 need not always exist given the morphisms f2 and g2 ([PP89]). Intuitively, the specification SPEC1 should contain all the sorts and operations of SPEC3 not contained in SPEC2 and the sorts and operations of SPEC0, i.e.,
S1 = S3 - $g2_S$(S2 - $f2_S$(S0)) and OP1 = OP3 - $g2_{OP}$(OP2 - $f2_{OP}$(OP0)).

Some conditions (such as "the sorts of each $N \in OP1$ must be in $S1$") must be satisfied for $(S1,OP1)$ to be a well defined signature. Similarly the obvious definition of $E1$ is $E3 - g2_E(E2 - f2_E(E0))$ and again to have a well defined specification $SPEC1 = (S1,OP1,E1)$, the equations in $E1$ cannot contain operator symbols not in $OP1$. We now formally state a necessary and sufficient condition for a pushout complement to exist.

2.3 Theorem (Gluing Condition)

If $f2 : SPEC0 \to SPEC2$ and $g2 : SPEC2 \to SPEC3$ are SPEC-morphisms and

$ID(g2)_S = \{s \in S2 : g2_S(s) = g2_S(s') \text{ for some } s' \in S2,\ s' \neq s\}$

$ID(g2)_{OP} = \{N \in OP2 : g2_{OP}(N) = g2_{OP}(N') \text{ for some } N' \in OP2,\ N' \neq N\}$

$DANG(g2) = \{s \in S2 : g2_S(s) \in sorts(N) \text{ for some } N \in OP3 - g2_{OP}(OP2)\}$.

Then the existence of $SPEC1$ such that $SPEC3 = SPEC1 +_{SPEC0} SPEC2$ is equivalent to the following three conditions

1) $f2_S(S0) \supset ID(g2)_S \cup DANG(g2)$

2) $f2_{OP}(OP0) \supset ID(g2)_{OP}$

3) $Eqn(S1,OP1) \supset E3 - g2_E(E2 - f2_E(E0))$

Note that SPEC1 need not be unique unless f2 is injective.

2.4 Definition (Module Specification)

An *algebraic module specification* MOD consists of four algebraic specifications (PAR, EXP, IMP, BOD) and four specification morphisms i, e (both injective), s and v satisfying

a) (syntactical correctness) the following diagram commutes

$$\begin{array}{ccc} PAR & \xrightarrow{e} & EXP \\ \downarrow i & & \downarrow v \\ IMP & \xrightarrow[s]{} & BOD \end{array}$$

b) (semantical correctness) the free functor $F_s : Alg(IMP) \to Alg(BOD)$ satisfies $V_s(F_s(A)) = A$ for all IMP-algebras A.

The <u>functorial semantics</u> SEM of MOD is the functor $SEM = V_v \cdot F_s : Alg(IMP) \to Alg(EXP)$.

2.5 Example

As an example of module specification, we give one whose semantics transforms an algebra of strings over a parameter alphabet defined with a binary operation of concatenation into another algebra of strings with two operations to add elements to the left and to the right of a string and adds it to an algebra of sets over the same alphabet.

The module MOD=(PAR, EXP, IMP, BOD) is given by

PAR = <u>sort</u> data

EXP = PAR + <u>sorts</u> string, set
<u>opns</u> CREATE : → set
INSERT : data string → set
NIL : → string
LADD : data string → string
RADD : string data → string
<u>eqns</u> INSERT(d1, INSERT(d2, x)) = INSERT(d2, INSERT(d1, x))

IMP = PAR + <u>sorts</u> string
<u>opns</u> NIL : → string
MAKE : data → string
CONC : string string → string
<u>eqns</u> CONC(NIL, x) = x = CONC(x, NIL)
CONC(x, CONC(y, z)) = CONC(CONC(x, y), z)

BOD = EXP ∪ IMP + <u>eqns</u> INSERT(d, INSERT(d, x)) = INSERT(d, x)
LADD(d, x) = CONC(MAKE(d), x)
RADD(x, d) = CONC(x, MAKE(d))

The specification morphisms i, e, s and v are just inclusions, trivially satisfying the syntactical correctnes condition. The semantical correctness is a consequence of the fact that BOD adds to IMP the sort set and its operations, with which it shares only PAR, and two equations <u>defining</u> new operators. Since the defining equations are explicit (and not recursive) and there are no equations of sort data, the free functor F_S is strongly persistent.

Before introducing the new match operation, which includes as special cases the operations of actualization, composition and union with respect to the parameter part, we briefly describe via an example the simple case of composition with identity matching.

Consider the module specification MOD' = (PAR', EXP', IMP', BOD') where

PAR' = IMP' = <u>sorts</u> data
EXP' = PAR' + <u>sorts</u> string
<u>opns</u> NIL : → string
MAKE : data → string

CONC : string string→ string

<u>eqns</u> CONC(NIL, x) = x = CONC(x, NIL)

CONC(x, CONC(y, z)) = CONC(CONC(x, y), z)

BOD' = EXP' + <u>opns</u> PLUS : string data → string

<u>eqns</u> MAKE(d) = PLUS(NIL, d)

CONC(x, PLUS (y,d)) = PLUS (CONC(x,y), d)

and the specification morphisms v', i', s' and e' are all inclusions.
This module provides as export an algebra of strings, which satisfies exactly the specification of the import of MOD. There is a perfect match between EXP' and IMP, which allows us to 'compose' the modules MOD and MOD' to obtain a new module MOD" = MOD • MOD' whose components are defined as

PAR" = PAR

IMP" = IMP' (= PAR' = PAR)

EXP" = EXP

BOD" = BOD ∪ BOD'

This resulting module transforms any set (IMP"-algebra) into an algebra of strings over that set (EXP-algebra) by first applying the functorial semantics of MOD' and then that of MOD (i.e., SEM" = SEM • SEM') .

The match operation deals with the more general situation where there is not a perfect match between the export E of one module and the import I of another one, but the two specifications overlap in part, say in M. The "unused" part of E (that is, the part of E not in M) becomes part of the overall export interface, while the "unsatisfied" part of I (that is hte part of I not in M) becomes part of the overall import interface. Just as the basic operations, in addition to the module specifications involved, need to specify parameter morphisms (for union) or an interface morphism (for the compositon) or an actual parameter and a parameter passing morphism (for the actualization), the match needs a "parametric part", which consists of a 'subpart' of the import interface of one module and of the export interface of another module and two 'fitting' morphisms. We call such data a <u>matching fork</u> and we formally define it next.

2.6 Definition (Matching Fork)

Given specification morphisms i1 : PAR1 → IMP1 and e2 : PAR2 → EXP2 , a <u>matching fork</u> for i1 and e2 consists of a specification MATCH and two specification morphisms m_I : MATCH→ IMP1 and m_E : MATCH→ EXP2 such that both IMP1 and EXP2 have pushout complements in MSPEC = $IMP1 +_{MATCH} EXP2$ with respect to PAR1 and PAR2 respectively. In other words, there exist specifications ACT1 and ACT2 such that $EXP2 +_{PAR2} ACT2 = EXP2 +_{MATCH} IMP1 = ACT1 +_{PAR1} IMP1$ as in the following diagram

$$\begin{array}{ccccccc} & & & \text{MATCH} & & & \\ & & \swarrow m_E & & m_I \searrow & & \\ \text{PAR2} & \xrightarrow{e2} & \text{EXP2} & & \text{IMP1} & \xleftarrow{i1} & \text{PAR1} \\ h2\downarrow & & & n_E \searrow \quad \swarrow n_I & & & \downarrow h1 \\ \text{ACT2} & & \xrightarrow[a2]{} & \text{MSPEC} & \xleftarrow[a1]{} & & \text{ACT1} \end{array}$$

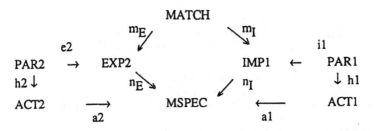

Intuitively, the existence of the pushout complement ACT1 requires that the part which EXP2 adds (in MSPEC) to IMP1 can share only part of PAR1 with IMP1. Also the only items of IMP1 which can be identified in MSPEC (because images by m_I of items in MATCH identified by m_E) must come from PAR1 (i.e., contained in the image of PAR1 under i1). Similarly for the conditions on the existence of ACT2, by symmetry.

2.7 Example

Recalling Example 2.5, let PAR2 = PAR, EXP2 = EXP and e2 : PAR2 → EXP2 the inclusion morphism. Also define

PAR1 =   sort data

IMP1 = **PAR1** +   sorts set, bintree
opns CREATE : → set
INSERT : data set → set
LEAF : data → bintree
LEFT : bintree data → bintree
RIGHT : data bintree → bintree
BOTH : bintree data bintree → bintree
eqns INSERT(d1, INSERT(d2, x))=INSERT(d2, INSERT(d1, x))

with i1: PAR1 → IMP1 also the inclusion.

A matching fork for the morphisms i1 and e2 consists of the specification

MATCH =   sorts data, set
opns CREATE : → set
INSERT : data set → set
eqns INSERT(d1, INSERT(d2, x))=INSERT(d2, INSERT(d1, x))

and the inclusion morphisms m_I : MATCH → IMP1 and m_E : MATCH → EXP2.

To check that the conditions of Definition 2.6 are satisfied, notice that the specification IMP1 can be considered the gluing $\underline{set} +_{\underline{data}} \underline{bintree}$ along $\underline{data}$ of the part defining the sorts and operations for binary trees and that defining sets. Similarly, EXP2 can be viewed as $\underline{string} +_{\underline{data}} \underline{set}$. Hence MSPEC = $(\underline{set} +_{\underline{data}} \underline{bintree}) +_{\underline{set}} (\underline{string} +_{\underline{data}} \underline{set})$ which simplifies to MSPEC = $\underline{string} +_{\underline{data}} \underline{set} +_{\underline{data}} \underline{bintree}$.

It is immediate to see now that ACT2 = bintree and ACT1 = string with inclusion morphisms a1 : ACT1 → MSPEC and a2 : ACT2 → MSPEC.

2.8 Definition (Match Operation)

Given two algebraic module specifications MODj=(PARj,EXPj,IMPj,BODj), j=1,2, and a matching fork M=(MATCH, m_I, m_E) for the morphisms i1 and e2, the match MOD1 $\#_M$ MOD2 of MOD1 and MOD2 via M is the module specification MOD3=(PAR3,EXP3,IMP3,BOD3, e3,i3,s3,v3), where the components, given the specifications ACT1 and ACT2 and the morphisms h1, h2, a1 and a2 as in 2.6, are constructed as follows

1) PAR3 is the pullback object of aj : ACTj → MSPEC, j=1,2, with morphisms p31 : PAR3 → ACT1 and p32 : PAR3 → ACT2

2) EXP3 = EXP1 $+_{PAR1}$ ACT1 is the pushout object of e1: PAR1 → EXP1 and h1 : PAR1 → ACT1 with c1 : ACT1 → EXP3 and e13 : EXP1 → EXP3

3) IMP3 = IMP2 $+_{PAR2}$ ACT2 is the pushout object of i2: PAR2 → IMP2 and h2 : PAR2 → ACT2 with c2 : ACT2 → IMP3 and i23 : IMP2 → IMP3

4) BOD3 = BOD1 $+_{MATCH}$ BOD2 is the pushout object of the morphisms $s1 \circ m_I$: MATCH → BOD1 and $v2 \circ m_E$: MATCH → BOD2 with bj : BODj → BOD3

If we call b3 : MSPEC → BOD3 the unique morphism induced by the universal property of MSPEC such that $b3 \circ n_I = b1 \circ s1$ and $b3 \circ n_E = b2 \circ v2$,

then $$b3 \circ a1 \circ h1 = b3 \circ n_I \circ i1 = b1 \circ s1 \circ i1 = b1 \circ v1 \circ e1 \quad \text{and}$$
$$b3 \circ a2 \circ h2 = b3 \circ n_E \circ e2 = b2 \circ v2 \circ e2 = b2 \circ s2 \circ i2.$$

5) $e3 = c1 \circ p31$: PAR3 → ACT1 → EXP3

6) $i3 = c2 \circ p32$: PAR3 → ACT2 → IMP3

7) v3 : EXP3 → BOD3 is the unique morphism induced by the universal property of EXP3 such that $v3 \circ e13 = b1 \circ v1$ and $v3 \circ c1 = b3 \circ a1$

8) s3 : IMP3 → BOD3 is the unique morphism induced by the universal property of IMP3 such that $s3 \circ i23 = b2 \circ s2$ and $s3 \circ c2 = b3 \circ a2$

The construction is summerized in the following diagram

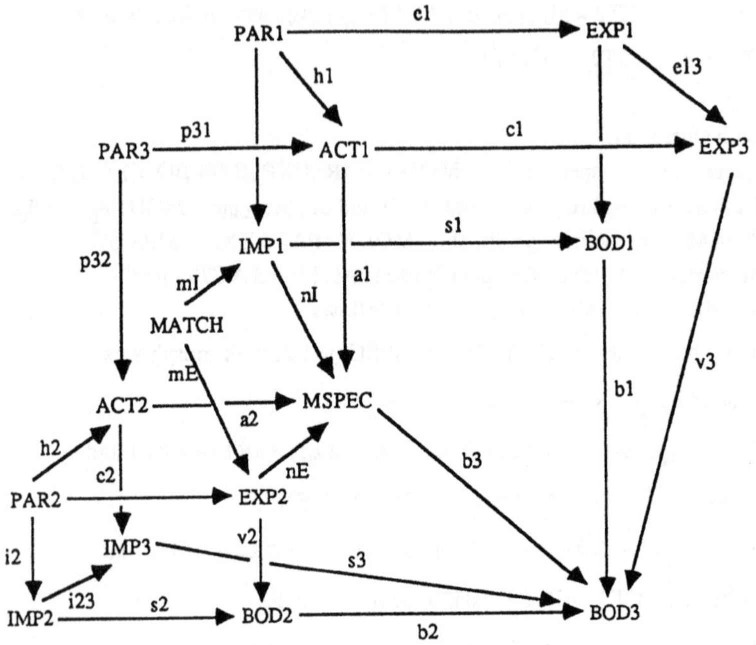

Interpretation

The part that two modules share, through their respective interfaces, is denoted by MATCH. This matching part of the import interface IMP1 and export interface EXP2 is used to glue the two bodies BOD1 and BOD2 : in BOD1, the "matched" subpart of IMP1 is replaced by BOD2. For the interfaces, ACT1 represents the "subpart" of EXP2 not used by the import IMP1 (the part 'used' is called MATCH) and therefore carried unchanged to the export of the resulting module by gluing it to EXP1 to form EXP3. Similarly, ACT2 represents the part of IMP1 not provided for by the export interface of MOD2 and therefore is carried through 'unused' to the import IMP3 of the resulting module by gluing it to IMP2. The specification ACT1 (containing PAR1) is part of EXP3 and represents the part provided by MOD2 not changed by MOD1; similarly ACT2 is part of IMP3 and is not changed by MOD1. Their "intersection" (pullback object of a1 and a2) is the parameter part of the resulting module, the part which is guaranteed (given the semantical correctness) not to change in the transformation form IMP3 to EXP3.

2.9 Example

Let MOD2 be the specification $\hat{MOD}$ of Example 2.5 and let MOD1=(PAR1,EXP1,IMP1,BOD1) be given by the specifications PAR1 and IMP1 of Example 2.7 to which we add

EXP1 = PAR1 + <u>sorts</u> bintree, set
<u>opns</u> LEAF : data → bintree
LEFT : bintree data → bintree
RIGHT : data bintree → bintree
BOTH : bintree data bintree → bintree
NODES : bintree → set

and

BOD1 = EXP1 ∪ IMP1 + <u>opns</u> ADD : set set → set
<u>eqns</u> ADD(CREATE, s) = s
ADD(INSERT(d,x), s) = INSERT(d, ADD(x,s))
NODES(LEAF(d)) = INSERT(d, CREATE)
NODES(LEFT(b,d)) = INSERT(d, NODES(b))
NODES(RIGHT(d,b)) = INSERT(d, NODES(b))
NODES(BOTH(b1,d,b2)) = INSERT(d, ADD(NODES(b1), NODES(b2)))

with the usual inclusion morphisms e2, i2, v2 and s2.
We have already seen a matching fork M for i1 and e2 in Example 2.7.
The match MOD1$\#_M$MOD2 constructed as in Definition 2.8, consists of

PAR3 = <u>**bintree**</u> $\times_{MSPEC}$ <u>**string**</u> = <u>sort</u> data
EXP3 = EXP1 $+_{PAR1}$ **ACT1 = PAR3 +** <u>sorts</u> string, bintree, set
<u>opns</u> LEAF : data → bintree
LEFT : bintree data → bintree
RIGHT : data bintree → bintree
BOTH : bintree data bintree → bintree
NODES : bintree → set
NIL : → string
LADD : data string → string
RADD : string data → string

IMP3 = IMP1 $+_{PAR2}$ **ACT2 = PAR3 +** <u>sorts</u> string, bintree
<u>opns</u> LEAF : data → bintree
LEFT : bintree data → bintree
RIGHT : data bintree → bintree
BOTH : bintree data bintree → bintree
NIL : → string
MAKE : data → string
CONC : string string → string

$$\underline{\text{eqns}} \qquad \text{CONC(NIL, x) = x = CONC(x, NIL)}$$
$$\text{CONC(x, CONC(y, z)) = CONC(CONC(x, y), z)}$$

BOD3 = BOD1 $+_{\text{MATCH}}$ **BOD2 = IMP3** $\cup$ **EXP3 +** <u>opns</u> ADD : set set → set

<u>eqns</u>

ADD(CREATE, s) = s
ADD(INSERT(d,x), s) = INSERT(d, ADD(x,s))
NODES(LEAF(d)) = INSERT(d, CREATE)
NODES(LEFT(b,d)) = INSERT(d, NODES(b))
NODES(RIGHT(d,b)) = INSERT(d, NODES(b))
INSERT(d, ADD(NODES(b1), NODES(b2))) = NODES(BOTH(b1,d,b2))
INSERT(d, x) = INSERT(d, INSERT(d, x))
LADD(d, x) = CONC(MAKE(d), x)
RADD(x, d) = CONC(x, MAKE(d))

2.10 Theorem (Correctness and Compositionality)

The match $MOD1\#_M MOD2$ of correct module specifications MOD1 and MOD2 with respect to the matching fork $M=(MATCH, m_I, m_E)$ is syntactically and semantically correct. Furthermore its semantics SEM3 is given by

$$SEM3 = (SEM1 +_{ID_{PAR1}} ID_{ACT1}) \circ (SEM2 +_{ID_{PAR2}} ID_{ACT2})$$

where with ID_{SPEC} we denote the identity functor on the category Alg(SPEC)

<u>Proof</u>

The syntactical correctness of $MOD1\#_M MOD2$ is straigthforward since
$v3 \circ e3 = v3 \circ c1 \circ p31 = b3 \circ a1 \circ p31 = b3 \circ a2 \circ p32 = s3 \circ c2 \circ p32 = s3 \circ i3.$
The proof of the semantical correctness and the compositionality of the semantics is quite involved if attempted directly. It will instead be a consequence of the correctness and compositionality of the semantics of the basic operations, once we show how to express the match in terms of composition and actualization.

2.11 Theorem (Match as Derived Operation)

Let MODj=(PARj,EXPj,IMPj,BODj), j=1,2, be module specifications, $M=(MATCH, m_I, m_E)$ a matching fork for e2 and i, and ACT1 and ACT2 as in 2.6, viewed as trivial parametrized specifications ACTj → ACTj. Then

$$MOD1\#_M MOD2 = act_{h1}(ACT1, MOD1) \bullet act_{h2}(ACT2, MOD2)$$

<u>Proof</u>

Let $MODj' = act_{hj}(ACTj, MODj)$ for j=1,2. Then

- the parameter of MOD1' • MOD2' is by definition the pullback of the two parameters with respect to the export of MOD2'. But $EXP2' = EXP2 +_{PAR2} ACT2$ = MSPEC and the parameters of MOD1' and MOD2' are ACT1 and ACT2, respectively, and thus their pullback is exactly PAR3

- the export of MOD1'•MOD2' is by definition that of MOD1' which is by definition of actualization $EXP1 +_{PAR1} ACT1 = EXP3$

- the import of MOD1'•MOD2' is that of MOD2' which is $IMP2 +_{PAR2} ACT2 = IMP3$

- finally the body BOD2' of MOD2' is $MSPEC +_{EXP2} BOD2$ and the body BOD1' of MOD1' is $MSPEC +_{EXP1} BOD1$. Hence the body of MOD1'•MOD2' is by definition of composition $BOD2' +_{MSPEC} BOD1' =$

$(BOD2 +_{EXP2} MSPEC) +_{MSPEC} (MSPEC +_{IMP1} BOD1) =$

$[BOD2 +_{EXP2} (EXP2 +_{MATCH} IMP1)] +_{(EXP2 +_{MATCH} IMP1)} [(EXP2 +_{MATCH} IMP1) +_{IMP1} BOD1] =$

$BOD2 +_{MATCH} BOD1$ by commutativity of colimits in Cat(SPEC) (see [PP86]).

Since the morphisms are induced by the universal property of pushouts, the morphisms of $MOD1 \#_M MOD2$ and MOD1' • MOD2' are the same. Notice that MSPEC is at the same time the export interface of $act_{h2}(MOD2,ACT2)$ and the import interface of $act_{h1}(MOD1,ACT1)$.

We can now complete the proof of Theorem 2.10 since both actualization and composition are correctness-preserving operations and the semantics SEMj' of the actualization MODj' = $act_{hj}(ACTj,MODj)$ is given by

$$SEMj' = SEMj +_{ID_{PARj}} ID_{ACTj}$$

In particular, each IMP3-algebra I3 can be decomposed uniquely into the amalgamated sum $I2 +_{P2} A2$ of algebras $I2 \in Alg(IMP2)$, $P2 \in Alg(PAR2)$ and $A2 \in Alg(ACT2)$. To I3 we can apply the semantics SEM2' of MOD2' to obtain the MSPEC-algebra $SEM2'(I2 +_{P2} A2) = SEM2(I2) +_{P2} A2$. This algebra, in turn, can be uniquely decomposed into the amalgamated sum $I1 +_{P1} A1$ with $I1 \in Alg(IMP1)$, $P1 \in Alg(PAR1)$ and $A1 \in Alg(ACT1)$ to which we can apply SEM1' to obtain an EXP3-algebra $E3 = SEM1'(I1 +_{P1} A1) = SEM1(I1) +_{P1} A1$.

Summarizing $SEM3(I3) = SEM1'(SEM2'(I3)) = SEM1'(SEM2(I2) +_{P2} A2) = SEM1'(I1 +_{P1} A1) = SEM1(I1) +_{P1} A1 = E3$.

In some special cases, the match operation reduces to some known operations. The simplest case consists of taking two module specifications MOD1 and MOD2 where IMP1=EXP2 and defining the match M with MATCH=IMP1=EXP2 and identity morphisms for m_I and m_E. The specifications ACT1 and ACT2 coincide with PAR1 and PAR2, respectively and thus

- $EXP3 = EXP1 +_{PAR1} ACT1 = EXP1 +_{PAR1} PAR1 = EXP1$
- $IMP3 = IMP2 +_{PAR2} ACT2 = IMP2 +_{PAR2} PAR2 = IMP2$
- $BOD3 = BOD1 +_{MATCH} BOD2 = BOD1 +_{IMP1} BOD2$
- PAR3 is the pullback object of $PAR1 \rightarrow IMP1$ and $PAR2 \rightarrow EXP2$

But these are exactly the four parts of the composition module of MOD1 and MOD2

Remark 1 If IMP1=EXP2 , then $\quad$ MOD1 $\cdot_{id}$ MOD2 = MOD1 $\#_{IMP1}$ MOD2

The restriction to the identity interface morphism for composition does not impose a loss of generality ([PP86]) because any composition can be rewritten as two compositions with identity.

A more general special case of the match operation allows us to model partial composition, in which only part of the import interface of MOD1 is mapped into the export interface of MOD2. The remaining part of IMP1 is added to the import IMP2 of MOD2 to form the import of the resulting module. As in the definition of the operation, itt is required that the overlap between the mapped and the unmapped parts of IMP1 be preserved by MOD2.

Remark 2 If IMP1 = EXP2 $+_{PAR2}$ ACT2 for some specification ACT2, then

MOD1 $\cdot p_h$ MOD2 = MOD1 $\#_M$ MOD2

where h is the identity on EXP2 and M = (PAR2, PAR2 $\rightarrow$ IMP1 , PAR2 $\rightarrow$ EXP2)

By reversing the roles of IMP1 and EXP2, it is possible to model the partial product of module specifications by using the match operation. In partial product, the part of the interface EXP2 not needed by IMP1 is added to EXP1 to form the export interface of the resulting module.

Remark 3 If EXP2 = IMP1 $+_{PAR1}$ ACT1 for some specification ACT1, then

MOD1 $*p_h$ MOD2 = MOD1 $\#_M$ MOD2

where h is the inclusion of IMP1 into EXP2 and M = (PAR1, PAR1 $\rightarrow$ IMP1, PAR1 $\rightarrow$ EXP2)

Since the match operation can be expressed as a derived operation using actualization, and actualization can be written as union it is no surprise that we can use match to express union with respect to the parameter part.

Remark 4 If PAR1 = PAR2 = PAR , then $\quad$ MOD1 $+_{PAR}$ MOD2 = MOD1 $\#_M$ MOD2

where M = (PAR , e2 : PAR $\rightarrow$ EXP2 , i1: PAR $\rightarrow$ IMP1)

In fact, MSPEC = IMP1 $+_{PAR}$ EXP2 for which it is clear that ACT1 = EXP2, ACT2 = IMP1 and therefore

- EXP3 = EXP1 $+_{PAR1}$ ACT1 = EXP1 $+_{PAR}$ EXP2
- IMP3 = IMP2 $+_{PAR2}$ ACT2 = IMP2 $+_{PAR}$ IMP1
- BOD3 = BOD1 $+_{MATCH}$ BOD2 = BOD1 $+_{PAR}$ BOD2
- PAR3 = the pullback object of PAR $\rightarrow$ IMP1 and PAR $\rightarrow$ EXP2 = PAR

It is also possible to express a simple actualization using the match operation.

Remark 5

If MOD1 = (Act, Act, Act, Act) and M = (PAR, e2 : PAR $\rightarrow$ EXP2, h: PAR $\rightarrow$ Act) then

$$act_h(ACT,MOD2) = MOD1 \#_M MOD2$$

where ACT is viewed as the trivial parameterized specification Act $\rightarrow$ Act.

3. RULE-BASED SYSTEM DESIGN

One of the main uses of the match operation is the design of modular systems based on "replacement rules" which substitute the import interface of a module with the export interface of the same module in a specification. The general realization problem addressed is the following:

> Given two specifications INIT and GOAL and a set LIB of module specifications, construct a module specification whose import and export interfaces are INIT and GOAL, respectively, and built by interconnecting only the modules of the given set.

An approach to solving this problem, introduced in [PP89, PP90] , consists of viewing the interfaces and parameter part of the modules in the library LIB as productions in an algebraic specification grammar [EPP90] and trying, starting from the initial specification INIT, to generate the goal specification GOAL using the productions. If the goal can be generated, the derivation sequence defines an interconnection of the realizations of the productions to produce a module specification whose interfaces are exactly INIT and GOAL. Each derivation is "translated" into an actualization, sequentially independent derivations into a union and sequentially dependent derivations into the match of the module realizing the production used in the derivation.

3.1 Definition (Production and Derivation)

A *SPEC-production* PRO = (IMP $\leftarrow$ PAR $\rightarrow$ EXP) consists of two injective specification morphisms i:PAR $\rightarrow$ IMP and e:PAR $\rightarrow$ EXP . A *direct derivation* from a specification L to a specification R via a SPEC-production PRO, denoted by PRO:L $\Rightarrow$ R, consists of a context specification CON and two pushouts in the category CATSPEC as in the diagram

$$\begin{array}{ccccc} & i & & e & \\ IMP & \leftarrow & PAR & \rightarrow & EXP \\ l\downarrow & & \downarrow c & & \downarrow r \\ L & \leftarrow & CON & \rightarrow & R \\ & j & & d & \end{array}$$

The middle specification PAR represents the part of the specification IMP left unchanged by the production : it provides the boundary between the part to be changed (IMP is replaced by EXP) and the context CON not affected by the production PRO. The production PRO is applicable to the specification L if L can be decomposed into the left hand side IMP of the production and a context (unchanged) specification CON, the two parts "glued" through PAR. The context CON is then glued to the right hand side EXP of PRO via PAR again. Given an occurrence of IMP in L, i.e., a specification morphism l : IMP → L, a context specification need not always exist ([PP89]) unless the specification morphism l satisfies the Gluing Condition of Theorem 2.3 with respect to i : PAR → IMP. If the Gluing Condition is satisfied, then the pushout complement CON exists and, by injectivity of i, it is unique (and so is R).

3.2 Example

The production PRO = (IMP ← PAR → EXP) with the specifications of Example 2.5 is applicable to the specification

L = <u>sorts</u> string, bintree, nat
<u>opns</u> ZERO : → nat
SUCC : nat → nat
LEAF : nat → bintree
LEFT : bintree nat → bintree
RIGHT : nat bintree → bintree
BOTH : bintree nat bintree → bintree
NIL : → string
MAKE : nat → string
CONC : string string → string
<u>eqns</u> CONC(NIL, x) = x = CONC(x, NIL)
CONC(x, CONC(y, z)) = CONC(CONC(x, y), z)

via the "occurrence" morphism l : IMP → L which maps the sort data into the sort nat and the other items by matching their names. The context specification

CON = <u>sorts</u> bintree, nat
<u>opns</u> ZERO : → nat
SUCC : nat → nat
LEAF : nat → bintree
LEFT : bintree nat → bintree
RIGHT : nat bintree → bintree
BOTH : bintree nat bintree → bintree

is then glued via PAR to EXP to produce the resulting specification

R = <u>sorts</u> string, bintree, nat, set
<u>opns</u> ZERO : → nat
SUCC : nat → nat

LEAF : nat → bintree
LEFT : bintree nat → bintree
RIGHT : nat bintree → bintree
BOTH : bintree nat bintree → bintree
NIL : → string
LADD : nat string → string
RADD : string nat → string
CREATE : → string
INSERT : nat set → set
eqns INSERT(n, INSERT(m, x))=INSERT(m, INSERT(n, x))

Productions can be combined to yield other productions whose applicability follows from that of the components. Furthermore, the result of a direct derivation using the composite production is equivalent to an appropriate combination of the results of the individual direct derivations.

3.3 Definition (Matched Production)

Given SPEC-productions PROj= (IMPj ← PARj → EXPj), j=1,2, and a matching fork M=(MATCH, m_I : MATCH → IMP1, m_E : MATCH → EXP2) for the morphisms e2: PAR2 → EXP2 and i1: PAR1 → IMP1, the *matched production* PRO2 $*_M$ PRO1 is the SPEC-production PRO3 = (IMP3 ← PAR3 → EXP3) as in the diagram

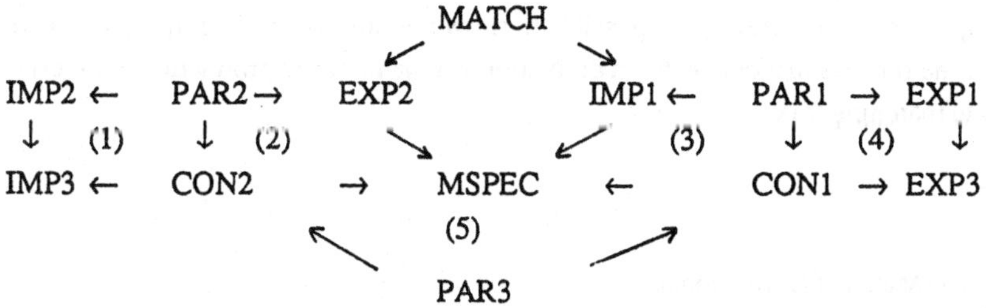

where MSPEC = EXP2 $+_{MATCH}$ IMP1 , (2) and (3) are the pushouts guaranteed by the definition of matching fork in 2.6, (1) and (4) the pushouts used to construct the left and right hand side of the composite production whose gluing part PAR3 is given by the pullback (5).

3.4 Example

Let PRO1= (IMP1 ← PAR1 → EXP1) be the production with the specifications of Example 2.9 and PRO2=(IMP2 ← PAR2 → EXP2) the production with IMP2 = IMP, PAR2 = PAR and EXP2= EXP as in Example 2.5. We have seen in 2.7 that

MATCH = sorts data, set
opns CREATE : → set
INSERT : data set → set
eqns INSERT(d1, INSERT(d2, x))= INSERT(d2, INSERT(d1, x))

with inclusion morphisms is a matching fork for e2 and i1 and

MSPEC = $\underline{\text{string}} +_{\underline{\text{data}}} \underline{\text{set}} +_{\underline{\text{data}}} \underline{\text{bintree}}$

The pushout complement of EXP2 with respect to MSPEC is CON2 = **bintree** and of IMP1 with respect to MSPEC is CON1 = **string**. Hence the matched production PRO2 $*_M$ PRO1 consists of

IMP3 = IMP2 $+_{PAR2}$ CON2 = IMP2 $+_{\underline{\text{data}}}$ $\underline{\text{bintree}}$
PAR3 = $\underline{\text{data}}$
EXP3 = EXP1 $+_{PAR1}$ CON1 = EXP1 $+_{\underline{\text{data}}}$ $\underline{\text{string}}$

Notice that this is exactly the interface of MOD1$\#_M$MOD2 of Example 2.9.

It is possible to replace a sequence of two or more derivations with one direct derivation, using only one production obtained by combining the productions used in the derivation sequence. With an appropriate adaptation of the Concurrency Theorem for Graph Grammars [ER80] to algebraic specifications, it is possible to show that the effect of a sequence of two derivations is the same as that of one direct derivation via the matched production with respect to an appropriate matching fork.

3.5 Theorem (Match of Derivations)

Given a sequence of direct derivations PRO2 : L ⇒ L' and PRO1 : L' ⇒ R, there exists a matching fork M such that PRO2 $*_M$ PRO1 : L ⇒ R.

Conversely, given a matching fork M and a direct derivation PRO2 $*_M$ PRO1 : L ⇒ R, there exists a specification L' such that PRO2 : L ⇒ L' and PRO1 : L' ⇒ R.

Proof

Consider the diagram

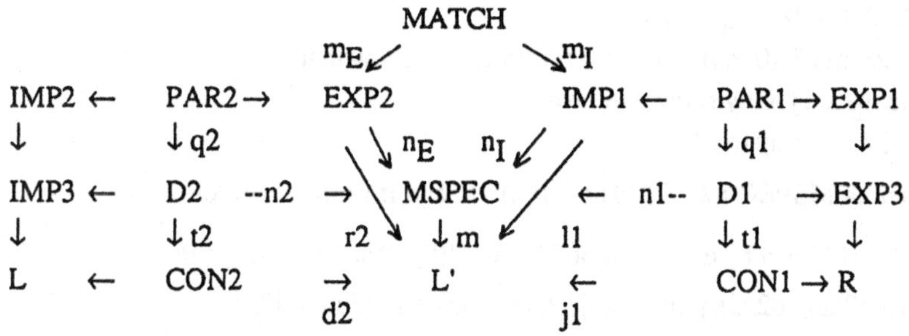

in which MATCH is defined as the pullback object of EXP2 and IMP1 with respect to L' and MSPEC = EXP2 $+_{MATCH}$ IMP1.

By the universal property of pushouts, there is a morphism m : MSPEC $\rightarrow$ L' such that EXP2 $\rightarrow$ MSPEC $\rightarrow$ L' = EXP2 $\rightarrow$ L' and IMP1 $\rightarrow$ MSPEC $\rightarrow$ L' = IMP1 $\rightarrow$ L'. Define D2 as the pullback of MSPEC $\rightarrow$ L' and CON2 $\rightarrow$ L' so that the morphism PAR2 $\rightarrow$ CON2 of the derivation PRO2 : L $\Rightarrow$ L' decomposes uniquely into PAR2 $\rightarrow$ D2 $\rightarrow$ CON2. Defining IMP3 = IMP2 $+_{PAR2}$ D2, the morphism IMP2 $\rightarrow$ L also decomposes into IMP2 $\rightarrow$ IMP3 $\rightarrow$ L. Symmetrically define D1 and EXP3.

<u>Fact1</u> m:MSPEC$\rightarrow$L' is injective up to n2, i.e., if m(x)=m(x') then x,x'$\in$ n2(D2) or x=x'

<u>Pf</u>

a) if x=n_E(y) and x'=n_E(y') for y,y'$\in$ EXP2, then r2(y)=r2(y') and therefore, by definition of L', y = e2(z), y' = e2(z') for z,z'$\in$ PAR2. Thus x = n_E(y) = n_E(e2(z)) = n2(q2(z)) $\in$ n2(D2). Similarly for x'.

b) if m(x)$\in$ L' - r2(EXP2), then m(x) = d2(y) $\in$ d2(CON2) and by definition of D2, x$\in$ n2(D2) and so x'$\in$ n2(D2)

c) if x=n_E(y2) , y2$\in$ EXP2, and x'=n_I(y1) , y1$\in$ IMP1, then r2(y2)=m(x)=m(x')=r1(y1) and thus y2=m_E(z) and y1=m_I(z) for some z$\in$ MATCH. But then x=n_E(y2)=n_E(m_E(z))=n_I(m_I(z))=n_I(y1)=x'.

Since by assumption L'=EXP2 $+_{PAR2}$ CON2 and e2 is injective, then PAR2 is the pullback of EXP2 and CON2 in L'. Since PAR2 $\rightarrow$ EXP2 $\rightarrow$ L'$\leftarrow$ CON2 and D2$\rightarrow$MSPEC$\rightarrow$L'$\leftarrow$ CON2 are both pullbacks, by standard properties of limits, also PAR2 $\rightarrow$ EXP2 $\rightarrow$ MSPEC$\leftarrow$ D2 is a pullback.

Fact2 MSPEC=EXP2 $+_{PAR2}$ D2

Pf by Lemma 3.10 in [PP90a], it is sufficient to show that

a) n2 and n_E are jointly surjective and

b) n_E is injective up to e2

For a), let $x \in$ MSPEC-n2(D2). Then $m(x) \in L'$ and if m(x)=d2(y) for some $y \in$ CON2, then by definition of D2, $x \in$ n2(D2) contrary to the choice of x. Since r2 and d2 are jointly surjective by construction of L', m(x)=r2(z) for some $z \in$ EXP2. Thus $m(n_E(z))=m(x)$. By Fact1, $n_E(z)=x$ or $x \in$ n2(D2).

For b), if $n_E(x)=n_E(x')$, then $r2(x)=m(n_E(x))=m(n_E(x'))=r2(x')$ and thus, since L'=EXP2 $+_{PAR2}$ CON2, $x,x' \in$ e2(PAR2) (since r2 is injective up to e2)

Now standard properties of colimits allow us to conclude that L'=MSPEC $+_{D2}$ CON2.

Define CON as the pullback object of CON2 $\rightarrow$ L' and CON1 $\rightarrow$ L' and PAR3 as the pullback object of D2 $\rightarrow$ MSPEC and D1 $\rightarrow$ MSPEC as in the diagram

$$\begin{array}{ccccc}
D2 & \rightarrow & MSPEC & \leftarrow & D1 \\
 & \nwarrow & & \nearrow & \\
\downarrow & & PAR3 \quad \downarrow & & \downarrow \\
CON2 & \rightarrow & \downarrow \quad L' & \leftarrow & CON1 \\
 & \nwarrow & & \nearrow & \\
 & & CON & &
\end{array}$$

By the universal property of pullbacks, there is a morphism c : PAR3 $\rightarrow$ CON such that PAR3 $\rightarrow$ CON $\rightarrow$ CON2 = PAR3 $\rightarrow$ D2 $\rightarrow$ CON2 and PAR3 $\rightarrow$ CON $\rightarrow$ CON1= PAR3 $\rightarrow$ D1 $\rightarrow$ CON1. In the diagrams

$$\begin{array}{ccccc}
PAR3 & \rightarrow & D2 & \rightarrow & CON2 \\
\downarrow & (1) & \downarrow & (2) & \downarrow \\
D1 & \rightarrow & MSPEC & \rightarrow & L'
\end{array}
\qquad
\begin{array}{ccccc}
PAR3 & \rightarrow & CON & \rightarrow & CON2 \\
\downarrow & (3) & \downarrow & (4) & \downarrow \\
D1 & \rightarrow & CON1 & \rightarrow & L'
\end{array}$$

(1) and (2), and hence (1)+(2), are pullbacks. But by definition of PAR3 and CON, (1)+(2) equals (3)+(4) and hence, since (4) is a pullback, so is (3). By symmetry we also have that PAR3 $\rightarrow$ CON $\rightarrow$ CON2 $\leftarrow$ D2 is a pullback.

Fact3 CON2 = D2 $+_{PAR3}$ CON

Pf It suffices to show ([PP90a], Lemma 3.10) that

a) CON → CON2 and D2 → CON2 are jointly surjective

b) t2 : D2 → CON2 is injective up to PAR → D2

For a), if x∈ CON2-t2(D2) then d2(x)∈ L'-m(MSPEC) and thus d2(x)=j1(y) for y∈ CON1. Hence by construction of CON, x=(CON → CON2)(z) for some z∈ CON.

For b), if t2(x)=t2(x'), then m(n2(x))=m(n2(x')) and therefore, by Fact1, n2(x), n2(x')∈ n1(D1). By definition of PAR3, x,x'∈ (PAR3 → D2)(PAR).

By symmetry, CON1=D1 $+_{PAR3}$ CON.

Now, since composition of pushouts is a pushout, we have

L = IMP3 $+_{D2}$ CON2 = IMP3 $+_{D2}$ (D2 $+_{PAR3}$ CON) = EXP3 $+_{PAR3}$ CON and

R = EXP3 $+_{D1}$ CON1 = EXP3 $+_{D1}$ (D1 $+_{PAR3}$ CON) = EXP3 $+_{PAR3}$ CON

which is equivalent to PRO2 $*_M$ PRO1 : L ⇒ R.

For the converse, consider the diagram for the direct derivation PRO2 $*_M$ PRO1 : L ⇒ R

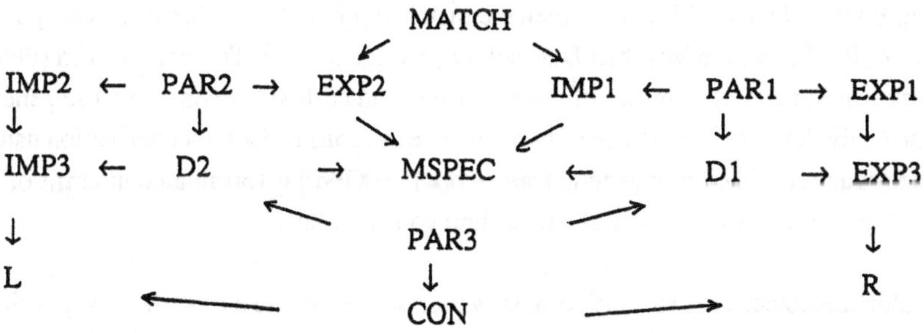

Define CON2=D2 $+_{PAR3}$ CON, CON1=D1 $+_{PAR3}$ CON and L' = MSPEC $+_{D2}$ CON2.

By the universal property of pushouts, there are morphisms

CON2 → L such that	CON → CON2 → L = CON → L
	D2 → IMP3 → L = D2 → CON2 → L
CON1 → L such that	CON → CON1 → R = CON → R
	D1 → EXP3 → R = D1 → CON1 → R
CON1 → L' such that	CON → CON1 → L' = CON → CON2 → L'
	D1 → CON1 → L' = D1 → MSPEC → L'

Then $L = IMP3 +_{D2} CON2$ since in the diagram

$$\begin{array}{ccccc} PAR3 & \rightarrow & D2 & \rightarrow & IMP3 \\ \downarrow & (1) & \downarrow & (2) & \downarrow \\ CON & \rightarrow & CON2 & \rightarrow & L \end{array}$$

(1) and (1)+(2) are pushouts. By symmetry $R = EXP3 +_{D1} CON1$. Hence $PRO2 : L \Rightarrow L'$ using the property that composition of pushouts is a pushout. By the conditions satisfied by $CON1 \rightarrow L'$ in the diagram

$$\begin{array}{ccccc} PAR3 & \rightarrow & D1 & \rightarrow & MSPEC \\ \downarrow & (1) & \downarrow & (2) & \downarrow \\ CON & \rightarrow & CON1 & \rightarrow & L' \end{array}$$

(1)+(2) and (1) are pushouts. Hence so is (2). By the fact that composed pushouts form pushouts, we have

$L' = MSPEC +_{D1} CON1 = (IMP1 +_{PAR1} D1) +_{D1} CON1 = IMP1 +_{PAR1} CON1$ and

$R = EXP3 +_{D1} CON1 = (EXP1 +_{PAR1} D1) +_{D1} CON1 = EXP1 +_{PAR1} CON1$

which is exactly $PRO1 : L' \Rightarrow R$.

This concludes the proof Theorem 3.5.

When EXP2 = IMP1 = MATCH, then the matched production of 3.3 is the composite production of [PP89] and the Match of Derivations result reduces to Theorem 3.11 in [PP90a] (see Remark 1 in Section 2). This proof is a simplified and ad-hoc version of a more general result of the equivalence of a sequence of two direct derivations and a direct derivation using a composite production. The more general framework [EHKP90] is formulated in terms of basic properties of the underlying category and of colimit constructions.

The ultimate objective is to translate a derivation sequence into a modular design using the operations on modules: we must be able to combine the realizations of the productions in a sequence to obtain a realization of the composite production. It is shown in [PP89, PP90a] that the composition of productions is realized by the composition of the realizations and that the amalgamation of productions is realized by the union of the module specifications which realize them. The new operation introduced in this paper is exactly what is needed for the matched production. If Int(MOD) denotes the visible part $IMP \leftarrow PAR \rightarrow EXP$ of MOD, then MOD *realizes* a production PRO if Int(MOD)=PRO.

3.6 Theorem (Realization of Matched Production)

Let MODj=(PARj,EXPj,IMPj,BODj), j=1,2, be module specifications and

M=(MATCH, m_I, m_E) a matching fork for e2:PAR2 → EXP2 and i1:PAR1 → IMP1. Then

$$Int(MOD1 \#_M MOD2) = Int(MOD2) *_M Int(MOD1)$$

Proof

Let MSPEC = EXP2 $+_{MATCH}$IMP1 and let ACT1 and ACT2 be such that MSPEC = EXP2 $+_{PAR2}$ACT2 = ACT $+_{PAR1}$ IMP1 as in Definition 2.6. By the definition (2.8) of Match operation, the interface of MOD1 $\#_M$ MOD2 consists of

- EXP3 = EXP1 $+_{PAR1}$ ACT1
- IMP3 = IMP2 $+_{PAR2}$ ACT2
- PAR3 is the pullback of aj : ACTj → MSPEC

By definition (3.3) of Matched Productions, the left hand side of PRO2 $*_M$ PRO1 is the amalgamation IMP2 $+_{PAR2}$ CON2 of the left hand side of PRO2 and the pushout complement CON2 of EXP2 in MSPEC. Since e2 is injective, the pushout complement is unique and therefore ACT2=CON2. Similarly, the right hand side of PRO2 $*_M$ PRO1 is the amalgamation EXP1 $+_{PAR1}$ CON1 with CON1 = ACT1. Finally, the gluing part of PRO2 $*_M$ PRO1 is by definition the pullback of the contexts CON1 and CON2 with respect to MSPEC, which is exactly the definition of the parameter part of MOD1 $\#_M$ MOD2.

We now have all the ingredients necessary to attain the objective stated at the beginning of this section. We can now design a modular interconnection, which uses only a predefined set of module specifications, to realize a given interface (INIT, GOAL) provided that it is possible to derive GOAL from INIT in a derivation sequence which uses only the interfaces of the predefined modules as productions.

3.7 Theorem (Realization of Derivation Sequences)

Let LIB be a set of module specifications and PROD the set of SPEC-productions corresponding to their interfaces. Given two specifications INIT and GOAL, and a derivation sequence INIT $\Rightarrow^*_{PROD}$ GOAL which uses only the productions in PROD, there exists a module specification MOD such that

a) the import interface of MOD is INIT
b) the export interface of MOD is GOAL
c) MOD is constructed by actualizing an appropriate interconnection of the module specifications in LIB

Proof

Let PROj : $L_j \Rightarrow R_j$, j=1,...,n, be the direct derivations in the derivation sequence INIT $\Rightarrow^*$ GOAL with L_1 = INIT, $L_{j+1} = R_j$ and R_n = GOAL. Also let MODj be the realization of PROj in LIB. For each adjacent pair of derivations (PRO, PRO') in the sequence use the Parallelism Theorem ([PP89]) and the Matching Theorem (3.5 above) as follows

- if (PRO,PRO') are sequentially independent, replace PRO : L $\Rightarrow$ R and PRO' : R $\Rightarrow$ R' with PRO+PRO' : L $\Rightarrow$ R'. The production PRO+PRO' is realized by MOD+MOD'
- if (PRO,PRO') are sequentially dependent, define a matching fork as in 3.5 and replace the sequence of the two direct derivations with a direct derivation $PRO*_M PRO'$: L $\Rightarrow$ R'. The production $PRO*_M PRO'$ is realized by $MOD'\#_M MOD$.

We then obtain one production PRO^* such that PRO^* : INIT $\Rightarrow$ GOAL in one direct derivation and the production PRO^* is realized by a module specification MOD^* constructed using union (+) , match (#) and the modules in LIB.

Since a direct derivation corresponds to actualization ([PP89]), if CON is the context of the direct derivation PRO^* : INIT $\Rightarrow$ GOAL, then MOD = act_c (CON, MOD^*).

4. CONCLUDING REMARKS

In this paper we have introduced the match operation between two module specifications as a generalization of the operation of composition, in that it requires that only part of the import of one module and the export of another module be identified. It has been shown that this operation guarantees the correctness of the result from that of its arguments and that the semantics of the resulting module specification is compositional. Match is not independent of the other operations on module specifications and in fact it is at the same time expressible in terms of composition and actualization (Theorem 2.11) and used to express both composition and actualization (end of Section 2). After reducing the problem of designing a modular system into the problem of deriving a specification in a production system ([PP89]), the match operation was motivated by the need to translate ANY derivation sequence into a modular design : previous results ([PP90a]) were restricted to derivation sequences of a particular type so that the resulting modular system could be built using only disjoint union and composition with identical interfaces, followed by actualization. The result in Theorem 3.7 provides the needed translation from derivations to systems. As there may be several derivation sequences from INIT to GOAL, there may be several modular systems to realize the objective. Some of these systems can be proven equivalent using the equivalence of derivation sequences (which correspond to the compatibility properties of the operations on module specifications).

Sometimes the specification GOAL cannot be generated from INIT using the given productions. A first step toward solving the problem is presented in [PP90b] where a modular system which realizes a subspecification of GOAL must be extended. Unfortunately, the extension ext(MOD) of a module specification does not guarantee the correctness of the result. More work needs to be done in analyzing the extension and the existence of a (correct) module specification, given its interfaces, with or without a predefined functorial semantics.

ACKNOWLDGEMENTS

This research was supported in part by the ESPRIT Basic Research Working Group 3264 and by CNR under "Progetto Finalizzato: Sistemi Informatici e Calcolo Parallelo"

REFERENCES

[BEPP87] E.K.Blum, H.Ehrig, F.Parisi-Presicce, Algebraic Specification of Modules and their Basic Interconnections, J. Comp. System Sci.34, 2/3 (1987) 239-339

[COMP89] B.Krieg-Bruckner, ed., A Comprehensive Algebraic Approach to System Specification and Development, ESPRIT BRWG 3264, Univ. Bremen, Bericht 6/89

[Ehr79] H.Ehrig, Introduction to the Algebraic Theory of Graph Grammars, Lect. Notes in Comp. Sci. 73 (1979) 1-69

[EFPB86] H.Ehrig, W.Fey, F.Parisi-Presicce, E.K.Blum, Algebraic Theory of Module Specifications with Constraint, invited, Proc MFCS, Lect. Notes in Comp. Sci. 233(1986) 59-77

[EHKP90] H.Ehrig, A.Habel, H.-J.Kreowski, F.Parisi-Presicce, Parallelism and Concurrency in High Level Replacement Systems, Tech.Univ.Berlin Technical Report 90-35, submitted

[EM85] H.Ehrig, B.Mahr, Fundamentals of Algebraic Specifications 1: Equations and Initial Semantics, EATCS Monographs on Theoret. Comp. Sci., vol 6, Springer-Verlag 1985

[EM90] H.Ehrig, B.Mahr, Fundamentals of Algebraic Specifications 2: Module Specifications and Constraints, EATCS Monographs on Theoret. Comp. Sci., vol. 21, Springer-Verlag 1990

[EPP90] H.Ehrig, F.Parisi-Presicce, Algebraic Specifications Grammars , to appear in Proc. 4th Intern. Workshop on Graph Grammars, Bremen (FRG), 1990

[ER80] H.Ehrig, B.Rosen, Parallelism and Concurrency of Graph Manipulations, Theoret. Comp. Sci. 11 (1980) 247-275

[EW85] H.Ehrig, H.Weber, Algebraic Specification of Modules, in "Formal Models in Programming" (E.J.Neuhold, G.Chronist, eds.) North-Holland 1985

[PP86] F.Parisi-Presicce, Inner and Mutual Compatibility of Basic Operations on Module Specifications, Proc. CAAP 86, Lect. Notes in Comp. Sci. 214 (1986) 30-44. Full Version : Tech.Univ.Berlin Technical Report 86-06, April 1986

[PP89] F.Parisi-Presicce, Modular System Design applying Graph Grammar Techniques, Proc. 16 ICALP, Lect.Notes in Comp.Sci. 372 (1989) 621-636

[PP90a] F.Parisi-Presicce, Foundations for a Rule-based Design of Modular Systems, to appear in Theor. Comp.Sci.

[PP90b] F.Parisi-Presicce, A Rule-Based Approach to Modular System Design, Proc. 12th Int.Conf.Soft.Eng., Nice(France) 1990, 202-211

TOWARDS OBJECT-ORIENTED ALGEBRAIC SPECIFICATIONS

Martin Große-Rhode

TU Berlin, FB 20, Sekr. FR 6-1
Franklinstr. 28/29, D-1000 Berlin 10
E-mail grosse-rhode@db0tui66.bitnet

Abstract

In order to model some features of object-oriented programming and system design algebraic and projection specifications (= process specifications) are combined in such a way, that declaration and manipulation of objects become basic features of specification. As class definitions algebraic module specifications with import and export interface, parameter and body part are used, with module interconnection mechanisms like union and extension to simulate strict inheritance.

1. Introduction

During the last years object-oriented programming and system design has become a feature of increasing importance. Within the discussion of object-orientedness some concepts evoluted, which , in addition, seem to be appropriate to enhance algebraic specification techniques. The aim of this paper is to integrate these concepts into algebraic specifications. On one hand, this could render algebraic specifications more suitable for larger applications, on the other hand, it would make it possible to support object-oriented programs with a specification with well-defined semantics.

This paper is meant to sketch an approach to 'object-oriented algebraic specifications', which combines algebraic specifications and algebraic process specifications in such a way that objects and dynamic behaviour can be specified.

The concepts from object-oriented programming which shall explicitly be integrated are :

- **objects as states:** Each object has a state; the collection of all object states is the state of the system: thus object-oriented algebraic specification introduces a notion of states.

- **objects for local behaviour:** The dynamic behaviour of objects of one class is specified by a process specification. The dynamic behaviour of the whole system consists of the clean integration of the behaviours of the objects.
Since each object is responsible for the safety of the data it manages, the local behaviours determine the global behaviour.

- **class definitions:** A class defines the type of an object of this class, thus can be considered as an object template. Modular algebraic specifications with import and export interface, parameter and body part serve as class definition in the framework of object-oriented algebraic specifications.

- **class combinators:** Classes can be combined to obtain composed or structured classes. This is modelled by "module operations" which are used to build up large structured modules from smaller components, preserving their semantics.

- **(strict) inheritance:** A class may inherit services and methods from another class. On the class definition level this corresponds to union, import actualization or extension of modules.

A typical problem concerning the first two topics, which often occurs within algebraic specifications is e.g. the following one: The terms *push(m, empty)* and *push(n, push(m, empty))* denote two states of a stack. How can one specify that they denote the states of <u>one</u> stack before and after the execution of the operation *push(n,_)*?

A central issue of 'object-oriented algebraic specifications' will be a syntactic means to identify objects such as stacks.

The approach towards 'object-oriented algebraic specifications' consists of the following integration of algebraic specification and (algebraic) process specification:

The system is separated into **static aspects**, such as
- the data types of the system
- the possible states of the objects
- the services the objects offer;

and **dynamic aspects**, such as
- processes
- execution of operations
- threads of control
- life cycles of objects.

The static aspects are specified by a modular algebraic specification (module specification, for short) as introduced in [EM 90]. The dynamic aspects are specified by an algebraic process specification, by which we mean a projection specification as introduced in [EPBRDG 88a/b] and [Gro 89].

Objects are introduced syntactically as an enrichment of the module specification describing the state of the system, whereby identifiers and initial states of the objects are declared. The semantics of the atomic events (=state changes) of the processes, specified in the projection specification, therefore consists in the syntactical modification of the underlying module specification. The semantics of a whole process can then be described as a tree- or graph-structure of algebras and transformations (atomic events), centered around the objects.

The integration of the two levels will be specified by the integration specification, which is a generic algebraic specification with fixed semantics.

One of main sources for this approach is the "reflexive semantics" as introduced in [GM 87], where the semantics of state changes is defined as a syntactic transformation of the state specification.

In the next section of this paper we will define the notions state specification (algebraic (module) specification), history specification (process specification) and integration specification, which have been described above. For sake of simplicity we only use simple (unstructured) algebraic specifications in that section. It will close with an example.

In the third section of this paper module specifications are considered as class definitions, which should replace the unstructured algebraic specifications in the second section. Furthermore, the interplay between module (state) specifications and histories (resp. processes) as introduced here will be considered.

2. Object-Oriented Algebraic Specification

2.1 State Specification and Atomic Events

To define our concept of 'object-oriented algebraic specification' we start with a simple algebraic specification SPEC = (Σ, E) (see [EM 85]), which serves as an abstract class definition. This means: the algebraic specification defines the abstract data types of the system, containing the admissible states of objects and messages to be interchanged. It does not, however, cover methods, threads of control etc., which belong to the dynamic aspects.

Now objects are introduced into SPEC as follows: The identifier of an object is added as a constant operation symbol $ob\colon \rightarrow sort$ to the specification; its state is defined by an equation $ob = term$ ($term \in T_\Sigma$, a ground term over the signature Σ), which is also added to the specification.

Thus to **create** an object means to add a declaration (*ob:* $\rightarrow$ *sort*) and a defining equation (*ob* = *term*) to the specification. A **manipulation** of an object is specified by replacing its defining equation *ob* = *term* by a new one *ob* = *term'* (*term'*$\in T_\Sigma$, i.e. *term'* does not contain object identifiers), which defines the new state of the object. The evaluation of a term containing the object identifiers thus depends on the current state of the specification. To **delete** an object its declaration and defining equation are removed from the specification.

We have thus defined three **atomic events** for the creation, manipulation and deletion of objects, where the second one assigns a new value to an already defined object. Since the underlying algebraic specification may be identified with the initial state of the system, where no object is defined, we will from now on refer to all algebraic specifications which occur as states as **state specifications.**

Semantically an atomic event corresponds to the distinction of data items: Creation of an object marks out one data item with a new identifier, which can be used for further computations. When the object is manipulated another data item is assigned to its identifier. Deletion of an object means the deletion of its identifier, not the deletion of the data item it denotes.

2.1.1 Example

Given a specification **stack(nat)** of stacks of natural numbers, the creation of a stack-object S1 with initial state *push(0, empty)* corresponds to the following enrichment

stack-state1 = **stack(nat)** +
<u>opns</u> S1: $\rightarrow$ stack
<u>eqns</u> S1 = push(0, empty)

Application of the operation *push(4, S1)* yields

stack-state2 = **stack(nat)** +
<u>opns</u> S1: $\rightarrow$ stack
<u>eqns</u> S1 = push(4, push(0, empty))

Note that the state of S1 in **stack-state2** is a term of **stack(nat)**, which gives the syntax for the admissible states. The operation applied to S1 may, of course, contain S1, i.e. is a term of **stack-state1**. The set of all atomic actions which can be executed in stack-state1 is the set of all (congruence classes) of terms over the signature of stack-state1 of sort stack.

Given a **stack(nat)**-algebra $A_{\mathbf{stack(nat)}}$ we obtain the following sequence of states:

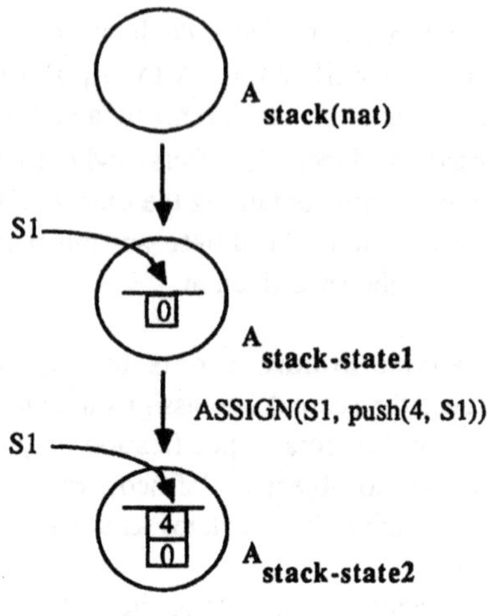

□

For the following complete definition of the atomic events let a large enough set of object identifiers ObId be given.

2.1.2 Definition (State Specification, Atomic Events)

1) Given a specification SPEC = (Σ, E) a <u>state specification</u> SPECSTATE (w.r.t. SPEC) is an enrichment of SPEC by
<u>opns</u> ob_i: → $sort_i$
<u>eqns</u> $ob_i = term_i$ $\quad (i \in I)$
where $ob_i \in$ ObId, $sort_i \in$ Sorts(Σ), $term_i \in T_\Sigma$, $(i \in I)$.

2) Given a state specification SPECSTATE = (ΣS, ES) w.r.t. SPEC = (Σ, E) the three atomic events CREATE, ASSIGN and DELETE are defined by

- CREATE(SPECSTATE, ob, t); ob ∈ ObId, $t \in T_{\Sigma S}$
  enriches SPECSTATE by
  <u>opns</u> ob: → s
  <u>eqns</u> ob = t'
  where *s* is the sort of *t* (which we suppose to be unique) and $t' \in T_\Sigma$ is a term congruent to *t* w.r.t. ES (*t'* is an admissible state).

- ASSIGN(SPECSTATE, ob, t); ob, $t \in T_{\Sigma S}$, ob an object identifier
  replaces the defining equation of *ob* in SPECSTATE by *ob* = *t'*, where $t' \in T_\Sigma$, $t' \equiv_{ES} t$.

- DELETE(SPECSTATE, ob); $ob \in T_{\Sigma S}$ an object identifier
  removes declaration and defining equation of *ob* from SPECSTATE.

Whenever an atomic events occurs as label of an arc between state specifications or if SPECSTATE is given by the context we will omit the first argument SPECSTATE.

□

2.2 Integration Specification

The three atomic events form the basis of the history specification, i.e. they are the actions which are performed by the processes. To specify this the **integration specification** is needed, which, syntactically, introduces CREATE(ob, t), ASSIGN(ob, t) and DELETE(ob) as terms of sort EVENT. Since these terms are always (implicitly) applied to a state specification the first argument SPECSTATE can again be omitted.

2.2.1 Definition (Integration Specification)

Given a specification SPEC = (S, OP, E) the corresponding integration specification INT-SPEC is defined by

INT-SPEC = SPEC +
sorts object-id, EVENT
opns ob_i: → object-id $(i \in I)$
CREATE: object-id s → EVENT
ASSIGN: object-id s → EVENT $(s \in S)$
DELETE: object-id → EVENT

Here the constants ob_i $(i \in I)$ specify a "large enough set" of object identifiers; ASSIGN(ob, t) and DELETE(ob) will be interpreted as empty events, if *ob* is not defined in the current state specification.

□

The definition of the integration specification yields a two stage semantics for the atomic events. On one hand they belong as terms to the initial algebra semantics of INT-SPEC, on the other hand they denote the transformation of state specifications described in 2.1 above.

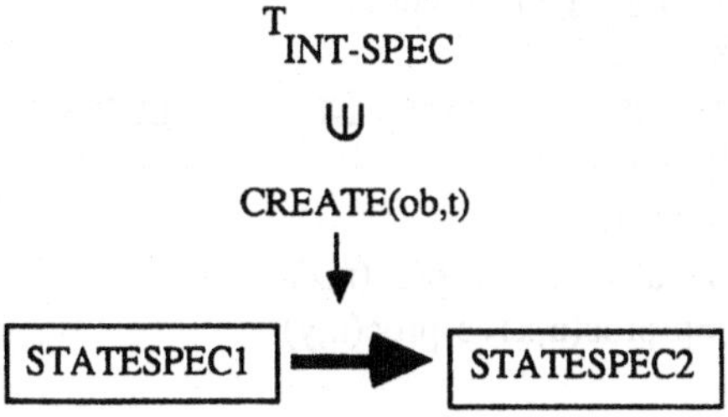

2.3 History Specification

The combination of atomic events to processes, which define life cycles of objects, threads of control, execution of operations etc. is specified in the **history specification.** It enriches the integration specification by operations for sequential, alternative and parallel composition, deadlock, communication etc. Its main sort is PROCESS, which specifies the dynamic behaviour of the system.

As history specifications we use projection specifications (as introduced in [EPBRDG 88a/b], [Gro 89], [GE 90]) which is an algebraic specification method for concurrent distributed systems. A projection specification is an algebraic specification which contains a projection operation p: $\mathbb{N}_1 \times$ PROCESS $\rightarrow$ PROCESS which decomposes a process Q into steps $Q_n := p(n, Q)$. Infinite processes are obtained as limits of sequences $(Q_n)_{n \in \mathbb{N}_1}$ where $p(n, Q_{n+1}) = Q_n$ for all n.

Let us first give an example of a simple projection specification **bpa** with events and processes, sequential and alternative composition. It is a specification of a *basic process algebra* (see [BK 86]). Since the projection has an $\mathbb{N}_1$ argument **bpa** has a **nat1** subspecification.

bpa = **nat1** +
  sorts event, proc
  opns a1,...,an : → event {elementary events}
    c : event → proc {coercion}
    +,·: proc proc → proc {choice,sequence}
    p-event : nat1 event → event {projection of sort event}
    p-proc : nat1 proc → proc {projection of sort proc}
  eqns for all x,y ,z in proc :
    x+x=x (idempotent)
    x+y=y+x (commutative)
    (x+y)+z=x+(y+z) (associative)
    (x·y)·z=x·(y·z) (associative)
    (x+y)·z=x·z+y·z (left distributive)
    for all n in nat1; for all a in event :
    p-event(n,a)=a
    for all n in nat1; for all a in event; for all x, y in proc :
    p-proc(n,c(a))=c(a)
    p-proc(1,c(a)·x)=c(a)
    p-proc(succ(n),c(a)·x)=c(a)·p-proc(n,x)
    p-proc(n,x+y)=p-proc(n,x)+p-proc(n,y)

A model for **bpa**, which is isomorphic to the complete initial **bpa**-algebra (the semantics of **bpa**), can be constructed as follows:

$A = \{a_1,...,a_n\}$ is a set of atomic events.

Process = TREE(A) is the set of all finite and infinite trees. The infinite trees are obtained by a completion of the (term generated) model of finite trees. Its elements are projective sequences of finite trees (projective means $p(n, t_{n+1}) = t_n$ for all n).

The arcs of a tree are labelled by events $a_i \in A$.

$t1 \cdot t2$ hangs t2 at each leaf of t1.

$t1 + t2$ identifies the roots of t1 and t2.

Thus for a history specification **bpa** (or an appropriate extension of **bpa**) can be used, the trees denoting trees of state specification transformations.

Again we have a two stage semantics of PROCESS terms: On one hand they belong as terms to the complete initial algebra semantics of the history specification, on the other hand they denote trees of state specification transformations.

To conclude this section we give an example for an "object-oriented algebraic specification", which specifies a small sample protocol. The example is taken from [WE 88], which motivated much of the ideas presented here.

2.3.1 Example

The sample protocol controls the communication of two partners R and L. A user program U (situated at one site) uses the protocol objects R and L to establish a communication connection that is subsequently used in the transfer of data between R and L.

In order to establish this communication connection the protocol objects R and L perform the following tasks:

(1) If U calls upon the services of L for data transfer L checks on the status variable c_1 continuously until L is available for the desired service (c_1=0).

→ procedure *transfer*

(2) L signals the desire to establish the connection to R (i.e. L issues a call to R).

→ procedure *pl1*

(3) R checks to whether it is ready to provide services for L (i.e. it checks on its status variable c_1 continuously until it is able to provide services to the other partner).

→ procedure *pr1*

(4) R signals its readiness to receive data from L after it becomes relieved from other services by issuing a call to the send-operation of L.

(5) L sends the data D to R (i.e. L issues a call to R and passes D to R).

→ procedure *send*

(6) R accepts the data D from L and terminates the data transfer (i.e. assigns D to the local variable r).

→ procedure *accept*

(7) Acknowledgements will be propagated back to the originator of the data transfer (i.e. returns for calls will be propagated back to U).
(8) The objects L and R will be relieved from the services and made available for new services (i.e. the status variable c_1 will be set to 0).
The whole data transfer task may then be described by the following invocation structure : U--->L--->R

The protocol objects may now be described as follows:

```
    LOC-OBJ (
E   transfer[D,A1,A2]
    pl1[D,A]
    send[A]
    pr1[A]
    accept[I] )
    constraints : pl1;send
                  pr1;accept
    ------------------------------
    proc transfer(D,A1,A2)
    call A1.pl1(D,A2)
B   end transfer

    proc pl1(D,A)
    when c1=0 do c1:=1 end
    I:=D
    call A.pr1(self)
    c1:=0
    end pl1

    proc send(A)
    call A.accept(I)
    end send

    proc pr1(A)
    when c1=0 do c1:=1 end
    call A.send
    c1:=0
    end pr1

    proc accept(I)
    r:=I
    end accept
    ------------------------------
    c1:=0
    I:=0
    r:=0
```

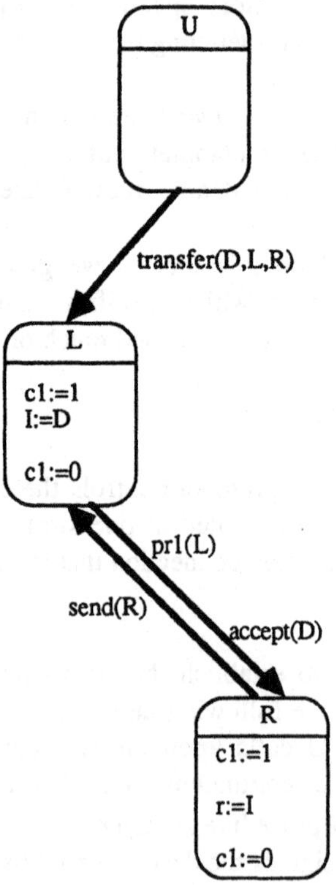

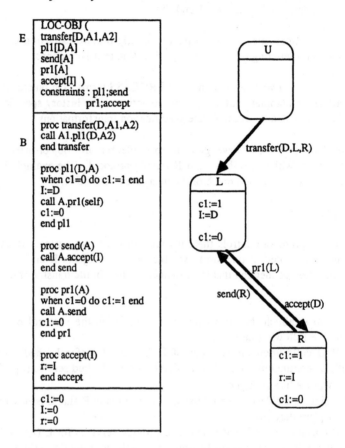

The object-oriented algebraic specification of the protocol now consisits of the following state, integration and history specification:

- *The module state specification LOCATION :*

The protocol objects are specified as triples of a state (vacant or occupied), parameters (data items to be transfered and addresses of other locations) and a service (the service the location actually executes). The services are the procedures given in the example.

We use a very abbreviated syntax here, meaning triples, enumeration types, lists etc with corresponding operations, as eg. projections, equality etc.

- *The integration specification* INT-SPEC
corresponding to LOCATION as given in 2.2.1.

- *The history specification PROTOCOL :*
The history specification contains sequential execution of events as indicated in the example above. It specifies a process CALL (for procedure call), EXECUTE (for the execution of the services listed in the LOC specification) and WAIT (checking on the status variable until the object is ready to offer a service). Note that the WAIT process may be infinite.
PROTOCOL is a variant of the basic process algebra specification **bpa** given in 2.3.

initial state specification :

LOCATION =
<u>sorts</u> location = status × parameters × service
status = {vacant, occupied}
parameters = data × list(location)
service = {transfer, pl1, pr1, send, accept, do-nothing}
<u>opns</u> ...

integration specification :

INT-SPEC = LOCATION +
<u>sorts</u> object-name = {U,L,R,...}
EVENT
<u>opns</u> CREATE : object-name location → EVENT
ASSIGN : object-name location → EVENT
DELETE : object-name → EVENT

history specification :

PROTOCOL = **pnatl** + INT-SPEC
<u>sorts</u> PROC
<u>opns</u> ε : → EVENT
_ : EVENT → PROC {coercion}
_•_ : PROC PROC→ PROC {sequential composition}
p-PROC : natl PROC → PROC {projection operation to define infinite processes}

CALL : location location service parameters → PROC
EXECUTE : location service parameters → PROC
WAIT : location → PROC

<u>eqns</u> CALL(l1,l2,s,p) = EXECUTE(l2,s,p)

EXECUTE(l1,transfer,<d,(l2,l3)>) = CALL(l1,l2,pl1,<d,(l3)>)

EXECUTE(l1,pl1,<d,(l2)>) =
WAIT(l1) • ASSIGN(l1,<status(l1),<d,(l2)>,pl1>) •
CALL(l1,l2,pr1,<d,(l1)>) •
ASSIGN(l1,<vacant,parameters(l1),service(l1)>)

EXECUTE(l1,pr1<d,(l2)>) = WAIT(l1) •
CALL(l1,l2,send,<data(l2),(l1)>) •
ASSIGN(l1,<vacant,parameters(l1),service(l1)>)

EXECUTE(l1,send,<d,(l2)>) = CALL(l1,l2,accept,<d,(l2)>)

EXECUTE(l1,accept,<d,(l2)>) = ASSIGN(l1<status(l1),<d,(l2)>,service(l1)>)

EXECUTE(l1,do-nothing,p) = ε

WAIT(l) = if occupied?(l)
then ε • WAIT(l)
else ASSIGN(l,<occupied,parameters(l),service(l)>)

{ equations for _•_ , p-PROC and ε }

Now the term
CREATE(l,<vacant,<d0,empty-list>,do-nothing>)
• CREATE(r,<vacant,<d0,empty-list>,do-nothing>)
• CREATE(u,<vacant,<d0,empty-list>,do-nothing>)
EXECUTE(u,transfer,<d1,(l,r)>)
for given data terms d0, d1
denotes the (behaviour of the) sample protocol.

A 'normal form' of this term, consisting of atomic events and their sequential composition only, can be depicted as follows. (It is, in fact, p-proc(5,T) with T = this term.)

LOCATION

↓ CREATE (U,<vacant, <d0,emptylist>,do-nothing>)

LOCATION +
opns U: → location
eqns U = <vacant,
<d0,emptylist>,
do-nothing>

↓ CREATE (L,<vacant, <d0,emptylist>,do-nothing>)

CREATE (R,<vacant, <d0,emptylist>,do-nothing>)

LOCATION +		
opns U: → location	L: → location	R: → location
eqns U = <vacant, <d0,emptylist>, do-nothing>	L = <vacant, <d0,emptylist>, do-nothing>	R = <vacant, <d0,emptylist>, do-nothing>

↓ ASSIGN (L,<occupied, <d0,emptylist>,do-nothing>)

LOCATION +		
opns U: → location	L: → location	R: → location
eqns U = <vacant, <d0,emptylist>, do-nothing>	L = <occupied, <d0,emptylist>, do-nothing>	R = <vacant, <d0,emptylist>, do-nothing>

↓ ASSIGN (L,<occupied, <d1,R>,pl1>)

LOCATION +		
opns U: → location	L: → location	R: → location
eqns U = <vacant, <d0,emptylist>, do-nothing>	L = <occupied, <d1,R>, pl1>	R = <vacant, <d0,emptylist>, do-nothing>

↓

. . .

□

3 Class Definition by Algebraic Module Specification

3.1 Single Modules / Simple Classes

In the previous section we have used algebraic specifications for the static part of the system description, which, essentially, means the attribute specification of a class definition of an object-oriented program. For such a class definition, however, more features are needed, as for instance explicit interfaces, an implementation part or body etc.

In the framework of algebraic specifications these features are covered by the notion of **module specifications** (or modular algebraic specifications).
Module specifications have been introduced in a series of papers and books (see eg. [EW 85], [WE 86], [BEP 87], [WE 88] and [EM 90]). Here we give a very short overview to indicate the most important features in comparison with class definitions.

A module specification MOD consists of four algebraic specifications PAR, EXP, IMP and BOD

MOD :

PAR	EXP
IMP	BOD

which are related by (inclusion) morphisms. The export EXP and the import IMP represent the interfaces of a module while the parameter PAR is a part common to both import and export interface. Note, that the import interface describes only a formal import, ie. the resources it requires rather than naming specific modules which provide these resources.

The semantics of a module specification MOD is given by the loose semantics of the specification PAR, EXP and IMP, a free construction F from import to body algebras which defines the BOD data and operations using the formal IMP data and operations, and the restriction of the body to the export, which hides the non-visisble parts of the body. The composition of free construction and restriction yields the **behaviour construction** from import to export algebras of the module MOD.

Thus we can use module specifiation as class definitions, covering the central requirements of object-oriented attribute specification.

The next step is to define the atomic events of state transformation (CREATE, ASSIGN and DELETE) for module specifications. We will present two alternative definitions here, which model different approaches to the use of module specifications.

3.1.1 1st alternative : Object manipulation through the export interface.

Since all manipulations and requests to objects are brought to the module through its export interface, this export has to provide the corresponding syntactical means, ie. at least the object identifiers have to be declared at the export interface. To show the properties of the object to the outside world also its defining equation becomes a part of the export.

Both declaration and defining equation are also added to the body, since it implements the export operations and therefor needs the information about the objects. (More formally: EXP is a subspecification of BOD, resp. there is a specification morphism from EXP to BOD.)

If *ob* belongs to an import sort (ie. *ob* is a 'formal object') its declaration and defining equation also enriches the import. Finally *ob* becomes a part of the parameter, if *ob* is passed through the module without manipulations, since PAR is a specified common part of import and export. Since module state specifications are abstract specifications of functionality and properties of a system the introduction of formal objects makes sense. For a formal object only type, functionality of services and the necessary requirements (equations) are specified, as for simple operations in the import and parameter section of a module specification.

Thus we obtain the following definition of the three atomic events on module state specifications:

Definition (Atomic events on module state specifications, 1st alternative)

1) Given a module specification MOD = (PAR,EXP,IMP,BOD)
   with PAR =(ΣP,EP), EXP =(ΣE,EE), IMP =(ΣI,EI), BOD =(ΣB,EB),
   a <u>module state specification</u> MODSTATE (w.r.t. MOD) consists of statespecifications
   MODSTATE = (PARSTATE,EXPSTATE,IMPSTATE,BODSTATE)
   with PARSTATE =(ΣPS,EPS), EXPSTATE =(ΣES,EES),
   IMPSTATE =(ΣIS,EIS), BODSTATE =(ΣBS,EBS),
   such that

- MODSTATE is a module specification, ie. there are specification morphisms (inclusions)

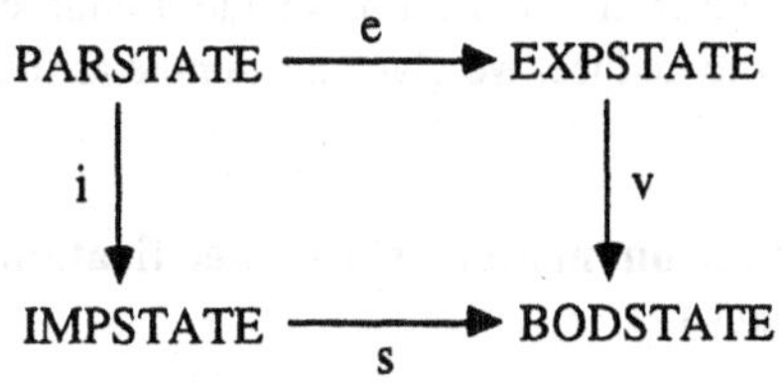

- and each part PAR$\subseteq$PARSTATE etc is an enrichment.
  (Compare definition 2.1.2 of state specifications.)

2) Given a module state specification
MODSTATE = (PARSTATE,EXPSTATE,IMPSTATE,BODSTATE) w.r.t. MOD = (PAR,EXP, IMP,BOD) the three atomic events CREATE, ASSIGN and DELETE are defined by

- CREATE(MODSTATE, ob, t); ob ∈ ObId, t ∈ $T_{\Sigma ES}$
enriches EXPSTATE and BODSTATE by
<u>opns</u> ob: → s
<u>eqns</u> ob = t'
where *s* is the sort of *t* (which we suppose to be unique) and *t'* ∈ $T_{\Sigma E}$ is a term congruent to *t* w.r.t. EES (*t'* is an admissible state).
The same enrichment is applied to IMPSTATE, if *s* (the sort of *t*) is an import sort, and to PARSTATE, if *s* is a parameter sort.

- ASSIGN(MODSTATE, ob, t); ob, t ∈ $T_{\Sigma ES}$, ob an object identifier
replaces the defining equation of *ob* in all parts of MODSTATE where it occurs by *ob* = *t'*, where *t'*∈ T_Σ, t' $\equiv_{EES}$ t.

- DELETE(MODSTATE, ob); ob ∈ $T_{\Sigma S}$ an object identifier
removes declaration and defining equation of *ob* from all parts of MODSTATE where they occurs.

If PARSTATE, EXPSTATE , IMPSTATE and BODSTATE are related by general specification morphisms, and not by inclusions, corresponding translations of declarations and defining equations of the objects have to be performed. □

3.1.2 2nd alternative : Hidden State / Single object appraoch

The single object approach works with exactly one object per sort, which is used to represent the current state of this sort. The object is only declared in the body, and all export operations which depend on the current state are implemented in the body using this object.

Instead of writing down the formal definition of the atomic events for the second alternative, which are easy to deduce, we give an example as illustration.

Example (Atomic events on module state specifications, 2nd alternative. A hidden stack)

We use the following module specification **stack(item)** of stacks of formal items, which defines an internal *stackobject*. This object is used to represent an internal state which is needed for the definition of the semantics of the export operations, but is not explicitly mentionend when called at the export interface. For real applications this saves a lot of unnecessary mentioning of contexts.

stack(item) =

PAR = IMP

EXP = PAR +
  sorts state
  opns top: → item
    pop : → state
    push : item → state

IMP =
  sorts item

BOD = EXP +
  sorts stack
  opns emptystack : → stack
    b-top : stack → item
    b-pop : stack → stack
    b-push : item stack → stack
    stackobject : → stack
    co : stack → state
  eqns top = b-top(stackobject)
    pop = co(b-pop(stackobject))
    push(i) = co(b-push(i,stackobject))
    {usual equations for b-top, b-pop, b-push}

Here the body implements the export operations, using the internal stackobject of the internal sort stack □

For both alternatives the definition of the integration specification remains the same, since the syntax of the atomic events has not changed; only the semantics (wrt. state specification transformations) has been redefined.

3.2 Inheritance via Module Interconnection

Now that interfaces and implementation part (= body) are modelled by module specifications, one central issue of class definitions, inheritance, is still missing. Looking at modular algebraic specification one sees, that inheritance corresponds to some of the interconnection mechanisms developed for modules, depending on what kind (or aspect) of inheritance is considered.

Here we present two interconnection mechanisms to model inheritance (see also the literature about modules, esp. [PP 85], [PP 86] and [EM 90]).

Composition

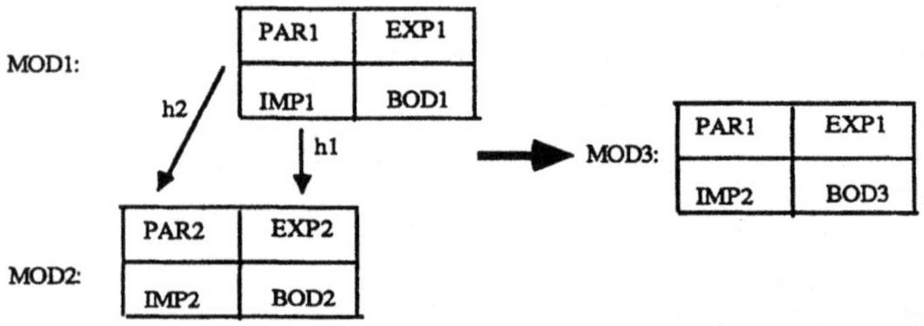

where h1 and h2 are passing morphisms and BOD3 = BOD1 $+_{IMP1}$ BOD2 is a pushout construction.

Union

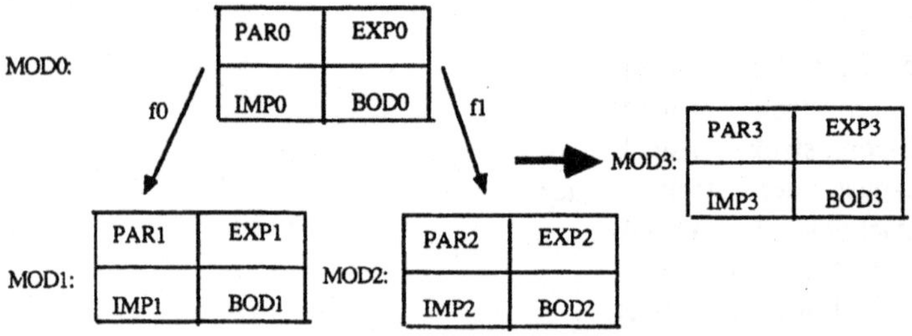

where f0 and f1 are "module specification morphisms" and SPEC3 = SPEC1 $+_{SPEC0}$ SPEC2 for SPEC = PAR, EXP, IMP, BOD are pushout constructions.

Since the result of an interconnection mechanism is defined as a simple module specification its semantics is defined as above. Note, however, that this definition of a resulting simple module specification is only needed to define its semantics and further interconnection with other modules. It is not necessary to carry out this 'flattening' (construction of the resulting simple module specification of an interconnection) for the specification of a system.

As main results for module specifications we can show that the basic interconnection mechanisms are operations on module specifications which are preserving correctness and which are compositional w.r.t. the semantics. This means that correctness of modular system specification can be deduced from correctness of its parts and its semantics can be composed from that of its components. Moreover, there are nice compatibility results between these operations which can be expressed by associativity, commutativity and distributivity results (see [BEP 87], [EW 85], [WE 86], and chapters 2, 3, 4, and 8 of [EM 89]).

In comparison with inheritance composition models 'imbedded' inheritance, where services from the imported module MOD2 are used to realize the services of MOD1, but are not shown in its export interface.
In the case of a union of MOD1 and MOD2 also all services from MOD2 belong to the united export interface, ie. MOD2 is completely open for further use

Altogether we have that specification and structuring mechanisms offered by module specifications to a large extent coincide with (object-oriented) class definition mechanisms.

4. Conclusion

The aim of this paper has been to sketch an approach to object-oriented algebraic specifications, to bring together advantages of algebraic specification techniques and object-orientedness. The ideas presented here, which to a certain extent are precisicions and developments of Goguen and Meseguer's approach using reflexive semantics, applied to module specifications as in [WE 88] should next be worked out with larger examples to see the directions for further developments. The use of identified processes as life cycles of objects and module specifications as class definitions, however, seems to be an appropriate approach.
Furthermore this approach should be compared with the works done by Ehrich/Sernadas [ESS89]. They take life cycles of objects and a general form of message passing as basic features to develop a categorical description of object-orientedness. Coming from very different starting points (integration of existing formalisms vs. development of a new basic category) one should try to find a meeting point in between.

References

[BEP87] E.K.Blum, H.Ehrig, F.Parisi-Presicce : Algebraic Specification of Modules and Their Basic Interconnections, in JCCS Vol.34, No.2/3, pp.293-339, 1987

[BK86] J.A.Bergstra, J.W.Klop: Algebra of Communicating Processes, in: CWI Monographs I Series, Proceedings of the CWI Symposium Mathematics and Computer Science, North-Holland, p. 89-138, Amsterdam 1986

[EM85] H.Ehrig, B.Mahr : Fundamentals of Algebraic Specifications 1 : Equations and Initial Semantics , Springer Verlag , Berlin-Heidelberg-NewYork-Tokyo 1985

[EM90] H.Ehrig, B.Mahr : Fundamentals of Algebraic Specifications 2 : Modules and Constraints, Springer Verlag , Berlin-Heidelberg-NewYork-Tokyo 1989

[EPBRDG88a] H.Ehrig, F.Parisi-Presicce, P.Boehm, C.Rieckhoff, C.Dimitrovici, M.Große-Rhode : Algebraic Data Type and Process Specifications Based on Projection Spaces , Springer LNCS 332, p.23-43, 1988

[EPBRDG88b] H.Ehrig, F.Parisi-Presicce, P.Boehm, C.Rieckhoff, C.Dimitrovici, M.Große-Rhode : Combining Data Type and Recursive Process Specifications using Projection Algebras , Theoretical Computer Science 71 (1990), 347-380

[ESS89] H.D.Ehrich, A.Sernadas, C.Sernadas : Objects, Object Types and Object Identification , in: Categorical Methods in Computer Science with Aspects from Topology, H.Ehrig, M.Herrlich, H.J.Kreowski G.Preuß (eds.), Springer LNCS 393, 1989

[EW85] H.Ehrig, H.Weber : Algebraic Specification of Modules, Proc. IFIP Work.Conference 85: The Role of Abstract Models in Programming, Wien 1985

[GM87] J.A.Goguen, J.Meseguer : Unifying Functional, Object-Oriented and Relational Programming with Logical Semantics. In : Research Directions in Object-Oriented Programming, ed. by B.Shriver and P.Wegner, pp 417-477, MIT Press 1987

[GE90] M.Große-Rhode, H.Ehrig : Transformation of Combined Data Type and Process Specifications Using Projection Algebras, in: J.W.deBakker, W.-P.deRoever, G.Rozenberg (eds): Stepwise Refinement of Distributed Systems, Springer LNCS 430 (1990), 301-339.
Also appeared as Technical Report No. 90/1, TU Berlin (1990)

[Gro89] M.Große-Rhode : Parameterized Data Type and Process Specifications Using Projection Algebras, in: Categorical Methods in Computer Science with Aspects from Topology, H.Ehrig, M.Herrlich, H.J.Kreowski G.Preuß (eds.), Springer LNCS 393, 1989

[PP 85] F.Parisi-Presicce : Union and Actualization of Module Specifications: Some Compatibility Results, Techn. Report USC 1985 and JCSS 35, 1(1987), 72-95

[PP 85] F.Parisi-Presicce : Inner and Mutual Compatibility of Basic Operations on Module Specifications, Proc. CAAP'86, LNCS 214(1986), 30-44. Full version : Techn. Report TU Berlin, FB 20, No. 86-06 (1986)

[WE86] H.Weber, H.Ehrig : Specification of Modular Systems, IEEE Transactions of Software Engineering, Vol.SE-12, no7,1986, pp.784-798

[WE88] H.Weber, H.Ehrig : Specification of Concurrently Executable Modules and Distributed Modular Systems, Proc. IEEE Workshop on Future Trends of Distr. Comp. Systems in the 1990's, HongKong 1988, pp.202-215

INDUCTIVE COMPLETION FOR TRANSFORMATION OF EQUATIONAL SPECIFICATIONS

Steffen Lange
Klaus P. Jantke
Technische Hochschule Leipzig,
FB Mathematik & Informatik
Postfach 66
7030 Leipzig

Abstract: The *Knuth-Bendix* completion procedure is a tool for algorithmically completing term rewriting systems which are operationally incomplete in the sense that the uniqueness of normal forms is not guaranteed. As the problem of operational completeness is undecidable, one may only expect a technique applicable to an enumerable number of cases. The *Knuth-Bendix* completion procedure may fail either by generating a critical pair which can not be oriented to form a new rewrite rule or by generating an infinite sequence of critical pairs to be introduced as new rewrite rules. The latter case is investigated. The basic idea is to invoke inductive inference techniques for abbreviating infinitely long sequences of rules by finitely many other rules. If simple syntactic generalization does not do, there will be automatically generated auxiliary operators. This is the key idea of the present paper. It contains a calculus of five learning rules for extending *Knuth-Bendix* completion procedures by inductive inference techniques. These rules are shown to be correct. The problem of completeness remains open.

Motivation

There are several models describing software development processes. Usually, there are different levels of specifications ranging from overall requirement specifications via functional requirement specifications, design specifications, and prototype/ executable specifications to program code. Our approach is focussed to the step from design specifications which are assumed to be intensionally complete to executable specifications required to be operationally complete. Up to now, the approach presented is restricted to equational specifications. We assume initial algebra semantics.

Knuth-Bendix completion [KnBe] is a standard methodology for transforming equational specifications into executable form. Unfortunately, it is restricted to a considerably small class of equational specifications, as equational theories with undecidable word problem can not be completed to a finite canonical rewrite system. The situation is even more complicated, because there exist equational theories with decidable word problem and without any equivalent finite canonical rewrite system (over the same signature). One of them is

$$a(b(a(X))) = \quad b(a(b(X)))$$

as it has been shown by *Kapur* and *Narendran* (cf. [KaNa]).

The present approach offers a methodology for completion which covers a considerably large number of cases out of the scope of *Knuth-Bendix* completion. Its power originates from taking signature enrichments into consideration. In a more general setting, the power of hidden functions for specifying abstract data types is already well-known. Our approach will be briefly illustrated using the example above.

Let us consider the following set of equations somehow equivalent to the original theory, which can be easily completed to a canonical rewrite system.

$$a(b(a(x))) = b(a(b(x)))$$
$$b(a(b(x))) = h(x)$$

The following canonical rewrite system forms the result of completing the given set of equations.

$$a(b(a(x))) \Rightarrow h(x)$$
$$b(a(b(x))) \Rightarrow h(x)$$
$$a(h(x)) \Rightarrow h(b(x))$$
$$b(h(x)) \Rightarrow h(a(x))$$

This illustrates that extending the underlying signature and the set of equations in an appropriate way may result in a finite canonical rewrite system which defines a rewrite relation equivalent to the original equational theory, when restricted to the original signature. The present papers deals with a detailed investigation of appropriate ways for extending equational specifications as above. One may imagine to extend the power of some *Knuth-Bendix* algorithm resp. program by procedures automatically providing the type of extensions sketched in the example before.

Introduction

The *Knuth-Bendix* completion procedure provides a method for transforming a given terminating but not confluent set of rewrite rules into a confluent rewrite system. Confluent and terminating (i.e. canonical) rewrite systems are desirable because they ensure that every term has a unique normal form and thus equalities between terms can be decided by simply comparing normal forms. Moreover, canonical rewrite systems provide an operational semantics for abstract data types within initial algebra semantics.

On the basis of a given set of rewrite rules, the *Knuth-Bendix* algorithm generates a confluent set of rewrite rules by repeatedly overlapping left-hand sides and adding any generated critical pair as new rewrite rule after orienting it w.r.t. a given termination ordering. This process terminates, if there are no more (non-identical) critical pairs, or if a critical pair is produced which can not be oriented by the given termination ordering. This process is said to diverge, if it generates an infinite set of new rewrite rules.

In [ThJa] the authors have introduced a new approach to solving divergence in the *Knuth-Bendix* completion algorithm. This approach emphasizes the idea to use inductive inference techniques (cf. [AnSm]) for improving the power of the *Knuth-Bendix* completion algorithm. In case it diverges, we try to find a finite set of rewrite rules being in some sense equivalent to the infinite sequence of generated rewrite rules. Inductive inference ideas will be applied within this approach in two ways: first, when generalizing a given infinite sequence (in fact, by processing only a finite initial segment), and second, when synthesizing auxiliary operators and sorts in order to rewrite a sequence into generalizable form.

The reader may assume the following scenario for relating our approach to the classical completion concept.

* Suppose a given equational specification E over some signature Σ assumed to be axiomatically complete with respect to some intended software module. In fact, E defines implicitly a certain congruence relation $=_E$.

* For transforming E into an operational complete form, its equations should be oriented to become rewrite rules. This yields some rewrite rule system R. If R is canonical, the work is done. Otherwise, it has to be completed.

* If *Knuth-Bendix* completion seems to diverge, our inductive completion rules are invoked. (Note that it is generally undecidable whether or not any given version of a *Knuth-Bendix* completion algorithm diverges. In [Herm] there have been investigated sufficient structural conditions for divergency. One may imagine that conditions of that type are checked. But one may also assume that, if a generated sequence of rewrite rules exceeds some size, the *Knuth-Bendix* completion processes is dovetailed with our approach proposed.) Our inductive completion rules may generate an extended rewrite rule system R', perhaps over some automatically extended signature Σ'. If R' is canonical, the work is done. Otherwise, the steps above are iterated.

* In case this iteration terminates, the implicitly given congruence relation $<\!-\!*\!-\!>_R$, on ground terms restricted to the original signature equals $=_E$, and the transformation into an operationally complete system of rewrite rules has been successful.

An Example

Consider the following rewrite rule system R. The signature contains the sort T with operators f,g,a,b having the corresponding arities $T \to T$, $T \to T$, $TT \to T$, and $TT \to T$, respectively.

(R1) f(a(x,g(y))) => a(f(x),y)
(R2) a(b(x,y),y) => y

The generated sequence of new critical pairs resp. new rewrite rules is

(A1) a(f(b(x,g(y))),y) => f(g(y))
(A2) a(f(f(b(x,g(g(y))))),y) => f(f(g(g(y))))
(A3) a(f(f(f(b(x,g(g(g(y))))))),y)
=> f(f(f(g(g(g(y))))))
(A4) a(f(f(f(f(b(x,g(g(g(g(y))))))))),y)
=> f(f(f(f(g(g(g(g(y))))))))

etc.

If we simply generalize this sequence by a single rule, for example a(f(w),y) => z , and if we add this new rule to the system R, we obtain a rewrite system which does not preserve the target equational theory. Consequently, we need a more sophisticated idea.

First of all, we introduce a new operator H for encoding the term f(b(x,g(y))) which is a common subterm of all left-hand sides. Additionally, we have to organize a counter for recognizing the number of occurrences of the operators f and g within the left-hand sides. Hence we have to add to the given signature a sort called *nat* with the usual operators with its indicated arities O: -> *nat* and S: *nat* -> *nat* . The new operator H has arity *nat T T* -> *T* .

The idea addressed above yields the rules

(R3)	f(b(x,g(y)))	=>	H(O,x,y)
(R4)	f(H(z,x,g(y)))	=>	H(S(z),x,y)

On the basis of the rewrite system { (R1) , (R2) , (R3) , (R4) } , we obtain the following sequence of new critical pairs resp. rewrite rules:

(B1)	a(H(O,x,y),y)	=>	f(g(y))
(B2)	a(H(S(O),x,y),y)	=>	f(f(g(g(y))))
(B3)	a(H(S(S(O)),x,y),y)	=>	f(f(f(g(g(g(y))))))
(B4)	a(H(S(S(S(O))),x,y),y)	=>	f(f(f(f(g(g(g(g(y))))))))

etc.

It is easy to see that the left-hand sides of this sequence can be generalized by the term a(H(z,x,y),y) . Unfortunately, it is again not desirable to generalize the whole sequence by a single rule like a(H(z,x,y),y) => f(w) . In this case, the relation between the left-hand sides and the right-hand sides would be lost.

Consequently, we need some way for describing this relationship. There is a rule for introducing a further operator G with arity *nat T T -> T*.

(R5) a(H(z,x,y),y) => f(G(z,x,y))

In the particular case under consideration, G is independent of its second argument. But this is not always the case. Therefore, we prefer this general form reflecting one of our inference rules introduced below. One could refine the corresponding rule by extracting sets of variables common to a list of terms. There are several refinements of this type. We decided to postpone those refinements to a later investigation.

By applying the *Knuth-Bendix* completion algorithm again, the following two critical pairs resp. rewrite rules will be generated.

(R6) f(G(O,x,y)) => f(g(y))
(R7) f(G(S(z),x,y)) => f(f(G(z,x,g(y))))

After that, the *Knuth-Bendix* completion algorithm terminates successfully.

To sum up, by introducing new operators H and G, and by introducing the concept of counting, we have produced a canonical term rewriting system R' = { (R1) , ... , (R7) } . Moreover, this new system is a conservative extension of the given rewrite system R , and it preserves the target equational theory.

Within the next chapter, we formalize the ideas addressed above. The first and the third inductive completion rule can be applied in order to introduce the new operators H and G, respectively, as outlined above.

Inductive Completion Rules

We assume a finite, heterogeneous and finitary signature Σ with a corresponding set X of variables. By $T(\Sigma,X)$ we denote the set of all well-formed terms over Σ and X. $T(\Sigma)$ denotes the subset of all variable-free terms.

A given rewrite system R defines the rewrite relation $\longrightarrow_R$, the transitive closure $-{*}\!\!\rightarrow_R$, and the corresponding equivalence relation $\leftarrow\!{*}\!\!\rightarrow_R$, as usual.

Throughout the whole paper, we assume that every given signature Σ contains at least the sort *nat* with the constant 0 and an operator S for the successor function. This assumption should help to simplify our inductive completion rules.

Let us assume that a given term rewriting system is terminating but not confluent. In this case, one can try the ***Knuth-Bendix*** completion algorithm for completing the given system. The completion algorithm generates critical pairs which are proposed as new rules. Within the present paper, we assume that it will be always possible to orient the critical pairs w.r.t. any given ordering without loosing termination. Other cases are out of the scope of our investigations. For avoiding additional complications, we assume that terms which occur in new rewrite rules are irreducible under the considered rewriting system.

Let us consider the case that the *Knuth-Bendix* completion algorithm generates for a given rewrite system R an infinite sequence of rewrite rules denoted by R^{ω} . If one wants to replace this infinite sequence by some finite set of rewrite rules, then such a replacement should at least preserve the equational theory defined by the original rewrite rule system R. It turns out that such a replacement may be based on a larger signature than the given system (cf. the example in the chapter before). Clearly, the replacement should exactly preserve the target equational theory on ground terms, when restricted to the original sorts. This notion is refered to as *conservative extension* (cf. [EhMa]).

Definition

Let R be a rewrite rule system over a given signature and R' be a finite enrichment of R (i.e. R' contains R). We call R' a *conservative extension* of R

iff $\forall t_1, t_2 \in T(\Sigma)$ (t_1 <-*->$_R$ t_2 iff t_1 <-*->$_{R'}$ t_2)

To sum up, if we try to replace an infinite sequence of rewrite rules by a finite set, we are looking for such replacements which yield conservative extensions of the given rewrite rule system.

The inductive completion rules of our calculus have, in general, the following structure:

Σ, R, $[R^{\omega}]_n$,

certain preconditions

$\Sigma \cup \Sigma'$, R $\cup$ R'

These inductive completion rules characterize how to extend the given signature Σ and the given rewrite rule system R, if some finite segment $[R^{\omega}]_n$ of the infinite sequence of rewrite rules in R^{ω} satisfies certain preconditions. The lower index n indicates the length of the initial segment of R^{ω} taken.

Before introducing the inductive completion rules in detail, we give some definitions which will be used as a basis for our rules. All of them abbreviate quite simple concepts, but make our rules below more readable.

For the sake of simplicity, we consider rewrite rules of the form l => r in R^{ω} as terms =>(l,r). That means, "=>" will be considered as an additional binary operator (which, by the way, is usually overloaded). Thus, we can restrict our investigations to infinite sequences of terms.

In the sequel, *Var*(t) denotes the set of variables contained in the term t. A substitution δ is a mapping from the set of variables X into the set of terms T(Σ) . Usually, δ is only specified on some finite set *Var*(t) . Substitutions are written in postfix notation, i.e. the result of applying δ to some term t is a term denoted by $t\delta$.

Definition

Suppose $[t_1,\dots,t_n]$ to be a finite list of terms.

Gen($[t_1,\dots,t_n]$) = t iff

(1) $\forall i \leq n \; \exists \delta_i \; (t\delta_i = t_i$, i.e. t generalizes $[t_1,\dots,t_n]$)

(2) $\forall$ t' (If t' generalizes $[t_1,\dots,t_n]$,

then $\exists \delta \; (t'\delta = t)$)

For *Gen*($[t_1,\dots,t_n]$) = t as above, *Sub*($[t_1,\dots,t_n]$) denotes the list of the corresponding substitutions $[\delta_1,\dots,\delta_n]$.

Definition

Suppose $[t_1,\dots,t_n]$ to be a finite list of terms.

Gen-Seq($[t_1,\dots,t_n]$) = $[g_1,\dots,g_{n-1}]$ iff

$\forall i \; (1 \leq i \leq n$ --> *Gen*($[t_i,t_{i+1}]$) = g_i)

Definition

Suppose $[t_1,\dots,t_n]$ to be a finite list of terms, and t to be a term with *Gen*($[t_1,\dots,t_n]$) = t. Assume $[\delta_1,\dots,\delta_n]$ to be the corresponding list of substitutions.

(1) *Var-Const*($[t_1,\dots,t_n]$,t) = { x / x $\in$ *Var*(t) and for all $i,j \leq n$ ($x\delta_i = x\delta_j$) }

(2) *Var-Change*($[t_1,\dots,t_n]$,t) = *Var*(t) — *Var-Const*($[t_1,\dots,t_n]$,t)

Definition

Suppose $[t_1,\dots,t_n]$ to be a finite list of terms, and t to be a term with *Gen*($[t_1,\dots,t_n]$) = t. Assume $[\delta_1,\dots,\delta_n]$ to be the corresponding list of substitutions.

Exact($[t_1,\dots,t_n]$,t) iff

(1) *Var-Change*($[t_1,\dots,t_n]$,t) = { z } with Sort(z) = *nat*

(2) $\forall i \; (1 \leq i \leq n$ --> $z\delta_i = s^{i-1}(0)$)

We are listing our learning rules developed. The first one has been applied in our example above. It resulted in introducing the auxiliary operator named H.

First Inductive Completion Rule

Σ , R , $[t_1,\ldots,t_n] \sqsubseteq R^\omega$,
assume x to be any variable not contained in any $Var(t_i)$,
$\exists p \; \exists u(x) \; \exists \beta \; \forall i \; (1 \leq i < n \; \longrightarrow t_{i+1|p} = u(x / t_{i|p}\beta))$,
$Var(t_{i|p}) = \{ y_1,\ldots,y_m \}$, for all i with $1 \leq i \leq n$,
$t_{1|p}$ is different from all $y_1,\ldots,y_m$

$\Sigma \cup \Sigma'$, R $\cup$ R' , where

$\Sigma' = \{$ <u>oprs</u>
H: *nat Sort*(y_1) ... *Sort*(y_m) -> *Sort*$(t_{1|p})\}$

$R' = \{ \quad t_{1|p} \Rightarrow H(0, y_1,\ldots,y_m)$,
$u(x / H(z, y_1,\ldots,y_m)\beta)$
$\Rightarrow H(S(z), y_1,\ldots,y_m) \quad \}$

It is always assumed that newly inserted operators are denoted by names not used before.

By $t_{|p}$ we denote the subterm of t at position p, as usual. If any u is a term containing a variable x, this is frequently expressed by u(x). Correspondingly, u(x/t) is the result of replacing x by t at each occurrence.

The second rule introduced here will be illustrated by a particular example in the following chapter. Its application will result in the introduction of an auxiliary operator named H, again.

Second Inductive Completion Rule

Σ , R , $[t_1,\dots,t_n] \sqsubseteq R^\omega$,
Gen-Seq($[t_1,\dots,t_n]$) $= [g_1,\dots,g_{n-1}]$,
$\exists p\ \exists \beta\ \forall i\ \ (1 \leq i \leq n-2 \ \ \text{-->}\ \ g_{i+1|p} = g_{i|p}\beta)$
Var($g_{i|p}$) $= \{ y_1,\dots,y_m \}$, for all i with $1 \leq i \leq n-1$,
$g_{1|p}$ is different from all $y_1,\dots,y_m$

$\Sigma \cup \Sigma'$, R $\cup$ R' , where
Σ' = { <u>oprs</u>
H: *nat Sort*(y_1) ... *Sort*(y_m) -> *Sort*($g_{1|p}$)}
R' = { $g_{1|p}$ => H(0, $y_1,\dots,y_m$) ,
u(x / H(z, $y_1,\dots,y_m$)β)
=> H(S(z), $y_1,\dots,y_m$) }

The reader may easily recognize the strong similarity between both inference rules introduced so far. Their common purpose is to insert auxiliary operators for rewriting an initial segment of an implicitly given sequence of rewrite rules into generalizable form. The preconditions of both rules formalize certain regularities basic for later generalization.

For shortening the following notation, we are introducing the notion of an acceptable sequence of terms.

Definition

A sequence of terms $[t_1,\dots,t_n]$ is said to be *acceptable*,

iff $\forall\, i,j \ (1 \le i,j \le n \ \text{-->}\ Var(t_i) = Var(t_j))$

As the two rules above, the following one is intended to prepare finite sequences of terms for generalization.

Third Inductive Completion Rule

Σ , R , $[{=>}(l_1,r_1)\ ,\ \dots\ ,\ {=>}(l_n,r_n)\ ] \subseteq R^{\omega}$,

$[l_1,\dots,l_n])$ is acceptable , $[r_1,\dots,r_n])$ is acceptable ,

$Gen(\ [{=>}(l_1,r_1)\ ,\ \dots\ ,\ {=>}(l_n,r_n)\ ]\ ) = {=>}(l,r)$,

$Exact([l_1,\dots,l_n\ ],l)$, $Var(l) = \{\ y_1,\dots,y_m\ \}$,

$Var\text{-}Change(\ [r_1,\dots,r_n\ ],r\ ) = \{\ y_1,\dots,y_k\ \} \subseteq \{\ y_1,\dots,y_m\ \}$

$\Sigma \cup \Sigma'$, R $\cup$ R' , where

Σ' = { <u>oprs</u>

G_j: *nat* $Sort(y_1)\ \dots\ Sort(y_m) \ \text{->}\ Sort(y_j)$

(for all $j \le k$) }

R' = { $l \ {=>}\ r\varphi$,

where $\varphi = [\ y_j/G_j(y_1,\dots,y_m)$, for all $j \le k]$ }

Although our fourth inductive completion rule below is of a particular interest, it has not been applied to the examples investigated in the present paper. It formalizes a situation where the regularities detected admit of rewriting without signature enrichments.

Fourth Inductive Completion Rule

Σ , R , [=>(l_1,r_1) , ... , =>(l_n,r_n)] $\equiv R^\omega$,
[=>(l_1,r_1) , ... , =>(l_n,r_n)] is acceptable ,
Gen([=>(l_1,r_1) , ... , =>(l_n,r_n)]) = =>(l,r) ,
Exact([l_1,...,l_n],l) , x is some variable not in *Var*(r_1) ,
$\exists$ u(x) $\exists\beta$ $\forall$ i (1 $\leq$ i < n --> r_{i+1} = u(x / $r_i\beta$) ,
Var-Change([l_1,...,l_n],l) = { z } ,φ = [z / S(z)]

Σ , R $\cup$ R' , where R' = { l_1 => r_1 , $l\varphi$ => $r\beta$ }

Our final fifth rule is doing generalizations as illustrated in the second example. Although this rule may be the simplest one, at least from a structural point of view, we preferred a presentation according to our scenario of of rewriting for generalization.

Fifth Inductive Completion Rule

Σ , R , [=>(l_1,r_1) , ... , =>(l_n,r_n)] $\equiv R^\omega$,
[=>(l_1,r_1) , ... , =>(l_n,r_n)] is acceptable ,
Gen([=>(l_1,r_1) , ... , =>(l_n,r_n)]) = =>(l,r) ,
Exact([=>(l_1,r_1) , ... , =>(l_n,r_n)] , =>(l,r))

Σ , R $\cup$ R' , where R' = { l => r }

These five inductive completion rules presented are reflecting our approach to appropriate extensions of the *Knuth-Bendix* completion algorithm. Before discussing problems of correctness, we are investigating an example in detail.

An Additional Example

Consider the following rewrite rule system R. The signature Σ contains a sort called *nat* with a constant O and the usual operators S , + , Diff (intended to describe successor, sum, and difference) having the arities *nat* -> *nat* , *nat nat* -> *nat* , and *nat nat* -> *nat* , respectively.

(R1) O + x => x
(R2) S(y) + x => S(y + x)
(R3) Diff(O,x) => O
(R4) Diff(y + x, y) => x

The generated sequence of critical pairs resp. rewrite rules is:

(A1) Diff(x,O) => x
(A2) Diff(S(y+x),S(y)) => x
(A3) Diff(S(x),S(O)) => x
(A4) Diff(S(S(y+x)),S(S(y))) => x
(A5) Diff(S(S(x)),S(S(O))) => x
(A6) Diff(S(S(S(y+x))),S(S(S(y)))) => x
(A7) Diff(S(S(S(x))),S(S(S(O)))) => x
(A8) Diff(S(S(S(S(y+x)))),S(S(S(S(y))))) => x
etc.

In order to apply our inductive completion rules to this sequence of rewrite rules, the sequence is partitioned in two subsequences: (A1) , (A3) , (A5) , (A7) , ... and (A2) , (A4) , (A6) , (A8) , ... For the moment, the question of how to divide a sequence into appropriate subsequences is an open problem. However, there are some useful heuristics.

Consider the second subsequence. An application of the second inductive completion rule has the following consequences. First of all, we have to introduce a new operator called H of arity *nat nat* -> *nat* . Second, we have to add the following new rules to the rewrite rule system R :

(R5) Diff(S(w),S(v)) => H(O,w,v)
(R6) H(z,S(w),S(v)) => H(S(z),w,v)

On the basis of the system R' = R ∪ { (R5) , (R6) }, we obtain the following sequence of new critical pairs resp. rewrite rules:

(B1) Diff(x,O) => x
(B2) H(S(O),y+x,y) => x
(B3) H(S(O),x,O) => x
(B4) H(S(S(O)),y+x,y) => x
(B5) H(S(S(O)),x,O) => x
(B6) H(S(S(S(O))),y+x,y) => x
(B7) H(S(S(S(O))),x,O) => x
(B8) H(S(S(S(S(O)))),y+x,y) => x
etc.

Obviously, each of the subsequences (B2) , (B4) , (B6) , ... and (B3) , (B5) , (B7) , ... , resp., can be generalized by a single rewrite rule. Formally, this generalization step will b realized by applying the fifth inductive completion rule to both subsequences.

(R7) H(z,y+x,y) => x
(R8) H(z,x,0) => x

If we apply the *Knuth-Bendix* completion algorithm to the new rewrite rule system R'' = R' ∪ {(R7) , (R8)} , the completion process terminates after generating the new rewrite rule (R9) successfully.

(R9) Diff(y,0) => y

The reader may easily check that the whole new rewrite rule system R''' = R'' ∪ { (R9) } is canonical and, moreover, a conservative extension of the given rewrite system R.

To sum up, under the assumption of a particular *Knuth-Bendix* completion algorithm together with a term ordering, the set of inference rules introduced define a deduction-like operator denoted by $\vdash_{gen}$. This allows to express the situation investigated in the present chapter by R $\vdash_{gen}$ R''' .

Correctness

Throughout this final part of the paper, we are discussing problems of correctness. First of all, we present a definition for the notion of correctness used.

<u>Definition</u>

An inductive completion rule is said to be *correct*, if and only if every application of this rule yields a conservative extension.

The next result forms a helpful basis for proving the correctness of our inductive completion rules.

<u>Theorem</u>

Suppose two rewrite rule systems R_1 and R_2 over the corresponding signatures Σ_1 resp. Σ_2 with $\Sigma_1 \subseteq \Sigma_2$.

Moreover, let us assume

(1) $(R_2)^{-1}$ is a canonical rewrite rule system.

(2) $\forall s \in S_1 \ \forall t \in T(\Sigma_2,X)_s$: The normal form of t w.r.t. $(R_2)^{-1}$ is contained in $T(\Sigma_1,X)_s$.

(3) $\forall t \in T(\Sigma_1,X)$: t is irreducible w.r.t. $(R_2)^{-1}$.

Under this assumption, it follows that the term rewriting system $R_1 \cup R_2$ is a conservative extension of the rewrite rule system R_1.

Notice that the system $(R_2)^{-1}$ above is built by simply changing the orientation of each rewrite rule in R_2. By $T(\Sigma_2,X)_s$ we denote the subset of all terms of sort *s* in $T(\Sigma_2,X)$. S_1 denotes the set of all sort names in Σ_1.

On the basis of this result, one can easily prove the following corollary. Within this proof, the rewrite rule system R' which will be generated by an application of an inductive completion rule plays the role of the rewrite rule system R_2 in the theorem above.

Theorem

The first, second, and third inductive completion rules are correct.

Additionally, these inductive completion rules have the particular property that there exists a general method for extending any given ordering to a termination ordering suitable for proving termination of the generated new rewrite rules.

Concerning the correctness of the fourth and fifth inductive completion rule, resp., one needs a more sophisticated approach.

Conclusions

There are several open problems left for further investigations. We are sketching some of them.

In the chapter above, we have only considered correctness of our first three inductive completion rules. A correctness concept for the other rules requires a consideration of the limiting process as a whole. The correctness of a generalization of a possibly infinite sequence of terms can not be described w.r.t. an initial segment of this sequence only. In a forthcoming paper, we intend to adopt the corresponding results from the classical recursion-theoretic inductive inference.

When developing any calculus, problems of completeness are usually attracting much attention. Despite the particular concept of completeness used, it is quite obvious that the set of inference rules introduced remains incomplete. It may be of a particular interest to develop calculi being complete for several classes of term rewriting systems. Up to now, it is still open how to characterize those problem classes appropriately.

First of all, we need a suitable concept of completeness. We are proposing the following approach. As a successful inductive completion as investigated above results in a finite canonical rewrite rule system, the underlying equational theory turns out to be decidable, a posteriori. Thus, one should call a set of inference rules complete, if for every decidable equational theory incompletely presented by a terminating but possibly not confluent term rewriting system there is a sequence of applications of these rules such that the ultimate result is a canonical system being a conservative extension of the given one.

From recursion-theoretic arguments, we know that such an extension always exists. It is still open whether or not there is a universal method for constructing a desired canonical conservative extension from any given rewrite rule system having such an extension.

Obviously, our techniques for introducing auxiliary operators are primitive recursive in structure. Therefore, we need another idea for introducing more general auxiliary operators. In other words, it seems to be necessary to find inductive completion rules reflecting the gist of the minimum operator.

Finally, when restricting our attention to primitive recursive rules, it arises the question whether this establishes a hierarchy similar to other primitive recursive hierarchies (in the sense of *Grzegorczyk*, e.g.).

Analogously to results in abstract data type theory, it seems possible to restrict the number of auxiliary operators to be introduced. But this may depend on the presence of certain rules reflecting the power of the minimum operator.

References

[AnSm] D. Angluin and C.H. Smith
Inductive Inference: Theory and Methods,
Computing Surveys 15 (1983) 3, 237-269

[EhMa] H. Ehrig and B. Mahr
Fundamentals of Algebraic Specifications 1,
EATCS Monographs on Theoretical Computer Science 6,
Springer-Verlag, 1985

[Herm] M. Hermann
Chain Properties of Rule Closures,
in: Proc. 6th STACS, B. Monien and R. Cori (eds.),
Paderborn, 1989, Springer-Verlag, Lecture Notes in
Computer Science 349, 1989, 339-347

[HuOp] G. Huet and D. Oppen
Equations and Rewrite Rules: A Survey,
in: Formal Language Theory: Perspectives and Open
Problems, R. Book (ed.), Academic Press, New York,
1980, 349-405

[KaNa] D. Kapur and P. Narendran
A Finite Thue System with Decidable Word Problem and Without Equivalent Finite Canonical System,
Theor. Comp. Sci. 35 (1985) 2&3, 337-344

[KnBe] D.E. Knuth and P.B. Bendix
Simple Word Problems in Universal Algebra,
in: Computational Algebra, J. Leach (ed.), Pergamon Press, 1970, 263-297

[Lang] St. Lange
Towards a Set of Inference Rules for Solving Divergence in Knuth-Bendix Completion,
in: Analogical and Inductive Inference, AII'89, Proc., K.P. Jantke (ed.), Springer-Verlag, Lecture Notes in Artificial Intelligence 397, 1989, 304-316

[ThJa] M. Thomas and K.P. Jantke
Inductive Inference for Solving Divergence in Knuth-Bendix Completion,
in: Analogical and Inductive Inference, AII'89, Proc., K.P. Jantke (ed.), Springer-Verlag, Lecture Notes in Artificial Intelligence 397, 1989, 288-303

A notion of implementation for the specification language *OBSCURE*

Thomas Lehmann
Universität des Saarlandes
FB14 Informatik
D–6600 Saarbrücken
e-mail: lehmann@cs.uni-sb.de

1 Introduction

In the beginning of the seventies abstract data types have been introduced with the goal to enhance security in the software development process. This work has been strongly influenced by the data type concepts in programming languages such as *CLU* ([LZ74]) and by the pioneering paper of Hoare ([Hoa72]). A lot of theoretical investigation has been made in the field of algebraic specifications of abstract data types starting with the initial algebra semantics of the ADJ group ([GTW78]). Alternatively other semantics for algebraic specifications have been studied, e.g. final semantics ([Wan79, Kam83]) or observational abstraction mechanisms ([GGM76]). Apart from the algebraic approach several authors suggested more constructive specification methods ([Car80, Kla84, Loe87]). Similarly to the development of programming languages, so called specification languages have been developed based on these methods, beginning with *CLEAR* ([BG80, San84]) and followed by *ACT ONE* ([EM85]), *ACT TWO* ([Fey88, EM90]), *OBJ2* ([FGJM85]), *OBJ3* ([GW88]), *PLUSS* ([Gau84, BGM87]) and *ASL* ([Wir86]).

In order to describe the process of developing concrete programs from abstract software specifications in the sense of stepwise refinement, several notions of implementation appeared in the literature. They study the question under which circumstances a specification is implemented by another one. The first concept proposed by [GTW78] for algebraic specifications has been extended by [EKMP82] and [Ehr82]. The approaches of [EK82] and [Lip83] considered implementations of parameterized specifications. More recent papers deal with notions of implementation in the context of loose specifications and mainly rely on the refinement concept of [SW83]. Examples are among others the work of Sannella and Tarlecki ([ST88]), Beierle and Voß ([BV85]), Schoett ([Sch86]) and Hennicker ([Hen89]).

The notion of implementation we will present here is based on the specification language *OBSCURE* whose semantics has been precisely described in [LL87]. *OBSCURE* provides tools to build up modules. The semantical behaviour of such a module is characterized by a function mapping algebras over its imported signature to algebras over its exported signature. The semantics is called *fixed* (in contrast with *loose* semantics), because for each imported algebra at most one exported algebra is admitted, whereas in a loose approach the semantical function maps an imported algebra to a *class* of exported algebras. Therefore the notion of implementation presented in this paper — although related to various approaches known from the literature — does not incorporate the refinement concept of [SW83] so far. In [Leh90] we discuss a possible extension of *OBSCURE* to loose semantics and transfer our notion of implementation to the new situation.

An implementation in our sense relates two *OBSCURE* modules. On the level of signatures this relation is characterized by morphisms connecting the imported and exported signatures of the module to be implemented with the corresponding signatures of the implementing module. On the level of algebras an implementation describes how a homomorphic relation between algebras over the imported signatures of the implementing and the implemented module can be extended to the corresponding exported algebras. The idea of such homomorphic relations, that will be called *representations* henceforth, occurs in many papers on abstract implementations and can already be found in the abstraction functions of [Hoa72].

We are especially interested in two different methods to combine implementations. The *vertical composition* of two implementations shows how from an implementation of a module m by a module m' and from an implementation of this module m' by a module m'' an implementation of m by m'' can be constructed. *Horizontal composition* relates implementations with the underlying specification language. Here we assume to be given modules $m_1, \ldots, m_r$ that can be combined to a module m using the specification building operations of *OBSCURE*. If moreover $m'_1, \ldots, m'_r$ are modules implementing $m_1, \ldots, m_r$, horizontal composition of implementations means that the combination m' of the modules $m'_1, \ldots, m'_r$ yields an implementation of the module m.

The paper is organized as follows. After a short introduction recalling several features of the specification language *OBSCURE* (Section 2), we define the notion of an implementation in Section 3 and illustrate the concept on a running example. Section 4 lists the main results, especially the vertical and horizontal composition properties, and provides an example using some of these results.

2 The specification language *OBSCURE*

This section presents a short introduction into the specification language *OBSCURE*. A more detailed version may be found in [LL87]. For the notions of signature, signature morphism and algebra we refer to the classical work of [EM85]. When dealing with formulas we always have formulas of first order predicate logic in mind with equality as the only predicate symbol. Given a signature Σ we denote its underlying set of sorts by $SOR(\Sigma)$ and the set of first order formulas over Σ containing variables from an (implicitly given) $SOR(\Sigma)$–sorted family X of infinite sets by $WFF(\Sigma)$.[1] For a formula w over Σ with variables from X, a Σ–algebra A and a (variable) assignment $\alpha : X \to A$ the satisfaction relation $A, \alpha \models w$ is defined as usual; we write $A \models w$ if $A, \alpha \models w$ holds for all assignments $\alpha : X \to A$.

It is our goal to describe the set **SPEC** of all *OBSCURE* specifications which is characterized by a *signature function* $\mathcal{S}$, assigning to each module its imported and exported signatures, and by a so called *meaning function* $\mathcal{M}$. $\mathcal{M}$ describes the semantical behaviour of the modules from **SPEC**, i.e. for each module m its semantics $\mathcal{M}(m)$ is a (possibly partial) function mapping algebras over the imported signature of m to algebras over its exported signature.

To define the set **SPEC** and the functions $\mathcal{S}$ and $\mathcal{M}$ we start from a given set **AtSPEC** of so called *atomic specifications* (*atomic modules*) and two functions $\mathcal{S}^0$ and $\mathcal{M}^0$ defined on **AtSPEC**. The function $\mathcal{S}^0$ maps each $m \in$ **AtSPEC** to a pair of signatures $\mathcal{S}^0(m) = (\mathcal{S}^0_i(m), \mathcal{S}^0_e(m))$. $\mathcal{S}^0_i(m)$ is called the *imported signature* and $\mathcal{S}^0_e(m)$ is called the *exported signature* of m. For $m \in$ **AtSPEC** the element $\mathcal{M}^0(m)$ denotes a partial function $\mathrm{Alg}_{\mathcal{S}^0_i(m)} \rightsquigarrow \mathrm{Alg}_{\mathcal{S}^0_e(m)}$ where Alg_Σ is the class of all Σ–algebras for a given signature Σ. The *inherited signature* $\mathcal{S}^0_i(m) \cap \mathcal{S}^0_e(m)$ for $m \in$ **AtSPEC** is abbreviated as $Isig(m)$ and the set $SOR(Isig(m))$ — the *inherited sorts* — as $I(m)$. Moreover we assume that each $\mathcal{M}^0(m)$ fulfills the following *persistency condition*:

$$\text{for each } \mathcal{S}^0_i(m)\text{–algebra } A \text{ such that } \mathcal{M}^0(m)(A) \text{ is defined we have}$$
$$\mathcal{M}^0(m)(A)_s = A_s \text{ for } s \in I(m) \text{ and}$$
$$f^{\mathcal{M}^0(m)(A)} = f^A \text{ for } s \in Isig(m).$$

The language **SPEC**, whose elements will be denoted as *specifications* or *modules* henceforth, is defined as a subclass of the set inductively generated over **AtSPEC** using the specification building operations

[1] Here we differ from the more general logical framework sketched in [LL87] in restricting our considerations to first order logic. We have chosen this restriction because in the context of implementations we only prove results for this kind of formulas.

of *OBSCURE*. These are given as follows: union of two modules, composition of two modules, forgetting sorts and operations from the exported signature of a module, renamings of the exported resp. imported signature of a module, axioms on the exported resp. imported signature of a module, a **subset**–operation in order to restrict carrier sets of exported algebras of a module and a **quotient**–operation that allows identification of elements in such carrier sets. The possible applications of each specification building operation are restricted by sets of so called *context conditions*. So **SPEC** is a *proper* subclass of the set inductively generated by **AtSPEC** and includes **AtSPEC** by definition. Simultaneously to the construction of **SPEC** we extend $\mathcal{S}^0$ and $\mathcal{M}^0$ to functions $\mathcal{S}$ and $\mathcal{M}$ defined on **SPEC**. Each $m \in$ **SPEC** will be mapped to a pair of signatures $\mathcal{S}(m) = (\mathcal{S}_i(m), \mathcal{S}_e(m))$ and to a partial function $\mathcal{M}(m) : \mathrm{Alg}_{\mathcal{S}_i(m)} \rightsquigarrow \mathrm{Alg}_{\mathcal{S}_e(m)}$. The notions of an inherited sort and an inherited signature defined above for atomic modules extend to arbitrary modules in the obvious way. As proved in [LL87], the persistency condition for $m \in$ **AtSPEC** guarantees, that the construction is well–defined and moreover that persistency holds for an arbitrary $m \in$ **SPEC**, i.e.:

for each $\mathcal{S}_i(m)$–algebra A such that $\mathcal{M}(m)(A)$ is defined we have
$\mathcal{M}(m)(A)_s = A_s$ for $s \in I(m)$ and
$f^{\mathcal{M}(m)(A)} = f^A$ for $s \in Isig(m)$.

We will here only explain those specification building operations, which are needed to formulate the results in Section 4. The complete description of the syntax and semantics of *OBSCURE* can be found in [LL87]. This paper also contains further comments to the different operations. The exact syntax and semantics of those specification building operations we use in this paper (including the context conditions) is given as follows:

(1) *Union of modules*
If $m_1, m_2 \in$ **SPEC** then

$$m_1 + m_2 \in \textbf{SPEC}$$

provided that

(*i*) $\mathcal{S}_e(m_1) \cap \mathcal{S}_e(m_2) \subseteq \mathcal{S}_i(m_1) \cap \mathcal{S}_i(m_2)$
(*ii*) $\mathcal{S}_e(m_1) \cap \mathcal{S}_i(m_2) \subseteq \mathcal{S}_i(m_1)$
(*iii*) $\mathcal{S}_e(m_2) \cap \mathcal{S}_i(m_1) \subseteq \mathcal{S}_i(m_2)$

In this case

$$\mathcal{S}(m_1 + m_2) = \mathcal{S}(m_1) \cup \mathcal{S}(m_2)$$

and

$$\mathcal{M}(m_1 + m_2)(A) = \mathcal{M}(m_1)(A|_{\mathcal{S}_i(m_1)}) \cup \mathcal{M}(m_2)(A|_{\mathcal{S}_i(m_2)})$$

iff $\mathcal{M}(m_1)(A|_{\mathcal{S}_i(m_1)})$ and $\mathcal{M}(m_2)(A|_{\mathcal{S}_i(m_2)})$ are both defined.[2]

(2) *Composition of modules*
If $m_1, m_2 \in$ **SPEC** then

$$m_1 \circ m_2 \in \textbf{SPEC}$$

provided that

(*i*) $\mathcal{S}_e(m_2) = \mathcal{S}_i(m_1)$
(*ii*) $\mathcal{S}_i(m_2) \cap \mathcal{S}_e(m_1) \subseteq \mathcal{S}_i(m_1)$

In this case

$$\mathcal{S}(m_1 \circ m_2) = (\mathcal{S}_i(m_2), \mathcal{S}_e(m_1))$$

and

$$\mathcal{M}(m_1 \circ m_2)(A) = \mathcal{M}(m_1)(\mathcal{M}(m_2)(A))$$

iff $\mathcal{M}(m_2)(A)$ and $\mathcal{M}(m_1)(\mathcal{M}(m_2)(A))$ are both defined.

[2]In all other cases $\mathcal{M}(m_1 + m_2)(A)$ is undefined. A similar remark holds for the other specification building operations.

(3) *Forgetting sorts and operations*
If $m \in \mathbf{SPEC}$ and lso is a list of sorts and operations then

$$lso \square m \in \mathbf{SPEC}$$

provided that

(*i*) $\mathcal{S}_e(m) \setminus lso$ (the sorts and operations obtained by removing from $\mathcal{S}_e(m)$ those listed in lso) forms a signature

In this case

$$\mathcal{S}(lso \square m) = (\mathcal{S}_i(m), \mathcal{S}_e(m) \setminus lso)$$

and

$$\mathcal{M}(lso \square m)(A) = \mathcal{M}(m)(A)|_{\mathcal{S}_e(m) \setminus lso}$$

iff $\mathcal{M}(m)(A)$ is defined.

(4) *Renaming of the exported signature*
If $m \in \mathbf{SPEC}$, Σ is a signature, $\rho_e : \mathcal{S}_e(m) \to \Sigma$ is a signature morphism and $\rho = (id(\mathcal{S}_i(m)), \rho_e)$ then

$$<\rho> m \in \mathbf{SPEC}$$

provided that

(*i*) $\rho_e|_{Isig(m)} = id(Isig(m))$ (ρ_e is the identity on $Isig(m)$)
(*ii*) ρ_e is injective
(*iii*) $\mathcal{S}_i(m) \cap \rho_e(\mathcal{S}_e(m)) \subseteq \mathcal{S}_e(m)$

In this case

$$\mathcal{S}(<\rho> m) = \rho(\mathcal{S}(m)) = (\mathcal{S}_i(m), \rho_e(\mathcal{S}_e(m)))$$

and

$$\mathcal{M}(<\rho> m)(A) = \mathcal{M}(m)(A)|_{\rho_e^{-1}}$$

iff $\mathcal{M}(m)(A)$ is defined. ($\rho_e^{-1} : \rho_e(\mathcal{S}_e(m)) \to \mathcal{S}_e(m)$ is the inverse of ρ_e and therefore also a signature morphism.)

(5) *Renaming of the imported signature*
If $m \in \mathbf{SPEC}$, Σ_i, Σ_e are signatures, $\rho_i : \mathcal{S}_i(m) \to \Sigma_i$ and $\rho_e : \mathcal{S}_e(m) \to \Sigma_e$ are signature morphisms and $\rho = (\rho_i, \rho_e)$, then

$$m <\rho> \in \mathbf{SPEC}$$

provided that

(*i*) $\rho_i|_{Isig(m)} = \rho_e|_{Isig(m)}$
(*ii*) ρ_e is injective on $\mathcal{S}_e(m) \setminus \mathcal{S}_i(m)$
(*iii*) $\rho_i(\mathcal{S}_i(m)) \cap \rho_e(\mathcal{S}_e(m) \setminus \mathcal{S}_i(m)) = \emptyset$

In this case

$$\mathcal{S}(m <\rho>) = \rho(\mathcal{S}(m)) = (\rho_i(\mathcal{S}_i(m)), \rho_e(\mathcal{S}_e(m))).$$

The algebra $\mathcal{M}(m<\rho>)(A)$ is defined iff $\mathcal{M}(m)(A|_{\rho_i})$ is defined, and then $\mathcal{M}(m<\rho>)(A)$ is the $\mathcal{S}_e(m<\rho>)$-algebra B given as follows:

$$B_{s'} = \mathcal{M}(m)(A|_{\rho_i})_s,$$

for $s \in SOR(\mathcal{S}_e(m))$ with $s' = \rho_e(s)$ and

$$f'^B = f^{\mathcal{M}(m)(A|_{\rho_i})}$$

if f is an operation from $\mathcal{S}_e(m)$ with $f' = \rho_e(f)$.

(6) *Axioms on the exported signature*
If $m \in$ **SPEC** and w is a formula then

$$\{w\}m \in \mathbf{SPEC}$$

provided that

(*i*) $w \in WFF(\mathcal{S}_e(m))$

In this case

$$\mathcal{S}(\{w\}m) = \mathcal{S}(m)$$

and

$$\mathcal{M}(\{w\}m)(A) = \mathcal{M}(m)(A)$$

iff $\mathcal{M}(m)(A)$ is defined and $\mathcal{M}(m)(A) \models w$. □

We now briefly comment these language constructs using the pictural illustration of Figure 1. It should be mentioned that the syntactical description of the renaming constructs (in (4) and (5)) slightly differs from the presentation given in [LL87]. We replace the renaming pairs ($lso1, lso2$) occurring there by the morphism ρ induced by them.

The construct "+" (in (1)) puts two modules together (cf. Figure 1(a)). It bears similarities with the construct "+" of *CLEAR* ([San84]), "and" of *ACT ONE* ([EM85]) and "union" of *ACT TWO* ([EM90]). The module signature of the module $m_1 + m_2$ is defined as the union of the imported resp. exported signatures of m_1 and m_2. For an algebra $A \in \mathrm{Alg}_{\mathcal{S}_i(m_1+m_2)}$ the corresponding exported algebra $\mathcal{M}(m_1 + m_2)(A)$ is defined as the union of the algebras $\mathcal{M}(m_1)(A|_{\mathcal{S}_i(m_1)})$ and $\mathcal{M}(m_2)(A|_{\mathcal{S}_i(m_2)})$. This union can be characterized by the equations

$$\mathcal{M}(m_1 + m_2)(A)|_{\mathcal{S}_e(m_j)} = \mathcal{M}(m_j)(A|_{\mathcal{S}_i(m_j)})$$

for $j = 1, 2$. A proof, that this construction yields a well-defined algebra $\mathcal{M}(m_1 + m_2)(A)$, is based on the context conditions (1)(*i*)–(*iii*) and may be found in [LL87]. Essentially, these conditions make sure that there are no "name clashes".

The construct "$\circ$" (in (2)) provides another way to combine two modules and can be compared with the enrich-construct of *CLEAR* and the composition construct of *ACT TWO*(cf. Figure 1(b)). The exported signature of $m_1 \circ m_2$ is identical with the exported signature of m_1, its imported signature coincides with the imported signtaure of m_2. The fact, that the signatures $\mathcal{S}_e(m_2)$ and $\mathcal{S}_i(m_1)$ are equal (condition (2)(*i*)), allows to define the meaning $\mathcal{M}(m_1 \circ m_2)$ as the functional composition of the meanings $\mathcal{M}(m_1)$ and $\mathcal{M}(m_2)$.

The next construct (s. (3)) allows to forget the sorts and operations listed in *lso* from the exported signature of a module m (cf. Figure 1(c)). In particular, it enables to get rid of "auxiliary" sorts and operations.

With the construct "$< \_ > \_$" (in (4)) it is possible to rename sorts and operations of the exported signature of a module m. It is especially useful in combination with the construct "+" for avoiding name clashes between two modules. The choice of the renaming morphism ρ as a pair of signature morphisms $(id(\mathcal{S}_i(m)), \rho_e)$ shows, that the imported signature of the module m is not affected by this kind of renaming. Figure 1(d) is an example for the export renaming. The exported sorts and/or operations a and c of the module m_1 are renamed into e and f, d is left unchanged. This renaming induces the pair of signature morphisms ρ in the picture.

Corresponding to the export renaming in (4) the construct "$\_ < \_ >$" in (5) allows to rename imported sorts and operations of a module. In contrast to (4) the import renaming may also change the exported signature of a module. Import renamings are useful in order to simulate actualization in the context of parameterized specifications (see [LL87] for further details).

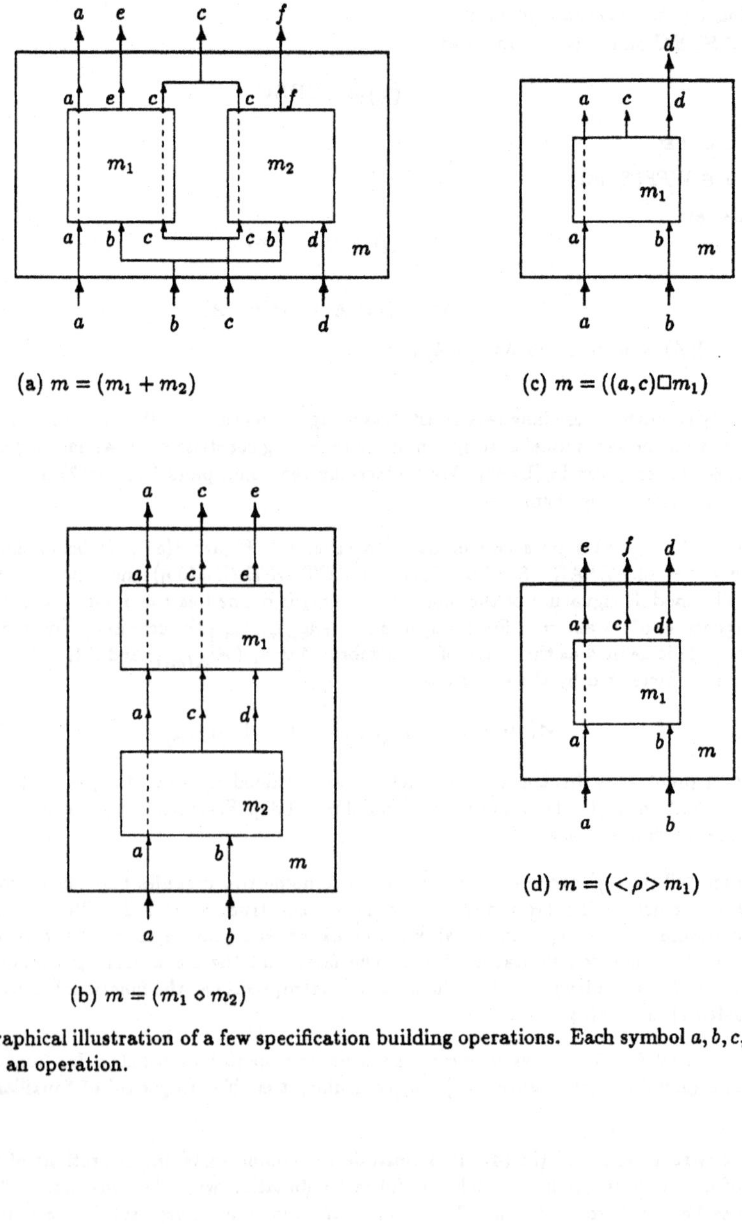

(a) $m = (m_1 + m_2)$

(c) $m = ((a, c)\Box m_1)$

(b) $m = (m_1 \circ m_2)$

(d) $m = (<\rho> m_1)$

Figure 1: Graphical illustration of a few specification building operations. Each symbol $a, b, c, \ldots$ stands for a sort or an operation.

OBSCURE provides the possibility to restrict the meaning of a module by the construct "{_}_" (s. (6)). If w is a formula over the exported signature of a module m, the meaning $\mathcal{M}(\{w\}m)$ is obtained by restricting the domain of $\mathcal{M}(m)$ to those algebras A whose exported algebras $\mathcal{M}(m)(A)$ satisfy w. The module signature is not changed by this construct.

Note, that the syntactic structure of the specifications in **AtSPEC** is left open. Instead each specification is characterized by the mappings $\mathcal{S}^0$ and $\mathcal{M}^0$ giving the module signatures and the meaning function as a mapping from imported algebras to exported algebras. This allows the choice of different specification methods for the description of the elements of **AtSPEC**, e.g. algebraic or algorithmic specifications. The algorithmic specification method assigns to an imported algebra A an exported algebra B whose carriers are built up using the carriers of A together with so called constructor operations specified in the module. The operations of B are given by recursive programs. A detailed version of the semantics is described in [Loe87]. Algebraically specified modules in our framework are modules whose exported operations are given by a set of conditional equations. If m is such an algebraically specified module, then the meaning $\mathcal{M}(m)$ assigns to an imported algebra of m its free extension if the persistency condition is satisfied. Otherwise the meaning is undefined.

We conclude this section by introducing the notion of a submodule. If $m, m' \in$ **SPEC** are modules, then m' is called a *submodule* of m if $\mathcal{S}_i(m') \subseteq \mathcal{S}_i(m)$ and $\mathcal{S}_e(m') \subseteq \mathcal{S}_e(m)$. Especially, if $m_1, m_2 \in$ **SPEC** such that $m_1 + m_2 \in$ **SPEC**, then both m_1 and m_2 are submodules of $m_1 + m_2$.

3 The notion of implementation

In this section we introduce the notion of implementation for the specification language *OBSCURE*. It is — roughly spoken — a relation on the set **SPEC**. More precisely, given modules $m, m' \in$ **SPEC** an implementation of the module m by the module m', as it will be formally presented in Definition 3.7, is based on the notion of

- a *module morphism* $\sigma : m \rightarrow m'$ and of
- a class $\mathcal{K}$ of σ–representations between imported algebras of m and m' for the given module morphism $\sigma : m \rightarrow m'$.

These notions are now made more precise and illustrated by a running example.

3.1 Module morphisms

Definition 3.1 Let $m, m' \in$ **SPEC** be modules. A *module morphism* $\sigma : m \rightarrow m'$ is a pair (σ_i, σ_e) of signature morphisms $\sigma_i : \mathcal{S}_i(m) \rightarrow \mathcal{S}_i(m')$ and $\sigma_e : \mathcal{S}_e(m) \rightarrow \mathcal{S}_e(m')$ that coincide on the inherited sorts and operations of m, i.e.

$$\sigma_i|_{Isig(m)} = \sigma_e|_{Isig(m)} \, . \qquad \square$$

This notion of a module morphism is similar to the notion of an interface specification morphism in ([EM90], Definition 5.13). The similarity is best seen if we additionally introduce the inherited signature $Isig(m)$ of a module m as the parameter interface (in the sense of [EM90]) into our module concept. The parameter part of the interface specification morphism is then given by the restriction $\sigma_i|_{Isig(m)}$ (resp. $\sigma_e|_{Isig(m)}$). The commutativity conditions in Definition 5.13 of [EM90] meet exactly our requirement that σ_i and σ_e shall coincide on the inherited signature of m.

Note that the specification building operations export and import renaming introduced in Section 2 induce module morphisms $\rho : m \rightarrow <\rho> m$ and $\rho : m \rightarrow m <\rho>$.

Example 3.1 We present two atomic modules SET and LIST specifying sets over the natural numbers resp. lists over the integers using the algebraic specification method with conditional equations.

```
MODULE SET IS
       IMPORTS SORTS nat, bool
               OPNS  true : → bool
                     false : → bool
                     =_nat : nat nat → bool
                     0 : → nat
                     succ : nat → nat
       CREATE  SORTS set
               OPNS  s-empty : → set
                     s-insert : set nat → set
                     s-member : nat set → bool
       SEMANTICS
       VARDEC  a, b : nat, s : set
       EQNS    s-insert(s-insert(s, a), a) = s-insert(s, a)
               s-insert(s-insert(s, a), b) = s-insert(s-insert(s, b), a)
               s-member(a, s-empty) = false
               s-member(a, s-insert(s, a)) = true
               IF (a =_nat b) = false THEN s-member(a, s-insert(s, b)) = s-member(a, s) FI
       ENDCREATE
END

MODULE LIST IS
       IMPORTS SORTS int, bool
               OPNS  true : → bool
                     false : → bool
                     =_int : int int → bool
                     0 : → int
                     succ : int → int
                     pred : int → int
       CREATE  SORTS list
               OPNS  l-empty : → list
                     l-insert : list int → list
                     l-member : int list → bool
       SEMANTICS
       VARDEC  a, b : int, s : list
       EQNS    l-member(a, l-empty) = false
               l-member(a, l-insert(s, a)) = true
               IF (a =_int b) = false THEN l-member(a, l-insert(s, b)) = l-member(a, s) FI
       ENDCREATE
END
```

As suggested by the notation we have
$\mathcal{S}_i(\text{SET}) = (\{nat,\ bool\},\ \{true,\ false,\ =_{nat},\ 0,\ succ\})$,
$\mathcal{S}_e(\text{SET}) = \mathcal{S}_i(\text{SET}) \cup (\{set\},\ \{\text{s-empty},\ \text{s-insert},\ \text{s-member}\})$,
$\mathcal{S}_i(\text{LIST}) = (\{int,\ bool\},\ \{true,\ false,\ =_{int},\ 0,\ succ,\ pred\})$ and
$\mathcal{S}_e(\text{LIST}) = \mathcal{S}_i(\text{LIST}) \cup (\{list\},\ \{\text{l-empty},\ \text{l-insert},\ \text{l-member}\})$.
The assignments

$$\begin{array}{lcl} bool & \longmapsto & bool \\ nat & \longmapsto & int \\ true & \longmapsto & true \\ false & \longmapsto & false \\ 0 & \longmapsto & 0 \\ succ & \longmapsto & succ \\ =_{nat} & \longmapsto & =_{int} \end{array}$$

define a signature morphism $\sigma_i : \mathcal{S}_i(\text{SET}) \to \mathcal{S}_i(\text{LIST})$. An extension of σ_i by

s-*empty*	$\longmapsto$	l-*empty*
s-*insert*	$\longmapsto$	l-*insert*
s-*member*	$\longmapsto$	l-*member*

yields a signature morphism $\sigma_e : \mathcal{S}_e(\text{SET}) \to \mathcal{S}_e(\text{LIST})$. The pair $\sigma = (\sigma_i, \sigma_e)$ describes a module morphism σ : SET $\to$ LIST. □

If $\sigma : m \to m'$ and $\sigma' : m' \to m''$ are module morphisms, their *composition* is defined componentwise yielding a module morphism $\sigma' \circ \sigma : m \to m''$. The restriction of a module morphism $\sigma : m \to m'$ to a submodule m'' of m is given by restricting σ_i to $\mathcal{S}_i(m'')$ and σ_e to $\mathcal{S}_e(m'')$. The result is the module morphism $\sigma|_{m''} : m'' \to m'$.

3.2 Representations

Definition 3.2 Let $m, m' \in$ **SPEC** be modules, $\sigma : m \to m'$ be a module morphism, $A \in \mathrm{Alg}_{\mathcal{S}_i(m)}$ and $B \in \mathrm{Alg}_{\mathcal{S}_i(m')}$ be algebras.
A family $r = (r_s)_{s \in SOR(\mathcal{S}_i(m))}$ of surjective partial functions $r_s : B_{\sigma_i(s)} \rightsquigarrow A_s$ is called *(σ-)representation of A by B* (also denoted $B \xrightarrow{r} A$) if for each operation $(f : s_1 \dots s_n \to s) \in \mathcal{S}_i(m)$

$$r_s(\sigma_i(f)^B(b_1, \dots, b_n)) = f^A(r_{s_1}(b_1), \dots, r_{s_n}(b_n))$$

holds for all $b_j \in B_{\sigma_i(s_j)}$ such that $r_{s_j}(b_j)$ is defined $(1 \le j \le n)$. The set of all σ-representations of A by B is denoted by $Rep_\sigma(B, A)$. □

By its very definition the notion of a σ-representation only depends on the imported component σ_i of a module morphism σ.

σ-representations are similar to partial homomorphisms known from the theory of partial algebras ([BW82]). But there is a little difference. A representation r of A by B (in our sense) is a $\mathcal{S}_i(m)$-homomorphism from $B|_{\sigma_i}$ to A (in the sense of [BW82]), if the equation

$$r_s(\sigma_i(f)^B(b_1, \dots, b_n)) = f^A(r_{s_1}(b_1), \dots, r_{s_n}(b_n))$$

also holds if some of the $r_{s_j}(b_j)$ are undefined. This means that in addition to the requirement of Definition 3.2 r_s has to be undefined on $\sigma_i(f)^B(b_1, \dots, b_n)$ as soon as one of the $r_{s_j}(b_j)$ is undefined. Note that the requirement

$$\text{“}\sigma_i(f)^B(b_1, \dots, b_n) \text{ is defined”}$$

in [BW82] is trivially fulfilled since we here deal with total algebras. This definedness property also guarantees that a σ-representation, which is a homomorphism, is automatically a weak homomorphism. Moreover it is a total homomorphism in the sense of [BW82], if all r_s are total functions.[3]

In the following we will consider arbitrary classes $\mathcal{K}$ of σ-representations, i.e. families $(\mathcal{K}(B, A))_{A \in \mathrm{Alg}_{\mathcal{S}_i(m)}, B \in \mathrm{Alg}_{\mathcal{S}_i(m')}}$ of sets $\mathcal{K}(B, A) \subseteq Rep_\sigma(B, A)$. Moreover we are interested in two special cases of such classes:

- The family $Rep_\sigma = (Rep_\sigma(B, A))_{A \in \mathrm{Alg}_{\mathcal{S}_i(m)}, B \in \mathrm{Alg}_{\mathcal{S}_i(m')}}$ — the class of *all* σ-representations
- The family Rtr_σ — the class of all *trivial* σ-representations — given by

$$Rtr_\sigma(B, A) = \begin{cases} \{id(A)\} & \text{if } A = B|_{\sigma_i} \\ \emptyset & \text{else} \end{cases}$$

where $A \in \mathrm{Alg}_{\mathcal{S}_i(m)}$, $B \in \mathrm{Alg}_{\mathcal{S}_i(m')}$ and $id(A)$ abbreviates the family of identities $(id(A_s))_{s \in SOR(\mathcal{S}_i(m))}$.

[3] For the notions of weak and total homomorphisms we refer to [BW82].

Example 3.2 Let SET, LIST and σ be given as in Example 3.1.
We choose a $\mathcal{S}_i$(SET)–Algebra A by $A_{nat} = \mathbf{N}_0$, $A_{bool} = \{\mathtt{tt}, \mathtt{ff}\}$ and interprete the operations as follows: $true^A = \mathtt{tt}$, $false^A = \mathtt{ff}$, $0^A = 0 \in \mathbf{N}_0$, $succ^A : \mathbf{N}_0 \to \mathbf{N}_0$ given by $succ^A(n) = n+1$, and the identity $(a {=_{nat}}^A b) = \mathtt{tt}$ holds iff $a = b$, where the last "=" stands for the usual equality in $\mathbf{N}_0$.
Let the $\mathcal{S}_i$(LIST)–Algebra B be given by $B_{int} = \mathbf{Z}$, $B_{bool} = A_{bool}$, $true^B = true^A$, $false^B = false^A$, $0^B = 0^A$. $succ$ and $pred$ are interpreted as the usual successor resp. predecessor on $\mathbf{Z}$ and $(a {=_{int}}^B b) = \mathtt{tt}$ holds iff $a = b$, the last "=" expressing the usual equality in $\mathbf{Z}$.
Assume $B \xrightarrow{r} A$ is a σ–representation. According to Definition 3.2 a σ–representation $B \xrightarrow{r} A$ must fulfill the following requirements:

i) $r_{bool}(\mathtt{tt}) = r_{bool}(true^B) = true^A = \mathtt{tt}$

ii) $r_{bool}(\mathtt{ff}) = r_{bool}(false^B) = false^A = \mathtt{ff}$

iii) $r_{nat}(0) = r_{nat}(0^B) = 0^A = 0$

iv) $r_{nat}(succ^B(x)) = succ^A(r_{nat}(x))$ if $r_{nat}(x)$ is defined

v) $r_{bool}(a {=_{int}}^B b) = (r_{nat}(a) {=_{nat}}^A r_{nat}(b))$ if $r_{nat}(a)$ and $r_{nat}(b)$ are defined.

It is easy to show that only one family of functions r satisfies these conditions, namely:

- $r_{bool} = id(A_{bool})$
- $r_{nat} : \mathbf{Z} \rightsquigarrow \mathbf{N}_0$ with $r_{nat}(z) = \begin{cases} z & \text{if } z \geq 0 \\ \text{undefined} & \text{else.} \end{cases}$ □

There is a natural way to combine two representations by building their function compositions componentwise. To make this notion more precise, let $m, m', m'' \in \mathbf{SPEC}$ be modules, $\sigma : m \to m'$ and $\sigma' : m' \to m''$ be module morphsims, $A \in \mathrm{Alg}_{\mathcal{S}_i(m)}$, $B \in \mathrm{Alg}_{\mathcal{S}_i(m')}$ and $C \in \mathrm{Alg}_{\mathcal{S}_i(m'')}$ be algebras and $r^1 \in Rep_\sigma(B, A)$ and $r^2 \in Rep_{\sigma'}(C, B)$ be representations. By definition, r^1 and r^2 are families of functions $r^1_s : B_{\sigma_i(s)} \rightsquigarrow A_s$ $(s \in SOR(\mathcal{S}_i(m)))$ and $r^2_{s'} : C_{\sigma'_i(s')} \rightsquigarrow B_{s'}$ $(s' \in SOR(\mathcal{S}_i(m')))$. With $r^2|_{\sigma_i}$ we denote the $SOR(\mathcal{S}_i(m))$–indexed family of functions $\left(r^2|_{\sigma_i}\right)_s = r^2_{\sigma_i(s)}$ $(s \in SOR(\mathcal{S}_i(m)))$, so we may componentwise form the composition $r^1 \circ r^2|_{\sigma_i}$ of the $SOR(\mathcal{S}_i(m))$–indexed families r^1 and $r^2|_{\sigma_i}$. A straightforward computation shows that this composition yields a $(\sigma' \circ \sigma)$–representation $C \xrightarrow{r} A$. We extend this notion to the composition of classes of representations in the following sense:

Definition 3.3 Let $m, m', m'' \in \mathbf{SPEC}$ be modules, $\sigma : m \to m'$, $\sigma' : m' \to m''$ be module morphisms and $\mathcal{K}_\sigma$ and $\mathcal{K}_{\sigma'}$ be classes of σ– resp. σ'–representations. We define the class $\mathcal{K}_{\sigma'} \circ \mathcal{K}_\sigma$ of $(\sigma' \circ \sigma)$–representations as follows:

$$\begin{aligned}(\mathcal{K}_{\sigma'} \circ \mathcal{K}_\sigma)(C, A) \;:=\; & \{r^1 \circ r^2|_{\sigma_i} \mid \exists B \in \mathrm{Alg}_{\mathcal{S}_i(m')} \text{ with } r^1 \in \mathcal{K}_\sigma(B, A) \\ & \text{and } r^2 \in \mathcal{K}_{\sigma'}(C, B)\}. \;\square\end{aligned}$$

We will now explain, how representations can be restricted to submodules. Let $m, m', m'' \in \mathbf{SPEC}$ be modules, $\sigma : m \to m''$ be a module morphism and m' be a submodule of m, then the restriction of a σ–representation $C \xrightarrow{r} B$ to m', where $C \in \mathrm{Alg}_{\mathcal{S}_i(m'')}$ and $B \in \mathrm{Alg}_{\mathcal{S}_i(m)}$, is given by the restriction of r to its $SOR(\mathcal{S}_i(m'))$–components.[4] We obtain a $(\sigma|_{m'})$–representation which we denote by $r|_{m'}$. This notion also naturally extends to classes of representations:

Definition 3.4 Let $m, m'' \in \mathbf{SPEC}$ be modules, $\sigma : m \to m''$ be a module morphism, $m' \in \mathbf{SPEC}$ be a submodule of m and $\mathcal{K}_\sigma$ be a class of σ–representations. The restriction $\mathcal{K}_\sigma|_{m'}$ of the class $\mathcal{K}_\sigma$ to the submodule m' is defined by

$$\begin{aligned}\mathcal{K}_\sigma|_{m'}(C, A) &= \bigcup \left\{ \{r|_{m'} \mid r \in \mathcal{K}_\sigma(C, B)\} \mid B \in \mathrm{Alg}_{\mathcal{S}_i(m)} \text{ with } A = B|_{\mathcal{S}_i(m')} \right\} \\ &= \left\{ r|_{m'} \mid \exists B \in \mathrm{Alg}_{\mathcal{S}_i(m)} \text{ with } A = B|_{\mathcal{S}_i(m')} \text{ and } r \in \mathcal{K}_\sigma(C, B) \right\}\end{aligned}$$

[4]Note the inclusion $\mathcal{S}_i(m') \subseteq \mathcal{S}_i(m)$ by definition of submodules.

for $C \in Alg_{S_i(m'')}$, $A \in Alg_{S_i(m')}$. □

We conclude this subsection with two results that are easy consequences from the definitions:

Proposition 3.1 If $m, m', m'' \in$ **SPEC** are modules and if $\sigma : m \to m'$, $\sigma' : m' \to m''$ are module morphisms, then

$$Rep_{\sigma' \circ \sigma} = Rep_{\sigma'} \circ Rep_{\sigma}.$$ □

Proposition 3.2 If $m, m', m'' \in$ **SPEC** are modules and if $\sigma : m \to m'$, $\sigma' : m' \to m''$ are module morphisms, then

$$Rtr_{\sigma' \circ \sigma} = Rtr_{\sigma'} \circ Rtr_{\sigma}.$$ □

3.3 Implementations

Our notion of implementation is based on a set of terms (cf. Definition 3.5) and on a method to manipulate these terms using module morphisms and representations (cf. Definition 3.6).

Definition 3.5 Let $m \in$ **SPEC** be a module and $A \in Alg_{S_i(m)}$ be an algebra. The $SOR(S_e(m))$–indexed family of sets of terms $\mathcal{B}(S_e(m), I(m), A)$ over the signature $S_e(m)$ with elements from A on inherited positions is inductively defined as follows:

a) $A_s \subseteq \mathcal{B}(S_e(m), I(m), A)_s$ for $s \in I(m)$

b) $c \in \mathcal{B}(S_e(m), I(m), A)_s$ for each constant $(c :\to s) \in S_e(m)$ and $s \in SOR(S_e(m))$

c) If $(f : s_1 \ldots s_n \to s) \in S_e(m)$ $(n \geq 1)$ and $t_i \in \mathcal{B}(S_e(m), I(m), A)_{s_i}$ $(1 \leq i \leq n)$ then $f(t_1, \ldots, t_n) \in \mathcal{B}(S_e(m), I(m), A)_s$. □

Example 3.3 With the notions from Example 3.1 and 3.2 one obtains:

- $succ(5) \in \mathcal{B}(S_e(\text{SET}), I(\text{SET}), A)_{nat}$
- $pred(pred(succ(-3))) \in \mathcal{B}(S_e(\text{LIST}), I(\text{LIST}), B)_{int}$
- $l\text{-}member(-2, l\text{-}insert(pred(4), l\text{-}empty)) \in \mathcal{B}(S_e(\text{LIST}), I(\text{LIST}), B)_{bool}$ □

Definition 3.6 Let $m, m' \in$ **SPEC** be modules, $\sigma : m \to m'$ be a module morphism, $A \in Alg_{S_i(m)}$, $B \in Alg_{S_i(m')}$ be algebras and $B \xrightarrow{r} A$ be a σ–representation. The $SOR(S_e(m))$–sorted family of mappings

$$(\sigma, r)^\sharp : \mathcal{B}(S_e(m), I(m), A) \to \mathcal{P}(\mathcal{B}(S_e(m'), I(m'), B))^5$$

transforming terms is inductively defined by:

a) For $a \in A_s$ $(s \in I(m))$:

$$(\sigma, r)^\sharp_s(a) := r_s^{-1}(\{a\}) = \{b \in B_{\sigma_i(s)} \mid r_s(b) = a\}$$

b) For each $(c :\to s) \in S_e(m)$:

$$(\sigma, r)^\sharp_s(c) = \{\sigma_e(c)\}$$

c) For $(f : s_1 \ldots s_n \to s) \in S_e(m)$, $t_i \in \mathcal{B}(S_e(m), I(m), A)_{s_i}$ $(1 \leq i \leq n)$:

$$(\sigma, r)^\sharp_s(f(t_1, \ldots, t_n)) := \sigma_e(f)\left((\sigma, r)^\sharp_{s_1}(t_1) \times \cdots \times (\sigma, r)^\sharp_{s_n}(t_n)\right).$$ □

Note, that for each $t \in \mathcal{B}(S_e(m), I(m), A)_s$ the set $(\sigma, r)^\sharp_s(t)$ is nonempty, because the representation r is surjective by definition.

[5] $\mathcal{P}(\mathcal{B}(S_e(m'), I(m'), B))_s$ $(s \in SOR(S_e(m)))$ is the set of all subsets of $\mathcal{B}(S_e(m'), I(m'), B)_s$.

Example 3.4 Using the notions of Example 3.1 and 3.2 one obtains:

$$(\sigma, r)^!_{set}(\text{s-insert}(\text{s-empty}, 3)) = \{\text{l-insert}(\text{l-empty}, 3)\}$$ □

For a term $t \in B(\mathcal{S}_e(m), I(m), A)_s$ $(s \in SOR(\mathcal{S}_e(m)))$ its evaluation $t^{\mathcal{M}(m)(A)}$ in the exported algebra $\mathcal{M}(m)(A)$ is defined in the usual way:
The $\mathcal{S}_e(m)$-operations occurring in t are interpreted in the $\mathcal{S}_e(m)$-algebra $\mathcal{M}(m)(A)$. The elements of A on inherited positions of t (which are also elements of $\mathcal{M}(m)(A)$ by persistency) are left unchanged. So the result $t^{\mathcal{M}(m)(A)}$ belongs to $\mathcal{M}(m)(A)_s$. This definition directly extends to sets of terms by

$$T^{\mathcal{M}(m)(A)} := \{t^{\mathcal{M}(m)(A)} \mid t \in T\}$$

for $T \subseteq B(\mathcal{S}_e(m), I(m), A)$.

We are now ready to present our notion of implementation:

Definition 3.7 Let $m, m' \in$ **SPEC** be modules, $\sigma : m \to m'$ be a module morphism and $\mathcal{K}$ be a class of σ-representations. The module m' *implements m with σ and 𝒦* (notation: $m' \xRightarrow{\sigma,\mathcal{K}} m$), if for each representation $B \xrightarrow{r} A$ in $\mathcal{K}$ the following conditions hold:

i) If $\mathcal{M}(m)(A)$ is defined, then $\mathcal{M}(m')(B)$ is defined too.

ii) If $\mathcal{M}(m)(A)$ is defined (and therefore $\mathcal{M}(m')(B)$ is defined too), then there exist partial functions

$$r'_s : \mathcal{M}(m')(B)_{\sigma(s)} \rightsquigarrow \mathcal{M}(m)(A)_s \quad (s \in SOR(\mathcal{S}_e(m)))$$

with

a) $r'_s = r_s$ if $s \in SOR(\mathcal{S}_i(m))$

b) For $t \in B(\mathcal{S}_e(m), I(m), A)_s$ $(s \in SOR(\mathcal{S}_e(m)))$:

$$r'_s(b) = t^{\mathcal{M}(m)(A)} \quad \text{for all } b \in (\sigma, r)^!_s(t)^{\mathcal{M}(m')(B)}$$

(Especially r'_s is totally defined on $(\sigma, r)^!_s(t)^{\mathcal{M}(m')(B)}$.) □

According to part ii) of Definition 3.7, r' may be considered as an *extension* of r.

We introduce two special cases of this notion of implementation depending on the underlying class $\mathcal{K}$ of σ-representations:
For $m' \xRightarrow{\sigma,Rep_\sigma} m$ we use the abbreviation $m' \xRightarrow{\sigma} m$, and we write $m' \xRightarrow{\sigma,\mathbf{tr}} m$ instead of $m' \xRightarrow{\sigma,Rtr_\sigma} m$.

Example 3.5 Let SET, LIST and σ be given as in Example 3.1. We want to prove that LIST implements SET with σ and Rep_σ, i.e. that LIST$\xRightarrow{\sigma}$SET holds. So let A and B be *arbitrary* $\mathcal{S}_i$(SET)– resp. $\mathcal{S}_i$(LIST)–algebras and $B \xrightarrow{r} A$ be a σ-representation. By definition of the semantics of algebraically specified atomic modules, the algebra $\mathcal{M}(\text{SET})(A)$, which we will abbreviate by A', is given by:

- $A'|_{\mathcal{S}_i(\text{SET})} = A$ (by persistency)
- $A'_{set} = \mathcal{P}_{\text{fin}}(A_{nat})$ (the set of finite subsets of A_{nat})
- s-empty$^{A'} = \emptyset$ (the empty set)
- s-insert$^{A'} : \mathcal{P}_{\text{fin}}(A_{nat}) \times A_{nat} \to \mathcal{P}_{\text{fin}}(A_{nat})$

$$\text{s-insert}^{A'}(M, n) = M \cup \{n\}$$

- $\text{s-member}^{A'} : A_{nat} \times \mathcal{P}_{fin}(A_{nat}) \to A_{bool}$

$$\text{s-member}^{A'}(n, M) = \begin{cases} true^A & \text{if } (n{=_{nat}}^A a) = true^A \text{ for some } a \in M \\ false^A & \text{else.} \end{cases}$$

Similarly the algebra $\mathcal{M}(\text{LIST})(B)$ which we will abbreviate by B' is given by

- $B'|_{\mathcal{S}_i(\text{LIST})} = B$ (by persistency)
- $B'_{list} = \{[b_1, \ldots, b_n] \mid b_i \in B_{int},\ 1 \le i \le n,\ n \ge 0\}$
- $\text{l-empty}^{B'} = [\,]$ (the empty list)
- $\text{l-insert}^{B'} : B'_{list} \times B_{int} \to B'_{list}$

$$\text{l-insert}^{B'}([b_1, \ldots, b_n], b) = [b_1, \ldots, b_n, b]$$

- $\text{l-member}^{B'} : B_{int} \times B'_{list} \to B_{bool}$

$$\text{l-member}^{B'}(b, [b_1, \ldots, b_n]) = \begin{cases} true^B & \text{if } (b{=_{int}}^B b_i) = true^B \\ & \text{for some } 1 \le i \le n \\ false^B & \text{else.} \end{cases}$$

According to Definition 3.7, we define the extension r' of r by

- $r'_{bool} = r_{bool}$
- $r'_{nat} = r_{nat}$
- $r'_{set} : B'_{list} \rightsquigarrow A'_{set}$

$$r'_{set}([b_1, \ldots, b_n]) = \begin{cases} \{r_{nat}(b_1), \ldots, r_{nat}(b_n)\} & \text{if all } r_{nat}(b_i) \text{ are defined} \\ \text{undefined} & \text{else.} \end{cases}$$

An inductive proof shows that r' indeed fulfills the requirements of Definition 3.7. □

4 Properties of implementations

4.1 Vertical composition

In this subsection we investigate the question, whether an implementation of a module m by a module m' and an implementation of m' by a module m'' can be combined in such a way, that the result is an implementation of m by m''. The next theorem answers this question affirmatively.

Theorem 4.1 Let $m, m', m'' \in$ **SPEC** be modules, $\sigma : m \to m'$ and $\sigma' : m' \to m''$ be module morphisms and $\mathcal{K}_\sigma$, $\mathcal{K}_{\sigma'}$ be classes of σ– resp. σ'–representations. If $m' \xrightarrow{\sigma, \mathcal{K}_\sigma} m$ and $m'' \xrightarrow{\sigma', \mathcal{K}_{\sigma'}} m'$ then $m'' \xrightarrow{\sigma' \circ \sigma, \mathcal{K}} m$, where $\mathcal{K} = \mathcal{K}_{\sigma'} \circ \mathcal{K}_\sigma$. □

Proof Let $A \in \text{Alg}_{\mathcal{S}_i(m)}$, $C \in \text{Alg}_{\mathcal{S}_i(m'')}$ be algebras and $C \xrightarrow{r} A$ be a representation in $\mathcal{K}$. By definition of $\mathcal{K}$ we find a $\mathcal{S}_i(m')$–Algebra B and representations $B \xrightarrow{r^1} A$ in $\mathcal{K}_\sigma$ and $C \xrightarrow{r^2} B$ in $\mathcal{K}_{\sigma'}$ such that

$r = r^1 \circ r^2|_{\sigma_i}$. If $\mathcal{M}(m)(A)$ is defined, then $\mathcal{M}(m')(B)$ is defined too, since m' implements m with σ and $\mathcal{K}_\sigma$. Now $\mathcal{M}(m'')(C)$ is defined, since m'' implements m' with σ' and $\mathcal{K}_{\sigma'}$.
According to our assumptions there exist families of partial functions $r^{1'} = (r_s^{1'})_{s \in SOR(\mathcal{S}_e(m))}$

$$r_s^{1'} : \mathcal{M}(m')(B)_{\sigma_e(s)} \rightsquigarrow \mathcal{M}(m)(A)_s \quad (s \in SOR(\mathcal{S}_e(m)))$$

and $r^{2'} = (r_{s'}^{2'})_{s' \in SOR(\mathcal{S}_e(m'))}$

$$r_{s'}^{2'} : \mathcal{M}(m'')(C)_{\sigma'_e(s')} \rightsquigarrow \mathcal{M}(m')(B)_{s'} \quad (s' \in SOR(\mathcal{S}_e(m'))),$$

extending r^1 and r^2 in the sense of Definition 3.7. Their composition $r' = r^{1'} \circ r^{2'}|_{\sigma_e}$ is a family of functions

$$r'_s : \mathcal{M}(m'')(C)_{(\sigma' \circ \sigma)_e(s)} \rightsquigarrow \mathcal{M}(m)(A)_s \quad (s \in SOR(\mathcal{S}_e(m))),$$

and it is not difficult to show that r' extends r in the sense of Definition 3.7. □

Applying Theorem 4.1 to the class of all representations and to the class of trivial representations, we obtain using Proposition 3.1 and 3.2:

Corollary 4.1 Let m, m', m'', σ and σ' be as in Theorem 4.1.

a) If $m' \stackrel{\sigma}{\Longrightarrow} m$ and $m'' \stackrel{\sigma'}{\Longrightarrow} m'$ then $m'' \stackrel{\sigma' \circ \sigma}{\Longrightarrow} m$.

b) If $m' \stackrel{\sigma, tr}{\Longrightarrow} m$ and $m'' \stackrel{\sigma', tr}{\Longrightarrow} m'$ then $m'' \stackrel{\sigma' \circ \sigma, tr}{\Longrightarrow} m$. □

4.2 Horizontal composition

In this subsection we investigate the compatibility of the notion of implementation with the specification building operations of *OBSCURE*. Let us consider for instance the union of modules, denoted by "+" in *OBSCURE*, and assume we are given modules $m_1, m'_1, m_2, m'_2 \in$ **SPEC**, such that the unions $m_1 + m_2$ and $m'_1 + m'_2$ are well formed modules from **SPEC**. Now the question arises how to construct an implementation of $m_1 + m_2$ by $m'_1 + m'_2$ from given implementations of m_j by m'_j $(j = 1, 2)$. Similar problems can be studied in the context of other specification building operations. In addition to a result for the union of modules, we will here also present theorems for the following constructions: composition of modules, forgetting of sorts and operations, renaming of the exported signature, renaming of the imported signature and axioms on the exported signature. Properties of this kind — also called *horizontal* composition properties in the literature ([GB80, Ehr89]) — are very useful with respect to the construction of implementations of larger modules from implementations of smaller ones.

4.2.1 Union of modules

Theorem 4.2 Let $m_1, m_2, m'_1, m'_2 \in$ **SPEC** be modules such that $m_1 + m_2$, $m'_1 + m'_2 \in$ **SPEC** and $\sigma = (\sigma_i, \sigma_e)$ be a pair of signature morphisms $\sigma_i : \mathcal{S}_i(m_1 + m_2) \to \mathcal{S}_i(m'_1 + m'_2)$ and $\sigma_e : \mathcal{S}_e(m_1 + m_2) \to \mathcal{S}_e(m'_1 + m'_2)$.

a) If the restrictions $\sigma|_{m_j}$ $(j = 1, 2)$ are module morphisms $m_j \to m'_j$,[6] then σ is a module morphism $m_1 + m_2 \to m'_1 + m'_2$.

b) In addition, let $\mathcal{K}$ be a class of σ-representations, then $\mathcal{K}|_{m_j}$ $(j = 1, 2)$ are classes of $(\sigma|_{m_j})$-representations, and $m'_1 + m'_2$ implements $m_1 + m_2$ with σ and $\mathcal{K}$, if m'_1 implements m_1 with $\sigma|_{m_1}$ and $\mathcal{K}|_{m_1}$ and if m'_2 implements m_2 with $\sigma|_{m_2}$ and $\mathcal{K}|_{m_2}$. □

[6] In this case especially $\sigma_i(\mathcal{S}_i(m_j)) \subseteq \mathcal{S}_i(m'_j)$ and $\sigma_e(\mathcal{S}_e(m_j)) \subseteq \mathcal{S}_e(m'_j)$ $(j = 1, 2)$ hold.

The proof of this theorem is rather technical and can be found in [Leh90]. Applications of Theorem 4.2 to the special classes Rep_σ and Rtr_σ yield the following corollary:

Corollary 4.2 Let $m_1, m_2, m'_1, m'_2, \sigma$ be as in Theorem 4.2.

a) As in Theorem 4.2.

b) If $m'_j \stackrel{\sigma|_{m_j}}{\Longrightarrow} m_j$ for $j = 1,2$ then $m'_1 + m'_2 \stackrel{\sigma}{\Longrightarrow} m_1 + m_2$.

c) If $m'_j \stackrel{\sigma|_{m_j},tr}{\Longrightarrow} m_j$ for $j = 1,2$ then $m'_1 + m'_2 \stackrel{\sigma,tr}{\Longrightarrow} m_1 + m_2$. □

4.2.2 Composition of modules

Definition 4.1 Let $m \in \mathbf{SPEC}$ be a module.

a) If $A \in \mathrm{Alg}_{\mathcal{S}_i(m)}$ is an algebra such that $\mathcal{M}(m)(A)$ is defined, then $\mathcal{M}(m)(A)$ is called *termgenerated (over A)*, if

$$\mathcal{M}(m)(A)_s = \{t^{\mathcal{M}(m)(A)} \mid t \in \mathcal{B}(\mathcal{S}_e(m), I(m), A)_s\}$$

for all $s \in SOR(\mathcal{S}_e(m))$.

b) The module m is called *termgenerated*, if for each $A \in \mathrm{Alg}_{\mathcal{S}_i(m)}$ such that $\mathcal{M}(m)(A)$ is defined the algebra $\mathcal{M}(m)(A)$ is termgenerated (over A). □

Theorem 4.3 Let $m_1, m_2, m'_1, m'_2 \in \mathbf{SPEC}$ be modules such that $m_1 \diamond m_2$, $m'_1 \diamond m'_2 \in \mathbf{SPEC}$ and $\sigma^j : m_j \to m'_j$ be module morphisms for $j = 1,2$ with $\sigma^1_i = \sigma^2_e$.
Then $\sigma = (\sigma^2_i, \sigma^1_e)$ is a module morphism $m_1 \diamond m_2 \to m'_1 \diamond m'_2$, and $m'_1 \diamond m'_2$ implements $m_1 \diamond m_2$ with σ and a class $\mathcal{K}$ of σ-representations if the following conditions hold:

i) m'_1 implements m_1 with $\mathcal{K}^1$ where $\mathcal{K}^1$ is a class of σ^1-representations fulfilling the following property:
If $A \in \mathrm{Alg}_{\mathcal{S}_i(m_2)}$ and $B \in \mathrm{Alg}_{\mathcal{S}_i(m'_2)}$ are given such that $\mathcal{M}(m_2)(A)$ and $\mathcal{M}(m'_2)(B)$ are defined, then a σ^1-representation $\mathcal{M}(m'_2)(B) \stackrel{r}{\to} \mathcal{M}(m_2)(A)$ belongs to $\mathcal{K}^1$ if there exists a σ^2-representation $B \stackrel{r'}{\to} A$ from $\mathcal{K}$ with $r'|_{I(m_2)} = r|_{I(m_2)}$.

ii) m'_2 implements m_2 with σ^2 and $\mathcal{K}$.

iii) For each $A \in \mathrm{Alg}_{\mathcal{S}_i(m_2)}$, such that there exists an algebra $B \in \mathrm{Alg}_{\mathcal{S}_i(m'_2)}$ with $\mathcal{K}(B, A) \neq \emptyset$, the algebra $\mathcal{M}(m_2)(A)$ is termgenerated if it is defined. □

Condition iii) in Theorem 4.3 is especially fulfilled if the module m_2 is termgenerated. Instead of giving a formal proof of this theorem, we only sketch some of the underlying ideas that may help to clarify the rather technical conditions i) and iii) above. It is our main task to extend a given representation $B \stackrel{r}{\to} A$ from $\mathcal{K}$ to a family of functions $(r^2_s)_{s \in SOR(\mathcal{S}_e(m_1 \diamond m_2))}$ with $r^2_s : \mathcal{M}(m'_1 \diamond m'_2)(B)_{\sigma^2_e(s)} \rightsquigarrow \mathcal{M}(m_1 \diamond m_2)(A)_s$ in the sense of Definition 3.7 ii). Using the fact that m'_2 implements m_2, we obtain an extension $\bar{r}$ of r which can be slightly modified to a σ^1-representation $\mathcal{M}(m'_2)(B) \stackrel{r^1}{\to} \mathcal{M}(m_2)(A)$. The required surjectivity of r^1 (cf. Definition 3.2) is a consequence of Condition iii). From the connection between $\mathcal{K}$ and $\mathcal{K}^1$ expressed in Condition i) we infer that r^1 belongs to $\mathcal{K}^1$. Since m'_1 implements m_1 with σ^1 and $\mathcal{K}^1$, we can extend r^1 to the family of functions r^2 we looked for.

If the class $\mathcal{K}^1$ is "sufficiently" large, the requirement in part i) of Theorem 4.3 is fulfilled. Trivially, this is always the case if $\mathcal{K}^1$ is the class Rep_{σ^1} of all σ^1-representations. Therefore we obtain in this special situation:

Corollary 4.3 Let m_1, m_2, m'_1, m'_2, σ^j, σ and $\mathcal{K}$ be as in Theorem 4.3, then $m'_1 \diamond m'_2$ implements $m_1 \diamond m_2$ with σ and $\mathcal{K}$, if m_2 is termgenerated and if the implementation relations $m'_1 \stackrel{\sigma^1}{\Longrightarrow} m_1$ and $m'_2 \stackrel{\sigma^2,\mathcal{K}}{\Longrightarrow} m_2$ hold. □

4.2.3 Forgetting sorts and operations

Theorem 4.4 Let $m, m' \in$ **SPEC** be modules, *lso*1 and *lso*2 be lists of sorts and operations and $\sigma : m \rightarrow m'$ be a module morphism such that $\sigma_e(S_e(m) \setminus lso1)$ is disjoint from *lso*2. Then $\sigma' := (\sigma_i, \sigma_e|_{S_e(m)\setminus lso1})$ is a module morphism $lso1\Box m \rightarrow lso2\Box m'$.
Moreover let $\mathcal{K}$ be a class of σ–representations, then $lso2\Box m'$ implements $lso1\Box m$ with σ' and $\mathcal{K}$ if m' implements m with σ and $\mathcal{K}$. □

The proof of this fact is an easy consequence from the definitions. Two special cases are listed in the following corollary:

Corollary 4.4 Let $m, m', lso1, lso2, \sigma$ and σ' be as in Theorem 4.4, then

a) $lso2\Box m' \overset{\sigma'}{\Longrightarrow} lso1\Box m$ if $m' \overset{\sigma}{\Longrightarrow} m$

b) $lso2\Box m' \overset{\sigma',tr}{\Longrightarrow} lso1\Box m$ if $m' \overset{\sigma,tr}{\Longrightarrow} m$. □

4.2.4 Renaming of the exported signature

Theorem 4.5 Let $m, m' \in$ **SPEC** be modules, Σ and Σ' be signatures, $\rho_e : S_e(m) \rightarrow \Sigma$ and $\rho'_e : S_e(m') \rightarrow \Sigma'$ be signature morphisms such that $<\rho>m$ and $<\rho'>m'$ are elements from **SPEC**, where ρ and ρ' are defined as the pairs $(id(S_i(m)), \rho_e)$ and $(id(S_i(m')), \rho'_e)$ resp. (cf. the formal definition of export renaming in (4) of Section 2).

a) If $\sigma : m \rightarrow m'$ is a module morphism, then σ', defined as (σ'_i, σ'_e) with $\sigma'_i = \sigma_i$ and $\sigma'_e = \rho'_e \circ \sigma_e \circ \rho_e^{-1}$, is a module morphism $<\rho>m \rightarrow <\rho'>m'$.

b) Under the assumptions of a), $<\rho'>m'$ implements $<\rho>m$ with σ' and $\mathcal{K}$, if m' implements m with σ and $\mathcal{K}$ for any class $\mathcal{K}$ of σ–(σ'–)representations. □

Note that σ– and σ'–representations coincide because of $\sigma'_i = \sigma_i$. The construction of σ' implies that the diagram

$$\begin{array}{ccc} m & \xrightarrow{\rho} & <\rho>m \\ \sigma\downarrow & & \downarrow\sigma' \\ m' & \xrightarrow[\rho']{} & <\rho'>m' \end{array}$$

commutes. In this situation, part b) of Theorem 4.5 shows, that an implementation of m by m' immediately yields an implementation of $<\rho>m$ by $<\rho'>m'$ without changing the underlying class of representations. Since the proof is rather technical, it will be omitted here.

Corollary 4.5 Let $m, m', \rho, \rho', \sigma$ and σ' be as in Theorem 4.5.

a) As in Theorem 4.5.

b) Under the assumptions of a) we have

   i) $<\rho'>m' \overset{\sigma'}{\Longrightarrow} <\rho>m$ if $m' \overset{\sigma}{\Longrightarrow} m$

   ii) $<\rho'>m' \overset{\sigma',tr}{\Longrightarrow} <\rho>m$ if $m' \overset{\sigma,tr}{\Longrightarrow} m$. □

4.2.5 Renaming of the imported signature

Theorem 4.6 Let $m, m' \in$ **SPEC** be modules, Σ_i, Σ_e, Σ'_i, Σ'_e be signatures, $\rho_i : S_i(m) \rightarrow \Sigma_i$, $\rho_e : S_e(m) \rightarrow \Sigma_e$, $\rho'_i : S_i(m') \rightarrow \Sigma'_i$ and $\rho'_e : S_e(m') \rightarrow \Sigma'_e$ be signature morphisms such that $m<\rho>$ and $m'<\rho'>$ are elements from **SPEC** where ρ and ρ' are defined as the pairs (ρ_i, ρ_e) and (ρ'_i, ρ'_e) resp.

a) If $\sigma : m \to m'$ is a module morphism and $\sigma' = (\sigma'_i, \sigma'_e)$ is a pair of signature morphisms $\sigma'_i : \mathcal{S}_i(m<\rho>) \to \mathcal{S}_i(m'<\rho'>)$ and $\sigma'_e : \mathcal{S}_e(m<\rho>) \to \mathcal{S}_e(m'<\rho'>)$, satisfying

$$\sigma' \circ \rho = \rho' \circ \sigma$$

then σ' is a module morphism $m<\rho> \to m'<\rho'>$.

b) Under the assumptions of a), $m'<\rho'> \overset{\sigma'}{\Longrightarrow} m<\rho>$ holds if $m' \overset{\sigma}{\Longrightarrow} m$ is satisfied and if $\rho_e : \mathcal{S}_e(m) \to \rho_e(\mathcal{S}_e(m))$ is surjective.

□

Note, we assume that the operations Ω of a signature $\Sigma = (S, \Omega)$ are given as a family $(\Omega_{w,s})_{w \in S^*, s \in S}$ of operations, where $\Omega_{w,s}$ consists of all operations with arity $w \to s$ in Ω. Correspondingly the operation component σ^{op} of a signature morphism $\sigma = (\sigma^{sort}, \sigma^{op}) : \Sigma \to \Sigma'$ is considered as a family $(\sigma^{op}_{w,s})_{w \in S^*, s \in S}$, where $\sigma^{op}_{w,s}$ is a function $\Omega_{w,s} \to \Omega'_{\sigma(w),\sigma(s)}$. *Surjectivity* of a signature morphism $\sigma : \Sigma \to \Sigma'$, as used in Theorem 4.6, means that the sort component and all operation components of σ are surjective. More precisely, let be $w \in S^*$, $s \in S$ and f' be an operation in Σ' with arity $\sigma(w) \to \sigma(s)$. The existence of an operation $f : w' \to s'$ ($w' \in S^*, s' \in S$) with $\sigma(f) = f'$ is *not* sufficient to establish surjectivity of σ; moreover, there must exist such an operation f with arity $w \to s$.

The results of Theorem 4.6 can be extended to arbitrary classes of representations as demonstrated in [Leh90].

4.2.6 Axioms on the exported signature

In this subsection we want to investigate the following question: Given an implementation of a module m by a module m' with a module morphism σ and a class $\mathcal{K}$ of σ-representations and given two formulas $w \in WFF(\mathcal{S}_e(m))$ and $w' \in WFF(\mathcal{S}_e(m'))$, when does $\{w'\}m'$ implement $\{w\}m$ (with σ and $\mathcal{K}$)? By inspection of Definition 3.7 it is easy to see that $m' \overset{\sigma,\mathcal{K}}{\Longrightarrow} \{w\}m$ holds as soon as $m' \overset{\sigma,\mathcal{K}}{\Longrightarrow} m$ is valid (in this special case w' is logical equivalent to "true"). More general, Theorem 4.7 expresses that $\{w'\}m' \overset{\sigma,\mathcal{K}}{\Longrightarrow} \{w\}m$ holds iff w is in some sense "stronger" than w' (cf. Theorem 4.7 ii)). In this theorem we obtain results for such formulas w where only variables from inherited sorts are allowed. The reason for this restriction lies in Lemma 4.1 that only deals with formulas of this kind. Under several restrictions on the module morphism σ, it is possible to extend Lemma 4.1 to arbitrary first order formulas and to enlarge correspondingly the set of fomulas considered in Theorem 4.7 (cf. [Leh90]).

Before presenting the results we have to introduce some technical notions. For a given signature Σ let $\mathcal{W}(\Sigma)$ be the subset of $WFF(\Sigma)$ consisting of all formulas whose variables belong to inherited sorts. A signature morphism $\sigma : \Sigma \to \Sigma'$ can be extended to a mapping $\bar{\sigma} : WFF(\Sigma) \to WFF(\Sigma')$ in the classical way. Given a module morphism $\sigma : m \to m'$ we denote the extension $\bar{\sigma}_e : WFF(\mathcal{S}_e(m)) \to WFF(\mathcal{S}_e(m'))$ of the export component $\sigma_e : \mathcal{S}_e(m) \to \mathcal{S}_e(m')$ by $\bar{\sigma}$. The following Lemma, whose proof can be found in [Leh90], is very important for our purposes.

Lemma 4.1 Assume $m, m' \in$ **SPEC** are modules, $\sigma : m \to m'$ is a module morphism and $B \overset{r}{\to} A$ is a total σ-representation with algebras $A \in \mathrm{Alg}_{\mathcal{S}_i(m)}$ and $B \in \mathrm{Alg}_{\mathcal{S}_i(m')}$, such that $\mathcal{M}(m)(A)$ and $\mathcal{M}(m')(B)$ are defined. If m' implements m with σ and $\{r\}$, such that there exists an injective extension r' of r in the sense of Definition 3.7, then for a formula $w \in \mathcal{W}(\mathcal{S}_e(m))$ the following holds:

$$\mathcal{M}(m)(A) \models w \iff \mathcal{M}(m')(B) \models \bar{\sigma}(w).$$ □

Definition 4.2 Let $m, m' \in$ **SPEC** be modules and $\sigma : m \to m'$ be a module morphism. A class $\mathcal{K}$ of σ-representations is *injective extendible*, if for each representation $B \overset{r}{\to} A$ from $\mathcal{K}$ ($A \in \mathrm{Alg}_{\mathcal{S}_i(m)}, B \in \mathrm{Alg}_{\mathcal{S}_i(m')}$), such that $\mathcal{M}(m)(A)$ and $\mathcal{M}(m')(B)$ are defined, there exists an injective extension $(r'_s)_{s \in SOR(\mathcal{S}_e(m))}$ with mappings $r'_s : \mathcal{M}(m')(B)_{\sigma_e(s)} \rightsquigarrow \mathcal{M}(m)(A)_s$ in the sense of Definition 3.7. □

The signatures of SET1' and LIST1' are given as follows:

- $\mathcal{S}_i(\text{SET1'}) = (\{el1, bool\}, \{true, false, =_{el1}\})$
- $\mathcal{S}_e(\text{SET1'}) = \mathcal{S}_i(\text{SET1'}) \cup (\{set\}, \{\text{s-}empty, \text{s-}insert1', \text{s-}member1'\})$
- $\mathcal{S}_i(\text{LIST1'}) = \mathcal{S}_i(\text{SET1'})$
- $\mathcal{S}_e(\text{LIST1'}) = \mathcal{S}_i(\text{LIST1'}) \cup (\{list\}, \{\text{l-}empty, \text{l-}insert1', \text{l-}member1'\})$.

The operation $=_{el1}$ has arity ($=_{el1}$: $el1\ el1 \rightarrow bool$) and s-*insert1'*, s-*member1'*, l-*insert1'* and l-*member1'* are obtained from s-*insert*, s-*member*, l-*insert* and l-*member* by renaming *el* to *el1* in their arities. In terms of the specification building operations of Section 2 we have SET1' = SET0 $<\rho>$ and LIST1' = LIST0 $<\rho'>$ where the module morphism ρ : SET0 $\rightarrow$ SET1' is given by the identity on *bool* extended by

$$\begin{array}{lcl} el & \longmapsto & el1 \\ =_{el} & \longmapsto & =_{el1} \\ set & \longmapsto & set \\ \text{s-}empty & \longmapsto & \text{s-}empty \\ \text{s-}insert & \longmapsto & \text{s-}insert1' \\ \text{s-}member & \longmapsto & \text{s-}member1'. \end{array}$$

The module morphism ρ' : LIST0 $\rightarrow$ LIST1' is obtained in a similar way. Choosing the module morphism $\bar{\sigma}^1$: SET1' $\rightarrow$ LIST1' as the identity on the imported signature extended by

$$\begin{array}{lcl} set & \longmapsto & list \\ \text{s-}empty & \longmapsto & \text{l-}empty \\ \text{s-}insert1' & \longmapsto & \text{l-}insert1' \\ \text{s-}member1' & \longmapsto & \text{l-}member1', \end{array}$$

we obtain $\rho' \circ \sigma^0 = \bar{\sigma}^1 \circ \rho$ and by Theorem 4.6

$$\text{LIST1'} \overset{\bar{\sigma}^1}{\Longrightarrow} \text{SET1'}.$$

In the next step we use an export renaming to rename the exported sort *set* of the module SET and the exported sort *list* of the module LIST.

```
MODULE SET1 IS
        SET1' E_RENAME SORTS set AS SORTS set1
                OPNS s-empty, s-insert1', s-member1' AS OPNS s-empty1, s-insert1, s-member1
END
```

```
MODULE LIST1 IS
        LIST1' E_RENAME SORTS list AS SORTS list1
                OPNS l-empty, l-insert1', l-member1' AS OPNS l-empty1, l-insert1, l-member1
END
```

The new operations have arities (s-*empty1* :$\rightarrow$ *set1*), (s-*insert1* : *set1 el1* $\rightarrow$ *set1*), (l-*empty1* :$\rightarrow$ *list1*), (l-*insert1* : *list1 el1* $\rightarrow$ *list1*), (l-*member1* : *el1 list1* $\rightarrow$ *list1*).

The signatures of SET1 and LIST1 are given by:

- $\mathcal{S}_i(\text{SET1}) = \mathcal{S}_i(\text{SET1'})$

- $\mathcal{S}_e(\text{SET1}) = \mathcal{S}_i(\text{SET1}) \cup (\{set1\}, \{\text{s-}empty1, \text{s-}insert1, \text{s-}member1\})$
- $\mathcal{S}_i(\text{LIST1}) = \mathcal{S}_i(\text{LIST1'})$
- $\mathcal{S}_e(\text{LIST1}) = \mathcal{S}_i(\text{LIST1}) \cup (\{list1\}, \{\text{l-}empty1, \text{l-}insert1, \text{l-}member1\})$.

By the export renamings above we have SET1 $=<\varphi>$ SET1' and LIST1 $=<\varphi'>$ LIST1', where φ : SET1' $\rightarrow$ SET1 is given as the identity on the imported signature and as

$$\begin{array}{lcl} set & \longmapsto & set1 \\ \text{s-}empty & \longmapsto & \text{s-}empty1 \\ \text{s-}insert1' & \longmapsto & \text{s-}insert1 \\ \text{s-}member1' & \longmapsto & \text{s-}member1 \end{array}$$

else. φ' : LIST1' $\rightarrow$ LIST1 is obtained analogously.

If the module morphism σ^1 : SET1 $\rightarrow$ LIST1 is defined as the extension of the identity on imported sorts and operations by

$$\begin{array}{lcl} set1 & \longmapsto & list1 \\ \text{s-}empty1 & \longmapsto & \text{l-}empty1 \\ \text{s-}insert1 & \longmapsto & \text{l-}insert1 \\ \text{s-}member1 & \longmapsto & \text{l-}member1, \end{array}$$

then we obtain $\varphi' \circ \tilde{\sigma}^1 = \sigma^1 \circ \varphi$ and LIST1$\stackrel{\sigma^1}{\Longrightarrow}$SET1 using Corollary 4.5 a).

In a similar way a combination of import renamings applied to SET0 and LIST0 results in new modules SET2 and LIST2 with a new imported sort *el*2 and new exported sorts *set*2 and *list*2 respectively. A module morphism σ^2 : SET2 $\rightarrow$ LIST2 is defined similarly to σ^1 and the implementation LIST2$\stackrel{\sigma^2}{\Longrightarrow}$SET2 is again infered from LIST0$\stackrel{\sigma^0}{\Longrightarrow}$SET0 with Theorem 4.6 and Corollary 4.5 a).

Finally, we form the unions

```
MODULE SET IS
        SET1 PLUS SET2
END


MODULE LIST IS
        LIST1 PLUS LIST2
END,
```

i.e. SET = SET1 + SET2 and LIST = LIST1 + LIST2, and obtain the following signatures:

- $\mathcal{S}_i(\text{SET}) = (\{el1, el2, bool\}, \{true, false, =_{el1}, =_{el2}\})$
- $\mathcal{S}_e(\text{SET}) = \mathcal{S}_i(\text{SET}) \cup (\{set1, set2\}, \{\text{s-}empty1, \text{s-}empty2, \text{s-}insert1, \text{s-}insert2, \text{s-}member1, \text{s-}member2\})$
- $\mathcal{S}_i(\text{LIST}) = \mathcal{S}_i(\text{SET})$
- $\mathcal{S}_e(\text{LIST}) = \mathcal{S}_i(\text{LIST}) \cup (\{list1, list2\}, \{\text{l-}empty1, \text{l-}empty2, \text{l-}insert1, \text{l-}insert2, \text{l-}member1, \text{l-}member2\})$.

Choosing σ : SET $\rightarrow$ LIST as

Theorem 4.7 Assume that m' implements m with σ and $\mathcal{K}$, where $\mathcal{K}$ is injective extendible and consists of total representations. Moreover let $w \in \mathcal{W}(\mathcal{S}_e(m))$ and $w' \in WFF(\mathcal{S}_e(m'))$ be formulas. Then the following statements are equivalent:

i) The module $\{w'\}m'$ implements $\{w\}m$ with σ and $\mathcal{K}$.

ii) If $B \in \mathrm{Alg}_{\mathcal{S}_i(m')}$ is an algebra, such that there exists a representation $B \xrightarrow{r} A$ from $\mathcal{K}$, where $\mathcal{M}(m)(A)$ is defined, then

$$\mathcal{M}(m')(B) \models \bar{\sigma}(w) \Longrightarrow \mathcal{M}(m')(B) \models w'. \qquad \square$$

Proof

i) $\Longrightarrow$ ii) Assume $\mathcal{M}(m')(B) \models \bar{\sigma}(w)$. Then by Lemma 4.1 $\mathcal{M}(m)(A) \models w$, i.e. $\mathcal{M}(\{w\}m)(A)$ is defined. Using $\{w'\}m' \overset{\sigma,\mathcal{K}}{\Longrightarrow} \{w\}m$ and Definition 3.7 i), we conclude that $\mathcal{M}(\{w'\}m')(B)$ is defined, i.e. $\mathcal{M}(m')(B) \models w'$ holds.

ii) $\Longrightarrow$ i) Let $A \in \mathrm{Alg}_{\mathcal{S}_i(\{w\}m)} = \mathrm{Alg}_{\mathcal{S}_i(m)}$ and $B \in \mathrm{Alg}_{\mathcal{S}_i(\{w'\}m')} = \mathrm{Alg}_{\mathcal{S}_i(m')}$ be algebras and $B \xrightarrow{r} A$ be a representation from $\mathcal{K}$. If $\mathcal{M}(\{w\}m)(A)$ is defined, then $\mathcal{M}(m)(A)$ is defined too and $\mathcal{M}(m)(A) \models w$ holds. Using the assumption $m' \overset{\sigma,\mathcal{K}}{\Longrightarrow} m$, the algebra $\mathcal{M}(m')(B)$ is defined and satisfies $\bar{\sigma}(w)$ by Lemma 4.1. By ii) we obtain $\mathcal{M}(m')(B) \models w'$, and therefore $\mathcal{M}(\{w'\}m')(B)$ is defined. This establishes part i) of Definition 3.7. Part ii) is an immediate consequence from the given implementation $m' \overset{\sigma,\mathcal{K}}{\Longrightarrow} m$. $\square$

Note that Condition ii) in Theorem 4.7 is especially fulfilled if the formula $\bar{\sigma}(w) \supset w'$ is valid in every exported algebra of the module m', so in this case an implementation $m' \overset{\sigma,\mathcal{K}}{\Longrightarrow} m$ automatically induces an implementation $\{w'\}m' \overset{\sigma,\mathcal{K}}{\Longrightarrow} \{w\}m$ by Theorem 4.7.

4.3 An example

This subsection illustrates several results for horizontal composition of modules (Section 4.2). We start with modules SET0 and LIST0 representing sets and lists over an imported sort *el* slightly modifying Example 3.1.

```
MODULE SET0 IS
        IMPORTS SORTS el, bool
                OPNS  true : → bool
                      false : → bool
                      =_el : el el → bool
        CREATE  SORTS set
                OPNS  s-empty : → set
                      s-insert : set el → set
                      s-member : el set → bool
        SEMANTICS
        VARDEC  a, b : el, s : set
        EQNS    s-insert(s-insert(s, a), a) = s-insert(s, a)
                s-insert(s-insert(s, a), b) = s-insert(s-insert(s, b), a)
                s-member(a, s-empty) = false
                s-member(a, s-insert(s, a)) = true
                IF (a =_el b) = false THEN s-member(a, s-insert(s, b)) = s-member(a, s) FI
        ENDCREATE
END
```

```
MODULE LIST0 IS
        IMPORTS SORTS el, bool
                OPNS  true : → bool
                      false : → bool
                      =_el : el el → bool
        CREATE  SORTS list
                OPNS  l-empty : → list
                      l-insert : list el → list
                      l-member : el list → bool
        SEMANTICS
        VARDEC  a, b : el, s : list
        EQNS    l-member(a, l-empty) = false
                l-member(a, l-insert(s, a)) = true
                IF (a =_el b) = false THEN l-member(a, l-insert(s, b)) = l-member(a, s) FI
        ENDCREATE
END
```

From the construction of the modules SET0 and LIST0 we infer

- $\mathcal{S}_i(\text{SET0}) = (\{el, bool\}, \{true, false, =_{el}\})$
- $\mathcal{S}_e(\text{SET0}) = \mathcal{S}_i(\text{SET0}) \cup (\{set\}, \{\text{s-empty}, \text{s-insert}, \text{s-member}\})$
- $\mathcal{S}_i(\text{LIST0}) = \mathcal{S}_i(\text{SET0})$
- $\mathcal{S}_e(\text{LIST0}) = \mathcal{S}_i(\text{LIST0}) \cup (\{list\}, \{\text{l-empty}, \text{l-insert}, \text{l-member}\})$.

Let σ^0 : SET0 → LIST0 be given by

set	⟼	*list*
s-empty	⟼	l-empty
s-insert	⟼	l-insert
s-member	⟼	l-member

and by the identity on the imported sorts and operations. It is not difficult to prove that $\text{LIST0} \overset{\sigma^0}{\Longrightarrow} \text{SET0}$ holds.

Using module constructions as union, import and export renamings it is our goal to form modules SET and LIST that build up sets resp. lists over two imported sorts *el*1 and *el*2 and to obtain an implementation of the module SET by the module LIST.

Renaming of the imported sort *el* results in

```
MODULE SET1' IS
        SET0 I_RENAME SORTS el AS SORTS el1
                      OPNS =_el AS OPNS =_el1
END
```

and

```
MODULE LIST1' IS
        LIST0 I_RENAME SORTS el AS SORTS el1
                       OPNS =_el AS OPNS =_el1
END
```

*set*1	$\longmapsto$	*list*1
*set*2	$\longmapsto$	*list*2
s-*empty*1	$\longmapsto$	l-*empty*1
s-*empty*2	$\longmapsto$	l-*empty*2
s-*insert*1	$\longmapsto$	l-*insert*1
s-*insert*2	$\longmapsto$	l-*insert*2
s-*member*1	$\longmapsto$	l-*member*1
s-*member*2	$\longmapsto$	l-*member*2

and as the identity on the imported signature, we obtain $\sigma|_{\text{SET1}} = \sigma^1$ and $\sigma|_{\text{SET2}} = \sigma^2$. Therefore LIST$\stackrel{\sigma}{\Longrightarrow}$SET by Corollary 4.2.

4.4 Reflexivity

In Section 4.2 we proved results showing e.g. how an implementation of $m_1 + m_2$ by $m_1' + m_2'$ may be constructed from given implementations of m_1 by m_1' and of m_2 by m_2'. Consider now the special case that the modules m_2 and m_2' are identical. In this situation we are looking for an implementation of $m_1 + m_2$ by $m_1' + m_2'$ built up from a given implementation of m_1 by m_1'. Since we want to apply Theorem 4.2, we have to prove, that the module m_2 implements itself with the identic module morphism $id(m_2) : m_2 \rightarrow m_2$ and an appropriate chosen class $\mathcal{K}$ of $id(m_2)$–representations. In general, it will be our aim to establish implementations $m \stackrel{id(m),\mathcal{K}}{\Longrightarrow} m$ for $m \in$ **SPEC** and large classes $\mathcal{K}$ of $id(m)$–representations ("reflexivity" of the implementation relation). As we have only weak restrictions on possible semantics for the modules, we cannot expect a result covering *all* modules from **SPEC** with a large class $\mathcal{K}$.

Theorem 4.8 For each module $m \in$ **SPEC** the relation $m \stackrel{id(m),tr}{\Longrightarrow} m$ holds. □

If one tries to extend Theorem 4.8 to larger classes $\mathcal{K}$, the problem arises that a representation $B \stackrel{r}{\rightarrow} A$ from $\mathcal{K}$ need not be extendible to a family r' of functions $r'_s : \mathcal{M}(m)(B)_s \rightsquigarrow \mathcal{M}(m)(A)_s$ ($s \in SOR(\mathcal{S}_e(m))$) in the sense of Definition 3.7. The following example shall illustrate this fact.

Example 4.1 Assume we are given a module $m \in$ **SPEC** with $\mathcal{S}_i(m) = (\{s\}, \emptyset)$ and $\mathcal{S}_e(m) = \mathcal{S}_i(m) \cup (\{s'\}, \{(f : s' \rightarrow s), (c :\rightarrow s')\})$.
Let A and B be $\mathcal{S}_i(m)$–algebras where A_s contains exactly two elements x and y and B_s exactly two elements z and w. The representation $B \stackrel{r}{\rightarrow} A$ shall be given by

$$\begin{array}{rccc} r_s : & B_s & \rightarrow & A_s \\ & z & \mapsto & x \\ & w & \mapsto & y. \end{array}$$

(Note that $\mathcal{S}_i(m)$ has no operations, so each surjective partial function $B_s \rightsquigarrow A_s$ leads to a representation by Definition 3.2.)
Now let $\mathcal{M}(m)(A)$ and $\mathcal{M}(m)(B)$ be the $\mathcal{S}_e(m)$–algebras given by:

- $\mathcal{M}(m)(A)_s = A_s$ and $\mathcal{M}(m)(B)_s = B_s$ (these equalities must hold because of the required persistency of our modules)
- $\mathcal{M}(m)(A)_{s'}$ consists of exactly one element p and $\mathcal{M}(m)(B)_{s'}$ of exactly one element q
- $c^{\mathcal{M}(m)(A)} = p$ and $c^{\mathcal{M}(m)(B)} = q$
- $f^{\mathcal{M}(m)(A)} : \mathcal{M}(m)(A)_{s'} \rightarrow \mathcal{M}(m)(A)_s$ maps p to y, and $f^{\mathcal{M}(m)(B)} : \mathcal{M}(m)(B)_{s'} \rightarrow \mathcal{M}(m)(B)_s$ maps q to z.

Put $t := f(c) \in \mathcal{B}(\mathcal{S}_e(m), I(m), A)_s$. By Definition 3.6 we obtain

$$(id, r)^! (t) = \{t\}$$

and

$$t^{\mathcal{M}(m)(A)} = f^{\mathcal{M}(m)(A)}(c^{\mathcal{M}(m)(A)}) = f^{\mathcal{M}(m)(A)}(p) = y$$

for the evaluation in $\mathcal{M}(m)(A)$ and

$$t^{\mathcal{M}(m)(B)} = f^{\mathcal{M}(m)(B)}(c^{\mathcal{M}(m)(B)}) = f^{\mathcal{M}(m)(B)}(q) = z$$

for the evaluation in $\mathcal{M}(m)(B)$. Assume there exist partial functions

$$r'_s : \mathcal{M}(m)(B)_s \rightsquigarrow \mathcal{M}(m)(A)_s$$

and

$$r'_{s'} : \mathcal{M}(m)(B)_{s'} \rightsquigarrow \mathcal{M}(m)(A)_{s'}$$

fulfilling the conditions ii) a) and b) of Definition 3.7. By b) we must have

$$r'_s(z) = r'_s(t^{\mathcal{M}(m)(B)}) = t^{\mathcal{M}(m)(A)} = y,$$

but by a)

$$r'_s(z) = r_s(z) = x,$$

which leads to a contradiction, because x and y are different. □

If the semantics of a module behaves sufficiently reasonable, reflexivity results for large classes $\mathcal{K}$ can be proved. We will here present such a result for algebraically specified modules.

Theorem 4.9 Let $m \in$ **SPEC** be an algebraically specified module and $\mathcal{K}$ be a class of total $id(m)$–representations, such that for $\mathcal{S}_i(m)$–algebras A and B the set $\mathcal{K}(B, A)$ is nonempty only if $\mathcal{M}(m)(A)$ and $\mathcal{M}(m)(B)$ are both defined. Then $m \xRightarrow{id(m),\mathcal{K}} m$ holds. □

The nonemptyness condition on $\mathcal{K}(B, A)$ guarantees that part i) in Definition 3.7 is satisfied. An example demonstrating the necessity of *total* representations in the theorem may be found in [Leh90]. A result similar to Theorem 4.9 holds for algorithmic specifications. Since an explanation of the underlying ideas needs some deeper knowledge about this specification method, we again refer to [Leh90] for an extensive discussion of this topic.

5 Concluding remarks

We introduced a notion of implementation for modules based on module morphisms and representation functions. In these aspects, our approach bears similarities with others known from the literature as we mentioned already in the introduction. In addition, the implementations should be compatible with the specification building operations of *OBSCURE* (horizontal composition), and we presented results for some constructions. Moreover transitivity of the implementation relation (vertical composition) turned out to be an immediate consequence from the definition of implementations. On the other hand, "good" reflexivity results depend on the underlying module semantics and do not hold in all cases.

With these results, it is now possible to study the *interaction* between horizontal and vertical composition of implementations, as suggested in [GB80]. For this purpose, Ehrig proposed an abstract framework ([Ehr89]), where specifications are considered as objects in a category whose morphisms consist of so called vertical transformations. These vertical transformations correspond to implementations in our approach. In [Leh90], we have shown how the results presented here can be embedded into this categorical framework.

As already mentioned in the introduction, it is also possible to generalize the notion of implementation to loose *OBSCURE* specifications. All composition results mentioned here also hold in the loose case — sometimes with slight modifications — except for the theorems dealing with exported axioms. Roughly spoken, the reason for this phenomenon stems from the fact, that the semantical behaviour of the specification building operation "exported axioms" in the loose semantics framework strongly differs from its behaviour in the case of fixed semantics. For a more detailed discussion we refer to [Leh90].

Acknowledgements. The author is grateful to Jacques Loeckx, Andreas Heckler and two anonymous referees for many suggestions on the subject of this paper.

References

[BV85] C. Beierle and A. Voß. Implementation specifications. *Recent Trends in Data Type Specification*, pp. 39 – 53, Proc. of the 3rd Workshop on Theory and Applications of Abstract Data Types, Springer, Informatik–Fachberichte 116, 1985.

[BGM87] M. Bidoit, M. Gaudel, and A. Mauboussin. *How to make algebraic specifications more understandable? — An experiment with the PLUSS specification language.* Int. Rep. 343, Univ. Paris-Sud, Apr. 1987.

[BW82] M. Broy and M. Wirsing. Partial abstract types. *Acta Inf.*, 18, pp. 47 – 64, 1982.

[BG80] R. Burstall and J. Goguen. The semantics of CLEAR, a specification language. In *Proc. 1979 Copenhagen Winter School*, pp. 292 – 332, Springer, LNCS 86, 1980.

[Car80] R. Cartwright. A constructive alternative to abstract data type definitions. *Proc. 1980 LISP Conf., Stanford Univ.*, pp. 46 – 55, 1980.

[Ehr82] H. Ehrich. On the theory of specification, implementation and parameterization of abstract data types. *JACM*, 29, pp. 206 – 227, 1982.

[Ehr89] H. Ehrig. The algebraic specification column. *EATCS - Bulletin*, 38, pp. 79 – 92, June 1989.

[EK82] H. Ehrig and H. Kreowski. Parameter passing commutes with implementation of parameterized types. In *Proc. of the 9th Coll. on Automata, Languages and Prog.*, pp. 197 – 211, Springer, LNCS 140, 1982.

[EKMP82] H. Ehrig, H. Kreowski, B. Mahr, and P. Padawitz. Algebraic implementation of abstract data types. *Theor. Comp. Sc.*, 20, pp. 209 – 263, 1982.

[EM85] H. Ehrig and B. Mahr. *Fundamentals of Algebraic Specification 1 — Equations and Initial Semantics.* Springer, 1985.

[EM90] H. Ehrig and B. Mahr. *Fundamentals of Algebraic Specification 2 — Module Specifications and Constraints.* Springer, 1990.

[Fey88] W. Fey. *Pragmatics, Concepts, Syntax, Semantics and Correctness notions of ACT TWO: An algebraic module specification and interconnection language.* Int. Rep. 1988/26, TU Berlin, 1988.

[FGJM85] K. Futatsugi, J. Goguen, J. Jouannaud, and J. Meseguer. Principles of OBJ2. In *Annual ACM Symposium on Principles of Programming Languages*, pp. 52 – 66, New Orleans, 1985.

[Gau84] M. Gaudel. *A first introduction to PLUSS.* Int. Rep., Univ. Paris–Sud, Dec. 1984.

[GGM76] V. Giarratana, F. Gimona, and U. Montanari. Observability concepts in abstract data type specifications. In *Proc. Math. Found. of Comp. Science 1976*, pp. 576 – 587, Springer, LNCS 45, 1976.

[GB80] J. Goguen and R. Burstall. *CAT, a system for the structured elaboration of correct programs from structured specifications.* Int. Rep. TR–CSL–118, Comp. Science Lab., SRI International, Menlo Park, 1980.

[GTW78] J. Goguen, J. Thatcher, and E. Wagner. An initial algebra approach to the specification, correctness and implementation of abstract data types. In *Current Trends in Programming Methodology IV*, pp. 80 – 149, Prentice-Hall, 1978.

[GW88] J.A. Goguen and T. Winkler. *Introducing OBJ3.* Int. Rep. SRI–CSL–88–9, Comp. Science Lab., SRI International, Menlo Park, 1988.

[Hen89] R. Hennicker. Implementation of parameterized observational specifications. In *Proc. of the Int. Joint Conf. on Theory and Pract. of Software Development*, pp. 290 – 305, Springer, LNCS 351, March 1989.

[Hoa72] C. Hoare. Proof of correctness of data representations. *Acta Inf.*, 1(4), pp. 271 – 281, 1972.

[Kam83] S. Kamin. Final data types and their specification. *ACM Trans. Prog. Lang. Syst.*, 5(1), pp. 97 – 123, 1983.

[Kla84] H. Klaeren. A constructive method for abstract algebraic software specification. *Theor. Comp. Sc.*, 30(2), pp. 139 – 204, 1984.

[Leh90] T. Lehmann. *Ein abstrakter Implementierungsbegriff für die Spezifikationssprache OBSCURE.* PhD thesis, Univ. Saarbrücken, Apr. 1990.

[LL87] T. Lehmann and J. Loeckx. The specification language of OBSCURE. In *Proc. of the 5th Workshop on Specification of Abstract Data Types*, pp. 131 – 153, Springer, LNCS 332, 1987.

[Lip83] U. Lipeck. *Ein algebraischer Kalkül für einen strukturierten Entwurf von Datenabstraktionen.* PhD thesis, Univ. Dortmund, 1983.

[LZ74] B. Liskov and S. Zilles. Programming with abstract data types. *SIGPLAN Notices*, 9(4), pp. 50 – 59, 1974.

[Loe87] J. Loeckx. Algorithmic specifications: a constructive specification method for abstract data types. *ACM Trans. Prog. Lang. Syst.*, 9(4), pp. 646 – 685, 1987.

[San84] D. Sannella. A set–theoretic semantics of CLEAR. *Acta Inf.*, 21(5), pp. 443 – 472, 1984.

[ST88] D. Sannella and A. Tarlecki. Specifications in an arbitrary institution. *Information and Computation*, 76, pp. 165 – 210, 1988.

[SW83] D. Sannella and M. Wirsing. A kernel language for algebraic specification and implementation. In *Proc. Int. Conf. on Found. of Comp. Theory*, pp. 413 – 427, Springer, LNCS 158, 1983.

[Sch86] O. Schoett. *Data Abstraction and the Correctness of Modular Programming.* PhD thesis, Univ. Edinburgh, 1986.

[Wan79] M. Wand. Final algebra semantics and data type expressions. *JCSS*, 19(1), pp. 27 – 44, 1979.

[Wir86] M. Wirsing. Structured algebraic specifications: a kernel language. *Theor. Comp. Sc.*, 42(2), pp. 124 – 249, 1986.

Model-theoretic specifications and back-and-forth equivalences

Gianfranco Mascari
I.A.C. (Istituto per le Applicazioni del Calcolo "M. Picone") - C.N.R.
Viale del Policlinico 137 - 00161 ROMA, ITALY.

Antonio Vincenzi
via Belvedere 17/1, 17012 ALBISSOLA MARE (Savona), ITALY.

Introduction.

Background on Logics. Today a 'logic' $\mathcal{L}$ can be defined essentially in three ways.

(1) The *model—theoretic approach* which uses as ingredients structures (data types) and formulas (elements of a specified abstract languages) related by a *satisfaction relation*

$\mathbf{M} \models \varphi \Leftrightarrow$ the property expressed by the formula φ correspond to a property of the structure $\mathbf{M}$.

(2) The *proof—theoretic approach,* in which a logic $\mathcal{L}$ is introduced by a purely syntactical definition which does not use the structures and relates the formulas by a *deduction relation*

$\varphi \vdash \psi \Leftrightarrow$ the theorem which has φ as hypothesis and ψ as thesis can be proved by using a fixed kind of axioms and rules.

(3) The *algebraic approach,* in which a logic $\mathcal{L}$ is introduced by a purely semantical definition (which does not uses the formulas) and relates structure by a *elementary equivalence relation*

$\mathbf{M} \equiv \mathbf{N} \Leftrightarrow$ $\mathbf{M}$ and $\mathbf{N}$ are two interchangeable examples of a given kind of mathematical objects

Relationships between the above approaches are given by *completeness theorems,* of the form:

$$\varphi \vdash \psi \iff \text{for every structure } \mathbf{M}, \text{ if } \mathbf{M} \models \varphi \text{ then } \mathbf{M} \models \psi,$$

and *duality theorems*, of the form:

$$\mathbf{M} \equiv \mathbf{N} \iff \text{for every formula } \varphi, \mathbf{M} \models \varphi \text{ if and only if } \mathbf{N} \models \varphi.$$

Aims. From the applicative point of view, the purely syntactical approach to logics is useful (and may be essential) to the study of *theorem provers,* whereas the model—theoretic and algebraic approaches are related to at least three features that arise in several areas of *Computer Science* :

Classification of structures: representing in a mathematical way the objects of interest (e.g. stacks, trees), by means of an equivalence relation (e.g. observational equivalence) between structures.

Expressiveness: characterizing a class of structures by a logical description (e.g. algebraic specification) and an equivalence relation between such structures by an elementary equivalence associated to a given logic.

Refinement: transformation of logical descriptions into "simpler" ones according to some measure of complexity, e.g. first order logic is simpler than infinitary logic with countable disjunctions and conjunctions.

Since in this paper we are interested only on the three above problems, we will use only the model—theoretic and algebraic approaches to logics.

Moreover, by defining a *model—theoretic specification* as class of *countable structures with countable vocabulary* (in which isomorphic structures are identified) and using the following *tools:*

(i) the *parametrization of model—theoretic specification* (i.e., the possibility to collect a model theoretic specification in a single structure by using additional sorts and predicates), and

(ii) the algebraic characterization of elementary equivalence by back and forth games (originated by Erenfeucht and Fraissé works), for which

$\mathbf{M} \equiv \mathbf{N} \iff$ the player *II* of a particular mathematical two—person game $G(\mathbf{M},\mathbf{N})$ has a winning strategy;

(iii) the following determination relation between back and forth games

$G_1 \rhd G_2 \Leftrightarrow$ for every winning strategy for player *II* in G_1 there exists a winning strategy for player *II* in G_2 .

we obtain some results concerning the classification, expressiveness, and refinement problems of model—theoretic specifications. Finally, we apply these results on three topics of applicative interest: the *bisimulation relation* between processes represented as appropriate labelled trees, the classification of figures of *Tarski elementary Eucliedean geometry*, and the classification of phrases of the *Barwise—Cooper* approach to Linguistics.

Related Works. The techniques, the results, and applications considered in this paper refer to the following areas.

(A) In the area of *Abstract Model Theory* an axiomatic approach to back—and—forth games has been developed principally by D.Mundici and summarized in MAKOWSKY—MUNDICI[1985, Section 5].

(B) In the area of *Formal Specification,* abstract data types i.e. isomorphism classes of (reachable) algebras are specified in a many sorted formalism which in the more general case is an institution. A general notion of observational equivalence corresponds to a form of elementary equivalence. References to such work include: BERGSTRA— TERLOUW[1983], BERTONI— MAURI—MIGLIOLI[1983], GOGUEN— BURSTALL[1985], MAIBAUM— VELOSO—SADLER [1985], MAKOWSKY[1984], MESEGUER[1990], SANNELLA— TARLECKI[1987], SANNELLA—SOKOLO-WSKI—TARLECKI[1990], WIRSING[1989], WIRSING—BROY[1989] .

(C) In the area of *First order Logics of Programs,* the countable infinitary logics have been proposed for expressing properties of programs as termination for various classes of programs and for comparing the various proposals. The back and forth games have been also used for such purpose.The references include: ABRUSCI—MASCARI[1989], ENGELER[1967], MAKOWSKY[1980], MEYER—TIURYN[1981], MEYER— TIURYN[1984], RASIOWA[1982], TIURYN[1984].

(D) In the area of *Concurrency,* one of the main interesting problem is that of the algebraic and logical characterizations (e.g. ASTESIANO— MASCARI—REGGIO—WIRSING[1985] HENNESSY— MILNER[1985], DENICOLA—FERRARI [1990]) of the bisimulation relation between precesses: as shown in *Paragraph 3.1*, this notion can be revised as a back—and—forth game between process trees.

(E) In the area of *Formal Languages* a distinction is made between languages of words and of trees (and of graphs): such a distinction corresponds to that of linear time and branching time in the area of *Propositional Modal and Temporal Logics of Programs*. A unified view of such issues is obtained by considering a word or a tree as a first order finite structure and a formal language as family of such structures. The logical characterization of formal languages and the so called functional completeness of some temporal logic can be studied by means of back and forth games. The references include: COURCELLE[1990], LADNER[1977], HAFNER[1986], PERRIN— PIN[1986], RESSAYE[1988], STRAUBING— THÉRIEN— THOMAS[1988] , THOMAS[1979].

(F) A recent development of Complexity Theory is that of *Descriptive Complexity* where the main issue is that of a logical characterization of a complexity class seen as a class of appropriate finite structures e.g. AJTAI— FAGIN[1990], BERMAN[1980], IMMERNAN[1989], IMMERMAN— KOZEN[1990], PANCONESI— RANJAN[1990], SPECKER[1988].

(G) In the area of *Database Systems and Computational Intelligence,* various extensions of first order logic have been studied e.g. CHANDRA— HAREL[1982], KOLAITIS— PAPADIMITRIOU [1990].

(H) A logical approach to *Geometry* exists since the fifties e.g. TARSKI[1959]. Recent work on pointless metric spaces seem also promising in this direction e.g. GERLA[1990]. Moreover knowledge representation formalisms are now considered for image representation e.g. REITER— MACKWORTH[1990].

(I) In the field of *Computational Linguistics,* the work presented in BARWISE— COOPER[1980], is one of the main starting point of the more recent work e.g. VAN BENTHEM[1986], FENSTAD[1989].

Note to the reader. The paper a short version of MASCARI— VINCENZI[199?], submitted to a Journal. To lack of space, we refer to the technical background of logics contained in (the first two and the last two chapters of) BARWISE— FEFERMAN[1985]. In particular, the *first—order logic* $\mathcal{L}_{\omega\omega}$, the *infinitary logics* $\mathcal{L}_{\omega_1\omega}$, $\mathcal{L}_{\omega_1\omega_1}$, and the *logics with Lindström—quantifiers* $\mathcal{L}_{\omega\omega}(Q_n)_{n<\omega}$ and $\mathcal{L}_{\omega_1\omega}(Q_n)_{n<\omega}$ are assumed. The proofs are omitted and the last to applications are only sketched. The extended version contains proofs and details. The original notions will be denoted by *.

Acknowledgment. The authors thank the referee, whose suggestions improved this paper in many aspects.

1. Basic notions.

***1.1 Model–theoretic specification and parametrizations**.** A *(model–theoretic) specification (relative to a vocabulary* τ*)* is a class

$$\mathcal{M} = \{\mathbf{M}_i \mid i \in I\}$$

of countable structures relative to a fixed countable vocabulary τ, closed under the usual model—theoretic operation of *renaming, contraction, restriction, relational version, pair expansion,* and *sum* (see, e.g., MAKOWSKY[1984]).

To obtain the parametrization of $\mathcal{M}$ we use a slight variation of a technique widely used in recursion theory (originated in Kleene's work), for which (e.g.) a class $\mathcal{F}$ of functions has a *parametrization theorem* when there is a function U such that for each $f \in \mathcal{F}$, some value c_f satisfies $U(c_f, x) = f(x)$ for all x.

Thus, given a model—theoretic specification $\mathcal{M} = \{\mathbf{M}_i \mid i \in I\}$ which we assume (by relational version construction) relative to the relation vocabulary vocabulary $\tau = (\mathbf{R}_j \mid j \in J)$, the *parametrization* of $\mathcal{M}$ is a two—sorted structure

$$\mathbf{Par}(\mathcal{M}) = (M, R_j^+, U, c_i \mid j \in J, i \in I)$$

relative to the vocabulary $\tau_{\text{par}} = \{s_{ind}, s_{data}, \mathbf{H}, \mathbf{c}_i, \mathbf{R}_j^+ \mid i \in I, j \in J\}$ in which

s_{ind} is the sort of indexes,

s_{data} is the sort of 'data',

$arity(\mathbf{H}) = \langle s_{ind}, s_{data}, \rangle$,

$arity(\mathbf{c}_i) = \langle s_{ind} \rangle$ for every $i \in I$,

$arity(\mathbf{R}_j^+) = \langle s_{ind}, arity(\mathbf{R}_j) \rangle$ for every $j \in J$,

and such that

$s_{ind}^{\mathbf{Par}(\mathcal{M})} = \{c_i \mid i \in I\}$,

for every $a \in M \setminus s_{ind}^{\mathbf{Par}(\mathcal{M})}$, there is $i \in I$ such that $H(c_i, a)$,

for every $i \in I$, $\mathbf{M}_i \cong (\{a \mid H(c_i, a)\}, R_j^+(c_i, -, \ldots, -) \mid j \in J)$.

We note that, under our assumption on model—theoretic specifications, parametrization always exists. Other aspects of parametrization can be found in the following

1.1.1 Example: a model–theoretic specification of labelled trees. (1) Let τ_{tree} be a single—sorted vocabulary consisting of a unary function symbol **f** and of a constant symbol **r**. A τ_{tree}—structure $\mathbf{T} = (T,f,r)$ is *tree—like* iff

(i) for every $x \in T$, $f(x) = x$ iff $x = r$,

(ii) f is surjective,

(iii) for every $x \in T$, there is an $n \in \omega$ such that $f^n(x) = r$,

where $f^n(x)$ is $f(..f(x)...)$ n times if $n > 0$ and x if $n = 0$ (cf. MAKOWSKY[1985, Definition 4.1.5]). The tree—like structures are a very useful way to represent the countable branching one—rooted trees, i.e. the trees usually used in computer science. We can look at its usefulness by making explicit some properties of a tree—like structure $\mathbf{T} = (T,f,r)$:

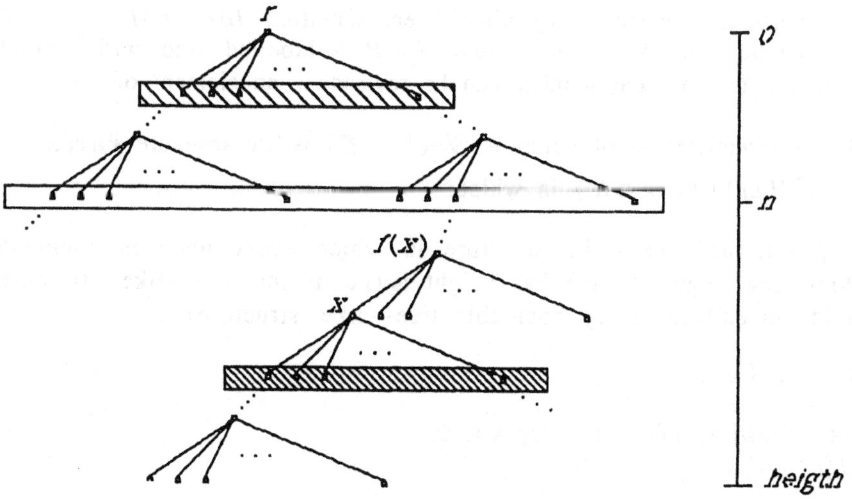

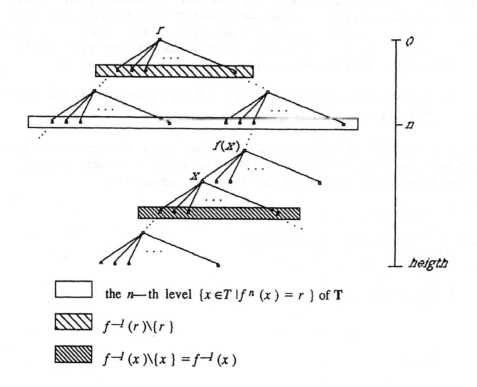

☐ the n—th level $\{x \in T \mid f^n(x) = r\}$ of **T**

▨ $f^{-1}(r)\setminus\{r\}$

▩ $f^{-1}(x)\setminus\{x\} = f^{-1}(x)$

where:

$f^{-1}(x)\setminus\{x\}$ is the set of the *immediate successors* $x \in T$,

$\{x \in T \mid f^n(x) = r\}$ is the *n—th level* of **T**,

$\sup\{n \in \omega \mid f^n(x) = r$ and $x \in T\}$ is the *height* of **T**,

$\sup\{|f^{-1}(x)\setminus\{x\}| \mid x \in T\}$ is the *branching* of **T**.

In this context, an *L—labelled tree* (i.e. a tree T in which every element is associated to some label $e \in L$) can be represented by a *L—labelled* tree—like structure $\mathbf{T}^L = \langle T,f,r,P_e \mid e \in L\rangle$ relative to a vocabulary $\tau_{\text{tree}}(\mathbf{P}_e \mid e \in L)$ with $\mathbf{P}_e$ unary relation symbol for any $e \in L$, in which

(v) if $e \neq e'$ then $P_e \cap P_{e'} = \emptyset$,

(vi) $T = \bigcup_{e \in L} P_e$.

i.e. the structure in which every P_e represent the nodes of T labelled by the same *e*. (We note that the conditions (4) and (5) extablish that $\{P_e \mid e \in L\}$ a *partition* of T and then define an equivalence relation over T.) $\mathcal{T}ree^L = \{\mathbf{T}^L{}_k \mid k \in K\}$ is the $\tau_{\text{tree}}(\mathbf{P}_a \mid a \in L)$—specification constituted by all L—labelled tree—like structures. On the other hand $\mathcal{T}ree^L$ is a very rich specification. In particular, since every binary representation *101...0,011...* of a real number can be revised as a countable $\{P_0, P_1\}$—labelled tree with branching *1* and height ω, any real number can be revised as an element of $\mathcal{T}ree^L$.

(2) The parametrization of $\mathcal{T}ree^L = \{\mathbf{T}^L{}_k \mid k \in K\}$ is the structure $\mathbf{Par}(\mathcal{T}ree^L) = (T,f,r,P_{ek}^{+},H,c_k \mid e \in L, k \in K)$ in which:

(i) (T,f,r) is the tree—like structure in which every node is countable—branching and every branch has height ω (i.e. is the tree—like structure in which is embeddable every countable tree—like structure),

(ii) $T \cap \{c_k \mid k \in K\} = \emptyset$,

(iii) the following hold for every $k \in K$:
$H(c_k,—) \cong T_k$

$P_{ek}^{+}(c_k,—) \cong P_{ek}(—)$ for every $k \in K, e \in L$.

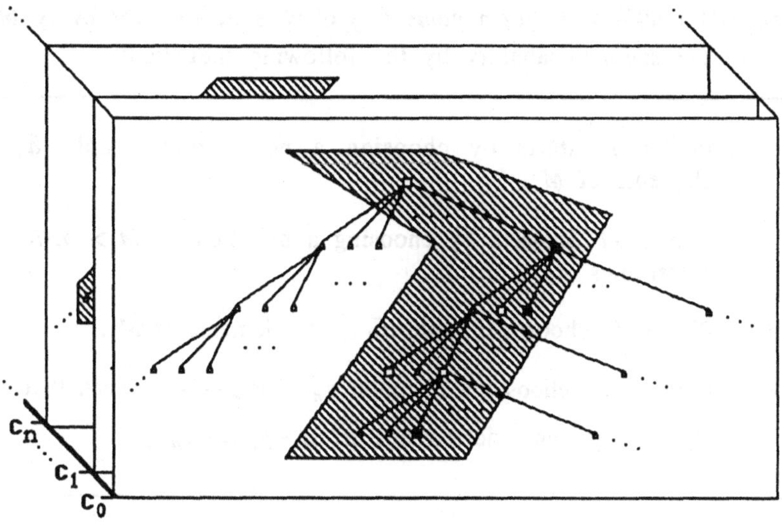

— s_{ind} Par($\mathcal{T}ree^{L}$) = $\{c_k \mid k \in K\}$

▨ $H(c_k,-) \cong T_k$ for some $k \in K$

□ ■ elements of $P_{e_k}{}^{+}(c_k,-) \cong P_{e_k}(-)$ for various $e \in L$

Since an infinitely—countable tree allows uncountably—many different labellings, $\mathcal{T}ree^{L}$ can be codified only by using uncountably—many new constant symbols. This fact shows that the parametrization of a model—theoretic specification can be an uncountable structure (and so not a model—theoretic specification).

1.2 Model–theoretic specifications, games, and logics.

1.2.1 Game of a specification. (Substantially HELLA[1989]). Let $\mathcal{K}$ be a be a class of structures and let $\mathbf{M} = (M,\ldots)$ and $\mathbf{N} = (N,\ldots)$ be two structures of $\mathcal{K}$ relative to the same vocabulary τ. As usual we assume τ relational. Then

(1) An injective function p is a *partial isomorphism from* $\mathbf{M}$ *into* $\mathbf{N}$, (in symbols $p : \mathbf{M} \rightarrowtail \mathbf{N}$), if $M \supseteq dom(p)$, $N \supseteq rng(p)$, and for every $\mathbf{R} \in \tau$ and every finite sequence $\bar{a}$ of elements of $dom(p)$,

$$\mathbf{R}^{\mathbf{M}}(\bar{a}) \quad \text{iff } \mathbf{R}^{\mathbf{N}}(p(\bar{a})).$$

(2) The *(general) back—and—forth game* $G_{\mathcal{K}}$ of $\mathcal{K}$ is defined for every **M**,**N** of $\mathcal{K}$ relative to the same vocabulary by the following induction:

Move I,0: Player *I* starts by choosing a non—empty tuple $\overline{a}_0$ of elements of M.

Move II,0: Player *II* answers by choosing a bijection $g_0 : M \rightarrowtail\!\!\!\twoheadrightarrow N$ and determines $p_0 = g_0 \upharpoonright \overline{a}_0$.

Move I,n+1: Player *I* chooses a tuple $\overline{a}_{n+1}$ of elements of M.

Move II,n+1: Player *II* chooses a bijection $g_{n+1} : M \rightarrowtail\!\!\!\twoheadrightarrow N$ such that $g_{n+1} \supseteq \bigcup_{i \leq n} p_i$ and determines $p_{n+1} = g_{n+1} \upharpoonright \overline{a}_{n+1}$.

Pictorially

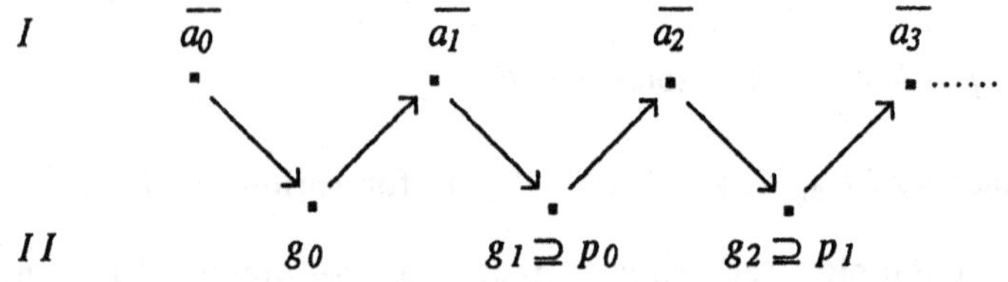

$p_0 = g_0 \upharpoonright \overline{a_0}$ $\quad p_1 = g_1 \upharpoonright \overline{a_1}$ $\quad p_2 = g_2 \upharpoonright \overline{a_2}$

The above game relative to **M**,**N** will be denoted $G_{\mathcal{M}}(\mathbf{M},\mathbf{N})$ (for short $G(\mathbf{M},\mathbf{N})$).

(3) After a countably—many pairs of moves, the player *II* is the *winner* of $G(\mathbf{M},\mathbf{N})$ if the partial function

$$\bigcup_{i<\omega} p_i : A \rightarrowtail B$$

is a partial isomorphism from **M** to **N**), otherwise the *winner* of $G(\mathbf{M},\mathbf{N})$ is *I*. (In particular *I* wins if there are no bijection from M to N).

(4) A *strategy h for player I (relative to* $G(\mathbf{M},\mathbf{N})$) consists of a function $n = h_{G(\mathbf{M},\mathbf{N})}$ which associates to every bijection $g : M \to N$ a tuple $\overline{a}$ of elements of M. *I follows h* if for each play $(\varnothing, g_1, g_2, \ldots)$ of *II*, the play of *I* is $(h(\varnothing), h(g_1), h(g_2), \ldots)$. Dually a *strategy for player II (relative to* $G(\mathbf{M},\mathbf{N})$) consists of a set—theoretic function $k = h_{G(\mathbf{M},\mathbf{N})}$ which associates to every $\overline{a}$

of elements of M a bijection $g:M \rightarrowtail\!\!\twoheadrightarrow N$. *II follows* k if for each play $(\bar{a}_0, \bar{a}_1 \bar{a}_2, \ldots)$ of I, the play of II is $(k(\bar{a}_0), k(\bar{a}_1), k(\bar{a}_2), \ldots)$.

(5) h is a *winning strategy for I* if, following h, I wins every play of $G(\mathbf{M},\mathbf{N})$ (and dually for II)

(6) $\mathbf{M} \sim_G \mathbf{N}$ means that there exists a winning strategy for II in the game $G(\mathbf{M},\mathbf{N})$.

1.2.2 Games and logics. Let $\mathcal{L}$ be a logic relative to a class $\mathcal{K}$ of structures and let $\equiv_{\mathcal{L}}$ its equivalence relation. Then $\mathcal{L}$ *is characterized* by a back—and—forth game G over $\mathcal{K}$ if, for every $\mathbf{M},\mathbf{N} \in \mathcal{K}$,

$$\mathbf{M} \equiv_{\mathcal{L}} \mathbf{N} \quad \Leftrightarrow \quad \mathbf{M} \sim_G \mathbf{N}.$$

If $\mathcal{K}$ is the class of all structures, the above characterization is global.

Since the above definition of back and forth games contains three parameters: the "complexity" of the object chosen by the player I (i.e. the length of the tuple $\bar{a}$), the "complexity" of the object chosen by the player II (the totality of partiality of the g 's), and the number of moves, by modifying these three parameters we can individuate some specialization of the general back—and—forth game by obtaining specific back and forth games which allow to characterize different logics. In the following we expresses in the unified way some of the characterization results contained in BARWISE—FEFERMAN[1985] and HELLA[1989]:

1.2.3 Unified characterization theorem. *The following logics are globally characterized by games individuated as follows:*

logic \ parameters	choices of player I	choices of player II	number of moves
$\mathcal{L}_{\omega_1\omega}(Q_n)_{n<\omega}$	$\bar{a}$ countable	$g:M \rightarrowtail\!\!\twoheadrightarrow N$	countable
$\mathcal{L}_{\omega_1\omega}(Q_n)$	$\bar{a}$ finite	$g:M \rightarrowtail\!\!\twoheadrightarrow N$	countable
$\mathcal{L}_{\omega\omega}(Q_n)$	$\bar{a}$ finite	$g:M \rightarrowtail\!\!\twoheadrightarrow N$	finite
$\mathcal{L}_{\omega_1\omega}$	a	$g:M \overset{<\omega}{\rightarrowtail} N$	countable

$\mathscr{L}_{\omega\omega}$	a	$g:M \overset{<\omega}{\rightarrowtail} N$	finite

(where $g:M \overset{<\omega}{\rightarrowtail} N$ is a partial function from the finite tuple of M into N with finite domain).

1.3 Local and global determination between games*. Let $\mathcal{M}$ be a model—theoretic specification.

(1) Let $\mathbf{M} = (M,\ldots)$ and $\mathbf{N} = (N,\ldots)$ be two structures of $\mathcal{M}$ and let $[X]^{\mathbf{M}}$ and $[Y]^{\mathbf{N}}$ be the substructures of $\mathbf{M}$ and $\mathbf{N}$ generated by $M \supseteq X$ and $N \supseteq Y$ respectively. Then $G(\mathbf{M},\mathbf{N})$ is *locally determined* by $G([X]^{\mathbf{M}},[Y]^{\mathbf{N}})$, in symbols

$$G([X]^{\mathbf{M}},[Y]^{\mathbf{N}}) \rhd G(\mathbf{M},\mathbf{N}),$$

if for every winning strategy for player *II* in $G([X]^{\mathbf{M}},[Y]^{\mathbf{N}})$ there exists a winning strategy for player *II* in $G(\mathbf{M},\mathbf{N})$.

(2) Let $\mathcal{K}$ be a class of structures closed under isomorphism and let G_1 and G_2 be two specialization of the general back—and—game relative to $\mathcal{K}$. G_1 *determines* G_2 *over* $\mathcal{K}$, in symbol

$$G_1 \rhd_{\mathcal{K}} G_2,$$

if for every $\mathbf{M},\mathbf{N} \in \mathcal{K}$ and every winning strategy for player *II* in $G_1(\mathbf{M},\mathbf{N})$ there exists a winning strategy for player *II* in $G_2(\mathbf{M},\mathbf{N})$.

1.3.1 Example: games over labelled trees. (1) Let $\mathbf{T} = (T,f,r,P_e \mid e \in L)$ and $\mathbf{T'} = (T',f',r',P'_e \mid e \in L)$ be two L—labelled trees. Since an injective function p from T to T' is a partial isomorphism if, for every $t_0, t_1 \in dom(p)$ the following hold

(i) $t_0 = t_1$ iff $p(t_0) = p(t_1)$,

(ii) $p(f(t_0)) = f'(p(t_0))$,

(iii) $p(r) = r'$,

(iv) $R_e(t_0)$ iff $R_e(p(t_0))$ for every $e \in L$.

Then every play of $G(\mathbf{T},\mathbf{T'})$ works as follows:

Move I,0: Player I choose an arbitrary non—empty tuple $\overline{t_0} \in T^{\leq\omega}$

Move II,0 Player II answers by choosing a bijection $g_0 : T \rightarrowtail\!\!\twoheadrightarrow T'$ such that the tuple $p_0 = g_0 \upharpoonright \overline{t_0}$ satisfies the conditions (1)—(3)

Move I,1 Player I chooses another non—empty tuple $\overline{t_1} \in T^{\leq\omega}$

... and so on, for ω time. If the Player II can choose any h_i such that p_i is a partial isomorphism from from **T** into **T'**, then it wins. Otherwise Player II wins.

2. Results

We now use the instruments introduced in the above section to study the classification, expressiveness, and refinement problems of model theoretic specifications.

As usual we assume the standard notions and results concerning the expressive power of the logics $\mathcal{L}_{\omega\omega}$, $\mathcal{L}_{\omega_1\omega}$, $\mathcal{L}_{\omega_1\omega_1}$, and and $\mathcal{L}_{\omega_1\omega}(Q_n)_{n<\omega}$ (summarized, e.g., in BARWISE— FEFERMAN[1985, II]).

2.1 *Expressiveness.* We add to the notions of *elementary, projective and relatively projective* $\mathcal{L}$ *— classes* the following one.

2.1.1 Definition*. A class $\mathcal{M}$ of structure (closed under isomorpjhisms) is *parametrically relatively projective in* $\mathcal{L}$ (or *PRPC in* $\mathcal{L}$) if **Par**($\mathcal{M}$) is *RPC* in $\mathcal{L}$

The properties of the *PRPC*$_{\mathcal{L}}$*— expressibility* are summarized in the following

2.1.2 Theorem* *In each logic* $\mathcal{L}$ *:*

(i) Each EC$_{\mathcal{L}}$*—expressible specification is PRPC*$_{\mathcal{L}}$*— expressible.*
(ii) There is a PRPC$_{\mathcal{L}}$*— expressible specification which is no RPC*$_{\mathcal{L}}$*— expressible.*

Its main application is the following

2.1.3 Expressiveness Theorem*. *Every model theoretic specification is PRPC—expressible in the logic* $\mathscr{L}_{\omega_1\omega_1}$.

2.2 Classification. Since the classification of a class of structures depends directly by the understanding logic, the relationships between logics determine the relationships between different classifications.

The relationships between logics are essentially of two types: these founded on the elementary equivalence(like the $<_{\equiv}$— relationships between logics or its $\mathcal{K}$— relativized version $<_{\equiv}{}^{\mathcal{K}}$) and these founded on the above EC,... classes (like the relation $<_{EC}$, see BARWISE— FEFERMAN[1985, II] for details). Then, starting by the following

2.2.1 Facts.

(1) $\mathscr{L}_{\omega\omega}(Q_n)_{n<\omega}$ *and* $\mathscr{L}_{\omega_1\omega}$ *restricted to countable structures are* $\equiv$*—equivalent.*

(2) $\mathscr{L}_1 \leqslant_{EC}{}^{\mathcal{K}} \mathscr{L}_2$ *implies, but is strictly stronger than* $\mathscr{L}_1 \leqslant_{\equiv}{}^{\mathcal{K}} \mathscr{L}_2$.

and adding the *PRPC*—relationships $<_{PRP}$,... to the above ones, we obtain the following version of the *expressiveness theorem*

2.2.2 Theorem*. $\mathscr{L}_{\omega_1\omega_1}$ *and* $\mathscr{L}_{\omega\omega}(Q_n)_{n<\omega}$ *restricted to countable structures are PRPC—equivalent;*

which allows to characterize also $\mathscr{L}_{\omega_1\omega_1}$ (restricted to countable structures) by the above back and forth games.

2.3 Refinement. Finally, we use the determination relation between games to refine the logic used to classify a class of specifications

2.3.1 Local Determination Theorem*. *Let $\mathcal{L}$ be a logic characterized by G, let* $\mathbf{M} = (M,...)$ *and* $\mathbf{N} = (N,...)$ *be two structures, and let* $M \supseteq X$, $N \supseteq Y$. *Then the following are equivalent:*

(i) $G([X]^{\mathbf{M}},[Y]^{\mathbf{N}}) \rhd G(\mathbf{M},\mathbf{N})$,

(ii) $[X]^{\mathbf{M}} \equiv_{\mathcal{L}} [Y]^{\mathbf{N}}$ *implies* $\mathbf{M} \equiv_{\mathcal{L}} \mathbf{N}$.

2.3.2 Fact*. *Let $\mathcal{K}$ be a model—theoretic specification, let G_i be a back—and—forth relative to $\mathcal{K}$ and let $\mathcal{L}_i$ be the logic characterized by G_i (i =1,2) over $\mathcal{K}$. Then the following are equivalent:*

(1) $G_1 \rhd^{\mathcal{K}} G_2$,

(2) $\mathcal{L}_2 \preccurlyeq_{\equiv}^{\mathcal{K}} \mathcal{L}_1$.

2.3.3 Theorem*. $\mathcal{L}_1 \preccurlyeq_{\equiv}^{\mathcal{K}} \mathcal{L}_2$ *over* $\mathcal{L}_1$*— elementary subclasses of* $\mathcal{K}$ *iff* $\mathcal{L}_1 \preccurlyeq_{PRPC}^{\mathcal{K}} \mathcal{L}_2$ *over* $\mathcal{L}_1$*— elementary subclasses of* $\mathcal{K}$.

Thus, denoting by $\mathcal{L}_1 \preccurlyeq_{\equiv}^{EC\,\mathcal{K}} \mathcal{L}_2$ and $\mathcal{L}_1 \preccurlyeq_{PRPC}^{EC\,\mathcal{K}} \mathcal{L}_2$ the relations $\mathcal{L}_1 \preccurlyeq_{\equiv}^{\mathcal{K}} \mathcal{L}_2$, $\mathcal{L}_1 \preccurlyeq_{PRPC}^{\mathcal{K}} \mathcal{L}_2$ restricted to the $\mathcal{L}_1$— elementary subclasses and using $\rhd^{EC\,\mathcal{K}}$ under the condition of the above fact, we can summarize the relationships between $\preccurlyeq_{\equiv}^{EC\,\mathcal{K}}$, $\preccurlyeq_{PRPC}^{EC\,\mathcal{K}}$ and $\rhd^{EC\,\mathcal{K}}$ as follows:

2.3.4 Refinement Theorem*. *If $\mathcal{L}_i$ is the logic characterized by G_i (i =1,2), then the following are equivalent:*

(1) $\mathcal{L}_1 \preccurlyeq_{\equiv}^{EC\,\mathcal{K}} \mathcal{L}_2$

(2) $\mathcal{L}_1 \preccurlyeq_{PRPC}^{EC\,\mathcal{K}} \mathcal{L}_2$

(3) $G_1 \rhd^{EC\,\mathcal{K}} G_2$.

3. Applications.

3.1 Local Determination of Bisimulation Games*. In this paragraph we consider the bisimulation relation studied in the area of semantics and logics of concurrent processes.

3.1.1 Processes and bisimulation. We begin by recalling that a *transition system* (which, in general is a labelled graph) generates a labelled tree which describe its behaviors, called *process*. The main relationship between processes (and then between transition system) is the so called *bisimulation* relation. (see, e.g. MILNER[1980], CLEAVELAND—HENNESSY [1989], and CLEAVELAND—PARROW—STEFFEN[1989]). We empathize that the transition system usually considered determine countable processes. More precisely, a *process* is a L—labelled tree **H** which possibly admits many labels for a given arc. $x \rightarrow^a y$ means that the nodes x and y are joined by an arc labelled by a. Let then two L—processes $\mathbf{H}_1$ and $\mathbf{H}_2$ relative to the set of nodes N_1 and N_2, respectively, and let $\simeq$ be an equivalence relation on $N_1 \cup N_2$. Then a $\simeq$— *bisimulation* is a relation $\approx$ on $N_1 \cup N_2$ which satisfy the following properties:

(B1) for any $m, n \in N_1 \cup N_2$, $m \approx n$ implies $x \simeq y$,

(B2) for any $m \in N_1$ such that $m \rightarrow^a m'$, $m \approx n$ with $n \in N_2$ implies that there is an $n' \in N_2$ such that $n \rightarrow^a n'$,

(B3) for any $n \in N_2$ such that $n \rightarrow^a n'$, $n \approx m$ with $m \in N_1$ implies that there is an $m' \in N_2$ such that $m \rightarrow^a m'$,

We note that $\approx$ acts both inside the two processes that between them and that $\approx$ restricted to any process is an equivalence relation in which every equivalence class is a path. Two processes $\mathbf{H}_1$ and $\mathbf{H}_2$ are *bisimilar* if there is a bisimulation $\approx$ such that $\mathbf{H}_1 \approx \mathbf{H}_2$.

3.1.2 Model–theoretic specification of processes. Since processes are countable objects, they fall in our model—theoretic context, where can be specified by a variation of the labelled tree. Thus define a *process tree* as a tree—like structure $\mathbf{T} = \langle T, f, r, P_a \mid a \in L \rangle$ such that, for every $x \in T$, $P_a(x)$ implies that

$P_a(f(x))$ or $P_a(y)$ for some $y \in f^{-1}(x) \setminus \{x\}$.

We note that, in this specification a "transition" $x \to^a x'$ is represented by a pair of nodes x, x' labelled by a, namely $P_a(x) \wedge \exists x' [x = f(x') \wedge P_a(x')]$. Moreover, nodes (and so arcs) can have many labels. The set of the transition trees in the specification $\mathcal{P}roc$ for processes. The parametrization of $\mathcal{P}roc$ is strictly analogous to that of the labelled trees considered in *1.1.1*.

3.1.3 Bisimulation game. Let $\mathbf{T}_1$ and $\mathbf{T}_2$ the process trees related to the precesses $\mathbf{H}_1$ and $\mathbf{H}_2$. We want individuate a relation between $\mathbf{T}_1$ and $\mathbf{T}_2$ which holds if and only if $\mathbf{H}_1$ and $\mathbf{H}_2$ are bisimilar. For this we first reduce $\mathbf{T}_1$ and $\mathbf{T}_2$ to the quotient structures determined by the action of the bisimulation inside them. More precisely, (since $\approx$ is an equivalence relations which preserves the paths) we assume that the *$\approx$-reduced* of a process tree $\mathbf{T}$ is the tree—like structure $\mathbf{T}[\approx] = \langle T' f', r', P'_a \mid a \in L \rangle$ such that

(1) $T' = T/\approx$,

(2) $f'([x]) = f(x)$ if x and $f(x)$ are not $\approx$-equivalent

$= f(f(x))$ otherwise,

(3) $P'_a([x])$ iff $P_a([y])$ for some $y \in [x]$,

(where $[x]$ is the $\approx$-equivalence class which contains x). We note that $\mathbf{T}[\approx]$ is a process tree. Then we show that

3.1.4 Fact. *Let $\mathbf{H}_1, \mathbf{H}_2$ be processes and $\mathbf{T}_1, \mathbf{T}_2$ be the associated process trees. Then the following are equivalent*

(1) $\mathbf{H}_1 \approx \mathbf{H}_2$.

(2) *Player II has a winning strategy for $G(\mathbf{T}_1[\approx], \mathbf{T}_2[\approx])$.*

3.1.5 Corollary. *In the above notations, if $G(\mathbf{T}_1[\approx], \mathbf{T}_2[\approx]) \rhd G(\mathbf{T}_1, \mathbf{T}_2)$, then the following are equivalent*

(1) $\mathbf{H}_1 \approx \mathbf{H}_2$.

(2) $\mathbf{T}_1 \equiv_{\mathcal{L}} \mathbf{T}_2$ *in some logic* $\mathcal{L}$.

3.1.6 Remarks. The previous considerations give a hint for an unified approach to three basic issues of concurrency by using model—theoretic methods:

- The mathematical modelling of processes by means of first—order structures (trees in the interleaving framework, partial orders in the true—concurrency framework).
- The operational equivalence between processes by means of a back—and—forth game equivalence on the above structures (by formulating the various equivalences between processes, including the various notions of testing, as such game equivalence on appropriate structures).
- The logical characterization à la Hennessy—Milner of such equivalences by means of general theorems *à la* Erenfeucht—Fraissé (propositional modal and temporal logics of processes being obtained by an appropriate coding of fragments of some model—theoretic logic).

3.2 Local Determination of Geometrical Games*. Working in the specification *Geom* constituted by the pairs (**E**,F) where **E** is a is a suitable three—dimensional model of the *Tarski Eulidean Elementary Geometry* ***EEG*** (see, e.g., Tarski[1959]) and F is a geometrical figure (i.e. a subset of E first—order definable with parameters in **E**), we prove that many notions of the combinatorial topology (like the topological dimension, the notions of topological complexes, and the boundary operator ∂) are parametrical expressible in *Geom* (see MASCARI—VINCENZI[199?]).

Then, defining ***homogeneous*** a geometrical figure F which is the smallest n—dimensional figure elementarily defined by a $(\tau_{geom})_{par}$—formula, we prove

3.2.1 Theorem*. *Let* F_i *be a geometrically homogeneous figures which does not coincides with* ∂F_i $(i = 1,2)$. *Then* $G(\partial F_1, \partial F_2) \rhd G(F_1, F_2)$.

which allow reduce the properties of a homogeneous F figure to the properties of ∂F and show that the remaining elements of F are indiscernibles in our geometrical context.

3.3 Global determination and linguistic games*. Working in the specification *Lang* (obtained as a pure model—theoretic version of the the Barwise— Cooper analysis of natural languages, see BARWISE— COOPER[1981] and MASCARI—VINCENZI[199?]) we consider the standard characterization of *Lang* given by the *ad hoc* Lindström logic $\mathcal{L}_{\omega\omega}(Q_{Lang})$. Since, $\mathcal{L}_{\omega\omega}(Q_{Lang})$ is *EC*— sublogic of $\mathcal{L}_{\omega\omega}(Q_n)_{n<\omega}$ it is also *PRPC*—equivalent (by *Expressiveness Theorem*) to some fragment of $\mathcal{L}_{\omega_1\omega_1}$. Rewriting this fact in its game—theoretic form, we have that any possible back and forth game G_{Lang} characterizing $\mathcal{L}_{\omega\omega}(Q_{Lang})$ over *Lang*, satisfies the following

3.3.1 Fact*. $G_{Lang} \rhd^{Lang} G_{\omega\omega}(Q_n)_{n<\omega}$.

which shows that, in G_{Lang}, player *I* chooses total bijections.

Conversely, the first—order expressibility of some fragment *Sublang* of *Lang*, (as in the case of left—continuous quantifiers, studied in VANBENTHEN[1986, Paragraph 2.3]), assumes the following game—theoretic form:

3.3.2 Fact*. $G_{\omega\omega} \rhd^{Sublang} G_{Lang}$.

References

Abrusci V.M., Mascari G.F.: A Logic of Recursion. *Information and Computation* 81 (1989) 168—226

Ajtai M., Fagin R/. (1990), Reachability is Harder for Directed than for Undirected Finite Graphs. *The Journal of Symbolic Logic* 55 (1990) 113—150.

Barwise K.J., Cooper R.: Generalized quantifiers and Natural Language. *Linguistics and Philosophy* 4 (1981)159—219.

Barwise J., Feferman S.: *Model Theoretic Logics*. Springer, Berlin (1985).

Bergstra J.A., Terlouw J.: Standard Model Semantics for DSL A Data Type Specification Language. *Acta Informatica* 19 (1983) 97—113.

Berman L.: The Complexity of Logical Theories. *Theoretical Computer Science* 11 (1980) 71—77.

Bertoni, A., Mauri G., Miglioli P.: Some uses of Model Theory to specify abstracts data types and to capture their recursiveness. *Fundamenta Informaticae*, VI.2 (1983).

Chandra A., Harel D.: Structures and Complexity of Relational Queris. *Journal of Computer and Systems Science* **25** (1982) 99—128.

Courcelle B.: The Monadic Second—Order Logic of Graphs. I. Recognizable Sets of Finite Graphs. *Information and Computation* **85** (1990) 12—75.

Cleaveland R., Hennessy M.: Testing Equivalence as a Bisimulation Equivalence. In: "Automatic Verification Methods for Finite State Systems (Sifakis J. ed.) *Lecture Notes in Computer Science* **407** Springer, Berlin 1989, 11—23,

Cleaveland R., Parrow M., Steffen B.: The Concurrency Worbench. In: "Automatic Verification Methods for Finite State Systems (Sifakis J. ed.) *Lecture Notes in Computer Science* **407**, Springer, Berlin 1989, 24—37, .

De Nicola R., Ferrari G.L.: Observational Logics and Concurrency Model. Technical Report TR—10/90 Università di Pisa (1990).

Fenstad J.E.: Logic and Natural Language Systems. In: H.—D. Ebbinghaus et al. eds: *Logic Colloquium '87* , North— Holland, Amsterdam 1989, 27—39.

Gerla G.: Pointless Metric Spaces. *The Journal of Symbolic Logic* **55** (1990) 207—219.

Goguen J.A. and Burstall R.M.: Institutions: Abstract Model Theory for Computer Science. *Report No. CSLI—85—30 Center for the Study of Language and Information, Stanford University* (1985).

Hafner T.: On the Expressive Completeness of CTL*. Technical Report. *Schriften zur Informatik und angewandten Mathematik* **123** (1986).

Hella L.: Definability Hierarchies of Generalized Quantifiers. *Annals of Pure and Applied Logic* **43** (1989) 235—271.

Hennessy M.C., Milner A.J.R.G.: Algebraic Laws for nondeterminism and concurrence. *Journal of the Association of Computing Machinery* **32** (1985) 137—161.

Immerman N.: Descriptive and Computational Complexity. *Proceedings of Symposia in Applied Mathematics*, Vol. 38, 75—91, Americal Mathematical Society, Providence (1989) 75—91.

Immerman N., Kozen D.: Definability with Bounded Number of Bound Variables, *Information and Computation* **83** (1989) 121—139.

Kolaitis P. and Papadimitriou C.H.: Some Computational Aspects of Circumscription, *Journal of the Association of Computing Machinery* **37** (1990) 1—14.

Ladner R.E.: Application of Model Theoretic Games to Discrete Linear Orders and Finite Automata. *Information and Control* **33** (1977) 281—303.

Maibaum T.S.E., Veloso P.A.S., Sadler M.R.: A Theory of Abstract Data Types for Program Development: Bridging the Gap? In: Ehrig H., Floyd C., Nivat M., Thatcher J. eds.: *TAPSOFT '85*, , Lecture Notes in Computer Science, Springer, Berlin 1985, Vol. 2°, 214—230.

Makowsky J.A.: Measuring the expressive power of dynamic logics: An application of abstract model theory. In: de Bakker W., van Leeuwen J. eds.:, *Automata, Languages and Programming*, , Lectures Notes in Computer Science 85, Springer, Berlin 1980, 409—421.

UNIVERSAL ALGEBRA IN HIGHER TYPES (Extended Abstract)

Karl Meinke
Department of Mathematics and Computer Science,
University College Swansea,
Singleton Park,
Swansea SA2 8PP,
Great Britain.
January 1991.

Abstract We develop the elementary theory of higher–order universal algebra using the non–standard approach to finite type theory introduced by Henkin. Basic results include: existence theorems for free and initial higher type algebras, a complete higher type equational calculus, and characterisation theorems for higher type equational and Horn classes.

0. INTRODUCTION.

In theoretical computer science, ***higher–order operations***, i.e. operations defined on sets of functions or sets of sets, arise quite naturally. Examples can be found in many branches of theoretical computer science, e.g. domain theory (Stoy [1977]), data type theory (Maibaum and Lucena [1980], Parsaye–Ghomi [1981], Möller [1987a], [1987b], Broy [1987], Möller et al [1988]), functional programming (Burstall et al [1980], Turner [1985], Harper et al [1986]) relational programming (Miller and Nadathur [1986]) and hardware verification (Gordon [1986], Meinke and Tucker [1988]). Such higher–order operations give rise to ***higher–order algebraic structures***. The theory of higher–order algebras turns out to be substantially different to the classical first–order theory as developed in e.g. Cohn [1965]. While a number of contributions to the theory of higher–order algebras exist in the literature, e.g. Poigné [1986], Möller [1987a], there appears to be no systematic treatment of the higher–order case. In this paper, we communicate the main results of a systematic theory of higher type universal algebra. An extended account of this theory will appear as Meinke [1991]. (See also Meinke [1990].)

The organisation of the paper is as follows: Section 1 introduces the basic concepts and terminology for higher type universal algebra. Section 2 establishes the role of extensionality and generalises the fundamental constructions and results for subalgebras, homomorphisms, quotient algebras, direct and reduced products. In Section 3 we consider free higher type algebras and generalise Birkhoff's Existence Theorem for free algebras in classes of algebras.

Section 4 introduces a sound and complete higher type equational calculus. Section 5 generalises the Variety and Quasivariety Theorems of Birkhoff and Malcev to higher types. Finally, in Section 6, we conclude with some general remarks about applications of the theory in computer science.

The prerequisites of this paper are a familiarity with elementary universal algebra and first-order model theory. (See for example Cohn [1965] or our own Meinke and Tucker [1991], and Chang and Keisler [1990].)

1. HIGHER TYPE ALGEBRAS.

We shall develop higher type universal algebra using the notation and terminology of many-sorted universal algebra. We adopt the notation of Meinke and Tucker [1991].

A set S of sorts is any non-empty set. As usual, S^* denotes the set of all words in the free monoid generated by S. The empty word is denoted by λ and $S^+ = S^* - \{ \lambda \}$ denotes the set of all non-empty words over S. An S-sorted signature Σ is an $S^* \times S$ indexed collection of disjoint sets $\Sigma = \{ \Sigma_{w,s} \mid w \in S^*, s \in S \}$. For the empty word λ and each sort $s \in S$, each element $c \in \Sigma_{\lambda,s}$ is a constant symbol of sort s. For each non-empty word $w = s(1) \ldots s(n) \in S^+$ and each sort $s \in S$, each element $f \in \Sigma_{w,s}$ is a function symbol of domain type w, codomain type s and arity n.

Let Σ be an S-sorted signature. An S-sorted Σ algebra is an ordered pair (A, Σ^A), consisting of an S-indexed collection $A = \{ A_s \mid s \in S \}$ of carrier sets A_s and an $S^* \times S$ indexed collection

$$\Sigma^A = \{ \Sigma^A_{w,s} \mid w \in S^*, s \in S \}$$

of sets of constants and algebraic operations. For each sort $s \in S$, $\Sigma^A_{\lambda,s} = \{ c_A \mid c \in \Sigma_{\lambda,s} \}$, where $c_A \in A_s$ is a constant that interprets c in A_s. For each $w = s(1) \ldots s(n) \in S^+$ and each sort $s \in S$, $\Sigma^A_{w,s} = \{ f_A \mid f \in \Sigma_{w,s} \}$, where $f_A : A^w \to A_s$ is an operation with domain $A^w = A_{s(1)} \times \ldots \times A_{s(n)}$ and codomain A_s which interprets f over A. As usual we let A denote both a Σ algebra and its S-indexed family of carrier sets.

We begin by giving rules of type formation for finite type theories.

1.1. Definition. A *type basis* B is a non-empty set. The *type hierarchy* $H(B)$ generated by a type basis B is the set $H(B) = \bigcup_{n \in \omega} H_n(B)$ of formal expressions built up inductively by

$$H_0(B) = B,$$

and

$$H_{n+1}(B) = H_n(B) \cup \{ (\sigma \times \tau), \ (\sigma \to \tau) \mid \sigma, \tau \in H_n(B) \}.$$

Each element $\sigma \in B$ is termed a *basic type*; each element $(\sigma \times \tau) \in H(B)$ is termed a *product type* and each element $(\sigma \to \tau) \in H(B)$ is termed a *function type*.

We can assign an *order* to each type $\sigma \in H(B)$ as follows. Each basic type $\sigma \in B$ has order 0. If $\sigma, \tau \in H(B)$ have order m and n respectively then $(\sigma \times \tau)$ has order $max\{ m, n \}$ and $(\sigma \rightarrow \tau)$ has order $max\{ m, n \} + 1$.

A ***type structure*** S over a type basis B is a subset $S \subseteq H(B)$, which is closed under subtypes in the sense that for any $\sigma, \tau \in H(B)$, if $(\sigma \rightarrow \tau) \in S$ or $(\sigma \times \tau) \in S$ then both $\sigma \in S$ and $\tau \in S$. We say that S is a ***basic type structure*** over B if, and only if, $S \subseteq B$. A type structure S over a basis B is said to be an ***nth–order type structure*** if, and only if, the order of each type $\sigma \in S$ is strictly less than n. If there is no bound $n \in \omega$ on the order of all types $\sigma \in S$ then we say that S is an ***ω–order type structure***. Clearly S is first–order if, and only if, S contains no function types.

The subtype closure property on type structures allows us to make definitions and prove statements, quantified over all members of a type structure, by induction on the complexity of types.

1.2. Definition. Let S be a type structure over a type basis B. An *S–typed signature* Σ is an S–sorted signature such that for each product type $(\sigma \times \tau) \in S$ we have two unary *projection operation symbols*

$$proj^{(\sigma\times\tau),\sigma} \in \Sigma_{(\sigma\times\tau),\sigma} \quad proj^{(\sigma\times\tau),\tau} \in \Sigma_{(\sigma\times\tau),\tau} \,.$$

Also for each function type $(\sigma \rightarrow \tau) \in S$ we have a binary *evaluation operation symbol*

$$eval^{(\sigma\rightarrow\tau)} \in \Sigma_{(\sigma\rightarrow\tau)\ \sigma,\tau} \,.$$

To avoid the problems associated with empty carrier sets, we always assume that an S–typed signature Σ allows the formation of a variable free term $t \in T(\Sigma)_\sigma$ for each $\sigma \in S$. If S is a basic type structure then an S–typed signature is just an S–sorted signature in the usual sense. In the sequel, when the subtypes σ and τ are clear, we let $proj^1$ and $proj^2$ denote the projection operation symbols $proj^{(\sigma\times\tau),\sigma}$ and $proj^{(\sigma\times\tau),\tau}$ respectively.

We can now introduce the intended interpretations of an S–typed signature Σ.

1.3. Definition. Let S be a type structure over a type basis B. Let Σ be an S–typed signature and A be an S–sorted Σ algebra. We say that A is *cumulative* if, and only if, for each product type $(\sigma \times \tau) \in S$ we have $A_{(\sigma\times\tau)} \subseteq A_\sigma \times A_\tau$, and for each function type $(\sigma \rightarrow \tau) \in S$ we have $A_{(\sigma\rightarrow\tau)} \subseteq [A_\sigma \rightarrow A_\tau]$, i.e. $A_{(\sigma\rightarrow\tau)}$ is a subset of the set of all (total) functions from A_σ to A_τ. We say that A is an *S–typed Σ algebra* if, and only if, A is cumulative and for each product type $(\sigma \times \tau) \in S$ the operations

$$proj_A^1 : A_{(\sigma\times\tau)} \rightarrow A_\sigma \quad proj_A^2 : A_{(\sigma\times\tau)} \rightarrow A_\tau$$

are the first and second *projection mappings* defined on each $a = (a_1, a_2) \in A_{(\sigma\times\tau)}$ by

$$proj_A^1(a) = a_1 \quad proj_A^2(a) = a_2;$$

furthermore, for each function type $(\sigma \to \tau) \in S$, $eval_A^{(\sigma\to\tau)} : A_{(\sigma\to\tau)} \times A_\sigma \to A_\tau$ is the *evaluation operation* on the function space $A_{(\sigma\to\tau)}$ defined by

$$eval_A^{(\sigma\to\tau)}(a, n) = a(n)$$

for each $a \in A_{(\sigma\to\tau)}$ and $n \in A_\sigma$. If A is an S–typed Σ algebra we say that A is *complete* if, and only if, for each product type $(\sigma \times \tau) \in S$ we have $A_{(\sigma\times\tau)} = A_\sigma \times A_\tau$, and for each function type $(\sigma \to \tau) \in S$ we have $A_{(\sigma\to\tau)} = [A_\sigma \to A_\tau]$.

We let $Alg(\Sigma)$ denote the class of all S–sorted Σ algebras and $Alg_{typ}(\Sigma)$ denote the subclass of all S–typed Σ algebras.

1.4. Example. Let S be a type structure over a type basis B. Let Σ be an S–typed signature and let $X = \{ X_\sigma \mid \sigma \in S \}$ be an S–indexed collection of disjoint sets X_σ of variable symbols of type σ. (We always assume that the sets X_σ are disjoint from each set $\Sigma_{w,s}$.) Define the *free S–typed Σ algebra* $\overline{T(\Sigma, X)}$ to be the S–typed Σ algebra with S–indexed family of carrier sets $\overline{T(\Sigma, X)} = \{ \overline{T(\Sigma, X)}_\sigma \mid \sigma \in S \}$, where

$$\overline{T(\Sigma, X)}_\sigma = \{ \bar{t} \mid t \in T(\Sigma, X)_\sigma \}.$$

We define each element $\bar{t} \in \overline{T(\Sigma, X)}_\sigma$ by induction on the complexity of types. For each basic type $\sigma \in S$ and each term $t \in T(\Sigma, X)_\sigma$ define $\bar{t} = t$. For each product type $(\sigma \times \tau) \in S$ and each term $t \in T(\Sigma, X)_{(\sigma\times\tau)}$ define

$$\bar{t} = (\overline{proj^1(t)}, \overline{proj^2(t)}).$$

For each function type $(\sigma \to \tau) \in S$ and each term $t \in T(\Sigma, X)_{(\sigma\to\tau)}$ define $\bar{t} : \overline{T(\Sigma, X)}_\sigma \to \overline{T(\Sigma, X)}_\tau$ on each $\bar{t}_0 \in \overline{T(\Sigma, X)}_\sigma$ by

$$\bar{t}\,(\bar{t}_0) = \overline{eval^{(\sigma\to\tau)}(t, t_0)}.$$

The constants and algebraic operations of $\overline{T(\Sigma, X)}$ are defined as follows. For each type $\sigma \in S$ and each constant symbol $c \in \Sigma_{\lambda,\sigma}$, define $c_{\overline{T(\Sigma,X)}} = \bar{c}$. For each type $\sigma \in S$, each $w = \sigma(1)\ldots\sigma(n) \in S^+$, any function symbol $f \in \Sigma_{w,\sigma}$ and any $t_1, \ldots, t_n \in T(\Sigma, X)^w$, define

$$f_{\overline{T(\Sigma,X)}}\,(\bar{t}_1, \ldots, \bar{t}_n) = \overline{f(t_1, \ldots, t_n)}.$$

Using the fact that $\bar{t}_0 = \bar{t}_1$ if, and only if, $t_0 = t_1$, it is easily verified that $\overline{T(\Sigma, X)}$ is a well defined S–typed Σ algebra. In Section 2 we shall see that $\overline{T(\Sigma, X)}$ arises as a special case of a general construction known as a *collapsing construction*.

2. CONSTRUCTIONS ON HIGHER TYPE ALGEBRAS.

In this section we begin by introducing the first–order condition of *extensionality* on S–sorted Σ algebras, for any type structure S and S–typed signature Σ. We show that the extensional Σ algebras are, up to isomorphism, precisely the S–typed Σ algebras. Extensionality is $\forall\exists$ axiomatisable but not universally axiomatisable. Thus, for example, the class of all extensional S–sorted Σ algebras is not closed under the formation of subalgebras. In the remainder of the section we identify those constructions on Σ algebras which impose or preserve extensionality.

In the sequel we consider a fixed, but arbitrarily chosen, type basis B, type structure S over B and S–typed signature Σ. To avoid the complications associated with algebras having empty carrier sets of some sort, we shall assume that for every type $\sigma \in S$ there exists a variable free Σ term of type σ. Let $X = \{ X_\sigma \mid \sigma \in S \}$ be an S–indexed collection of disjoint, infinite sets X_σ of variables of sort σ. Recall the definition of the S–sorted first–order language $\mathcal{L}(\Sigma, X)$, over Σ and X. If S is an nth–order (respectively ω–order) type structure then $\mathcal{L}(\Sigma, X)$ is said to be an nth–order (respectively ω–order) language. The observation that a higher–order language can be viewed as a many–sorted, first–order language, admitting first–order (but typed) models, is the essential idea behind the completeness theorem of Henkin [1950] for finite type theory. Recall too the satisfaction relation $\models$ between Σ algebras and $\mathcal{L}(\Sigma, X)$ formulas, and the inference relation $\vdash$ between $\mathcal{L}(\Sigma, X)$ theories and formulas, obtained via the many–sorted first–order predicate calculus. If $\Phi \subseteq \mathcal{L}(\Sigma, X)$ is any set of formulas then $Alg(\Sigma, \Phi)$ denotes the class $\{ A \in Alg(\Sigma) \mid A \models \Phi \}$ of all models of Φ, and $Alg_{typ}(\Sigma, \Phi)$ denotes the class $\{ A \in Alg_{typ}(\Sigma) \mid A \models \Phi \}$ of all S–typed models of Φ.

2.1. Definition. Define the set $\mathbf{Ext} = \mathbf{Ext}_\Sigma$ of *extensionality axioms* over Σ to be the set of all $\mathcal{L}(\Sigma, X)$ sentences of the form

$$\forall x \forall y \Big(\forall z \big(eval^{(\sigma\to\tau)}(x, z) = eval^{(\sigma\to\tau)}(y, z) \big) \Rightarrow x = y \Big),$$

for each function type $(\sigma \to \tau) \in S$, where $x, y \in X_{(\sigma\to\tau)}$, $z \in X_\sigma$, together with all $\mathcal{L}(\Sigma, X)$ sentences of the form

$$\forall x \forall y \Big(proj^1(x) = proj^1(y) \ \wedge\ proj^2(x) = proj^2(y) \Rightarrow x = y \Big),$$

for each product type $(\sigma \times \tau) \in S$, where $x, y \in X_{(\sigma\times\tau)}$.

We say that a Σ algebra A is *extensional* if, and only if, $A \models \mathbf{Ext}$. We let $Alg_{Ext}(\Sigma)$ denote the class $Alg(\Sigma, \mathbf{Ext})$ of all extensional Σ algebras, and $Alg_{Ext}(\Sigma, \Phi)$ denote the class $Alg(\Sigma, \Phi \cup \mathbf{Ext})$ for any set $\Phi \subseteq \mathcal{L}(\Sigma, X)$ of formulas.

Clearly every S–typed Σ algebra is extensional. However if A is an S–sorted Σ algebra and $A \models \mathbf{Ext}$ it does not follow that A is an S–typed Σ algebra. Nevertheless, under the assumption of extensionality, the following construction gives an S–typed Σ algebra $\overline{A}$ which is isomorphic to A.

2.2. Definition. Let A be an extensional S–sorted Σ algebra. The *collapse* of A is the S–typed Σ algebra $\overline{A}$ with S–indexed family of carrier sets $\overline{A} = \{ \overline{A}_\sigma \mid \sigma \in S \}$, where

$$\overline{A}_\sigma = \{ \overline{a} \mid a \in A_\sigma \}.$$

We define each element $\overline{a} \in \overline{A}_\sigma$ by induction on the complexity of types. For each basic type $\sigma \in S$ and each $a \in A_\sigma$, define $\overline{a} = a$. For each product type $(\sigma \times \tau) \in S$ and each $a \in A_{(\sigma\times\tau)}$, define

$$\overline{a} = (\ \overline{proj^1_A(a)},\ \overline{proj^2_A(a)}\ ).$$

For each function type $(\sigma \rightarrow \tau) \in S$ and each $a \in A_{(\sigma\rightarrow\tau)}$, define $\overline{a} : \overline{A}_\sigma \rightarrow \overline{A}_\tau$ on each $\overline{a_0} \in \overline{A}_\sigma$ by

$$\overline{a}\,(\,\overline{a_0}\,) = \overline{eval_A^{(\sigma\rightarrow\tau)}(a,\,a_0)}.$$

The constants and algebraic operations of $\overline{A}$ are defined as follows. For each type $\sigma \in S$ and each constant symbol $c \in \Sigma_{\lambda,\,\sigma}$, define

$$c_{\overline{A}} = \overline{c_A}.$$

For each $\sigma \in S$, each $w = \sigma(1)\ldots\sigma(n) \in S^+$, each function symbol $f \in \Sigma_{w,\,\sigma}$ and for any $a_1, \ldots, a_n \in A^w$, define

$$f_{\overline{A}}\,(\,\overline{a_1}, \ldots, \overline{a_n}\,) = \overline{f_A(a_1, \ldots, a_n)}.$$

2.3. Lemma. *Let A be an extensional S–sorted Σ algebra. Then $A \cong \overline{A}$.*

An immediate consequence of Lemma 2.3 is the following representation theorem for extensional Σ algebras, first proved by Mostowski for models of set theory. (See for example Jech [1978].)

2.4. Collapsing Theorem. (Mostowski) *Let A be an S–sorted Σ algebra. Then A is isomorphic to an S–typed Σ algebra if, and only if, A is extensional.*

From the Collapsing Theorem it follows that, for the purposes of algebra, the general model theory and first–order model theory of finite type theory are equivalent. General model theory is simply based on a standard representation of extensional Σ algebras as S–typed Σ algebras. This observation has several immediate consequences.

2.5. Corollary. *Let Φ be any set of $\mathcal{L}(\Sigma, X)$ formulas. Then every Σ algebra $A \in Alg(\Sigma,\ \Phi \cup \mathbf{Ext})$ is isomorphic to an S–typed Σ algebra $B \in Alg_{typ}(\Sigma, \Phi)$.*

The Completeness Theorem for finite type theory is an immediate consequence of the Completeness Theorem for the many–sorted first–order predicate calculus and Corollary 2.5.

2.6. Completeness Theorem. (Henkin [1950]) *Let Φ be any set of $\mathcal{L}(\Sigma, X)$ formulas and let $\phi \in \mathcal{L}(\Sigma, X)$ be any formula. Then*

$$\Phi \cup \mathbf{Ext} \vdash \phi \Leftrightarrow Alg_{typ}(\Sigma, \Phi) \models \phi.$$

In the remainder of this section we wish to identify those basic algebraic constructions which impose or preserve extensionality. Such constructions will be used to prove the existence of free algebras in classes of extensional algebras and to establish characterisation theorems for equational and equational Horn theories of finite type.

Let A be a Σ algebra. Recall the definition of a Σ subalgebra of A. We write $B \leq A$ if B is a Σ subalgebra of A. A Σ algebra A is said to be minimal (or reachable or term generated) if, and only if, A has no proper Σ subalgebra. If K is any class of Σ algebras then $Min(K)$ denotes the subclass of all minimal members of K,

$$Min(K) = \{\ A \in K \mid A \text{ is minimal }\ \}.$$

Of course $Min(K)$ may be empty. However if K is non–empty and closed under the formation of Σ subalgebras then every $A \in K$ has a minimal subalgebra $B \leq A \in K$ and in this case $Min(K)$ is non–empty.

We next observe that extensionality is $\forall\exists$ axiomatisable. The extensionality axiom for a product type $(\sigma \times \tau) \in S$ is universal while the extensionality axiom for a function type $(\sigma \rightarrow \tau) \in S$ has the prenex normal form

$$\forall x \forall y \exists z (\ eval^{(\sigma\rightarrow\tau)}(x,\ z) = eval^{(\sigma\rightarrow\tau)}(y,\ z) \Rightarrow x = y\ ) \qquad (1).$$

It is easily shown that the class of all extensional Σ algebras need not be closed under the formation of Σ subalgebras. Thus extensionality is $\forall\exists$ axiomatisable but not universally axiomatisable. This observation leads us to formulate a more restricted notion of subalgebra and the corresponding closure condition on a class K of Σ algebras.

2.7. Definition. Let A and B be Σ algebras. We say that A is an *extensional* Σ *subalgebra* of B if, and only if, $A \leq B$ and $A \models$ **Ext**. If A is an extensional Σ subalgebra of B we write $A \leq_{Ext} B$.

Let K be any class of Σ algebras. We say that K is *closed under the formation of extensional* Σ *subalgebras* if, and only if, for any A, $B \in Alg(\Sigma)$, if $A \in K$ and $B \leq_{Ext} A$ then $B \in K$.

Clearly $Alg_{Ext}(\Sigma)$ is closed under the formation of extensional Σ subalgebras.

Let $A = \{\ A(i) \mid i \in I\ \}$ be an I–indexed family of Σ algebras, for some (possibly empty) indexing set I. Recall the definition of the direct product $\Pi A = \Pi_{i\in I} A(i)$. Observe that the extensionality sentence (1) above is an $\forall\exists$ Horn sentence. Furthermore the extensionality axiom for each product type $(\sigma \times \tau)$ is a universal Horn sentence. Indeed both types of formulas are strict or positive Horn sentences. Since Horn formulas are preserved under the formation of direct products, it follows that the direct product of any set of extensional Σ algebras is extensional.

More interesting is the case of homomorphic images and quotient algebras. Let A and B be Σ algebras. Recall the definition of a Σ homomorphism $\phi : A \rightarrow B$, from A to B.

It is easily shown that the class of all extensional Σ algebras need not be closed under the formation of homomorphic images. This observation leads us to formulate a more restricted notion of homomorphic image and the corresponding closure condition on a class K of Σ algebras.

2.8. Definition. Let A and B be Σ algebras. We say that B is an *extensional homomorphic image of* A if, and only if, B is a homomorphic image of A and $B \models$ **Ext**.

Let K be any class of Σ algebras. We say that K is *closed under the formation of extensional homomorphic images* if, and only if, for any $A \in K$ and $B \in Alg(\Sigma)$, if B is an extensional homomorphic image of A then $B \in K$.

Obviously $Alg_{Ext}(\Sigma)$ is closed under the formation of extensional homomorphic images. Note that if $K \subseteq Alg_{Ext}(\Sigma)$ is any extensional class closed under the formation of extensional homomorphic images then K is closed under the formation of isomorphic images.

Let A be a Σ algebra. Recall the definition of a Σ congruence $\equiv$ on A and the usual construction of the quotient algebra $A/\equiv$. We let $Con(A)$ denote the set of all Σ congruences on a Σ algebra A. Just as the class $Alg_{Ext}(\Sigma)$, of all extensional Σ algebras, need not be closed under the formation of homomorphic images, so $Alg_{Ext}(\Sigma)$ need not be closed under the formation of quotients. Which congruences on a Σ algebra A yield extensional quotient algebras? To answer this question we introduce the following extensionality condition for Σ congruences.

2.9. Definition. Let A be a Σ algebra and $\equiv$ be a Σ congruence on A. Then $\equiv$ is an *extensional* Σ *congruence* on A if, and only if, $\equiv$ satisfies the following two conditions: (i) for each product type $(\sigma \times \tau) \in S$ and any $a, b \in A_{(\sigma\times\tau)}$, if $proj_A^1(a) \equiv_\sigma proj_A^1(b)$ and $proj_A^2(a) \equiv_\tau proj_A^2(b)$ then $a \equiv_{(\sigma\times\tau)} b$; and, ($ii$) for each function type $(\sigma \to \tau) \in S$ and any $a, b \in A_{(\sigma\to\tau)}$, if $eval_A^{(\sigma\to\tau)}(a, n) \equiv_\tau eval_A^{(\sigma\to\tau)}(b, n)$ for all $n \in A_\sigma$ then $a \equiv_{(\sigma\to\tau)} b$. We let $Con_{Ext}(A)$ denote the set of all extensional Σ congruences on A.

A class K of Σ algebras is said to be *closed under the formation of extensional quotients* if, and only if, for any Σ algebra A, if $A \in K$ and $\equiv$ is an extensional Σ congruence on A then $A/\equiv \in K$.

Clearly, for any extensional Σ algebra A, the null congruence, i.e. the S-indexed family $\{ =_\sigma \mid \sigma \in S \}$ of equality relations $=_\sigma$ on A_σ, is an extensional Σ congruence on A. For any Σ algebra A, the unit congruence $A^2 = \{ A_\sigma \times A_\sigma \mid \sigma \in S \}$ is an extensional Σ congruence on A. Thus for any Σ algebra A the set $Con_{Ext}(A)$ is non-empty. We can now characterise those congruences on a Σ algebra A which yield quotient algebras that are extensional.

2.10. Theorem. *Let A be a Σ algebra and $\equiv$ be a Σ congruence on A. Then $A/\equiv$ is extensional if, and only if, $\equiv$ is extensional.*

2.11. Proposition. *Let A be a Σ algebra, B be an extensional Σ algebra and $\phi : A \to B$ be a Σ epimorphism. Then the kernel $\equiv^\phi$ of ϕ is an extensional Σ congruence on A.*

2.12. Proposition. *Let K be any class of Σ algebras which is closed under the formation of isomorphic images. Then K is closed under the formation of extensional homomorphic images if, and only if, K is closed under the formation of extensional quotients.*

Recall that if $\equiv^\theta$ and $\equiv^\phi$ are congruences on a Σ algebra A such that $\equiv^\theta \subseteq \equiv^\phi$ then we can form the factor congruence $\equiv^{\phi/\theta}$ on $A/\equiv^\theta$ defined by

$$(a/\equiv^\theta) \ \equiv_\sigma^{\phi/\theta} \ (b/\equiv^\theta) \quad \Leftrightarrow \quad a \equiv_\sigma^\phi b.$$

2.13. Proposition. *Let A be a Σ algebra. Let $\equiv^\theta$ be a Σ congruence on A and $\equiv^\phi$ be an extensional Σ congruence on A such that $\equiv^\theta \subseteq \equiv^\phi$. Then $\equiv^{\phi/\theta}$ is an extensional Σ congruence on $A/\equiv^\theta$.*

2.14. Proposition. *Let A be a Σ algebra and $\{ \equiv^i \mid i \in I \}$ be non-empty set of extensional Σ congruences on A. Then $\bigcap_{i\in I} \equiv^i$ is an extensional Σ congruence on A.*

2.15. Definition. Let A be a Σ algebra and $X = \{ X_\sigma \subseteq A_\sigma \times A_\sigma \mid \sigma \in S \}$ be any S-indexed collection of sets of ordered pairs. The *extensional Σ congruence generated by* X is the congruence

$$cg_A^{Ext}(X) = \bigcap \{ \equiv \in Con_{Ext}(A) \mid X \subseteq \equiv \}.$$

The existence of $cg_A^{Ext}(X)$ is guaranteed since the unit congruence on A contains X. The extensionality of $cg_A^{Ext}(X)$ follows from Proposition 2.14. Clearly if $X \subseteq Y$ then $cg_A^{Ext}(X) \subseteq cg_A^{Ext}(Y)$. Also for any extensional Σ congruence $\equiv$ on A, $cg_A^{Ext}(\equiv)$ is $\equiv$. We leave it to the reader to complete the proof that $Con_{Ext}(A)$ is a complete lattice, for any Σ algebra A. Note that in general $Con_{Ext}(A)$ is not a sublattice of $Con(A)$, the lattice of all Σ congruences on A, since the supremum in $Con(A)$ of a family of extensional congruences need not be extensional.

Recall the definitions of a filter F on a non-empty set I, an ultrafilter U on I and the reduced product of a non-empty I-indexed set $A = \{ A(i) \mid i \in I \}$ of Σ algebras by a filter F. Since **Ext** is a set of first-order sentences, it follows that the class $Alg_{Ext}(\Sigma)$, of all extensional Σ algebras, is closed under the formation of ultraproducts. In fact, since **Ext** is a set of $\forall\exists$ Horn sentences, the class $Alg_{Ext}(\Sigma)$ is closed under the formation of reduced products.

3. FREE HIGHER TYPE ALGEBRAS.

Let K be any class of Σ algebras. Let F be any Σ algebra (not necessarily in K) and let $X \subseteq F$ be any S-indexed collection of subsets of F. Recall that F is said to be free for K on X if, and only if, for each algebra $A \in K$ and each S-indexed collection of mappings

$\alpha : X \to A$ there exists a unique Σ homomorphism $\bar{\alpha} : F \to A$ which agrees with α on X. The S-indexed set X is termed the set of (collections of) free generators for F, and F is said to be freely generated by X. If $F \in K$ and F is free for K on X then we say that F is free in K on X. If F is free for (respectively in) K on $\emptyset$ then there exists a unique Σ homomorphism from F to each algebra $A \in K$ and F is said to be initial for (respectively in) K. Recall the category theoretic dual concept of a final algebra. If F is free for K on $X \subseteq F$ and $\alpha : X \to A$ is any mapping then we let $\overline{\alpha} : F \to A$ denote the unique homomorphic extension of α. We shall consider the existence and construction of free extensional Σ algebras.

3.1. Proposition. *For any S-indexed set $X = \{ X_\sigma \mid \sigma \in S \}$ of sets X_σ of variables,*

$$T(\Sigma, X) \models \mathbf{Ext}.$$

Thus $T(\Sigma, X)$ is free in $Alg_{Ext}(\Sigma)$ on X, in particular $T(\Sigma)$ is initial in $Alg_{Ext}(\Sigma)$.

Clearly every unit Σ algebra is extensional and hence final in $Alg_{Ext}(\Sigma)$.

Recall the concrete construction of free Σ algebras for a non-empty class K of Σ algebras. Let $X = \{ X_\sigma \mid \sigma \in S \}$ be any S-indexed collection of sets of variables. Define the S-indexed family of binary relations $\equiv^K = \{ \equiv^K_\sigma \mid \sigma \in S \}$ on $T(\Sigma, X)$ as follows. For any $\sigma \in S$ and $t, t' \in T(\Sigma, X)_\sigma$ define

$$t \equiv^K_\sigma t'$$

if, and only if, $\overline{\alpha}_\sigma(t) = \overline{\alpha}_\sigma(t')$ for every $A \in K$ and every assignment $\alpha : X \to A$. Let $T_K(\Sigma, X) = T(\Sigma, X)/\equiv^K$. A basic result of universal algebra is that $T_K(\Sigma, X)$ is free for K on X. Furthermore, by a result of Birkhoff [1935], a sufficient condition for $T_K(\Sigma, X)$ to be a member of K, i.e. free in K on X, is that K be closed under the formation of isomorphic images, subalgebras and direct products. Unfortunately, as we have already observed in Section 2, classes of extensional Σ algebras need not be closed under the formation of Σ subalgebras. Which classes of extensional Σ algebras contain free algebras? We must examine the construction of free algebras more carefully.

3.2. Definition. Let K be any non-empty class of Σ algebras. Let $X = \{ X_\sigma \mid \sigma \in S \}$ be any S-indexed collection of sets of variables. Define the S-indexed family of binary relations $\approx^K = \{ \approx^K_\sigma \mid \sigma \in S \}$ on $T(\Sigma, X)$ by

$$\approx^K = \bigcap \{ \equiv \in Con_{Ext}\big(T(\Sigma, X)\big) \mid T(\Sigma, X)/\equiv \text{ embeds in some } A \in K \}.$$

3.3. Lemma. *There exists an S-indexed family κ of cardinals such that for every S-indexed family X of sets of variables and every non-empty class K of extensional Σ algebras, if $|X| \geq \kappa$ then $\equiv^K$ and $\approx^K$ are identical extensional Σ congruences on $T(\Sigma, X)$.*

3.4. Corollary. *There exists an S-indexed family κ of cardinals such that for every S-indexed family X of sets of variables and every non-empty class K of extensional Σ algebras, if $|X| \geq \kappa$ then $T_K(\Sigma, X)$ is extensional and free for K on X.*

The careful construction of $\approx^K$ allows a suitable weakening of the closure conditions on K under which K admits $T_K(\Sigma, X)$.

3.5. Theorem. *There exists an S–indexed family κ of cardinals such that for every S–indexed family X of sets of variables and every non–empty class K of extensional Σ algebras which is closed under the formation of isomorphic images, non–empty direct products and extensional subalgebras, if $|X| \geq \kappa$ then*

$$T_K(\Sigma, X) \in K.$$

In particular, in the case where S and each $\Sigma_{w,\sigma} \in \Sigma$ are at most countably infinite, the proof of Lemma 3.3 indicates that there exists a free extensional Σ algebra $T_K(\Sigma, X) \in K$ on *countably infinite* generator sets X_σ when K satisfies the closure conditions of Theorem 3.5. However the lower bound on κ given by the cardinality of Σ and S is not necessarily optimal. For example, we shall see in Section 4 that if K is an extensional equational class it suffices that $\kappa_\sigma = \aleph_0$ for each $\sigma \in S$, irrespective of the cardinality of Σ and S.

Unfortunately Theorem 3.5 provides no information about the existence of initial algebras. Proposition 3.1 indicates that the class $Alg_{Ext}(\Sigma)$ admits an initial algebra, namely $T(\Sigma)$. However this turns out to be unusual; most subclasses of $Alg_{Ext}(\Sigma)$, for example subclasses satisfying some set E of equations, do not admit initial algebras. Nevertheless a subclass $K \subseteq Alg_{Ext}(\Sigma)$ satisfying the closure conditions of Theorem 3.5, which admits a *minimal* algebra, does admit a minimal algebra which approximates the properties of an initial model. The important observation is the following.

3.6. Lemma. *Let K be any non-empty class of minimal, extensional Σ algebras. Then $\equiv^K$ and $\approx^K$ are identical extensional Σ congruences on $T(\Sigma)$.*

Let K be any class of Σ algebras. Recall that $Min(K) = \{ A \in K \mid A \text{ is minimal } \}$.

3.7. Corollary. *Let K be any non–empty class of extensional Σ algebras. If K admits a minimal algebra then $T_{Min(K)}(\Sigma)$ is initial for $Min(K)$.*

We shall term $T_{Min(K)}(\Sigma)$ the *initial extensional model* to emphasise the fact that it is initial in a much weaker sense.

3.8. Theorem. *Let K be any non–empty class of extensional Σ algebras which is closed under the formation of isomorphic images, non–empty direct products and extensional subalgebras. If K admits a minimal algebra then $T_{Min(K)}(\Sigma)$ is initial in $Min(K)$.*

4. HIGHER TYPE EQUATIONAL LOGIC.

The completeness theorem for single–sorted equational logic is due to Birkhoff [1935]. The problems of the many–sorted case, i.e. the possibility of an empty carrier set for some sort, and a solution were considered in Goguen and Meseguer [1982]. We avoid the problems of the many–sorted case here by the simple assumption that we can form a closed Σ term of each type $\sigma \in S$.

The Completeness Theorem 2.6 provides a sound and complete calculus for finite type theories with respect to extensional models. However, in Theorem 2.6 the extensionality axioms of **Ext** must be added to the axiom system Φ, and these are clearly not equations. Furthermore, in general, for any equational theory E there is no purely equational extension $E \subseteq E'$ such that $Alg(\Sigma, E') = Alg(\Sigma, E \cup \mathbf{Ext})$, since the homomorphic image of an extensional algebra need not be extensional. We show that, even in the absence of an equational axiomatisation of extensionality, it is possible to extend the deduction rules of equational logic with new rules which are sound and complete with respect to extensional Σ, E algebras.

In the remainder of this section let $X = \{ X_\sigma \mid \sigma \in S \}$ be an S–indexed collection of disjoint, infinite sets X_σ of variable symbols of type σ. We let $Eqn(\Sigma, X)_\sigma$ denote the set of all equations over Σ and X of type σ and $Eqn(\Sigma, X) = \bigcup_{\sigma \in S} Eqn(\Sigma, X)_\sigma$. A class K of Σ algebras is said to be an *extensional equational class* if, and only if, $K = Alg_{Ext}(\Sigma, E)$ for some equational theory $E \subseteq Eqn(\Sigma, X)$. If K is any class of Σ algebras then $Eqn_K(\Sigma, X) = \{ e \in Eqn(\Sigma, X) \mid K \models e \}$ denotes the equational theory of K.

4.1. Definition. The deduction rules of *higher type equational logic* are the following.
(i) For any type $\sigma \in S$ and any term $t \in T(\Sigma, X)_\sigma$,

$$\frac{}{t = t}$$

is a *reflexivity* rule.

(ii) For any type $\sigma \in S$ and any terms $t_0, t_1 \in T(\Sigma, X)_\sigma$,

$$\frac{t_0 = t_1}{t_1 = t_0}$$

is a *symmetry* rule.

(iii) For any type $\sigma \in S$ and any terms $t_0, t_1, t_2 \in T(\Sigma, X)_\sigma$,

$$\frac{t_0 = t_1, \quad t_1 = t_2}{t_0 = t_2}$$

is a *transitivity* rule.

(iv) For each type $\sigma \in S$, any terms $t, t' \in T(\Sigma, X)_\sigma$, any type $\tau \in S$, any variable symbol $x \in X_\tau$ and any terms $t_0, t_1 \in T(\Sigma, X)_\tau$,

$$\frac{t = t', \quad t_0 = t_1}{t[x/t_0] = t'[x/t_1]}$$

is a *substitution* rule.

(v) For each product type $(\sigma \times \tau) \in S$ and any terms $t_0, t_1 \in T(\Sigma, X)_{(\sigma\times\tau)}$,

$$\frac{proj^1(t_0) = proj^1(t_1), \quad proj^2(t_0) = proj^2(t_1)}{t_0 = t_1}$$

is a *projection* rule.

(vi) For each function type $(\sigma \to \tau) \in S$, any terms $t_0, t_1 \in T(\Sigma, X)_{(\sigma\to\tau)}$ and any variable symbol $x \in X_\sigma$ not occurring in t_0 or t_1,

$$\frac{eval^{(\sigma\to\tau)}(t_0, x) = eval^{(\sigma\to\tau)}(t_1, x)}{t_0 = t_1}$$

is an *evaluation* rule.

The deduction rules of higher type equational logic induce an inference relation $\vdash$ between equational theories $E \subseteq Eqn(\Sigma, X)$ and equations $e \in Eqn(\Sigma, X)$, defined by $E \vdash e$ if, and only if, there exists a proof of e from E using the deduction rules of higher type equational logic.

Recall that the proof of Birkhoff's Completeness Theorem rests on the construction of an equationally generic model, namely the term algebra $T(\Sigma, X)$ factored by the relation of provable equivalence between terms. To establish a similar completeness result for higher type equational logic, let $E \subseteq Eqn(\Sigma, X)$ be any set of equations over Σ and X. Define the S–indexed family $\equiv^E = \{ \equiv^E_\sigma \mid \sigma \in S \}$ of binary relations $\equiv^E_\sigma$ on the term algebra $T(\Sigma, X)$ by

$$t \equiv^E_\sigma t' \Leftrightarrow E \vdash t = t',$$

for each type $\sigma \in S$ and any terms $t, t' \in T(\Sigma, X)_\sigma$.

4.2. Lemma. *Let $E \subseteq Eqn(\Sigma, X)$ be any equational theory. Then $\equiv^E$ is an extensional Σ congruence on $T(\Sigma, X)$.*

4.3. Completeness Theorem. *Let $E \subseteq Eqn(\Sigma, X)$ be any equational theory. For any equation $e \in Eqn(\Sigma, X)$,*

$$E \vdash e \Leftrightarrow Alg_{Ext}(\Sigma, E) \models e.$$

Note that a higher–order inequational calculus and its completeness theorem can be found in Möller [1987b], from which Theorem 4.3 can be derived as a special case.

For any equational theory $E \subseteq Eqn(\Sigma, X)$, the class $Alg_{Ext}(\Sigma, E)$ admits a minimal model, namely the unit algebra $\mathbf{1}(\Sigma)$. Thus by Theorem 3.8 and the closure properties of equational classes, $Alg_{Ext}(\Sigma, E)$ admits an initial extensional model $I_{Ext}(\Sigma, E) = T_{Min(K)}(\Sigma)$, where $K = Alg_{Ext}(\Sigma, E)$, which is initial in the class of all minimal, extensional models of E. However the higher type equational calculus need not be complete, even for ground zero-order equations, with respect to the initial extensional model $I_{Ext}(\Sigma, E)$. We can choose S, Σ and an equational theory $E \subseteq Eqn(\Sigma, X)$ so that for some zero-order type $\sigma \in S$ and ground equation $e \in Eqn(\Sigma, X)_\sigma$ we have $I_{Ext}(\Sigma, E) \models e$ but $E \not\vdash e$. An example can be constructed from any ω-incomplete first-order equational theory over Σ. In practise, most recursive equational theories, e.g. theories of arithmetic, are ω-incomplete. It follows from this incompleteness that the relation of provable equivalence $\equiv^E$ need not be an extensional Σ congruence on the ground term algebra $T(\Sigma)$. Thus we cannot usually construct $I_{Ext}(\Sigma, E)$ as the quotient algebra $T(\Sigma)/\equiv^E$, as is done in first-order equational logic. To solve both of these problems we must resort to an infinitary calculus.

4.4. Definition. For each function type $(\sigma \to \tau) \in S$ and any terms $t_0, t_1 \in T(\Sigma, X)_{(\sigma\to\tau)}$,

$$\frac{\{\ eval^{(\sigma\to\tau)}(t_0, t) = eval^{(\sigma\to\tau)}(t_1, t)\ \mid t \in T(\Sigma)_\sigma\ \}}{t_0 = t_1}$$

is an (infinitary) *ω-evaluation rule.*

Let $\vdash_\omega$ denote the inference relation between equational theories $E \subseteq Eqn(\Sigma, X)$ and equations $e \in Eqn(\Sigma, X)$, defined by $E \vdash_\omega e$ if, and only if, there exists an infinitary proof of e from E using the rules of higher type equational deduction and the ω-evaluation rules. Clearly if $E \vdash_\omega e$ then $A \models e$ for every minimal extensional Σ, E algebra A. Define the S-indexed family $\equiv^{E,\omega} = \{\ \equiv^{E,\omega}_\sigma\ \mid \sigma \in S\ \}$ of binary relations $\equiv^{E,\omega}_\sigma$ on the term algebra $T(\Sigma)$ by

$$t \equiv^{E,\omega}_\sigma t' \Leftrightarrow E \vdash_\omega t = t'$$

for each type $\sigma \in S$ and any terms $t, t' \in T(\Sigma)_\sigma$.

4.5. Proposition. *Let $E \subseteq Eqn(\Sigma, X)$ be any equational theory. Then $\equiv^{E,\omega}$ is an extensional Σ congruence on $T(\Sigma)$.*

4.6. Lemma. *Let $E \subseteq Eqn(\Sigma, X)$ be any equational theory and $K = Alg_{Ext}(\Sigma, E)$. Then $T(\Sigma)/\equiv^{E,\omega} \cong T_{Min(K)}(\Sigma)$, and hence $T(\Sigma)/\equiv^{E,\omega}$ is initial in $Min(K)$.*

Thus the infinitary higher type equational calculus, using the ω-evaluation rules, gives us a syntactic construction of the initial extensional model of a higher type equational theory. The infinitary calculus is also ground equationally complete with respect to this model.

4.7. Theorem. *Let $E \subseteq Eqn(\Sigma, X)$ be any equational theory and $e \in Eqn(\Sigma, X)$ be any ground equation. Then*

$$E \vdash_\omega e \Leftrightarrow T(\Sigma)/\equiv^{E,\omega} \models e.$$

5. CHARACTERISATION THEOREMS.

As is well known, the classes of models axiomatisable by syntactic subclasses of first–order formulae can often be characterised in terms of their model theoretic closure properties. The first result of this kind, the Variety Theorem of Birkhoff [1935], asserts that the equationally axiomatisable classes of algebras are precisely the varieties of algebras, i.e. the classes closed under homomorphic images, subalgebras and direct products. The Quasivariety Theorem of Malcev [1973], asserts that the Horn axiomatisable classes of algebras are precisely the quasivarieties of algebras, i.e. the classes closed under isomorphic images, subalgebras, non–empty direct products and ultraproducts. We shall consider generalisations of both these results for higher type algebras.

5.1. Definition. Let K be any class of Σ algebras. Then K is an *extensional variety* if, and only if, $K \models$ **Ext** and K is closed under the formation of extensional homomorphic images, extensional subalgebras and direct products.

5.2. Proposition. *Let K be an extensional variety.*

(i) There exists an S–indexed set κ of cardinals such that for any S–indexed collection X of sets of variables, with $|X| \geq \kappa$, we have

$$T_K(\Sigma, X) \in K.$$

(ii) $Min(K)$ is non–empty and hence $T_{Min(K)}(\Sigma)$ is initial in $Min(K)$.

5.3. Extensional Variety Theorem. *Let K be any class of Σ algebras. Then K is an extensional variety if, and only if, K is an extensional equational class.*

A (universal) equational Horn formula over Σ and X is an $\mathcal{L}(\Sigma, X)$ formula of the form

$$\neg e_1 \vee \neg e_2 \vee \ldots \vee \neg e_n \qquad (i)$$

or

$$\neg e_1 \vee \neg e_2 \vee \ldots \vee \neg e_n \vee e_{n+1} \qquad (ii).$$

Equational Horn formulas of the form (ii) are often known as positive or strict equational Horn formulas or conditional equations. We let $Hcl(\Sigma, X)$ denote the set of all equational Horn formulas over Σ and X. A class K of Σ algebras is said to be an *extensional equational Horn class* if, and only if, $K = Alg_{Ext}(\Sigma, \Phi)$ for some equational Horn theory $\Phi \subseteq Hcl(\Sigma, X)$. Similarly, K is said to be an *extensional conditional equational class* if, and only if, $K = Alg_{Ext}(\Sigma, \Phi)$ for some conditional equational theory $\Phi \subseteq Hcl(\Sigma, X)$. If K is any class of Σ algebras then $Hcl_K(\Sigma, X) = \{ \phi \in Hcl(\Sigma, X) \mid K \models \phi \}$ denotes the equational Horn theory of K.

5.4. Proposition. *Let K be an extensional equational Horn class. Then K is an extensional conditional equational class if, and only if, K admits unit Σ algebras.*

5.5. Definition. Let K be any class of Σ algebras. Then K is an *extensional quasivariety* if, and only if, $K \models$ **Ext** and K is closed under the formation of isomorphic images, extensional subalgebras, non–empty direct products and ultraproducts.

5.6. Proposition. *Let K be a non–empty extensional quasivariety. There exists an S–indexed set κ of cardinals such that for any S–indexed collection X of sets of variables with $|X| \geq \kappa$ we have*

$$T_K(\Sigma, X) \in K.$$

We shall consider the existence of initial extensional algebras in extensional quasivarieties separately.

5.7. Extensional Quasivariety Theorem. *Let K be any class of Σ algebras. Then K is an extensional quasivariety if, and only if, K is an extensional equational Horn class.*

5.8. Corollary. *Let K be any class of Σ algebras. Then K is an extensional conditional equational class if, and only if, K is an extensional quasivariety which admits unit algebras.*

Finally we turn to the question of the existence of initial extensional algebras in extensional quasivarieties. By definition, quasivarieties (i.e. equational Horn classes) are closed under the formation of subalgebras and thus we are always guaranteed the existence of a minimal model in any non–empty quasivariety. By contrast, a non–empty extensional quasivariety K need not admit any minimal models. The reason for this is that K may be the class of all models of an ω–inconsistent theory.

5.9. Example. Consider the type basis $B = \{ \ nat \ \}$, the second–order type structure $S = \{ \ nat, \ (nat \rightarrow nat) \ \}$ and the S–typed signature Σ with $0 \in \Sigma_{\lambda, nat}$ and $s, f, g \in \Sigma_{\lambda, (nat \rightarrow nat)}$. Let Φ be the equational Horn theory consisting of the equations

$$eval^{(nat \rightarrow nat)}(f, t) = eval^{(nat \rightarrow nat)}(g, t)$$

for each closed term $t \in T(\Sigma)_{nat}$, together with the Horn formula

$$f \neq g.$$

Then $\Phi \cup$**Ext** is consistent and has an extensional model. However $\Phi \cup$**Ext** is ω–inconsistent and has no minimal model.

The situation for extensional quasivarieties with respect to initial extensional algebras can be summarised as follows.

5.10. Theorem. *Let K be a non–empty extensional quasivariety.*

(i) If K is an extensional conditional equational class then $Min(K)$ is non–empty and hence $T_{Min(K)}(\Sigma)$ is initial in $Min(K)$.

(ii) $Min(K)$ is non–empty (and hence $T_{Min(K)}(\Sigma)$ is initial in $Min(K)$) if, and only if, $K = Alg_{Ext}(\Sigma, \Phi)$ where Φ is an equational Horn theory and $\Phi \cup \mathbf{Ext}$ is ω–consistent.

6. CONCLUDING REMARKS.

In this paper our aim has been to set out the elementary theory of higher type universal algebra. We shall conclude with a few remarks about the the applications of this theory in computer science.

With a small number of exceptions, e.g. Malcolm [1973], the general model theory of finite type theory has received little attention in mathematical logic where it arose. Perhaps this is because mathematical practise has presented few examples of structures which can be formalised as general models. The higher–order concepts arising in areas such as number theory, analysis or topology, mostly call for true second–order or higher–order model theory (widely regarded as intractable with present model theoretic methods, see for example Barwise and Feferman [1985]), or at best the model theory of weak second–order or infinitary logic.

By contrast computer science is relatively rich in examples of structures which fit into the framework of general models. For example, the semantics of any deterministic programming language, which assigns functions as the denotations of programs, can be formulated as the *minimal* subalgebra of the appropriate function space, generated by applying the denotations of programming constructs (operators) to the denotations of atomic programs (functions). In the metamathematics of programming logics, *countable* subalgebras of function spaces arise naturally as non–standard models which support completeness and independence results. We hope to report further on both these observations in future work.

It is a pleasure to acknowledge the hospitality offered by the Forschungs Institut für Mathematik, ETH Zürich, while carrying out this research, in particular we are grateful for the help and encouragement of Professor E. Engeler. We should also like to acknowledge the financial support for this work given by the Royal Society and the Science and Engineering Research Council, under their European Research Fellowship Scheme. We are also grateful for helpful comments received from B. Möller and H. Simmons during preparation of the final draft of this paper.

REFERENCES.

J. Barwise and S. Feferman (eds), Model–Theoretic Logics, (Springer Verlag, Berlin, 1985).

G. Birkhoff, On the structure of abstract algebras, Proc. Cambridge Phil. Soc. 31 (1935) 433-454.

M. Broy, Equational specification of partial higher–order algebras, in: M. Broy (ed) Logic of programming and calculi of discrete design, (Springer Verlag, Berlin, 1987).

R. Burstall, D. MacQueen and D. Sanella, Hope: an experimental applicative language, in: Proceedings, First LISP Conference, Stanford University, 1980, 136–143.

C.C. Chang and H.J. Keisler, Model Theory, third edition, (North Holland, Amsterdam, 1990).

P.M. Cohn, Universal Algebra, (Harper and Row, New York, 1965).

J.A. Goguen and J. Meseguer, Completeness of many–sorted equational logic, Association for Computing Machinery SIGPLAN Notices 17 (1982) 9–17.

M. Gordon, Why higher–order logic is a good formalism for specifying and verifying hardware, in: G. Milne and P.A. Subrahmanyam, (eds) Formal aspects of VLSI design, (North Holland, Amsterdam, 1986).

R. Harper, D. MacQueen and R. Milner, Standard ML, Technical Report ECS–LFCS–86–2, Department of Computer Science, University of Edinburgh, 1986.

L. Henkin, Completeness in the theory of types, J. Symbolic Logic 2 (1950) 81–91 .

T. Jech, Set theory, (Academic Press, New York, 1978).

G. Kreisel and J.L. Krivine, Elements of mathematical logic: model theory, (North Holland, Amsterdam, 1967).

T.S.E. Maibaum and C.J. Lucena, Higher–order data types, International Journal of Computer and Information Sciences 9, (1980) 31–53.

A.I. Malcev, Algebraic Systems, (Springer Verlag, Berlin, 1973).

W.G. Malcolm, Application of higher–order ultraproducts to the theory of local properties in universal algebras and relational systems, Proc. London Math. Soc. 3 (1973) 617–637.

K. Meinke, Universal algebra in higher types, to appear in: Theoretical Computer Science, 1991.

K. Meinke, Subdirect representation of higher type algebras, Report CSR 14–90, Department of Mathematics and Computer Science, University College of Swansea, 1990.

K. Meinke and J.V. Tucker, The scope and limits of synchronous concurrent computation, in: F. H. Vogt, (ed) Concurrency '88, Lecture Notes in Computer Science 335 (Springer Verlag, Berlin, 1988) 163–180.

K. Meinke and J.V. Tucker, Universal algebra, to appear in: S. Abramsky, D. Gabbay and T.S.E. Maibaum, (eds) Handbook of Logic in Computer Science, (Oxford University Press, Oxford, 1991).

D.A. Miller and G. Nadathur, Higher–order logic programming, Departmental Report MS–CIS–86–17, University of Pennsylvania, Department of Computer and Information Science, 1986.

B. Möller, Algebraic specifications with higher–order operators, in: L.G.L.T. Meertens (ed) Program specification and transformation, (North Holland, Amsterdam, 1987a).

B. Möller, Higher–order algebraic specifications, Facultät für Mathematik und Informatik, Technische Universität München, Habilitationsschrift, 1987b.

B. Möller, A. Tarlecki and M. Wirsing, Algebraic specifications of reachable higher–order algebras, in: D. Sannella and A. Tarlecki (eds), Recent Trends in Data Type Specification, Lecture Notes in Computer Science 332,(Springer Verlag, Berlin, 1988) 154–169.

K. Parsaye–Ghomi, Higher–order abstract data types, Department of Computer Science, University of California at Los Angeles, PhD thesis, (1981).

A. Poigné, On specifications, theories and models with higher types, Information and Control 68, (1986) 1–46.

J.E. Stoy, Denotational semantics: the Scott–Strachey approach to programming language theory (MIT Press, Cambridge, Massachusetts, 1977).

D. Turner, Miranda: a non–strict functional language with polymorphic types, in: J–P. Jouannaud (ed) Functional programming languages and computer architectures, Lecture Notes in Computer Science 201, (Springer Verlag, Berlin, 1985).

Clausal Rewriting: Applications and Implementation

Robert Nieuwenhuis
Fernando Orejas

Universidad Politécnica de Cataluña
Dept. Lenguajes y Sistemas Informáticos
Pau Gargallo 5, E-08028 Barcelona, Spain
E-mail: eanieuw@ebrupc51 (bitnet)

Abstract: The techniques of clausal rewriting and clausal completion provide several theorem proving methods in theories expressed by clauses having at most one positive equality literal and without negative equality literals. The clausal completion procedure consists of a form of ordered superposition, combined with the powerful clausal rewriting technique for simplification and deletion of redundant axioms, and has been described and proved correct in [NO90]. In this note we outline several applications of these techniques, such as efficient prototyping, checking sufficient completeness properties and theorem proving in partial specifications. Furthermore, some methods used in the implementation of these techniques are described and their correctness is proved.

1. Introduction

Knuth-Bendix completion [KB 70] has been applied to theorem proving in theories involving equality, including the full first order case [HR 89], [BG 90a]. In [NO 90] we proved the correctness of the *clausal completion procedure*, consisting of a form of ordered superposition, combined with the powerful clausal rewriting technique for simplification and deletion of redundant axioms. This clausal completion procedure is proved to provide several theorem proving techniques for the language of *restricted equality clauses*: clauses of the form $(t = t') \vee l_1 \vee \ldots \vee l_n$ or $l_1 \vee \ldots \vee l_n$, where $l_1, \ldots, l_n$ are positive or negative non-equality literals. The associated models are the first order interpretations. Therefore, this work in fact establishes a link between conditional rewriting and first order logic.

The most important advantage of clausal completion when compared with traditional conditional completion, the one that makes it behave well in practice, is that our kind of models allow to use more powerful simplification and elimination rules for axioms. In particular, *conditional* critical pairs can be proved effectively and thus eliminated if convergent, which is well-known to be a crucial aspect of conditional completion procedures.

The main purpose of this paper is to describe and prove correct three additional applications of the methods of clausal rewriting and completion. First, it is shown how sufficient completeness properties can be checked by clausal rewriting. Second, we show that recursive conditional rewriting with complete systems of clausal rewrite rules is,

This work has been partially supported by the ESPRIT Project PROSPECTRA ref. no. 390, under subcontract with Alcatel SESA.

under certain conditions, an efficient method for term evaluation and therefore, for rapid prototyping. A third application of clausal completion, theorem proving in partial logic, through a correct translation into restricted equality clauses, is given.

Furthermore, our implementation (in Quintus-Prolog) of clausal rewriting and completion is described, including some aspects used to increase its efficiency. Complete systems of clausal rewrite rules have been obtained efficiently for many non-trivial examples. The system has also been integrated at the University of Dortmund as a part of the CEC system [GS 90].

The organization of this paper is as follows. This introduction is the first section. Then, after introducing some notation, we give an overview of the clausal rewriting and completion techniques, and we state the main results proved in [NO 90]. Sections 4 and 5 describe the results on sufficient completeness and prototyping, and section 6 introduces our technique for dealing with partial specifications. In section seven, we give a very short description of the system implementing these techniques. Finally, in an appendix some examples are shown.

2. Terminology and notations

By ***restricted equality clauses*** we mean general clauses without negative equality literals and with at most one positive equality literal. Literals will be denoted from now on by $l, c, d, \ldots$; clauses will be denoted by $A, C, D, \ldots$; sets of clauses will be denoted by symbols $\mathcal{A}, \mathcal{M}, \mathcal{C} \ldots$, etc. Clauses are considered to be (finite) multisets of literals (i.e. deduction is performed "modulo" associativity and commutativity of $\vee$), where *true* is the smallest literal. Void sorts are supposed not to exist. Substitutions are denoted by σ, σ', etc, and their application to a term t by $t\sigma$. Occurrences in terms are denoted by u, u', and their concatenation is denoted by $u \cdot u'$. The expression $t[s]$ means that s is a subterm of t, and $t[s][s']$ denotes the fact that s and s' are disjoint subterms of t. If u is an occurrence of a subterm s in a term t, then t/u denotes s, and $t[u \leftarrow t']$ (or just $t[t']$) denotes the result of the replacement in t of the subterm at occurrence u by t'. The expression $E \doteq E'$ denotes ambiguously $E = E'$ and $E' = E$. The left and right hand sides of rules are denoted by lhs and rhs respectively. The set of variables of a term T is denoted by $vars(T)$.

3. An overview of Clausal Rewriting and Completion

In this section we will briefly describe the methods of clausal rewriting and completion. The main results on termination and on completeness of different proof methods are stated. The theorems of this section are proved in detail in [NO 90].

3.1. The clausal rewriting relation

As said, in this framework valid sentences may be seen as conditional equations of the form $T \Rightarrow t = t'$ or simply T, where T is any boolean sorted term. These sentences are expressed in this paper by clauses of the form $(t = t') \vee l_1 \vee \ldots \vee l_n$ or $l_1 \vee \ldots \vee l_n$, where $l_1, \ldots, l_n$ are positive or negative non-equality literals. Equivalently, our logic may be seen as an extension of full clausal logic allowing the use, within every clause, of at most one positive equality literal. Clausal rewrite rules are oriented forms of these axioms, written $(L \rightarrow R) \vee l_1 \vee \ldots \vee l_n$. These rules are *reductive* or *simplifying* in the sense of [Kap 85], i.e. $L \gg R, l_1, \ldots, l_n$, where $\gg$ is the multiset extension of a given simplification ordering $>$.

By applying a clausal rewrite step on a clause, a set of clauses is obtained: if $(L \rightarrow R) \vee l_1 \vee \ldots \vee l_n$ is a rewrite rule and the clause C rewrites into C' using $L \rightarrow R$ with a substitution σ (in the usual sense), then C can be rewritten into the clauses: $\{ C' \vee l_1\sigma \vee \ldots \vee l_n\sigma,\ C \vee \neg l_1\sigma, \ldots, C \vee \neg l_n\sigma \}$.

In these steps, the last n clauses are called *complementary*, since they correspond to the cases that are complementary w.r.t. the condition of the rule. Thus, in clausal rewriting the condition is treated by a kind of case analysis on its literals. In steps with a rewrite rule corresponding to an axiom without equality literal, some *maximal* literal is used as left hand side, and the literal *true* is used as right hand side. The rest of the literals form the condition of the rule in these steps.

A clause C is proved by clausal rewriting using a set of rules if there is a *clausal rewrite tree* with C as root, other clauses as inner nodes, where the children of each node D are the clauses obtained by a rewrite step on D, and where every leaf is a tautology.

Example 1: Below we show a simple example of such a clausal rewrite tree for the clause $P(f(a))$, using the rules: 1) $(\ f(x) \rightarrow b\ ) \vee Q(x)$, 2) $\neg Q(a) \rightarrow$ *true* and 3) $(\ P(b) \rightarrow$ *true* $) \vee Q(a)$. The negations '$\neg$' are denoted by unary minus '-' operators, and the disjunctions $\vee$ are denoted by v.

```
                            P(f(a))
                          /    |  1)
                         /     |
              P(b) v Q(a)       P(f(a)) v -Q(a)
               /       |                 |
              /    3)  |                 |  2)
             /         |                 |
  true v Q(a)    P(b) v Q(a) v -Q(a)    P(f(a)) v true
```

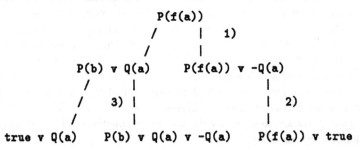

This type of rewriting has an obvious risk of non-termination, even if the rules are reductive. We have solved this problem by proving that clausal rewriting is finitely terminating (without loosing its completeness properties) if certain *useless* useless steps are not allowed. These forbidden steps are the ones creating some complementary clause $C \vee l$ by a step on a clause C, where the literal l already belongs to an ancestor of C. Obviously, rewriting on tautologies is also unnecessary.

Theorem 2: There is no infinite clausal rewrite tree without useless steps of a clause C using a finite set of rules.

As said, this kind of rewriting provides some additional deductive power due to the fact that the associated models are the ones of first order logic. In our framework, from $P(x) \Rightarrow (t = t')$ and $\neg P(x) \Rightarrow (t = t')$ we are able to infer $(t = t')$, whereas within conditional equational logic, from $P(x) = true \Rightarrow (t = t')$ and $P(x) = false \Rightarrow (t = t')$ it would not be sound to infer $(t = t')$, since models with more than two boolean values may not satisfy the equation. In fact, by using the two conditional equations as conditional rewrite rules it would be impossible to prove $(t = t')$, since these rules could not be applied without being one of the conditions provably true.

3.2. Clausal completion

In [NO 90] it is shown that, given a set $\mathcal{A}$ of (unoriented) axioms, for every clause C which is a valid consequence of $\mathcal{A}$, there exists a proof by *clausal deduction* using axioms of $\mathcal{A}$. Clausal deduction is a kind of "equational" version of clausal rewriting. The same type of proof trees are used, but the children of each node are obtained by different proof steps. On one hand, the axioms of $\mathcal{A}$ (which are unoriented restricted equality clauses) can be used in any direction, that is, axioms without equality literal can be applied using any of its literals as left hand side, and axioms with equality literal can be applied using any side of this equality as left hand side. Moreover, some additional steps are allowed: ***duplication*** of literals, i.e. $C \vee l \vee l$ is (unique) child of $C \vee l$, and ***case analysis*** steps, where the clauses $C \vee l_1 \vee \ldots \vee l_n$, $C \vee \neg l_1, \ldots, C \vee \neg l_n$ are children of a clause C, for any set of literals $l_1, \ldots, l_n$.

Theorem 3: The clausal deduction proof method is sound and complete for restricted equality clauses.

Clausal completion consists of a *fair* application of inference rules transforming the sets of unoriented axioms $\mathcal{A}$ and clausal rewrite rules $\mathcal{R}$. There are inference rules for orienting axioms into rules, for deleting and simplifying axioms, and for computing certain additional axioms (*critical pairs*) which are consequences of rules. The inference rules are as follows:

(BCC1) Orienting an axiom:

$$\frac{(\mathcal{A} \cup \{a\}, \mathcal{R})}{(\mathcal{A}, \mathcal{R} \cup \{r\})} \quad \text{if } r \text{ is obtained by orienting } a$$

(BCC2) Adding clausal critical pair:

$$\frac{(\mathcal{A}, \mathcal{R})}{(\mathcal{A} \cup \{a\}, \mathcal{R})} \quad \text{if } a \text{ is a critical pair between two rules in } \mathcal{R}$$

(BCC3) Simplifying an axiom:

$$\frac{(\mathcal{A} \cup \{a\}, \mathcal{R})}{(\mathcal{A} \cup \{a_0, \ldots, a_m\}, \mathcal{R})} \quad \begin{array}{l} \text{if } \{a\} \rightarrow^*_{\mathcal{R}} \{a_0, \ldots, a_m\} \\ \text{and } \{a\} > \{a_0, \ldots, a_m\} \end{array}$$

(BCC4) Deleting a trivial axiom:

$$\frac{(\mathcal{A} \cup \{a\}, \mathcal{R})}{(\mathcal{A}, \mathcal{R})} \quad \text{if } a \text{ is a tautology}$$

During completion, the sets of axioms and rules are transformed in such a way, that any proof by clausal deduction can be transformed into a clausal rewrite proof after a finite number of applications of these inference rules. In [NO 90] the formalism of proof orderings [BDH 86] is used in order to prove this fact: first a well-founded ordering $>_p$ on proofs is defined, and then it is shown that any non-rewrite proof can be simplified w.r.t. $>_p$ during completion.

The additional axioms that are computed during completion are the equivalent in clausal completion to the well-known critical pairs in unconditional and conditional completion. The clausal critical pairs computed correspond to (a restriction to our language of) strict superposition [BG 90b] and ordered factoring.

The beforementioned *fairness* conditions needed in completion are that (i) any axiom must be oriented, simplified or deleted sooner or later, and (ii) that any critical pair between rules must be considered as an axiom at some point of the completion procedure. These conditions imply that there is a possibility of *failure* of the process, since it may happen that some axiom with an equality literal can never be oriented, and perhaps never be treated at all. Fortunately, axioms without equality literal can always be oriented.

Another characteristic of clausal completion is that the simplification of an axiom by clausal rewriting does not supply simpler axioms in general. Therefore it is necessary to restrict simplification to those cases in which an axiom a is simplified by rewriting with clausal rewrite rules into a set of *simpler* axioms $\{a_1, \ldots, a_n\}$.

The inference rule for deletion of axioms allows to eliminate every tautology, since it can be shown that these axioms are unnecessary in order to obtain rewrite proofs.

We now summarize the main results obtained in [NO 90]. In what follows, C and $\mathcal{A}$ are supposed to be a restricted equality clause and a set of restricted equality clauses respectively. A completion procedure is supposed to be given a set of axioms $\mathcal{A}$ (and an ordering $>$) as input. If it terminates, it produces a set of rules $\mathcal{R}$. Otherwise, if it does not fail, it generates an infinite sequence of sets of rules.

Theorem 4: Let *CCP* be a clausal completion procedure with input $\mathcal{A}$ such that $\mathcal{A} \models C$. If *CCP* does not fail, it will generate after a finite number of steps a set of rules $\mathcal{R}$ such that there is a rewrite proof for C using $\mathcal{R}$.

A particular case is the following application for refutational theorem proving:

Theorem 5: Let *CCP* be a clausal completion procedure with input $\mathcal{A}$ such that $\mathcal{A} \models \Box$. If *CCP* does not fail, it will generate after a finite number of steps the empty clause $\Box$ as a critical pair.

Definition 6: A clausal rewrite rule is called *deterministic* if every maximal literal contains all the variables of the rule.

Now suppose the completion procedure terminates, producing as output a *complete* system of clausal rewrite rules $\mathcal{R}$. If $\mathcal{R}$ contains only deterministic rules then it is decidable whether a clause C is a valid consequence of $\mathcal{R}$ or not:

Theorem 7: If $\mathcal{R}$ is a complete set of deterministic rules, then $\mathcal{R} \models C$ if, and only if, every clausal rewrite tree without useless steps of C using $\mathcal{R}$ has only tautologies as leafs.

This system $\mathcal{R}$ can also be used for refutational theorem proving in an efficient way, because no inferences have to be computed between its rules.

General clauses $C \vee D$, where D contains the negative equality literals of the clause, can also be proved by a combination of refutation and rewriting. This is done by running completion on $\mathcal{R}$ and the Skolemized negated literals of D (which are restricted equality clauses). If the empty clause is generated, then D, and therefore $C \vee D$ has been proved. Otherwise, the clause C, with the same Skolemizing substitution applied to it, can be proved or disproved in a consequence-finding way by the system obtained.

Finally, there are some other proof methods for both general and restricted equality clauses using deterministic and undeterministic rules. For example, there is a semidecision procedure for restricted equality clauses if completion does not terminate nor fail and generates only deterministic rules.

4. Checking sufficient completeness

In this section we show how complete systems of clausal rewrite rules can be used in order to check sufficient completeness of (parameterized) log-specifications, i.e. parameterized specifications axiomatized by restricted equality clauses. Let $(SP_1, SP_2) = ((S_1, \Sigma_1, \mathcal{A}_1), (S_2, \Sigma_2, \mathcal{A}_2))$ be a parameterized specification (with $SP_1 \subseteq SP_2$), where the sets of axioms $\mathcal{A}_1$ and $\mathcal{A}_2$ can be expressed by the complete systems of deterministic clausal rewrite rules $\mathcal{R}_1$ and $\mathcal{R}_2$ respectively. We assume that the ordering $>$ in which $\mathcal{R}_1$ and $\mathcal{R}_2$ are contained is compatible with the specification hierarchy, i.e. terms in T_{Σ_1} are small in the sense that $t > t'$ for every t in $T_{\Sigma_2}(X_{s_1})_{s_1}$ and t' in $T_{\Sigma_1}(X_{s_1})$, whenever $vars(t) \supset vars(t')$. Note that $\mathcal{R}_1$ is not necessarily contained in $\mathcal{R}_2$.

Our goal is to prove or disprove the following sufficient completeness property for this kind of parameterized specifications. It holds, roughly speaking, if for every term t in $T_{\Sigma_2}(X_{s_1})_{s_1}$ there exist conditions $C_1, \ldots, C_n$ which cover all the cases, such that under each condition C_i, the term t is equivalent to a term t_i in $T_{\Sigma_1}(X_{s_1})$:

Definition 8: A parameterized log-specification (SP_1, SP_2) with $SP_1 = (S_1, \Sigma_1, \mathcal{A}_1)$ and $SP_2 = (S_2, \Sigma_2, \mathcal{A}_2)$ is sufficiently complete iff for every term t in $T_{\Sigma_2}(X_{s_1})_{s_1}$ there are terms $t_1 \ldots t_n$ in $T_{\Sigma_1}(X_{s_1})$ and clauses $C_1 \ldots C_n$ which are disjunctions of literals from $T_{\Sigma_1}(X_{s_1})_{bool}$ such that $SP_2 \vdash (t = t_i) \vee C_i$ and $SP_1 \vdash \neg C_1 \vee \ldots \vee \neg C_n$.

Definition 9: The *scheme set* for a sort s is the set of terms containing (i) the constants of sort s and (ii) for every operator $f: s_1 \times \ldots \times s_n \rightarrow s$, the term $f(x_1, \ldots, x_n)$ where x_i is a variable of sort s_i for $i \leq i \leq n$.

Definition 10: A term t is said to be *solvable* iff (i) t is in $T_{\Sigma_1}(X_{s_1})$ or else (ii) t can be reduced in one rewrite step with k different rules with conditions $D_1, \ldots, D_k$ such that $SP_1 \vdash \neg D_1 \vee \ldots \vee \neg D_k$.

Definition 11: A term t can be *expanded* into terms $t_1, \ldots, t_n$ iff these terms are obtained by replacing in t a variable of sort s_2 in $S_2 - S_1$, by each of the n terms of the scheme set of s_2.

We now describe an algorithm which has the property that, if the specification is *not* sufficiently complete, then it stops saying so, while in case of sufficient completeness it may stop saying so or run forever. It works by effectively enumerating all possible terms that could cause non-sufficient completeness. Therefore, we suppose that it will behave *fairly*, e.g. by storing the unsolved terms in a queue, and by expanding terms in breadth-first order. This method generalizes the technique described in [BR 90] to the parameterized specification case by using clausal rewriting.

```
U := the union of the scheme sets for every sort in S1
while there is some unsolved term t in U do
   if t is solvable, then remove it from U.
   else
      if t can be expanded into t1,...,tn, then replace it in U by t1,...,tn
      else stop with output "no sufficient completeness"
      endif
   endif
endwhile
stop with output "sufficient completeness"
```

Theorem 12: (i) The specification SP_2 is sufficiently complete w.r.t. SP_1 iff the previous algorithm stops with output "sufficient complete" or loops forever, and (ii) the specification SP_2 is not sufficiently complete w.r.t. SP_1 iff the algorithm stops with output "not sufficiently complete".

Proof. We will prove the part (i) of the theorem, which implies the second part. For the implication $\Longrightarrow$, suppose SP_2 is sufficiently complete. Then for every term t in $T_{\Sigma_2}(X_{s_1})_{s_1}$ there are terms $t_1 \ldots t_n$ in $T_{\Sigma_1}(X_{s_1})$ and clauses $C_1 \ldots C_n$ which are disjunctions of literals from $T_{\Sigma_1}(X_{s_1})_{bool}$ such that $SP_2 \vdash (t = t_i) \vee C_i$ and $SP_1 \vdash \neg C_1 \vee \ldots \vee \neg C_n$.

We will show that this implies that every term t must be solvable. As the axioms of SP_2 are expressed by a complete deterministic system $\mathcal{R}_2$, all the clauses $(t = t_i) \vee C_i$ have proofs by clausal rewriting with $\mathcal{R}_2$.

If the term t is already equal to t_i, then it is solvable. Otherwise, we have $t > t_i$, since t is in $T_{\Sigma_2}(X_{s_1})_{s_1}$ and the t_i are in $T_{\Sigma_1}(X_{s_1})$. Then there must be some rule which is applicable to t, since not every C_i can be provable, because $SP_1 \vdash \neg C_1 \vee \ldots \vee \neg C_n$. After applying all possible steps, with conditions $D_1, \ldots, D_k$, to the term t, we obtain p complementary clauses of the form $(t = t_i) \vee C_i \vee E_j$, for $1 \leq j \leq p$, where the literal $(t = t_i)$ cannot be used any more. Since in every model at least one C_i must be false, $SP_1 \vdash E_1 \wedge \ldots \wedge E_p$ must hold. By distributivity, $\neg D_1 \vee \ldots \vee \neg D_k$ can be obtained.

The proof for $\Longleftarrow$ proceeds by induction on the size of t under the ordering $>$. We prove that, if a term t can be reduced, then it has no instances that could cause a lack of sufficient completeness. This is obviously the case if t is in $T_{\Sigma_1}(X_{s_1})$. Otherwise, by applying all k possible steps to t with conditions $D_1,\ldots,D_k$ s.t. $SP_1 \vdash \neg D_1 \vee \ldots \vee \neg D_k$, a set of terms $t'_1,\ldots,t'_k$ is obtained. By the induction hypothesis, for each of these t'_j exist conditions $C_{j_1},\ldots,C_{j_n}$ and terms $t_{j_1},\ldots,t_{j_n}$ in $T_{\Sigma_1}(X_{s_1})$, such that for $1 \leq j \leq n$ we have $SP_2 \vdash (t_j = t_{j_q}) \vee C_{j_q}$ and $SP_1 \vdash \neg C_{j_1} \vee \ldots \vee \neg C_{j_n}$. But then we have the same property for t by taking the terms t_{j_q} and conditions $D_j \vee C_{j_q}$. ∎

Note that, under the presence of constructors, the search for terms that could cause a lack of sufficient completeness can be optimized by considering only schemes built by constructors.

5. Efficient prototyping

In "classical" term rewriting, reducing a ground term into its normal form using a canonical system is usually considered to be equivalent to "evaluate" the term. The reason is that the model specified by the rewrite system is supposed to be the *initial* model, in which values are congruence classes of ground terms. The unique normal form associated to each congruence class can be seen as its canonical representative. This idea is the basis of many systems that provide prototyping through specification "execution".

In our case, we can do something similar for specifications that have an initial model (this is not the case in general). Let $\mathcal{R}$ be a canonical set of deterministic clausal rewrite rules that corresponds to the axioms of a clausal specification SP, i.e. a specification axiomatized by first order clauses with equality. Then SP has an initial model if, and only if, it is consistent and for every predicate P and ground terms $t_1,\ldots,t_n$ it holds that $P(t_1,\ldots,t_n)$ is provably true or else it is provably false (i.e. $\neg P(t_1,\ldots,t_n)$ is provably true) by the given set of axioms.

Below we show how systems obtained by clausal completion, which in general behaves much better in practice w.r.t. termination and efficiency than classical conditional completion, can be used for term evaluation by recursive conditional rewriting. This method of recursive rewriting consists of rewriting by applying the conclusion of a conditional rewrite rule only if previously the condition has been proved, whereas in clausal rewriting the evaluation of the condition is postponed in some sense. In general, recursive conditional rewriting is more efficient if the conditions can indeed be proved.

Let SP be a clausal specification having an initial model. Furthermore assume SP is axiomatized by a complete set of deterministic clausal rules $\mathcal{R}$. Then we can obtain a unique canonical representative for every ground term (and, indeed, for every congruence class) by recursive conditional rewriting using the rules of $\mathcal{R}$. This means that a rule $(L \rightarrow R) \vee c_1 \vee \ldots \vee c_m$ can be applied to a term t with $t/u = L\sigma$ if the condition holds for the substitution σ, that is, for every literal c_i in the condition $\neg c_i\sigma$ evaluates to *true* . After doing this, the term t can be rewritten into $t[u \leftarrow R\sigma]$.

Lemma 13: Recursive conditional rewriting with complete deterministic systems of clausal rewrite rules is finitely terminating.

Proof. Since $L \gg R, l_1, \ldots, l_n$ for every rule, in this process the terms treated by both the recursive evaluation of the condition and the rewrite process itself become smaller after each step. ∎

Now we will prove that, under the assumptions given above, recursive conditional rewriting is indeed enough for what we need for term evaluation.

Theorem 14: Let SP be a clausal specification having an initial model, and let SP be axiomatized by a canonical set of deterministic clausal rules $\mathcal{R}$. A ground literal l is equivalent to *true* in SP iff it evaluates to *true* by recursive conditional rewriting with $\mathcal{R}$. Moreover, every ground term can be reduced into a unique normal form by recursive conditional rewriting.

Proof. If l is a non-equality literal, then the proof proceeds by induction on the size of l. If there is some step applicable to l such that the condition holds, then a smaller literal l' is obtained, for which, by the induction hypothesis, a recursive rewrite proof exists. Otherwise, we will derive a contradiction from the fact that there is a proof P by clausal rewriting for l, where in P first all possible steps on l are applied.

Note that in all these steps there is at least one c_i such that $\neg c_i$ does not evaluate into *true*, i.e. $\neg c_i$ is equivalent to *false* . After applying these n steps applicable to l, there must be a complementary clause of the form $l \vee \neg c_1, \vee \ldots \vee \neg c_n$, where every $\neg c_i$ is equivalent to *false*. In the proof of this clause, the literal l is not used any more, since l is not *true* and, by reductivity, no literal $\neg l$ can be obtained from steps on literals which are smaller than l. But, if l is not used any more, then there must be a proof for $\neg c_1, \vee \ldots \vee \neg c_n$ which is impossible, because this clause is equivalent to *false*.

A consequence is that, for every term t such that the smallest representative of its equivalence class is t', by recursive conditional rewriting there must be a proof for the equality $t \doteq t'$, and therefore, t must be reducible into t' by recursive conditional rewriting. ∎

The previous theorem also implies that, under the given assumptions, recursive conditional rewriting with complete systems of clausal rewrite rules is confluent.

6. Theorem proving for partial specifications

The technique described here is based on a sound and complete translation from partial into total presentations. This translation process and also some simplifications on the total specification obtained, are provided by the system. The kind of specifications we deal with are ***partial clausal specifications***, i.e. specifications in which functions may be partial and where formulae take the form $l_1 \vee \ldots \vee l_n$, where each l_i is of the form $P(t_1, \ldots, t_n)$, $\neg P(t_1, \ldots, t_n)$, $Def(t)$, $\neg Def(t)$, or (at most for one literal) $t_1 = t_2$.

A (partial) model A is considered to satisfy (i) $P(t_1, \ldots, t_n)$, (ii) $\neg P(t_1, \ldots, t_n)$, (iii) $Def(t)$, (iv) $\neg Def(t)$ or (v) $t_1 = t_2$ iff, respectively, for every substitution σ of the variables involved by (defined) values of A, (i) $P(t_1, \ldots, t_n)\sigma$ holds in A, (ii) $P(t_1, \ldots, t_n)\sigma$ does not hold in A ($t_i\sigma$ is undefined for some i, or else for every i, $t_i\sigma$ is defined in A and $P(t_1, \ldots, t_n)\sigma$ is false in A), (iii) $t\sigma$ is defined in A, (iv) $t\sigma$ is not

defined in A, (v) $t_1\sigma$ and $t_2\sigma$ are both undefined in A or they are both defined and equal.
Here *Def* is considered to be a built-in (meta) predicate to specify function definedness. Note that the interpretation given to equality is the so-called strong interpretation, which is considered to be more difficult to prove than the other possible interpretations [AC 89].

Example: The following set of axioms would define stacks of natural numbers:
axioms for all $n : nat;\ s : stack \Rightarrow$

$pop(push(s,n)) = s$	$Def(push(s,n))$
$top(push(s,n)) = n$	$isempty(s) \vee Def(pop(s))$
$isempty(emptystack)$	$\neg isempty(s) \vee \neg Def(pop(s))$
$\neg isempty(push(s,n))$	$isempty(s) \vee Def(top(s))$
$Def(emptystack)$	$\neg isempty(s) \vee \neg Def(top(s))$

end;

Given a partial specification $PSP = (\Sigma, \mathcal{A})$, its transformation is defined as follows. We replace the built-in *Def* (meta) predicates by "normal" *def* predicates for every sort. Then we transform specifications in such a way that every (total) model of the transformed specification could be seen as a model of the original (partial) specification by *forgetting* or *eliminating* from the total model the values that should be undefined according to the *def* predicates. The new axioms $\mathcal{A}'$ are defined as the union of two different sets:

$$\mathcal{A}' = Strict(\Sigma) \cup Transf(\mathcal{A})$$

where the first one specifies that functions are considered strict (in case of non-strictness, obviously, this set would have to be modified or even suppressed):

$$Strict(\Sigma) = \{\ def(x_i) \vee \neg def(f(x_1,\ldots,x_n)) \mid f\colon s_1 \times \ldots \times s_n \rightarrow s,\quad i=1\ldots n\ \}$$

The second set, $Transf(\mathcal{A})$, is obtained by a transformation of $\mathcal{A}$ in which every old axiom may be transformed into several new ones:

$$Transf(l_1 \vee \ldots \vee l_n) = \{\ C_1 \vee \ldots \vee C_n \mid C_i \in auxtransf(l_i)\ \ \forall i \in 1\ldots n\ \}$$

i.e. the clauses in $Transf(l_1 \vee \ldots \vee l_n)$ are different combinations of the clauses C_i obtained by applying the following auxiliary transformation on each literal l_i:

1. If l is of the form $P(t_1,\ldots,t_n)$ then
   $auxtransf(l) = \{\ l \vee \neg def(x_1) \vee \ldots \vee \neg def(x_m)\ \}$, where $\{x_1,\ldots,x_m\} = vars(l)$.
2. If l is of the form $\neg P(t_1,\ldots,t_n)$ then
   $auxtransf(l) = \{\ l \vee \neg def(t_1) \vee \ldots \vee \neg def(t_n)\ \}$
3. If l is of the form $t_1 = t_2$, then a set of three clauses is obtained:
   $auxtransf(l) =$
   $$\{\ \neg def(t_1) \vee \neg def(x_1) \vee \ldots \vee \neg def(x_n) \vee def(t_2),$$
   $$def(t_1) \vee \neg def(y_1) \vee \ldots \vee \neg def(y_m) \vee \neg def(t_2),$$
   $$\neg def(t_1) \vee \neg def(t_2) \vee t_1 = t_2\ \}$$
   where $\{x_1,\ldots,x_n\} = vars(t_2) - vars(t_1)$ and $\{y_1,\ldots,y_m\} = vars(t_1) - vars(t_2)$.

4. If l is or of the form $Def(t)$ then
   $auxtransf(l) = \{\ def(t) \vee \neg def(x_1) \vee \ldots \vee \neg def(x_m)\ \}$, where $\{x_1, \ldots, x_m\} = vars(t)$.
5. If l is or of the form $\neg Def(t)$ then
   $auxtransf(l) = \{\ \neg def(t)\ \}$.

Note that the three clauses of case 3. express the facts that: if t_1 is defined so is t_2, if t_2 is defined so is t_1, and if both are defined then $t_1 = t_2$. The result of this transformation is a (total) clausal specification. Therefore, all the techniques described in this paper can be applied to it.

Example: The previous partial stack specification would yield after some trivial simplifications the following (total) specification:

axioms for all $x : nat; s : stack \Rightarrow$

$\neg def(s) \vee \neg def(x) \vee pop(push(s,x)) = s$
$\neg def(s) \vee \neg def(x) \vee def(pop(push(s,x)))$
$\neg def(s) \vee \neg def(x) \vee top(push(s,x)) = x$
$\neg def(s) \vee \neg def(x) \vee def(top(push(s,x)))$
$isempty(emptystack)$
$\neg def(s) \vee \neg def(x) \vee \neg isempty(push(s,x))$
$def(emptystack)$
$\neg def(s) \vee \neg def(x) \vee def(push(s,x))$
$\neg isempty(s) \vee \neg def(pop(s))$
$isempty(s) \vee \neg def(s) \vee def(pop(s))$
$\neg isempty(s) \vee \neg def(top(s))$
$isempty(s) \vee \neg def(s) \vee def(top(s))$
$def(s) \vee \neg def(push(s,x))$
$def(x) \vee \neg def(push(s,x))$
$def(s) \vee \neg def(pop(s))$
$def(s) \vee \neg def(top(s))$

end;

In [NNOS 89] it is proved that the previous transformation Tr is sound and complete in the following sense. For every partial clausal specification PSP we have:

$$PartialModels(PSP) \models C \iff Models(Tr(PSP)) \models Tr(C)$$

7. An experimental implementation

The clausal completion procedure has been implemented under Quintus-Prolog. The main reason for using Prolog is that it provides efficiency and flexibility, since features such as operations on terms, unification and variable management are already provided by the language in an efficient way.

As said, the completion procedure can be any fair application of the inference rules of Clausal Completion. Below, a very basic version of such an algorithm is given. It only simplifies axioms before orienting them. The data structures used in this algorithm are three queues: one for axioms and two for rules: the "old" ones, which already have been used to compute critical pairs, and the "new" ones. The usual operations are assumed on queues: ***empty-queue***, ***take-first***, ***add*** and ***is-empty***. The basic operations used in the algorithm are the following:

- ***simplification***$(a,\mathcal{R})$, which returns a set of axioms obtained by simplifying the axiom a with the rules of the set $\mathcal{R}$.

- *orient*(a), which returns the rule obtained by orienting the axiom a.
- *critical-pairs*(r,$\mathcal{R}$), which returns all axioms which are critical pairs between the rule r and the rules in $\mathcal{R}$.

```
𝒜 := queue of initial axioms
ℛ_old := empty-queue
ℛ_new := empty-queue
while not is-empty(𝒜) or not is-empty(ℛ_new) do
   while not is-empty(𝒜) do
      a := take-first(𝒜)
      S := simplification(a,ℛ_old ∪ ℛ_new)
      while not is-empty(S) do
         r := orient(take-first(S))
         add(r,ℛ_new)
      endwhile
   endwhile
   r := take-first(ℛ_new)
   add( critical-pairs(r,ℛ_old), 𝒜 )
   add(r,ℛ_old)
endwhile
```

Note that this procedure guarantees the fairness of the completion process. First, by organizing axioms and rules into queues, and second, by simplifying (in a finitely terminating manner) the axioms just before converting them into rules.

One of the basic operations of clausal completion is the orientation of axioms into rewrite rules. As said, this is done by choosing one side of an equality literal as left hand side and by checking for reductivity or by marking one or more literals as *maximal* ones. The system provides implementations of two different simplification orderings for this purpose. The most simple and fast one is the Recursive Path Ordering (RPO) [Der 87]. Another more powerful one is the ordering KNS [KNS 85]. These orderings on terms work by lifting a well-founded ordering on operator symbols, which can be defined totally or partially by the user before starting the completion process, but can also be supplied on demand by the system. When the system needs more information in order to orient an axiom it can give suggestions to the user about how to extend the ordering on operator symbols. The user can supply this information interactively.

Now we outline some techniques that have been used in the implementation to speed up the rewriting and completion processes. One of these methods is to group together rewrite rules into the so-called *c-rules*, which are groups of rewrite rules with the same left hand side. This grouping together has many advantages from an efficiency point of view. As we will see, it increases the speed of the rewriting process and also the superposition process.

For instance, if we have the following rewrite rules:

$(L \rightarrow R_1) \vee C_1$

...

$(L \to R_n) \vee C_n$

where C_i for $i = 1 \ldots n$ is the disjunction of the rest of the literals in these rules, then they are grouped together in the following c-rule:

$$[L, (R_1, C_1), \ldots, (R_n, C_n), D_1, \ldots, D_m]$$

where $\{D_1, \ldots, D_m\}$ is the clausal form of $\neg(C_1 \wedge \ldots \wedge C_n)$, called the *complementary condition* of the c-rule. These c-rules are applied to a clause C as follows: If we have $C/u = L\sigma$, we obtain a set of clauses

$$\{\ C[u \leftarrow R_1\sigma] \vee C_1\sigma,\ \ldots,\ C[u \leftarrow R_n\sigma] \vee C_n\sigma,\ \ C \vee D_1\sigma,\ \ldots,\ C \vee D_m\sigma\ \}$$

That is, application of c-rules is done by detecting in a clause *one* single subterm that matches with the left hand side L of the c-rule. Then, by simply replacing this subterm by all right hand sides and adding the conditions, *all* the new clauses are obtained. The complementary conditions are computed in completion time when building the c-rules. Therefore, theorem proving with complete systems spends no time on this matter. This can be seen as "doing more things at compile time and less things at run time".

This rewriting process is obviously correct and also more efficient than applying the rules separately, since it consists in applying more than one step at the same time. Note that if the c-rule contains only one rewrite rule $(L \to R) \vee c_1 \vee \ldots \vee c_m$, then the set $\{D_1, \ldots, D_m\}$ is $\{\neg c_1, \ldots, \neg c_m\}$ and the rewrite step with the c-rule is exactly the same as in the normal case.

Also critical pairs can be computed more efficiently using the c-rule representation. Suppose we have two c-rules including n and m single rules respectively. Then, by computing once a superposition between the two left hand sides we obtain $n * m$ critical pairs by simply replacing subterms.

The simplification process of axioms, which uses an important part of the time of the completion process, is done using some additional rules for clause simplification and tautology detection, such as the elimination of repetitions of literals. These rules are built-in and directly expressed by Prolog clauses.

8. Conclusions

We have given an overview of the techniques of clausal rewriting and completion, including the main results on theorem proving using these methods as proved in [NO 90]. Three main additional applications of our methods have been outlined and proved correct. First we have shown how sufficient completeness properties can be checked by clausal rewriting. Second, we have shown that recursive conditional rewriting with complete systems of clausal rewrite rules is an efficient method for term evaluation and therefore, for rapid prototyping. A third application of clausal completion, theorem proving in partial logic, through a correct translation into restricted equality clauses, has been described, and illustrated by an example. An implementation of clausal rewriting and completion has been described, including some aspects used to increase its efficiency. Our methods have been illustrated by several examples.

Acknowledgement: The authors would like to thank Albert Rubio for his work on the implementation and his comments on the theory.

9. References

[AC 89] E. Astesiano, M. Ceroli. On the existence of initial models for partial (high-order) conditional specifications, in Proc. TAPSOFT '89, vol 1, J. Diaz, F. Orejas (eds.) Springer Lect. Notes in Comp. Sc. 351 (1989) pp. 74-88.

[BDH 86] L. Bachmair, N. Dershowitz, J. Hsiang: Orderings for equational proofs. In Proc. Symp. Logic in Computer Science, 346-357, Boston (Massachusetts USA), 1986.

[BG 90a] L. Bachmair, H. Ganzinger: On restrictions of ordered paramodulation with simplification. In Proc. 10th Int. Conf. on Automated Deduction. LNCS. To appear.

[BG 90b] L. Bachmair, H. Ganzinger: Completion of First Order Clauses with Equality By Strict Superposition. To appear in proc. Second Int. Workshop on Conditional and Typed Term Rewriting. LNCS, 1990.

[BR 90] W. Bousdira, J-L. Remy: On sufficient Completeness of Conditional Specifications. To appear in proc. Second Int. Workshop on Conditional and Typed Term Rewriting. LNCS, 1990.

[Der 87] N. Dershowitz: Termination of rewriting. Journal of Symbolic Computation, 69-116, 1987.

[GS 90] H. Ganzinger, R Schäfers: System support for order-sorted Horn clause specifications. In Proc. 12th Int. Conf. on Software Engineering. Nice. pp. 150-159. 1990.

[HR 89] J. Hsiang, M. Rusinowitch: Proving refutational completeness of theorem proving strategies: The transfinite semantic tree method. Submitted for publication.

[KB 70] D.E. Knuth, P.B. Bendix: Simple word problems in universal algebras. J. Leech, editor, Computational Problems in Abstract Algebra, 263-297, Pergamon Press, Oxford, 1970.

[Kap 85] S. Kaplan: Fair conditional term rewriting systems: unification, termination and confluence. Recent Trends in Data Type Specification, Springer IFB 116 (1985).

[KNS 85] D. Kapur, P. Narendran, G. Sivakumar: A path Ordering for Proving Termination of Term Rewrite Systems. LNCS 186, 173-187, 1985.

[NOR 90] R. Nieuwenhuis, F. Orejas, A. Rubio: TRIP: an implementation of clausal rewriting. In Proc. 10th Int. Conf. on Automated Deduction. Kaiserslautern 1990, LNCS 449, pp 667-668.

[NO 90] R. Nieuwenhuis, F. Orejas: Clausal Completion. To appear in proc. Second Int. Workshop on Conditional and Typed Term Rewriting. (LNCS) Montreal 1990.

[Nie 90] R. Nieuwenhuis: Theorem proving in first order logic with equality by clausal rewriting and completion. PhD thesis, UPC Barcelona, 1990.

[NNOS 89] M. Navarro, P. Nivela, F. Orejas, A. Sánchez: Translating partial into total specifications, Research Report LSI-89-21 Dept. Lenguajes y Sistemas Informáticos, UPC, 1989.

Appendix

Here we show two examples of applications of the clausal completion procedure. The negations '¬' are denoted by unary minus '-' operators, and the disjunctions by 'v'.

A first –very simple– example consists of a set of initial axioms specifying natural numbers with =< and *max*, and ordered lists of natural numbers with maximum. The system of rules obtained by running the completion procedure on this input is showed below. Note that the totality axiom for =< (rule number 10) has been deduced during the completion procedure:

```
Initial axioms:
 1) 0=<A
 2) -(s(A)=<0)
 3) -(s(A)=<s(B))  v   A=<B
 4) s(A)=<s(B)  v  -(A=<B)
 5) A=<A
 6) A=<s(A)
 7) -(A=<B)  v    A=<s(B)
 8) max(A,B)=B   v  -(A=<B)
 9) max(A,B)=A   v    A=<B
 10) A=<max(A,B)
 11) A=<max(B,A)
 12) ordered(nil)
 13) ordered(cons(A,nil))
 14) -(A=<B)  v  -ordered(cons(A,C))  v    ordered(cons(B,cons(A,C)))
 15) A=<B    v  -ordered(cons(B,cons(A,C)))
 16) insert(A,nil)=A
 17) insert(A,cons(B,C))=cons(A,cons(B,C))  v  -(B=<A)
 18) insert(A,cons(B,C))=cons(B,insert(A,C))  v    B=<A
 19) maxlst(nil)=0
 20) maxlst(cons(A,B))=A    v  -(maxlst(B)=<A)
 21) maxlst(cons(A,B))=maxlst(B)   v    maxlst(B)=<A

Completion successfully terminated.  Final system of rules:

 1) (( 0=<A --> true ))
 2) (( -(s(A)=<0) --> true ))
 3) (( -(s(A)=<s(B)) --> true )) v  A=<B
 4) (( s(A)=<s(B) --> true )) v  -(A=<B)
 5) (( A=<A --> true ))
 6) (( A=<s(A) --> true ))
 7) (( A=<s(B) --> true )) v  -(A=<B)
 8) (( max(A,B) --> B )) v  -(A=<B)
 9) (( max(A,B) --> A )) v  A=<B
 10) (( A=<B   v   B=<A --> true ))
 11) (( ordered(nil) --> true ))
 12) (( ordered(cons(A,nil)) --> true ))
 13) (( ordered(cons(A,cons(B,C))) --> true )) v  -ordered(cons(B,C)) v -(B=<A)
 14) (( -ordered(cons(A,cons(B,C))) --> true )) v  B=<A
 15) (( insert(A,nil) --> A ))
 16) (( insert(A,cons(B,C)) --> cons(A,cons(B,C)) )) v  -(B=<A)
 17) (( insert(A,cons(B,C)) --> cons(B,insert(A,C)) )) v  B=<A
 18) (( maxlst(nil) --> 0 ))
 19) (( maxlst(cons(A,B)) --> A )) v  -(maxlst(B)=<A)
 20) (( maxlst(cons(A,B)) --> maxlst(B) )) v  maxlst(B)=<A
 21) (( -(s(A)=<B) --> true )) v  A=<B

time spent: 3.016 sec.
```

The second example is the system of rules obtained by running the completion procedure on the total stack specification of section 6:

```
Completion successfully terminated.

Final system of rules:

1) (( pop(push(A,B)) --> A )) v [ -def(A)  v  -def(B) ]
2) (( top(push(A,B)) --> B )) v [ -def(B)  v  -def(A) ]
3) (( is_empty(empty) --> true ))
4) (( -is_empty(push(A,B)) --> true )) v [ -def(B)  v  -def(A) ]
5) (( def(empty) --> true ))
6) (( def(push(A,B)) --> true )) v [ -def(B)  v  -def(A) ]
7) (( -def(pop(A)) --> true )) v [ -is_empty(A) ]
8) (( def(pop(A)) --> true )) v [ is_empty(A)  v  -def(A) ]
9) (( -def(top(A)) --> true )) v [ -is_empty(A) ]
10) (( def(top(A)) --> true )) v [ is_empty(A)  v  -def(A) ]
11) (( -def(top(A)) --> true )) v [ is_empty(A)  v   def(A) ]
12) (( -def(pop(A)) --> true )) v [ is_empty(A)  v   def(A) ]
13) (( -def(push(A,B)) --> true )) v [ def(A) ]
14) (( -def(push(A,B)) --> true )) v [ -def(A)  v   def(B) ]

time spent: 1.850 sec.
```

Constraints for Behavioural Specifications

F. Orejas, P. Nivela
Dept. de Llenguatges i Sistemes Informàtics
Universitat Politècnica de Catalunya
Pau Gargallo 5, (08028) Barcelona, SPAIN

Abstract

Behavioural specifications with constraints for the incremental development of algebraic specifications are presented. The behavioural constraints correspond to the completely defined subparts of a given incomplete behavioural specification. Moreover, the *local* observability criteria used within a behavioural constraint can differ from the global criteria used in the behavioural specification. This is absolutely needed because, otherwise, some constructions could involve only non-observable sorts and therefore have trivial semantics. Finally, the extension and completion operations for refining specifications are defined. The extension operations correspond to horizontal refinements and build larger specifications on top of existing ones in a conservative way. The completion operations correspond to vertical refinements, they *add detail* to an incomplete behavioural specification and they do restrict the class of models.

1. Introduction

In [OSC 89] we presented a formal framework for the incremental development of algebraic specifications. The main ideas of this approach are:

1. The possibility of dealing with incomplete specifications at any stage of the development process. *Incompleteness* means that there may be not enough equations for defining the operations of the specification or there may be not enough operations to generate all the "values" of a certain sort. It is our believe that any approach for formalizing the specification development process from informal requirements should be capable of dealing with such kind of incomplete specifications. The reason is that, on the one hand, informal requirements are usually incomplete (even inconsistent) and, as a consequence, the specifier must take *design* decisions within the development process that would make the final specification complete and consistent. On the other hand prematurely taking these decisions may cause severe problems if it is later discovered that these decisions were inadequate from the customer point of view. This may mean in practice that all the work done since the inadequate decision could be wasted. The way of handling this incompleteness in this approach was by means of algebraic specifications with constraints [Rei 80, BG 80]. The constraints correspond to the completely defined subparts of a given incomplete specification. The corresponding semanticsis then loose, accepting as

models all algebras satisfying the axioms and all constraints of the specification. A related approach, in this context, is the pioneering concept of *canon* [Rei 80] which essentially coincides with our notion of incomplete specification but allowing also to deal with partial operations and algebras. Even more related than the work of Reichel is the work on the design of the specification language Look [ETLZ 82], in which many technical and methodological ideas of [OSC 89] could be found. However, the results obtained in [OSC 89] go beyond the ones used for the semantic definition of Look and, in fact, some open problems were solved.

2. Related with the notion of incomplete specification is the idea of developing specifications by means of horizontal and vertical refinements. In more classical approaches in the field of algebraic specification (e.g. [GB 80]) specifications are developed only by horizontal refinements (i.e. extensions), while vertical refinements were considered only for the development of implementations. In our context, vertical refinements are the operations by which we *add detail* to an incomplete specification, i.e. vertical refinements make the specifications more complete. At the semantic level this is seen as a restriction on the class of models. Our notion of vertical refinement coincides with the notion used by Sannella and Wirsing and Sannella and Tarlecki to define implementations [SW 83, ST 87a, ST 87b], eventhough the aims are different because they are more interested with the development of programs from specifications. In fact, most of the methodological ideas underlying our approach and theirs are the same. However, there is a fundamental difference in the sense that they are only concerned with what happens at the model level and never try to obtain compatibility results or even to describe their ideas at the specification level. In this sense, our approach can be considered an extension and a complement of theirs, in that one of our main aims is to obtain this kind of compatibility results. We can also say that, in some sense, our methodological ideas about the incremental development of specifications may be found in the specification language Larch (the connection to Look has already been established). However the lack of precise formal semantics (to our knowledge) make difficult a comparison at the technical level. Anyhow, our approach could be seen as providing the adequate framework for writing such a semantic definition.

3. The way of handling incomplete specifications and the *interaction* of horizontal and vertical refinements make useless, in our approach, the use of (explicitly) parameterized specifications. The reason is that every incomplete specification may be seen as implicitly parameterized by its incomplete subspecifications. In particular, the abovementioned interaction of horizontal and vertical refinement allows to substitute any incomplete subspecification of a given specification by a more complete one in a way that generalizes parameter passing in the more standard approaches [EM 85]. In fact, the results obtained in our approach generalize all classical results on parameter passing by just requiring a limited form of persistency.

Being convinced that the notions of behaviour and observability are critical with respect to the semantics of software specifications, from the very beginning we wanted to express all the framework in the behavioural setting defined in [NO 88] and [ONE 89] (for related approaches to behavioural specifications see e.g. [HW 85, MG 85, ST 87a, Rei 81]). However there seemed to be a technical problem: in the standard case most of the results and semantics constructions were obtained making heavy use of the Amalgamation Lemma for specifications with constraints [Ehr 89] but, on the other hand, in [ONE 89] it was shown that Amalgamation Lemma was only possible (under certain reasonable restrictions) for pushout diagrams involving behaviour specification morphisms, but not when involving the so called *view specification morphisms*. Now the problem was that because of the need of having different observability criteria within the same specification (certain sorts are considered non-observable at the global level but may be considered locally observable within a constraint) there was a need of dealing with this view morphisms that would cause all the troubles.

Fortunately, we were able to provide the adequate definitions, both from the methodological (we think) and from the technical point of view, that would allow us to obtain all the needed results. To do that, we had to generalize the Amalgamation and Extension Lemmas for behaviour specification morphisms and the Extension Lemma for view morphisms for the case of specifications with constraints. Also, we had to develop a very restricted version of the Amalgamation for view morphisms that would only apply to free algebras. But, once this was done, must of the proofs and constructions from [OSC 89] could be directly translated to the new setting, with some exception in which a use of the Amalgamation Lemma in [OSC 89] was now translated into the use of the Extension Lemma for view morphisms. This experience apparently showed that, in fact, the whole approach could be parameterized being independent of any arbitrary Specification Logic or Institution [GB 85], as long as a reasonble amount of basic constructions (amalgamation and extensions) are provided. In this sense, we think that this could be done by extending some preliminary results that were presented in [EPO 89].

Most of the related work (that we know) to our framework has already been mentioned: it mainly has to do with the *standard* setting as defined in [OSC 89]. With respect to the new aspects presented in this paper, i.e. the handling of behaviour constraints, the only related work we know is from Reichel [Rei 87]. However there are big differences between the two approaches not only in the aims, since the kind of results we obtain are of different nature of the ones obtained by him, but also technical in two senses: a) our notion of behavioural equivalence is stronger, since algebras that only differ on non-observable junk would be not equivalent for him but they would be for us, b) on the very notion of constrained specification because, according to his approach, observability in a behavioural canon is global, i.e. a sort can either be observable or non-observable in the whole specification while, for us, a sort may be non observable at the global level but may be considered observable locally within a constraint. The reason for this is that, otherwise, some constraints could involve only non-observable sorts and therefore have trivial semantics.

The organization of the paper is as follows: in the next section we provide the basic definitions and notation about behavioural specifications. In the third section we present the main basic tools to be used for proving all the results: we provide the Amalgamation and Extension Lemmas for behavioural specifications slightly generalized with respect to the version of [OSC 89]. Also, we give the restricted version of the Amalgamation Lemma for the view case that was mentioned above. In section 4, we define our concept of behaviour specification with constraints and we specialize some results of the previous section to this setting. Finally, in section 5, the operations for refining specifications are defined and the main results are obtained.

2. Behavioural Semantics

In this section a summary of the behavioural framework is given. For more details see [Niv 87, NO 88, ONE 89].

2.1 Basic Behavioural Concepts

Given a signature $\Sigma = (S, \Omega)$ a **behaviour signature** $B\Sigma$ is a triple $B\Sigma = (Obs, S, \Omega)$ with $Obs \subseteq S$. The sorts in Obs are called **observable sorts.** A behaviour signature determines a set of observable computations which will provide its observable behaviour. A **computation** is a term in $T_\Sigma(X_{Obs})$ where $X_{Obs} = \{X_s\}_{s \in Obs}$ is a family of observable variables. A computation of observable sort, that is, in $T_\Sigma(X_{Obs})_s$ with $s \in Obs$, is called an **observable computation.** Analogously, a **computation over a Σ-algebra** A is a term in $T_\Sigma(A_{Obs})$. A computation of observable sort, that is, in $T_\Sigma(A_{Obs})_s$ with $s \in Obs$, is called an **observable computation over** A.

We may associate two categories of models to every behaviour signature $B\Sigma$: the well-known category $Alg(\Sigma)$ of Σ-algebras and Σ-homomorphisms, and the category $Beh(B\Sigma)$ which defines behavioural semantics. In this category objects are Σ-algebras as in $Alg(\Sigma)$ but morphisms are different. To avoid confusion from now on morphisms in $Alg(\Sigma)$ will be called Σ-homomorphisms while morphisms in $Beh(B\Sigma)$ will be called Σ-behaviour morphisms.

A **Σ-behaviour morphism** $f: A \to B$ between two Σ-algebras A and B is an Obs-indexed family of mappings $f = \{f_s\}_{s \in Obs}$ preserving all the observable computations, that is, for every $t \in T_\Sigma(A_{Obs})_s$, $s \in Obs$, it holds that $f_s(\varepsilon_A(t)) = \varepsilon_B(f^\#_s(t))$ where $f^\#: T_\Sigma(A_{Obs}) \to T_\Sigma(B_{Obs})$ is the unique Σ-homomorphism which extends f and ε_A is the evaluation of terms in A, i.e. the unique Σ-homomorphism extending the inclusion of A_{Obs} into A. Σ-algebras together with Σ-behaviour morphisms form the category **Beh(BΣ)**.

If Obs coincides with S then $Beh(B\Sigma)$ is exactly the same as $Alg(\Sigma)$ and if there are no observable sorts in Σ then Σ-behaviour homomorphisms are empty sets.

A Σ-behaviour morphism f establishes a relationship between the observable computations t over A and $f^\#(t)$ over B in such a way that it is compatible with their results $\varepsilon_A(t)$ in A and $\varepsilon_B(f^\#(t))$ B respectively. Thus an Obs-indexed family $f = \{f_s\}_{s \in Obs}$ is a Σ behaviour morphism if these observable computations over A yield in B the same value as in A, up to the transformation determined by f. If the converse holds, that is, if all the observable computations over B yield in A the same value as in B up to the transformation determined by f, and f itself is a bijection then A and B give the same answers to the same questions, that is, they *show the same observable behaviour*. Hence behavioural equivalence is characterized by isomorphism in the category $Beh(B\Sigma)$. In particular, isomorphism in $Beh(B\Sigma)$ coincides with the notion of behavioural equivalence from [MG 85, HW 85, SW 83, ST 85].

A Σ-behaviour morphism f such that f_s is bijective for every s in Obs is a Σ-behaviour isomorphism in the category Beh (BΣ).

Two Σ-algebras A and B are **behaviourally equivalent**, denoted $A \equiv_{B\Sigma} B$, if there exists a Σ-behaviour isomorphism $f: A \to B$ between them. Behavioural equivalence is an equivalence relation between Σ-algebras and every equivalence class is called a **behaviour**.

A **Σ-context over the sort** s is a term $c[z] \in T_\Sigma(X_{Obs} \cup \{z\})_{s'}$ with $s' \in Obs$ and $sort(z) = s$. By c[t] we denote the **application of the context over** t, that is, $\bar{\sigma}(c[z])$ where σ is the assigment $\sigma: X_{Obs} \to T_\Sigma(X_{Obs})$ defined by $\sigma(z) = t$ and $\sigma(x) = x$ for every x in X_{Obs}. Analogously, a **Σ-context over the sort** s **for a Σ-algebra** A is a term $c_A[z] \in T_\Sigma(A_{Obs} \cup \{z\})_{s'}$ with $s' \in Obs$ and $sort(z) = s$.

A Σ-algebra A **behaviourally satisfies** the Σ-equation e: $\lambda Y.t_1 = t_2$, denoted by $A \models_B e$, if A satisfies $\lambda X_{Obs}.c[\bar{\sigma}(t_1)] = c[\bar{\sigma}(t_2)]$ for every Σ-context c[z] over the sort of e and every assignment $\sigma: Y \to T_\Sigma(X_{Obs})$.

A **behaviour presentation** BP is a 4-tuple, BP = (Obs, S, Ω, E) where BΣ = (Obs, S, Ω) is a behaviour signature and E a set of Σ-equations. **Beh(BP)** is the full subcategory of Beh(BΣ) of all Σ-algebras which behaviourally satisfy the equations in E. In what follows we will also denote BP by BP = (Obs, P) with P = (S, Ω, E), Obs $\subseteq$ S and Σ = (S, Ω), where P is called a **presentation**. We will indistinctly write $A \equiv_{B\Sigma} B$ or $A \equiv_{BP} B$.

2.2 Presentation morphisms and their associated functors

The relationships that can be established between two behaviour presentations BP1 = (Obs1, P1) and BP2 = (Obs2, P2) are as usual defined by *presentation morphisms* h : BP1 $\to$ BP2, that is, a signature morphism h : Σ1 $\to$ Σ2 such that E2 |- h(E1). But now it is necessary to make the relationship between the observability criteria of BP1 and BP2 explicit. If the observable sorts are preserved, then h is said to be a *weak presentation morphism*. If the non observable sorts are preserved then h is called a *view presentation morphism*. Finally, a *behaviour presentation morphism* preserves both the observable and the non observable sorts.

Definition 2.2.1

Let BP1 = (Obs1, P1) and BP2 = (Obs2, P2) be two behaviour presentations and h: P1 $\to$ P2 a presentation morphism. We say that h: BP1 $\to$ BP2 is a

a) **weak presentation morphism** if h(Obs1) $\subseteq$ Obs2

b) **view presentation morphism** if h(S1-Obs1) $\subseteq$ S2-Obs2

c) **behaviour presentation morphism** if h(Obs1) $\subseteq$ Obs2 and h(S1-Obs1) $\subseteq$ S2-Obs2

The associated categories are the following:

a) **Weak-BP** is the category of behaviour presentations and weak presentation morphisms. The usual pushout constructions in **P** can be extended in a simple way to pushouts in **Weak-BP**.

b) **BP** is the category of behaviour presentations and behaviour presentation morphisms. Obviously, pushouts in the category **BP** are defined in the same way as in **Weak-BP**.

c) **View-BP** is the category of behaviour presentations and view presentation morphisms. Pushout constructions are easily obtained by using the ones of the non observable sorts (in the category of **Sets**).

For every weak presentation morphism h: BP1 $\to$ BP2 (resp. behaviour presentation morphism) there is a forgetful functor BU_h: Beh(BP2) → Beh(BP1) defined as usual.

Every weak presentation morphism h (resp. behaviour presentation morphism) has an associated free functor $BFree_h$, which is left adjoint to the forgetful functor BU_h, and is defined by

$$BFree_h(A) = T_{\Sigma 2}(A_{Obs1})/\equiv_{h(obs\text{-}eq(A))+E2}$$

where the values $a \in A_s$ are interpreted as values of sort h(s).

If Obs1 = S1 then $BFree_h(A)$ is the usual free construction for every P1-algebra A.

The behavioural equivalence relation may be extended uniformly from algebras to functors, that is, behavioural equivalence of functors coincides with natural isomorphism. If F and F' are two functors from Beh(BP1) to Beh(BP2) we will say that F and F' are behaviourally equivalent if they are naturally isomorphic, which will be denoted by F ≡ F'. Therefore, we immediately have that any functor behaviourally equivalent to a free functor is also free.

However, if h is a view presentation morphism then it has no associated forgetful functor. The reason is that there can be less observable sorts in Obs2 than in Obs1. This means that when *forgetting* over a BP2-behaviour morphism $f = \{f_s : A2_s \to A2'_s\}_{s \in Obs2}$ there can exist some sort s ∈ Obs1 such that h(s) ∉ Obs2 and therefore $f_{h(s)}$ would not be defined. Passing from BP2 to BP1 behaviours can be done by a functor $View_h$, called *view functor*, which builts up a BP1-behaviour morphism from a BP2-behaviour morphism and describes how the models of Beh(BP2) are *seen* from the BP1 *point of view*. First of all a special realization of the behaviour of an algebra A2 in Beh(BP2) is constructed. This realization belongs to the category Alg(P2⁺) and is behaviourally equivalent to A2, in in such a way that BP2-behaviour morphisms can be extended to usual $P2^+$ homomorphisms. After that a forgetful functor from Alg($P2^+$) to Beh(BP1) is applied to this realization.

Definition 2.2.2

Let BP = (Obs, P) with P = (S, Ω, E) be a behaviour presentation. The presentation P* **behaviourally derived from** BP is defined as $P^* = (S, \Omega, E^*)$ where E* is the set of all observable properties deduced from E, that is, $E^* = \{t_1 = t_2 \mid t_1, t_2 \in T_\Sigma(X_{Obs})_s, s \in Obs, E \vdash t_1 = t_2\}$.

A Σ-algebra A belongs to Beh(BP) if and only if A belongs to Alg(P^*).

Definition 2.2.3

Let h: BP1 → BP2 be a view presentation morphism, $BP2^+$ the behaviour presentation given by $BP2^+ = (Obs2 + h(Obs1), P2^+)$ with $P^+ = P^* + (\emptyset, \emptyset, h(E1))$. Let h^+: BP1 → $BP2^+$ be the behaviour presentation morphism defined as h on sorts and operations, and let η be the weak presentation inclusion η: $BP2^* \to BP2^+$.

The h(E1)-realization functor $R_{h(E1)}$ is defined by the composition of functors $R_{h(E1)} = BFree_\eta \cdot Id$, where Id is the identity functor between the categories Beh(BP2) and Beh($BP2^*$).

Proposition 2.2.4

$R_{h(E1)}(A2)$ is behaviourally equivalent to A2 for every algebra A2 in Beh(BP2).

Definition 2.2.5

Let BP1 = (Obs1, P1) and BP2 = (Obs2, P2) be two behaviour presentations with P1 = (S1, Ω1, E1) and P2 = (S2, Ω2, E2). Let h: BP1 → BP2 be a view presentation morphism.

The functor $View_h$: Beh(BP2) → Beh(BP1), called **view functor associated to** h, is defined as $View_h = BU_{h^+} \circ R_{h(E1)}$

2.3 Pushout constructions

When putting together two behaviours BP2 and BP3 with a common sub-behaviour BP1 it may happen that the resulting behaviour BP4 is not the right combination of BP1 and BP2 behaviours because the observable computations of BP2 and BP3 may be combined to cause side effects in the observable computations of BP4.

This means that not every pushout diagram {BP4, i2, h2} = po {BP1, BP2, BP3, i1, h1} of the form

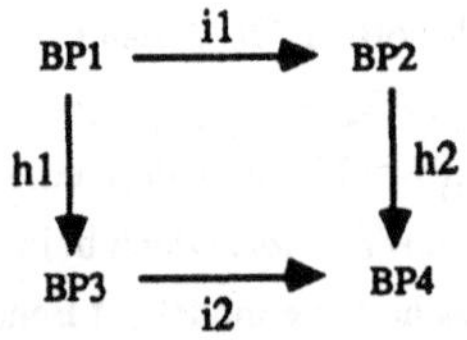

with the involved presentation morphisms being any of the previous three kinds, will be useful when dealing with behavioural semantics. This kind of discontinuity, if allowed, originates several undesired effects being the most important one the incompatibility of the semantic constructs used at the presentation and model levels. This problem is overcome if the pushout satisfies the *observation preserving property*. We say that an observable computation $t \in T_\Sigma(X_{Obs})_{Obs}$ is **minimal** if no subterm of t different from a variable is an observable computation.

Definition 2.3.1

A pushout diagram {BP4, i2, h2} = po {BP1, BP2, BP3, i1, h1} in the category **BP** or in **Weak-BP** satisfies the **observation preserving property** if, for any set X_{Obs4} of observable variables, for every minimal observable computation $t \in T_{\Sigma 4}(X_{Obs4})$ and for every $s \in S4 - Obs4$ being the sort of a non observable subterm of t, it holds that $s \in S4 - i2 \circ h1(S1)$.

If a pushout satisfies the observation preserving property then every minimal observable computation t belongs either to $T_{h2(\Sigma 2)}(X_{Obs2})$ or to $T_{i2(\Sigma 3)}(X_{Obs3})$.

When dealing with the category **View-BP** we need a slightly different version of the observation preserving property, as we will see in the proof of the existence of the extension lemma.

Definition 2.3.2

A pushout diagram {BP4, i2, h2} = po {BP1, BP2, BP3, i1, h1}in the category **View-BP** with i1, i2 behaviour presentation morphisms of **BP**, satisfies the **observation preserving property** if the diagram $\{P4^+, i2^+, h2^+\} = po\ \{P1, P2, P3^+, i1, h1^+\}$ satisfies the observation preserving property in **BP**.

So, also in this case, every minimal observable computation $t \in T_{\Sigma 4}(X_{Obs4})$ belongs either to $T_{h2(\Sigma 2)}(X_{Obs2})$ or to $T_{i2(\Sigma 3)}(X_{Obs3})$.

The observation preserving property of all the pushouts diagrams in this paper is assumed. For this reason we will not explicitly state this porperty.

3. Behavioural Amalgamation and Extension properties

This section describes the amalgamation and extension properties that can be obtained in each of the categories **BP** and **View-BP** (unfortunately, in the category **Weak-BP** in general there are neither Amalgamation nor Extension Lemmas). First, we will state the Amalgamation Lemma associated to the category **BP** (its proof can be found in [ONE 89]). Then we will see a slight generalization, with respect to [ONE 89], of the Extension Lemmas associated to the categories **BP** and **View-BP**. Finally, we will present a restrictive (with respect to free algebras) version of the Amalgamation Lemma for **View-BP**. This restrictive version is caused by the problem that, in general, in **View-BP** there are no appropriate amalgamated sums. Nevertheless, that restrictive version is sufficient for our purposes in the following sections.

Definition 3.1 (Behavioural Amalgamation)

Let {BP4, i2, h2} = po {BP1, BP2, BP3, i1, h1}be a pushout diagram in **BP**.

1. For all algebras A3 ∈ Beh(BP3), A2 ∈ Beh(BP2) and A1 ∈ Beh(BP1) such that $BU_{h1}(A3) = A1 = BU_{i1}(A2)$ the **behavioral amalgamated sum** of A3 and A2 with respect to A1, denoted by $A4 = A3 +_{A1} A2$, is the algebra in Beh(BP4) defined by $A4 = A3 +_{A1} A2$ where $+_{A1}$ denotes the usual amalgamation in categories of algebras.

2. For all behaviour morphisms h3: A3 → B3 in Beh(BP3), h2: A2 → B2 in Beh(BP2) and h1: A1 → B1 in Beh(BP1) with $BU_{h1}(f3) = f1 = BU_{i1}(f2)$ the **behavioral amalgamated sum** of f3 and f2 with respect to f1, denoted by $f4 = f3 +_{f1} f2$, is the BP4-behaviour morphism defined for every s in S4 as $f4_s$ = **if** s ∈ i2(S3) **then** $f3_s$ **else** $f2_s$.

Lemma 3.2 (Behavioural Amalgamation Lemma)

Let {BP4, i2, h2} = po {BP1, BP2, BP3, i1, h1} be a pushout diagram in **BP**.

1. Given algebras A3 ∈ Beh(BP3), A2∈ Beh(BP2) and A1∈ Beh(BP1) such that $BU_{h1}(A3) = A1 = BU_{i1}(A2)$ the behavioural amalgamation $A4 = A3 +_{A1} A2$ is the unique algebra in Beh(BP4) which satisfies $A3 = BU_{i2}(A4)$ and $A2 = BU_{h2}(A4)$.

Conversely, every A4 ∈ Beh(BP4) has a unique representation $A4 = A3 +_{A1} A2$ where $A3 = BU_{i2}(A4)$, $A2 = BU_{h2}(A4)$ and $A1 = BU_{h1}(A3) = BU_{i1}(A2)$.

2 Given behaviour morphisms h3: A3 $\rightarrow$ B3 in Beh(BP3), h2: A2 $\rightarrow$ B2 in Beh(BP2) and h1: A1 $\rightarrow$ B1 in Beh(BP1) with $BU_{h1}(f3) = f1 = BU_{i1}(f2)$ the behavioural amalgamation $f4 = f3 +_{f1} f2$ is the unique homomorphism satisfying $f3 = BU_{i2}(f4)$ and $f2 = BU_{h2}(f4)$.

Conversely, every BP4-behaviour morphism f4: A4 $\rightarrow$ B4 has a unique representation $f4 = f3 +_{f1} f2$ where $f3 = BU_{i2}(f4)$, $f2 = BU_{h2}(f4)$ and $f1 = BU_{h1}(f3) = BU_{i1}(f2)$.

Definition 3.3

Let BP1, BP2 be two behaviour presentations and h: BP1 $\rightarrow$ BP2 a (weak) behaviour presentation morphism and let **A** be a subcategory of Beh(BP1). A functor G: Beh(BP1) $\rightarrow$ Beh(BP2) is (strongly) persistent relative to **A** iff for every A in **A** $A = BU_h(G(A))$.

Lemma 3.4 (Behaviour Extension Lemma)

Let {BP4, i2, h2} = po {BP1, BP2, BP3, i1, h1} be a pushout diagram in **BP**. Let **A3** and **A1** be subcategories of Beh(BP3) and Beh(BP1) respectively such that BU_{h1}(**A3**) is included in **A1**. Finally, let F: Beh(BP1) $\rightarrow$ Beh(BP2) be a strongly persistent functor relative to **A1**.

1. There exists a unique (up to isomorphism) persistent relative to **A3** functor F': **A3** $\rightarrow$ Beh(BP4) such that $BU_{h2} \circ F' = F \circ BU_{h1}$ which moreover is defined by

(i) $F'(A3) = A3 +_{A1} F(A1)$ for every A3 in **A3** with $A1 = BU_{h1}(A3)$
(ii) $F'(f3) = f3 +_{f1} F(f1)$ for every f3 in **A3** with $f1 = BU_{h1}(f3)$

2. If F restricted to **A1** is a free functor with respect to BU_{i1} then F' is free w.r.t. BU_{i2}.

Proof Sketch

1. Trivially, F' is a functor as defined by i) and ii) and, by construction, is persistent relative to **A3** and is an extension of F.

2. Suppose B4 $\in$ Beh(BSPEC4) and f: A3 $\rightarrow$ $BU_{i2}(B4) \in$ **A3**, then let $A1 = BU_{h1}(A3)$, $B2 = BU_{h2}(B4)$ and $f' = BU_{h1}(f)$. Since F_{i1} is free then there is a unique g': F(A1) $\rightarrow$ B2 in Beh(BSPEC2) such that $BU_{i1}(g') = f'$. Taking $g = f +_{f'} g$ we have that g: F'(A3) $\rightarrow$ B4 and $BU_{i2}(g) = f$. Moreover, the Behavioural Amalgamation Lemma implies the uniqueness of g. []

It is not always possible to define amalgamated sums for pushouts in the category **View-BP**. For instance, consider the following behaviour presentations

bpres BP1 = **obs sorts** s1, s2 **ops** a: $\rightarrow$ s1 **end bpres**
bpres BP2 = **obs sorts** s1, s2, s3 **ops** a: $\rightarrow$ s1, g: s1 s3 $\rightarrow$ s2 **end bpres**
bpres BP3 = **obs sorts** s1 **non obs sorts** s2 **ops** a: $\rightarrow$ s1 **end bpres**
bpres BP4 = **obs sorts** s1, s3 **non obs sorts** s2 **ops** a: $\rightarrow$ s1, g: s1 s3 $\rightarrow$ s2 **end bpres**

The algebra $A4 = \{ \{a\}_{s1}, \{b\}_{s3}, \{g(a, b)\}_{s2} \}$ cannot be properly decomposed as an amalgmated sum. The algebras A2 and A3 should be defined by $A2 = View_{h2}(A4) = \{ \{a\}_{s1}, \{b\}_{s3}, \{g(a, b)\}_{s2} \}$ and $A3 = BU_{i2}(A4) = \{ \{a\}_{s1}, \{g(a, b)\}_{s2} \}$. But then $View_{h1}(A3) = \{ \{a\}_{s1}, \emptyset_{s2} \}$ and $BU_{i1}(A2) = \{ \{a\}_{s1}, \{g(a, b)\}_{s2} \}$ which are not equal.

However, in the view case we have a restricted version of the Extension Lemma that will allow us to express an amalgamation decomposition for the subclass of algebras which are free constructions.

Lemma 3.5 (View Extension Lemma)

Let {BP4, i2, h2} = po {BP1, BP2, BP3, i1, h1}be pushout diagram in **View-BP** with i1and i2 behaviour presentation morphisms. Let A3 and A1 be subcategories of Beh(BP3) and Beh(BP1) respectively such that $View_{h1}(A3)$ is included in A1. If $BFree_{i1}$ is persistent relative to A1 then

(i) $BFree_{i2}$ is persistent relative to A3

(ii) $BFree_{i2}$, with respect to algebras is A3, is an extension of $BFree_{i1}$, that is, $BFree_{i1} \circ View_{h1}(A3) \equiv_{BP2} View_{h2} \circ BFree_{i2}(A3)$, for every A3 in A3.

Proof

We can consider the following presentation diagram (1)

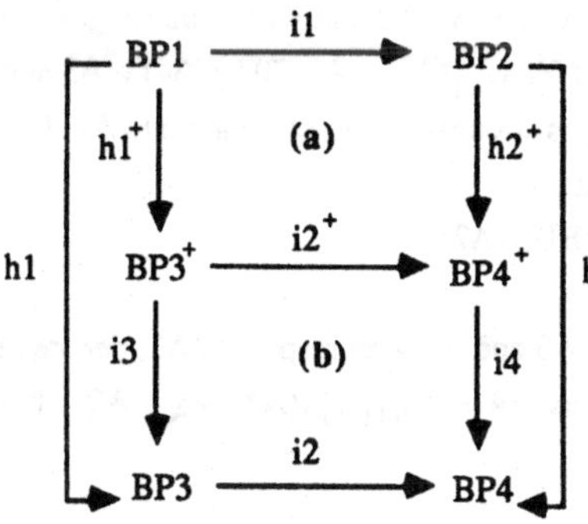

where BP3+ is the presentation BP3+ = (Obs3+h1(Obs1), $P3^*$+h1(E1)), BP4+ is the presentation BP4+ = (Obs4+h2(Obs2), $P4^*$+h2(E2)), h1+ and h2+ are defined (on sorts and operations) as h1 and h2, and i3 and i4 are the inclusion morphisms i3: $BP3^* \rightarrow BP3^+$, i4: $BP4^* \rightarrow BP4^+$.

Its corresponding semantic diagram (2) is

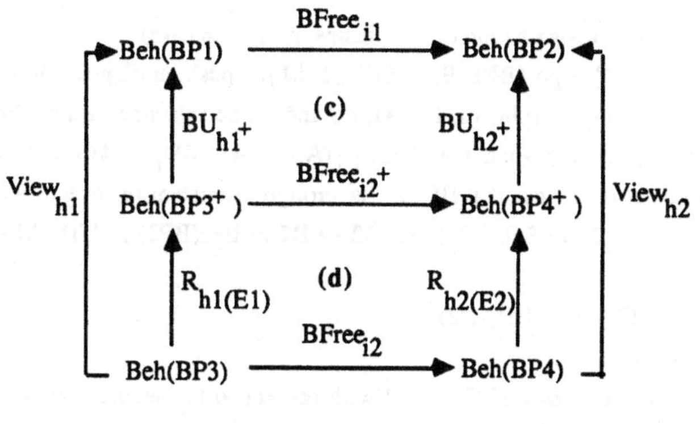

The functor $BFree_{i2+}$ is an extension of $BFree_{i1}$ by the Behaviour Extension Lemma (applied to the subdiagram (a) which is a pushout in **BP**). Moreover, $R_{h1(E1)}$ is in fact a free functor. Since the composition of free functors is also a free functor we have that $BFree_{i2+} \circ R_{h1(E1)}$ and $R_{h2(E2)} \circ BFree_{i2}$ are naturally isomorphic and therefore

$$BFree_{i1} \circ View_{h1} \equiv_{BP2} View_{h2(E2)} \circ BFree_{i2}$$

The relative persistency of $BFree_{i1}$ implies the relative persistency of $BFree_{i2+}$ by the Behaviour Extension Lemma. Moreover, the relative persistency of $BFree_{i2+}$ implies the relative persistency of $BFree_{i2}$ since the former can be seen as a realization of the latter. []

By having this version of the Extension Lemma, it is possible to represent (up to behavioural equivalence) the subclass algebras in Beh(BP4) which are free constructions over algebras of Beh(BP3) as amalgamated sums of appropriate algebras in Beh(BP3) and Beh(BP2).

Definition 3.6 (View Amalgamation of algebras in the free case)

Let {BP4, i2, h2} = po {BP1, BP2, BP3, i1, h1}be a pushout diagram in **View-BP** with i1and i2 behaviour presentation morphisms. Let **A**1, **A**3 and **A**4 be subcategories of Beh(BP1), Beh(BP3) and Beh(BP4) respectively such that $View_{h1}$(**A**3) = **A**1, BU_{i2}(**A**4) = **A**3 and $View_{h2}$(**A**4) = $Free_{i1}$(**A**1). Let us also suppose that $BFree_{i1}$ is strongly persistent relative to **A**1. For all algebras A3 ∈ **A**3, A2 ∈ Beh(BP2) and A1 ∈ **A**1 such that

(i) $View_{h1}(A3) = A1 = BU_{i1}(A2)$

(ii) $A2 = BFree_{i1}(A1)$

the **view amalgamated sum** of A3 and A2 with respect to A1, denoted by $A4 = A3 \oplus_{A1} A2$, is the algebra in Beh(BP4) defined as $A4 = R_{h1(E1)}(A3) +_{A1} A2$ where $+_{A1}$ denotes behaviour amalgamation.

To see that this definition has sense let us consider consider the above presentation diagrams (1) and (2). The algebra $R_{h1(E1)}$ is in Beh(BP3$^+$) and satisfies $BU_{h1+}(A3) = A1 = BU_{i1}(A2)$. Therefore $A4 = R_{h1(E1)}(A3) +_{A1} A2$ is an algebra in Beh(BP4$^+$) and also in Beh(BP4).

The same argument allows to define the amalgamation of behaviour morphisms as stated in the following definition.

Definition 3.7 (View Amalgamation of morphisms in the free case)

Let {BP4, i2, h2} = po {BP1, BP2, BP3, i1, h1}be pushout diagram in **View-BP** with i1 and i2 behaviour presentation morphisms. Let **A**1, **A**3 and **A**4 be subcategories of Beh(BP1), Beh(BP3) and Beh(BP4) respectively such that $View_{h1}$(**A**3) = **A**1, BU_{i2}(**A**4) = **A**3 and $View_{h2}$(**A**4) = $Free_{i1}$(**A**1). Let us also suppose that $BFree_{i1}$ is strongly persistent relative to **A**1. For all behaviour morphisms h3: A3 → B3 in Beh(BP3), h2: A2 → B2 in Beh(BP2) and h1: A1 → B1 in Beh(BP1) such that

(i) $View_{h1}(f3) = f1 = BU_{i1}(f2)$

(ii) $f2 = BFree_{i1}(f1)$

the **view amalgamated sum** of f3 and f2 with respect to f1, denoted by $f4 = f3 \oplus_{f1} f2$, is the BP4-behaviour morphism defined by $f4 = R_{h1(E1)}(f3) +_{f1} f2$.

Lemma 3.8 (View Amalgamation Lemma in the free case)

Let {BP4, i2, h2} = po {BP1, BP2, BP3, i1, h1} be pushout diagram in **View-BP** with i1and i2 behaviour presentation morphisms. Let A1, A3 and A4 be subcategories of Beh(BP1), Beh(BP3) and Beh(BP4) respectively such that $View_{h1}(A3) = A1$, $BU_{i2}(A4) = A3$ and $View_{h2}(A4) = Free_{i1}(A1)$. Moreover, assume that $Free_{i1}$ is persistent relative to A1. Then:

1. Given algebras A3 ∈ A3, A2 ∈ Beh(BP2) and A1 ∈ A1 such that

 (i) $A2 = BFree_{i1}(A1)$

 (ii) $View_{h1}(A3) = A1 = BU_{i1}(A2)$

the view amalgamation sum $A4 = A3 \oplus_{A1} A2$ is a free construction w.r.t. A3.

Moreover, for every A4 ∈ Beh(BP4) it holds that $A4 \equiv_{BP4} R_{h1(E1)}(A3) +_{A1} A2$, where $A3 = BU_{i2}(A4)$, $A2 = View_{h2}(A4)$ and $A1 = View_{h1}(A3) = BU_{i1}(A2)$.

2 Given behaviour morphisms h3: A3 → B3 in A3, h2: A2 → B2 in Beh(BP2) and h1: A1→ B1 in A1 with

 (i) $f2 = BFree_{i1}(f1)$

 (ii) $View_{h1}(f3) = f1 = BU_{i1}(f2)$

the view amalgamation sum $f4 = f3 \oplus_{f1} f2$ satisfies that $f4 = Free_{i2}(f3)$.

Moreover, every BP4-behaviour morphism f4: A4 → B4 is naturally isomorphic to $R_{h1(E1)}(f3) +_{f1} f2$ where $f3 = BU_{i2}(f4)$, $f2 = View_{h2}(f4)$ and $f1 = View_{h1}(f3) = BU_{i1}(f2)$.

Proof

Since the diagram (a) is pushout in **BP** we have by the Behaviour Extension Lemma that $Free_{i2}+$ is an extension of $Free_{i1}$ which moreover is given by $Free_{i2}+(B) = B +_{B1} Free_{i1}(B1)$ where $B1 = BU_{h1}+(B)$. Thus in particular $Free_{i2}+(R_{h1(E1)}(A3)) = R_{h1(E1)}(A3) +_{A1} Free_{i1}(A1) =$
$= R_{h1(E1)}(A3) +_{A1} A2 = A4$.

The algebra A4 is a free construction w.r.t. A3 because by the View Extension Lemma $Free_{i2}$ is also an extension of $Free_{i2}+$.

The same argument is valid for morphisms.

4. Behaviour Constraints

As it was said in the introduction, our aim is to deal with incomplete behavioural specifications by means of constraints. The idea will be that a specification consists of a *global* presentation that includes all the sorts, operations and equations that have been declared up to a certain point and a set of constraints that characterize the completely defined subparts of the given specification. These constraints work as the standard free or generating constraints [BG 80, Rei 80] but only up to behavioural equivalence. That is, the use of standard free generating constraints allows to restrict the class of models of a given specification by considering acceptable only those models that satisfy that a certain subpart of the model has been freely constructed from another subpart. In our framework, making use of the existence of free constructions for categories of behaviours [NO 88] that work like the standard free constructions, but up to behavioural equivalence, we define our constraints by means of these behaviour free constructions. In this sense, intuitively, a model of a given specification satisfies a behaviour constraint if some part of this model is behaviourally equivalent to what can be obtained aplying a free construction to another subpart. It must be said that in fact, the situation is a little more complicated, as we will see later, because the *local* observability criteria used within the constraint need not to coincide with the global criteria used in the specification. However, before considering this problem let us, first, see an standard simple example of what we may consider an incomplete behaviour specification.

```
bspec Val_eq = enrich Bool  with
                            obs sorts val, bool
                            opns  eq: val x val → bool
                            eqns  eq(X,X) = true
                                  eq(X,Y) = eq(Y,X)
                                  (eq(X,Y) and eq(Y,Z)) ⊃ eq(X,Z) = true
end bspec

bspec Set = enrich val_eq defining
                            non-obs sorts set
                            opns  Ø: set
                                  add: set x val → set
                                  _∈_ : val x set → bool
                            eqns  add(add(S,X),Y) = add(add(S,Y),X)
                                  X∈ Ø = false
                                  X∈ add(S,Y) = (X∈ S) or eq(X,Y)
end bspec

bspec Choose = enrich  Set  with
                            opns  choose: set → val
                            eqns  choose(add(S,X))∈ add(S,X)
end bspec
```

According to our framework, the specification Choose is an incomplete specification with two completely defined subparts: the booleans and the sets of values. On the other hand, in Choose the sort val and the operations eq and choose are considered to be incompletely defined. The semantics of this specification is going to be loose, i.e. all (behavioural) models of the specification satisfying the constraints will be considered admissible. In particular, this means that admissible models will be those that their Boolean part coincides with the standard boolean algebra of two elements and whose Set part behaves as finite sets of elements taken from the sort val. Note that this means that, if the Set part are sequences of values, this will be an admissible model, even if it is not a model in the standard sense (it does not satisfy the commutativity property for add).

Now, in order to define the *proper* notion of behaviour constraints we have to take into account that, as said above, observability in constraints must be *local* and not *global* in the following sense: In the standard framework that we defined in [OSC 89] the presentations defining the constraint on a given specification were contained in the *global presentation.* Here, asking for this inclusion would not be sensible, in general, because it could happen that none of the sorts involved in the constraint is observable and, as a consequence, the semantics of the constraint would be trivial. This means that some sorts should be considered locally observable within the constraint even if, at the global level, they are not observable. This also means that, in order to define constraint satisfaction, i.e. to describe how some parts of the models of the given specification are freely constructed (up to behavioural equivalence) from another part of the model, the forgetful functor cannot be used to *obtain* these parts. Instead, a View functor will have to be used.

Definition 4.1

A **behaviour constraint** BC is a pair of behaviour presentations (BP1, BP1') such that Obs1 = S1 and BP1 $\subseteq$ BP1'.

Given a presentation BP, a **behaviour constraint** BC = (BP1, BP1') is **defined on** BP if 1) BP1' *view included* in BP, i.e. P1' $\subseteq$ P and S1-Obs1' $\subseteq$ S-Obs, and 2) for every sort s1 in Obs1'-Obs1 we have that s1 is in Obs.

An algebra A $\in$ Beh(BP) **satisfies** a behaviour constraint (BP1, BP1') on BP, denoted A = (BP1, BP1') if

$$(A|_{BP1})|^{BP1'} \equiv_{BP1'} A|_{BP1'}$$

Notation:

We will shortly write $\equiv$ instead of $\equiv_{BP}$ if Bp is clear from the context. From now on, we will denote by $\_|_{BP}$: Beh(BP') $\rightarrow$ Beh(BP) and $\_|^{BP'}$: Beh(BP) $\rightarrow$ Beh(BP') the forgetful functor and the free functor respectively which are associated to the inclusion BP $\subseteq$ BP'. Moreover, if BP is view included in BP' then $\_|_{BP}$: Beh(BP') $\rightarrow$ Beh(BP) will denote the View functor associated to this view inclusion.

The previous definitions reflect the above discussion. In particular, condition 1) states our choice with respect to local observability within a constraint, i.e. we have considered that when stating a constraint (BP1, BP1') all sorts in BP1 could be used to observe the behaviour of the objects *created* by the constraint. On the other hand, condition 2) states that all sorts introduced by the constraint should be observable if and only if they are observable at the global level. The reason for this is that we are considering that constraints are the way of completely defining the sorts and operations introduced by them, i.e. the sorts and operations that are in BP1'-BP1. Therefore, if this is the complete definition of these sorts, their observability should also be defined by the constraint, i.e. the observability of these sorts should be the same within the constraint and at the global level.

Now, we can define our concept of behaviour (incomplete) specification as a presentation, including all the sorts, operations and equations of interest at this point and a set of constraints defining the complete parts of this specification. The semantics of such specification is, obviously, loose.

Definition 4.2

A **behaviour specification** BSP is a pair <BP, ζ> where BP is a behaviour presentation and ζ is a set of behaviour constraints on BP. The **semantics** of a behaviour specification BSP is defined by the following class of models

$$\text{Mod(BSP)} = \{A \in \text{Beh(BP)} \mid A \models \zeta\}$$

As in [OSC 89] and other related approaches (e.g. [ST 87b]) no special notion of specification (internal) correctness is used apart of consistency, i.e. the class of models of a given specification should not be empty.

As said above the basic constructions needed for adequately defining the operations for building specifications are the amalgamation and extension lemmas. The amalgamation lemma we present here is just an extension of the one in section 3., in the sense that it applies to specifications (with constraints) and not only presentations. On the other hand, the extension lemma is a special case of the view extension lemma from section 3., just considering that the subcategories of algebras on which we build the extension are the ones defined by the constraints.

In what follows we will define these lemmas with respect to pushouts in which all morphisms are inclusions or view inclusions. The reasons for this restriction is, on the one hand, simplicity and, on the other, that with the exception of some constructions at the end of the paper, that need that two of the arrows of a pushout be what it is called a refinement morphism, we only need inclusions.

Pushouts of specifications will not be explicitly defined although they are what it is expected, i.e. the pushout of the global presentations and if, we are just dealing with inclusions, the union of the sets of constraints.

Lemma 4.3 (Behaviour Amalgamation Lemma with Constraints)

Let BSPi = (BPi, ζi), i=1..4, be two specifications such that BSP4 is the pushout of BSP2 and BSP3 with respect to BSP1. Then

$$Mod(BSP4) = Mod(BSP2) +_{Mod(BSP1)} Mod(BSP3)$$

Moreover, amalgamation has the following universal property: If $A4 = A2 +_{A1} A3$ (resp. $h4 = h2 +_{h1} h3$) then A4 is the unique algebra (resp. h4 is the unique homomorphism) satisfying $A4|_{P2} = A2$ and $A4|_{P3} = A3$. (resp. $h4|_{P2} = h2$ and $h4|_{P3} = h3$).

Proof

By making use of the Behaviour Amalgamation Lemma, it is only necessary to prove that if $A4 = A2 +_{A1} A3$, and Ai is in Mod(BSPi), i=1,3, then A4 satisfies every constraint in BSP4. Now, let (BP, BP') be a constraint in BSP4. This means that there there is an i (i=1,2 or 3) such that (BP, BP') is in BSPi. But then we have:

$$A4|_{BP}|^{BP'} = A4|_{BPi}|_{BP}|^{BP'} = Ai|_{BP}|^{BP'} = Ai|_{BP'} = A4|_{BPi}|_{BP'} = A4|_{BP'}$$

[]

In order to state the Extension Lemma we need, we will first define the notion of relative persistency that is adequate here.

Definition 4.4

Given a specification BSP = <BP, ζ>, a behaviour constraint BC = (BP1, BP1'), with

BP1 $\subseteq$ BP, is **persistent relative to** BSP if for any A in Mod(BSP) it holds that

$$(A|_{BP1}|^{BP1'})|_{BP1} = A|_{BP1}$$

Please note that we do not assume BP1' to be included in BP.

Lemma 4.5 (Extension Lemma with Constraints)

Let BSP be a specification, BSP = <BP, ζ>, and BC be a behaviour constraint, BC = (BP1, BP2), such that BP1 is view included in BP and BP$\cap$BP2 = BP1 and let BP+BP2 denote the result specification of the pushout diagram

$$\begin{array}{ccc} BP1 & \longrightarrow & BP2 \\ \downarrow & & \downarrow \\ BP & \longrightarrow & BP+BP2 \end{array}$$

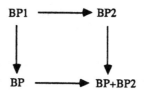

then if (BP1, BP2) is persistent relative to BSP we have that (BP, BP+BP2) is persistent relative to BSP and the associated free functor $\_|^{BP+BP2}$: Beh(BP) $\rightarrow$ Beh(BP+BP2) is an extension of $\_|^{BP2}$: Beh(BP1) $\rightarrow$ Beh(BP2) for BSP-models, that is for every A in Mod(BSP):

$$A|_{BP1}|^{BP2} = A|^{BP+BP2}|_{BP2}$$

Moreover, Mod(BSP)$|^{BP+BP2} \subseteq$ Mod(<BP+BP2, $\zeta \cup \{$(BP1, BP2)$\}$>) and for every algebra A4 (respectively behaviour homomorphism h4) in Mod(BSP4) we have that A4 (resp. h4) is naturally isomorphic to $A4|_{BP}|^{BP+BP2}$ (respectively $h4|_{BP}|^{BP+BP2}$).

Proof

Immediate from the view extension lemma and from the view amalgamation lemma for the free case just considering that the subcategories A1, A3 and A4 of Beh(BP1), Beh(BP3) and Beh(BP4) are the ones that satisfy the constraints of BSP. []

5. Main results

Now that we have the basic results needed (amalgamation and extension lemmas) we will extend the results presented in [OSC 89] to the behaviour case. These results concern the whole process of building a specification. In particular, first we will see that if a specification is completely defined then its semantics coincides with the initial behaviour semantics [Niv 87, NO 88], i.e. the final result of the development process has what we consider the proper behaviour semantics of a specification. Then, we will present the three basic operations for extending a specification (horizontal refinements) and show that we can define compatible semantics both at the model level and at the specification level. Finally, we introduce the notion of vertical refinement and show a horizontal composition theorem that may be seen as a generalization of parameter passing as defined in [EM 85] for the standard case and in [Niv 87, NO 88] for the behaviour case.

The notion of completeness of a specification is, as in [OSC 89] based on two properties 1) every sort and operation is defined in some constraint and 2) there is no circularity among constraints. The absence of circularity is needed as it shows the following example:

Let BP0, BP0', BP1, BP1' and BP be

```
bspec BP0 = obs sorts s1 end bspec

bspec BP0'= obs sorts s1, s2
            ops f: s1 → s2
end bspec

bspec BP1 =obs sorts s2 end bspec

bspec BP1'=   obs sorts s1, s2
              ops g: s2 → s1
end bspec

bspec BP =  obs sorts s1, s2
            ops f: s1 → s2
                g: s2 → s1
end bspec
```

and let BSP be (BP, {(BP0, BP0'), (BP1, BP1')}). In BSP every sort and operation seems to be defined on some constraint, but this is not really true. In fact, the constraints only say that elements of sorts s1 must be a copy of elements of sort s2 and vice-versa. Absence of this kind of circularity allows to avoid this kind of situations. Certainly, circularity is not by itself a problem (for instance, in the previous example another constraint could have existed really defining the elements of sorts s1 and s2). However, for simplicity, we have adopted this restricted notion together with the additional restriction that every sort or operation is defined by a unique constraint. Nevertheless the next theorem would also apply for not so strong restrictions.

Definition 5.1

A specification BSP = <BP, ζ> is **complete** iff the following two conditions hold:

a) **Complete definition**: for every $s \in S$ there exists a unique $(BP1, BP2) \in \zeta$ such that $s \in S2-S1$ and for every $op \in \Omega$ there exists a unique $(BP1, BP2) \in \zeta$ such that $op \in \Omega2-\Omega1$.

b) **No circularity**: the transitive closure of the relation <, defined by $(BP1, BP2) < (BP3, BP4)$ if there exists $s \in S3$ such that $s \in S2-S1$ or there exists $op \in \Omega3$ such that $op \in \Omega2 - \Omega1$, is a strict partial order on ζ.

Theorem 5.2

Let BSP = <BP, ζ> be a consistent behaviour specification, then if BSP is complete we have

$$Mod(BSP) = \{A \in Alg(BP) / A \equiv_{BP} T_{BP}\}$$

where T_{BP} is the initial BP-algebra.

Proof

Let $BC_0, BC_1, ..., BC_n$ be a topological sort of ζ with respect to the partial order defined by condition b. that is $BC_i < BC_j$ implies $i<j$. Note that BC_0 must have the form $(\emptyset, BP_0)$. Let $BSP_0 = <BP_0,\zeta_0>, ..., BSP_n = <BP_n,\zeta_n>$ be the following sequence of specifications:

$$BSP_0 = <BP_0, (\emptyset,BP_0)>$$
$$BSP_{i+1} = <BP_{i+1},\zeta_i \cup \{ (BP'_{i+1},BP''_{i+1}) \}>$$

where $BC_{i+1} = (BP'_{i+1},BP''_{i+1})$ and BP_{i+1} denotes the result of the pushout

$$\begin{array}{ccc} BP'_{i+1} & \longrightarrow & BP''_{i+1} \\ \downarrow & & \downarrow \\ BP & \longrightarrow & BP_{i+1} \end{array}$$

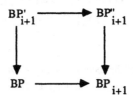

Note that for every i, j, with $i \leq j$, if s is in $S''_i - S'_i$ then s is observable in BP''_i iff s is observable in BP_j. Now, we will prove by induction that for every i:

1. BC_i is persistent relative to BSP_{i-1}. In the case $i = 0$ we consider BC_i to be persistent (persistent relative to the empty specification), which trivially is since $BC_0 = (\emptyset,BP_0)$.

2. $T_{BPi} \in Mod(BSP_i)$

3. If A, $B \in Mod(BSP_i)$ then $A \equiv_{BSP_i} B$.

It should be clear that, if 1., 2. and 3. hold for every i, then the theorem is true since, by construction, $BSP_n \subseteq BSP$ and in addition, by condition a., $\Sigma_n = \Sigma$ and $\zeta_n = \zeta$. Then, $Mod(BSP) \subseteq Mod(BSP_n)$. But if $Mod(BSP_n)$ only contains algebras which are isomorphic to T_{BPn} and Mod(BSP) cannot be empty, since it is assumed to be consistent, then $Mod(BSP) = Mod(BSP_n)$ and $T_{BPn} \equiv_{BP} T_{BP}$.

If $i = 0$ then, as it was said above, condition 1. trivially holds. Also, conditions 2. and 3. are obviously satisfied since the only BP_0-algebras that satisfy the behaviour constraint $(\emptyset,BP_0)$ are exactly the algebras which are isomorphic to T_{BP0}.

Assume $i = j+1$. To prove that BC_{j+1} is persistent relative to BSP_j we have to prove that:

$$T_{BPj} \mid_{BP'j+1} \mid^{BP''_{j+1}} \mid_{BP'j+1} \equiv T_{BPj} \mid_{BP'j+1}$$

Now, if BSP is consistent there should be an A such that $A \in Mod(BSP)$, but since T_{BPj} is the only BP_j-algebra satisfying the behaviour constraints in ζ_j, this means that $A \mid_{BPj} \equiv T_{BPj}$. On the other hand, A must also satisfy the behaviour constraint BC_{j+1}, therefore:

$$A|_{BP'j+1}|^{BP''j+1} \equiv A|_{BP''j+1}$$

but this implies that:

$$T_{BPj}|_{BP'j+1}|^{BP''j+1} \equiv A|_{BPj}|_{BP'j+1}|^{BP''j+1} \equiv A|_{BP''j+1}$$

and therefore:

$$T_{BPj}|_{BP'j+1}|^{BP''j+1}|_{BP'j+1} \equiv A|_{BP''j+1}|_{BP'j+1} = A|_{BP'j+1} \equiv T_{BPj}|_{BP'j+1}$$

Now, to prove 2. it is enough to notice that, since (BP'_{j+1},BP''_{j+1}) is persistent relative to BSP_j, according to the Extension Lemma $T_{BPj}|^{BP_{j+1}}$ is in $Mod(BSP_{j+1})$. But, $T_{BPj}|^{BP_{j+1}} \equiv T_{BPj+1}$.

Finally, 3 is also a consequence of the Extension Lemma. On one hand we have that all algebras in $Mod(BSP_j)$ are isomorphic which implies that all algebras in $Mod(BSP_j)|_{BP'j+1}$ are also isomorphic and, therefore, so it happens with algebras in $Mod(BSP_j)|_{BP'j+1}|^{BP''j+1}$. On the other, from the Extension Lemma we have that:

$$Mod(<BP_{j+1},\zeta_j \cup \{BC_{j+1}\}>) = Mod(BSP_j) \oplus_{Beh(BP'j+1)} (Beh(BP'_{j+1})|^{BP''j+1})$$

then, from the Amalgamation Lemma [EM85], we have that all algebras in $Mod(<BP_{j+1},\zeta_j \cup \{BC_{j+1}\}>)$ are also isomorphic. []

The next thing to study, as said above, are the basic operations that we define for building a specification. We consider two kinds of them: extension operations and completion operations. Extension operations, which correspond to horizontal refinements, build larger specifications on top of existing ones in a conservative way. That is, we assume that if BSP2 extends BSP1 then the models of BSP2, when forgetting the new sorts and operations coincide exactly with the models of BSP1. This means that we assume that extension operations do not add additional detail on existing sorts and operations, i.e. there is no restriction on the class of models. On the other hand, completion operations, which correspond to vertical refinements, do restrict the class of models of the refined specification. Since completion operations may also add new sorts, operations and equations to a existing specification, it happens that extensions are a special case of vertical refinements. Then, we could ask about the need of this distinction. The reason is mainly methodological, we believe that a specifier should always be conscious of when s/he is adding new things or when is s/he adding detail or completing a previously existing specification. This also happens in many specification languages (e.g. the *protecting* case for enrichment declaration in OBJ [FGJ 85]). In particular, the language GSBL developped following the ideas introduced in [OSC 89] makes heavy use of this distinction in order to enhance the incremental construction of specifications. Moreover, at a more technical level, knowing that some specifications are extensions, in our sense, of some subspecifications allows to assure, for free the correctness (i.e. consistency) of the result specification after applying certain operations. For instance this happens when *combining* specifications or when doing a horizontal composition of vertical refinements.

Definition 5.3

Given specifications BSP1 and BSP2, BSP2 is a **loose extension** of BSP1 if

a) $BSP1 \subseteq BSP2$

b) $Mod(BSP1) = Mod(BSP2)|_{BP1}$

We consider three basic operations for defining loose extensions: **enrich defining**, **enrich with** and **combine**. Their semantics, at the specification level is given below.

The operation **enrich defining** adds to a given specification new sorts and operations together with a constraint defining them. That is, given a specification $BSP = \langle BP, \zeta \rangle$ and a constraint $C = (BP1, BP2)$ such that $BP1 \subseteq BP$, **enrich defining** creates a new specification $\langle BP+BP2, \zeta \cup \{C\} \rangle$, where BP+BP2 denotes, as in the Extension Lemma (cf. 4.5) the pushout of BP and BP2 over BP1.

The operation **enrich with** adds new sorts and operations without any new constraint. That is, given a specification $BSP = \langle BP, \zeta \rangle$, where $BP = ((S, Op), E)$, and a triple $(S1, Op1, E1)$, such that $BP1 = ((S+S1, Op+Op1), E+E1)$ is a presentation and where + denotes disjoint union, **enrich with** creates the new specification $\langle BP1, \zeta \rangle$.

Finally, the operation **combine** puts together two specifications whithout duplicating their common part. That is, given specifications BSP1, BSP2 and BSP3, such that BSP2 and BSP3 are loose extensions of BSP1, the combination of BSP2 and BSP3 over BSP1 is defined as the result of the pushout:

$$\begin{array}{ccc} BSP1 & \longrightarrow & BSP2 \\ \downarrow & & \downarrow \\ BSP3 & \longrightarrow & BSP4 \end{array}$$

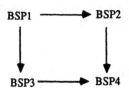

The semantics of these three operations could also be defined at the model level as follows:

$$Mod(\textbf{enrich} \langle BP, \zeta \rangle \textbf{ defining } (BP1,BP2)) = \{A \,/\, \exists\, A' \in Mod(\langle BP, \zeta \rangle),\ A \equiv A'|^{P+P2}\}$$

$$Mod(\textbf{enrich} \langle BP, \zeta \rangle \textbf{ with } (B\Sigma,E)) = Mod(\langle BP, \zeta \rangle) +_{Mod(\langle BP, \emptyset \rangle)} Mod(\langle BP+(B\Sigma,E), \emptyset \rangle)$$

$$Mod(\textbf{combine } BSP2 \textbf{ and } BSP3 \textbf{ wrt } BSP1) = Mod(BSP2) +_{Mod(BSP1)} Mod(BSP3)$$

This model level definitions are compatible with the previous ones because of the Amalgamation and Extension Lemmas seen in the previous section. It may be noted that these definitions are essentially the same as the ones given in [OSC 89] except for the case of the **enrich defining** operation. The reason is that in [OSC 89] this operation was defined in terms of amalgamated sums, while here, because this operation involves some view inclusions, this would not be possible in general. As a consequence, in this paper, we have defined the meaning of that operation by means of the closure, under behavioural equivalence (behavioural isomorphy) of the extensions of the models of the enriched specification.

In what follows, we will study the correctness of these three operations, i.e. under which conditions these operations define loose extensions. The simplest case is the **combine** operation, since the result BSP4 of the combination of two specifications, BSP2 and BSP3, that are loose extensions of BSP1 is always a loose extension of BSP2 and BSP3:

Theorem 5.4

Let BSP1, BSP2 and BSP3 be three consistent specifications such that BSP2 and BSP3 are loose extensions of BSP1 and BSP2$\cap$BSP3 = BSP1, and let BSP4 be the result of the pushout:

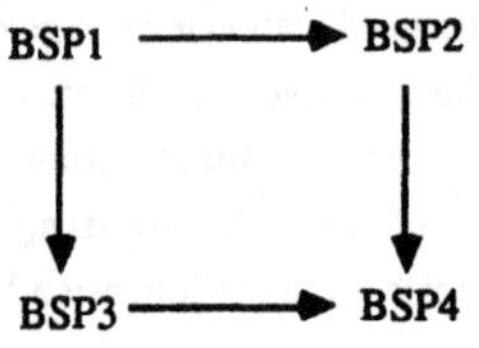

then BSP4 is a loose extension of BSP2 and BSP3.

Proof

The proof is almost trivial: w.l.o.g., let us prove that BSP4 is a loose extension of BSP2. Let A2 be in Mod(BSP2), then we know that A1 = A2 $|_{BP1}$ is in Mod(BSP1) and, since BSP3 is an extension of BSP1, there should be an A3 in Mod(BSP3) such that A1 = A3 $|_{BP1}$. Then, by the Amalgamation Lemma, we have that A4 = A2 $+_{A1}$ A3 is in Mod(BSP4). []

The case of **enrich defining** is also quite simple. It depends on the relative persistency of the new constraint with respect to the enriched specification:

Theorem 5.5

Given a specification BSP = <BP, ζ> and a constraint C = (BP1, BP2) such that BP1 $\subseteq$ BP and BP2$\cap$BP = BP1, and let BP+BP2 be the result of the pushout:

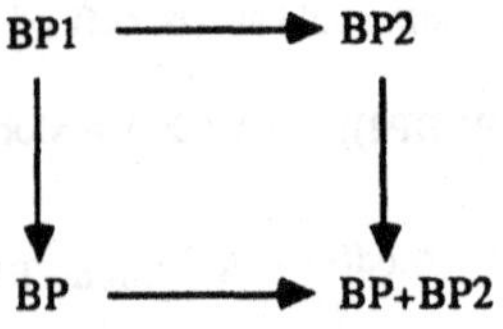

then BSP' = <BP+BP2, $\zeta \cup \{C\}$> is a loose extension of BSP iff C is persistent relative to BSP.

Proof

If BSP' is a loose extension of BSP this means that for every BP-algebra A such that A $\models \zeta$ there is a BP+BP2-algebra B such that B $\models \zeta \cup \{C\}$ and B $|_{BP}$ = A. Now, if B satisfies C this means that:

$$B|_{BP1}|^{BP2} = B|_{BP2}$$

but this implies that:

$$B|_{BP1}|^{BP2}|_{BP1} = B|_{BP2}|_{BP1} = B|_{BP1}$$

and therefore:

$$A|_{BP1}|^{BP2}|_{BP1} = B|_{BP1}|^{BP2}|_{BP1} = B|_{BP1} = A|_{BP1}$$

Conversely, if (BP1,BP2) is persistent relative to BSP, by the Extension Lemma proved above, we know that for every $A \in Mod(BSP)$ it holds that $A|^{BP+BP2} \in Mod(BSP')$ and $A|^{BP+BP2}|_{BP} = A$. []

Finally, the correctness of the enrich with operation is the most complicated case. Here, as in [OSC 89] we will just give a sufficient condition which we think can handle many situations. Essentially, it says that an enrichment of this kind over a specification BSP is a loose extension if we can provide a constraint persistent relatively to BSP, *defining completely* the enrichment. We think that this is a reasonable condition for many situations since, often, the reason of adding some sorts or operations without defining them completely is that we do not want to take a decision of choosing among several possible alternatives.

Corollary 5.6

Given a specification BSP = <BP, ζ>, and a presentation BP1, such that $BP \subseteq BP1$, then BSP1 = <BP1, ζ> is a loose extension of BSP if there exists a constraint C = (BP2,BP3), such that $BP2 \subseteq BP$, $BP1 \subseteq BP3$ and (BP2,BP3) is persistent relative to BSP.

Proof

If there is a constraint (BP2, BP3) such that $BP2 \subseteq BP$, $BP1 \subseteq BP3$ and (BP2, BP3) is persistent relative to BSP, then using the previous theorem we know that BSP' = <BP+BP3, $\zeta \cup \{C\}$> is a loose extension of BSP. But, $Mod(BSP')|_{BP1} \subseteq Mod(BSP1)$ thus BSP1 is a loose extension of BSP.[]

The second kind of refinements we consider are vertical refinements. A vertical refinement consists on *adding detail* to a specification, in our case completing the given specification or, similarly, restricting its class of models. In this sense, it seems reasonable to consider vertical refinements as some class of specification morphism. As in [OSC 89] we have considered a definition which is more restrictive than it, perhaps, could be. In particular, we have restricted *refinement morphisms* to translate constraints injectively. The reason for this is, mainly, methodological. According to our approach a constraint represents a part of a specification completely defined. In this sense, it seems reasonable to think that when we are completing a specification the already completed parts should remain *untouched.* A similar restriction is taken in [ETLZ82] but, apparently, just for technical reasons.

Definition 5.7

A refinement morphism f: <BP1, ζ1> $\rightarrow$ <BP2, ζ2> is a behaviour presentation mophism f: BP1 $\rightarrow$ BP2, satisfying:

a) f is injective on constrained sorts and operations, that is for every constraint (BP, BP') in ζ1, if $s1, s2 \in S'-S$ (resp. $op1, op2 \in \Omega' - \Omega$) then f(s1) = f(s2) implies s1 = s2 (resp. f(op1) = f(op2) implies op1 = op2)

b) $f(\zeta 1) \subseteq \zeta 2$.

Facts 5.8

1. Obviously, the composition of vertical refinements is a vertical refinement. Therefore, vertical composition trivially holds.

2. If f: $<BP1, \zeta 1> \rightarrow <BP2, \zeta 2>$ is a refinement morphism then $Mod(<BP2,\zeta 2>)|_{BP1} \subseteq Mod(<BP1, \zeta 1>)$. This is a consequence of the restriction imposing f to be injective on $\zeta 1$.

3. There are pushouts (amalgamations) associated to categories of specifications (models) with refinement morphisms (the associated forgetful functors). In particular, the proof of existence of amalgamations, in this case, would be just a slight generalization of the one given in the previous section.

The main operation for defining vertical refinements is presented in the following theorem. In particular, it shows how we can substitute, within a specification, an incomplete part by a more complete one. Specifically, it states how a vertical refinement of a given specification BSP1 induces a vertical refinement on any loose extension of BSP1. This fact has several interpretations. On one hand, the theorem states, in our framework, the horizontal composition property [GB80], namely, that the order in which we perform vertical and horizontal refinements is not important. On the other, it shows that in our framework there is no need for parameterization, since any specification BSP2 may be seen as having as implicit parameters all specifications BSP1 loosely extended by BSP2. Then, this induced vertical refinement may be seen as a generalized form of parameter passing. The relation of our construction to parameter passing is very similar to the one found by B. Meyer [Mey86], at the programming language level, between genericity and inheritance, showing that inheritance may be seen as a generalization of genericity. Indeed, as it is shown in [CO88], our notion of vertical refinement may be seen, from a methodological standpoint, as an inheritance relation defined at the specification level. Obviously, this kind of inheritance relation has nothing to do with the subtyping (or subsorting) relation also studied in the literature [GM83].

Theorem 5.9

Let BSP1 and BSP2 be consistent behaviour specifications such that BSP2 is a loose extension of BSP1, and let f be a refinement morphism, f: BSP1 $\rightarrow$ BSP3, for a given specification BSP3 such that BSP1 = BSP2$\cap$BSP3. The result of substituting BSP1 by BSP3 in BSP2 is the specification BSP4 = $<BP4, \zeta 4>$ defined by the pushout:

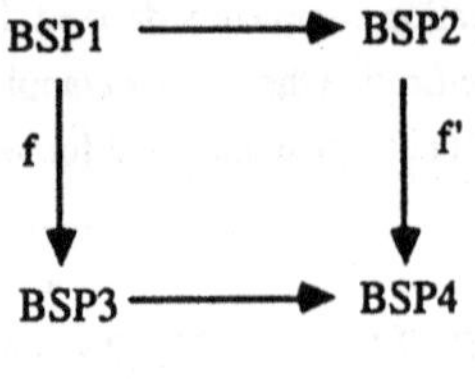

then we have:

1. BSP4 is a loose extension of BSP3
2. BSP3 is consistent iff BSP4 is consistent

Proof

1.We know that $Mod(BSP4) = Mod(BSP3) +_{Mod(BSP1)} Mod(BSP2)$. Then, if $Mod(BSP3) = \emptyset$, so is Mod(BSP4). Now, given an A∈Mod(BSP3), we have that $A|_{BP1}$∈Mod(BSP1). But, if BSP2 is a loose extension of BSP1, there is a B∈Mod(BSP2) such that $B|_{BP1} = A|_{BP1}$. Then, by defining $B' = A +_{A|_{BP1}} B$ we have that B'∈Mod(BSP4) and $B'|_{BP3} = A$.

2. Is an immediate consequence of 1., since if BSP4 is a loose extension of BSP3, then Mod(BSP3) is not empty iff Mod(BSP4) is not empty.[]

In the previous theorem, the fact that BSP2 is a loose extension of BSP1, i.e. $Mod(BSP2)|_{BP1} = Mod(BSP1)$, is absolutely needed to guarantee the consistency of BSP4. The situation is similar to the need of persistency to assure the correctness of parameter passing:

Theorem 5.10

Let BSP1 and BSP2 be specifications such that BSP1 ⊆ BSP2, then if BSP2 is not a loose extension of BSP1 there is a consistent specification BSP3 such that BSP2∩BSP3 = BSP1 and a refinement morphism f: BSP1 → BSP3 such that the result, BSP4, of the associated pushout diagram:

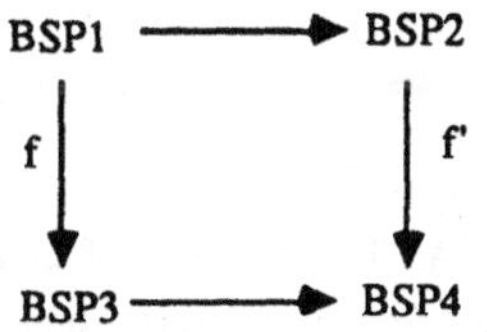

is not consistent.

Proof

If BSP2 is not a loose extension of BSP1 this means that there is an A1∈Mod(BSP1) such that for every A2∈Mod(BSP2) $A2|_{BP1}$ is not isomorphic to A1. Let BSP3 = <BP3, ζ3>, where BP3 is the presentation obtained by adding to BP1 all the values from A1 as constants of the appropriate sorts and all the equations satisfied by A1, and ζ3 is obtained by adding to ζ1 the constraint (∅, BP3). Obviously, Mod(BSP3) = {B∈Beh(BP3) / $B|_{BP1} \cong A1$}.
Now, Mod(BSP4) = ∅, for

$$Mod(BSP4) = Mod(BSP3) +_{Mod(BSP1)} Mod(BSP2)$$

and

$$\{A \in Mod(BSP2) \,/\, A|_{BP1} \in Mod(BSP3)|_{BP1}\} = \varnothing \quad []$$

6. Conclusions

We have presented an approach for formalizing the specification development process from informal requirements which is capable of dealing with incomplete specifications. Moreover, it also takes into account the notions of behaviour and observability which are critical with respect to the semantics of software specifications. The way of handling this incompleteness is by means of behavioural specifications with constraints, which correspond to the completely defined subparts of a given incomplete specification. The concept of behavioural constraint allows to deal with different observability criteria within the same behavioural specification (certain sorts are considered non-observable at the global level but may be considered locally observable within a constraint) which is a need from a methodological point of view. The corresponding semantics is loose, accepting as models all algebras behaviourally satisfying the axioms and the behavioural constraints, obtaining compatibility results with respect to the operations of horizontal and vertical refinement. The *interaction* of horizontal and vertical refinements allows to substitute any incomplete subspecification of a given specification by a more complete one, in a way that generalizes the standard behavioural parameter passing by requiring a limited form of persistency in the behavioural sense.

To achieve that, a generalization of the Amalgamation and Extension Lemmas for behaviour specification morphisms, the Extension Lemma for view morphisms and a version of the Amalgamation Lemma for view morphisms for free algebras have been obtained.

Acknowledgements

This work has been partially supported by the C.E.C. in the Esprit Basic Research Working Group COMPASS.

7. References

[BG 80] Burstall, R.M.; Goguen, J.A. The semantics of Clear, a specification language, Proc. Copenhagen Winter School on Abstract Software Specification, Springer LNCS 86, pp. 292-332, 1980.

[CO 88] Clerici, S.; Orejas, F. GSBL: an algebraic specification language based on inheritance, Proc. Europ. Conf. on Object Oriented Programming, (Oslo, 1988), Springer LNCS.

[Ehg 89] Ehrig, H. A categorical concept of constraints for algebraic specifications, Proc. Int. Workshop on Categorical Methods in Computer Science with Aspects from Topology, Springer LNCS 332, (1989).

[EM 85] Ehrig, H., Mahr, B.Fundamentals of algebraic specification 1, EATCS Monographs on Theor. Comp. Sc., Springer Verlag, 1985.

[EPO 89] Ehrig, H., Pepper, P. , Orejas, F. On recent trends in algebraic specification, Proc. ICALP 89, Springer LNCS 372, (1989), 263-289.

[ETLZ 82] Ehrig, H., Thatcher, J.W., Lucas, P., Zilles, S.N. Denotational and initial algebra semantics of the algebraic specification language LOOK, Draft Rep. IBM Res., 1982.

[FGJM 85] Futatsugi, K. Goguen, J.A., Jouannaud, J.P., Meseguer, J. Principles of OBJ 2, Proc. POPL 85, ACM (1985), 221-231.

[GB 80] Goguen, J.A., Burstall, R.M. CAT, a system for the structured elaboration of correct programs from structured specifications, Tech. Report CSL-118, Comp. Sc. Lab., SRI Int., 1980.

[GB 85] Goguen, J.A., Burstall, Institutions: Abstract Model Theory for Computer Science, CSLI Rep. 85-30, 1985.

[HW 85] R. Hennicker, M. Wirsing, Observational Specification: A Birkhoff-Theorem , Recent Trends in Data Type Specification, Informatik-Fachberichte, Springer 116 (1985) 119-135.

[MG 85] J. Meseguer, J. A. Goguen, Initiality, induction and computability, Algebraic Methods in Semantics, M. Nivat and J. Reynolds (eds.), Cambridge Univ. Press (1985) 459-540.

[Mey 86] B. Meyer, Genericity versus Inheritance, Proc. ACM conf. Object-Oriented Programming Syst, Languages, and Applications, ACM, New York, 1986, pp. 391-405

[Niv 87] Mª P. Nivela, Semántica de Comportamiento en Lenguajes de Especificación, PhD. Thesis, Facultat d'Informàtica, Universitat Politècnica de Catalunya, Barcelona (1987).

[NO 88] Mª P. Nivela, F. Orejas, Initial Behaviour Semantics for Algebraic Specifications, Proc. 5th Workshop on Algebraic Specifications of Abstract Data Types, Gullane 1987, Springer LNCS 332, (1988) 184-207.

[ONE 89] F. Orejas, Mª P. Nivela, H. Ehrig, Semantical constructions for categories of behavioural specifications, Proc. International Workshop on Categorical Methods in Computer Science with Aspects from Topology, Berlin 1988, Springer LNCS 332, (1989) 220-243.

[OSC 89] F. Orejas, V. Sacristan, S. Clerici, Development of Algebraic Specifications with Constraints, Proc. International Workshop on Categorical Methods in Computer Science with Aspects from Topology, Berlin 1988, Springer LNCS 332, (1989)

[Rei 80] H. Reichel, Initially restricting algebraic theories, Proc. MFCS 80, Springer LNCS 88 (1980), pp. 504-514.

[Rei 81] H. Reichel, Behavioural equivalence - a unifying concept for initial and final specification methods, Proc. 3rd Hungarian Computer Science Conf., Budapest (1981) 27-39.

[Rei 84] H. Reichel, Behavioral validity of equations in abstract data types, Contributions to General Algebra 3, Proc.of the Vienna Conference, Verlag B. G. Teubner, Stuttgart (1985) 301-324.

[Rei 87] H. Reichel, Initial Computability, Algebraic Specifications and Partial Algebras, Int. Series of Monographs on Comp. Sc, Oxford Science Publ., 1987.

[SW 83] D. Sannella, Wirsing, M., A kernel language for algebraic specification and implementation. Proc. Intl. Conf. on Foundations of Computation Theory Sweden. Springer LNCS 158 (1983) 413-427.

[ST 87a] D. Sannella, A. Tarlecki, On observational equivalence and algebraic specification. J. Comp. and Sys. Sciences 34, pp. 150-178 (1987).

[ST 87b] D. Sannella, A. Tarlecki Toward formal development of programs from algebraic specifications: implementations revisited. Proc. Joint Conf. on Theory and Practice of Software Development, Pisa, Springer LNCS 249, pp. 96-110 (1987).

ENTITIES: AN INSTITUTION FOR DYNAMIC SYSTEMS

GIANNA REGGIO

DIPARTIMENTO DI MATEMATICA - UNIVERSITA' DI GENOVA
VIA L.B. ALBERTI 4, 16132 GENOVA, ITALY

INTRODUCTION

In this paper we introduce the entity framework (entity algebras and entity specifications) and show, also with the help of several examples, how they can be used for formally modelling and specifying dynamic systems.

Entity algebras are structures devised as formal models for both data types, processes and objects, thus allowing to give integrated abstract specifications of processes, data types and objects. They are a subclass of partial algebras with predicates, having the following features:

- some sorts correspond to dynamic elements, that we call *entities*; dynamics is represented by the possibility of performing labelled transitions;
- entities may have subcomponent entities together with usual (static) subcomponents; it is important to notice that the structure of an entity is not fixed, as the binary parallelism with interleaving of CCS or the record-like structure of usual objects, but is definable by giving appropriate operations and axioms;
- entities have *identities* in such a way that it is possible to retrieve entity subcomponents depending on their identities and to describe sharing of subcomponents.

Moreover the structure of each entity can be represented graphically in a way that makes *sharing* explicit.

Correspondingly to this model level, it is possible to define *entity specifications*; which are just the correspondent in the entity field of the usual specifications of abstract data types and can be used to formally specify dynamic systems. Using entity specifications we can abstractly describe how it is structured a dynamic system, give properties about its activity and the activity of its dynamic subcomponents; for example we can require for a certain entity that the order of the subcomponents is not relevant, that it must always terminate its activity, that its subcomponents interact in a synchronous way and so on.

However using this kind of entity specifications, called *specifications in the small*, we cannot formalize "very" abstract properties about the structure of classes of dynamic systems; for example we cannot specify the class of all "simple" dynamic systems (ie, that cannot be decomposed in several other entities interacting between them) and the class of all systems where no entity is shared between several others. To handle these cases it is possible to use a kind of ultra loose entity specifications, called *entity specifications in the large*. To enlighten the distinction between specifications in the small and in the large consider the well-known firing squad problem (see [DHJW]): for specifying one system which represents a possible solution of the problem we use an entity specification in the small; while for specifying the class of all systems representing solutions of the problem we use an entity specification in the large.

In this paper we consider only entity specifications in the small and give a brief hint of specifications in the large, while a full treatment of them can be found in [AR2]. We show that the specifications in the small constitute an institution; give conditions ensuring the existence of the initial model and show that has inter-

Work partially funded by COMPASS-Esprit-BRA-W.G. n 3264, by CNR-PF-Sistemi Informatici e Calcolo Parallelo and by a grant ENEL/CRA (Milano Italy).

esting properties about the dynamics and the structure (it is characterized by the minimum amount of activity and by the simpler structure).

Since entity specifications are particular algebraic specifications of abstract data types, we can extend to them various notions and results about classical specifications (eg, structured and hierarchical specifications, observational/behavioural semantics, implementation and so on); usually these extensions are adequate for coping with the particular features of entities. Here we only consider the notion of implementation (see [W]) and show that its extension to entity specifications is reasonable.

Because of their characteristics (dynamics, structure, identities) entity algebras and specifications could be used for modelling and specifying object systems; in this paper we just give an example, but do not handle this topic in a general way (for more about that see [Dragon]).

The basic algebraic institution we use in the paper is that of partial algebras with predicates; see [GM] for the institution of algebras with predicates and [BW] for the institution of partial algebras; the institution of partial algebras with predicates can be found in [AC]; note that the combination of the two institutions does not pose particular problems.

The problem of the development of an integrated algebraic framework for the specification of concurrent systems has been treated in previous papers about the SMoLCS methodology, see for example [AR], [AR1], [AGR]; the SMoLCS specifications of concurrent systems could be considered as particular entity specifications in the small. Recently it has been considered also the problem of using algebraic techniques for the formal modelling and specifications of classical object-oriented systems, see for example [BZ] and [FB]; a very recent paper of Meseguer [M] tries to offer a unifying and integrated framework for the specifications of dynamic system based on rewriting. Since the technical framework of all these approaches is quite different from the present one, it is not easy to make a comparison; some special effort should be made for investigating their relationship.

In sect. 1 and 2 we introduce entity algebras and entity specifications in the small and show their features; these sections include complete examples. Entity specifications in the large are shortly introduced in sect. 3. The proofs are omitted and will appear in [AR2].

1 ALGEBRAS FOR DYNAMIC ENTITIES

Entity algebras are particular partial algebras with predicates used for modelling dynamic concurrent and object-oriented systems; "particular" means that they always have certain sorts, operations and predicates, whose interpretations must respect some conditions. These special algebraic ingredients are used for:

- representing dynamic systems (for example, processes) and their activity;
- determining whether such systems are simple or structured, and, in the second case, allowing to describe their structure (eg, fix the number of dynamic subcomponents),
- determining the identity of such systems

and so on.

In the paper we abbreviate "signature with predicates" and "partial algebra with predicates" with "psignature" and "palgebra".

1.1 Entity signatures

Entity signatures are particular psignatures where some sorts correspond to the usual static values and some other correspond to dynamic elements (entities), their identities and their "cores". Each entity is completely determined by its identity and its core. The sorts corresponding to cores of entities, ie, whose elements are the cores of entities, are called *dynamic sorts*. In an entity signature for each dynamic sort there exist some special sorts, operations and predicates; precisely, given a dynamic sort s:

- a sort, ent(s), of entities (dynamic elements) with cores of type s (shortly entities of type s);
- a sort, ident(s), of identities of the elements of ent(s);
- an operation building the elements of ent(s)
  $\_ : \_ : \text{ident}(s) \times s \to \text{ent}(s)$
  which taken an identity and a core returns an entity;
- a sort, lab(s), of labels for the transitions of the elements of ent(s);
- a predicate describing the activity of the elements of ent(s) by means of labelled transitions
  $\_ \overset{-}{\longrightarrow} \_ : \text{ent}(s) \times \text{lab}(s) \times \text{ent}(s)$.

Notice that here and in the following we use operations and predicates with mixfix syntax; the symbol "_" denotes the places of the arguments.

For giving an entity signature it is sufficient to give the basic sorts, distinguishing the ones which correspond to the cores of dynamic elements (dynamic sorts), while we can omit the special components; thus we have the following definition.

Def. 1.1

- An *entity signature* (or simply *signature*) is a 4-tuple $E\Sigma = (D, S, OP, PR)$ such that:
  - D and S are two disjoint sets
    (the basic sorts; those in D correspond to the cores of dynamic elements and are called *dynamic sorts*);
  - $(D^E \cup S, OP, PR)$ is a psignature, where
    $D^E = D \cup (\cup_{s \in D} \{ \text{ent}(s), \text{lab}(s), \text{ident}(s) \})$
    (the sorts having form ent(s) are called *entity sorts*).
- $E\Sigma^E$ is the psignature $(D^E \cup S, OP^E, PR^E)$, where:
  - $OP^E = OP \cup \{ \_ : \_ : \text{ident}(s) \times s \to \text{ent}(s) \mid s \in D \}$,
  - $PR^E = PR \cup \{ \_ \overset{-}{\longrightarrow} \_ : \text{ent}(s) \times \text{lab}(s) \times \text{ent}(s) \mid s \in D \}$.□

Notation: in the following $E\Sigma$ will be a generic entity signature (D, S, OP, PR) and Dsorts($E\Sigma$) will denote the set of the dynamic sorts of $E\Sigma$. Moreover we will write

sorts $s_1, \ldots, s_n$
dsorts $d_1, \ldots, d_m$
opns $Op_1, \ldots, Op_k$
preds $Pr_1, \ldots, Pr_h$

for denoting the entity signature $(\{ d_1, \ldots, d_m\}, \{ s_1, \ldots, s_n\}, \{ Op_1, \ldots, Op_k\}, \{ Pr_1, \ldots, Pr_h\})$.

1.2 Entity algebras

Given an entity signature $E\Sigma$, an $E\Sigma$-entity algebra is a particular $E\Sigma^E$-palgebra, but not all $E\Sigma^E$-palgebras are suitable as entity algebras; the interpretations of the special sorts, operations and predicates must respect some conditions. Consider indeed the entity signature ΣS

dsorts nat, stack
opns $0 : \to \text{nat}$
Succ: nat $\to$ nat
$\alpha, \beta, \ldots$: ident(nat)
Empty: $\to$ stack
Push: ent(nat) $\times$ stack $\to$ stack
Pop: ent(stack) $\to$ ent(stack)
$\Gamma, \Psi, \ldots$: ident(stack)

and let AS be a ΣS^E-palgebra; for example, it may happen that in AS:

- $AS \models \alpha: 0 = \beta: 1$ and $AS \models \alpha \neq \beta$ (entities with different identities are identified);

– AS $\models \Gamma$: Empty $\xrightarrow{1}$ Ψ: Empty and AS $\models \Gamma \neq \Psi$
(an entity changes its identity performing a transition);

– there exists $v \in AS_{ent(nat)}$ and for all $id \in AS_{ident(nat)}$, $n \in AS_{nat}$ $v \neq id :^{AS} n$
(we cannot determine the identity and the core of an entity);

– AS $\models 0 \neq 1$ and the interpretation of Γ: Push(α: 0, Push(α: 1, Empty)) in AS is defined
(an entity has two different subentities with the same identity).

Obviously an $E\Sigma^E$-palgebra where one of the above properties holds cannot be considered an entity algebra.

To define formally which $E\Sigma^E$-palgebras are entity algebras, we need some technical definitions and for clarity we first illustrate them on an example.

Given an $E\Sigma^E$-palgebra and an element of entity sort, say e, we can find out the possible "views" of the dynamic structure of e by showing which are its dynamic subcomponents (ie, entity subcomponents) and how they are put together.

Consider a term-generated ΣS^E-palgebra BS, where sorts and operations are interpreted in the obvious way: $BS_{nat} = \mathbb{N}$, $BS_{ent(nat)} = \{ \alpha, \beta, \dots \} \times BS_{nat}$, $BS_{stack} = BS_{ent(nat)}^{*}$, $BS_{ent(stack)} = \{ \Gamma, \Psi, \dots \} \times BS_{stack}$ and so on.

Here and in the following $Symb^{ALG}$, the interpretation in an algebra ALG of Symb, either a predicate or an operation symbol, will be simply written Symb and analogously for ground terms, thus t^{ALG} will be written t.

The element

e = Γ: Push(α: 0, Push(β: 1, Empty))

represents an entity of type stack with identity Γ and core Push(α: 0, Push(β: 1, Empty)), which has two *subentities* of type nat, represented respectively by α: 0 and β: 1, organized in a stack. Thus e could be viewed as

$\Gamma : \lambda\, e_1, e_2.$ (Push(e_1, Push(e_2, Empty)))(α: 0, β: 1),

where the function

(*1) $\lambda\, e_1, e_2.$ Push(e_1, Push(e_2, Empty)): $BS_{ent(nat)} \times BS_{ent(nat)} \to BS_{stack}$

represents the way the entities α: 0, β: 1 are *composed* (ie, organized in a stack) to build up the compound entity e.

The entities α: 0, β: 1 are in some sense "simple" (ie, without subcomponents); indeed the zero-ary functions

(*2) 0, 1: $\to BS_{nat}$

say that they are not built by composing other entities.

Graphically this *way of viewing the dynamic structure* of e can be represented by

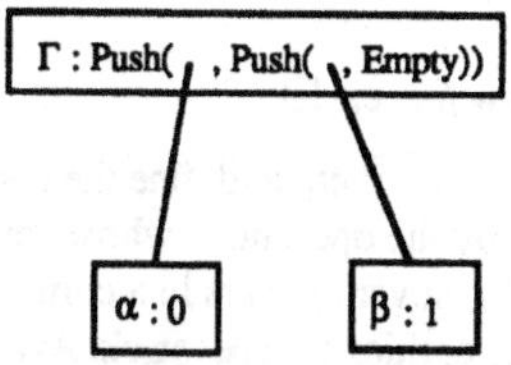

where the term with holes "Push(, Push(, Empty))" stands for the function (*1). Notice that

represent the *views of the dynamic structures* of the two entities α: 0 and β: 1 (they have no subcomponents).

The functions like (*1) and (*2), which describe how some entities are put together to get the core of compound entities, are called *entity composers*; while the structures pictorially represented above by graphs are called *entity views*; both notions are formally given in def. 1.2 and 1.3.

The entity composers such as (1*) and (2*) correspond to open terms on ΣS; however we are not restricted to term-generated algebras, since, as usual we can use a new signature obtained by adding zero-ary operations for all junk elements (recall that $v \in ALG_s$ is a *junk* element iff there does not exist a ground term t s.t. $v = t^{ALG}$).

$E\Sigma^J$ is the psignature

enrich $E\Sigma^E$ **by** $\{ Op_v : \rightarrow s \mid s \in Sorts(E\Sigma^E), v \in A_s$ junk $\}$;

and A^J the term-generated $E\Sigma^J$-palgebra obtained from A by interpreting each Op_v as v.

Def. 1.2 Let A be an $E\Sigma^E$-palgebra. The set $EC(E\Sigma, A)$ of the *entity composers* on $E\Sigma$ and A is the set of functions

$\{ \lambda\, e_1, \ldots, e_n.\ t^{A^J, [e_1/x_1, \ldots, e_n/x_n]} \mid t \in (T_{E\Sigma^J}(X))_s$
$Var(t) = \{ x_1 : ent(s_1), \ldots, x_n : ent(s_n) \}$, for some $s, s_1, \ldots, s_n \in Dsorts(E\Sigma)$ and
$x_1, \ldots, x_n$ are the only subterms of t of entity sort $\}$. □

Notice that entity composers are given at a "semantic level" not at a "syntactical level", ie they are composition of operation interpretations of the algebra not terms.

Notation: given $ec \in EC(E\Sigma, A)$, if ec is a function from $A_{ent(s_1)} \times \ldots \times A_{ent(s_n)}$ into A_s, then we simply write $ec: ent(s_1) \times \ldots \times ent(s_n) \rightarrow s$.

Def. 1.3

- The set $EV(E\Sigma, A)$ of the *entity views* of an $E\Sigma^E$-palgebra A is the subset of ordered trees with nodes labelled by couples consisting of an entity identity and an entity composer for entity of the same sort (such sort is the sort of the view) inductively defined as follows:

  for all $ec: ent(s_1) \times \ldots \times ent(s_n) \rightarrow s \in EC(E\Sigma, A)$ with $n \geq 0$, $id \in A_{ident(s)}$ and $ev_1, \ldots, ev_n \in EV(E\Sigma, A)$ having sorts respectively $s_1, \ldots, s_n$

  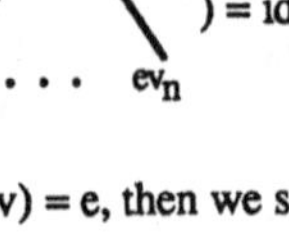

  $\in EV(E\Sigma, A)$.

- With each entity view there is associated an element of entity sort, defined in the following way:

  V(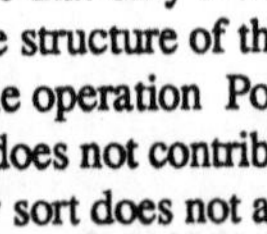

) $= id : ec(V(ev_1), \ldots, V(ev_n)) \in \cup_{s \in Dsorts(E\Sigma)} A_{ent(s)}$;

  if $V(ev) = e$, then we say that ev *is a view for* e. □

Notice that only the operations having sort s contribute to define the composers for entities of sort $ent(s)$, ie, the structure of the entities is determined by the operations whose result sort is the core sort; for example the operation Pop, having sort ent(stack), never appears in a composer for entities of sort ent(stack), ie, it does not contribute to the structure of the entities of type stack. Also note that in general an element of entity sort does not admit a unique view of its structure as it is shown in the following (see sect. 1.3).

We need also the following terminology.

Assume that A is an $E\Sigma^E$-palgebra, $e \in \cup_{s \in Dsorts(E\Sigma)} A_{ent(s)}$ and $ev \in EV(E\Sigma, A)$.

- e is a *(proper) subentity* of ev iff there exists a (proper) subtree of ev which is a view for e.
- ev is *simple* iff it is a tree of depth 1.
- e *has identity* id or *is identified by* id iff e = id: v for some v.
- ev is *sound* iff for all subentities of ev e' and e", if e' and e" have the same identity, then e' = e".

Def. 1.4 An $E\Sigma$-*entity algebra* (or simply $E\Sigma$-*algebra)* is an $E\Sigma^E$-palgebra EA such that for all $s \in Dsorts(E\Sigma)$

- $EA_{ent(s)} \subseteq EA_{ident(s)} \times EA_s$(*) and $(\_:\_ : ident(s) \times s \to ent(s))^{EA} = \lambda\, id, x. <id, x>$;
- if $EA \models e \xrightarrow{1} e'$, then e and e' have the same identity;
- all elements of $EA_{ent(s)}$ have at least a view and only sound views.

The class of all $E\Sigma$-algebras is denoted by $eAlg_{E\Sigma}$. □

Notice that the last property requires that usually the interpretations in EA of some operations (eg, the entity builder operations _ : _) are partial functions.

Fact 1.5 shows that def. 1.4 is reasonable.

Fact 1.5 Let EA be an $E\Sigma$-algebra and $e \in EA_{ent(s)}$ for some s sort of $E\Sigma$,

i) e has one and only one identity;

ii) if e' and e" are two distinct subentities of a view for e, then e' and e" have different identities;

iii) if e has identity id, then a view for e cannot have a proper subentity identified by id. □

Instead the following properties show that our definition of entity algebras is not too restrictive and allows to formally describe several interesting situations.

For example, it is possible to give an $E\Sigma$-algebra EA and $e, e' \in EA_{ent(s)}$ for some s sort of $E\Sigma$ s.t.:

- $EA \models e \xrightarrow{1} e'$ and e, e' have views with a different number of subentities (dynamic creation and termination of subentities);
- e has several different views also with different subentities (different ways to put together (different) groups of entities are semantically equivalent);
- there exists a view for e where two distinct subentities have the same subentity (sharing of subentities).

1.3 An Example: Distributed Concurrent Calculi

In this section we define a particular algebra DC (and some variations) and use them to enlighten the most relevant features of entity algebras.

DC represents a simple distributed concurrent calculus. In DC we have sequential processes which evolve in an interleaving way and interact between them by handshaking communication; Nil, _ . _ and _ +_ are the combinators for expressing the sequential processes and _ || _ is the parallel combinator.

Let $D\Sigma$ be the following entity signature:

(*) More precisely $EA_{ent(s)}$ is isomorphic to a subset of $EA_{ident(s)} \times EA_s$.

dsorts proc, prog — processes and programs
opns Tau, Alpha, Beta, ... → lab(proc) — process actions
$\overline{\_}$: lab(proc) → lab(proc) — complementary operation on actions
Nil: → proc
_ . _ : lab(proc) × proc → proc
_ + _ : proc × proc → proc
α, β, ... : → ident(proc)
_: ent(proc) → prog
_ || _ : prog × prog → prog
_ : lab(proc) → lab(prog)
Γ, Ψ, ... : → ident(prog)

DC is a term-generated DΣ-algebra such that:

- its carriers are subsets of the quotient of the ground terms on DΣ modulo the congruence generated by the equations $\overline{\overline{l}} = l$ for $l \neq$ Tau, $\overline{\text{Tau}} =$ Tau and those corresponding to the fact that + and || are commutative, associative and that Nil, id: Nil for all id are their identities;
- its operations are defined in the obvious way;
- the transition relation predicates (——> for processes and ===> for programs) are defined by the following inductive rules, where p: proc, ep: ent(proc), id: ident(proc), a: lab(proc), pg: prog, pid: ident(prog).

$$\frac{}{\text{id: a . p} \xrightarrow{a} \text{id: p}} \qquad \frac{\text{id: } p_1 \xrightarrow{a} \text{id: } p_1'}{\text{id: } p_1 + p_2 \xrightarrow{a} \text{id: } p_1'}$$

$$\frac{\text{ep} \xrightarrow{a} \text{ep}'}{\text{ep} \overset{a}{\Longrightarrow} \text{ep}'} \qquad \frac{\text{pid: } pg_1 \overset{a}{\Longrightarrow} pg_1'}{\text{pid: } pg_1 \parallel pg_2 \overset{a}{\Longrightarrow} \text{pid: } pg_1' \parallel pg_2}$$

$$\frac{\text{pid: } pg_1 \overset{a}{\Longrightarrow} pg_1' \quad \text{pid: } pg_2 \overset{\overline{a}}{\Longrightarrow} pg_2'}{\text{pid: } pg_1 \parallel pg_2 \overset{\text{Tau}}{\Longrightarrow} \text{pid: } pg_1' \parallel pg_2'} \quad a \neq \text{Tau}$$

Different ways of composing some entities together may be equivalent

epg = Γ: (α: Tau . Nil || β: Gamma . Nil) ∈ $DC_{ent(prog)}$

is an example of an entity whose structure may be seen in two different ways; indeed epg is also equal to
Γ: (β: Gamma . Nil || α: Tau . Nil);

the two views of epg are graphically represented by

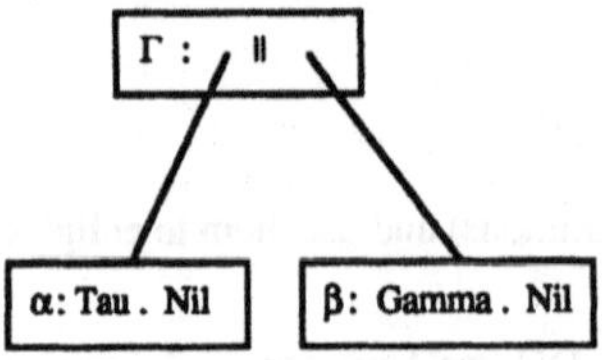

and

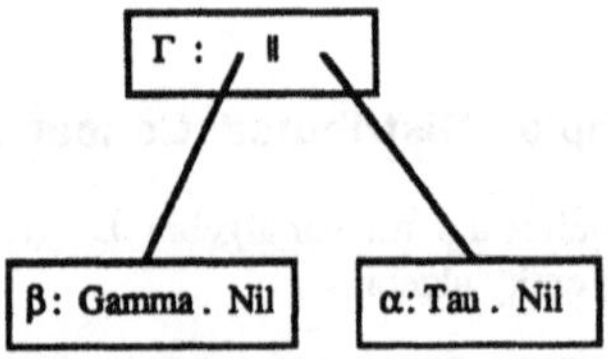

That means that in DC programs the order of the processes put in parallel is not relevant.

Compositions of different groups of entities may be equivalent

It is possible that different views of an entity can differ also for the number of dynamic subentities, as it is shown by the entity epg' = Γ: α: Nil; indeed epg' is also equal to

Γ: α: Nil || β: Nil , Γ: α: Nil || β: Nil || γ: Nil

and to any number of Nil processes put in parallel (recall that processes having form id: Nil are identities for the operation ||).

Various views of the structure of epg' are graphically represented by:

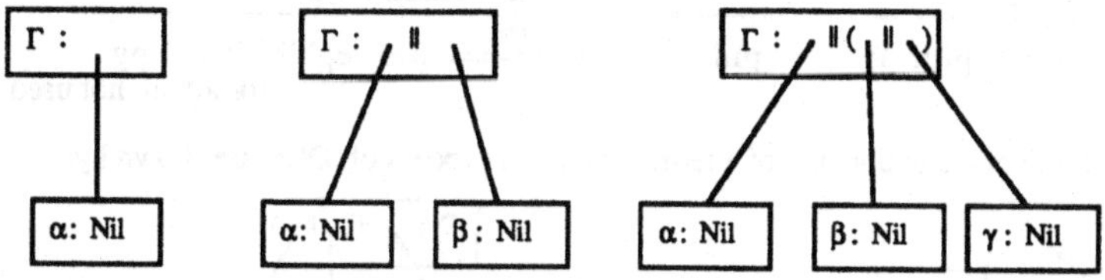

Thus in the DC programs the processes which cannot perform any action (id: Nil) do not matter.

Not all operations contribute to the entity composers

Here we consider a calculus DC_1 differing from DC only for having an operation for extracting from a program a process with a given identity,

Get: ent(prog) × ident(proc) → ent(proc),

whose interpretation is given by

Get(pid: id: p || ep_1 ... || ep_n, id) = id: p

Get(pid: id_1: p_1 || ... || id_n: p_n, id, p') undefined if id $\neq$ id_i for i = 1, ..., n.

The set of entity composers on DC_1 is the same of those on DC.

Sharing of subentities

Here we consider a calculus DC_2 differing from DC only for having a multilevel parallelism instead of a flat one; we just take a new signature $D\Sigma_2$ obtained from DΣ by replacing the operation _ || _ with
_ ||| _: ent(prog) × ent(prog) → prog,
and give a $D\Sigma_2$-algebra DC_2 in the same way of DC. In this case an entity of sort prog has either one subentity of sort proc or two subentities of the same sort prog.

epg" = Γ: [Ψ: (Ω: pg_1 ||| Λ: pg_2) ||| Δ: (Ω: pg_1 ||| Θ: pg_3)],

is an entity where the subentity represented by Ω: pg_1 is shared between the subentities identified by Ψ and Δ; its structure is graphically represented by

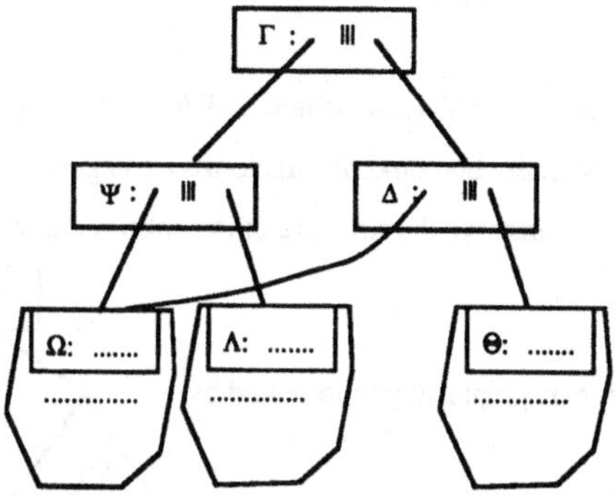

Entities may terminate and new entities may be created

Here we consider a calculus DC_3 differing from DC only for allowing the termination and the creation of processes. We just take a new signature $D\Sigma_3$ obtained from DΣ by adding the operations

Terminate: $\rightarrow$ lab(proc) and Create: proc $\rightarrow$ lab(proc),

and DC_3 is defined as DC; the transitions due to the new actions are given by

$$\frac{ep \xrightarrow{\text{Terminate}} ep'}{pid: ep \parallel pg \xrightarrow{\text{Tau}} pid: pg} \qquad \frac{ep \xrightarrow{\text{Create(p)}} ep'}{pid: ep \parallel pg \xrightarrow{\text{Tau}} pid: ep' \parallel id: p \parallel pg}$$

for all id not used in pg

Graphically an example of a creation and of a termination of a process of DC_3 are shown by:

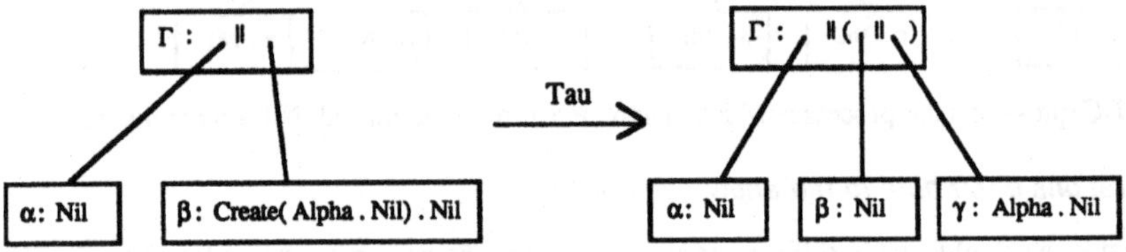

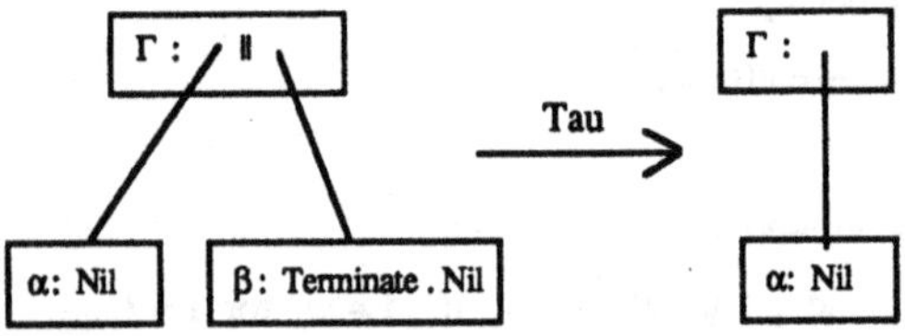

1.4 Entity homomorphisms

Since entity algebras are particular palgebras, we take as homomorphisms between entity algebras the total strengthening homomorphisms between palgebras (see [AC]) and will show that they have good properties. Recall that a total strengthening homomorphism between two palgebras $h: A \rightarrow B$ is a family of total functions $h_s: A_s \rightarrow B_s$ s.t.

- for all Op and $a_1, \ldots, a_n \in A$
  if $Op^A(a_1, \ldots, a_n)$ is defined, then $Op^B(h_{s_1}(a_1), \ldots, h_{s_n}(a_n))$ is defined and
  $h_s(Op^A(a_1, \ldots, a_n)) = Op^B(h_{s_1}(a_1), \ldots, h_{s_n}(a_n))$;
- for all Pr and all $a_1, \ldots, a_n \in A$
  if $Pr^A(a_1, \ldots, a_n)$ holds, then $Pr^B(h_{s_1}(a_1), \ldots, h_{s_n}(a_n))$ holds.

Def. 1.6 Let EA and EA' be two EΣ-algebras; a total strengthening homomorphism between $E\Sigma^E$-palgebras

$h: EA \rightarrow EA'$

is an *entity homomorphism* from EA into EA' (still written $h: EA \rightarrow EA'$). □

It is easy to see that $eAlg_{E\Sigma}$ with the entity homomorphisms forms a category (still denoted by $eAlg_{E\Sigma}$).

Entity homomorphisms in some sense preserve the structure of the entities but can enrich it as prop. 1.7 shows; if a view of the structure of e is graphically represented by

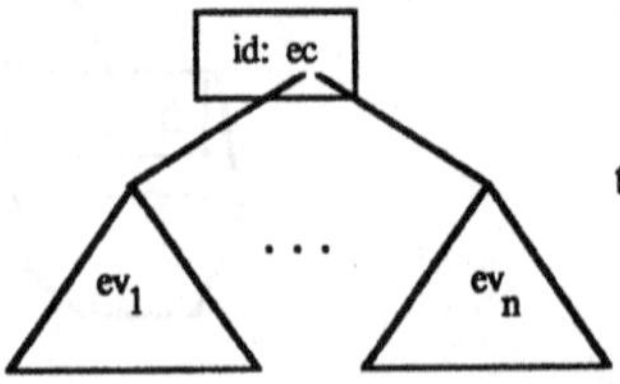

then

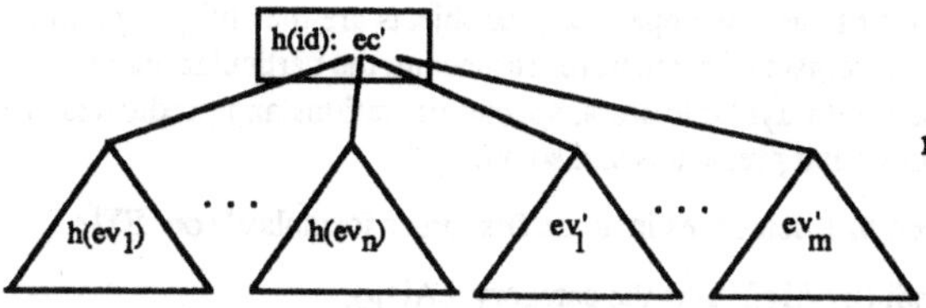

represents a view of the structure of h(e).

Thus, for example,

- if e has only simple views, then h(e) could have a non-simple view;
- if h(e) has only simple views, then e has only simple views.

Prop. 1.7 Assume $h: EA \rightarrow EA'$ and e, e' elements of entity sort in EA, if e' is a subentity of some view for e, then h(e') is a subentity of some view for h(e) (the vice versa does not hold). □

Using entity homomorphisms we can speak of initial elements in a class of entity algebras and the following proposition shows their properties.

Prop. 1.8 Let C be a class of EΣ-algebras and $I \in C$ be initial in C; then

1) $I \models t = t'$ iff ($EA \models t = t'$ for all $EA \in C$) where "=" stands for strong equality;

2) for all predicates Pr of EΣ
   $I \models Pr(t_1, \ldots, t_n)$ iff ($EA \models Pr(t_1, \ldots, t_n)$ for all $EA \in C$), thus in particular
   - $I \models e \xrightarrow{1} e'$ iff ($EA \models e \xrightarrow{1} e'$ for all $EA \in C$)
     in I each entity has in some sense the minimum amount of activity,
   - $I \models D(t)$ iff ($EA \models D(t)$ for all $EA \in C$)
     I is minimally defined;

3) for all terms of entity sort et, et'
   et is a subentity of et' in I iff (et is a subentity of et' in EA for all $EA \in C$). □

Notice that 1) implies that two entity views ev and ev' are equivalent in I, ie. $I \models V(ev) = V(ev')$, iff (they are equivalent in all $EA \in C$).

2 ENTITY SPECIFICATIONS IN THE SMALL

Correspondingly to the model level introduced in the previous section we can define *entity specifications* in the same way as it is done for the usual specifications of abstract data types: a specification is a couple (EΣ, Ax), where Ax is a set of formulas on EΣ and the validity is the usual validity in palgebras; and we have that this framework constitutes an institution (see [GB]).

To such specifications could be given either an initial or a loose semantics; in the first case we give conditions for its existence, while in the latter we show how the usual notion of implementation for abstract data type specifications can be extended to the entity specifications.

2.1 Entity specifications in the small

We define the *institution of entities in the small*

e = (**ESign**, eSen, eAlg, $\overset{e}{\models}$)

where:

- ESign is the category of the entity signatures (see the appendix); its objects are the entity signatures and its morphisms are the subclass of the morphism of psignatures respecting the particular features related to entities (eg, dynamic sorts are sent into dynamic sorts, special operations and predicates are sent into the corresponding special operations and predicates and so on);
- eSen is the sentence functor (see the appendix); sentences in *e* are first order formulas(*) on $E\Sigma^E$;
- eAlg is the algebra functor (see the appendix); eAlg(EΣ) is the category $eAlg_{E\Sigma}$;
- $\overset{e}{\models}$ is the satisfaction relation defined by

  $EA \overset{e}{\models}_{E\Sigma} \vartheta$ iff $EA \overset{P}{\models}_{E\Sigma^E} \vartheta$,

  where $\overset{P}{\models}_\Sigma$ is the satisfaction relation in the institution of palgebras with existential equality, ie,

  $A \overset{P}{\models}_\Sigma t = t'$ iff t^A and t'^A are both defined and equal, thus the formula $t = t$ requires that the interpretation of t must be defined; in the following we will write $D(t)$ instead of $t = t$.

Theorem 2.1 e = (ESign, eSen, eAlg, $\overset{e}{\models}$) is an institution. □

Thus we can define an *entity specification (in the small)* as a couple

ESP = (EΣ, Ax)

where EΣ is an entity signature and $Ax \subseteq eSen(E\Sigma)$; the class of the *models* of ESP, denoted by eMod(ESP), is

$\{ EA \mid EA$ is an $E\Sigma^E$-palgebra and $EA \overset{e}{\models} \vartheta$ for all $\vartheta \in Ax \}$.

To investigate the properties of entity specifications (existence of the initial model, of a sound and complete deductive system and so on), we first note that the class of the models of an entity specification ESP = (EΣ, Ax) is the class of the models of a (partial with predicates) specification $ESP^P = (E\Sigma^E, Ax \cup eAxioms(E\Sigma))$, where

$eAxioms(E\Sigma) = \cup_{s \in Dsorts(E\Sigma)}$

(a) $\{ \exists\, id, x \,.\, e = id{:}\, x,$

(b) $id{:}\, x = id'{:}\, x' \supset id = id' \wedge x = x',$

(c) $id{:}\, x \xrightarrow{l} id'{:}\, x \supset id = id' \mid id, id'{:}\ ident(s),\ l{:}\ lab(s),\ x, x'{:}\ s,\ e{:}\ ent(s) \} \cup$

(d) $\{ D(tid{:}\, tv) \wedge tid' = tid'' \supset tv' = tv'' \mid$
$tid{:}\, tv \in T_{E\Sigma}(X)_{ent(s)},\ tid'{:}\, tv',\ tid''{:}\, tv''$ are subterms of $tid{:}\, tv \}$.

Lemma 2.2 $eMod(ESP) = PMod(ESP^P)$,
where PMod denotes the class of models of a (partial with predicates) specification. □

Partial specifications with predicates whose axioms are (existential) positive conditional formulas have particular nice properties. Recall that a positive conditional formula has form

$\wedge_{1 \le i \le n}\ \alpha_i \supset \alpha,$

where α and α_i for $i = 1, \ldots, n$ are atoms and atoms are formulas of the form either $Pr(t_1, \ldots, t_n)$ with

---

(*) The set of the *first order formulas* on a predicate signature Σ and X (a Sorts(Σ)-sorted family of variables), indicated by $F_\Sigma(X)$, is inductively defined as follows:

- $t = t' \in F_\Sigma(X)$ for all $t, t' \in (T_\Sigma(X))_s$, $s \in Sorts(\Sigma)$;
- $Pr(t_1, \ldots, t_n) \in F_\Sigma(X)$ for all $Pr{:}\ s_1 \times \ldots \times s_n \in Preds(\Sigma)$, $t_i \in (T_\Sigma(X))_{s_i}$ $i = 1, \ldots, n$;
- if $\vartheta, \vartheta' \in F_\Sigma(X)$ and $x \in X$, then $\neg \vartheta$, $\vartheta \supset \vartheta'$, $\exists x \,.\, \vartheta \in F_\Sigma(X)$;
- if for all $i = 1, \ldots, n$ $\vartheta_i \in F_\Sigma(X)$, then $\wedge_{i = 1, \ldots, n} \vartheta_i \in F_\Sigma(X)$.

Morover, $t \ne t'$, $\forall x \,.\, \vartheta$, $\vee_{i \in I} \vartheta_i$, $\exists! x \,.\, \vartheta$, $\vartheta \equiv \vartheta'$ are defined as abbreviations as usual.

Pr predicate or $t = t'$. In particular for such specifications there exist the initial model and a deductive system which is sound a complete w.r.t. the class of the models. If the signature of the specification Σ is such that $(T_\Sigma)_s \neq \emptyset$ for all sorts s, this system can be obtained, as in [C], by considering a system which is sound and complete for the total case and modifying it as follows: suppress reflexivity of equality; allow substitution of t for x only when t is defined (rule SUB below); add rules to assert that operations and predicates are strict (rules STRICT below).

Such system is given by the following rules, where D(t) stands for $t = t$:

$$\frac{t = t'}{t' = t} \qquad \frac{t = t' \quad t' = t''}{t = t''}$$

$$\frac{D(Op(t_1, \ldots, t_n)) \qquad t_i = t_i' \ (i = 1, \ldots, n)}{Op(t_1, \ldots, t_n) = Op(t_1', \ldots, t_n')}$$

$$\frac{Pr(t_1, \ldots, t_n) \qquad t_i = t_i' \ (i = 1, \ldots, n)}{Pr(t_1', \ldots, t_n')}$$

$$\frac{(\wedge_{i = 1, \ldots, n}\, \vartheta_i) \supset \vartheta \qquad \vartheta_i \ (i = 1, \ldots, n)}{\vartheta}$$

(STRICT) $$\frac{D(Op(t_1, \ldots, t_n))}{D(t_i)} \qquad \frac{Pr(t_1, \ldots, t_n)}{D(t_i)}$$

(SUB) $$\frac{\vartheta[x] \quad D(t)}{\vartheta[t]}.$$

In the following we write $SP \vdash \vartheta$, if ϑ can be proved in the above system starting from the axioms of SP.

Theorem 2.3 Let $ESP = (E\Sigma, Ax)$ be an entity specification such that

0) for all sorts s $(T_{E\Sigma})_s \neq \emptyset$,

1) Ax is a set of positive conditional formulas,

2) for all $te \in (T_{E\Sigma})_{ent(s)}$ s.t. $ESP \vdash D(te)$
there exist $tid \in (T_{E\Sigma})_{ident(s)}$, $tv \in (T_{E\Sigma})_s$ s.t. $ESP \vdash te = tid\text{: } tv$,

then:

i) $ESP^P \vdash \alpha$ iff ($EA \models \alpha$ for all $EA \in eMod(ESP)$) for all atoms α;

ii) there exists the initial element of eMod(ESP), denoted by I_{ESP};

iii) $I_{ESP} \models \alpha$ iff $ESP^P \vdash \alpha$ for all atoms α. □

2.2 Some Examples

2.2.1 A specification of a class of objects

We give a specification describing an object-oriented version of the data type consisting of queues of integers; precisely we give a specification of a class queue whose objects are queues of objects of class int (just integers).

Let INT be the specification of a class of objects corresponding to integers with the entity sort ent(int) and we assume that each entity of sort ent(int) is simple.

The specification SPQ corresponding to the class queue is

enrich INT **by**
dsorts queue
opns
Empty: → queue (total)
Get: queue → ident(int)
Remove: ent(queue) → ent(queue)
Put: ent(int) × queue → queue
Γ, Ψ, ... : → ident(queue) (total)
* _ . Empty: ident(queue) → lab(queue) (total)
* _ = _ . Get: ident(int) × ident(queue) → lab(queue) (total)
* _ . Remove: ident(queue) → lab(queue) (total)
* _ . Put(_): ident(queue) × ent(int) → lab(queue) (total)
* Queue : lab(int) → lab(queue)
– defines the labels corresponding to sending a method to a subcomponent of class int
preds
_ Diff _ : ident(queue) × ident(queue)
Unused: queue × ident(int)
-- checks whether a queue has not an integer component with a certain identity
axioms
0 Γ Diff Ψ ...

1 Get(Put(id: i, Empty)) = id
2 D(Get(q)) ⊃ Get(Put(ei, q)) = Get(q)

3 Remove(id: Put(ei, Empty)) = id: Empty
4 Remove(id: q) = id: q' ⊃ Remove(id: Put(ei, q)) = id; Put(ei, q')

5 Unused(id, Empty)
6 id Diff id' ∧ Unused(id, q) ⊃ Unused(id, Put(id': i, q))

7 Unused(id, q) ⊃ D(Put(id: i, q))

-- sending a method to an element of class queue

8 id: q $\xrightarrow{\text{id . Empty}}$ id: Empty
9 D(Put(ei, q)) ⊃ id: q $\xrightarrow{\text{id . Put(ei)}}$ id: Put(ei, q)
10 D(Remove(id: q)) ⊃ id: q $\xrightarrow{\text{id . Remove}}$ Remove(id: q)
11 Get(q) = id' ⊃ id: q $\xrightarrow{\text{id' = id . Get}}$ id: q

-- sending a method to a subcomponent of class int

12 ei $\xrightarrow{1}$ ei' ⊃ id: Put(ei, q) $\xrightarrow{\text{Queue(l)}}$ id: Put(ei', q)
13 id: q $\xrightarrow{\text{Queue(l)}}$ id: q' ⊃ id: Put(ei, q) $\xrightarrow{\text{Queue(l)}}$ id: Put(ei, q')

In this specification we have that:

- the sort ent(queue) corresponds to the class queue;
- the entities of sort ent(queue) represent the objects of the class queue;
- the operations having either as result and/or as argument the sorts queue and ent(queue) (Empty, Put, Remove and Get) correspond to the methods of the class queue (Get, whose result sort is different from queue and ent(queue), corresponds to a method returning some result);
- the activity of the entities of sort ent(queue) is the result of the application of some methods, thus their transitions are labelled by message sendings (method applications in object-oriented jargon) defined by the operations marked with *.

Notice how in this specification the structure and the methods of the class queue have been abstractly specified. Since Empty and Put are the only operations of sort queue we have that each object of class queue has n ($n \geq 0$) subcomponent objects of class int arranged in a row. Axiom 7 requires that no object of class int may appear in two different places in the same queue. Axioms 1, ..., 4 say that the methods Get and Remove respectively returns an identification of and removes the last element of the row.

Axioms 8, ..., 11 describe the dynamic effects of the method applications; while axioms 12 and 13 describe the application of a method of the class int to some subcomponent.

2.2.2 Non-lazy processes with handshaking communications

Here we give the specification NLP (for Non-Lazy Process) of the concurrent systems with exactly the following properties:

- the active components of the systems are processes of "the same kind" and there are no "passive components";
- each component process is identified by a unique name;
- the component processes exchange messages (not further specified) between them in a handshaking way and that is the only kind of interaction between the processes; moreover each process sending a message states the name of receivers, analogously a process receiving a message states the name of the senders;
- there are no mutual exclusion requirements on the process actions (ie, whatever number of processes can perform internal actions and whatever number of disjoint couples of processes can exchange messages between them simultaneously);
- no component process can be lazy;
- processes can neither be created nor terminate.

Note that here we are abstractly specifying handshaking and nonlaziness, not just giving a particular system having such properties.

PROC =
sorts message
dsorts process
opns Tau: $\rightarrow$ lab(process)
SEND, REC: ident(process) $\times$ ident(process) $\times$ message $\rightarrow$ lab(process)
axioms
$ep \xrightarrow{l} ep' \supset l = Tau \vee (\exists\, pi, pi', m \,.\, l = SEND(pi, pi', m) \vee l = REC(pi, pi', m))$

The sort message is static, its element are usually values; while process is a dynamic sort, its elements are the cores of the dynamic elements corresponding to the process components of the systems.

NLP =
enrich PROC **by**
dsorts system
opns $\emptyset$: $\rightarrow$ system
_ : ent(process) $\rightarrow$ system
_ | _ : system $\times$ system $\rightarrow$ system (comm., assoc.)
Tau : $\rightarrow$ lab(system)
preds _ $\Longrightarrow$ _ : system $\times$ system
-- auxiliary predicate used for defining the properties of the transitions of the entities of sort system
axioms

1) $D(id{:}\ s) \supset (\exists\, ep \,.\, s = ep) \vee (\exists\, s_1, s_2 \,.\, D(id{:}\ s_1) \wedge D(id{:}\ s_2) \wedge s = s_1 \mid s_2)$
2) $ep \xrightarrow{Tau} ep' \supset ep \Longrightarrow ep'$
3) $ep_1 \xrightarrow{SEND(pi, pi', m)} ep_1' \wedge ep_2 \xrightarrow{REC(pi', pi, m)} ep_2' \supset ep_1 \mid ep_2 \Longrightarrow ep_1' \mid ep_2'$
4) $s_1 \Longrightarrow s_1' \wedge s_2 \Longrightarrow s_2' \supset s_1 \mid s_2 \Longrightarrow s_1' \mid s_2'$
5) $si{:}\ s \xrightarrow{l} si{:}\ s' \supset$
5.1) $l = Tau \wedge$
5.2) $\exists\, s_1, s_2, s_1' \,.\, (s = s_1 \mid s_2 \wedge s_1 \Longrightarrow s_1' \wedge s' = s_1' \mid s_2 \wedge$
5.3) $\nexists\, s_3, s_3', s_4 \,.\, s_2 = s_3 \mid s_4 \wedge s_3 \Longrightarrow s_3')$

Axiom 1) requires that the only subcomponents of the system states are processes specified by PROC arranged in parallel by the "|" operator; that means, for example, that a model of this specification cannot have either additional processes or buffers to handle the communications between the component processes.

Axioms 2), 3) and 4) define the auxiliary predicate ==>, which describes partial moves of groups of processes (combinations of internal actions and of handshaking communications).

Axiom 5) requires that:

- the whole system is closed (5.1);
- the only transitions of the system are caused by a combination of process internal actions and process communications (5.2), thus processes can interact between them only by exchanging messages in a handshaking way;
- no process can idle (5.3);

but note that these axioms do not specify what is the policy to be followed when some conflict arises; thus this specification admits models where the conflicts are solved by allowing nondeterministically all the possible choices, by using priorities associated with the processes and so on. Moreover axiom 5) also requires that a process can neither be created nor terminate.

The structure of the entities of sort system can be graphically represented by:

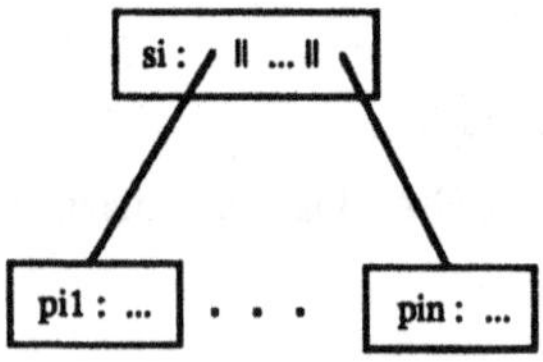

2.3 Implementation of Entity Specifications

Here we try to extend to the case of entity specifications the well-known general notion of implementation for algebraic specifications of Wirsing (see [W]); we have chosen this notion since it has been proved well adequate in the case of usual specifications.

For Wirsing a specification SP *is implemented by another specification* SP_1 *via* f, where f is a function from specifications into specifications built by composing specification operations (as enrich, rename, export, hide and so on) iff

$$Mod(f(SP_1)) \subseteq Mod(SP).$$

The function f describes how the elements of the sorts, the operations and the predicates of SP can be obtained from those of SP_1; while requiring the inclusion of the classes of models instead of the coincidence allows SP_1 to be a "refinement" of SP, ie, "things" not specified in SP are made more precise in SP_1.

This notion is very general but it includes as particular cases (ie, when f has a particular form) the various notions presented in the literature as implementation by rename-forget-restrict-identify or implementation by behavioural abstraction (see [W]).

Def. 2.4 Let ESP = $(E\Sigma, Ax)$ and $ESP_1 = (E\Sigma_1, Ax_1)$ be two entity specifications and f a function from specifications with signature $E\Sigma$ into specifications with signature $E\Sigma_1$ built by composing specification operations.

ESP *is implemented by* ESP_1 *via* f (written ESP $\rightsquigarrow^f ESP_1$) iff $EMod(f(ESP_1)) \subseteq EMod(ESP)$. □

As examples we give two implementations of the entity specification NLP defined in sect. 2.2.2.

First we give a specification SYSTEM describing a particular concurrent calculus similar to Milner's SCCS having all the properties required by the specification NLP. In SYSTEM the elements of the static sort message and of the dynamic sort process (the cores of the system components) are completely defined (specifications CHAN and BEH); moreover the proper axioms of SYSTEM precisely define the activity of the systems.

CHAN = **sorts** chan
opns Alpha, Beta, ... : $\to$ chan (total)

BEH =
enrich CHAN **by**
dsorts beh
opns SEND, REC: ident(beh) $\times$ ident(beh) $\times$ chan $\to$ lab(beh)
Tau: $\to$ lab(beh)
Nil: $\to$ beh
_?_ . _, _!_ . _: chan $\times$ ident(beh) $\times$ beh $\to$ beh
_+_: beh $\times$ beh $\to$ beh (comm., assoc.)
δ _: beh $\to$ beh

axioms

$$bi': ch\ !\ bi\ .\ b \xrightarrow{SEND(bi',\ bi,\ ch)} bi': b$$

$$bi': ch\ ?\ bi\ .\ b \xrightarrow{REC(bi',\ bi,\ ch)} bi': b$$

$$bi: b_1 \xrightarrow{l} bi: b_1' \supset bi: b_1 + b_2 \xrightarrow{l} bi: b_1'$$

$$bi: \delta\, b \xrightarrow{Tau} bi: \delta\, b$$

$$bi: b \xrightarrow{l} bi: b' \supset bi: \delta\, b \xrightarrow{l} bi: b'$$

SYSTEM =
enrich BEH **by**
dsorts system
opns
$\emptyset$: $\to$ system
_ : ent(beh) $\to$ system
_ | _ : system $\times$ system $\to$ system (comm., assoc.)
Tau : $\to$ lab(system)

axioms

$$eb \xrightarrow{Tau} eb' \supset si: eb \xRightarrow{Tau} si: eb'$$

$$eb_1 \xrightarrow{SEND(ch,\ bi,\ bi')} eb_1' \wedge eb_2 \xrightarrow{REC(ch,\ bi',\ bi)} eb_2' \supset si: eb_1 \mid eb_2 \xRightarrow{Tau} si: eb_1' \mid eb_2'$$

$$si: eb_1 \xRightarrow{Tau} si: eb_1' \wedge si: eb_2 \xrightarrow{Tau} si: eb_2' \supset si: eb_1 \mid eb_2 \xRightarrow{Tau} si: eb_1' \mid eb_2'$$

SYSTEM is an implementation of NLP, indeed changing the sort names chan, beh into message, process, hiding the operations Alpha, Beta, ..., Nil, ?, ! , +, δ and defining the auxiliary predicate $\Longrightarrow$ we get a new specification, whose models are included into the models of NLP. Formally NLP $\leadsto^f$ SYSTEM, where

f = λ X . **hide** { Alpha, Beta, ..., Nil, !, ?, +, δ } **in**
enrich X[process/beh, message/chan] **by**
preds _ $\Longrightarrow$ _: system $\times$ system
axioms

$$si: es \xRightarrow{l} si: es' \supset es \Longrightarrow es'$$

The notion of implementation of def. 2.4 allows also that simple entities are implemented by structured entities having several dynamic subcomponents, as it is shown by specifications as NLP2, given below, where the entities of type process are implemented by groups of other entities interacting between them.

NLP2 = **enrich** NLP **by**
dsorts agent
opns _: ent(agent) $\to$ process
_ ||| _: ent(agent) $\times$ process $\to$ process
axioms ...

In this case NLP $\leadsto^f$ NLP2, where f is just the hiding of the dynamic sort agent and the operation |||.

The structure of the entities of sort system in NLP2 is graphically represented by:

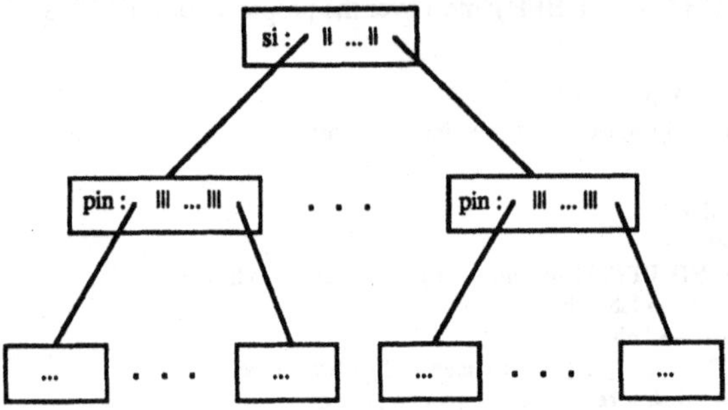

3 FURTHER DEVELOPMENTS: ENTITY SPECIFICATIONS IN THE LARGE

Entity specifications in the small allow us to do a lot of things: for example we can formally represent object-systems where subcomponents are shared, specify concurrent systems by giving very abstract properties about their activity and so long; but they do not allow us to write down specifications whose axioms only require some very abstract properties about the structure of the entities but do not completely describe such structure; ie, we do not want to fix which are the operations for composing entities together and give their properties (as we have done in NLP), but just require some properties of the resulting structure.

This point is very important for keeping the level of the specifications very abstract.

Consider the following paradigmatic situations: we want to give an entity specification requiring one of the following conditions:

i) each entity of sort s is simple, ie, it has not entity subcomponents (eg, each process of type s is sequential, each object of type s has no object attributes);

ii) each entity of sort s has exactly two simple subentities (eg, each process of type s consists of the parallel composition of two sequential processes);

iii) each entity of sort s has either a subentity satisfying P or a subentity satisfying Q (P and Q predicates) but not both (eg, each process of type s has either a subcomponent which is a printer or a modem but not both);

but we do not want to completely describe the entities of sort s.

Situations of this kind can arise when we want to give only very abstract properties of some dynamic system without fully defining its structure. Think, for example, of giving the requirements for a net of personal computers just saying how many people must be able to work simultaneously and how many resources they may have, without specifying anything about the use of servers, bridges and so on; or also of specifying the firing squad problem (see [DHJW]).

To solve this problem we can define a new kind of entity specifications, called *entity specifications in the large*, whose axioms allow to express properties on the dynamic structure of the entities without fully describing such structure.

The idea is to introduce some special predicates "_ Are-Sub _" for checking which are the subcomponents of the entities; these predicates, given a set of entities es and an entity e of a certain sort, return true iff es is the set of all subentities (proper and not) of e w.r.t. some view.

Using these predicates the properties i), ii) and iii) may be formalized by the following formulas.

i) es Are-Sub e $\supset$ es = { e }

ii) es Are-Sub e $\supset \exists e_1, e_2 \,.\, e_1 \neq e_2 \neq e \wedge es = \{ e_1, e_2, e \}$

iii) es Are-Sub e $\supset \exists e' \,.\, e' \in es \wedge e \neq e' \wedge (P(e') \vee Q(e')) \wedge \neg (P(e') \wedge Q(e'))$

The axioms of these new entity specifications are the first order formulas on a new signature $E\Sigma^{ST}$, obtained by enriching $E\Sigma$. The validity of one of these new formulas, say ϑ, in an $E\Sigma$-entity algebra EA is defined as the validity of ϑ in a particular $E\Sigma^{ST}$-palgebra, EA^{ST}, which is an extension of EA:

$$EA \overset{E}{\models}_{E\Sigma} \vartheta \text{ iff } EA^{ST} \overset{P}{\models}_{E\Sigma^{ST}} \vartheta.$$

Also for entity specifications in the large it is possible give a corresponding institution

$$\mathbf{E} = (\mathbf{ESign}, \text{ESen}, \text{EAlg}, \overset{E}{\models})$$

where **ESign** is defined in the appendix, $\text{ESen}(E\Sigma) = \text{eSen}(E\Sigma^{ST})$ and

$$\text{EAlg}(E\Sigma) = \{ EA \mid EA \text{ is an } E\Sigma'\text{-algebra for some } E\Sigma' \text{ s.t. } E\Sigma \subseteq E\Sigma' \}$$

Here for lack of room we cannot further justify the definition of EAlg and prove that $\mathbf{E}$ is truly an institution (see [AR2] for a full treatment).

APPENDIX

The Category of Entity Signatures

Def. A.1 Given an entity signature $E\Sigma$, $s \in \text{Sorts}(E\Sigma^E)$ is *entity-reaching* iff for some dynamic sort s' there exists a term t of sort ent(s') having a subterm of sort s. □

Def. A.2 Given two entity signatures $E\Sigma$ and $E\Sigma'$, an *entity signature morphism* ϕ is a psignature morphism (see [AC]) $\phi: E\Sigma^E \to E\Sigma'^E$ such that:

a1) $\phi(\text{Dsorts}(E\Sigma)) = \text{Dsorts}(E\Sigma')$;

a2) for all $s \in \text{Dsorts}(E\Sigma)$
$\phi(\text{ent}(s)) = \text{ent}(\phi(s))$,
$\phi(\text{lab}(s)) = \text{lab}(\phi(s))$,
$\phi(\text{ident}(s)) = \text{ident}(\phi(s))$,
$\phi(\_ : \_ : \text{ident}(s) \times s \to \text{ent}(s)) = \_ : \_ : \text{ident}(\phi(s)) \times \phi(s) \to \text{ent}(\phi(s))$,
$\phi(\_ \xrightarrow{\ \_\ } \_ : \text{ent}(s) \times \text{lab}(s) \times \text{ent}(s)) = \_ \xrightarrow{\ \_\ } \_ : \text{ent}(\phi(s)) \times \text{lab}(\phi(s)) \times \text{ent}(\phi(s))$;

a3) for all $s' \in \text{Dsorts}(E\Sigma')$
$\phi^{-1}(\{ \text{ent}(s') \})$(*) $= \{ \text{ent}(s) \mid s \in \phi^{-1}(\{ s' \}) \}$,
$\phi^{-1}(\{ \text{lab}(s') \}) = \{ \text{lab}(s) \mid s \in \phi^{-1}(\{ s' \}) \}$,
$\phi^{-1}(\{ \text{ident}(s') \}) = \{ \text{ident}(s) \mid s \in \phi^{-1}(\{ s' \}) \}$,
$\phi^{-1}(\{ \_ : \_ : \text{ident}(s') \times s' \to \text{ent}(s') \}) = \{ \_ : \_ : \text{ident}(s) \times s \to \text{ent}(s) \mid s \in \phi^{-1}(\{ s' \}) \}$,
$\phi^{-1}(\{ \_ \xrightarrow{\ \_\ } \_ : \text{ent}(s') \times \text{lab}(s') \times \text{ent}(s') \}) =$
$\{ \_ \xrightarrow{\ \_\ } \_ : \text{ent}(s) \times \text{lab}(s) \times \text{ent}(s) \mid s \in \phi^{-1}(\{ s' \}) \}$;

a4) $\phi^{-1}(\{ Op \}) \neq \emptyset$
for all $Op: s_1 \times \ldots \times s_n \to s \in \text{Opns}(E\Sigma^E)$ with s entity-reaching. □

Conditions a2 and a3 require that ϕ sends the special elements of $E\Sigma$ into the corresponding special elements of $E\Sigma'$; while a1 (a4) requires that all dynamic sorts (dynamic operations, ie those which build the entity composers) of $E\Sigma'$ are image w.r.t. ϕ of some dynamic sort (dynamic operation) of $E\Sigma$.

(*) If $f: A \to B$ is a function, then f^{-1} indicates the function from $\mathcal{P}(B)$ into $\mathcal{P}(A)$ defined by $f^{-1}(\mathcal{B}) = \{ a \mid f(a) \in \mathcal{B} \}$.

If there exists an entity signature morphism $\phi: E\Sigma_1 \to E\Sigma_2$, then in some sense $E\Sigma_1$ and $E\Sigma_2$ may be used to describe dynamic systems with a similar structure.

Fact A.3 Entity signatures and entity signature morphisms form a category denoted by **ESign**. □

The Institution of Entity Algebras in the Small e

e = (**ESign**, eSen, eAlg, $\overset{e}{\models}$)

We recall that P = (**PSign**, PSen, PAlg, $\overset{P}{\models}$) is the institution of palgebras with first order formulas (see [AC]).

- **The signature category**

  ESign is given above.

- **The sentence functor**

  eSen: **ESign** $\to$ **Set**

is the functor defined by:
- on objects: $\text{eSen}(E\Sigma) = \text{PSen}(E\Sigma^E)$;
- on morphisms: $\text{eSen}(\phi: E\Sigma \to E\Sigma') = \text{PSen}(\phi: E\Sigma^E \to E\Sigma'^E)$;

it is trivial to see that eSen is a functor.

- **The algebras functor**

  eAlg: **ESign** $\to$ **Cat**^{OP}

is the functor defined by:

- on objects: $\text{eAlg}(E\Sigma) = \text{eAlg}_{E\Sigma}$ ($\text{eAlg}_{E\Sigma}$ is a category, see fact 1.10);
- on morphisms: $\text{eAlg}(\phi: E\Sigma \to E\Sigma')$ is the restriction of $\text{PAlg}(\phi: E\Sigma^E \to E\Sigma'^E)$ to $\text{eAlg}_{E\Sigma'}$.

Fact A.4 ensures that PAlg(ϕ)(EA) is an EΣ-algebra; moreover, since entity homomorphisms (in the small) are just phomomorphisms and PAlg is a functor, it is easy to see that eAlg is a functor.

Fact A.4 PAlg(ϕ)(EA) is an EΣ-algebra. □

- **The satisfaction relation**

For all entity signatures EΣ, $\overset{e}{\models}_{E\Sigma} \subseteq |\text{eAlg}(E\Sigma)| \times \text{eSen}(E\Sigma)$ is defined by

$EA \overset{e}{\models}_{E\Sigma} \vartheta$ iff $EA \overset{P}{\models}_{E\Sigma^E} \vartheta$.

Acknowledgement. This paper grew out of some common work with Prof. E. Astesiano on further developments of the SMoLCS approach. I wish to thank him for constant inspiration and encouragement.

REFERENCES

[AC] Astesiano E.; Cerioli M. "Commuting between Institutions via Simulation", Internal Report Dipartimento di Matematica Università di Genova n. 5, June 1990.

[AGR] Astesiano, E.; Giovini, A.; Reggio, G. "Data in a concurrent environment", in (Vogt, F. ed.) *Proc Concurrency '88 (International Conference on Concurrency, Hamburg, FRG October 1988)*, Berlin, Springer Verlag, 1988 (Lecture Notes in Computer Science n.335), pp. 140-159.

[AR] Astesiano, E.; Reggio, G. "An Outline of the SMoLCS Methodology", (Venturini Zilli, M. ed.) *Mathematical Models for the Semantics of Parallelism, Proc. Advanced School on Mathematical Models of Parallelism*, Berlin, Springer Verlag, 1987 (Lecture Notes in Computer Science n. 280), pp. 81-113.

[AR1] Astesiano, E.; Reggio, G. "SMoLCS-Driven Concurrent Calculi", *Proc. TAPSOFT'87*, vol.1, Berlin, Springer Verlag, 1987 (Lecture Notes in Computer Science n. 249), pp. 169–201.

[AR2] Astesiano, E.; Reggio G. *Entity Institutions: Frameworks for Dynamic Systems*, in preparation.

[BW] Broy, M.; Wirsing, M. "Partial abstract data types", *Acta Informatica* 18 (1982), 47-64.

[BZ] Breu, R.; Zucca, E. "An algebraic compositional semantics of an object-oriented notation with concurrency", in (Veni Madhavan, C. E. ed.) *Foundations of Software Technology and Theoretical Computer Science (Proc. of the Ninth conference, Bangalore, India)*, 1989, Berlin, Springer Verlag, (Lecture Notes in Computer Science n. 405).

[C] Cerioli M. "A sound and equationally-complete deduction system for partial conditional (higher order) types" Proc. 3rd Italian Conf. on Theoretical Comp. Sci. Mantova 1989, World Scientific Pub. pp 164 - 175.

[DHJW] Denvir B.T.; Harwood W. T.; Jackson M.I.; Wray M.J. *Proc. of the Workshop on The Analysis of Concurrent Systems, Cambridge, 1983*, Berlin, Springer Verlag, 1985 (Lecture Notes in Computer Science n. 207).

[Dragon] Astesiano E.; Breu R. Hennicker R.: Reggio G.; Wirsing M.; Zucca E. *A Theory of Reuse and its Applications to Object Oriented Environments*, Deliverable of the DRAGON project, June 1990.

[GB] Goguen J.A.; Burstall R. M. "Introducing Institutions", *Logics of Programming*, Berlin, Springer Verlag, 1983 (Lecture Notes in Computer Science n. 164).

[GM] Goguen, J.A.; Meseguer, J. "Models and Equality for Logical Programming", *Proc. TAPSOFT'87*, vol.2, Berlin, Springer Verlag, 1987 (Lecture Notes in Computer Science n. 249), pp. 1-22.

[M] Meseguer J. *Rewriting as a Unified Model of Concurrency*, draft, 1990.

[FB] Fiadeiro J.; Maibaum T. "Describing, Structuring and Implementing Objects", Draft, presented at the REX School/Workshop on Foundations of Object-Oriented Languages, May, 1990.

[W] Wirsing M. "Algebraic Specifications", *Handbook of Theoretical Computer Science, Vol. B*, North-Holland, 1990.

A 2–Category Approach to Critical Pair Completion

Horst Reichel
Fakultät für Informatik
Institut für Theoretische Informatik
TU Dresden, Mommsenstr. 13, Dresden, O-8027

1 Introduction

In 1987 B.Buchberger introduced a *Critical Pair Completion Algorithm Schema* which unifies the Resolution Procedure of Robinson, the algorithm for polynomial ideals, i.e. the Buchberger Algorithm, and the Knuth–Bendix Algorithm. This unification was done in an informal way. In the same year D. Rydeheard and J.G. Stell, see [RS 87], developed a categorical treatment of euqational proofs and unification algorithms, based on 2-categories. Thus, the question arises wether the categorical framework of 2–categories can also be used to deal with the critical pair completion procedure. In the following we will show that ordered 2–categories with products form a suitable formal framework and that one can give the informal unification of Buchberger a formal setting. This can ruther easily be done and so this paper is more or less only an exercise in applying the framework of 2-categories.

It is worth to mention that recently 2–categories have been comming in use for different purposes in theoretical computer science. A.J. Power uses 2–categories as an abstract formulation for rewrite systems, see [Po 89], E. Moggi investigates program modules within the formal framework of 2-categories, see [Mo 89]. In [Se 87] a 2–categorical approach for modelling computations is suggested. But, also in pure category theory 2–categories are subject of increasing interest, see for instance the investigation on accessible categories by M. Makkai and R.Paré in [MP 89]. By the following illustrative application of 2–categories to the critical pair completion we hope to support the increasing interest in the formal framework of 2–categories.

2 Basic concepts and notions of 2–categories

In 2-categories three kinds of objects are distinguished which will be called *0–cells, 1–cells,* and *2–cells* respectively.

The most familiar example of a 2–category in pure category theory is the category of small categories, where small categories form the 0–cells, functors between small categories form the 1–cells, and natural transformations between functors finally form the 2–cells. From point of view of equational logic 0–cells may be interpreted as types, atomic types or Cartesian products of atomic types, 1–cells may be interpreted as terms or more generally as substitutions of free variables by terms, and 2–cells correspond to directed equations, i.e. rewrite rules. This interpretation is the conceptual backgound of D.Rydeheard and J.G.Stell and also of the present paper.

For a detailed introduction into the formal framework of 2–categories the reader is referred to [RS 87] or [Po 89]. We will use the following typograpical representations:

- 0–cells: A
- 1–cells: $f : A \longrightarrow B$
- 2–cells: $\alpha : f \Longrightarrow g : A \longrightarrow B$

The 0–cells together with the 1–cells form a usual category with respect to the ***horizontal composition*** of 1–cells which will be denoted by the infix binary operation symbol $\circ$:

$f : A \longrightarrow B, g : B \longrightarrow C$ give rise to the horizontal product of 1–cells $g \circ f : A \longrightarrow B$.

In the two examples above the horizontal composition corresponds to the composition of functors and substitutions respectively. Beside the horizontal composition of 1–cells for any two 0–cells A, B one gets a category where the 1–cells $f : A \longrightarrow B$ form the objects and where the ***vertical composition*** of 2-cells forms the partial binary multiplication:

$$\alpha : f \Longrightarrow g : A \longrightarrow B \text{ and } \beta : g \Longrightarrow h : A \longrightarrow B$$

give rise to the vertical product of 2–cells

$$\alpha \oplus \beta : f \Longrightarrow h : A \longrightarrow B.$$

In the two examples the vertical composition corresponds to the compostion of natural transformations and to the composition of rewrite rules.

Both compositions are associative and have left and right units denoted by $id(A)$, $id(B)$, and $id(f)$, $id(g)$ respectively.

The horizontal composition can be extended to the compostion of 1–cells and 2–cells:

$$f : A \longrightarrow B, \quad \alpha : g \Longrightarrow h : B \longrightarrow C, \quad j : C \longrightarrow D$$

gives rise to the following horizontal products of 1–cells and 2–cells:

$$\begin{aligned} \alpha \circ f : g \circ f &\Longrightarrow h \circ f : A \longrightarrow C \\ j \circ \alpha : j \circ g &\Longrightarrow j \circ h : B \longrightarrow D \\ j \circ (\alpha \circ f) = (j \circ \alpha) \circ f : j \circ g \circ f &\Longrightarrow j \circ h \circ f : A \longrightarrow B \end{aligned}$$

The last product is an example of a ***whisker*** introduced by A.J.Power using whiskers as conceptual units for a calculus of computation within 2–categories.

Finally there is a *horizontal composition of 2-cells*:

$$\alpha : f_1 \Longrightarrow g_1 : A \longrightarrow B, \quad \beta : f_2 \Longrightarrow g_2 : B \longrightarrow C$$
$$\text{give rise to} \quad \beta \circ \alpha : f_2 \circ f_1 \Longrightarrow g_2 \circ g_1 : A \longrightarrow C.$$

The horizontal composition of 2-cells can be expressed by the vertical composition of whiskers:

$$\beta \circ \alpha = (\beta \circ f_1) \oplus (g_2 \circ \alpha) = (f_2 \circ \alpha) \oplus (\beta \circ g_1).$$

An important property relating vertical and horizontal composition of 2-cells is the *interchange law*:

$$(\beta_1 \circ \alpha_1) \oplus (\beta_2 \circ \alpha_2) = (\beta_1 \oplus \beta_2) \circ (\alpha_1 \oplus \alpha_2)$$

where

$$\alpha_1 : f_1 \Longrightarrow f_2 : A \longrightarrow B,$$
$$\alpha_2 : f_2 \Longrightarrow f_3 : A \longrightarrow B,$$
$$\beta_1 : g_1 \Longrightarrow g_2 : B \longrightarrow C,$$
$$\beta_2 : g_2 \Longrightarrow g_3 : B \longrightarrow C$$

is assumed.

3 Ordered 2–Categories with Products

To deal with equational logic one needs categories with additional structure. It was F.W.Lawvere, see [La 63], who characterized algebraic theories as categories with products. Therefore, it is not surprising that we will need 2–categories with products.

3.1.Definition: We speak of a *2–category with products* if

1. for any 0–cells A, B there is a 0–cell $A \times B$ and there are 1–cells $fst_{A,B} : A \times B \longrightarrow A$, $scd_{A,B} : A \times B \longrightarrow B$;

2. for any two 1–cells $f : C \longrightarrow A$, $g : C \longrightarrow B$ there is exactly one 1–cell $\langle f, g\rangle : C \longrightarrow A \times B$ with $fst_{A,B} \circ \langle f, g\rangle = f$ and $scd_{A,B} \circ \langle f, g\rangle = g$; and $\langle f, g\rangle \circ h = \langle f \circ h, g \circ h\rangle$ for each $h : D \longrightarrow C$;

3. For any two 2–cells $\alpha_1 : f_1 \Longrightarrow g_1 : C \longrightarrow A$, $\alpha_2 : f_2 \Longrightarrow g_2 : C \longrightarrow B$ there is exactly one 2–cell $\langle \alpha_1, \alpha_2\rangle : \langle f_1, f_2\rangle \Longrightarrow \langle g_1, g_2\rangle : C \longrightarrow A \times B$ with $fst_{A,B} \circ \langle \alpha_1, \alpha_2\rangle = \alpha_1$, $scd_{A,B} \circ \langle \alpha_1, \alpha_2\rangle = \alpha_2$ and $\langle \alpha_1, \alpha_2\rangle \circ h = \langle \alpha_1 \circ h, \alpha_2 \circ h\rangle$ for each $h : D \longrightarrow C$;

4. The category of 0–cells and 1–cells has a terminal object.♠

We will illustrate the introduced notion by means of the theory of groups. In the framework of 2–categories an algebraic theory is a freely generated 2–category with products. The different kinds of elements, basic types or sorts, correspond to the freely generating

0–cells (in case of group theory there is only one sort), the basic operations correspond to the freely generating 1–cells, and the required equations correspond with a choosen direction to the freely generating 2–cells. Models of algebraic theories are now product preserving 2–functors. If we choose the category of sets as the domain of functorial interpretation, where we understand this ordinary category as a 'discrete 2–category', which means that beside unites there are no other 2–cells, then any two 1–cells connected by a 2–cell have to be interpreted identically in each model. In contrast to the framework of algebraic theories in the sense of Lawvere we have now within theories an explicit presentation of equations. Thus, the choosen domain of functorial interpretation , which has now to be a 2–category, gives a semantic interpretation to directed equations, which constitute the 2–cells of the algebraraic theory.

In order to improve the readability we will use a notation which is oriented on 2–categories with finite products and not only with binary products as defined above. Additionally, we use a homogenious theory, so that there is only one freely generating 0–cell, which will be denoted by 1, an n-fold product of 1 will be denoted by n, and the i-th projection by $x_i^n : n \longrightarrow 1$. Thus, the projection x_1^1 coincides with the identity of the 0-cell 1.

With this conventions the algebraic theory of groups is given by the following freely generating 0–cells, 1–cells and 2–cells:

0–cells: 1 ,
1–cells: $e : 0 \longrightarrow 1$,
$inv : 1 \longrightarrow 1$,
$mult : 2 \longrightarrow 1$,
2–cells: $\alpha_1 : mult \circ \langle e, id \rangle \Longrightarrow id : 1 \longrightarrow 1$,
$\alpha_2 : mult \circ \langle inv, id \rangle \Longrightarrow \langle \rangle \circ e : 1 \longrightarrow 1$,
$\alpha_3 : mult \circ \langle mult \circ \langle x_1^3, x_2^3 \rangle, x_3^3 \rangle \Longrightarrow mult \circ \langle x_1^3, mult \circ \langle x_2^3, x_3^3 \rangle\rangle : 3 \longrightarrow 1$.

In the traditional notation the three freely generating 2–cells correspond to the equations

$$mult(e, x) = x, \quad mult(inv(x), x) = e,$$

$$mult(mult(x, y), z) = mult(x, mult(y, z))$$

directed from left to right.

In order to reflect the notion of a termination ordering in the framework of 2-categories we give the following definition:

3.2 Definition: We speak of an *ordered 2–category* if there is given a partial ordering $\leq$ on the set of 1–cells satisfying the following conditions:

1. $f \leq g$ implies $f : A \longrightarrow B$, $g : A \longrightarrow B$, i.e. comparable 1–cells have common source and target 0–cells;
2. $f \leq g$, $f, g : A \longrightarrow B$, $j : C \longrightarrow A$, $h : B \longrightarrow D$ imply $h \circ f \circ j \leq h \circ g \circ j$;
3. $\alpha : f \Longrightarrow g : A \longrightarrow B$ implies $f \leq g$. ♠

Intuitively, ordered 2–categories are a weakening of the concept of 2–categories, since they may be identified with those 2–categories that have at most one 2–cell between any two 1–cells.

4 Critical Pair Completion in 2–Categories

In the critical pair completion algorithm schema of B.Buchberger the key construction is the following operation:

> Unification of the left hand sinde of a rewrite rule α with a subterm of a given term t and subsequent application of the generated instance of the rewrite rule.

This construction was transformed into the framework of 2–categories with products by D.Rydeheard and has been called

narrowing a 2–cell α against a 1–cell t.

This construction may be visualized by the following diagram:

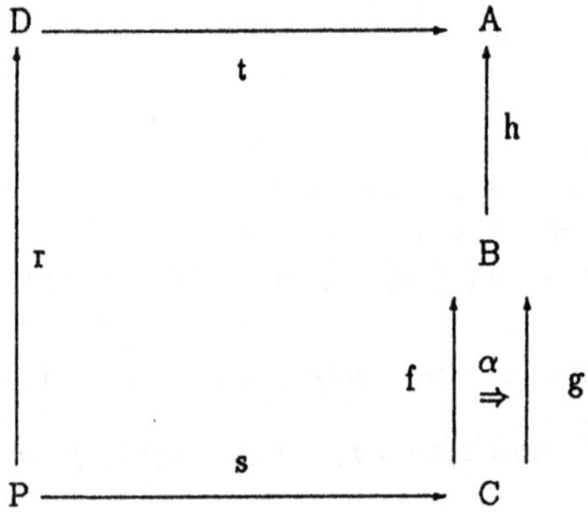

A 2–cell $\alpha : f \Longrightarrow g : C \longrightarrow B$ can be narrowed against a 1–cell $t : D \longrightarrow A$ if

1. t can be factored by B, i.e. if there are 1–cells $t' : D \longrightarrow B, h : B \longrightarrow A$ with $t = h \circ t'$;
2. there exists a pullback $r : P \longrightarrow D, s : P \longrightarrow C$ of $t : D \longrightarrow A$ and $h \circ f : C \longrightarrow A$.

The result of narrowing $\alpha : f \Longrightarrow g : C \longrightarrow B$ against $t : D \longrightarrow A$ with respect to the prefix (of t) $h : B \longrightarrow A$ is the 1–cell $h \circ g \circ s : P \longrightarrow A$.

The intuitive aim of the critical pair completion algorithm schema is the conversion of the following implication:

> If there is a 2–cell $\alpha : f \Longrightarrow g$ in an algebraic theory T, formalized as a 2–category, then f and g have to be interpreted identically by each functorial interpretation of T in the domain of interpretation SET.

The CPC algorithm schema trys to extend the set of 2-cells in **T** in such a way that finally two 1-cells f, g will be interpreted identically if and only if there is a 2-cell $\alpha_1 : f \Longrightarrow g$ or $\alpha_2 : g \Longrightarrow f$.

Thus, if $\alpha : f \Longrightarrow g$, $\beta : t \Longrightarrow u$ are 2-cells and α can be narrowed against t w.r.t. h and with the pullback 1-cells r, s then $u \circ r$ and $h \circ g \circ s$ are 1-cells which will also be interpreted identically in each functorial interpretation. If neither a 2-cell $\delta_1 : u \circ r \Longrightarrow h \circ g \circ s$ nor $\delta_2 : h \circ g \circ s \Longrightarrow u \circ r$ exists, then this pair is called a *critical pair*. It depends on the given termination ordering on the 1-cells wether $\delta_1 : u \circ r \Longrightarrow h \circ g \circ s$ or $\delta_2 : h \circ g \circ s \Longrightarrow u \circ r$ will be produced by the CPC algorithm schema as an additional 2-cell.

In order to improve the readability we introduce the *direct product* $\alpha \times \beta$ of 2-cells: For any two 2-cells $\alpha : f \Longrightarrow g : A \longrightarrow B$, $\beta : h \Longrightarrow j : C \longrightarrow D$ the 2-cell $\alpha \times \beta : f \times h \Longrightarrow g \times j : A \times C \longrightarrow B \times D$, is uniquely determined by $fst_{B,D} \circ (\alpha \times \beta) = \alpha \circ fst_{A,C}$, $scd_{B,D} \circ (\alpha \times \beta) = \beta \circ scd_{A,C}$, i.e. $\alpha \times \beta = \langle \alpha \circ fst_{A,C}, \beta \circ scd_{A,C} \rangle$.

The direct product of 2-cells opens the way to investigate *parallel rewriting*. But, we will not follow this line in the present paper.

Using the example of the 2-categorical theory of groups we discuss at first the 2-cell $\alpha_2 \times id(x_1^1)$, which is constructed by pairing of the two 2-cells $\alpha_2 \circ x_1^2$ and $id(x_1^1) \circ x_2^2$. Thus, it holds

$$\alpha_2 \circ x_1^2 : mult \circ \langle inv, x_1^1 \rangle \circ x_1^2 \Longrightarrow e \circ \langle\rangle \circ x_1^2 : 2 \longrightarrow 1,$$

$$id(x_1^1) \circ x_2^2 : x_1^1 \circ x_2^2 \Longrightarrow x_1^1 \circ x_2^2 : 2 \longrightarrow 1,$$

what can be simplified to

$$\alpha_2 \circ x_1^2 : mult \circ \langle inv \circ x_1^2, x_1^2 \rangle \Longrightarrow e \circ \langle\rangle \circ x_1^2 : 2 \longrightarrow 1,$$

$$id(x_1^1) \circ x_2^2 = id(x_2^2) : x_2^2 \Longrightarrow x_2^2 : 2 \longrightarrow 1.$$

So that

$$(\alpha_2 \times id(x_1^1)) : \langle mult \circ \langle inv, x_1^1 \rangle \circ x_1^2, x_1^1 \circ x_1^2 \rangle \Longrightarrow \langle e \circ \langle\rangle \circ x_1^2, x_1^1 \circ x_1^2 \rangle : 2 \longrightarrow 2$$

and simplified

$$(\alpha_2 \times id(x_1^1)) : \langle mult \circ \langle inv \circ x_1^2, x_1^2 \rangle, x_2^2 \rangle \Longrightarrow \langle e \circ \langle\rangle \circ x_1^2, x_2^2 \rangle : 2 \longrightarrow 2.$$

The 2-cell $mult \circ (\alpha_2 \times id(x_1^1))$ represents a rewrite rule applicable to the left subterm of a term with main operator *mult*.

The 2-cell $\alpha = (\alpha_2 \times id(x_1^1))$ can now be narrowed against the 1-cell $t = mult \circ \langle mult \circ \langle x_1^3, x_2^3 \rangle, x_3^3 \rangle : 3 \longrightarrow 1$, being the source 1-cell of the 2-cell α_3 with respect to the prefix $h = mult$ and with the pullback s and r given by $s = id(2)$ and $r = \langle inv \circ x_1^2, x_1^2, x_2^2 \rangle : 2 \longrightarrow 3$.

The narrowing of $(\alpha_2 \times id(x_1^1))$ against the left hand side of α_3 generates the critical pair

$$(mult \circ \langle inv \circ x_1^2, mult \circ \langle x_1^2, x_2^2 \rangle \rangle, mult \circ \langle e \circ \langle\rangle \circ x_1^2, x_1^2 \rangle)$$

which corresponds to the directed equation

$$mult(inv(x), mult(x, y)) \Rightarrow mult(e, y).$$

Using an instance of the identity axiom represented by the 2–cell

$$\alpha_1 \circ x_1^2 : mult \circ \langle e \circ \langle\rangle \circ x_1^2, x_1^2 \rangle \Longrightarrow x_1^2 : 2 \longrightarrow 1$$

one could narrow the 2–cell

$$(mult \circ (\alpha_2 \times id(x_1^1))) \oplus (\alpha_1 \circ x_1^2)$$

against t as above w.r.t. $id(1)$ and in this case one would generate the the additional 2–cell

$$\eta : mult \circ \langle inv \circ x_1^2, mult \circ \langle x_1^2, x_2^2 \rangle\rangle \Longrightarrow x_2^2 : 2 \longrightarrow 1.$$

It turns out that the basic constructions for the CPC algorithm schema within the formal framework of 2–categories with products are:

- the pullback construction in the category of 0–cells and 1–cells;
- decomposition of 1–cells with respect to the horizontal composition of 1–cells;
- decomposition of 2–cells with respect to the direct product or w.r.t. the pairing construction of 2–cells.

5 Conclusions

The categorical presentation of the CPC algorithm scheme exposes the essential ingredients of the CPC algorithm scheme which are independent from the syntacic surface. This insight is a sufficient basis to transfer the CPC algorithm scheme to other formalisms. In mathematics on the metalevel only product types have been used so far. But, in recently used higher order formalisms the function type came additionally into use.

There are serious reasons to use also other types on the metalevels of formal systems. Those types could be lists or trees for instance. Since the above described decomposition properties are probably satisfied for all those type constructions which can be formalized as parameterized abstract data types without equations effecting the constructors,in the generalisation of the CPC algorithm scheme one has to focus the attention only on the pullback construction in the resulting category of types and terms.

REFERENCES:

[Bu 89] Buchberger,B.: History and Basic Features of the Critical- Pair/ Completion Procedure. J.Symbolic Computation (1987), 3,3-38.

[La 63] Lawvere,F.W.: Functorial semantics of algebraic theories. Proc. Nat. Ac. Sci. 50, 869-872 (1963).

[Mo 89] Moggi,E.: A Category-theoretic Account of Program Modules. Proc. Category Theory and Computer Science, Manchester 1989,Lecture Notes in Computer Science, 389, Springer - Verlag,1989

[MP 89] Makkai,M. and Paré,R.: Accessible Categories: The Foundations of Categorical Model Theory. Contemporary Mathematics, Vol.104, AMS, Providence,Rhode Island,1989.

[Po 89] Power,A.J.: An Abstract Formulation for Rewrite Systems. Proc. Category Theory and Computer Science, Manchester 1989, Lecture Notes in Computer Science, 389, Springer - Verlag,1989.

[RS 87] Rydeheard,D.E., and Stell,J.G.: Foundations of Equational Deduction: A Categorical Treatment of Equational Proofs and Unification Algorithms. Proc. Category Theory and Computer Science, Edingurgh, 1987, Lecture Notes in Computer Science, 283, Springer-Verlag, 1987.

[Se 87] Seely,R.A.G.: Modelling computations - a 2-categorical approach. Proc. 2nd Symp. on Logic in Comp.Science, Ithaca,New York, IEEE Publications 1987.

A kernel specification formalism with higher-order parameterisation*

Donald Sannella† Andrzej Tarlecki‡

Abstract

A specification formalism with parameterisation of an arbitrary order is presented. It is given a denotational-style semantics, accompanied by an inference system for proving that an object satisfies a specification. The inference system incorporates, but is not limited to, a clearly identified type-checking component.

Special effort is made to carefully distinguish between parameterised specifications, which denote functions yielding classes of objects, and specifications of parameterised objects, which denote classes of functions yielding objects. To deal with both of these in a uniform framework, it was convenient to view specifications, which specify objects, as objects themselves, and to introduce a notion of a specification of specifications.

The formalism includes the basic specification-building operations of the ASL specification language. This choice, however, is orthogonal to the new ideas presented. The formalism is also institution-independent, although this issue is not explicitly discussed at any length here.

1 Introduction

The most basic assumption of work on algebraic specification is that software systems are modelled as algebras. The signature of the algebra gives the names of data types and of operations, and the algebra itself gives the semantics of the particular realisations of these data types and operations in the system. Consequently, to specify a software system viewed in this way means to give a signature and define a class of algebras over this signature, that is, describe a class of admissible realisations of the types and operations.

The standard way to give a specification of a system in work on algebraic specification is to present a list of axioms over a given signature and describe in this way the properties that the operations of the system are to satisfy. This view of algebraic specification is perhaps the simplest possible, but has a number of disadvantages. Most notably, any specification of a real software system given in this style would comprise a very long, unstructured, and hence unmanageable list of axioms.

An obvious solution to this problem is to devise a *specification language* to build specifications in a structured fashion, using some *specification-building operations* to form complex specifications by putting together smaller and presumably well-understood pieces. The need for structure in specifications is universally recognized, and mechanisms for structuring specifications appear in all modern algebraic specification languages including CLEAR [BG 80], CIP-L [Bau 85], ASL [SW 83], [Wir 86], ACT ONE [EM 85], PLUSS [BGM 89] and the Larch Shared Language [GHW 85].

An important structuring mechanism is *parameterisation*. A parameterised specification P may be applied to any non-parameterised specification SP_{arg} fitting a certain signature Σ_{par} (or parameter specification SP_{par}) to yield a specification $P(SP_{arg})$. Hence, parameterised specifications are transformations mapping (argument) specifications to (result) specifications. A standard example is

*Much of the material presented here has been included in a very preliminary form in Section 6 of [SST 90].

†LFCS, Department of Computer Science, University of Edinburgh, Edinburgh, Scotland.

‡Institute of Computer Science, Polish Academy of Sciences, Warsaw, Poland.

a specification *Stack-of-X* which takes a specification of stack elements and produces a specification of stacks containing those elements. All the specification languages mentioned above provide a parameterisation mechanism, although the exact technicalities vary considerably[1]. In some algebraic specification frameworks, parameterisation is implicit in the sense that no distinction is made between parameterised and non-parameterised specifications (see for example LOOK [ETLZ 82], ASPIK [Voß 85] and the unified algebra framework [Mos 89a], [Mos 89b]) but the idea is the same.

Quite similarly, adequate structuring mechanisms are needed to organise programs to facilitate their development and understanding (and to enable separate compilation of program components). Many modern programming languages, beginning with Simula [DMN 70] and including Modula-2 [Wirth 88], CLU [Lis 81], Ada [Ada 80] and Standard ML [MTH 90] provide some notion of a program module to allow the programmer to structure the code being written. Again, an important structuring mechanism here is parameterisation. A parameterised program module F (an ML functor [MacQ 86], cf. [Gog 84]) may be applied to any non-parameterised program module A_{arg} matching a given import interface A_{par}. The result is a non-parameterised program module $F(A_{arg})$, a version of F in which the types and functions in A_{par} have been instantiated to the matching types and functions in A_{arg}. An example of a parameterised program module is a parser module which takes a lexical analyser module as argument. Since we model programs as algebras, such parameterised program modules are naturally modelled as functions mapping (argument) algebras to (result) algebras, i.e., algebras parameterised by other algebras. Somewhat informally, we will refer to such objects as *parametric algebras* (cf. *algebra modules* in OBSCURE [LL 88]). It is important to realise that such parametric algebras model self-contained programming units, and hence may correspond to independent programming tasks in the process of development of a software system.

A common drawback of the specification languages mentioned above is that they are predominantly concerned with specifications of non-parametric algebras without any provision for the structuring mechanisms used to construct complex programs (algebras) in a modular way. In particular, they do not provide any explicit concept of a specification of parametric algebras. In some specification frameworks this comes in, but only implicitly as an alternative interpretation of the concept of parameterised specification used in the formalism. For example, the "parameterised specifications" of ACT ONE [EM 85] are interpreted both as means of transforming specifications, i.e., parameterised specifications in our sense, and as a description of a certain functor on algebras, i.e., of a parametric algebra in our sense. Unfortunately, this dual view of "parameterised specifications" imposes in effect a requirement that the structure of a program implementing a specification, composed of (possibly parametric) algebras, must follow the structure of the specification, composed of (possibly parameterised) specifications. This not only violates the principle that a requirements specification is to describe the *what* without indicating the *how* of the system, but also is not acceptable from a practical point of view (see [FJ 90] for a realistic example of a specification with a structure entirely different from the structure of a software system it describes). We have discussed this issue in much detail in [SST 90], where our conclusion was summarised by the following slogan:

$$\text{parameterised (program specification)} \neq \text{(parameterised program) specification}$$

In short, we want a specification language where one can formulate both parameterised specifications on one hand and specifications of parameterised programs on the other.

Another idea for which we have argued in [SST 90] is an extensive use of higher-order parameterisation. Higher-order parameterisation arises not only because higher-order parametric algebras and their specifications are natural to consider from the semantic point of view, but more importantly because they are desirable from the methodological point of view: the use of higher-order parameterisation gives more flexibility in the process of systematic software development. In our opinion,

[1] In particular, the phrase "parameterised specification" has been reserved in some work on algebraic specification (see e.g. [Ehr 82] or [EKTWW 84]) for a formal object (a pair of specifications) which determines a parameterised specification in our sense via so called "parameter passing". We could not think of a better phrase to name "specifications that are parameterised by other specifications", hence the terminological clash.

this issue again has not been given proper attention in the specification languages mentioned above. Some parameterisation mechanisms used there may be straightforwardly extended to higher-order (for example, such a possibility exists in COLD–K [FJKR 87] and has been considered for ASL [SW 83], [ST 88]). We believe that all the benefits of higher-order parameterisation come to light only in the context of a careful distinction between parameterised specifications and specifications of parametric algebras.

In this paper we present our first attempt to incorporate the two methodological ideas sketched above into a specification language. We propose here a specification formalism which builds on the simple yet powerful specification-building operations of ASL (this choice is not essential for the development presented in this paper) and incorporates a parameterisation mechanism capable of describing parametric algebras of an arbitrary order and their specifications, as well as parameterised specifications of an arbitrary order. It was possible to use a single parameterisation mechanism in all these situations because our formalism gives arbitrary specifications the status of first-level objects. Thus, specifications which are primarily used to specify "simpler" objects of the language, are themselves treated also as objects, which in turn may be specified, passed as arguments to functions and arise as results of function application.

The parameterisation mechanism added is inspired by the λ-abstraction mechanism of typed λ-calculi (thus, it generalises the original parameterisation mechanism of ASL [SW 83], [ST 88]). It is important to realise that although the objects of the formalism we propose look like typed λ-expressions, the underlying intuition is slightly different. We like the phrase ***specified*** ***λ-calculus*** as a possible indication of the difference. In typed λ-calculi, the admissible arguments of a function defined by a λ-expression are described just by stating their required type; it is intuitively expected that it will be easy to determine statically whether or not application of such a function to an argument is well-formed. This is in contrast with the situation in specified λ-calculi such as the formalism we propose: the admissible arguments are specified here rather than just being characterised by a type, and so a full-blown verification process is required to determine well-formedness of application.

The paper is organised as follows. Section 2 lists the usual algebraic prerequisites we assume the reader to be familiar with and recalls, for the sake of completeness of the definitions given later, the specification-building operations of ASL. A brief informal description of the language we propose, including its syntax, is given in Section 3. A denotational-style semantics of the language is in Section 4. Section 5 studies the well-formedness and verification of the objects of the language. We point out that the two are necessarily intertwined, and present a formal system to derive judgements of the form $Obj : SP$ stating that an object Obj satisfies a specification SP. Some basic properties of the system are then proved in the second part of the section. Although it is impossible to determine well-formedness of objects of the language using purely "static" type-checking technology, the verification process as presented in Section 5 contains an intuitively clear type-checking component. We introduce a notion of type appropriate for our language in Section 6, and then use it to separate this "type-checking" component from the verification process. Finally, a summary of the topics presented in the paper and some discussion of directions for further work is given in Section 7.

2 Preliminaries

Throughout the paper we assume that the reader is familiar with the basic concepts of logic and universal algebra. In particular we will freely use the notions of: algebraic many-sorted signature, usually denoted by Σ, Σ', Σ_1, etc.; algebraic signature morphism $\sigma : \Sigma \to \Sigma'$; Σ-algebra; Σ-homomorphism; Σ-isomorphism; Σ-equation; first-order Σ-sentence (the set of all Σ-sentences will be denoted by $Sen(\Sigma)$); and satisfaction relation between Σ-algebras and Σ-sentences. These all have the usual definitions (see e.g. [ST 88]) and a standard, hopefully self-explanatory notation is used to write them down. We will also use the standard notation and concepts of λ-calculus, in particular, free and bound occurrences of variables, substitution, β-reduction etc., cf. [Bar 84].

For any signature Σ, the class of all Σ-algebras is denoted by $Alg(\Sigma)$. We will identify this with the category of Σ-algebras and Σ-homomorphisms whenever convenient. If $\sigma : \Sigma \to \Sigma'$ is a signature morphism then $\_|_\sigma : Alg(\Sigma') \to Alg(\Sigma)$ is the reduct functor defined in the usual way (the notation $\_|_\Sigma$ is sometimes used when σ is obvious).

The most essential feature of any specification formalism is that every specification SP over a given signature Σ (we will say that SP is a Σ-specification) unambiguously determines a class of Σ-algebras (sometimes referred to as *models* of the specification) $[\![SP]\!] \in Pow(Alg(\Sigma))$[2]. See [ST 88] for a more extensive discussion of the semantics of specifications.

As a starting point for the presentation of specifications in this paper, we recall here the simple yet powerful specification-building operations defined in [ST 88] (with the slight difference that signatures are regarded as specifications in their own right here with **impose** Φ **on** Σ in place of $\langle\Sigma, \Phi\rangle$). These were in turn based on the ASL specification language [SW 83], [Wir 86]. Even though the particular choice of specification-building operations is not important for the purposes of this paper, we give here their full formal definitions to make the paper self-contained. We refer the reader to [ST 88] for a full explanation of the motivation, intuitive understanding and technical machinery behind these definitions.

- If Σ is a signature, then Σ is a Σ-specification with the semantics:

$$[\![\Sigma]\!] = Alg(\Sigma)$$

- If SP is a Σ-specification and Φ is a set of Σ-sentences, then **impose** Φ **on** SP is a Σ-specification with the semantics:

$$[\![\textbf{impose } \Phi \textbf{ on } SP]\!] = \{A \in [\![SP]\!] \mid A \models \Phi\}$$

- If SP is a Σ-specification and $\sigma : \Sigma' \to \Sigma$ is a signature morphism, then **derive from** SP **by** σ is a Σ'-specification with the semantics:

$$[\![\textbf{derive from } SP \textbf{ by } \sigma]\!] = \{A|_\sigma \mid A \in [\![SP]\!]\}$$

- If SP is a Σ-specification and $\sigma : \Sigma \to \Sigma'$ is a signature morphism, then **translate** SP **by** σ is a Σ'-specification with the semantics:

$$[\![\textbf{translate } SP \textbf{ by } \sigma]\!] = \{A' \in Alg(\Sigma') \mid A'|_\sigma \in [\![SP]\!]\}$$

- If SP and SP' are Σ-specifications, then $SP \cup SP'$ is a Σ-specification with the semantics:

$$[\![SP \cup SP']\!] = [\![SP]\!] \cap [\![SP']\!]$$

- If SP is a Σ-specification and $\sigma : \Sigma' \to \Sigma$ is a signature morphism, then **minimal** SP **wrt** σ is a Σ-specification with the semantics:

$$[\![\textbf{minimal } SP \textbf{ wrt } \sigma]\!] = \{A \in [\![SP]\!] \mid A \text{ is minimal in } Alg(\Sigma) \text{ w.r.t. } \sigma\}^3$$

  where a Σ-algebra A is *minimal w.r.t.* σ if it has no non-trivial subalgebra with an isomorphic σ-reduct (cf. [ST 88]).

- If SP is a Σ-specification, then **iso-close** SP is a Σ-specification with the semantics:

$$[\![\textbf{iso-close } SP]\!] = \{A \in Alg(\Sigma) \mid A \text{ is isomorphic to } B \text{ for some } B \in [\![SP]\!]\}$$

[2] $Pow(X)$, for any class X, denotes the "class of all subclasses" of X. This raises obvious foundational difficulties. We disregard these here, as they may be resolved in a number of standard ways. For example, for the purposes of this paper we could assume that algebras are built within an appropriate universal set, and deal with sets, rather than classes, of algebras.

- If SP is a Σ-specification, $\sigma : \Sigma \to \Sigma'$ is a signature morphism and Φ' is a set of Σ'-sentences, then **abstract** SP **wrt** Φ' **via** σ is a Σ-specification with the semantics:

$$[\![\textbf{abstract } SP \textbf{ wrt } \Phi' \textbf{ via } \sigma]\!] = \{A \in Alg(\Sigma) \mid A \equiv^{\sigma}_{\Phi'} B \text{ for some } B \in [\![SP]\!]\}$$

where $A \equiv^{\sigma}_{\Phi'} B$ means that A is observationally equivalent to B w.r.t. Φ' via σ. The concept of observational equivalence used here covers as special cases the different notions of behavioural equivalence with respect to a set of observable sorts which appear in the literature. The set Φ' contains formulae over Σ (with "free variables" introduced by σ) intended to characterise the relevant aspects of the "behaviour" of Σ-algebras. If no free variables are involved (σ is the identity morphism on Σ) then $A \equiv^{\sigma}_{\Phi'} B$ holds iff A and B satisfy exactly the same sentences from Φ'. (See [ST 87], [ST 88] for details.)

The above definitions were given in [ST 88] in the framework of an arbitrary *institution* [GB 84]. This means that the specification-building operations defined above are actually independent of the underlying logical system, that is, of the particular definitions of the basic notions of signature, algebra, sentence and satisfaction relation. This is an important advantage: we can use the operations in an arbitrary logical system (formalised as an institution) without having to redefine them each time we decide to modify the underlying notions; see [GB 84] and [ST 88] for a discussion of this issue.

3 Introducing the language

The specification formalism we develop in this paper extends in an essential way the kernel specification language presented in [ST 88] by adding a simple yet powerful parameterisation mechanism which allows us to define and specify parametric algebras of arbitrary order, as well as extending the mechanism in [ST 88] for defining first-order parameterised specifications to the higher-order case. This is achieved by viewing specifications on one hand as specifications of objects such as algebras or parametric algebras, and on the other hand as objects themselves to which functions (i.e. parameterised specifications) may be applied. Consequently, the language allows specifications to be specified by other specifications, much as in CLEAR [BG 80] or ACT ONE [EM 85] parameterisation where the parameter specification specifies the permissible argument specifications.

The view of specifications as objects enables the use of a uniform parameterisation mechanism, functions defined by means of λ-abstraction, to express both parameterised specifications and parametric algebras. There is also a uniform specification mechanism to specify such functions, Π-abstraction (Cartesian-product specification, closely related to the dependent function type constructor in e.g. NuPRL [Con 86]). This may be used to specify (higher-order) parametric algebras as well as (higher-order) parameterised specifications. There is no strict separation between levels, which means that it is possible to intermix parameterisation of objects and parameterisation of specifications, obtaining (for example) algebras which are parametric on parameterised specifications or specifications which are parameterised by parametric algebras. We have not yet explored the practical implications of this technically natural generalisation.

The language does not include notation for describing algebras, signatures, signature morphisms, or sets of sentences. Such notation must be provided separately, for example as done for ASL in [Wir 86]. The definition of the language is independent of this notation; moreover, it is essentially *institution independent*, with all the advantages indicated in [GB 84], [ST 88].

The language has just one syntactic category of interest, which includes both specifications and

[3] This is slightly different from the definition in [ST 88].

objects that are specified, with syntax as follows:

Object =	*Signature*		*Simple specifications*
	| **impose** *Sentences* **on** *Object*		
	| **derive from** *Object* **by** *Signature-morphism*		
	| **translate** *Object* **by** *Signature-morphism*		
	| *Object* ∪ *Object*		
	| **minimal** *Object* **wrt** *Signature-morphism*		
	| **iso-close** *Object*		
	| **abstract** *Object* **wrt** *Sentences* **via** *Signature-morphism*		
	| Π *Variable*:*Object*. *Object*		*Other specifications*
	| {*Object*}		
	| **Spec**(*Object*)		
	| *Variable*		*Other objects*
	| *Algebra-expression*		
	| λ *Variable*:*Object*. *Object*		
	| *Object*(*Object*)		

As usual, we have omitted the "syntax" of variables. The other syntactic categories of the language above are algebra expressions, signatures, sets of sentences and signature morphisms — as mentioned above, the details of these are not essential to the main ideas of this paper and we assume that they are provided externally. Algebra expressions may contain occurrences of object variables. We will assume, however, that variables do not occur in signatures, signature morphisms and sentences, which seems necessary to keep the formalism institution-independent. This requirement may seem overly restrictive, as it seems to disallow the components of a particular algebra to be used in axioms; one would expect to be able to write something like $\Pi X{:}\Sigma.\,(\ldots X.op \ldots)$. Fortunately, using the power of the specification-building operations included in the language, it is possible to define a more convenient notation which circumvents this restriction (see Appendix A in [SST 90]).

We have used the standard notation for Π- and λ-objects to suggest the usual notions of a free and of a bound occurrence of a variable in a term of the language, as well as of a closed term. As usual, we identify terms which differ only in their choice of bound variable names. We define substitution of objects for variables in the usual way: $Obj[Obj'/X]$ stands for the result of substituting Obj' for all free occurrences of X in Obj in such a way that no unintended clashes of variable names take place. This also defines the usual notion of β-reduction between objects of the language: $(\ldots(\lambda X{:}SP.\, Obj)(Obj')\ldots) \rightarrow_\beta (\ldots Obj[Obj'/X]\ldots)$. Then, $\rightarrow_\beta^*$ is the reflexive and transitive closure of $\rightarrow_\beta$.

The first eight kinds of specifications listed above (simple specifications) are taken directly from [ST 88] (see Section 2). The particular choice of these eight operations is orthogonal to the rest of the language and will not interfere with the further development in this paper. The other three kinds of specifications are new. Π-abstraction is used to specify parametric objects. To make this work, it must be possible to use objects in specifications. The {_} operation provides this possibility by allowing objects to be turned into (very tight) specifications. The next clause allows a specification which defines a class C of objects to be turned into a specification which defines the class of specifications defining subclasses of C. This is compatible with the use of parameter specifications in parameterised specifications as in CLEAR and ACT ONE. For example, the declaration **proc** $P(X : SP) = \ldots$ in CLEAR introduces a parameterised specification P, where the parameter (or *requirement*) specification SP describes the admissible arguments of P. Namely, if SP defines a class of objects $C = [\![SP]\!]$ then P may be applied to argument specifications SP_{arg} defining a subclass of C, i.e. such that $[\![SP_{arg}]\!] \subseteq [\![SP]\!]$ (we disregard the parameter fitting mechanism). In our formalism this would be written as $P \equiv \lambda X{:}\mathbf{Spec}(SP). \ldots$.

The syntax of other objects is self-explanatory.

The richness of the language may lead to some difficulty in recognizing familiar concepts which appear here in a generalised form. The following comments might help to clarify matters:

- A specification is (an object which denotes) a class of objects. If the objects of this class are algebras, then this specification is a specification in the usual sense.
- ΠX:....... denotes a class of mappings from objects to objects. If these objects are algebras, then this is a class of parametric algebras, i.e. a specification of a parameterised program.
- λX:....... denotes a mapping from objects to objects. If these objects are specifications in the usual sense, then this is a parameterised specification.

The semantics of the language, presented in the next section, gives more substance to the informal comments above concerning the intended denotations of certain phrases.

As pointed out above, we assume that the sublanguage of expressions defining algebras is to be supplied externally (with a corresponding semantics — see Section 4). Even under this assumption, it would be possible to include institution-independent mechanisms for building algebras from other algebras (amalgamation, reduct, free extension, etc.) in the language, which could lead to a powerful and uniform calculus of specified modular programs. This is an interesting possibility for future work but it is outside the scope of this paper.

4 Semantics

We have chosen the syntax for objects in the language so that their semantics should be intuitively clear. We formalise it by defining for any environment ρ, which assigns meanings to variables, a partial function $[\![\_]\!]\rho$ mapping an object Obj to its meaning $[\![Obj]\!]\rho$. It is defined below by structural induction on the syntax of objects. The use of the meta-variable SP instead of Obj in some places below is intended to be suggestive (of objects denoting object classes, used as specifications) but has no formal meaning. This convention will be used throughout the rest of the paper.

Simple specifications:

$[\![\Sigma]\!]\rho = Alg(\Sigma)$
$[\![\textbf{impose } \Phi \textbf{ on } SP]\!]\rho = \{A \in [\![SP]\!]\rho \mid A \models \Phi\}$
    if $[\![SP]\!]\rho \subseteq Alg(\Sigma)$ and $\Phi \subseteq Sen(\Sigma)$ for some signature Σ
$[\![\textbf{derive from } SP \textbf{ by } \sigma]\!]\rho = \{A|_\sigma \mid A \in [\![SP]\!]\rho\}$
    if $[\![SP]\!]\rho \subseteq Alg(\Sigma)$ and $\sigma : \Sigma' \to \Sigma$ is a signature morphism for some signatures Σ and Σ'
... *similarly for the other forms, based on the semantics given in Section 2* ...

Other specifications:

$[\![\{Obj\}]\!]\rho = \{[\![Obj]\!]\rho\}$
    if $[\![Obj]\!]\rho$ is defined
$[\![\Pi X{:}SP.\ SP']\!]\rho = \Pi_{v\in[\![SP]\!]\rho}[\![SP']\!]\rho[v/X]$[4,5]
    if $[\![SP]\!]\rho$ is a class of values and for each $v \in [\![SP]\!]\rho$, $[\![SP']\!]\rho[v/X]$ is a class of values
$[\![\textbf{Spec}(SP)]\!]\rho = Pow([\![SP]\!]\rho)$
    if $[\![SP]\!]\rho$ is a class of values

Other objects:

$[\![X]\!]\rho = \rho(X)$
$[\![A]\!]\rho = \ldots$ *assumed to be given externally* $\ldots$
$[\![\lambda X{:}SP.\,Obj]\!]\rho = \{\langle v \mapsto [\![Obj]\!]\rho[v/X]^5\rangle \mid v \in [\![SP]\!]\rho\}$
if $[\![SP]\!]\rho$ is a class of values and for each $v \in [\![SP]\!]\rho$, $[\![Obj]\!]\rho[v/X]$ is defined
$[\![Obj(Obj')]\!]\rho = [\![Obj]\!]\rho([\![Obj']\!]\rho)$
if $[\![Obj]\!]\rho$ is a function and $[\![Obj']\!]\rho$ is a value in the domain of this function

In the above definition, it is understood that a condition like "$[\![SP]\!]\rho \subseteq Alg(\Sigma)$" implicitly requires that $[\![SP]\!]\rho$ is defined. An object's meaning is undefined unless the side-condition of the appropriate definitional clause holds.

It is easy to see that the semantics of an object of the language depends only on the part of the environment which assigns meanings to variables which occur free in the object. In particular, the meaning of a closed object is independent from the environment. That is, for any closed object Obj and environments ρ and ρ', $[\![Obj]\!]\rho$ is defined if and only if $[\![Obj]\!]\rho'$ is defined and if they are defined then $[\![Obj]\!]\rho = [\![Obj]\!]\rho'$. This allows us to omit the environment when dealing with the semantics of closed objects and write simply $[\![Obj]\!]$ to stand for $[\![Obj]\!]\rho$ for any environment ρ whenever Obj is closed.

Of course, the above remark is true only provided that the sublanguage of algebra expressions and its semantics assumed to be given externally have this property. In the following, we will take this for granted. We will also assume that the sublanguage satisfies the following substitutivity property: for any algebra expression A, variable X and object Obj, for any environment ρ such that $v = [\![Obj]\!]\rho$ is defined, $[\![A[Obj/X]]\!]\rho$ is defined if and only if $[\![A]\!]\rho[v/X]$ is defined, and if they are defined then they are the same. This ensures that the following expected fact holds for our language (the standard proof by induction on the structure of objects is omitted):

Fact 4.1 For any objects Obj, Obj' and variable X, for any environment ρ such that $v' = [\![Obj']\!]\rho$ is defined, $[\![Obj[Obj'/X]]\!]\rho$ is defined if and only if $[\![Obj]\!]\rho[v'/X]$ is defined, and if they are defined then

$$[\![Obj[Obj'/X]]\!]\rho = [\![Obj]\!]\rho[v'/X]$$

□

Corollary 4.2 β-reduction preserves the meaning of objects. That is, for any objects Obj and Obj' such that $Obj \rightarrow^*_\beta Obj'$, for any environment ρ, if $[\![Obj]\!]\rho$ is defined then so is $[\![Obj']\!]\rho$ and $[\![Obj]\!]\rho = [\![Obj']\!]\rho$. □

The above semantics is overly permissive in comparison with the semantics given to simple specifications in Section 2 and [ST 88] in the sense that it assigns meanings to some specifications which would be considered ill-formed according to the definitions given there. This is caused by the "polymorphic" character of the empty class of algebras. For example, if SP is an inconsistent Σ-specification (i.e., assuming SP is closed, $[\![SP]\!] = \emptyset$) then **impose** Φ **on** SP has a well-defined meaning (the empty class of algebras) even if Φ is a set of sentences over a signature which is completely unrelated to Σ. Generalising the treatment in Section 2 in the present context is possible via the notion of type to be introduced in Section 6. However, the use of specifications (rather than signatures and types) to constrain formal parameters makes such a type system insufficiently descriptive to ensure well-formedness of specifications. For this, full-blown verification, rather than just type-checking, is required. We will discuss this issue in more detail in the following sections.

[4] Π on the right-hand side of this definition denotes the usual Cartesian product of an indexed family of sets. That is, $\Pi_{x\in S}C_x$ is the set of all functions with domain S mapping any $x \in S$ to an element of C_x.

[5] As usual, $\rho[v/X]$ is the environment which results from ρ by assigning v to the variable X (and leaving the values of other variables unchanged).

The reader might feel uneasy about the fact that we have not actually defined here any domain of values, the elements of which are assigned to objects of the language as their meanings. A naive attempt might have been as follows:

$$Values = Algebras \mid Pow(Values) \mid Values \rightharpoonup Values$$

Clearly, this leads to serious foundational problems, as the recursive domain definition involves "heavy recursion" (cf. [BT 83]) and hence cannot have a set-theoretic solution (even assuming that we consider here a set *Algebras* of algebras built within a fixed universe). However, since the formalism we introduce is not intended to cater for any form of self application of functions or non-well-foundedness of sets, the equation above attempts to define a domain of values of objects which is undesirably rich. The well-formed[6] objects of the language can easily be seen to form a hierarchy indexed by "types" (see Section 6). Thus, we can define a corresponding cumulative hierarchy of sets of values, and then define the domain of the meanings of objects as the union of sets in the hierarchy, much in the style of [BKS 88] (see [BT 83] where the idea of using hierarchies of domains in denotational semantics is discussed in more detail). Another, less "constructive", possibility is to work within a fixed universal set of values of objects containing the "set" of all algebras [Coh 81].

5 Proving satisfaction

We are interested in determining whether or not given objects satisfy given specifications. We use the formal judgement $Obj : SP$ to express the assertion that a closed object Obj satisfies a closed specification SP, i.e. that $[\![Obj]\!] \in [\![SP]\!]$, and generalise it to $X_1 : SP_1, \ldots, X_n : SP_n \vdash Obj : SP$ stating the assertion that an object Obj satisfies a specification SP in the *context* $X_1 : SP_1, \ldots, X_n : SP_n$, i.e. under the assumption that objects $X_1, \ldots, X_n$ satisfy specifications $SP_1, \ldots, SP_n$, respectively. The inference rules listed below allow us to derive judgements of this general form. For the sake of clarity, though, we have decided to make contexts implicit in the rules and rely on the natural deduction mechanism of introducing and discharging assumptions (all of the form $X : SP$ here) to describe the appropriate context manipulation. For example, in (R2) below, $[X : SP]$ is an assumption which may be used to derive $SP' : \mathbf{Spec}(SP'')$, but is discharged when we apply the rule to derive its conclusion. Whenever necessary, we will use the phrase "the current context" to refer to the sequence of currently undischarged assumptions. We say that an environment ρ is *consistent* with a context $X_1 : SP_1, \ldots, X_n : SP_n$ if for $i = 1, \ldots, n$, $\rho(X_i) \in [\![SP_i]\!]\rho$.

Simple specifications:

$$\frac{\Sigma \text{ signature}}{\Sigma : \mathbf{Spec}(\Sigma)} \qquad \frac{SP : \mathbf{Spec}(\Sigma) \quad \Phi \subseteq Sen(\Sigma)}{\mathbf{impose}\ \Phi\ \mathbf{on}\ SP : \mathbf{Spec}(\Sigma)}$$

$$\frac{SP : \mathbf{Spec}(\Sigma') \quad \sigma : \Sigma \to \Sigma'}{\mathbf{derive\ from}\ SP\ \mathbf{by}\ \sigma : \mathbf{Spec}(\Sigma)} \qquad \frac{SP : \mathbf{Spec}(\Sigma) \quad \sigma : \Sigma \to \Sigma'}{\mathbf{translate}\ SP\ \mathbf{by}\ \sigma : \mathbf{Spec}(\Sigma')}$$

$$\frac{SP : \mathbf{Spec}(\Sigma) \quad SP' : \mathbf{Spec}(\Sigma)}{SP \cup SP' : \mathbf{Spec}(\Sigma)} \qquad \frac{SP : \mathbf{Spec}(\Sigma) \quad \sigma : \Sigma' \to \Sigma}{\mathbf{minimal}\ SP\ \mathbf{wrt}\ \sigma : \mathbf{Spec}(\Sigma)}$$

$$\frac{SP : \mathbf{Spec}(\Sigma)}{\mathbf{iso\text{-}close}\ SP : \mathbf{Spec}(\Sigma)} \qquad \frac{SP : \mathbf{Spec}(\Sigma) \quad \Phi' \subseteq Sen(\Sigma') \quad \sigma : \Sigma \to \Sigma'}{\mathbf{abstract}\ SP\ \mathbf{wrt}\ \Phi'\ \mathbf{via}\ \sigma : \mathbf{Spec}(\Sigma)}$$

[6] An intuitive understanding of the notion of well-formedness involved is sufficient here (we hope) — we introduce it formally in Section 5.

Other specifications:

$$\frac{Obj : SP}{\{Obj\} : \mathbf{Spec}(SP)} \tag{R1}$$

$$\frac{SP : \mathbf{Spec}(SP_{any}) \qquad \begin{matrix}[X : SP] \\ SP' : \mathbf{Spec}(SP'')\end{matrix}}{\Pi X{:}SP.\, SP' : \mathbf{Spec}(\Pi X{:}SP.\, SP'')} \tag{R2}$$

$$\frac{SP : \mathbf{Spec}(SP')}{\mathbf{Spec}(SP) : \mathbf{Spec}(\mathbf{Spec}(SP'))} \tag{R3}$$

λ-expressions:

$$\frac{SP : \mathbf{Spec}(SP_{any}) \qquad \begin{matrix}[X : SP] \\ Obj : SP'\end{matrix}}{\lambda X{:}SP.\, Obj \; : \; \Pi X{:}SP.\, SP'} \tag{R4}$$

$$\frac{Obj : \Pi X{:}SP.\, SP' \qquad Obj' : SP}{Obj(Obj') : SP'[Obj'/X]} \tag{R5}$$

$$\frac{Obj : SP \qquad SP \rightarrow_{\beta}^{*} SP'}{Obj : SP'} \tag{R6}$$

$$\frac{Obj : SP \qquad SP' : \mathbf{Spec}(SP_{any}) \qquad SP' \rightarrow_{\beta}^{*} SP}{Obj : SP'} \tag{R7}$$

Trivial inference:

$$\frac{Obj : SP_{any}}{Obj : \{Obj\}} \tag{R8}$$

"Cut"

$$\frac{Obj : SP \qquad SP : \mathbf{Spec}(SP')}{Obj : SP'} \tag{R9}$$

Semantic inference:

$$\frac{SP : \mathbf{Spec}(\Sigma) \qquad [\![A]\!]\rho \in [\![SP]\!]\rho \text{ for all } \rho \text{ consistent with the current context}}{A : SP} \quad \text{(R10)}$$

$$\frac{SP, SP' : \mathbf{Spec}(\Sigma) \qquad [\![SP]\!]\rho \subseteq [\![SP']\!]\rho \text{ for all } \rho \text{ consistent with the current context}}{SP : \mathbf{Spec}(SP')} \quad \text{(R11)}$$

Some of these rules involve judgements (Σ signature, $\Phi \subseteq Sen(\Sigma)$, $\sigma : \Sigma \rightarrow \Sigma'$) which are external to the above formal system. This is a natural consequence of the fact that the language does not include any syntax for signatures, sentences, etc. More significantly, there are two rules which involve model-theoretic judgements, referring to the semantics of objects given above.

Following the usual practice, in the sequel we will simply write "$Obj : SP$" meaning "$Obj : SP$ is derivable".

The rules labelled *Simple specifications* characterise the well-formedness of Σ-specifications built using the underlying specification-building operations included in the language. They directly incorporate the "syntactic" requirements of Section 2 on the use of these operations. Rules (R1), (R2) and (R3) play a similar role for the other specification-forming operations: singleton specification, Cartesian-product specification and **Spec**(_), respectively. Notice, however, that their specifications are given here in a form which is as tight as possible. For example, for any $SP : \mathbf{Spec}(\Sigma)$ and $Obj : SP$, rule (R1) allows us to deduce $\{Obj\} : \mathbf{Spec}(SP)$ rather than just $\{Obj\} : \mathbf{Spec}(\Sigma)$.

The rules related to λ-expressions and their applications to arguments are quite straightforward. Rules (R4) and (R5) are the usual rules for λ-expression introduction and application, respectively. The assumption $SP : \mathbf{Spec}(SP_{any})$ in rule (R4) asserts the well-formedness of the specification SP (see also (R2), (R7), (R8)). Whenever the meta-variable SP_{any} is used below, it will play the same role as part of a well-formedness constraint. Notice that in order to prove $\lambda X{:}SP.\, Obj : \Pi X{:}SP.\, SP'$, we have to prove $Obj : SP'$ "schematically" for an arbitrary unknown $X : SP$, rather than for all values in the class $[\![SP]\!]\rho$ (for the appropriate environments ρ).

Rules (R6) and (R7) embody a part of the observation that β-reduction preserves the semantics of objects (Corollary 4.2). Rule (R6) allows for β-reduction and rule (R7) for well-formed β-expansion of specifications. A particular instance of the latter is

$$\frac{Obj' : SP'[Obj/X] \qquad (\lambda X{:}SP.\, SP')(Obj) : \mathbf{Spec}(SP_{any})}{Obj' : (\lambda X{:}SP.\, SP')(Obj)}$$

That is, in order to prove that an object satisfies a specification formed by applying a parameterised specification to an argument, it is sufficient to prove that the object satisfies the corresponding β-reduct.

However, we have not incorporated full β-equality into our system; rules (R6) and (R7) introduce it only for specifications. In particular, we have not included the following rule, which would allow well-formed β-expansion of objects:

$$\frac{Obj : SP \qquad Obj' : SP_{any} \qquad Obj' \rightarrow^{*}_{\beta} Obj}{Obj' : SP}$$

An instance of this would be:

$$\frac{Obj_1[Obj_2/X] : SP \qquad (\lambda X{:}SP_2.\, Obj_1)(Obj_2) : SP_{any}}{(\lambda X{:}SP_2.\, Obj_1)(Obj_2) : SP}$$

Hence, in order to prove that a structured object $(\lambda X{:}SP_2.\, Obj_1)(Obj_2)$ satisfies a specification SP, it would suffice to show that the object is well-formed and to prove that its β-reduct $Obj_1[Obj_2/X]$

satisfies the specification. We think that this is not methodologically desirable: a proof of correctness of a program should follow the structure of the program, without any possibility of flattening it out. So, to prove $(\lambda X{:}SP_2.\,Obj_1)(Obj_2) : SP$ we have to find an appropriate specification for the parameterised program $\lambda X{:}SP_2.\,Obj_1$, say $\lambda X{:}SP_2.\,Obj_1 : \Pi X{:}SP_2.\,SP_1$ such that $SP_1[Obj_2/X] = SP$ (actually, $SP_1[Obj_2/X] : \mathbf{Spec}(SP)$ is sufficient).

The other part of β-equality for objects, β-reduction, although not derivable in the system, is admissible in it[7]:

Lemma 5.1 The following rule is an admissible rule of the system

$$\frac{Obj : SP \qquad Obj \rightarrow^*_\beta Obj'}{Obj' : SP}$$

Proof (sketch) It is sufficient to consider the case $Obj \rightarrow_\beta Obj'$ (then the more general case follows by easy induction on the length of the reduction sequence). We will need an additional lemma:

> **Lemma 5.2** The following rule is an admissible rule of the system
>
> $$\frac{Obj : SP \qquad \begin{array}{c}[X : SP]\\ Obj' : SP'\end{array}}{Obj'[Obj/X] : SP'[Obj/X]}$$
>
> **Proof (idea)** By obvious induction on the derivation of $Obj' : SP'$, by inspection of the rules of the system. □

The proof now is by induction on the derivation of $Obj : SP$. The only essential case is that of rule (R5) where a β-reduct may be introduced. So, in (R5) let Obj be $\lambda X{:}SP_1.\,Obj_1$, and suppose that $\lambda X{:}SP_1.\,Obj_1 : \Pi X{:}SP.\,SP'$ and $Obj' : SP$. We can assume that $\lambda X{:}SP_1.\,Obj_1 : \Pi X{:}SP.\,SP'$ has been derived using (R4): we can show that no generality is lost since (R4) is the only rule introducing λ-expressions. Hence, we have that $Obj_1 : SP'$ under the assumption $X : SP$. Thus, by Lemma 5.2, $Obj_1[Obj'/X] : SP'[Obj'/X]$, which is what we need to show. All the other cases of the inductive proof are easy; for example:

(R1): What we have to show is that whenever $Obj : SP$ and $\{Obj\} \rightarrow_\beta Obj'$ then $Obj' : \mathbf{Spec}(SP)$. Since $\{Obj\} \rightarrow_\beta Obj'$, Obj' has to be of the form $\{Obj''\}$ where $Obj \rightarrow_\beta Obj''$. By the inductive assumption, $Obj : SP$ and $Obj \rightarrow_\beta Obj''$ imply $Obj'' : SP$, and so using the same rule we derive $\{Obj''\} : \mathbf{Spec}(SP)$.

(R6): One of the assumptions of the rule is $Obj : SP$. Hence, by the inductive assumption, $Obj' : SP$, and so using the same rule we can conclude that indeed $Obj' : SP'$.

□

It might be interesting to enrich the system by the β-reduction rule for objects given in the above lemma, or even more generally by some "operational semantics rules" for (the computable part of) the object language. This, however, would be quite orthogonal to the issues of object specification considered in this paper. Therefore, to keep the system as small and as simple as possible, the rule is not included in the system.

Rules (R8) and (R9) embody trivial deductions which should be intuitively straightforward. Notice that $SP : \mathbf{Spec}(SP')$, as in the premise of (R9), asserts that specification SP imposes at least the same requirements as SP'.

[7] A rule is *admissible* in a deduction system if its conclusion is derivable in the system provided that all its premises are derivable. This holds in particular if the rule is *derivable* in the system, that is, if it can be obtained by composition of the rules in the system.

Rules (R10) and (R11) refer directly to the semantics of objects. They embody the semantic verification process which is a necessary component of inference in the above formal system. These rules are deliberately restricted to the non-parametric case, since this is the point at which an external formal system is required; parameterisation is handled by the other rules. We do not attempt here to provide a formal system for proving the semantic judgements $[\![A]\!]\rho \in [\![SP]\!]\rho$ and $[\![SP]\!]\rho \subseteq [\![SP']\!]\rho$ for all environments ρ consistent with the current context. This is an interesting and important research topic, which is however separate from the main concerns of this paper; some preliminary considerations and results on this may be found in e.g. [ST 88] and [Far 89]. It is not possible to give a set of purely "syntactic" inference rules which is sound and complete with respect to the semantics above because of the power of the specification mechanisms included in the language (this is already the case for the subset of the language excluding parameterisation, presented in Section 2).

As mentioned earlier, to make the rules as clear and readable as possible, the presentation of the system omits a full formal treatment of contexts. In particular, we should add two rules to derive judgements that a context is well-formed (here, $\langle\rangle$ is the empty context):

$$\frac{}{\langle\rangle \text{ is a well-formed context}}$$

$$\frac{\Gamma \text{ is a well-formed context} \qquad X \text{ is not in } \Gamma \qquad \overset{[\Gamma]}{SP : \mathbf{Spec}(SP_{any})}}{\Gamma, X : SP \text{ is a well-formed context}}$$

and then axioms $X_1 : SP_1, \ldots, X_n : SP_n \vdash X_k : SP_k$, for $k = 1, \ldots, n$, where $X_1 : SP_1, \ldots, X_n : SP_n$ is a well-formed context. It is important to realise that contexts are *sequences*, rather than sets, and so we allow the variables $X_1, \ldots, X_k$ to occur in SP_{k+1}.

We will continue omitting contexts throughout the rest of the paper. All the definitions and facts given below (as well as above) are correctly stated for closed objects only, but are meant to be naturally extended to objects in a well-formed context. This will be done explicitly only within proofs where it is absolutely necessary. Similarly, we will omit in the following the environment argument to the semantic function for objects; all the environments thus implicitly considered are assumed to be consistent with the corresponding context. We hope that this slight informality will contribute to the readability of the paper without obscuring the details too much.

The following theorem expresses the soundness of the formal system above with respect to the semantics given earlier.

Theorem 5.3 For any object *Obj* and specification *SP*, if $Obj : SP$ is derivable then $[\![Obj]\!] \in [\![SP]\!]$ (that is, $[\![SP]\!]$ is defined and is a class of values and $[\![Obj]\!]$ is defined and is a value in this class).

Proof (sketch) By induction on the length of the derivation and by inspection of the rules. A complete formal proof requires, of course, a careful treatment of free variables and their interpretation (cf. the remark preceding the theorem). Thus, for example, rule (R4) really stands for:

$$\frac{\Gamma \vdash SP : \mathbf{Spec}(SP_{any}) \qquad \Gamma, X : SP \vdash Obj : SP' \qquad X \text{ is not in } \Gamma}{\Gamma \vdash \lambda X{:}SP.\, Obj : \Pi X{:}SP.\, SP'}$$

where Γ is a context. In the corresponding case of the inductive step we can assume that

1. $[\![SP]\!]\rho \in [\![\mathbf{Spec}(SP_{any})]\!]\rho$ for all environments ρ consistent with context Γ, and
2. $[\![Obj]\!]\rho \in [\![SP']\!]\rho$ for all environments ρ consistent with context $\Gamma, X : SP$

and then we have to prove that $[\![\lambda X{:}SP.\, Obj]\!]\rho \in [\![\Pi X{:}SP.\, SP']\!]\rho$ for all environments ρ consistent with context Γ. That is, taking into account the semantics of λ- and Π-expressions as given in Section 4, we have to prove that for all environments ρ consistent with context Γ

- $[\![SP]\!]\rho$ is defined and is a class of values — which follows directly from assumption (1) above, and then
- for all values $v \in [\![SP]\!]\rho$,
  - $[\![Obj]\!]\rho[v/X]$ is defined,
  - $[\![SP']\!]\rho[v/X]$ is defined and is a class of values, and
  - $[\![Obj]\!]\rho[v/X] \in [\![SP']\!]\rho[v/X]$,

  which in turn follow directly from assumption (2) above.

The cases corresponding to the other rules of the system require similar, straightforward but tedious analysis. Notice that the proofs about the rules concerning application and β-reduction, (R5), (R6) and (R7), crucially depend on Fact 4.1 and Corollary 4.2. □

It is natural to ask if the above formal system is also complete with respect to the semantics. It turns out not to be complete. One reason for incompleteness is that the formal system does not exploit the semantical consequences of inconsistency. For example, for any inconsistent specification SP we have that $[\![SP]\!] \in [\![\mathbf{Spec}(SP_{any})]\!]$ for any SP_{any} such that $[\![SP_{any}]\!]$ is a class of values. The corresponding formal judgement $SP : \mathbf{Spec}(SP_{any})$ is not derivable when (for example) SP and SP_{any} are simple specifications over different signatures. If the formal parameter specification in a λ- or Π-expression is inconsistent then similar difficulties arise (cf. [MMMS 87] for a discussion of the related issue of "empty types" in typed λ-calculi). This topic deserves further study; it might be that the system is complete when inconsistencies are excluded and perhaps some additional restrictions on the objects and specifications involved are imposed (although the deliberate omission of a rule allowing for well-formed β-expansion of objects makes this unlikely).

Definition 5.4 An object Obj is *well-formed* if $Obj : SP$ for some SP. □

This also defines the well-formed specifications since specifications are objects.

Checking whether an expression in the language is well-formed must in general involve "semantic" verification as embodied in rules (R10) and (R11). In fact, checking the well-formedness of objects is as hard as checking if they satisfy specifications: $Obj : SP$ if and only if $(\lambda X{:}SP.\ (\text{any constant}))(Obj)$ is well formed.

An easy corollary to the soundness theorem is the following:

Corollary 5.5 Any well-formed object Obj has a well-defined meaning $[\![Obj]\!]$. □

Since specifications do not form a separate syntactic category of the language, in the above discussion we have used the term "specification" and the meta-variable SP rather informally, relying on an intuitive understanding of the role of the objects of the language. This intuitive understanding may be made formal as follows:

Definition 5.6 An object SP is called a *specification* if for some SP_{any}, $SP : \mathbf{Spec}(SP_{any})$. □

Corollary 5.7 The meaning of a specification is a class of values: if $SP : \mathbf{Spec}(SP_{any})$ then $[\![SP]\!] \subseteq [\![SP_{any}]\!]$. □

Note that this covers ordinary Σ-specifications, specifications of (higher-order) parametric algebras, specifications of (higher-order) parameterised specifications, etc. The following theorem shows that this is indeed consistent with our previous informal use of the term.

Theorem 5.8 If $Obj : SP$ then SP is a specification.

Proof We prove that $SP : \mathbf{Spec}(SP_{any})$ for some SP_{any} by induction on the derivation of $Obj : SP$, by inspection of the rules of the system:

Simple specifications: The rules for simple specifications cause no problem. For any signature Σ, $\mathbf{Spec}(\Sigma)$ is indeed a specification as we have $\mathbf{Spec}(\Sigma) : \mathbf{Spec}(\mathbf{Spec}(\Sigma))$, which may be derived by using the rule introducing Σ, and then the rule of **Spec(_)**-introduction (R3).

(R1): By the inductive assumption we have $SP : \mathbf{Spec}(SP_{any})$, from which we can derive $\mathbf{Spec}(SP) : \mathbf{Spec}(\mathbf{Spec}(SP_{any}))$.

(R2): We need the following lemma:

Lemma 5.9 If an object $\mathbf{Spec}(SP)$ is well-formed then SP is a specification.

Proof We proceed by induction on a derivation of the well-formedness of $\mathbf{Spec}(SP)$, by inspection of the possible last rules in the derivation:

(R3): Clearly, we have here $SP : \mathbf{Spec}(SP')$ as the assumption for the use of this rule.

(R6), (R7), (R8), (R9): Let Obj be $\mathbf{Spec}(SP)$. One of the premises of each of these rules implies the well-formedness of $\mathbf{Spec}(SP)$ and so the inductive assumption implies that SP is a specification.

(R11): As in the previous case, but take SP to be $\mathbf{Spec}(SP)$. (In fact, this case is vacuous since $\mathbf{Spec}(SP) : \mathbf{Spec}(\Sigma)$ is not derivable anyway.)

Notice that only the first case of the above was essential: it is sufficient to analyse only the rules that may be used to "build" objects of the form we consider (the **Spec(_)**-introduction rule (R3) in this case). We have relied on a similar remark in the proof of Lemma 5.1. □

By the inductive assumption (of the proof of the theorem) we have that under the assumption $X : SP$, $\mathbf{Spec}(SP'')$ is well-formed, and so using the above lemma we conclude that $SP'' : \mathbf{Spec}(SP'_{any})$. Hence, we can derive $\Pi X{:}SP.\, SP'' : \mathbf{Spec}(\Pi X{:}SP.\, SP'_{any})$, and then $\mathbf{Spec}(\Pi X{:}SP.\, SP'') : \mathbf{Spec}(\mathbf{Spec}(\Pi X{:}SP.\, SP'_{any}))$.

(R3): By the inductive assumption, $\mathbf{Spec}(SP') : \mathbf{Spec}(SP_{any})$, which entails $\mathbf{Spec}(\mathbf{Spec}(SP')) : \mathbf{Spec}(\mathbf{Spec}(SP_{any}))$.

(R4): By the inductive assumption we have that under the assumption $X : SP$, $SP' : \mathbf{Spec}(SP'_{any})$, and so we can derive $\Pi X{:}SP.\, SP' : \mathbf{Spec}(\Pi X{:}SP.\, SP'_{any})$.

(R5): The inductive assumption implies that $\Pi X{:}SP.\, SP'$ is well-formed. We prove that this implies that SP' is a specification under the assumption $X : SP$. The proof is by induction on the derivation of the well-formedness of $\Pi X{:}SP.\, SP'$, by inspection of the possible last rules used in the derivation. As in the proof of Lemma 5.9, it is sufficient to analyse the Π-introduction rule (R2). Since what we need is one of the assumptions for the applicability of this rule, we can indeed conclude that $SP' : \mathbf{Spec}(SP'')$ under the assumption $X : SP$. Hence, by Lemma 5.2 we conclude that $SP'[Obj'/X] : \mathbf{Spec}(SP''[Obj'/X])$.

(R6): By the inductive assumption applied to one of the premises of this rule, SP is a specification. Thus, since $SP \rightarrow^*_\beta SP'$, by Lemma 5.1 it follows that SP' is a specification as well.

(R7): Trivial.

(R8): From the premise of the rule, we can directly derive $\{Obj\} : \mathbf{Spec}(SP_{any})$.

(R9): By the inductive assumption, from the premise of the rule it follows that $\mathbf{Spec}(SP')$ is well-formed. Thus, by Lemma 5.9, SP' is a specification.

(R10): Trivial.

(R11): From the premise $SP' : \mathbf{Spec}(\Sigma)$, we derive $\mathbf{Spec}(SP') : \mathbf{Spec}(\mathbf{Spec}(\Sigma))$.

This completes the proof of the theorem. □

It is perhaps surprising how long and relatively complicated the proof of an intuitively rather obvious fact has become here. Unfortunately, this seems to be typical of many proofs dealing with "syntactic" properties of λ-calculi.

6 Type-checking

Inference in the system presented in the previous section has a purely "type-checking" component on which the "verification" component is in a sense superimposed. We try to separate this "type-checking" process below. The concept of type we use must cover signatures (as "basic types" of algebras) and "arrow types" (types of functions) which would be usual in any type theory, as well as "specification types" which are particular to the formalism presented here: as we have stressed before, the type of a specification is distinct from the type of objects the specification specifies.

Definition 6.1 The class of types $\mathcal{T}$ is defined as the least class such that:

- for any signature Σ, $\Sigma \in \mathcal{T}$;
- for any types $\tau_1, \tau_2 \in \mathcal{T}$, $\tau_1 \rightarrow \tau_2 \in \mathcal{T}$; and
- for any type $\tau \in \mathcal{T}$, $\mathbf{Spec}(\tau) \in \mathcal{T}$.

□

Under the standard notational convention that arrow types of the form $\tau \rightarrow \tau'$ stand for Π-types of the form $\Pi X{:}\tau.\,\tau'$ where X does not actually occur in τ', types as defined above are well-formed specifications.

We define type $\mathit{Type}(\mathit{Obj})$ for an object Obj of our system by induction as follows:

Simple specifications:

$$\frac{\Sigma \text{ signature}}{\mathit{Type}(\Sigma) = \mathbf{Spec}(\Sigma)} \qquad \frac{\mathit{Type}(SP) = \mathbf{Spec}(\Sigma) \qquad \Phi \subseteq \mathit{Sen}(\Sigma)}{\mathit{Type}(\mathbf{impose}\ \Phi\ \mathbf{on}\ SP) = \mathbf{Spec}(\Sigma)}$$

... and similarly for other simple specifications ...

Other specifications:

$$\frac{\mathit{Type}(\mathit{Obj}) = \tau}{\mathit{Type}(\{\mathit{Obj}\}) = \mathbf{Spec}(\tau)} \qquad \frac{\mathit{Type}(SP) = \mathbf{Spec}(\tau)}{\mathit{Type}(\mathbf{Spec}(SP)) = \mathbf{Spec}(\mathbf{Spec}(\tau))}$$

$$\frac{\mathit{Type}(SP) = \mathbf{Spec}(\tau) \qquad \begin{matrix}[\mathit{Type}(X) = \tau] \\ \mathit{Type}(SP') = \mathbf{Spec}(\tau')\end{matrix}}{\mathit{Type}(\Pi X{:}SP.\,SP') = \mathbf{Spec}(\tau \rightarrow \tau')}$$

λ-expressions:

$$\frac{\mathit{Type}(SP) = \mathbf{Spec}(\tau) \qquad \begin{matrix}[\mathit{Type}(X) = \tau] \\ \mathit{Type}(\mathit{Obj}) = \tau'\end{matrix}}{\mathit{Type}(\lambda X{:}SP.\,\mathit{Obj}) = \tau \rightarrow \tau'} \qquad \frac{\mathit{Type}(\mathit{Obj}) = \tau \rightarrow \tau' \qquad \mathit{Type}(\mathit{Obj}') = \tau}{\mathit{Type}(\mathit{Obj}(\mathit{Obj}')) = \tau'}$$

Algebra expressions:

$$\frac{A \text{ is an algebra expression denoting a } \Sigma\text{-algebra}}{\mathit{Type}(A) = \Sigma}$$

Note that the semantic inference rules (R10), (R11), the trivial inference rule (R8), the "cut" rule (R9), and the β-reduction and β-expansion rules (R6) and (R7), which do not introduce new well-formed objects, do not have counterparts in the above definition.

Clearly, the above definition depends on a judgement whether or not an algebra expression denotes an algebra over a given signature. We will assume that such "type-checking" of algebra expressions is defined externally in such a way that it is consistent with the semantics (i.e., if A is a well-formed algebra expression denoting a Σ-algebra then indeed $[\![A]\!] \in Alg(\Sigma)$). Moreover, we will assume that it is substitutive: if A is an algebra expression denoting a Σ-algebra under an assumption $Type(X) = \tau$ then for any object Obj with $Type(Obj) = \tau$, $A[Obj/X]$ is an algebra expression denoting a Σ-algebra as well.

The above rules (deliberately) do not define $Type(Obj)$ for all object expressions of our language. However, if a type is defined for an object, it is defined unambigously. An object Obj is *roughly well-formed* if its type $Type(Obj)$ is defined. There are, of course, roughly well-formed objects that are not well-formed. The opposite implication holds, though:

Theorem 6.2 $Type(Obj)$ is well-defined for any well-formed object Obj. In particular:

1. If $Obj : SP$ then $Type(SP) = \mathbf{Spec}(Type(Obj))$.
2. If SP is a specification then $Type(SP) = \mathbf{Spec}(\tau)$ for some type τ.
3. If $Obj : \Pi X{:}SP.\, SP'$ then $Type(Obj) = \tau \rightarrow \tau'$, where $Type(SP) = \mathbf{Spec}(\tau)$, for some types τ and τ'.

Proof The first part of the theorem follows by induction on the length of the derivation (we sketch this proof below). The other two parts follow directly from this.

Let us first rephrase the first part of the theorem taking contexts describing free variables explicitly into account, which is perhaps not entirely obvious here:

1′. If $Obj : SP$ is derivable under assumptions $X_1 : SP_1, \ldots, X_n : SP_n$ where $Type(SP_1) = \mathbf{Spec}(\tau_1), \ldots, Type(SP_n) = \mathbf{Spec}(\tau_n)$, then $Type(SP) = \mathbf{Spec}(Type(Obj))$ under the assumptions $Type(X_1) = \tau_1, \ldots, Type(X_n) = \tau_n$.

Now, we prove this part of the theorem by induction on the derivation of $Obj : SP$, by inspection of the rules:

Simple specifications: The rules for simple specifications cause no problem, since using the inductive assumption we conclude that each well-formed specification SP in the conclusion of these rules has type $Type(SP) = \mathbf{Spec}(\Sigma)$, and $Type(\mathbf{Spec}(\Sigma)) = \mathbf{Spec}(\mathbf{Spec}(\Sigma))$.

(R1): By the inductive assumption we have $Type(SP) = \mathbf{Spec}(Type(Obj))$, hence $Type(\mathbf{Spec}(SP)) = \mathbf{Spec}(Type(SP)) = \mathbf{Spec}(\mathbf{Spec}(Type(Obj))) = \mathbf{Spec}(Type(\{Obj\}))$.

(R2): We need the following lemma:

Lemma 6.3 If $\mathbf{Spec}(SP)$ has a type then SP has a type of the form $\mathbf{Spec}(\tau)$.

Proof Obvious, since the only way to derive a type for $\mathbf{Spec}(SP)$ is using the rule

$$\frac{Type(SP) = \mathbf{Spec}(\tau)}{Type(\mathbf{Spec}(SP)) = \mathbf{Spec}(\mathbf{Spec}(\tau))}$$

which requires that indeed $Type(SP) = \mathbf{Spec}(\tau)$ for some type τ. □

By the inductive assumption (of the proof of the theorem) under the assumption $Type(X) = \tau$ where $Type(SP) = \mathbf{Spec}(\tau)$, $\mathbf{Spec}(SP'')$ has a type, and so using the above lemma we conclude that $Type(SP'') = \mathbf{Spec}(\tau'')$ for some type τ''. Hence, we can derive $Type(\Pi X{:}SP.\, SP'') = \mathbf{Spec}(\tau \rightarrow \tau'')$, and then $Type(\mathbf{Spec}(\Pi X{:}SP.\, SP'')) = \mathbf{Spec}(\mathbf{Spec}(\tau \rightarrow \tau''))$.

On the other hand, by the inductive assumption again, under the assumption $Type(X) = \tau$, $Type(\mathbf{Spec}(SP'')) = \mathbf{Spec}(Type(SP'))$. Hence, $\mathbf{Spec}(\mathbf{Spec}(\tau'')) = \mathbf{Spec}(Type(SP'))$, and so $Type(SP') = \mathbf{Spec}(\tau'')$. Thus, $Type(\Pi X{:}SP.\, SP') = \mathbf{Spec}(\tau \rightarrow \tau'')$, which completes the proof in this case.

(R3): By the inductive assumption, $\mathbf{Spec}(Type(SP)) = Type(\mathbf{Spec}(SP'))$, which easily implies $\mathbf{Spec}(Type(\mathbf{Spec}(SP))) = Type(\mathbf{Spec}(\mathbf{Spec}(SP')))$.

(R4): By the inductive assumption, using Lemma 6.3, we have that $Type(SP) = \mathbf{Spec}(\tau)$ for some type τ, and then under the assumption $Type(X) = \tau$, $Type(SP') = \mathbf{Spec}(\tau')$ where $\tau' = Type(Obj)$. Thus, we can derive both $Type(\lambda X{:}SP.\, Obj) = \tau \rightarrow \tau'$ and $Type(\Pi X{:}SP.\, SP') = \mathbf{Spec}(\tau \rightarrow \tau')$

(R5): The inductive assumption implies that $Type(SP) = \mathbf{Spec}(\tau)$ where $\tau = Type(Obj')$, and that $Type(\Pi X{:}SP.\, SP') = \mathbf{Spec}(Type(Obj))$. Since there is only one rule which allows us to derive a type for the Π-expression, by a direct analysis of this rule we can conclude that under the assumption $Type(X) = \tau$, $Type(SP') = \mathbf{Spec}(\tau')$ for some type τ'. Moreover, $Type(\Pi X{:}SP.\, SP') = \mathbf{Spec}(\tau \rightarrow \tau')$, which implies $Type(Obj) = \tau \rightarrow \tau'$. Hence, we can derive $Type(Obj(Obj')) = \tau'$.

Lemma 6.4 For any object Obj', variable X and type τ, if $Type(Obj') = \tau'$ under the assumption $Type(X) = \tau$, then for any object Obj such that $Type(Obj) = \tau$, we have $Type(Obj'[Obj/X]) = \tau'$.

Proof By obvious induction on the derivation of $Type(Obj') = \tau'$, by inspection of the clauses in the definition of $Type(\_)$. □

Hence, by the above lemma we conclude that $Type(SP'[Obj'/X]) = \mathbf{Spec}(\tau')$, which completes the proof in this case.

(R6): We need the following lemma:

Lemma 6.5 β-reduction preserves types of objects. That is, for any object Obj such that $Type(Obj) = \tau$, if $Obj \rightarrow_\beta^* Obj'$ then $Type(Obj') = \tau$.

Proof (sketch) It is sufficient to show the lemma for $Obj \rightarrow_\beta Obj'$. The proof proceeds by induction on the derivation of the type of Obj. The only non-trivial case is that of application, where a β-reduct may be introduced. So, assume that Obj is a roughly well-formed object of the form $(\lambda X{:}SP.\, Obj_1)(Obj_2)$. Then, for some types τ and τ', $Type((\lambda X{:}SP.\, Obj_1)(Obj_2)) = \tau'$, $Type(\lambda X{:}SP.\, Obj_1) = \tau \rightarrow \tau'$, $Type(Obj_2) = \tau$, $Type(SP) = \mathbf{Spec}(\tau)$ and under the assumption $Type(X) = \tau$, $Type(Obj_1) = \tau'$. Hence, by Lemma 6.4, $Type(Obj_1[Obj_2/X]) = \tau'$, which is what is needed in this case. □

Now, by the inductive assumption applied to one of the premises of the rule we have that $\mathbf{Spec}(Type(Obj)) = Type(SP)$. Then, since $SP \rightarrow_\beta^* SP'$, by the above lemma we have indeed $\mathbf{Spec}(Type(Obj)) = Type(SP')$.

(R7): Similarly as in the previous case.

(R8), (R9), (R10), (R11): Easy use of the inductive assumption.

□

The above theorem states that a necessary condition for an object to satisfy a specification is that both are roughly well-formed and the type of the object is consistent with the type of the specification. Of course, nothing like the opposite implications holds. As pointed out earlier, proving that an object satisfies a specification must involve a verification process as embodied in the two rules of semantic inference.

One might now expect that any well-formed object *Obj* "is of its type", i.e. $Obj : Type(Obj)$. This is not the case, though. The problem is that both λ- and Π-expressions include parameter *specifications* rather than just parameter *types*, and so functions denoted by λ-expressions and specified by Π-expressions have domains defined by specifications, not just by types. This is necessary for methodological reasons: we have to be able to specify permissible arguments in a more refined way than just by giving their types. However, as a consequence, objects denoted by λ- and Π-expressions in general do not belong to the domain defined by their types, and so we cannot expect that such expressions would "typecheck" to their types.

To identify the purely "type-checking" component in our system we have to deal with objects where parameter specifications are replaced by their types. Formally, for any roughly well-formed object *Obj*, its version *Erase*(*Obj*) with parameter specifications erased is defined by induction as follows:

Specifications:

$$
\begin{aligned}
Erase(\Sigma) &=_{def} \Sigma \\
Erase(\textbf{impose } \Phi \textbf{ on } SP) &=_{def} \textbf{impose } \Phi \textbf{ on } Erase(SP)
\end{aligned}
$$

... *and similarly for other simple specifications* ...

$$
\begin{aligned}
Erase(\{Obj\}) &=_{def} \{Erase(Obj)\} \\
Erase(\Pi X{:}SP.\, SP') &=_{def} \Pi X{:}\tau.\, Erase(SP') \\
&\qquad \text{where } Type(SP) = \mathbf{Spec}(\tau) \\
Erase(\mathbf{Spec}(SP)) &=_{def} \mathbf{Spec}(Erase(SP))
\end{aligned}
$$

Other objects:

$$
\begin{aligned}
Erase(A) &=_{def} A \\
Erase(\lambda X{:}SP.\, Obj) &=_{def} \lambda X{:}\tau.\, Erase(Obj) \\
&\qquad \text{where } Type(SP) = \mathbf{Spec}(\tau) \\
Erase(Obj(Obj')) &=_{def} Erase(Obj)(Erase(Obj'))
\end{aligned}
$$

We have chosen here to define $Erase(A) = A$ for all algebra expressions A. Alternatively, we could leave this case out again, and require a definition to be provided externally. For example, one might want that $Erase(A[Obj/X]) = Erase(A[Erase(Obj)/X])$ (which would not necessarily hold under the above definition). The only property we need is that if A is an algebra expression denoting a Σ-algebra then so is $Erase(A)$.

Theorem 6.6 For any roughly well-formed object *Obj*, $Erase(Obj) : Type(Obj)$ (hence, *Erase*(*Obj*) is well-formed).

Proof (idea) Again, the extension to objects with free variables is not entirely clear. What we mean is: if $Type(Obj) = \tau$ under the assumptions $Type(X_1) = \tau_1, \ldots, Type(X_n) = \tau_n$ then $Erase(Obj) : Type(Obj)$ under the assumptions $X_1 : \tau_1, \ldots, X_n : \tau_n$. This may be proved by straightforward induction on the derivation of the type of *Obj*. □

Joining this with Theorem 6.2, we conclude that a necessary condition for an object to satisfy a specification is that the version of the object where parameter specifications have been "rounded up" to parameter types has a type which is consistent with the type of the specification. This necessary condition embodies the purely type-checking component of any proof that an object satisfies a specification.

Corollary 6.7 For any roughly well-formed object Obj, $Type(Erase(Obj)) = Type(Obj)$.
Proof This follows directly from Theorems 6.6 and 6.2 since for any type τ, $Type(\tau) = \mathbf{Spec}(\tau)$, which may easily be established by an obvious induction on the structure of types. □

The above corollary, when the equality is read from right to left, may be viewed as an alternative definition of the type of a roughly well-formed object. The type-checking of $Erase(Obj)$ may be performed within the original system separately from the semantic verification part, without any reference to the meanings of objects and specifications. We present below the corresponding proper fragment of the original system:

Simple specifications:

$$\frac{\Sigma \text{ signature}}{\Sigma : \mathbf{Spec}(\Sigma)} \qquad \frac{SP : \mathbf{Spec}(\Sigma) \qquad \Phi \subseteq Sen(\Sigma)}{\mathbf{impose}\ \Phi\ \mathbf{on}\ SP : \mathbf{Spec}(\Sigma)}$$

... *and just as before for other simple specifications* ...

Other specifications:

$$\frac{Obj : \tau}{\{Obj\} : \mathbf{Spec}(\tau)} \qquad \frac{\begin{array}{c}[X:\tau]\\ SP' : \mathbf{Spec}(\tau')\end{array}}{\Pi X{:}\tau.\, SP' : \mathbf{Spec}(\tau \rightarrow \tau')} \qquad \frac{SP : \mathbf{Spec}(\tau)}{\mathbf{Spec}(SP) : \mathbf{Spec}(\mathbf{Spec}(\tau))}$$

λ-expressions:

$$\frac{\begin{array}{c}[X:\tau]\\ Obj : \tau'\end{array}}{\lambda X{:}\tau.\, Obj : \tau \rightarrow \tau'} \qquad \frac{Obj : \tau \rightarrow \tau' \qquad Obj' : \tau}{Obj(Obj') : \tau'}$$

Algebra expressions:

$$\frac{A \text{ is an algebra expression denoting a } \Sigma\text{-algebra}}{A : \Sigma}$$

We hope that a comparison of the above with the system presented in Section 5 should clearly illustrate the intuitive difference between typed λ-calculi, like the one above, and "specified" λ-calculi, like the one in Section 5.

7 Concluding remarks

Spurred by the methodological considerations in [SST 90], we have presented an institution-independent specification formalism which provides a notation for parameterised specifications and specifications of parametric objects of an arbitrary order, as well as any mixture of these concepts. The formalism incorporates the kernel specification-building operations described in [ST 88] based on those in the ASL specification language [SW 83], [Wir 86]. The basic idea was to treat specifications, which specify objects, as objects themselves. This collapsing together of the two levels, that of objects and that of their specifications, led (perhaps surprisingly) to a well-behaved inference system for proving that an object satisfies a specification with a clearly identified formal type-checking component (cf. [SdST 90] where the formal type-checking component of Extended ML is given).

The formalism presented deals explicitly with two levels of objects involved in the process of software development: programs (viewed as algebras) and their specifications (viewed as classes of algebras) — both, of course, arbitrarily parameterised. Aiming at the development of an institution-independent framework, we decided to omit from our considerations yet another level of objects involved, namely that of algebra components (such as data values and operations on them). In particular institutions, however, it may be interesting to explicitly consider this level as well, and to intermix constructs for dealing with this level with those for the other two levels mentioned above. This would lead to entities such as algebras parametric on data values, specifications parameterised by functions on data, functions from algebras and specifications to data values, etc.

Just as the kernel ASL-like specification formalism it builds on, the presented system is too low-level to be directly useful in practice. We view it primarily as a kernel to be used as a semantic foundation for the development of more user-friendly specification languages. An example of such a more user-oriented framework is the Extended ML specification language [ST 85] which comes together with a program development methodology as presented in [ST 89]. The formalism described in this paper provides adequate foundations for Extended ML. Indeed, one of the main stimuli for its development was our inability to express the semantics of the current version of Extended ML directly in terms of the kernel specification-building operations in ASL: Extended ML functor specifications are specifications of parametric objects, and these were not present in ASL. The task of writing out a complete institution-independent semantics of Extended ML in terms of the specification formalism presented here remains to be done. We expect that some technicalities, like those which arise in connection with ML type inheritance, will cause the same problems as in [ST 89]. Some others, like the use of behavioural equivalence and the concept of functor stability in the Extended ML methodology, although directly related to the **abstract** operation in the formalism presented here, require further study in this more general framework. Finally, properties of ML functors such as persistency, which cause difficulties in other specification formalisms, will be easy to express here.

Of course, the formal properties of the system need much further study. For example, it seems that the "cut" rule should be admissible (although not derivable) in the remainder of the system. The standard properties of β-reduction, such as the Church-Rosser property and termination (on well-formed objects) should be carefully proven, probably by reference to the analogous properties of the usual typed λ-calculus. For example, the termination property of β-reduction on the well-formed objects of the language should follow easily from the observation that the *Erase* function as defined in Section 6 preserves β-reduction, which allows us to lift the corresponding property of the usual typed λ-calculus to our formalism. The system is incomplete, as pointed out earlier. It would be useful to identify all the sources of this incompleteness, for example by characterising an interesting subset of the language for which the system is complete. One line of research which we have not followed (as yet) is to try to encode the formalism we present here in one of the known type theories (for example, Martin-Löf's system [NPS 90], the calculus of constructions [CH 88] or LF [HHP 87]). It would be interesting to see both which of the features of the formalism we propose would be difficult to handle, as well as which of the tedious proofs of some formal properties of our formalism (cf. the proofs sketched for Theorems 5.8 and 6.2) would turn out to be available for free under such an encoding.

Acknowledgements: We are grateful to Stefan Sokołowski for his collaboration on [SST 90] leading to the development of an early version of the formalism presented here. Thanks to Jordi Farrés, Cliff Jones and Stefan Kahrs for helpful comments on a draft of [SST 90], and to Jan Bergstra for a question on β-reduction which led to the current version of the system. Thanks to an anonymous referee for comments on a draft of this paper which helped to improve the presentation.

This research was supported by the University of Edinburgh, the University of Bremen, the Technical University of Denmark, the University of Manchester, and by grants from the Polish Academy of Sciences, the (U.K.) Science and Engineering Research Council, ESPRIT, and the Wolfson Foundation.

8 References

[Note: LNCS n = Springer Lecture Notes in Computer Science, Volume n]

[Ada 80] *The Programming Language Ada: Reference Manual.* LNCS 106 (1980).

[Bar 84] H.P. Barendregt. *The Lambda Calculus: Its Syntax and Semantics* (second edition). North-Holland (1984).

[Bau 85] F.L. Bauer *et al* (the CIP language group). *The Wide Spectrum Language CIP-L.* LNCS 183 (1985).

[BGM 89] M. Bidoit, M.-C. Gaudel and A. Mauboussin. How to make algebraic specifications more understandable? An experiment with the PLUSS specification language. *Science of Computer Programming* 12, 1–38 (1989).

[BT 83] A. Blikle and A. Tarlecki. Naive denotational semantics. *Information Processing 83, Proc. IFIP Congress '83* (ed. R. Mason), Paris. North-Holland, 345–355 (1983).

[BKS 88] A.M. Borzyszkowski, R. Kubiak and S. Sokołowski. A set-theoretic model for a typed polymorphic λ-calculus. *Proc. VDM-Europe Symp. VDM — The Way Ahead*, Dublin. LNCS 328, 267–298 (1988).

[BG 80] R.M. Burstall and J.A. Goguen. The semantics of CLEAR, a specification language. *Proc. of Advanced Course on Abstract Software Specification*, Copenhagen. LNCS 86, 292–332 (1980).

[Coh 81] P.M. Cohn. *Universal Algebra.* Reidel (1981).

[Con 86] R.L. Constable *et al. Implementing Mathematics with the Nuprl Proof Development System.* Prentice-Hall (1986).

[CH 88] T. Coquand and G. Huet. The calculus of constructions. *Information and Computation* 76 (1988).

[DMN 70] O.-J. Dahl, B. Myrhaug and K. Nygaard. Simula 67 common base language. Report S-22, Norwegian Computing Center, Oslo (1970).

[Ehr 82] H.-D. Ehrich. On the theory of specification, implementation, and parametrization of abstract data types. *Journal of the Assoc. for Computing Machinery 29*, 206–227 (1982).

[EKTWW 84] H. Ehrig, H.-J. Kreowski, J. Thatcher, E. Wagner and J. Wright. Parameter passing in algebraic specification languages. *Theoretical Computer Science* 28, 45–81 (1984).

[EM 85] H. Ehrig and B. Mahr. *Fundamentals of Algebraic Specification I: Equations and Initial Semantics.* Springer (1985).

[ETLZ 82] H. Ehrig, J.W. Thatcher, P. Lucas and S.N. Zilles. Denotational and initial algebra semantics of the algebraic specification language LOOK. Report 84-22, Technische Universität Berlin (1982).

[Far 89] J. Farrés-Casals. Proving correctness of constructor implementations. *Proc. 14th Symp. on Mathematical Foundations of Computer Science*, Porąbka-Kozubnik. LNCS 379, 225–235 (1989).

[FJKR 87] L.M.G. Feijs, H.B.M. Jonkers, C.P.J. Koymans and G.R. Renardel de Lavalette. Formal definition of the design language COLD-K. METEOR Report t7/PRLE/7, Philips Research Laboratories (1987).

[FJ 90] J.S. Fitzgerald and C.B. Jones. Modularizing the formal description of a database system. *Proc. VDM'90 Symp. VDM and Z — Formal Methods in Software Development*, Kiel. LNCS 428, 189–210 (1990).

[Gog 84] J.A. Goguen. Parameterized programming. *IEEE Trans. Software Engineering SE-10*, 528–543 (1984).

[GB 84] J.A. Goguen and R.M. Burstall. Introducing institutions. *Proc. Logics of Programming Workshop*, Carnegie-Mellon. LNCS 164, 221–256 (1984).

[GHW 85] J.V. Guttag, J.J. Horning and J. Wing. Larch in five easy pieces. Report 5, DEC Systems Research Center, Palo Alto, CA (1985).

[HHP 87] R. Harper, F. Honsell and G. Plotkin. A framework for defining logics. *Proc. 2nd IEEE Symp. on Logic in Computer Science*, Cornell, 194–204 (1987).

[LL 88] T. Lehmann and J. Loeckx. The specification language of OBSCURE. *Recent Trends in Data Type Specification, Selected Papers from the 5th Workshop on Specification of Abstract Data Types*, Gullane, Scotland. LNCS 332, 131–153 (1988).

[Lis 81] B.H. Liskov *et al. CLU Reference Manual.* LNCS 114 (1981).

[MacQ 86] D.B. MacQueen. Modules for Standard ML. In: R. Harper, D.B. MacQueen and R. Milner. Standard ML. Report ECS-LFCS-86-2, Univ. of Edinburgh (1986).

[MMMS 87] A.R. Meyer, J.C. Mitchell, E. Moggi and R. Statman. Empty types in polymorphic lambda calculus. *Proc. 14th ACM Symp. on Principles of Programming Languages*, 253–262; revised version in *Logical Foundations of Functional Programming* (ed. G. Huet), Addison-Wesley, 273–284 (1990).

[MTH 90] R. Milner, M. Tofte and R. Harper. *The Definition of Standard ML.* MIT Press (1990).

[Mos 89a] P. Mosses. Unified algebras and modules. *Proc. 16th ACM Symp. on Principles of Programming Languages*, Austin, 329–343 (1989).

[Mos 89b] P. Mosses. Unified algebras and institutions. *Proc. 4th IEEE Symp. on Logic in Computer Science*, Asilomar, 304–312 (1989).

[NPS 90] B. Nordström, K. Petersson and J.M. Smith. *Programming in Martin-Löf's Type Theory: An Introduction.* Oxford Univ. Press (1990).

[SdST 90] D. Sannella, F. da Silva and A. Tarlecki. Syntax, typechecking and dynamic semantics for Extended ML (version 2). Draft report, Univ. of Edinburgh (1990). Version 1 appeared as Report ECS-LFCS-89-101, Univ. of Edinburgh (1989).

[SST 90] D. Sannella, S. Sokołowski and A. Tarlecki. Toward formal development of programs from algebraic specifications: parameterisation revisited. Report 6/90, Informatik, Universität Bremen (1990).

[ST 85] D. Sannella and A. Tarlecki. Program specification and development in Standard ML. *Proc. 12th ACM Symp. on Principles of Programming Languages*, New Orleans, 67–77 (1985).

[ST 87] D. Sannella and A. Tarlecki. On observational equivalence and algebraic specification. *J. Comp. and Sys. Sciences 34*, 150–178 (1987).

[ST 88] D. Sannella and A. Tarlecki. Specifications in an arbitrary institution. *Information and Computation 76*, 165–210 (1988).

[ST 89] D. Sannella and A. Tarlecki. Toward formal development of ML programs: foundations and methodology. Report ECS-LFCS-89-71, Univ. of Edinburgh (1989); extended abstract in *Proc. Colloq. on Current Issues in Programming Languages*, Joint Conf. on Theory and Practice of Software Development (TAPSOFT), Barcelona. LNCS 352, 375–389 (1989).

[SW 83] D. Sannella and M. Wirsing. A kernel language for algebraic specification and implementation. *Proc. Intl. Conf. on Foundations of Computation Theory*, Borgholm, Sweden. LNCS 158, 413–427 (1983).

[Sch 86] O. Schoett. Data abstraction and the correctness of modular programming. Ph.D. thesis, Univ. of Edinburgh (1986).

[Voß 85] A. Voß. Algebraic specifications in an integrated software development and verification system. Ph.D. thesis, Universität Kaiserslautern (1985).

[Wir 86] M. Wirsing. Structured algebraic specifications: a kernel language. *Theoretical Computer Science* 42, 123–249 (1986).

[Wirth 88] N. Wirth. *Programming in Modula-2* (third edition). Springer (1988).

Extended ML: Past, present and future

Donald Sannella* Andrzej Tarlecki†

Abstract

An overview of past, present and future work on the Extended ML formal program development framework is given, with emphasis on two topics of current active research: the semantics of the Extended ML specification language, and tools to support formal program development.

1 Introduction

The ultimate goal of work on program specification is to establish a practical framework for the systematic production of correct programs from requirements specifications via a sequence of verified-correct development steps. Such a framework should be fully formal and based on sound mathematical foundations in order to guarantee the correctness of the resulting program with respect to the original specification. The program development activity must be supported by computer-based tools which remove the burden of clerical work from the user and eliminate the possibility of human error.

Extended ML is a framework for the formal development of programs in the Standard ML functional programming language from high-level specifications of their required input/output behaviour. It strongly supports "development in the large", producing modular programs consisting of an interconnected collection of generic and modular units. The Extended ML framework includes a methodology for formal program development which establishes a number of ways of proceeding from a given specification of a programming task towards a program. Each such step (modular decomposition, etc.) gives rise to one or more proof obligations which must be discharged in order to establish the correctness of that step.

The Extended ML language is a wide-spectrum language which encompasses both specifications and executable programs in a single unified framework. It is a simple extension of the Standard ML programming language in which axioms are permitted in module interfaces and in place of code in module bodies. This allows all stages in the development of a program to be expressed in the Extended ML language, from the initial high-level specification to the final program itself and including intermediate stages in which specification and program are intermingled.

Formally developing a program in Extended ML means writing a high-level specification of a generic Standard ML module and then refining this specification top-down by means of a sequence (actually, a tree) of development steps until an executable Standard ML program is obtained. The development has a tree-like structure since one of the ways to proceed from a specification is to decompose it into a number of smaller specifications which can then be independently refined further. In programming terms, this corresponds to implementing a program module by decomposing it into a number of independent sub-modules. The end-product is an interconnected collection of generic Standard ML modules, each with a complete and accurate specification of its interface with the rest of the system. The explicit interfaces enable correct reuse of the individual modules in other systems, and facilitate maintainability by making it possible to localize the effect on the system of subsequent changes in the requirements specification.

*LFCS, Department of Computer Science, University of Edinburgh, Edinburgh, Scotland.
†Institute of Computer Science, Polish Academy of Sciences, Warsaw, Poland.

This paper is intended as a report on the status of work on Extended ML with emphasis on two topics of current active research: the semantics of the Extended ML language, and tools to support program development. In an attempt to make the paper self-contained, a brief introduction to formal program development in Extended ML is included in Section 2. Past work on the theoretical underpinnings of Extended ML is summarized in Section 3. Current work on the semantics of Extended ML is discussed in Section 4, and plans for tools to support formal program development are outlined in Section 5.

2 An introduction to Extended ML

The aim of this section is to briefly outline the main ideas of Extended ML. Three topics are discussed: the Standard ML functional programming language, which is the target of formal program development and on which the Extended ML wide-spectrum language is based; the Extended ML wide-spectrum language; and the Extended ML formal program development methodology. This outline is necessarily brief, and readers with no prior knowledge of Extended ML will probably find it helpful to consult the references given below.

2.1 Standard ML

Standard ML consists of two sub-languages: the Standard ML "core language" and the Standard ML "module language". The core language provides constructs for programming "in the small" by defining a collection of types and values of those types. The module language provides constructs for programming "in the large" by defining and combining a number of self-contained program units. These sub-languages can be viewed as more or less independent since there are relatively few points of contact between the sub-languages.

A complete formal semantics of Standard ML is in [MTH 90]; see [MT 90] for valuable explanatory prose. The features of the language are introduced at a more tutorial level in [Wik 87] (core language only), [MacQ 86a] and [Tof 89] (module language only), [Har 89], and [Rea 89].

2.1.1 The Standard ML core language

The Standard ML core language is a strongly typed functional programming language. It has a flexible type system including polymorphic types, disjoint union, product and (higher-order) function types, and user-defined abstract and concrete types. Programs written in the core language look very similar to programs in Hope [BMS 80], Miranda [BW 88] or Haskell [HW 89]. The following example of an Standard ML program uses most of the main features of the Standard ML core language:

```
datatype (''a,'b) alist = default of ''a -> 'b
                        | cons of ''a * 'b * (''a,'b) alist

type dictionary = (string,string) alist

exception novalue

val empty = default(fn a => raise novalue)

fun lookup(a,default f) = f a
  | lookup(a,cons(a1,b,l)) = if a=a1 then b else lookup(a,l)

fun isin(a,l) = (lookup(a,l); true) handle novalue => false

exception conflict
```

```
fun add(a,b,default f) = cons(a,b,default f)
  | add(a,b,cons(a1,b1,l)) = if a=a1 then raise conflict
                             else cons(a1,b1,add(a,b,l))

fun remove(a,default f) = let fun g a1 = if a=a1
                                         then raise novalue
                                         else f a1
                          in default g
                          end
  | remove(a,cons(a1,b1,l)) = if a=a1 then l
                              else cons(a1,b1,remove(a,l))
```

Features which are not used include: record types, user-defined abstract types (more flexibly provided by the Standard ML module language), exceptions which pass values, and input/output. Also not used are references and assignment, which are available in Standard ML but which are not taken into account in work on Extended ML.

Conceptually, every value in Standard ML is represented as a term consisting of a *constructor* applied to a number of sub-terms, each of which in turn represents another value. In the above program, `default` is a unary constructor (of type `(''a -> 'b) -> (''a,'b) alist`) and `cons` is a ternary constructor (of type `''a * 'b * (''a,'b) alist -> (''a,'b) alist`). Constructor functions are uninterpreted; they just construct. There is no need to define a lower-level representation of `alists` in terms of lists, arrays, pointers, etc.

Functions are defined by a sequence of one of more equations, each of which specifies the value of the function over some subset of the set of possible argument values, as above. This subset is described by a *pattern* (a term containing constructors and variables only, without repeated variables) on the left-hand side of the equation. The pattern is thereby used for case selection and variable binding. The patterns on the left-hand side of equations should normally be disjoint and should exhaust the possibilities given in the definition of the argument type(s).

Certain types are designated by ML as *equality types*. See [MTH 90] for the exact definition; roughly, only types whose definitions involve abstract types or function types are excluded. The function `= : ''a * ''a -> bool` is the built-in equality function; the type variable `''a` can only be instantiated to equality types (in contrast to `'a` which can be instantiated to any type) which prevents values of non equality types from being tested for equality.

2.1.2 The Standard ML module language

The Standard ML module language provides mechanisms which allow large Standard ML programs to be structured into self-contained program units with explicitly-specified interfaces. Under this scheme, interfaces (called *signatures*) and their implementations (called *structures*) are defined separately. Every structure has a signature which gives the names of the types and values defined in the structure. Structures may be built on top of existing structures, so each one is actually a *hierarchy* of structures, and this is reflected in its signature. *Functors* are "parameterized" structures; the application of a functor to a structure yields a structure. A functor has an input signature describing structures to which it may be applied, and an output signature describing the structure which results from such an application. It is possible, and sometimes necessary to allow interaction between different parts of a program, to declare that certain substructures (or just certain types) in the hierarchy are identical or *shared*.

The following is a simple example of a modular Standard ML program for sorting a list of values of arbitrary type, provided an order relation on that type is supplied.

```
signature PO =
   sig
      type elem
      val le : elem * elem -> bool
   end

signature SORT =
   sig
      structure Elements : PO
      val sort : Elements.elem list -> Elements.elem list
   end

functor Sort(X : PO) : SORT =
   struct
      structure Elements = X
      fun insert(a,[]) = [a]
        | insert(a,b::l) = if Elements.le(a,b) then a::b::l
                           else b::insert(a,l)
      fun sort [] = []
        | sort(a::l) = insert(a,sort l)
   end

structure IntPO : PO =
   struct
      type elem = int
      val le = op <=
   end

structure SortInt = Sort(IntPO)
```

This defines a functor called `Sort` which may be applied to any structure matching the signature `PO` (such as `IntPO`), whereupon it will yield a structure (above, `SortInt`) matching the signature `SORT`. In order for the definition of `Sort` to be correctly typed, the body of `Sort` must define a structure containing a substructure called `Elements` which matches `PO`, and a function called `sort` with the type given. The function `SortInt.sort` may be applied to the list `[11,5,2,8]` to yield `[2,5,8,11]`. Since the function `insert` is not mentioned in the output signature `SORT`, it is considered local to the body of `Sort` and does not appear in the structure `SortInt`. The body of `Sort` makes no reference to other functors but of course it is possible to define new functors by building on top of existing functors.

Signatures serve both to impose constraints on the bodies of structures/functors and to restrict the information which is made available externally about the types and functions which are defined in structure/functor bodies. Only the information which is explicitly recorded in the signature(s) of a structure/functor is available externally.[1] This is vital to allow parts of a large software system to be developed and maintained independently.

Multi-argument functors are treated as single-argument functors in which the input signature requires a structure with multiple substructures. The functor below takes two structures matching `PO` and produces another structure matching `PO`:

[1]This is not quite true in Standard ML; see [ST 89] for more discussion on this point.

```
functor Lexicographic(structure X : PO
                      structure Y : PO) : PO =
   struct
      type elem = X.elem * Y.elem
      fun le((x,y),(x',y')) = if X.le(x,x')
                              then if X.le(x',x) then Y.le(y,y') else true
                              else false
   end

structure BoolPO : PO =
   struct
      type elem = bool
      fun le(x,y) = (not x) orelse y
   end

structure Lex = Lexicographic(structure X = IntPO
                              structure Y = BoolPO)
```

The function Lex.le is an order relation on $\langle$`int` $\times$ `bool`$\rangle$-pairs, where `Lex.le((2,true),(2,false))` is `false`.

When multi-argument functors are defined, it is sometimes necessary to declare that certain components of the argument structures are common to both structures. This is done using a *sharing constraint*. For example, changing the heading of `Lexicographic` to:

```
functor Lexicographic(structure X : PO
                      structure Y : PO
                      sharing type X.elem = Y.elem) : PO = ...
```

would restrict application to structures having the indicated types in common. In some cases (not this one) such a restriction is necessary to ensure that the functor body is well-typed for all admissible parameter structures.

It is possible to use sharing constraints to make explicit the fact that parts of the argument structure of a functor are inherited by the result structure. This information can be added to the heading of the `Sort` functor above as follows:

```
functor Sort(X : PO) : sig include SORT
                           sharing Elements = X
                       end = ...
```

The declaration `include SORT` has the same effect as repeating the declarations in the signature `SORT` above. The sharing constraint `sharing Elements = X` asserts that the substructure `Elements` of the result structure is identical to the argument structure.

2.2 The Extended ML wide-spectrum language

Extended ML is a vehicle for the systematic formal development of programs from specifications by means of individually-verified steps. Extended ML is called a *wide-spectrum* language since it allows all stages in the formal development process to be expressed in a single unified framework, from the initial high-level specification to the final program itself and including intermediate stages in which specification and program are intermingled. The eventual product of the formal development process is a modular program in Standard ML, and thus Standard ML is the executable sub-language of Extended ML. Earlier stages in the development of such a program are incomplete modular programs in which some parts are only specified by means of axioms rather than defined in an executable fashion by means of ML code. The use of axioms allows more information to be provided in signatures (properties may be specified which are required to hold of any structure matching that signature), and less information to be provided in structure/functor bodies (since axioms are permitted in place of ML code).

In the Standard ML module language, a signature acts as an interface to a program unit (structure or functor) which serves to mediate its interactions with the outside world. The information in a signature is sufficient for the use of Standard ML as a programming language, but when viewed as an interface specification a signature does not generally provide enough information to permit proving program correctness (for example). To make signatures more useful as interfaces of structures in program specification and development, we allow them to include axioms which put constraints on the permitted behaviour of the components of the structure. An example of such a signature is the following more informative version of the signature PO from the last section:

```
signature PO =
   sig
      type elem
      val le : elem * elem -> bool
      axiom forall x => le(x,x)
      axiom forall x,y => (le(x,y) andalso le(y,x) implies x=y)
      axiom forall x,y,z => (le(x,y) andalso le(y,z) implies le(x,z))
   end
```

This includes the previously-unexpressible precondition which IntPO must satisfy if Sort(IntPO) is to behave as expected, namely that IntPO.le is a partial order on IntPO.elem.

Formal specifications can be viewed as abstract programs. Some specifications are so completely abstract that they give no hint of an algorithm, while other specifications are so concrete that they amount to programs (e.g. Standard ML function definitions, which are just equations of a certain special form which ensures that they are executable). In order to allow different stages in the evolution of a program to be expressed in a single framework, we allow structures to contain a mixture of ML code and non-executable axioms. Functors can include axioms as well since they are simply parameterized structures. For example, a stage in the development of the functor Sort in the last section might be the following:

```
functor Sort(X : PO) : sig include SORT
                           sharing Elements = X
                       end =
   struct
      structure Elements : PO = X
      fun member(a:Elements.elem,l:Elements.elem list) = ? : bool
      axiom forall a => member(a,[]) = false
      axiom forall a,l => member(a,a::l) = true
      axiom forall a,b,l => (a<>b implies member(a,b::l) = member(a,l))
      fun isordered(l:Elements.elem list) = ? : bool
      axiom forall l =>
                isordered l = forall a,b,l1,l2,l3 =>
                                 (l = l1@[a]@l2@[b]@l3 implies Elements.le(a,b))
      fun insert(a:Elements.elem,l:Elements.elem list) = ? : Elements.elem list
      axiom forall a,l => member(a,insert(a,l))
      axiom forall a,l =>
                isordered l
                   implies
                      (exists l1,l2 =>
                          l1 @ l2 = l
                          andalso insert(a,l) = l1@[a]@l2
```

```
                                  andalso forall a1 =>
                                          (member(a1,l1) implies Elements.le(a1,a))
                                  andalso forall a2 =>
                                          (member(a2,l2) implies Elements.le(a,a2)))
        fun sort [] = []
          | sort(a::l) = insert(a,sort l)
      end
```

In this functor declaration, the function **sort** has been defined in an executable fashion in terms of **insert** which is so far only constrained by axioms. As in Standard ML, the functions **member**, **isordered** and **insert** are not visible outside the functor body since they do not appear in the output signature of **Sort**. The functions **member** and **isordered** are only used to specify **insert**. At some stage in the development of executable code for **insert**, **member** and **isordered** will no longer be used (presumably). At this point, their specifications can be omitted from the body of **Sort** without the need to develop executable code for them (although first it must be shown that their specifications are consistent with the code developed for **insert** and **sort**, in order to ensure the correctness of this step).

Functions and constants which are not defined in an executable fashion are declared using the special place-holder expression ? as in the example above. This is necessary in order to declare the type of the function or constant which would normally be inferred from an executable definition by the ML system. The same construct can be used to declare a type when its representation in terms of other types has not yet been selected. It is also useful at the earliest stage in the development of a functor or structure when no body has been supplied:

```
    functor Sort(X : PO) : sig include SORT
                                sharing Elements = X
                           end = ?
```

The Extended ML language is the result obtained by extending Standard ML as indicated above. That is, axioms are allowed in signatures and in structures, and the place-holder ? is allowed in place of the expression (type expression, value expression, or structure expression) on the right-hand side of declarations. A more complete introduction to the Extended ML language appears in [San 91]; a tutorial introduction is [San 87]. More discussion of the motivation behind Extended ML may be found in [ST 85]. [SdST 90] defines the concrete syntax and some aspects of the semantics of Extended ML. A difference with respect to these earlier papers is that following recent work on the semantics of Extended ML (see Section 4) we have dropped the restriction to a simple subset of Standard ML; we now aim to cover all of Standard ML except for references and assignment.

The examples above use the notation of first-order equational logic to write axioms (where equality may be used in axioms on *all* types, not just on equality types as in Standard ML executable code). This choice is to a large extent arbitrary since the formal underpinnings of Extended ML are mostly independent of the choice of logic. It is natural to choose a logic which has the Standard ML core language as a subset; this way, the development process comes to an end when all the axioms in structure and functor bodies are expressed in this executable subset.

The role of signatures as interfaces suggests that they should be regarded as descriptions of the externally observable behaviour of structures. This amounts to not distinguishing between *behaviourally equivalent* implementations in which all computations produce the same observable results. Validity of implementations is defined in Extended ML in terms of satisfaction of axioms up to behavioural equivalence with respect to an appropriate set of observable types. The details of this may be found in [ST 89]. This is reflected in the proof obligations which are incurred in the course of Extended ML program development (see the next section) where *behavioural consequence* ($\models_{OBS}$) is used in place of ordinary consequence ($\models$).

2.3 The Extended ML development methodology

The starting point of formal development is a high-level requirements specification of a software system. The concept of a Standard ML functor corresponds to the informal notion of a self-contained software system. A functor may be built by composing other functors and so the scale of such a system may vary from small (like the examples above) to very large. In Extended ML, a specification of a software system is a functor with specified interfaces. The initial high-level specification will be a functor of the form:

```
functor F(X : SIG) : SIG' = ?
```

where `SIG` and `SIG'` are Extended ML signatures containing axioms. At later stages of development, a functor specification may include a body which is not yet composed of executable code. This is still a specification of a software system, but one in which some details of the intended implementation have been supplied.

Any non-executable Extended ML functor specification, i.e. a functor specification having a body consisting only of the placeholder ? or having a non-trivial body which is however not yet composed entirely of executable code, is regarded as a specification of a programming task. The task which is specified is (in the case of ?) to fill in a body which satisfies the functor interfaces, or (in the case of a body containing axioms) to fill in a body which satisfies the axioms in the current body.

Given a specification of a programming task, there are three ways to proceed towards a program which satisfies the specification:

Decomposition step: Decompose the functor into a composition of "smaller" functors, which are then regarded as separate programming tasks in their own right.

Coding step: Provide a functor body in the form of an abstract program containing type and value declarations and a mixture of axioms and code to define them.

Refinement step: Further refine an abstract program by providing a more concrete (but possibly still non-executable) version which fills in some of the decisions left open by the more abstract version.

Decomposition steps may be seen as programming (or program design) "in the large", while coding and refinement steps are programming "in the small".

Each of the three kinds of step gives rise to one or more proof obligations which can be generated mechanically from the "before" and "after" versions of the functor. The details of each kind of step are given below. Each proof obligation is a condition of the form:

$$SP_1 \cup \cdots \cup SP_n \models_{OBS} SP$$

where $SP_1, \ldots, SP_n, SP$ are Extended ML signatures or structure expressions and *OBS* is a set of observable types (a subset of the types of *SP*). Discharging such a proof obligation requires showing that the axioms and definitions in *SP* logically follow from the axioms and definitions in $SP_1, \ldots, SP_n$, up to behavioural equivalence with respect to *OBS*. Since behavioural consequence is a weakening of ordinary logical consequence, it is sufficient to show that $SP_1 \cup \cdots \cup SP_n \models SP$ which is generally easier to show (if it holds). A step is correct if all the proof obligations it incurs do in fact hold. An executable Standard ML program which is obtained via a sequence of correct steps from an Extended ML specification of requirements is guaranteed to satisfy that specification.

Decomposition step Given an Extended ML functor of the form:

```
functor F(X0 : SIG0) : SIG0' = ?
```

we may proceed by introducing a number of additional functors:

```
functor G1(X1 : SIG1) : SIG1' = ?
    ⋮
functor Gn(Xn : SIGn) : SIGn' = ?
```

and replacing the definition of F with the definition:

```
functor F(X0 : SIG0) : SIG0' = strexp
```

where *strexp* is a structure expression which involves the functors G1, ..., Gn (and possibly other already completed functors and structures). The developments of G1, ..., Gn may then proceed separately.

The new definition of F is required to be a well-formed Extended ML functor definition. A number of proof obligations are incurred, one for each point in the expression *strexp* where two modules come into contact. This includes the point where the result delivered by *strexp* is returned as the result of F. In particular:

1(a). If the result of an application of G*j* is used in a context which demands a structure of signature *SIG*, then it is necessary to prove that SIG*j*' $\models_{OBS}$ *SIG*, where *OBS* is an appropriate subset of the types of *SIG*.

1(b). If the result of an application of an already completed functor H is used in a context which demands a structure of signature *SIG*, then it is necessary to prove that *SIG'* $\models_{OBS}$ *SIG*, where *OBS* is an appropriate subset of the types of *SIG* and *SIG'* is the output signature of H.

2(a). If any explicit structure expression *strexp'* is used in *strexp* in a context which demands a structure of signature *SIG*, then it is necessary to prove that *strexp'* $\models_{OBS}$ *SIG*, where *OBS* is an appropriate subset of the types of *SIG*. (Note that *strexp* itself is such a structure expression, where the context demands a structure of signature SIG0'.)

2(b). If any structure identifier S is used in *strexp* in a context which demands a structure of signature *SIG*, then it is necessary to prove that *SIG'* $\models_{OBS}$ *SIG*, where *OBS* is an appropriate subset of the types of *SIG* and *SIG'* is the signature associated with S. (Note that the parameter X0 is such a structure identifier, associated with the signature SIG0.) □

Coding step Given an Extended ML functor of the form:

```
functor F(X : SIG) : SIG' = ?
```

we may proceed by replacing the definition of F with the definition:

```
functor F(X : SIG) : SIG' = strexp
```

where *strexp* is a well-formed Extended ML functor body. This incurs a single proof obligation:

$$\text{SIG} \cup \textit{strexp} \models_{OBS} \text{SIG'}$$

where *OBS* is an appropriate subset of the types of SIG', in addition to any proof obligations arising from the use of structures within *strexp*. □

Refinement step Given an Extended ML functor of the form:

```
functor F(X : SIG) : SIG' = strexp
```

we may proceed by replacing the definition of F with the definition:

```
functor F(X : SIG) : SIG' = strexp'
```

where *strexp'* is a well-formed Extended ML functor body. This incurs a single proof obligation:

$$\mathtt{SIG} \cup \mathit{strexp}' \models_{OBS} \mathit{strexp}$$

where *OBS* is an appropriate subset of the types of *strexp*, in addition to any proof obligations arising from the use of structures within *strexp'*. □

See [ST 89] for more details, in particular concerning the set *OBS* of observable sorts appearing in the above proof obligations. [ST 89] and [San 91] contain examples of the application of all three kinds of step during the process of developing a software system from a specification.

3 Past work

A considerable volume of theory relevant to the enterprise of formal development of Standard ML programs from Extended ML specifications has accumulated during the past several years. The purpose of this section is to indicate the relevant theory which exists and to mention some topics which have not yet been sufficiently investigated.

One compelling reason for focusing on the development of Standard ML programs, apart from the powerful and convenient Standard ML modularization mechanisms outlined in the previous section, is that Standard ML is without doubt the most rigorously formalized full-scale programming language in existence today. Standard ML possesses a formal semantics [MTH 90] which completely defines all aspects of the language. Draft versions of this semantics have been widely studied over a period of several years, leading to a high degree of confidence in its accuracy and integrity. A number of important properties of the semantics have been proved [Tof 88], [MT 90]. The formal semantics provides the basis for reasoning about Standard ML programs, which is required in order to prove that a program satisfies an Extended ML specification. Compatibility between the formal semantics of Standard ML and of Extended ML is required to simplify the transition between Extended ML and Standard ML; for example, the semantics of modules must be compatible in order to ensure that when an Extended ML program development task (an Extended ML functor specification) is decomposed into simpler tasks, the composition of Standard ML functors fulfilling these tasks will be well-formed and will fulfill the original task.

Other important theory concerning Standard ML includes a large body of work on various aspects of Standard ML's polymorphic type system and related type systems, beginning with [Mil 78]. Type-theoretic studies of the Standard ML module system include [MacQ 86b] and [MH 88]; the latter has been reformulated in category-theoretic terms and modified in [HMM 90]. The theorem-proving systems Edinburgh LCF [GMW 79] and Cambridge LCF [Pau 87] implement versions of the logic PPλ (polymorphic predicate λ-calculus) which can be used for reasoning about programs written in a subset of the Standard ML core language. A number of good implementations of SML exist, see e.g. Standard ML of New Jersey [AM 87]. Although as yet few environmental tools for Standard ML programming have been produced (debuggers, etc.), work on these is underway.

A very important problem in the context of Standard ML which has not yet been solved is that of proving properties of programs in the full Standard ML language. Obtaining an appropriate correctness logic and proof system for the core language alone will not be an easy task because of the number of interacting features present in the language (polymorphism, user-defined types, higher-order functions, equality types, non-terminating functions, exceptions, references, input/output, etc.). Ensuring soundness of any such system with respect to the semantics of Standard ML is another important but difficult problem. Once a sound proof system is available for the core language, extending it to the module language should be a less arduous task, although the problem of checking soundness remains difficult. Ideas in [SB 83] about proof in the context of structured specifications should be relevant to such an extension. A natural extension to the Standard ML module system is to permit higher-order functors. Although this is not included in the semantics of the language, recent work has demonstrated that such an extension would be semantically unproblematic. Some of the implications of such an extension on Extended ML have already been considered [SST 90]; see [KS 91] for a description of the SPECTRAL specification language, which extends Extended ML with higher-order functors, dependent types and object-oriented inheritance.

Work on Extended ML proper has so far concentrated almost exclusively on issues of semantics, correctness and foundations. Some of these issues have proved to be more subtle than was thought at first, which means that the treatment of certain aspects has changed significantly in the process of further investigation. The first work on Extended ML was [ST 85] which provided an introduction to the Extended ML language and outlined some ideas concerning its semantics. An early goal of work on Extended ML was to maintain independence from the choice of logical language to be used for writing axioms; since executable definitions are taken to be a subset of axioms, this also results in independence from the choice of target programming language. A suitable formalisation of the notion of logic is provided in the theory of *institutions* [GB 84]. An institution comprises not only a language for writing axioms but also a notion of signature (different from Standard ML or Extended ML signature), a notion of model, and a satisfaction relation between models and axioms. Several unpublished drafts of an institution-independent denotational semantics of Extended ML were written early in 1986. The semantics described a translation of Extended ML into institution-independent ASL [ST 88a]. An outline of the principles of this semantics appeared in [ST 86]. The semantics itself was never finalized since the design of Standard ML was not yet fixed at this point in time, and frequent subsequent changes to the semantics would have been required to keep it in line with changes in the Standard ML language.

The Extended ML methodology for formal program development was introduced in [ST 89], with results demonstrating that any program obtained from a requirements specification using the methods presented will be correct with respect to that specification. This work required a revision of the treatment of behavioural equivalence along lines suggested by [Sch 86], and accordingly the correctness results in [ST 89] are subject to the assumption that the Standard ML language is *stable* (roughly speaking, functors preserve behavioural equivalence). The methodology and results concerning correctness are in principle institution-independent, but they have not yet been explicitly formulated in these terms. In order to provide a basis for the first work on tools, [SdST 90] defines the concrete syntax, static semantics and dynamic semantics of Extended ML (instantiated to an institution of first-order equational logic) as an extension to the semantics of Standard ML, ignoring the role of axioms beyond requiring them to be syntactically well-formed and well-typed. The language described is substantially different from that described in the 1986 version of the Extended ML semantics because of the changes to the Standard ML languages since then. The revised semantics of Extended ML discussed in Section 4 is a major extension of this to deal fully with the effect of axioms, and to encompass the full Standard ML language apart from references and assignment.

The foundations of Extended ML are based on a theory of algebraic specifications developed in the context of the ASL kernel specification language. This theory includes the semantics of ASL and its properties [SW 83], [Wir 86], its extension to the framework of an arbitrary institution [ST 88a], work on observational and behavioural equivalence in algebraic specifications [ST 87], on implementation of specifications [ST 88b], on first-order and higher-order parameterization [SST 90], [ST 91], and on theorem proving [SB 83], [ST 88a] and proofs of model class containment [Far 89], [Far 90], [Far 91] in the context of structured specifications. All of this theory is relevant to Extended ML, although translating results from the level of ASL to the level of Extended ML is a non-trivial task. Some work on related approaches is also relevant, e.g. work on PLUSS [Bid 89], which is also based on ASL, and the theory of module algebra [BHK 90] together with related work on the $\lambda\pi$-calculus [FJKR 87]. Results concerning logical relations and data abstraction [Mit 86] are related to the correctness of the Extended ML formal program development methodology. However, much of the "classical" theory of algebraic specifications such as described in [EM 85] is not applicable in the context of Extended ML because of the restriction to (conditional) equations and the different methods used for structuring specifications.

A number of examples of Extended ML specifications have been written and formal program developments carried out in spite of the difficulty in using Extended ML in the absence of appropriate support tools. These include examples of complete formal developments in [ST 85], [ST 89], [HK 90],

[San 91] and case studies done by students at Edinburgh and elsewhere, and a large Extended ML specification of a Standard ML typechecker in [MS 90]. A case study in the formal development of a standardized protocol using a combination of Extended ML and CCS [Mil 89] has also been carried out [SGM 89].

The above discussion has mentioned some issues which remain to be resolved. This includes the question of whether Standard ML (minus references and assignment) is stable or not; the answer is almost certainly yes, but the proof of this result will be difficult. If the answer should turn out to be no, this would indicate a worrying flaw in the design of Standard ML rather than a failure of Extended ML. Once the revised semantics of Extended ML is finished, it will be necessary to check that it is fully compatible with the semantics of Standard ML. It would also be desirable to eventually give an institution-independent version of this semantics in order to facilitate application to other programming languages. We lack a proof system for the language of Extended ML axioms; this should not be a surprise since such a system would be practically the same as a proof system for the Standard ML core language (minus references and assignment). Extending such a proof system to all of Extended ML is similar to the problem of extending a proof system for the Standard ML core language to the module language. Given a semantics of Extended ML by translation to ASL, such as the 1986 draft semantics, the proof rules for ASL in [ST 88a] would be applicable.

An important problem concerns practical methods for proving behavioural consequence. A number of methods for establishing behavioural consequence are available. These include: methods described in [ST 89], which apply only to conditional equational specifications of a certain kind; methods developed for VDM for proving the correctness of data reification [Jon 86]; correspondences [Sch 86]; and context induction [Hen 90]. The ease of use of these different methods is in inverse proportion to the number of cases of interest which they cover. This suggests that the best approach is to use a collection of methods, applying the simpler and less powerful methods (starting with ordinary consequence, which is a sufficient condition for behavioural consequence) before trying the more inconvenient but more powerful methods.

Finally, a range of tools to support formal program development in Extended ML is required. Work on these has just begun; see Section 5 for current plans.

4 Semantics

Active work is currently in progress on a new semantics of Extended ML. The aim of this section is to discuss some aspects of this work: why it is necessary, what decisions have been made so far, and what problems have arisen. The semantics of Extended ML is not yet complete, and so some of the details in the following may change in the final version.

As was mentioned in the last section, a draft semantics of Extended ML has been in existence since 1986. This semantics described an institution-independent translation from Extended ML into the ASL kernel specification language. Its principles (primarily, the technicalities required to make the translation from Extended ML to ASL institution independent) were outlined in [ST 86]. The most fundamental difference between these two languages is that Extended ML provides convenient and fairly elaborate mechanisms for handling sharing of components (see Section 2.1.2), while such mechanisms are completely absent in ASL for the sake of simplicity. The translation from Extended ML to ASL is largely a matter of making these mechanisms explicit. The semantics of institution-independent ASL [ST 88a] assigns to every well-formed specification a signature and a class of models over that signature. Composing the translation from Extended ML to ASL with the semantics of ASL therefore associates a signature and a class of models with every well-formed Extended ML signature and structure.

In 1986 the design of Standard ML was not yet fixed. The draft semantics of Extended ML was written by reference to a draft of [MacQ 86a]. In the process of writing the semantics, certain gaps and ambiguities in [MacQ 86a] came to light, making it necessary (through discussion with MacQueen and with ML implementors) to guess the intended semantics of some constructs. During 1986–1989 the Standard ML language evolved in response to problems discovered by implementors and by users, diverging in many respects from the guesses made in the Extended ML semantics and even from some details which were explicitly treated in [MacQ 86]. The formal semantics of Standard ML [MTH 90] was written during this time. Now that the semantics of Standard ML is finished, complete implementations of it are available, and work on tools to support the use of Extended ML is beginning (see Section 5), it is appropriate to revise the semantics of Extended ML to make it fully compatible with Standard ML.

Faced with the job of producing a semantics for Extended ML which is consistent with the semantics of Standard ML, there seem to be two options:

1. Revise the 1986 draft of the Extended ML semantics to take account of changes in Standard ML.

2. Introduce the features of Extended ML into the semantics of Standard ML [MTH 90].

Each of these two options has advantages and disadvantages. The main advantage of (1) is that the revision is a matter of detail which does not involve a radical departure from our previous approach. The semantics then remains institution-independent. Its main disadvantage is that establishing consistency with [MTH 90] is extremely difficult since the styles of the two semantics are radically different. An advantage of (2) is that consistency is almost automatic by construction. Furthermore, it is relatively easy to include features of ML like polymorphic types and exceptions by extending the treatment in [MTH 90]. Although an advantage of an institution-independent semantics is that such features are in principle easily integrated afterwards by instantiation to an appropriate institution, defining an institution covering all the features of Standard ML would be a technically difficult task which would involve redoing much of the Standard ML semantics in a different form. A further advantage of (2) is that it would be easy to keep up with any changes to Standard ML (although none are expected, at least in the short term) since these will be reflected in future editions of [MTH 90]. We have chosen (2) in spite of some short-term disadvantages which are discussed at the end of this section. We aim to cover almost the full Standard ML language, including polymorphism, higher-order functions, exceptions and non-terminating functions, but excluding references and assignment.

The semantics of Standard ML in [MTH 90] is given in the style of structured operational semantics [Plo 81], presented as system of inference rules. It is split into static semantics, which covers type inference (102 rules) and dynamic semantics, which covers evaluation (91 rules), with 3 rules to make the connection between the two. Considering that Standard ML is a general-purpose language with a wide range of advanced features and that the semantics completely defines all aspects of the language, the semantics is quite elegant and compact.

For each language construct the Standard ML semantics contains one or more static rules and one or more dynamic rules which define its meaning. A typical example is the semantics of declarations of the form `local` $strdec_1$ `in` $strdec_2$ `end`, where $strdec_1$ and $strdec_2$ (and `local` ... `end`) are *structure-level declarations*. The relevant rule in the static semantics is the following:

$$\frac{B \vdash strdec_1 \Rightarrow E_1 \qquad B \oplus E_1 \vdash strdec_2 \Rightarrow E_2}{B \vdash \texttt{local}\ strdec_1\ \texttt{in}\ strdec_2\ \texttt{end} \Rightarrow E_2}$$

The meta-variables B, E_1 and E_2 stand for static environments giving the "static" properties (types, signatures etc.) associated with currently accessible names of types, values, exceptions, structures, signatures and functors. This rule says that $strdec_2$ is elaborated in an environment containing previously-defined types, values, etc. together with the types etc. declared in $strdec_1$, but that the declarations in $strdec_1$ do not themselves contribute to the resulting environment. The rule for this construct in the dynamic semantics is:

$$\frac{B \vdash strdec_1 \Rightarrow E_1 \qquad B + E_1 \vdash strdec_2 \Rightarrow E_2}{B \vdash \texttt{local}\ strdec_1\ \texttt{in}\ strdec_2\ \texttt{end} \Rightarrow E_2}$$

In the dynamic semantics the meta-variables B, E_1 and E_2 stand for dynamic environments containing *bindings* for value names, exception names, structure names, signature names and functor names.

Types are fully handled in the static semantics so type names do not appear in environments at this level; if static elaboration is successful then no type errors can occur during dynamic evaluation. This rule has a similar meaning to the corresponding static rule; the difference is that it deals with values rather than with types. (The above explanation and the discussion below gloss over some of the details of the semantics which are not essential to the discussion, such as the difference between the meta-variables B and E and the difference between $B + E$ and $B \oplus E$.)

As an example of the application of these rules, consider the following Standard ML program fragment:

```
local
    datatype t = mkt of int  }
    val a = 4                } strdec1
in
    fun f x = x*2            }
    val v = mkt(f a)         } strdec2
end
```

Static elaboration proceeds as follows. Suppose that B_0 is the initial static environment of built-in types and values; then

$$B_0 \vdash \mathit{strdec}_1 \Rightarrow (\mathit{TE}_1, \mathit{VE}_1)$$

where TE_1 is the type environment $\mathit{TE}_1 = \{\mathtt{t} \mapsto (t_0, \{\mathtt{mkt} \mapsto \mathtt{int} \text{ -> } t_0\})\}$ and VE_1 is the (static) value environment $\mathit{VE}_1 = \{\mathtt{mkt} \mapsto \mathtt{int} \text{ -> } t_0, \mathtt{a} \mapsto \mathtt{int}\}$ Here, t_0 is a unique internal name for `t` which ensures that it is not confused with other types in the program named `t`, and $\{\mathtt{mkt} \mapsto \mathtt{int} \text{ -> } t_0\}$ gives the constructors for that type. The result also includes empty environments of exceptions and structures; such empty environments will usually be omitted below. Continuing,

$$B_0 \oplus (\mathit{TE}_1, \mathit{VE}_1) \vdash \mathit{strdec}_2 \Rightarrow \mathit{VE}_2$$

where VE_2 is the value environment $\mathit{VE}_2 = \{\mathtt{f} \mapsto \mathtt{int} \text{ -> } \mathtt{int}, \mathtt{v} \mapsto t_0\}$. Putting these together gives

$$B_0 \vdash \mathtt{local}\ \mathit{strdec}_1\ \mathtt{in}\ \mathit{strdec}_2\ \mathtt{end} \Rightarrow \mathit{VE}_2$$

Notice that `a`, `t` and `mkt` are not available in the resulting environment. The type `t` is hidden even though there is a value (`v`) having that type.

As for dynamic evaluation, if B'_0 is the initial dynamic environment of built-in values, then

$$B'_0 \vdash \mathit{strdec}_1 \Rightarrow \mathit{VE}'_1$$

where VE'_1 is the (dynamic) value environment $\mathit{VE}'_1 = \{\mathtt{mkt} \mapsto \mathtt{mkt}, \mathtt{a} \mapsto 4\}$. The type `t` does not appear in this result, but the constructor `mkt` does. Then,

$$B'_0 + \mathit{VE}'_1 \vdash \mathit{strdec}_2 \Rightarrow \mathit{VE}'_2$$

where VE'_2 is the value environment $\mathit{VE}'_2 = \{\mathtt{f} \mapsto (\mathtt{x} \Rightarrow \mathtt{x*2}, \ldots), \mathtt{v} \mapsto (\mathtt{mkt}, 8)\}$. Here, $(\mathtt{x} \Rightarrow \mathtt{x*2}, \ldots)$ is a *closure*; the missing component is the declaration-time environment of the function `f` (this is omitted here since it is unimportant for this example). The value bound to `v` demonstrates the fact that constructors in Standard ML are uninterpreted. Putting these two inferences together gives

$$B'_0 \vdash \mathtt{local}\ \mathit{strdec}_1\ \mathtt{in}\ \mathit{strdec}_2\ \mathtt{end} \Rightarrow \mathit{VE}'_2$$

As in the static semantics, `a` and `mkt` are not available in the resulting environment.

The semantics of Extended ML is comprised of three main parts: static semantics, dynamic semantics and "verification" semantics. The role of the static semantics is to define the class of well-formed phrases, the same as in Standard ML, and the static semantic rules for Extended ML are largely the same as those for Standard ML. The role of the dynamic semantics is to define the effect of running a "program" which may contain components which have been specified but not yet defined in an executable fashion. The effect will be the same as in Standard ML, provided the undefined components are not used; otherwise an exception is raised. The dynamic semantic rules for Extended ML are largely the same as those for Standard ML.

In the static and dynamic semantics of Extended ML, axioms are treated as formal comments which are typechecked but have no other effect. The role of the verification semantics is to define the effect of these axioms, which involves computing the class of models corresponding to each structure, signature and functor. The classes of models computed correspond (roughly speaking) to the results produced by the composition of the 1986 semantics of Extended ML and the semantics of ASL. The division between the static and verification semantics of Extended ML is not so clean as the division between the static and dynamic semantics, since the interpretation of quantifiers in axioms, which takes place in the verification semantics, depends strongly on type information collected by the static semantics (see below). This makes the verification semantic rules a little messy; since most of the discussion below has nothing to do with this issue, the messiness will be suppressed wherever possible.

The static and dynamic semantic rules for local declarations in Extended ML are exactly the same as the corresponding rules in the static and dynamic semantics of Standard ML which have already been discussed above. The rule in the verification semantics is:

$$\frac{J \vdash \mathit{strdec}_1 \Rightarrow \mathcal{M}_1 \qquad \text{for each } M_1 \in \mathcal{M}_1,\quad J + M_1 \vdash \mathit{strdec}_2 \Rightarrow \mathcal{M}_2[M_1]}{J \vdash \texttt{local}\ \mathit{strdec}_1\ \texttt{in}\ \mathit{strdec}_2\ \texttt{end} \Rightarrow \{(\varphi_1 + \varphi_2, E_2) \mid (\varphi_1, E_1) \in \mathcal{M}_1, (\varphi_2, E_2) \in \mathcal{M}_2[(\varphi_1, E_1)]\}}$$

The meta-variable M_1 stands for a *model*, $\mathcal{M}_1$ and $\mathcal{M}_2[M_1]$ stand for classes of models, and J stands for an *interpretation*, which is a model together with a signature and dynamic functor environment. Models here are much more concrete than algebras as traditionally used in work on algebraic specifications, built from the formal entities used in the semantics of Standard ML, although the purpose is the same. In place of a collection of carrier sets, a model contains a *realisation* (meta-variables φ_1 and φ_2 above) which gives a set of constructors for each type. In place of a set of functions, a model additionally contains a dynamic environment (meta-variables E_1 and E_2 above). This binds function names to closures rather than to arbitrary mathematical functions, and binds (constant) value names to Standard ML values. The advantage of using this concrete notion of model rather than algebras is that evaluation of an expression in a model is defined directly via the dynamic semantics (taking exceptions, higher-order functions, etc. into account) rather than by some other means. The above rule says that the result of `local` strdec_1 `in` strdec_2 `end` is a class of models which is obtained by combining realisations from models of strdec_1 with corresponding models of strdec_2. Although the types declared in strdec_1 are no longer accessible in the result, it is necessary to keep track of their "carriers" in order to interpret quantifiers over types which depend on such types. The premise "for each $M_1 \in \mathcal{M}_1, \ldots$" should be interpreted as a conjunction of premises, one for each $M_1 \in \mathcal{M}_1$. Since $\mathcal{M}_1$ may be infinite, we are really dealing here with infinitary rules.

As an example of the application of this rule, consider the following Extended ML fragment (compare this with the Standard ML example above):

```
local
   datatype t = mkt of int                         }
   val a:int = ?                                   } strdec1
   axiom a<5 andalso a>2                           }
in
   fun f (x:int) = ?:int                           }
   axiom forall x => abs(f x) = abs(x) * 2         } strdec2
   val v = mkt(f a)                                }
end
```

Static elaboration and dynamic evaluation have the same results as for the previous example in Standard ML. As for the verification semantics, if J_0 is the initial interpretation of built-in types and values, then

$$J_0 \vdash \mathit{strdec}_1 \Rightarrow \{M_1, M_2\}$$

where M_1 is a model containing the realisation $\varphi_1 = \{t_0 \mapsto (t_0, \{\texttt{mkt} \mapsto \texttt{int->}\ t_0\})\}$ and the value environment $\{\texttt{mkt} \mapsto \texttt{mkt}, \texttt{a} \mapsto 3\}$, and M_2 is a model containing φ_1 and the value environment $\{\texttt{mkt} \mapsto \texttt{mkt}, \texttt{a} \mapsto 4\}$ (compare VE'_1 above). These are the only two models containing the realisation generated by the declaration of **t** and an interpretation of **a** which satisfies the axiom.[2] The second premise determines two classes of models, $\mathcal{M}_2[M_1]$ and $\mathcal{M}_2[M_2]$. $\mathcal{M}_2[M_1]$ is the result of evaluating strdec_2 under the interpretation of strdec_1 given by M_1, which yields $\{M_{1_1}, M_{1_2}, \ldots\}$ where M_{1_1} is a model containing the empty realisation (no new types are introduced) and the value environment $\{\texttt{f} \mapsto (\texttt{x => x*2}, \ldots), \texttt{v} \mapsto (\texttt{mkt}, 6)\}$, M_{1_2} is a model containing the empty realisation and the value environment $\{\texttt{f} \mapsto (\texttt{x => ~x*2}, \ldots), \texttt{v} \mapsto (\texttt{mkt}, -6)\}$, etc. $\mathcal{M}_2[M_2]$ is the result of evaluating strdec_2 under the interpretation of strdec_1 given by M_2, which yields $\{M_{2_1}, M_{2_2}, \ldots\}$ where M_{2_1} is a model containing the empty realisation and the value environment $\{\texttt{f} \mapsto (\texttt{x => x*2}, \ldots), \texttt{v} \mapsto (\texttt{mkt}, 8)\}$, M_{2_2} is a model containing the empty realisation and the value environment $\{\texttt{f} \mapsto (\texttt{x => ~x*2}, \ldots), \texttt{v} \mapsto (\texttt{mkt}, -8)\}$, etc. Putting these together as the rule requires gives

$$J_0 \vdash \texttt{local}\ \mathit{strdec}_1\ \texttt{in}\ \mathit{strdec}_2\ \texttt{end} \Rightarrow \{M'_{1_1}, M'_{1_2}, \ldots, M'_{2_1}, M'_{2_2}, \ldots\}$$

where M'_{1_n} is obtained by combining the realisation in M_1 (i.e. φ_1) with M_{1_n} and M'_{2_n} is obtained by combining the realisation in M_2 (also φ_1) with M_{2_n}. So for example, M'_{2_1} is the model $(\varphi_1, \{\texttt{f} \mapsto (\texttt{x => x*2}, \ldots), \texttt{v} \mapsto (\texttt{mkt}, 8)\})$ (compare VE'_2 above).

The ideas of the Extended ML program development methodology presented in Section 2.3 are reflected in the verification semantics of Extended ML structure and functor bindings. We will briefly comment on structure bindings; functor bindings are similar, *mutatis mutandis*. The Standard ML dynamic semantic rule for a structure binding *strid* : *sigexp* = *strexp* is the following:

$$\frac{B \vdash \mathit{strexp} \Rightarrow E \qquad \mathrm{Inter}\, B \vdash \mathit{sigexp} \Rightarrow I}{B \vdash \mathit{strid} : \mathit{sigexp} = \mathit{strexp} \Rightarrow \{\mathit{strid} \mapsto E \downarrow I\}}$$

Here, $\mathrm{Inter}\, B \vdash \mathit{sigexp} \Rightarrow I$ computes the "interface" I of *sigexp*, the set of (value, exception and structure) names in *sigexp*, and $E \downarrow I$ restricts E to the names in I. The result is a dynamic structure environment where *strid* is bound to a restricted view of the structure E obtained by evaluating *strexp*. The dynamic semantic rule in Extended ML is the same; a simplified version of the corresponding verification semantic rule in Extended ML is the following:

$$\frac{\begin{array}{c} J \vdash \mathit{strexp} \Rightarrow \mathcal{M} \qquad J \vdash \mathit{sigexp} \Rightarrow \mathcal{M}' \\ \text{for each } M \in \mathcal{M},\ \exists M' \in \mathcal{M}' .\ M \text{ "fits" } M' \end{array}}{J \vdash \mathit{strid} : \mathit{sigexp} = \mathit{strexp} \Rightarrow \{(\varphi', \{\mathit{strid} \mapsto E'\}) \mid (\varphi', E') \in \mathcal{M}'\}}$$

Here, M "fits" M' means that an appropriately restricted version of M is behaviourally equivalent to M' with respect to an appropriate set of observable types. The precise details of this are too complicated to be explained without reference to more of the Extended ML semantics. This requirement corresponds to one of the proof obligations which is incurred by a decomposition step, namely 2(a) in Section 2.3. The result of a structure binding is a class of models, one for each possible model of the structure. A very important point here is that the class of possible models of the structure is taken to be $\mathcal{M}'$ (the models of the interface *sigexp*) rather than $\mathcal{M}$ (the models of the body *strexp*). This may seem worryingly inaccurate: *sigexp* may allow more models than *strexp*, and the models

[2] This is not quite true; an infinite number of similar models would be obtained by interpreting **mkt** as a closure such as (**x => mkt x**,...) or (**x => if true then mkt x else mkt(x+1)**,...).

of *strexp* need only be behaviourally equivalent to models of *sigexp*. This choice has strong methodological motivations. First, in reasoning about a structure we should only need to use those of its properties which are recorded in its interface. Additional properties which the structure happens to satisfy are to be ignored since they are accidents of the particular choice of implementation. This choice is the reason why proof obligation 2(b) incurred by a decomposition step (see Section 2.3) refers to the signature *SIG'* associated with a structure identifier rather than requiring the actual class of models of the structure to be determined. Second, the "inaccuracy" caused by the use of behavioural equivalence is justified by [Sch 86] and [ST 89]. The name "verification" semantics comes from the fact that "idealized" classes of models are computed, for the sake of verification of interfaces. By the way, if there is some model of *strexp* which fits no model of *sigexp*, then (since there is no other rule for this form of structure binding) the structure binding fails to evaluate and so is regarded as ill-formed from the viewpoint of the verification semantics. This is similar to the failure of an ill-typed expression to elaborate according to the static semantics. Both forms of failure are caught by rules for handling programs (sequences of top-level declarations) — these are the rules which make the connection between the static, dynamic and verification semantics.

One of the advantages of building a semantics of Extended ML starting with the semantics of Standard ML is that features of Standard ML like polymorphism, higher-order functions and exceptions are relatively easy to integrate. Concretely, this means that the type system of Standard ML is already able to cope with these features and that corresponding semantic objects are already defined together with appropriate basic operations to manipulate them. Seen within the institutional framework, the signatures and the models of the institution are fixed; a problem which remains is the choice of the logical language appropriate for writing axioms which specify the properties of the components of these models and the definition of satisfaction of an axiom by a model. The design of this language and its semantics involves making choices which are difficult to assess properly without substantial experience with examples. We have attempted to make choices which seem natural from the standpoint of the semantics of Standard ML. Further, we have attempted to maximize expressive power, and to avoid making certain common specification idioms unduly awkward to write.

Syntactically, it is convenient to take axioms to be closed expression of type `bool`, with the syntax of such expressions extended by (higher-order) universal and existential quantifiers and equality over values of arbitrary type. The interpretation of quantifiers is not entirely obvious, especially in the presence of polymorphic types; this topic will be discussed below. There is a choice with the interpretation of equality since the evaluation of an expression may diverge or generate an exception. We have chosen to use a weak version of equality (cf. existence equations [Rei 87]); if exp_1 and exp_2 are two closed expressions of the same type, then $exp_1 = exp_2$ is `true` in a model M iff the values of exp_1 and exp_2 in M are defined, are not exceptions, and are equal. If exp_1 diverges or raises an exception, then so does $exp_1 = exp_2$. If this is not the case but exp_2 diverges or raises an exception, then so does $exp_1 = exp_2$. This definition also holds if exp_1 and exp_2 are of functional type, or are data values containing embedded functions, except that we have to decide what kind of equality to use on function values. We have chosen to use here a strong version of extensional equality; two functions are equal in a model M iff for all well-typed arguments they produce either equal values in M or else both are undefined or both produce the same exception. A (postfix) definedness predicate called `terminates` is provided; as with $D(exp)$ in [BW 82], *exp* `terminates` is `true` in a model M if the value of *exp* is defined in M and is `false` in M if the value of *exp* is undefined in M. If the value of *exp* in M is an exception then the value of *exp* `terminates` is `true`. In contrast to $D(exp)$ in [BW 82], *exp* `terminates` is not definable as $exp = exp$, since the value of the latter formula is undefined (rather than `false`) if the value of *exp* is undefined. One could supply a similar predicate to test whether an expression produces an exception or not (and to test which exception is produced); this, however, is already expressible in Standard ML. For example, the expression:

```
(exp ; false) handle _ => true
```

is `true` in M if the value of *exp* in M is an exception, is `false` if the value of *exp* in M is defined but not an exception, and is undefined otherwise.

From the above discussion it is clear that a multiple-valued logic is being used. Besides the usual `true` and `false`, the value of a closed expression of type `bool` can be undefined or one of a possibly infinite number of exceptions. However, at the level of axioms, this does not complicate matters: an axiom *exp* is satisfied by a model M iff the value of *exp* in M is `true`. Any other result means that the axiom *exp* is not satisfied by M.

There are at least two complications concerning the interpretation of quantifiers, both involving the domain of quantification. Since only *ML-representable* types and values are available as components of models, it seems natural that the domain of quantification should include only such values. Only computable functions are representable in Standard ML; thus the following axiom, which specifies a function `alwayshalts : (int -> int) -> bool` to solve the halting problem for (computable) functions of type `int -> int`, will not be satisfied by any model:

```
forall g:int->int => alwayshalts g = (forall x:int => (g x) terminates)
```

The other complication involves the domain of quantification of quantifiers over polymorphic types. For example, what is specified by the following axiom?

```
forall (l:'a list,l':'a list) => length(l@l') = length l + length l'
```

If `l` and `l'` are really meant to range over values of type `'a list` only, then this axiom only says that

```
length([]@[]) = length [] + length []
```

since `[]` is the only value of this type (in Standard ML)! This is probably not what was intended. The interpretation we have been considering is to take the value of a quantified formula to be `true` if its value is `true` for all instantiations of the types of the quantified variables (including the identity instantiation and other instantiations containing type variables)[3], and `false` if its value is `false` for all such type instantiations. If its value is `true` for some instantiations and `false` for others, then the result is undefined. (Quantifiers range only over well-defined values, excluding exceptions and undefined.) This means that the value of the following expression is undefined:

```
forall x:'a => forall l:'a list => [x]@l = l@[x]
```

(it is vacuously `true` for the identity instantiation, is `true` when `'a` is instantiated to any type having just one value (examples are the built-in type `unit` and the type `'a list`) and is `false` when `'a` is instantiated to any type having more than one value). This seems to be the best choice of interpretation, taking into account complications involved with nested quantifiers and quantifiers occurring in negative positions. A similar choice is taken for equality of functions of polymorphic type. Another possibility would have been to explicitly quantify type variables, but we prefer to avoid this if possible since it seems to be in conflict with the spirit of ML where types are left implicit whenever possible.

In a quantified expression, the domain of quantification depends critically on the type(s) of the quantified variable(s), as we have seen. This is the source of the (one-way) interaction between the static and verification semantics of Extended ML; the static semantics is responsible for determining the most general types of all variables and expressions, and the verification semantics is responsible for evaluating quantified formulae (and other expressions in axioms). Dynamic recomputation of types is necessary to make the examples of quantification above and the following example work as intended:

```
fun ispermutation(l,l') = forall x => count(x,l) = count(x,l')
```

where `count : 'a * 'a list -> int` counts the number of occurrences of a value in a list. Another slightly more bizarre example is the following:

```
fun onlyvalue x = forall y => x=y
```

[3] It might be more appropriate to take only ground instantiations of type variables, as in [GP 89].

The function **onlyvalue** tests whether or not the given value is the only value of its type. For example, **onlyvalue 3** is **false** and **onlyvalue ()** is **true** (where **()** is the unique value of type **unit**). However, **onlyvalue []** is undefined since the quantifier ranges over **'a list**, and as we have seen there is a single value of type **'a list** but many values of its type instances (**int list**, **unit list**, etc.). Adding an explicit (monomorphic) type qualification to **[]** changes this result; **onlyvalue([]:int list)** is **false**.

The above discussion leaves completely open the question of proving theorems about Extended ML specifications. Any proof system for Extended ML would have to be shown sound with respect to the semantics sketched above. Although this semantics is in some sense very much more "concrete" than the 1986 version, it is still model-based rather than theory-based and so establishing the soundness of a proof system will not be an easy task (completeness is unachievable since **datatype** definitions correspond to data constraints — see [MS 85]). Although the way that we have dealt with polymorphism is somewhat unusual, the inference rules for type instantiation in PPλ [GMW 79], [Pau 87] seem to remain sound. We have not yet thought about inference rules for the version of equality discussed above, and the impact of higher-order functions and exceptions on the rest of the logic is not clear. It might be necessary to revise our decisions concerning the interpretation of equality, quantification, etc. if we discover that the versions we have chosen cause grave problems for theorem proving. This is a delicate area, where seemingly minor changes can have dramatic consequences [Coq 86]. The inference rules supplied in [ST 88a] for the specification-building operations of ASL should be applicable to Extended ML since the basic elements are similar (e.g., **local** corresponds to a combination of **translate**, $\cup$ and **derive**, and substructures in signatures correspond to a combination of $\cup$ and **translate**). For example, the following inference rule may be derived from the ASL inference rules for **translate**, $\cup$ and **derive**, assuming no name conflicts occur between $strdec_1$ and $strdec_2$ (here, $\vdash$ stands for provability, which is intended to be sound with respect to satisfaction, $\models$):

$$\frac{strdec_1 \cup strdec_2 \vdash exp \qquad exp \text{ contains no names from } strdec_1}{\texttt{local } strdec_1 \texttt{ in } strdec_2 \texttt{ end} \vdash exp}$$

This rule is sound, but more is needed. In order to prove the correctness of development steps when the signatures involved use **local**, a different approach is required; see [Far 90] for some methods developed in the ASL context which are relevant to this problem. The use of infinitary rules in the verification semantics of Extended ML should not cause substantial additional difficulties, since it corresponds more or less directly to the use of quantification over model classes in the semantics of ASL.

Our choice to build the semantics of Extended ML by modifying the semantics of Standard ML has at least two disadvantages. One is that the resulting semantics is not institution-independent. This means that the logical language to be used in writing axioms is fixed, along with the target language to be used for writing code. If we are interested only in the development of Standard ML programs, this is not such a serious disadvantage since the logical language we intend to provide is powerful enough to cover all the features of Standard ML. Of course, it might turn out that our definition of satisfaction is not the most convenient one, but then the main problem is how to redefine satisfaction in an appropriate way (and the provision of a sound proof system for the new version of satisfaction). If we are interested in applying the methods of Extended ML in the context of other programming languages (an obvious candidate is Prolog with modularization facilities added [SWa 87]) then the advantages of an institution-independent approach are more apparent. Another disadvantage is that the semantics will not be ASL-based. This will make the theory and methods developed in the context of ASL more difficult to transfer to the Extended ML context. It should not be difficult to overcome both of these disadvantages. Once we have finished a semantics of Extended ML and convinced ourselves that it is fully compatible with the semantics of Standard ML, it will be time to consider how to factor the definitions via ASL and which parts of the semantics depend on the institution at hand.

5 Extended ML support tools

The eventual practical feasibility of formal program development hinges on the availability of computer-aided tools to support various development activities. This is necessary both because of the sheer amount of (mostly clerical) work involved and because of the need to avoid the possibility of human error.

Now that most of the theoretical underpinnings of Extended ML seem to be in place, the time seems ripe to turn attention to an Extended ML support system which will allow the ideas to be tested in practice. Some ideas concerning appropriate components for such a system and how they might assist in the program development process are outlined below. What follows is a more or less unstructured collection of ideas rather than a complete system design. More definite ideas will crystallize once the first components of the system are in use. Highest priority will be placed on completing three components: the front end (Extended ML parser and typechecker), adapting a theorem prover for use with Extended ML, and the verification condition generator. Even a primitive system consisting of just these three components will be of enormous help in carrying out case studies in formal program development.

As is to be expected, the Extended ML support system will be written in Standard ML. This will enable us to exploit the fact that the Extended ML language is a relatively minor modification of Standard ML by adapting components of the Standard ML of New Jersey compiler (itself written in ML) for our purposes. It will also allow us to experiment with the use of the techniques we advocate in developing the components of the system itself.

User interface

A very important feature of any system is its user interface. With powerful workstations and bit-mapped screens, windows, pop-up menus, structure editing, hypertext, etc. it is possible to produce a very flashy interface, although the effort involved is considerable. Our guiding principle here is to exploit other people's work as far as possible by adapting and integrating existing user interfaces as appropriate rather than investing our own effort, at least in the forseeable future.

The syntax and type system of Extended ML is intentionally very close to that of Standard ML and so the Standard ML parser and typechecker will be useable for the front end of the system with only minor modifications. One further great advantage of adopting a specification language which is a variant of Standard ML is that we will be able to take advantage of the environmental tools for Standard ML (structure editors, etc.) which will shortly be emerging.

This takes care of the user interface for those aspects of program development involving the text of specifications and programs. The most important thing which this leaves out is theorem proving. We expect to adapt some existing theorem prover (see below) which will come with its own user interface.

Module library

The task of constructing specifications and developing programs is greatly eased if we have available a large library of commonly-used specifications (for example, of standard data types like sets, stacks and queues and standard functions like sorting and searching), each with one or more correct implementations. Then most of the effort can be devoted to those aspects which are unique to the problem at hand.

A support system would incorporate a library of Standard ML modules (structures and functors — mainly the latter) each associated with its interface specification and with cross references to other modules in the library on which it depends and which depend on it. The cross references would be used to provide a version control mechanism to ensure that everything is kept consistent when specifications and modules in the library are changed. This library will grow as the system is used to develop new modules. In many cases it will be advantageous to retain the entire development history of a module as advocated in [SS 83], rather than just the module and its interface specification; this will come in handy in cases where modification of an existing module to suit some new purpose is required.

Making friends with specifications

A Standard ML system provides various ways of experimenting with programs in an interactive fashion — functors may be applied to structures and functions may be applied to various values, expression evaluation may be timed, etc. In this way it is possible to test that a program is suitable for some purpose.

We need to provide suitable facilities for users to experiment with specifications in order to understand their consequences and to gain confidence that they reflect what is desired. This is especially important given the role of a specification as the starting point of the program development process, and the amount of work involved in formally developing a program from a specification. The parser and typechecker mentioned above will at least ensure that specifications are syntactically well-formed and free from type errors, but this is only a start.

If a specification consists only of universally quantified equations or conditional equations, then under certain conditions term rewriting may be used to evaluate expressions. This fact is used to justify interest in specification languages in which the expressive power is restricted so as to guarantee that all specifications are executable. We regard such restrictions as much too strong (cf. [HJ 89]) — the step from a non-executable statement of required behaviour to an executable algorithm (even a very high-level one) is too difficult and too fundamental to be ignored. However, it makes sense to take advantage of the technology developed in systems like OBJ [GW 88] and RAP [Hus 85] to allow specifications which happen to be in the required form to be tested. The consequences of specifications not in this form can be explored using a theorem prover (see below); instead of asking for the value of an expression $f(c)$ we can try to prove a theorem of the form $f(c) = d$ where d is the value we expect $f(c)$ to have.

In addition, tools will be needed to check for certain properties of specifications (sufficient completeness, consistency etc.). Some of these properties may be checked automatically while checking others requires the use of a theorem prover. Properties like consistency are very desirable to ensure peace of mind, albeit not actually required for correctness (an inconsistent specification cannot be refined to a program, so no incorrect program will be produced). If properties such as sufficient completeness are present then certain stages of the program development process are simplified.

Verification condition generator

According to the formal program development methodology presented in [ST 89] and outlined in Section 2.3, developing Standard ML functors from Extended ML requirements specifications (functor headings) involves three kinds of steps: decomposition steps, coding steps, and refinement steps. Each kind of development step involves constructing one or more specifications and verifying that certain well-formedness conditions hold, and that certain relationships between specifications hold. Some of these conditions are entirely syntactic, corresponding more or less to signature matching in Standard ML, and would be handled automatically. Others involve proving theorems and would be recorded for later attention.

The conditions required may be generated automatically from proposed development steps. It is natural to make this a side-effect of the usual Standard ML signature matching process, since the conditions depend to a large extent on information concerning sharing between types which is determined in the course of signature matching.

Agenda of outstanding tasks

During program development, progress is made on a variety of fronts:

1. Functor headings are implemented in terms of other functors.

2. Abstract programs are written and refined, sometimes producing executable code.

3. Proof obligations incurred during (1) and (2) are discharged.

The final program is guaranteed to be executable and correct with respect to the original specification once all of these tasks are completed. Some mechanism is required to keep track of those tasks which remain, perhaps enforcing some loose control on the order in which they are attacked. For example, to avoid wasted effort it makes sense to attack a set of accumulated proof obligations top-down (e.g. discharging those incurred by early development steps before those incurred by later ancillary development steps) rather than bottom-up.

Behavioural consequence

The proof obligations which arise as a result of development steps will in general involve proving that certain specifications entail other specifications *up to behavioural equivalence* rather than "literally". As discussed in Section 3, a number of methods are available for establishing behavioural consequence, where the simplest methods only work in some cases but the most general methods are difficult to use. In most cases literal entailment will suffice and so nothing more than a theorem prover as described below will be needed. For those cases where proper behavioural consequence is involved, some extra machinery is required to apply each of the methods available, generating proof-theoretic sufficient conditions which may be passed to the theorem prover.

Theorem prover

We expect to use some existing theorem prover as the proof engine for this system, rather than developing a new theorem prover from scratch. The currently most promising candidates are Isabelle [Pau 86], [PN 90] and Lego [Bur 89], [LPT 89]. Any existing theorem prover would have to be enriched to cope with the modular structure of specifications along the lines described in [SB 83], cf. [Far 89], [Far 90], [Far 91].

The small examples of formal program development in Extended ML which have been attempted so far suggest that 90% or more of the proof obligations which arise will be trivial to establish, either because (for example) the input interface of one functor is syntactically identical to the output interface of another, or because any proof involved is immediate. Such proof obligations could be discharged automatically by a background job while the user is busy with other tasks. The remaining ones inevitably involve more or less complex induction proofs. This suggests that the methods described in [BM 88], which can be cast in the form of LCF-style proof strategies [Ste 90], might be able to handle many of them automatically. This would leave only a few hard proofs which would be tackled interactively. Limited experience with a theorem prover for the CLEAR specification language suggests that the modular structure of specifications makes it easier to discover proofs [San 82].

Changing one's mind

The formal development of realistic programs will not proceed in practice without backtracking, mistakes and iteration, and Extended ML does not remove the possibility of unwise design decisions. In particular, it is difficult to get specifications right and so during the program development process some specifications will change several times in more or less significant ways. It will be important to salvage as much as possible of a development in progress when such changes are made.

Certain changes to specifications do not affect the correctness of a development in progress at all provided that an appropriate relation between the old specification and the new specification can be shown to hold. Alternatively, if the modified specification provides the interface between functors arising during the decomposition process, then the correctness of the development is preserved if it is possible to re-establish the correctness of the functors involving that interface.

Salvaging a major part of the development in progress under more radical alterations to specifications should be possible if the system keeps track of interdependencies, not only at the level of modules in the library but also at the level of the verification of individual interfaces (for example, matching a structure against a signature involves matching its substructures against the corresponding subsignatures). Even when a specification changes in a radical way, most of the specifications on which it depends and which depend on it will remain unchanged. The system could check which of the earlier interfaces still match and flag those which do not, making a distinction between an interface which must itself be shown to match and one which will match once certain interfaces on which it depends are shown to match.

Reusing existing program modules

An often-cited advantage of equipping program modules with specified interfaces is that it enables such modules to be reused in the development of other systems. As the library becomes more and more full of modules which were useful as components in previous systems, new systems are supposed to become easier to build. The effort involved in ensuring that such a module is correct with respect to its interface specification can thus be justified not only with reference to the system currently under development but also with reference to possible future projects.

The methodology described in Section 2.3 and the module library mentioned above support such reuse. The discussion above concerning altering specifications also applies here, allowing existing modules to be changed to fit modified interface specifications, provided enough information is retained in the library about the development history of the module. But as the library grows it will become difficult to identify potentially useful modules. Any process of matching a requirement specification against the modules in the library which involves theorem proving or non-trivial user interaction seems doomed to failure once the library grows to a significant size. Probably screening the modules in the library by means of some crude mechanism such as keyword search is the most cost-effective way of separating the potential wheat from the chaff.

Changing to a new institution

The first version of the support system will be specialised to developing Standard ML programs from specifications containing axioms written using the logical language described in Section 4. If necessary, simplifications may be adopted; for example, the first version of the theorem prover will no doubt be unable to deal fully with exceptions and/or higher-order quantifiers. As described earlier, the ideas embodied by Extended ML apply in the context of an arbitrary logical system (*institution* [GB 84]) and so ultimately we expect the system to support any form of axioms and any suitable target programming language. But in order to achieve a well-engineered general system it is necessary to first gain some experience with a more specialised system such as the one we propose. In the process of building this system we hope to gain a more concrete understanding of the extent to which components like those described above can be implemented in an institution-independent way.

Acknowledgements: Thanks to Mike Fourman, Robin Milner, Brian Monahan and Mads Tofte for useful discussions on aspects of Section 4, and to Stefan Kahrs, Ed Kazmierczak, Jim Hook and an anonymous referee for helpful comments on a draft of this paper. This research was supported by the Universities of Edinburgh, Bremen and Manchester, and by grants from the Polish Academy of Sciences, the (U.K.) Science and Engineering Research Council, ESPRIT, and the Wolfson Foundation.

6 References

[Note: LNCS n = Springer Lecture Notes in Computer Science, Volume n]

[AM 87] A. Appel and D. MacQueen. A Standard ML compiler. *Proc. Conf. on Functional Programming and Computer Architecture*, Portland. LNCS 274 (1987).

[BHK 90] J. Bergstra, J. Heering and P. Klint. Module algebra. *Journal of the Assoc. for Computing Machinery* 37(2), 335–372 (1990).

[Bid 89] M. Bidoit. PLUSS, un langage pour le développement de spécifications algébriques modulaires. Thèse d'Etat, Université Paris-Sud, Orsay (1989).

[BW 88] R. Bird and P. Wadler. *Introduction to Functional Programming*. Prentice-Hall (1988).

[BM 88] R. Boyer and J. Moore. *A Computational Logic Handbook*. Academic Press (1988).

[BW 82] M. Broy and M. Wirsing. Partial abstract data types. *Acta Informatica* 18(1), 47–64 (1982).

[Bur 89] R. Burstall. Computer-assisted proof for mathematics: an introduction, using the Lego proof system. *Proc. IAM Conf. on The Revolution in Mathematics Caused by Computing*, Brighton (1989).

[BMS 80] R. Burstall, D. MacQueen and D. Sannella. HOPE: an experimental applicative language. *Proc. 1980 LISP Conference*, Stanford, 136–143 (1980).

[Coq 86] T. Coquand. An analysis of Girard's paradox. *Proc. IEEE Symp. on Logic in Computer Science*, Cambridge (1986).

[EM 85] H. Ehrig and B. Mahr. *Fundamentals of Algebraic Specification 1: Equations and Initial Semantics*. EATCS Monographs on Theoretical Computer Science, Vol. 6. Springer (1985).

[Far 89] J. Farrés-Casals. Proving correctness of constructor implementations. *Proc. 1989 Symp. on Mathematical Foundations of Computer Science*. LNCS 379, 225–235 (1989).

[Far 90] J. Farrés-Casals. Proving correctness w.r.t. specifications with hidden parts. *Proc. 2nd Intl. Conf. on Algebraic and Logic Programming*, Nancy. LNCS 463, 25–39 (1990).

[Far 91] J. Farrés-Casals. Verification in ASL and Related Specification Languages. Ph.D. thesis, Univ. of Edinburgh, to appear (1991).

[FJKR 87] L. Feijs, H. Jonkers, C. Koymans and G. Renardel de Lavalette. Formal definition of the design language COLD-K. METEOR Report t7/PRLE/7, Philips Research Lab., Eindhoven (1987).

[GB 84] J. Goguen and R. Burstall. Introducing institutions. *Proc. Logics of Programming Workshop*, Carnegie-Mellon. LNCS 164, 221–256 (1984).

[GW 88] J. Goguen and T. Winkler. Introducing OBJ3. Research report, SRI International (1988).

[GMW 79] M. Gordon, R. Milner and C. Wadsworth. *Edinburgh LCF*. LNCS 78 (1979).

[GP 89] M. Gordon and A. Pitts. The HOL logic. Part II of *The HOL System: Description*. DSTO Australia and SRI International (preliminary version), November 1989.

[Har 89] R. Harper. Introduction to Standard ML. Report ECS-LFCS-86-14, Univ. of Edinburgh. Revised edition (1989).

[HMM 90] R. Harper, J. Mitchell and E. Moggi. Higher-order modules and the phase distinction. *Proc. 17th ACM Symp. on Principles of Programming Languages* (1990).

[HJ 89] I. Hayes and C. Jones. Specifications are (not necessarily) executable. *Software Engineering Journal* 4(6), 320–338 (1989).

[Hen 90] R. Hennicker. Context induction: a proof principle for behavioural abstractions. *Proc. Intl. Symp. on Design and Implementation of Symbolic Computation Systems*, Capri. LNCS 429, 101-110 (1990).

[HK 90] J. Hook and R. Kieburtz. Key Words in Context: an example. Technical Report CSE-90-012, Oregon Graduate Institute (1990).

[HW 89] P. Hudak and P. Wadler *et al.* Report on the functional programming language Haskell. Report CSC/89/R5, Univ. of Glasgow (1989).

[Hus 85] H. Hußmann. Rapid prototyping for algebraic specifications: RAP system user's manual. Report MIP-8504, Universität Passau (1985).

[Jon 86] C. Jones. *Systematic Software Development Using VDM*. Prentice-Hall (1986).

[KS 91] B. Krieg-Brückner and D. Sannella. Structuring specifications in-the-large and in-the-small: higher-order functions, dependent types and inheritance in SPECTRAL. *Proc. Joint Conf. on Theory and Practice of Software Development*, Brighton, April 1991. LNCS, to appear (1991).

[LPT 89] Z. Luo, R. Pollack and P. Taylor. How to use Lego (a preliminary user's manual). Report LFCS-TN-27, Univ. of Edinburgh (1989).

[MacQ 86a] D. MacQueen. Modules for Standard ML. In: Report ECS-LFCS-86-2, Univ. of Edinburgh (1986).

[MacQ 86b] D. MacQueen. Using dependent types to express modular structure: experience with Pebble and ML. *Proc. 13th ACM Symp. on Principles of Programming Languages* (1986).

[MS 85] D. MacQueen and D. Sannella. Completeness of proof systems for equational specifications. *IEEE Transactions on Software Engineering* SE-11, 454–461 (1985).

[MS 90] C. Meldrum and A.W. Smith. Design of an SML to Ten15 compiler. Harlequin Ltd. (1990).

[Mil 78] R. Milner. A theory of type polymorphism in programming. *Journal of Computer and System Sciences* 17, 348–375 (1978).

[Mil 89] R. Milner. *Communication and Concurrency.* Prentice-Hall (1989).

[MT 90] R. Milner and M. Tofte. *Commentary on Standard ML.* MIT Press (1990).

[MTH 90] R. Milner, M. Tofte and R. Harper. *The Definition of Standard ML.* MIT Press (1990).

[Mit 86] J. Mitchell. Representation independence and data abstraction. *Proc. 13th ACM Symp. on Principles of Programming Languages* (1986).

[MH 88] J. Mitchell and R. Harper. The essence of ML. *Proc. 15th ACM Symp. on Principles of Programming Languages* (1988).

[Pau 86] L. Paulson. Natural deduction proof as higher-order resolution. *Journal of Logic Programming* 3, 237–258 (1986).

[Pau 87] L. Paulson. *Logic and Computation: Interactive Proof with Cambridge LCF.* Cambridge Univ. Press (1987).

[PN 90] L. Paulson and T. Nipkow. Isabelle tutorial and user's manual. Report 189, Cambridge University (1990).

[Plo 81] G. Plotkin. A structural approach to operational semantics. Report DAIMI FN-19, Aarhus University (1981).

[Rea 89] C. Reade. *Elements of Functional Programming.* Addison-Wesley (1989).

[Rei 87] H. Reichel. *Initial Computability, Algebraic Specifications, and Partial Algebras.* Oxford Univ. Press (1987).

[San 82] D. Sannella. Semantics, Implementation and Pragmatics of CLEAR, a Program Specification Language. Ph.D. thesis CST-17-82, Univ. of Edinburgh (1982)

[San 87] D. Sannella. Formal specification of ML programs. *Jornadas Rank Xerox Sobre Inteligencia Artificial Razonamiento Automatizado*, Blanes, Spain, 79–98 (1987).

[San 91] D. Sannella. Formal program development in Extended ML for the working programmer. *Proc. 3rd BCS/FACS Workshop on Refinement*, Hursley Park, January 1990. LNCS, to appear (1991).

[SB 83] D. Sannella and R. Burstall. Structured theories in LCF. *Proc. 8th Colloq. on Trees in Algebra and Programming*, L'Aquila, Italy. LNCS 159, 377–391 (1983).

[SdST 90] D. Sannella, F. da Silva and A. Tarlecki. Syntax, typechecking and dynamic semantics for Extended ML (version 2). Draft report, Univ. of Edinburgh (1990). Version 1 appeared as Report ECS-LFCS-89-101, Univ. of Edinburgh (1989).

[SST 90] D. Sannella, S. Sokołowski and A. Tarlecki. Toward formal development of programs from algebraic specifications: parameterisation revisited. Report 6/90, Univ. of Bremen (1990).

[ST 85] D. Sannella and A. Tarlecki. Program specification and development in Standard ML. *Proc. 12th ACM Symp. on Principles of Programming Languages*, New Orleans, 67–77 (1985).

[ST 86] D. Sannella and A. Tarlecki. Extended ML: an institution-independent framework for formal program development. *Proc. Workshop on Category Theory and Computer Programming*, Guildford. LNCS 240, 364–389 (1986).

[ST 87] D. Sannella and A. Tarlecki. On observational equivalence and algebraic specification. *Journal of Computer and System Sciences* 34, 150–178 (1987).

[ST 88a] D. Sannella and A. Tarlecki. Specifications in an arbitrary institution. *Information and Computation* 76, 165–210 (1988).

[ST 88b] D. Sannella and A. Tarlecki. Toward formal development of programs from algebraic specifications: implementations revisited. *Acta Informatica* 25, 233–281 (1988).

[ST 89] D. Sannella and A. Tarlecki. Toward formal development of ML programs: foundations and methodology. *Proc. Joint Conf. on Theory and Practice of Software Development*, Barcelona. LNCS 352, 375–389 (1989). Full version as Report ECS-LFCS-89-71, Univ. of Edinburgh (1989).

[ST 91] D. Sannella and A. Tarlecki. A kernel specification formalism with higher-order parameterisation. *Proc. 7th Workshop on Specification of Abstract Data Types*, Wusterhausen, GDR; LNCS, this volume (1991).

[SWa 87] D. Sannella and L. Wallen. A calculus for the construction of modular Prolog programs. *Proc. 1987 IEEE Symp. on Logic Programming*, San Francisco, 368–378 (1987); to appear in *Journal of Logic Programming.*

[SW 83] D. Sannella and M. Wirsing. A kernel language for algebraic specification and implementation. *Proc. 1983 Intl. Conf. on Foundations of Computation Theory*, Borgholm, Sweden. LNCS 158, 413–427 (1983).

[SS 83] W. Scherlis and D. Scott. First steps towards inferential programming. *Information Processing '83*, 199–212. North-Holland (1983).

[Sch 86] O. Schoett. Data Abstraction and the Correctness of Modular Programming. Ph.D. thesis CST-42-87, Univ. of Edinburgh (1987).

[Ste 90] A. Stevens. An Improved Method for the Mechanisation of Inductive Proof. Ph.D. thesis, Univ. of Edinburgh (1990).

[SGM 89] T. Stroup, N. Götz and M. Mendler. Stepwise refinement of layered protocols by formal program development. *Proc. 9th Conf. on Protocol Specification, Testing, and Verification*, North-Holland (1989).

[Tof 88] M. Tofte. Operational Semantics and Polymorphic Type Inference. Ph.D. thesis CST-52-88, Univ. of Edinburgh (1988).

[Tof 89] M. Tofte. Four lectures on Standard ML. Report ECS-LFCS-89-73, Univ. of Edinburgh (1989).

[Wik 87] Å. Wikström. *Functional Programming Using Standard ML.* Prentice-Hall (1987).

[Wir 86] M. Wirsing. Structured algebraic specifications: a kernel language. *Theoretical Computer Science* 42, 123–249 (1986).

Dependent Types Considered Necessary for Specification Languages *

T. Streicher, M. Wirsing
Fakultät für Mathematik und Informatik
Universität Passau, Postfach 2540
D-8940 Passau, FRG

Abstract

The aim of this paper is to show that the concept of dependent type is necessary and appropriate for a specification language. This is examplified by expressing the type SPEC of all specifications, two different approaches to parameterization, and (a simple variant of) Weber's and Ehrig's module specifications. In particular the formalization of the parameterization concepts gives the solution to the open problem, how to combine the theory of institutions with the lambda calculus approach to parameterization.

1. Introduction

Formal specifications are an approach to describe data structures in an abstract, implementation independent way. For the description of large data structures and of systems of data structures it is necessary to compose specifications from smaller ones. This has led to the introduction of specification languages such as CLEAR [BG1, 2], Larch [GHW], OBJ [FGJM], ACT [EM], [WE] and ASL [SW], [ST].

The intended meaning of a specification is a class of structures (or sometimes a category of structures) over some signature and, therefore, any specification language can be understood as a calculus for building and manipulating classes of structures. Therefore a specification language should be able to speak about signatures, classes of structures of certain signatures and the relations between these objects.

---

* This work has been partially sponsored by Forwiss (Bayer. Forschungszentrum für Wissensbasierte Systeme), the ESPRIT-working group COMPASS and the DFG-project SPECTRUM.

As in many cases the form of the axioms is restricted to equations or Horn formulas one often speaks of *algebraic* specifications. But as the expressive power of such logical calculi is very restricted one often wants to use stronger logical systems such as full first order logic or higher order logic. Typically one wants to use strong logics for high level specifications and weaker logics for low level specifications as they should already have some algorithmic nature.

Therefore already in [BG2], Burstall and Goguen remark that the specification-building operations should be independent from the specific choice of the underlying logic (such as equational logic, Horn logic, first order logic, higher-order logic etc.) used for writing basic specifications. In order to express this generality Burstall and Goguen have introduced the concept of an *institution*, a notion which intends to describe axiomatically (actually in the language of category theory) the notion of language and structure. The kernel of a good specification language should be independent from the choice of a specific institution but instead a specification language should be *parametric* w.r.t. to one or more institutions.

The idea of interpreting algebraic specifications over arbitrary institutions has already been investigated in [ST]. But, as they have remarked themselves, there are problems with expressing the concept of parameterized data type. In the literature one can distinguish two main approaches to parameterization : the pushout approach [TWW], [EKTWW], [E] and λ-abstraction [SW], [ST].

In both cases, instantiation of a parameterized specification consists in giving an actual parameter specification together with a signature morphism that relates the symbols occurring in the formal parameter with those occurring in the actual parameter. Then the result is either defined via the pushout of the underlying signature morphism of the actual parameter and the signature morphism relating the formal parameter to the specification body or via a kind of β-reduction. Hence, the signature of an instantiated parameterized data type not only depends on the signature of the actual parameter, but also on the signature morphism relating the signature of the formal parameter with the signature of the actual parameter and thus parameterization of specifications cannot be defined via λ-abstraction in simply typed λ-calculus, but needs the more refined concept of dependent type in order to express that the type of the result of a function depends on its argument.

Furthermore, categorical notions and especially the notion of an institution can be expressed easily using dependent types. One assumes that there is a type Sign of signatures and a *family of types* Struct(Σ) indexed over $\Sigma \in$ Sign. Moreover, Sign and Struct(Σ) are not simply types but they carry the structure of a category which can also be expressed using the concept of dependent types. Actually we shall not use the categorical structure on Struct(Σ), but we heavily use the categorical structure of Sign.

The aim of this paper is to show that the concept of dependent type is necessary and appropriate for formally expressing the manipulation of algebraic specifications. We exemplify this by expressing the type SPEC of all specifications, the two different approaches to parameterization, and

Weber's and Ehrig's [WE] module specifications. In particular, our formalization of the parameterization concepts gives a solution to the open problem how to combine the theory of institutions with the λ-calculus approach to parameterization.

The paper is organized as follows. In section 2, the concepts of dependent types are presented informally. As an example we express in the language of dependent types that the type Sign carries the structure of a category. In section 3, we specify the concept of pushout for the category Sign in the language of dependent types. In section 4, the type SPEC of all loose specifications is defined as the sum of a family of types. In section 5, the two approaches to parameterization of specifications (pushout and λ-calculus) are defined and compared in the framework of dependent types. For the pushout approach, a parameterized loose specification is defined as a pair consisting of a signature morphism mapping the formal parameter signature to the result signature and a class of structures over the result signature. To our knowledge, this approach to loose parameterized specifications and their corresponding instantiation mechanism via a pushout construction (although not very difficult) is new. The λ-calculus approach to parameterization is more general than the pushout approach (as shown by an example) and it can be expressed directly in the language of dependent types in such a way that it extends the formalizations of [SW], [ST], [W]. In the rest of the section we discuss the concept of a parameterized algebra in its relation to the concept of parametrized specification as introducd in [SST]. In section 6, a (slightly simplified) description of module specifications [WE] is given in the language of dependent types. Section 7 closes with some final remarks.

2. Manipulating Specifications Using Dependent Types

In this section we shall give a quick and informal introduction to the concept of dependent types and use it for expressing the categorical aspects of signatures.

Dependent types have been introduced into Logic and Computer Science by the work of deBruijn on the AUTOMATH project and most prominently by Martin-Löf in his Intuitionistic Type Theory [M-L]. Following suggestions of D. Scott who emphasized that dependent types are necessary in order to axiomatize category theory, R. Dyckhoff has extended Martin-Löf's Intuitionistic Type Theory and developed basic categorical notions and theorems in this language, see [Dy]. Our exposition essentially follows the ideas of Dyckhoff.

The intended interpretation of the concepts used is that *types* are interpreted as *sets* and *families of types* are interpreted as *families of sets indexed over some other set called index set.* As we do *not* use any impredicative features, as e.g. in the Calculus of Constructions [CH], the straightforward set-theoretic interpretation is not misleading and does not cause any inconsistencies. Throughout the paper we neglect foundational problems concerning the size of collections as index types will always be sets, i.e. we never quantify over proper classes.

One of the most important notions in theories of dependent types is the notion of *context*. A context Γ is an expression of the form $x_1: A_1, \ldots, x_n: A_n$ where the A_i are type expressions and for i with $1 \leq i \leq n$ the type expression A_i depends at most on the variables declared before, i.e. $x_1, \ldots, x_{i-1}$.

Another basic notion is the one of a *judgement* relative to some context Γ. There are four forms of judgement :

- $\Gamma \vdash A$ **type** — A is a type w.r.t. context Γ
- $\Gamma \vdash A = B$ — A and B are equal types w.r.t. context Γ
- $\Gamma \vdash t \in A$ — t is an object of type A w.r.t. context Γ
- $\Gamma \vdash t = s \in A$ — t and s are equal objects of type A w.r.t. context Γ.

As an introductory example we describe signatures on a very abstract level (the one of institutions, cf. [GB]) as a category.

First, we assume that there exists a type of signatures denoted by Sign. This assumption is expressed in the language of type theory as

(1) $\vdash$ Sign **type**.

For any objects $\Sigma 0, \Sigma 1 \in$ Sign one can introduce the type Sign_Mor($\Sigma 0$,$\Sigma 1$) of *signature morphisms from* $\Sigma 0$ *to* $\Sigma 1$. This is expressed in the language of type theory as

(2) $\Sigma 0, \Sigma 1$: Sign $\vdash$ Sign_Mor($\Sigma 0$,$\Sigma 1$) **type**.

Of course, $\Sigma 0, \Sigma 1$: Sign abbreviates $\Sigma 0$: Sign, $\Sigma 1$: Sign. We shall use this convention for the rest of the paper.

Furthermore, we assume that the type Sign and the family of types Sign_Mor together form a *category of signatures*. That means that one has an operation for composing morphisms and for any object in Sign_Ob one has an associated identity morphism. Using the concept of function type (where $A \rightarrow B$ denotes the type of functions from A to B) this can be expressed in type theory as follows.

We assume

(3) $\Sigma 0$: Sign $\vdash$ id($\Sigma 0$) $\in$ Sign_Mor($\Sigma 0$,$\Sigma 0$) and

(4) $\Sigma 0, \Sigma 1, \Sigma 2$: Sign $\vdash$ Sign_comp($\Sigma 0$,$\Sigma 1$,$\Sigma 2$) $\in$
Sign_Mor($\Sigma 1$, $\Sigma 2$) $\rightarrow$ Sign_Mor($\Sigma 0$,$\Sigma 1$) $\rightarrow$ Sign_Mor($\Sigma 0$, $\Sigma 2$)

One of the most important notions in theories of dependent types is the notion of *context*. A context Γ is an expression of the form $x_1: A_1, \dots, x_n: A_n$ where the A_i are type expressions and for i with $1 \le i \le n$ the type expression A_i depends at most on the variables declared before, i.e. $x_1, \dots, x_{i-1}$.

Another basic notion is the one of a *judgement* relative to some context Γ. There are four forms of judgement :

- $\Gamma \vdash A$ **type** — A is a type w.r.t. context Γ
- $\Gamma \vdash A = B$ — A and B are equal types w.r.t. context Γ
- $\Gamma \vdash t \in A$ — t is an object of type A w.r.t. context Γ
- $\Gamma \vdash t = s \in A$ — t and s are equal objects of type A w.r.t. context Γ.

As an introductory example we describe signatures on a very abstract level (the one of institutions, cf. [GB]) as a category.

First, we assume that there exists a type of signatures denoted by Sign. This assumption is expressed in the language of type theory as

(1) $\vdash$ Sign **type** .

For any objects $\Sigma 0, \Sigma 1 \in$ Sign one can introduce the type Sign_Mor(Σ0,Σ1) of *signature morphisms from* $\Sigma 0$ *to* $\Sigma 1$. This is expressed in the language of type theory as

(2) $\Sigma 0, \Sigma 1$: Sign $\vdash$ Sign_Mor(Σ0,Σ1) **type** .

Of course, $\Sigma 0, \Sigma 1$: Sign abbreviates $\Sigma 0$: Sign, $\Sigma 1$: Sign. We shall use this convention for the rest of the paper.

Furthermore, we assume that the type Sign and the family of types Sign_Mor together form a *category of signatures*. That means that one has an operation for composing morphisms and for any object in Sign_Ob one has an associated identity morphism. Using the concept of function type (where $A \rightarrow B$ denotes the type of functions from A to B) this can be expressed in type theory as follows.

We assume

(3) $\Sigma 0$: Sign $\vdash$ id(Σ0) $\in$ Sign_Mor(Σ0,Σ0) and

(4) $\Sigma 0, \Sigma 1, \Sigma 2$: Sign $\vdash$ Sign_comp(Σ0,Σ1,Σ2) $\in$
Sign_Mor(Σ1, Σ2) $\rightarrow$ Sign_Mor(Σ0,Σ1) $\rightarrow$ Sign_Mor(Σ0, Σ2)

satisfying the following constraints :

(5) "identity morphisms are neutral w.r.t. composition"

(a) $\Sigma0, \Sigma1$: Sign, σ : Sign_Mor($\Sigma0,\Sigma1$) $\vdash$ Sign_comp($\Sigma0,\Sigma0,\Sigma1$)(σ)(id($\Sigma0$)) = σ
$\in$ Sign_Mor($\Sigma0,\Sigma1$)

(b) $\Sigma0, \Sigma1$: Sign, σ : Sign_Mor($\Sigma0,\Sigma1$) $\vdash$ Sign_comp($\Sigma0,\Sigma1,\Sigma1$)(id($\Sigma1$))(σ) = σ
$\in$ Sign_Mor($\Sigma0,\Sigma1$)

(6) "composition of morphisms is associative"

$\Sigma0, \Sigma1, \Sigma2, \Sigma3$: Sign, σ_1 : Sign_Mor($\Sigma0,\Sigma1$), σ_2 : Sign_Mor($\Sigma1,\Sigma2$), σ_3 : Sign_Mor($\Sigma2,\Sigma3$) $\vdash$
Sign_comp($\Sigma0,\Sigma2,\Sigma3$)(σ_3)(Sign_comp ($\Sigma1,\Sigma2,\Sigma3$)(σ_2)(σ_1)) =
Sign_comp($\Sigma0,\Sigma1,\Sigma3$) (Sign_comp($\Sigma1,\Sigma2,\Sigma3$)(σ_3)(σ_2))(σ_1) $\in$ Sign_Mor($\Sigma0,\Sigma3$).

For the purposes of this paper it is not necessary to be very explicit about the way how signatures are denoted. It is sufficient simply to assume that signatures form a category. For a way of expressing first-order signatures in the language of type theory see e.g. [TBG].

For Sign_comp($\Sigma0,\Sigma1,\Sigma2$)(σ_2)(σ_1) we will often write rather sloppily $\sigma_2 \circ \sigma_1$ as is usually done in category theory.

3. Pushouts

A concept which is needed for the description of parameterized data types and instantiations thereof is the *pushout* of two signature morphisms with common source.

Informally, that means that for any signatures $\Sigma0, \Sigma1, \Sigma2$ and signature morphism $\sigma_1 : \Sigma0 \rightarrow \Sigma1$, $\sigma_2 : \Sigma0 \rightarrow \Sigma2$ there is a signature Po(σ_1,σ_2) and signature morphisms po_1(σ_1,σ_2) : $\Sigma1 \rightarrow$ Po(σ_1,σ_2) and po_2(σ_1,σ_2) : $\Sigma2 \rightarrow$ Po(σ_1,σ_2) such that po_1(σ_1,σ_2) $\circ\, \sigma_1$ = po_2(σ_1,σ_2) $\circ\, \sigma_2$

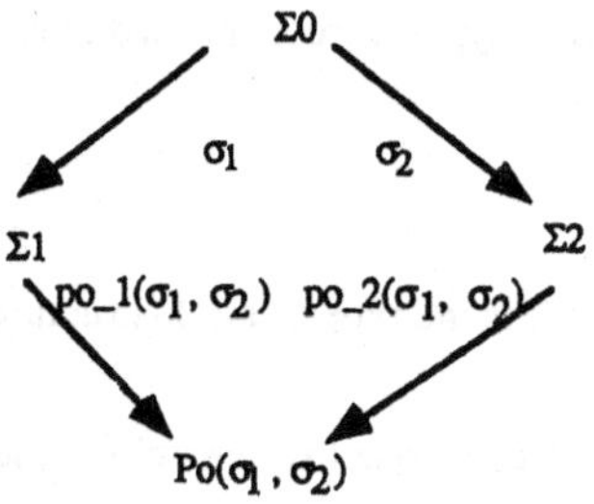

Diag. 1

and some (co)universality condition is satisfied : for any signature $\Sigma 3$ and signature morphisms $\sigma_3 : \Sigma 1 \rightarrow \Sigma 3$ and $\sigma_4 : \Sigma 2 \rightarrow \Sigma 3$ with $\sigma_3 \circ \sigma_1 = \sigma_4 \circ \sigma_2$ there exists a *unique* signature morphism $\sigma : Po(\sigma_1,\sigma_2) \rightarrow \Sigma 3$ with the property that $\sigma \circ po\_1(\sigma_1,\sigma_2) = \sigma_3$ and $\sigma \circ po\_2(\sigma_1,\sigma_2) = \sigma_4$.

In the type theoretic formalism this can be expressed as follows.

(7) " $Po(\sigma_1,\sigma_2)$ is a signature"

$\Sigma 0, \Sigma 1, \Sigma 2 : Sign, \sigma_1 : Sign\_Mor(\Sigma 0, \Sigma 1), \sigma_2 : Sign\_Mor(\Sigma 0, \Sigma 2) \vdash Po(\sigma_1,\sigma_2) \in Sign$

(8) " $po\_i(\sigma_1,\sigma_2)$ is a signature morphism from Σi to $Po(\sigma_1,\sigma_2)$ for $i=1, 2$ "

(a) $\Sigma 0, \Sigma 1, \Sigma 2 : Sign, \sigma_1 : Sign\_Mor(\Sigma 0, \Sigma 1), \sigma_2 : Sign\_Mor(\Sigma 0, \Sigma 2)$
$\vdash po\_1(\sigma_1,\sigma_2) \in Sign\_Mor(\Sigma 1, Po(\sigma_1,\sigma_2))$

(b) $\Sigma 0, \Sigma 1, \Sigma 2 : Sign, \sigma_1 : Sign\_Mor(\Sigma 0, \Sigma 1), \sigma_2 : Sign\_Mor(\Sigma 0, \Sigma 2)$
$\vdash po\_2(\sigma_1,\sigma_2) \in Sign\_Mor(\Sigma 2, Po(\sigma_1,\sigma_2))$.

The (co)universality can be expressed in a similar way in the type theoretic formalism. But as we do not need it for the purposes of this paper we omit the details.

4. Structures of a signature and the type SPEC of all specifications

In this section, we associate with any signature Σ the type Struct(Σ) whose objects are considered as the structures (or algebras) over the signature Σ and we construct the type SPEC whose objects are the specifications.

For this purpose we assume to be given a family of types Struct indexed over Sign :

(9) Σ : Sign $\vdash$ Struct(Σ) **type** .

Intuitively, for any signature Σ the type Struct(Σ) is the type of all Σ-structures (or Σ-algebras).

Any signature morphism $\sigma \in$ Sign_Mor(Σ0,Σ1) gives rise to a renaming function Struct(σ) in the reverse direction mapping Struct(Σ1) to Struct(Σ0) :

(10) Σ0, Σ1 : Sign, σ : Sign_Mor(Σ0, Σ1) $\vdash$ Struct(σ) $\in$ Struct(Σ1) $\rightarrow$ Struct(Σ0) .

The notion of institution introduced in [GB] is more comprehensive in the sense that for any signature Σ Struct(Σ) is not simply a type, but carries the structure of a category and, correspondingly, Struct(σ) extends to a functor from Struct(Σ1) to Struct(Σ0). But as already mentioned in the introduction we do not need this additional categorical structure for the purposes of our paper and therefore omit it.

In [SW], [W] the semantics of a *loose algebraic specification* is given by a signature Σ and a subclass $\mathcal{M}$ of Struct(Σ). Thus, the type SPEC considered as basic in ASL appears to be definable in our framework as

SPEC = (Σ Σ : Sign) $\wp$(Struct(Σ)),

where $\wp$(M) denotes the type of all subclasses of the class M and we allow comprehension to build elements of $\wp$(M). We use for any *object* A of type $\wp$(M) the notation ext(A) to denote the *type* of all objects in M contained in the subclass A. The notation (Σ x : A)B(x) is interpreted as the disjoint sum of a family of classes and pr_1 and pr_2 denote the projections on the first and second component, respectively, see [M-L]. It makes sense to apply projection functions to elements of (Σ x : A)B(x) as this type consists of all pairs <a,b> such that a is an object of type A and b is an object of type B[a/x]. In the same way the disjoint sum of a family of sets is defined in naive set theory !

Although it is not our main concern here we sketch how to construct basic objects of type SPEC. Assume that for any Σ of type Sign we are given a type Form(Σ) of formulas over signature Σ and a predicate $\models_\Sigma$ on Struct(Σ) and $\wp$(Form(Σ)) with the intuitive meaning that M $\models_\Sigma \Phi$ iff all formulas in Φ are satisfied w.r.t M. Now we may introduce an operator **spec** _ , _ **end** ; given a signature Σ and Φ of type $\wp$(Form(Σ)) it gives the object **spec** Σ , Φ **end** which by definition is equal to <Σ, { M $\in$ Struct(Σ) : M $\models_\Sigma \Phi$ }>.

This example shows that it is crucial to distinguish between objects of type Form(Σ) which are *formulas of specifications* and *assertions* like $M \models_\Sigma \Phi$ which by no means can be considered as objects of some type.

In [W] for a signature Σ the set $\wp$(Struct(Σ)) has been endowed with a cpo structure where for $\mathcal{M}_1, \mathcal{M}_2 \in \wp(\text{Struct}(\Sigma))$ $\mathcal{M}_1 \sqsubseteq \mathcal{M}_2$ iff $\mathcal{M}_2$ is a subclass of $\mathcal{M}_1$, which intuitively means that a specification is more defined than another iff it excludes more models, i.e. is less liberal.

One can extend this idea to SPEC but one has to generalize the partial order to a category. If $<\Sigma_1,\mathcal{M}_1>$, $<\Sigma_2,\mathcal{M}_2> \in$ SPEC then a *specification morphism* from $<\Sigma_1,\mathcal{M}_1>$ to $<\Sigma_2,\mathcal{M}_2>$ is a signature morphism $\sigma : \Sigma_1 \to \Sigma_2$ such that for all $M \in \mathcal{M}_2$ it holds that Struct(σ)(M) $\in \mathcal{M}_1$. Of course, identity specification morphisms are induced by identity signature morphisms and composition of specification morphisms is inherited from the composition of signature morphisms.

If the category of signatures has arbitrary colimits (which is the case for most categories of signatures studied in the literature such as first order and higher order signatures), then the category of specifications and specification morphisms has arbitrary colimits as well and thus generalizes the concept of a cpo. One can prove that the standard specification-building operations as studied e.g. in ASL induce functors over SPEC which respect colimits of directed diagrams.

5. Dependent Types for Expressing Parameterized Specifications

In this section, we first discuss informally the concept of parameterized specification and then show how to express the pushout approach to parameterized specifications in a λ-calculus with dependent types. Then we show that the λ-calculus approach is more general than the pushout approach. Finally we discuss the concept of parameterized algebra and explain in which sense parameterized specifications can be understood as specifications of classes of parameterized algebras.

5.1 Informal discussion

Informally, a parameterized specification is a function mapping specifications to specifications, see [W]. A typical example is the parameterized specification which takes a specification of data over some fixed parameter signature Σ_{DATA} with a specified sort data as an argument and produces the specification over signature $\Sigma_{LIST\text{-}OF\text{-}DATA}$ of the type of lists with elements of sort data. In this case, the signature Σ_{DATA} of the parameter and the signature $\Sigma_{LIST\text{-}OF\text{-}DATA}$ of the result specification are related by an embedding of signatures, as new sorts and operations are added to the parameter signature and the sorts and operations of the parameter signature are left unchanged.

More generally, we can assume that the parameter and the result signature are related by an arbitrary signature morphism which is not necessarily an embedding. Thus, the notion of parameterized specification can be given as a pair consisting of this signature morphism and the class of models of the body specification. If one has constraints on the parameter it is no problem to formulate these in terms of the signature of the body : one restricts the models of the body specification to that subclass which consists of exactly those models of the body specification whose restriction along the signature morphism gives models satisfying the parameter constraints.

Thus a loose parameterized specification is given by a signature morphism $\sigma_{par} : \Sigma_{par} \to \Sigma_{body}$ and a subclass $\mathcal{M}_{body}$ of $Struct(\Sigma_{body})$. The signature Σ_{par} is called the signature of the formal parameter and Σ_{body} is called the signature of the (body of the) parameterized specification or result signature (cf. [BGGN]). For any $M \in \mathcal{M}_{body}$ the corresponding parameter part is $Struct(\sigma_{par})(M)$.

A parameter constraint can be expressed by choosing additionally a subclass $\mathcal{M}_{par}$ of $Struct(\Sigma_{par})$. This is equivalent to restricting $\mathcal{M}_{body}$ to $\mathcal{M}_{body} \cap Struct(\sigma_{par})^{-1}(\mathcal{M}_{par})$, i.e. to those structures in $\mathcal{M}_{body}$ whose restriction along σ_{par} is in $\mathcal{M}_{par}$ as well.

From the point of view of the λ-calculus approach the intended meaning of the parameterized specification is a map F from $\wp(Struct(\Sigma_{par}))$ to $\wp(Struct(\Sigma_{body}))$ which behaves as follows :

$$F(\mathcal{M}) = \{ M \in \mathcal{M}_{body} : Struct(\sigma_{par})(M) \in \mathcal{M} \} = Struct(\sigma_{par})^{-1}(\mathcal{M}) \cap \mathcal{M}_{body}$$

for all $\mathcal{M} \in \wp(Struct(\Sigma_{par}))$.

The drawback of this point of view is that the parameterized specification accepts only those specifications as arguments whose underlying signature coincides with the signature Σ_{par} of the formal parameter. (This is the approach of SML [MQ]).

But in general we want to accept specifications as arguments of parameterized specifications, whose underlying signatures are not identical with the signature of the formal parameter but *contain it in some sense* . E.g. we want to instantiate the parameterized specification LIST-OF-DATA by any specification with a distinguished sort of data. This example shows that an actual parameter has to be given as a specification SP *together* with a signature morphism from the signature of the formal parameter to the signature of the actual parameter SP. The signature of the instantiation of the parameterized specification must contain the signatures of the body of the parameterized specification *and* of the actual parameter. Of course, if the signature morphisms relating the formal parameter to the body of the parameterized specification and to the actual parameter are not both embeddings then there have to be made some identifications on sort and operation symbols of the disjoint union of the signatures of the body and the actual parameter.

This can be expressed on an abstract level by considering the pushout of the underlying signature morphism of the parameterized specification and the signature morphism which relates the formal to the actual parameter.

5.2 Formulating the pushout approach by λ-calculus with dependent types

An *actual parameter* is given by a subclass $\mathcal{M}_{act}$ of Struct(Σ_{act}) (denoting the actual parameter specification) and a signature morphism $\sigma_{act} : \Sigma_{par} \rightarrow \Sigma_{act}$ relating the formal parameter signature Σ_{par} with the signature Σ_{act} of the formal parameter.

The specification corresponding to the *instantiated parameterized specification* has the signature $Po(\sigma_{par},\sigma_{act})$ and the corresponding class of models contains exactly those structures M in $Struct(Po(\sigma_{par},\sigma_{act}))$ such that $Struct(po\_1(\sigma_{par},\sigma_{act}))(M) \in \mathcal{M}_{body}$ and $Struct(po\_2(\sigma_{par},\sigma_{act}))(M) \in \mathcal{M}_{act}$.

One can see immediately that the roles of the parameterized specification and of the actual parameter are *symmetric* . This is a difference to the situation when one considers function application : in that case the role of the function and the role of the argument are *not symmetric* .

The more primitive concept underlying the concept of a parameterized specification in the pushout approach seems is the *amalgamation of two specifications over a shared part* (cf. [EM], [ST]). The operation of amalgamation can be expressed formally in the language of dependent types as follows :

$$\Gamma \vdash \langle Po(\sigma_{par},\sigma_{act}), \{ M \in Struct(Po(\sigma_{par},\sigma_{act})) : \phi(\mathcal{M}_{act}) \}\rangle \in SPEC$$

where Γ is an abbreviation for the context

$$\Sigma_{par}, \Sigma_{body} : Sign, \mathcal{M}_{body} : \wp(Struct(\Sigma)), \sigma_{par} : Sign\_Mor(\Sigma_{par},\Sigma_{body}),$$
$$\Sigma_{act} : Sign, \mathcal{M}_{act} : \wp(Struct(\Sigma_{act})), \sigma_{act} : Sign\_Mor(\Sigma_{par},\Sigma_{act})$$

and $\phi(\mathcal{M})$ is an abbreviation for the formula

$$Struct(po\_1(\sigma_{par},\sigma_{act}))(M) \in \mathcal{M}_{body} \wedge Struct(po\_2(\sigma_{par},\sigma_{act}))(M) \in \mathcal{M} .$$

Remark : The situation seems to be easier if one allows for signature morphisms only embeddings. Then the category of signatures collapses down to a sup-semi-lattice and the instantiation of a parameterized specification with an actual parameter does not anymore depend on the signature morphism $\sigma_{act} : \Sigma_{par} \rightarrow \Sigma_{act}$ as it is already determined uniquely by Σ_{act} whenever it exists. Anyway the problem remains that the operation of instantiation is only *partially defined*, i.e. one can only instantiate specifications $\langle \Sigma_{act},\mathcal{M}_{act}\rangle$ such that Σ_{par} can be embedded into Σ_{act}. That already would cause some severe problems as partial lambda calculus itself, although an interesting topic for research, is a rather involved concept and still we would not have achieved full generality.

5.3 λ-calculus with dependent types is more expressive than pushouts

The above notion of parameterization is not adequate for parameterized specifications (understood from the point of view of λ-abstraction) which forget parts of the signature of the formal parameter. Consider the following example. Let $\Sigma_{par} = <\{s1,s2\},\{\}>$ be a signature consisting of two sorts s1 and s2 and no function symbols and let $\Sigma_{body} = <\{s1\},\{\}>$ be the subsignature of Σ_{par} where s2 is not "exported". In a specification language such as ASL (cf. [SW],[ST],[W]) the corresponding parameterized specification can be denoted by the term

$$(\lambda SP : SPEC(\Sigma_{par}))\ \textbf{derive}\ SP\ \textbf{from}\ \iota$$

where ι is the inclusion of Σ_{body} into Σ_{par} (for an arbitrary specification SP over signature Σ' and σ : Sign_Mor(Σ,Σ')) the term **derive** SP **from** σ denotes the specification $< \Sigma , \{Struct(\sigma)(M) : M \in pr_2(SP)\}>$).

If one tries to understand the parameterized specification above according to the pushout approach then there arises the problem that the relation between Σ_{par} and Σ_{body} cannot be described by a (total) signature morphism from Σ_{par} to Σ_{body}. Intuitively, it should be described by the "*partial* signature morphism" mapping s1 to itself and undefined for s2. But the notion of partial signature morphism is quite unclear and we shall solve the problem in another more general way by defining a notion of parameterized specification which subsumes both the λ-abstraction and the pushout approach by extending the specification framework with the concept of dependent type.

Thus we define a parameterized specification with parameter Σ_{par} to be a definable object of type

$$(\Pi\ SP : SPEC)(\Pi\sigma_{act} : \text{Sign-Mor}(\Sigma_{par}, pr_1(SP)))\ SPEC$$

where a type $(\Pi x : A)B(x)$ is interpreted as the product of the family of sets B(x) indexed over the set A, see e.g. [M-L].

Explicit forms of parameterized specifications are terms of the form

$$(\lambda\ SP : SPEC)(\lambda\sigma_{act} : \text{Sign-Mor}(\Sigma_{par}, pr_1(SP)))\ E$$

where E is an expression of type SPEC w.r.t. the context

$SP : SPEC, \sigma_{act} : \text{Sign-Mor}(\Sigma_{par}, pr_1(SP))$.

In particular, the pushout approach to parameterized specifications can be expressed in the framework of ASL extended with the concept of dependent types. Assume that a parameterized specification is given by a signature morphism $\sigma_{par} : \text{Sign\_Mor}(\Sigma_{par}, \Sigma_{body})$ and a subclass $\mathcal{M}_{body}$ of $\text{Struct}(\Sigma_{body})$. Then the corresponding parameterized specification in explicit form is given by the following term :

$$(\lambda\ SP : SPEC)\ (\lambda\ \sigma_{act} : \text{Sign-Mor}(\Sigma_{par}, pr_1(SP)))$$
$$< Po(\sigma_{par},\sigma_{act}) ,$$
$$\{ M \in \text{Struct}(Po(\sigma_{par},\sigma_{act})) : \text{Struct}(po\_1(\sigma_{par},\sigma_{act}))(M) \in \mathcal{M}_{body} \wedge$$
$$\text{Struct}(po\_2(\sigma_{par},\sigma_{act}))(M) \in pr_2(SP)\ \} > .$$

In terms of ASL (see [W], but extended with dependent types) the term above could be rewritten as

$$(\lambda\ SP : SPEC)\ (\lambda\ \sigma_{act} : \text{Sign-Mor}(\Sigma_{par}, pr_1(SP)))$$
$$\textbf{translate} < \Sigma_{body}, \mathcal{M}_{body} > \textbf{by}\ po\_1(\sigma_{par},\sigma_{act})\ +\ \textbf{translate}\ SP\ \textbf{by}\ po\_2(\sigma_{par},\sigma_{act})$$

where for $\sigma \in \text{Sign\_Mor}(pr_1(SP), \Sigma)$ the expression **translate SP by** σ denotes the specification $< \Sigma, \{ M \in \text{Struct}(\Sigma) : \text{Struct}(\sigma)(M) \in pr_2(SP) \}$.

This shows that although semantically adequate and mathematically pleasing the pushout approach to parameterization leads to clumsy and uncomfortable syntactic representations of specifications : the operations Po, po_1 and po_2 are rather complicated to describe as they take rather unperspicious quotients of sums of signatures. But in practically relevant situations one can usually replace these heavy syntactic manipulations by simpler ones which do the same job (cf. [EM]).

5.4 Parameterized algebras vs. parameterized specifications

Introducing concepts of dependent types into a specification language has the advantage that the distinction between *parameterized specifications* and *parameterized algebras* (as introduced recently in [SST]) arises in a most natural way.

Intuitively, a parameterized algebra A does not map specifications to specifications but it maps algebras to algebras. If we consider simply typed λ-calculus then a parameterized specification P is an object of type $\wp(\text{Struct}(\Sigma_{par})) \rightarrow \wp(\text{Struct}(\Sigma_{body}))$ whereas a parameterized algebra A is an object of type $\mathrm{Struct}(\Sigma_{par}) \rightarrow \mathrm{Struct}(\Sigma_{body})$.

Usually parameterized specifications P are *additive* , i.e. P respects arbitrary unions. This means that P is uniquely determined by its behavior on singleton arguments. Thus additive parameterized specifications P are in a 1-1-correspondence with maps $Q : \mathrm{Struct}(\Sigma_{par}) \rightarrow \wp(\mathrm{Struct}(\Sigma_{body}))$ (called families of specifications indexed by algebras). For any for $Q : \mathrm{Struct}(\Sigma_{par}) \rightarrow \wp(\mathrm{Struct}(\Sigma_{body}))$ we define an additive parameterized specification P by associating with any $\mathcal{M} \in \wp(\mathrm{Struct}(\Sigma_{par}))$ the specification $P(\mathcal{M}) = \{M' \in Q(M) : M \in \mathcal{M}\}$. Of course, any additive parameterized specification can be obtained from an appropriate unique Q in this way.

Any $Q : \mathrm{Struct}(\Sigma_{par}) \rightarrow \wp(\mathrm{Struct}(\Sigma_{body}))$ is a family of classes indexed by a class. Therefore it is meaningful to look at the collection of choice functions for Q, i.e. those parameterized algebras $A : \mathrm{Struct}(\Sigma_{par}) \rightarrow \mathrm{Struct}(\Sigma_{body})$ choosing for any $M \in \mathrm{Struct}(\Sigma_{par})$ a structure $A(M) \in Q(M)$. Obviously, such a choice function cannot exist if $Q(M)$ is empty for some $M \in \mathrm{Struct}(\Sigma_{par})$. This problem can be avoided by requiring A to be defined only for those arguments $M \in \mathrm{Struct}(\Sigma_{par})$ for which Q(M) is nonempty and undefined otherwise. This suggests the following notion.

We say that a partial function $A : \mathrm{Struct}(\Sigma_{par}) \longrightarrow_{part} \mathrm{Struct}(\Sigma_{body})$ *realizes* $Q: \mathrm{Struct}(\Sigma_{par}) \rightarrow \wp(\mathrm{Struct}(\Sigma_{body}))$ iff for any $M \in \mathrm{Struct}(\Sigma_{par})$ the application $A(M)$ is defined iff $Q(M)$ is nonempty and if $A(M)$ is defined then $A(M) \in Q(M)$.

The condition that Q(M) is nonempty is called the *parameter constraint of* Q. These parameter constraints are essential for parameterized algebras as in general there is no natural way to choose an algebra out of $\mathrm{Struct}(\Sigma_{body})$ in order to totalize a partial function A realizing Q.

E.g. in the initial algebra approach to abstract data types one considers only that choice functions which choose for any Σ_{par}-algebra the generated free Σ_{body}-algebra provided it leaves the Σ_{par}-algebra unchanged (persistence!). In general such a choice need not be possible for any actual parameter. Thus in the initial algebra approach it is often necessary and helpful to impose restrictions on the actual parameters such that for all actual parameters satisfying the parameter restriction the choice can be done in a natural way.

In contrast, when considering loose semantics for specifications (as in CLEAR, ASL etc.) it is not essential to impose parameter restrictions. As if one instantiates for the formal parameter an actual parameter which cannot be consistently extended such that it satisfies the specification of the body as well, then one gets the inconsistent specification as the result, which can be considered as a natural choice for an error element. Thus in the case of parameterized specifications one can totalize in a natural way !

The concepts studied above can be extended to our more general framework incorporating dependent types in the following way.

A *family of specifications parameterized by* Σ_{par}*- algebras* is an object Q of type

$$(\Pi\ \Sigma : \text{Sign})(\Pi\ M : \text{Struct}(\Sigma))(\Pi\ \sigma : \text{Sign\_Mor}(\Sigma_{par}, \Sigma))\ \text{SPEC}.$$

So in a first attempt (just as above for the nondependent case) one would like to say that a parameterized algebra for the family Q of specifications parameterized by Σ_{par}- algebras is an object A of type

$$(\Pi\ \Sigma : \text{Sign})(\Pi\ M : \text{Struct}(\Sigma))(\Pi\ \sigma : \text{Sign-Mor}(\Sigma_{par}, \Sigma))\ \text{ext}(E)$$

where E is an abbreviation for $pr_2(Q(\Sigma)(M)(\sigma))$.

The obvious disadvantage of that formalization is that A is forced to be defined for all arguments of Q. But as Q may deliver inconsistent (i.e. empty) specifications for certain arguments we want the parameterized algebra A to be defined only for those arguments where Q gives a consistent specification as its result.

This suggests to define A as an object of type

$$(\Pi\ \Sigma : \text{Sign})\ (\Pi\ M : \text{Struct}(\Sigma))\ (\Pi\ \sigma : \text{Sign-Mor}(\Sigma_{par}, \Sigma))$$
$$((\text{ext}(E) \to N_0) \to N_0) \to \text{ext}(E)$$

where N_0 denotes the *empty type*.

It is straightforward to see that for an arbitrary type B the type $(B \to N_0) \to N_0$ is empty if B is empty and contains exactly one element otherwise, namely the unique function defined on the empty domain. This may seem tricky but is quite in accordance with the practice in naive set theory where one also has that there exists exactly one function with an empty domain of definition. More generally this practice is justified by the logical law that quantification over empty sets always gives true propositions which in turn can be derived from the *ex falso quodlibet* assumption in classical *and* in constructive logic.

6. Module Specifications

A notion quite related to, but more refined than the notion of parameterized specification is the notion of *module specification* developed by Ehrig et. al., see e.g. [WE]. For reasons of simplicity, we consider a somewhat restricted notion of module specification which does not contain a parameter part.

A module specification is given by two signature morphisms $\sigma_{imp} : \Sigma_{imp} \to \Sigma$ and $\sigma_{exp} : \Sigma_{exp} \to \Sigma$ and a subclass $\mathcal{M}$ of $\text{Struct}(\Sigma)$. Such a module specification maps an actual parameter given by a signature morphism $\sigma_{act} : \Sigma_{imp} \rightarrow \Sigma_{act}$ and a subclass $\mathcal{M}_{act}$ of $Struct(\Sigma_{act})$ to a specification with signature Σ_{exp} in a way which can be described in terms of dependent types as follows :

$$
\begin{aligned}
&(\lambda\ \Sigma_{act} : Sign)\ (\lambda\ \mathcal{M}_{act} : \wp(Struct(\Sigma_{act})))\ (\lambda\ \sigma_{act} : Sign\_Mor(\Sigma_{imp}, \Sigma_{act})) \\
&\quad < \Sigma_{exp}, \{\ M \in Struct(\Sigma_{exp}) : \ (\exists\ M' : Struct(Po(\sigma_{act}, \sigma_{imp})) \\
&\qquad\qquad Struct(po\_1(\sigma_{act}, \sigma_{imp}))(M') \in \mathcal{M}_{act} \text{ and} \\
&\qquad\qquad Struct(po\_2(\sigma_{act}, \sigma_{imp}) \circ \sigma_{exp})(M') = M\ \}\ > .
\end{aligned}
$$

The following diagram may be helpful in understanding the rather complicated term above.

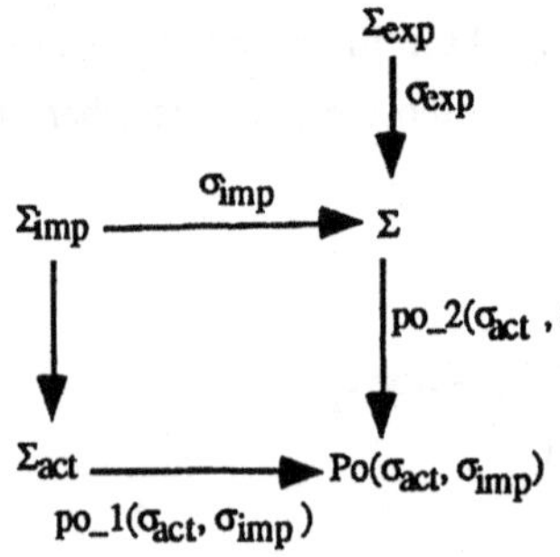

In ASL-like notation one would write

$(\lambda\ \Sigma_{act} : Sign)\ (\lambda\ \mathcal{M}_{act} : \wp(Struct(\Sigma_{act})))\ (\lambda\ \sigma_{act} : Sign\_Mor(\Sigma_{imp}, \Sigma_{act}))$

derive

translate $< \Sigma_{act}, \mathcal{M}_{act} >$ **by** $po\_1(\sigma_{act}, \sigma_{imp})$ +

translate $< \Sigma_{body}, \mathcal{M}_{body} >$ **by** $po\_2(\sigma_{act}, \sigma_{imp})$

by $po\_2(\sigma_{act}, \sigma_{imp}) \circ \sigma_{exp}$.

7. Concluding Remarks

In the previous sections we have shown how the use of dependent types allows to express the notion of an institution in a framework allowing λ-abstraction. This makes it possible to combine the generality of institutions with the λ-calculus approach to parameterization. That way several main concepts of algebraic specification languages such as pushout parameter passing and module specifications are expressible.

Hence, this work suggests a suitable extension of ASL: the use of dependent types as a concept which allows to express parameterization by λ-abstraction and subsumes the pushout approach to parameterization as a special case. It would be worthwhile for future investigations to be more explicit about syntactic details of this extended specification language and to study an axiomatization of the underlying type theory as we have introduced quite liberally concepts such as powertypes and comprehension which are not present in the traditional calculi of dependent types. But as we have never referred to some impredicative principles such as quantification over all types we are quite optimistic that the calculus of dependent types used in this paper can be given a semantics based on naive set theory.

Acknowledgements

We would like to thank the anonymous referee for careful reading of a draft version of the paper and a lot of hints to improve presentation.

References

[BG1] R. Burstall, J. Goguen *Putting theories together to make specifications* . Proc. 5th Internat. Joint Conf. on Artificial Intelligence, Cambridge Mass., pp. 1045-1058, 1977.

[BG2] R. Burstall, J. Goguen *The semantics of CLEAR, a specification language.* In: D. Bjorner (ed.): Proc. Advanced Course on Abstract Software Specifications. Lecture Notes in Computer Science. 86, Springer, Berlin, pp. 292-323, 1980.

[BGGN] M. Breu, M. Broy, T. Grünler, F. Nickl *PAnndA-S Semantics* Passau, 1989.

[CH] Th. Coquand, G. Huet *The Calculus of Constructions* . Information and Computation 76, pp. 95-120, 1988.

[Dy] R. Dyckhoff *Category Theory as an extension of Martin-Löf Type Theory.* Department of Computational Science, University of St. Andrews, Techn. Report CS/85/3, 1985.

[E] H.-D. Ehrich *On the theory of specification, implementation and parameterization of abstract data types.* J. ACM 29(1), pp. 206-277, 1982.

[EKTWW] H. Ehrig, H.-J. Kreowski, J. Thatcher, E. Wagner, J. Wright *Parameterized data types in algebraic specification languages (short version).* In: J. de Bakker, J. van Leuwen (eds.): Proc. 7th Internat. Coll. on Automata, Languages and Programming. Lecture Notes in Computer Science 85, Springer, Berlin, pp. 157-168, 1980.

[EM] H. Ehrig, B. Mahr *Fundamentals of Algebraic Specifications I* . EATCS Monographs on Theoretical Computer Science 6, Springer, Berlin, 1985.

[FGJM] K. Futatsugi, J. Goguen, J.-P. Jouannaud, J. Meseguer *Principles of OBJ-2* . Proc. POPL 1985, pp. 52-66, 1985.

[GB] J. Goguen, R. Burstall *Introducing Institutions.* Proc. Logics of Programming Workshop, Carnegie-Mellon, Lecture Notes in Computer Science 164, Springer, Berlin, pp. 221-256, 1984.

[GHW] J. Guttag, J. Horning, J. Wing *Larch in Five Easy Pieces.* Digital, Systems Research Center, Palo Alto, California, 1985.

[M-L] P. Martin-Löf *Intuitionistic Type Theory.* Bibliopolis, Naples, 1984.

[MQ] D. MacQueen *Using Dependent Types to Express Modular Structure.* In Proc. 13-th ACM Symp. on Principles of Programming Languages, pp. 277-286, 1986.

[ST] D. Sannella, A. Tarlecki *Specifications in Arbitrary Institutions.* Information and Computation 76, pp. 165-210, 1988.

[SST] D. Sannella, S. Sokolowski, A. Tarlecki *Toward formal development of programs from algebraic specifications : parameterisation revisited.* Draft, 1990.

[SW] D. Sannella, M. Wirsing *A kernel language for algebraic specification and implementation* . In: M. Karpinsky (ed.): Coll. on Foundations of Computation Theory, Lecture Notes in Computer Science 158, Springer, Berlin, pp. 413-427, 1983.

[TBG] R. Burstall, J. Goguen, A. Tarlecki *Some Fundamental Algebraic Tools for the Semantics of Computation. Part III : Indexed Categories.* ECS-LFCS-88-60, Techn. Report, Univ. Edinburgh, 1988.

[Th] J. Thatcher, E. Wagner, J. Wright *Data type specification : Parameterization and the power of specification techniques.* TOPLAS 4, pp. 711-773, 1982.

[WE] H. Weber, H. Ehrig *Programming in the large with algebraic module specifications.* H.J. Kugler (ed.): Proc. IFIP, 10th World Computer Congress. North Holland, Amsterdam, pp. 675-684, 1986.

[W] M. Wirsing *Algebraic Specifications.* In *Handbook of Theoretical Computer Science* Volume B, *Formal Models and Semantics* ed. J.van Leeuwen, Elsevier, Amsterdam, pp.675-788, 1990.

Generic Types in a Language for Data Directed Design

Eric G. Wagner
Computer Science Principles
Mathematical Sciences Department
IBM Research Division, T. J. Watson Research Center
Yorktown Heights, NY 10598 / USA
CSNET: Wagner@ibm.com

1 Introduction

The essential idea of data directed design is that the emphasis in program design should be on data types rather than on procedures. This idea underlies much of the work on object oriented programming [5], [6], some of the earlier work on "modular programming" [7], [11], and also the more theoretical work on the algebraic specification of data types [3], [2]. A good presentation the motivation behind the data directed approach is given in [6].

The framework provided by universal algebra and elementary category has been widely used to provide abstract approaches to data directed design. In particular, this framework has been used in the specification of data types, parameterized data types, and modules [2], [1]. While systems, e.g., OBJ [4], have been developed that permit one to "run" such specifications on computers, the specifications are still a long way from being what many computer programmers would call "real code". One result of this is that the many constructions that have been developed in the algebraic/categorical setting for such things as "passing parameters" to generic types, and generally building new types from old, do not seem relevant to the writers of "real code".

The aim of this paper is to show that those constructions, and others, can be carried out with "real code" at the level of abstract syntax. We show that many "real programming' practices such as

- Building new classes and methods (types and procedures) from ones defined earlier.
- Defining generic classes (parameterized types) and instantiating them.
- Polymorphic operators such as $\texttt{identity}_{\mathrm{D}}$, $\texttt{if-then-else}_{\mathrm{D}}$, and $\texttt{double}_{\mathtt{f},\mathrm{D}}$.
- Importation of previously defined classes into the specifications of new classes.
- Controlling exportation of methods from class specifications.
- Constructing generic classes from non-parameterized classes.

are easily specifiable in terms of categorical constructions in suitable categories of "programs". While the categories and the details of the constructions differ from those employed in algebraic specifications, the constructions are very similar at the categorical level – in brief, pushouts are again the key. We believe that category theory provides a natural framework of explicating and suggesting programming language constructs at both the algebraic and code levels.

Our approach is to employ these categorical constructions in the setting provided by a particular programming language, namely the language $\mathbf{LD}^3$ originally introduced in [9] and further discussed in [8] and [10]. We will carry out our constructions in the context of various categories of $\mathbf{LD}^3$

programs. However it should become apparent that much of what we do is completely independent of $\mathbf{LD}^3$, that is, similar categories could be readily developed for many other languages. None-the-less, $\mathbf{LD}^3$ lends itself to this kind of treatment because it is highly extensible (it is easy to define new classes and methods) and it is highly encapsulated (the "private part" of a class k, the data $\iota(k)$, $\tau(k)$, and $\xi(k)$, see below, is not accessible from outside of the class).

An important aspect is that we build the new constructions "on top of the underlying language". That is, $\mathbf{LD}^3$ as originally specified [9], does not have parameterized classes, or importation and exportation, etc., and we introduce these concepts as constructions on programs in the original language. In effect, we exploit the the mathematical structure of the original language to develop a meta-language over the original language.

The essential idea is to introduce categories in which the objects are programs and the morphisms provide means for identifying the names (identifiers, tokens) in one program with those in another program in an appropriate manner. Several different, but related, categories are employed so that we can specify different levels of information about a program. Briefly, the category **PUB** only specifies the names of the objects, and the names and arity of the methods in the class-system (program) and thus corresponds to the public part of the class-system; the category **TSM** gives a complete specification including the form (structure) of the objects and the bodies and local variables for the methods, and thus combines the public and the private part of the class-system; the category **PSM** gives partial specifications, in that some information concerning the form of objects, method bodies, or local variables, may be missing. What these categories do for us, especially in combination, is to provide a framework in which we can put pieces of programs together, identify parts we wish to have identified, distinguish parts we wish to have distinguished, hide parts we want to hide, parameterize parts as desired, and so on.

Section 2 of the paper reviews some fundamental concepts and notations. Section 3 provides a brief introduction to the language $\mathbf{LD}^3$, and the concept of a class-system. In Section 4 we define three different categories in which the objects are class-systems, and give some basic results on the properties of these categories. These categories are employed, in Section 5, to define the concept of a generic class-system, and two examples of generic class-systems are given. The instantiation of generic class-systems is defined in terms of pushouts in Section 6. Similar constructions are used in Section 8 to define extensions and importations of class-systems. Finally, in Section 8, we give a more extended example, and provide a treatment of exportation. Concluding remarks are given in Section 9.

2 Mathematical and Notational Preliminaries

Let ω denote the set of natural numbers, $\omega = \{0, 1, 2, \cdots\}$. For $n \in \omega$ let $[n] = \{1, 2, \cdots, n\}$, so, in particular $[0] = \emptyset$. Given any set S, define a *string ϕ on S of length n* to be a mapping $\phi : [n] \to S$. Let S^n denote the set of all strings on S of length n, and let S^* denote the set of all strings on S, so $S^* = \bigcup\langle S^n \mid n \in \omega\rangle$. We write ε_S for the unique string, $\varepsilon_S : [0] \to S$, on S of length 0, and we drop the subscript when there is no ambiguity.

With this definition of string, we see that a *string-of-strings on S* is well-defined as a map $u : [n] \to S^*$ for some $n \in \omega$. We will use the informal notation "$(v_1)(v_2)\cdots(v_n)$ " to denote a string-of-strings $u :\to S^*$ where $u(i) = v_i \in S^*$ for $i = 1, \ldots, n$. If $v_i = \varepsilon_S$ we write (v_i) as ( ), rather than as (ε_S). Let $(S^*)^*$ denote the set of all strings-of-strings on S.

Given a string u we write $|u|$ to denote the length of u. Given a string $v \in K^*$ and $i \in [|v|] = \{1, \ldots, |v|\}$, we write v_i for the ith component of v. Given $w \in (K^*)^*$ and suitable i and j we generally write $w_{i,j}$, rather than $(w_i)_j$, for the jth component of the ith component of w.

Given sets S_1 and S_2 and a mapping $f : S_1 \to S_2$ let

$$f^* : S_1^* \to S_2^*$$
$$\phi \mapsto f \bullet \phi$$

and let

$$f^{**} : (S_1^*)^* \to (S_2^*)^*$$
$$\phi \mapsto f^* \bullet \phi.$$

Fact 2.1 *Let* $f : S_1 \to S_2$ *and* $g : S_2 \to S_3$, *then*

$$g^* \bullet f^* = (g \bullet f)^*$$

and

$$g^{**} \bullet f^{**} = (g \bullet f)^{**}.$$

□

We shall write **Set** to denote the category of sets and total functions, and **Pfn** to denote the category of sets and partial functions. Given two sets A, and B, we write $\bot_{A,B} : A \to B$ for the everywhere undefined partial function from A to B. When the source and target are evident from context we will just write $\bot$.

We use square brackets, $[,\ldots,]$ to denote *coproduct mediators*, i.e, given sets $A_1,\ldots,A_n$, with coproduct object $A_1 + \cdots + A_n$ and coproduct injections $\iota_i : A_i \to (A_1 + \cdots + A_n)$, $i = 1,\ldots,n$, then for any set B and family of mappings $(f_i : A_i \to B \mid i = 1,\ldots,n)$, we write $[f_1,\ldots,f_n]$ for the unique mapping $f : (A_1 + \cdots + A_n) \to B$ such that $f \bullet \iota_i = f_i$ for each $i = 1,\ldots,n$.

3 LD^3: A Language for Data Directed Design

In this section we will give the precise syntax, and an informal, incomplete semantics of the language, **LD^3**, that we use to put our results in a relatively concrete context. This language is related to object oriented languages such as SMALLTALK but differs in several important respects. In **LD^3** an object is either a *nil object* or an *instantiated object* where an instantiated object will have a value which is an element of a sum of products of "classes" rather than of just a product of classes as in SMALLTALK. The use of sums of products of classes makes it much easier to extend the language, indeed it enables us to start without any conventional built-in types. Two, the primitive operations used in methods fall into two classes, public and private. Each class k has private operations (NEW, CASE, CHANGE, ASSIGN and ACCESS) which can only be used within methods belonging to that class, and public operations (NIL, INST, CALL and ;) that can be used in methods of any class. This provides a firm basis for encapsulation. Three, we use a method calling paradigm in which a "message is sent" to a class rather than to an object – this lets us avoid the problems that object-oriented languages have with multi-argument functions. For a much more detailed look at this language, including both an intuitive overview and a complete, formal development of its semantics, see [9] or [10].

Definition 3.2 A specification of a *class-system* consists of the following data:

K, a set (of *class names*).

Σ, a set (of *method names*).

$\alpha : \Sigma \to K \times K^* \times K$. If $\sigma \in \Sigma$, and $\alpha(\sigma) = \langle k, u, t\rangle$ then σ *belongs* to the class k, has $|u|$ *parameters* where the ith parameter, $\mathrm{P}_{\sigma,i}$, is of class u_i, and σ *returns* a value of class t.

$\iota : K \to (K^*)^*$. If $\iota(k) = v_1 \cdots v_n \in (K^*)^*$ with $v_i = v_{i,1} \cdots v_{i,n_i} \in K^*$, then the class k is of *form* $\iota(k)$, has n *summands* the jth of which, $\mathrm{T}_{\sigma,i}$, for $j \in \{1,\ldots,n\}$ having n_j *components* the ith of which, for $i \in \{1,\ldots,n_j\}$, being of class $v_{j,i}$.

$\tau : \Sigma \to K^*$. If $\tau(\sigma) = w$, then the method σ has $|w|$ *temporaries (local variables)*, the ith of which is of class w_i.

$\xi : \Sigma \rightarrow Expr = \bigcup(Expr_{k,\sigma} \mid k \in K, \sigma \in \Sigma)$, where if $\alpha(\sigma) = \langle s, u, k\rangle$ then $\xi(\sigma) \in Expr_{k,\sigma}$, as defined below:

For each $k \in K$ and $\sigma \in \Sigma$ we will define a set, $Expr_{k,\sigma}$, of *k-σ-expressions*. Intuitively a k-σ-expression is an expression, or block of code, that returns an object of class k and can be used as a subexpression in $\xi(\sigma)$. Write $e : \langle k, \sigma\rangle$ for $e \in Expr_{k,\sigma}$. The set of k-σ-expressions is then given by the following deductive rules.

$$\mathtt{NIL}_k : \langle k, \sigma\rangle$$

$$\frac{\alpha(\sigma) = \langle h, u, s\rangle,\ i \in [|u|],\ u_i = k}{\mathtt{P}_{\sigma,i} : \langle k, \sigma\rangle}$$

$$\frac{i \in [|\tau(\sigma)|],\ \tau(\sigma)_i = k}{\mathtt{T}_{\sigma,i} : \langle k, \sigma\rangle}$$

$$\frac{e_1 : \langle j, \sigma\rangle,\ e_2 : \langle k, \sigma\rangle}{e_1 ; e_2 : \langle k, \sigma\rangle}$$

$$\frac{e_0 : \langle j, \sigma\rangle,\ e_1 : \langle k, \sigma\rangle,\ e_2 : \langle k, \sigma\rangle}{\mathtt{INST}_j(e_0, e_1, e_2) : \langle k, \sigma\rangle}$$

$$\frac{i \in [|\tau(\sigma)|],\ \tau(\sigma)_i = k,\ e_i : \langle k, \sigma\rangle}{\mathtt{ASSIGN}_{\sigma,i}(e_1) : \langle k, \sigma\rangle}$$

$$\frac{\rho \in \Sigma,\ \alpha(\rho) = \langle t, w, k\rangle,\ (\forall i \in [|w|])(e_i : \langle w_i, \sigma\rangle)}{\mathtt{CALL}_{t,\rho}(e_1, \ldots, e_{|w|}) : \langle k, \sigma\rangle}$$

$$\frac{\alpha(\sigma) = \langle k, u, k\rangle,\ i \in [|\iota(k)|]}{\mathtt{NEW}_{k,i} : \langle k, \sigma\rangle}$$

$$\frac{\alpha(\sigma) = \langle h, u, s\rangle,\ e_0 : \langle h, \sigma\rangle,\ (\forall i \in [|\iota(h)|])(e_i : \langle k, \sigma\rangle)}{\mathtt{CASE}_h(e_0, e_1, \ldots, e_{|\iota(h)|}) : \langle k, \sigma\rangle}$$

$$\frac{\alpha(\sigma) = \langle k, u, s\rangle,\ i \in [|\iota(k)|],\ (\forall j \in [|\iota(k)_i|])(e_j : \langle \iota(k)_{i,j}, \sigma\rangle),\ e_0 : \langle k, \sigma\rangle}{\mathtt{CHANGE}_{k,i}(e_0, e_1, \ldots, e_{|\iota(k)_i|}) : \langle k, \sigma\rangle}$$

$$\frac{\alpha(\sigma) = \langle h, u, s\rangle,\ e_0 : \langle h, \sigma\rangle,\ i \in [|\iota(h)|],\ j \in [|\iota(h)_i|],\ \iota(h)_{i,j} = k}{\mathtt{ACCESS}_{h,i,j}(e_0) : \langle k, \sigma\rangle}$$

□

For fixed K, Σ, α, ι, and τ, these rules can be reduced to a context free grammar. The semantics of $\mathbf{LD^3}$ may be briefly, if inadequately, sketched as follows:

$\mathtt{NIL}_k$ is the nil-object of class k.

$\mathtt{P}_{\sigma,i}$ is the ith parameter of method σ.

$T_{\sigma,i}$ is a temporary (local) variable used in method σ to hold a value of class k.

$e_1 ; e_2$ is the usual "semi-colon" operator.

$\mathtt{INST}_j(e_0, e_1, e_2)$: If e_0 evaluates to a nil-object then evaluate e_2, otherwise evaluate e_1.

$\mathtt{ASSIGN}_{\sigma,i}(e_1)$: Assign the result of evaluating e_1 to the ith temporary variable of σ.

$\mathtt{CALL}_{t,\rho}(e_1, \ldots, e_p)$: Call the method ρ and pass it the result of evaluating the expressions e_1 through e_p.

$\mathtt{NEW}_{k,i}$: Create a new instance of an object of class k and initialize it to the all nil tuple for summand i.

$\mathtt{CASE}_h(e_0, e_1, \ldots, e_n)$: If e_0 evaluates to a tuple in the ith summand of h then the expression e_i is evaluated.

$\mathtt{CHANGE}_{k,i}(e_0, e_1, \ldots, e_p)$: Changes the value of the object of class k resulting from evaluating e_0 to the n-tuple for summand i resulting from evaluating e_1 through e_p.

$\mathtt{ACCESS}_{h,i,j}(e_0)$: Returns the jth component of the ith summand of the object of class k resulting from evaluating the expression e_0.

Example 3.3 Here is an example of a class-system specification written using just the above formal syntax – the abstract syntax of the language. We follow this example with a somewhat more sugared version of the syntax and a redo of this example in that more sugared syntax.

In this example we define two classes, *NAT* and *BOOL*. The key to the definitions is the form of the classes, i.e.,

$$\iota(NAT) = (\,)(NAT$$
$$\iota(BOOL) = (\,)(\,).$$

The idea is that we are defining *NAT*, the set of natural numbers, as the solution to the equation

$$NAT \cong (1 + NAT),$$

and we are defining *BOOL*, the set of booleans, as the solution to the equation

$$BOOL \cong 1 + 1,$$

where **1** denotes a singleton set (one element set). These equations correspond informally to saying "a natural number is either 0 or it is the successor of a natural number", and that "a boolean is either *true* or *false*".

$K = \{NAT,\ BOOL\}$

$\Sigma = \{zero,\ succ,\ pred,\ add,\ true,\ false,\ and, not,\ leq,\ eq\}$

$\alpha(zero) = \langle NAT,\ \varepsilon,\ NAT\rangle$
$\alpha(succ) = \alpha(pred) = \langle NAT,\ NAT,\ NAT\rangle$
$\alpha(add) = \langle NAT,\ NAT \cdot NAT,\ NAT\rangle$
$\alpha(true) = \alpha(false) = \langle BOOL,\ \varepsilon,\ BOOL\rangle$
$\alpha(and) = \langle BOOL,\ BOOL \cdot BOOL,\ BOOL\rangle$
$\alpha(not) = \langle BOOL,\ BOOL,\ BOOL\rangle$
$\alpha(leq) = \alpha(eq) = \langle NAT,\ NAT \cdot NAT,\ BOOL\rangle$

$\iota(NAT) = (\,)(NAT)$

$\iota(BOOL) = (\,)(\,)$

$\tau(zero) = \tau(pred) = \tau(add) = \tau(leq) = \tau(eq) = \tau(true) = \tau(false) = \tau(and) = \tau(not) = \emptyset$
$\tau(succ) = \{NAT\}$

$\xi(zero) = \mathtt{NEW}_{NAT,1}$
$\xi(succ) = \mathtt{ASSIGN}_{succ,1}(\mathtt{NEW}_{NAT,2})\text{;}\,\mathtt{CHANGE}_{NAT,2}(\mathtt{T}_{succ,1},\ \mathtt{P}_{succ,1})$
$\xi(pred) = \mathtt{CASE}_{NAT}(\mathtt{P}_{pred,1},\ \mathtt{P}_{pred,1},\ \mathtt{ACCESS}_{NAT,2,1}(\mathtt{P}_{pred,1}))$
$\xi(add) = \mathtt{CASE}_{NAT}(\mathtt{P}_{add,2},\ \mathtt{P}_{add,1},\ \mathtt{CALL}_{NAT,add}(\ \mathtt{CALL}_{NAT,succ}(\mathtt{P}_{add,1}),\ \mathtt{CALL}_{NAT,pred}(\mathtt{P}_{add,2})))$
$\xi(true) = \mathtt{NEW}_{BOOL,1}$
$\xi(false) = \mathtt{NEW}_{BOOL,2}$
$\xi(and) = \mathtt{CASE}_{BOOL}(\mathtt{P}_{and,1},\ \mathtt{CASE}_{BOOL}(\mathtt{P}_{and,2}, \mathtt{CALL}_{BOOL,true}, \mathtt{CALL}_{BOOL,false}),$
$\quad \mathtt{CALL}_{BOOL,false}).$
$\xi(not) = \mathtt{CASE}_{BOOL}(\mathtt{P}_{BOOL,1}, \mathtt{CALL}_{BOOL,false}, \mathtt{CALL}_{BOOL,true}).$
$\xi(leq) = \mathtt{CASE}_{NAT}(\mathtt{P}_{leq,1}, \mathtt{CALL}_{BOOL,true}, \mathtt{CASE}_{NAT}(\mathtt{P}_{leq,2}, \mathtt{CALL}_{BOOL,false},$
$\quad \mathtt{CALL}_{NAT,leq}(\mathtt{CALL}_{NAT,pred}(\mathtt{P}_{leq,1}), \mathtt{CALL}_{NAT,pred}(\mathtt{P}_{leq,2})))).$
$\xi(eq) = \mathtt{CALL}_{BOOL,and}(\mathtt{CALL}_{NAT,leq}(\mathtt{P}_{eq,1}, \mathtt{P}_{eq,2}), \mathtt{CALL}_{NAT,leq}(\mathtt{P}_{eq,2}, \mathtt{P}_{eq,1})).$

□

The above formal specification provides what we need for our mathematical work, but clearly some sugaring is needed to make programs readable. Here is one example of a sugaring of the language. Compilers have been written for both the formal syntax and this sugared version.

Pi	for	$\mathtt{P}_{\sigma,i}$ (that is, for example, P4 for $\mathtt{P}_{\sigma,4}$)
Ti	for	$\mathtt{T}_{\sigma,i}$
Ti:= e_1	for	$\mathtt{ASSIGN}_{\sigma,i}(e_1)$
$\rho(e_1,\ldots,e_p)$	for	$\mathtt{CALL}_{k,\rho}(e_1,\ldots,e_p)$
$e_0.\mathrm{i}\langle e_1,\ldots,e_p\rangle$	for	$\mathtt{CHANGE}_{k,i}(e_0,e_1,\ldots,e_p)$
e_0.i.j	for	$\mathtt{ACCESS}_{k,i,j}(e_0)$
NEW.i	for	$\mathtt{NEW}_{k,i}$

Example 3.4 Here, again, is the class-system for *BOOL* and *NAT*, but using the above sugaring and additional sweetening as explained in the comments "/*···*/".

CLASS-SYSTEM *NAT-BOOL*
classes
    NAT   /* $NAT \in K$ */
    BOOL   /* $BOOL \in K$ */
form
    NAT : ( )(*NAT*)   /* $\iota(NAT) = (\,)(NAT)$ */
    BOOL : ( )( )   /* $\iota(BOOL) = (\,)(\,)$ */
methods
    NAT::*zero*:*NAT*;   /* $zero \in \Sigma,\ \alpha(zero) = \langle NAT, \varepsilon, NAT\rangle$ */
        NEW.1.   /* $= \xi(zero)$ */

    NAT::*succ*(P1:*NAT*):*NAT*;   /* $succ \in \Sigma,\ \alpha(succ) = \langle NAT, NAT, NAT\rangle$ */
        |T1:*NAT*| /* $\tau(succ) = NAT$ */
        T1:=NEW.1;T1.2⟨P1⟩.   /* $= \xi(succ)$ */

    NAT::*pred*(P1:*NAT*):*NAT*;
        CASE(P1, P1, P1.2.1).

```
NAT::add(P1, P2:NAT):NAT;
    CASE( P2, P1, add( succ(P1), pred(P2))).

BOOL::true:BOOL;
    NEW.1.

BOOL::false:BOOL;
    NEW.2.

BOOL::and(P1,P2:BOOL):BOOL;
    CASE(P1, CASE(P2, true, false), false).

BOOL::not(P1:BOOL):BOOL;
    CASE(P1, false, true).

NAT::leq(P1,P2:NAT):BOOL;
    CASE(P1, true, CASE(P2, false, leq(pred(P1), pred(P2)))).

NAT::eq(P1,P2:NAT):BOOL;
    and(leq(P1, P2), leq(P2, P1)).
```

end CLASS-SYSTEM

□

4 The Categories

We define three categories in which the objects are class-systems. We start with at the category corresponding to "the public view of class-system specifications" where we do not see the "inner details" given by ι, τ, and ξ.

Definition 4.5 Given truncated class-system specifications $\Gamma_i = \langle K_i, \Sigma_i, \alpha_i \rangle$, $i = 1, 2$, we define a *public class-system morphism* from Γ_1 to Γ_2 as a quadruple

$$\langle \Gamma_1,\ f_\Sigma : \Sigma_1 \to \Sigma_2,\ f_K : K_1 \to K_2,\ \Gamma_2 \rangle$$

such that, where $f_K^* : K_1^* \to K_2^*$ is defined from f_K as in Section 1, that

$$\alpha_2 \bullet f_\Sigma = (f_K \times f_K^* \times f_K) \bullet \alpha_1.$$

i.e., the following diagram commutes

$$\begin{array}{ccc} \Sigma_1 & \xrightarrow{\ f_\Sigma\ } & \Sigma_2 \\ \downarrow \alpha_1 & & \downarrow \alpha_2 \\ K_1 \times K_1^* \times K_1 & \xrightarrow[f_K \times f_K^* \times f_K]{} & K_2 \times K_2^* \times K_2 \end{array}$$

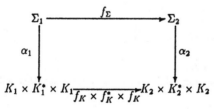

Define **PUB** to be the category of truncated class-systems together with the public class-system morphisms between them. □

Notation 4.6 Since we will often need morphisms of the form $f \times f^* \times f : K_1 \times K_1^* \times K_1 \to K_2 \times K_2^* \times K_2$ induced by morphisms $f : K_1 \to K_2$ it will be convenient to use the notation

$$\overline{K_i} \text{ for } K_i \times K_i^* \times K_i$$
$$\text{and}$$
$$\overline{f} \text{ for } f \times f^* \times f.$$

Fact 4.7 *If* $f : K_1 \to K_2$ *and* $g : K_2 \to K_3$ *then*

$$\overline{g} \bullet \overline{f} \;=\; \overline{(g \bullet f)} : \overline{K_1} \to \overline{K_3}.$$

Proof: This is an immediate consequence of Fact 2.1. □

Definition 4.8 Given class-system specifications $\Gamma_i = (K_i, \Sigma_i, \alpha_i, \iota_i, \tau_i, \xi_i)$, $i = 1, 2$, we define a *total class-system morphism* from Γ_1 to Γ_2 as a public class-system morphism $\langle \Gamma_1,\ f_\Sigma : \Sigma_1 \to \Sigma_2,\ f_K : K_1 \to K_2,\ \Gamma_2 \rangle$ with the additional properties that, where f_K^{**} is defined from f_K as in Section 1, $\iota_2 \bullet f_K = f_K^{**} \bullet \iota_1$, and $\tau_2 \bullet f_K = f_K^{*} \bullet \tau_1$, that is, the following diagrams commute

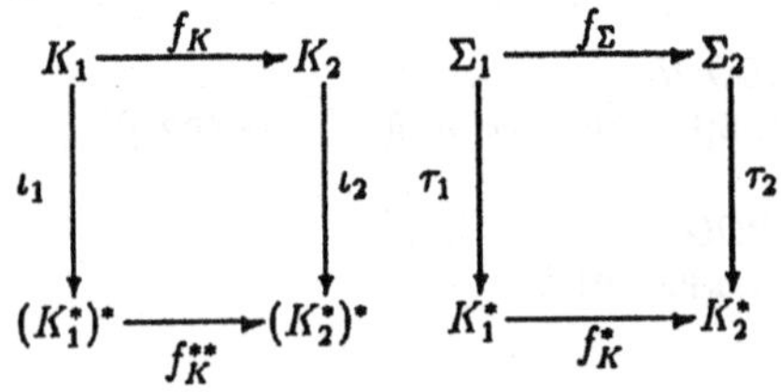

and, in addition, where f_{Expr} is inductively defined from f_K and f_Σ as follows:

$$
\begin{array}{c}
f_{Expr} : Expr_1 \to Expr_2 \\
\mathtt{NIL}_k \mapsto \mathtt{NIL}_{f_K(k)} \\
\mathtt{P}_{\sigma,i} \mapsto \mathtt{P}_{f_\Sigma(\sigma),i} \\
\mathtt{T}_{\sigma,i} \mapsto \mathtt{T}_{f_\Sigma(\sigma),i} \\
\mathtt{INST}_j(e_0, e_1, e_2) \mapsto \mathtt{INST}_{f_K(j)}(f_{Expr}(e_0), f_{Expr}(e_1), f_{Expr}(e_2)) \\
\mathtt{ASSIGN}_{\sigma,i}(e_1) \mapsto \mathtt{ASSIGN}_{f_\Sigma(\sigma),i}(f_{Expr}(e_1)) \\
\mathtt{CALL}_{\iota,\rho}(e_1, \ldots, e_p) \mapsto \mathtt{CALL}_{f_K(\iota), f_\Sigma(\rho)}(f_{Expr}(e_1) \ldots f_{Expr}(e_p)) \\
\mathtt{NEW}_{k,i} \mapsto \mathtt{NEW}_{f_K(k),i} \\
\mathtt{CASE}_h(e_0, e_1, \ldots e_n) \mapsto \mathtt{CASE}_{f_K(h)}(f_{Expr}(e_0), f_{Expr}(e_1), \ldots, f_{Expr}(e_n)) \\
\mathtt{CHANGE}_{k,i}(e_0, e_1, \ldots e_n) \mapsto \mathtt{CHANGE}_{f_K(k),i}(f_{Expr}(e_0), f_{Expr}(e_1), \ldots, f_{Expr}(e_n)) \\
\mathtt{ACCESS}_{h,i,j}(e_0) \mapsto \mathtt{ACCESS}_{f_K(h),i,j}(f_{Expr}(e_0)).
\end{array}
$$

that the diagram,

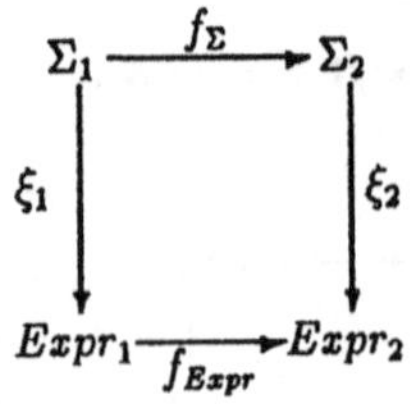

commutes, i.e., $f_{Expr} \bullet \xi_1 = \xi_2 \bullet f_\Sigma$.

Define **TSM** to be the category of (total) class-systems together with the total class-system morphisms between them. □

Lemma 4.9 *If* $f : \Gamma_1 \to \Gamma_2$ *and* $g : \Gamma_2 \to \Gamma_3$ *then* $(g \bullet f)_{Expr} \;=\; g_{Expr} \bullet f_{Expr}$. □

Definition 4.10 Define a *partial class-system* to be a tuple $\Gamma = \langle K, \Sigma, \alpha, \iota, \tau, \xi \rangle$, where the maps ι, τ, and ξ are partial mappings. This is not quite as simple as it may first appear. According to Definition 3.2, $\xi : \Sigma \rightarrow Expr$ where the definition of $Expr$ depends heavily on the definitions of ι and τ. For example, if $k \in K$ but $\iota(k)$ is undefined, then the number of arguments of $\mathtt{CASE}_k$ is also undefined. Similarly, for $\sigma \in \Sigma$, whether or not $\mathtt{T}_{\sigma,i}$ is defined depends on how $\tau(\sigma)$ is defined. Indeed the only primitives that are necessily defined are $\mathtt{NIL}_k$, $\dot{;}$, $\mathtt{INST}_k$, and $\mathtt{CALL}_{k,\sigma}$. In light of this, we will say that a partial class-system is *well-formed* iff for every $\sigma \in \Sigma$, $\xi(\sigma)$ is well-defined, that is, only employs primitives that are supported by the definitions of ι and τ. Where, for example, the primitive $\mathtt{CASE}_k$ is supported by ι iff $\iota(k)$ is defined. A partial class-system that is not well-formed will be said to be *ill-formed*. We will see, in Section 7, that ill-formed partial class-systems can be useful. However, unless otherwise stated, "partial class-system" should be taken to mean "well-formed partial class-system".

Given partial class-systems $\Gamma_i = \langle K_i, \Sigma_i, \alpha_i, \iota_i, \tau_i, \xi_i \rangle$, $i = 1, 2$, a *partial class-system morphism* from Γ_1 to Γ_2 is given by a quadruple

$$\langle \Gamma_1,\ f_\Sigma : \Sigma_1 \rightarrow \Sigma_2,\ f_K : K_1 \rightarrow K_2,\ \Gamma_2 \rangle$$

where f_Σ and f_K are total mappings such that, the diagrams for α, ι, τ and ξ partial-commute, that is

$$\overline{f_K} \bullet \alpha_1 \sqsubseteq \alpha_2 \bullet f_K$$

$$f_K^{**} \bullet \iota_1 \sqsubseteq \iota_2 \bullet f_K$$

$$f_K^{*} \bullet \tau_1 \sqsubseteq \tau_2 \bullet f_\Sigma$$

and

$$f_{Expr} \bullet \xi_1 \sqsubseteq \xi_2 \bullet f_\Sigma,$$

where "$\sqsubseteq$" denotes the usual partial order on partial functions, and where the "$\times$" in the definition of $\overline{f_K}$ and $\overline{f_\Sigma}$ is the cartesian product rather than the categorical product from **Pfn**.

Let **PSM** denote the category of partial class-systems and the morphisms between them. □

The proofs of the following results, in the form of an appendix to this paper, are available from the author.

Proposition 4.11 *The categories* **PUB** *and* **TSM** *have binary coproducts.* □

Corrollary 4.12 *The category* **PSM** *has binary coproducts.* □

Proposition 4.13 *The categories* **PUB** *and* **TSM** *have coequalizers* □

Unfortunately this result does not extend to **PSM**, that is:

Fact 4.14 *The category* **PSM** *does not have all coequalizers and pushouts.* □

Proposition 4.15 *The category* **TSM** *is a subcategory of the the category* **PSM** *and this inclusion preserves colimits.* □

However, as we will show in the next section, **PSM** has pushouts even for certain non-total morphisms. In particular, it has the pushouts we will need for parameter passing.

We end this section with a simple result that provides some necessary notation.

Proposition 4.16 *The forgettful functor* : $\mathcal{U}$: **PSM** $\rightarrow$ **PUB** *such that* $\mathcal{U}(\langle K, \Sigma, \alpha, \iota, \tau, \xi \rangle) = \langle K, \Sigma, \alpha \rangle$ *has a left adjoint* $\mathcal{F}$: **PUB** $\rightarrow$ **PSM** *where* $\mathcal{F}(\langle K, \Sigma, \alpha \rangle) = \langle K, \Sigma, \alpha, \emptyset, \emptyset, \emptyset \rangle$ *i.e., if* $\Gamma_0 = \langle K, \Sigma, \alpha \rangle \in$ **PUB** *take* $\mathcal{F}(\Gamma_0) = \langle K, \Sigma, \alpha, \emptyset, \emptyset, \emptyset \rangle$, *then for any* $\Gamma \in |$**PSM**$|$, *and* $f : \Gamma_0 \rightarrow \mathcal{U}(\Gamma)$ *there exists a unique* $\widehat{f} : \mathcal{F}(\Gamma_0) \rightarrow \Gamma$ *such that* $\mathcal{U}(\widehat{f}) = f$. □

5 Generic Class-Systems

The key concept is the following:

Definition 5.17 A *generic class-system*, S, is specified by the data

$$K_0,\ K_1,\ \Sigma_0,\ \Sigma_1,\ \alpha_0,\ \alpha_1,\ \iota_1,\ \tau_1,\ \xi_1$$

where, if $\gamma_K : K_0 \to (K_0 + K_1)$ and $\gamma_\Sigma : \Sigma_0 \to (\Sigma_0 + \Sigma_1)$ are coproduct injections in **Pfn**, then

$$\Gamma_0 \ = \ \langle K_0,\ \Sigma_0,\ \alpha_0 \rangle$$

is a truncated class-system (called the *parameters of* S) and

$$\Gamma_1 \ = \ \langle K_0 + K_1,\ \Sigma_0 + \Sigma_1,\ [\overline{\gamma_K} \bullet \alpha_0,\ \alpha_1],\ [\bot,\ \iota_1],\ [\bot,\ \tau_1],\ [\bot,\ \xi_1] \rangle$$

is a well-formed partial class-system (called the *parameterized part of* S). □

Fact 5.18 *It follows from the above definition that*

$\alpha_0 : K_0 \to \overline{K_0}$ *and is a total mapping.*

$\alpha_1 : K_1 \to \overline{(K_0 + K_1)}$,

$\iota_1 : K_1 \to ((K_0 + K_1)^*)^*$,

$\tau_1 : \Sigma_1 \to (K_0 + K_1)^*$,

and

$\xi_1 : \Sigma_1 \to Expr_{\Gamma_1}$,

where the maps ι_1, τ_1, *and* ξ_1 *may be partial functions. Furthermore,*

$\gamma \ = \ \langle \gamma_K,\ \gamma_\Sigma \rangle : \Gamma_0 \to \mathcal{U}(\Gamma_1)$

in **PUB**, *and so, by Proposition 4.16,*

$\hat{\gamma} : \mathcal{F}(\Gamma_0) \to \Gamma_1$

in **PSM**. *We leave the proofs to the reader.* □

In light of the above we will frequently denote a generic class-system by the data $\langle \Gamma_0,\ \Gamma_1,\ \gamma \rangle$.
Here two examples of generic class-systems presented in an extension of the sugared syntax given in section 3.

Example 5.19 Our first example is the familiar parameterized stack, *PSTACK*. The only parameter is the class D, and the end result is supposed to be a stack-of-D.

```
GENERIC CLASS – SYSTEM PSTACK /* = parameterized stack */

  parameters
     D      /* Γ0 = ({D}, ∅, ∅) */
  classes
     STACK     /* K1 = {STACK}, */
  form
     STACK : ( )(STACK · D)     /* ι1(STACK) = ( )(STACK · D) */

  methods    /* Σ1 = {makestk, pop, push} */

     STACK :: makestk( ) : STACK;       /* α1(makestk) = (STACK, ε, STACK) */
        NEW.1.     } = ξ(makestk)

     STACK :: pop(P1 : STACK) : D;      /* α1(pop) = (STACK, STACK, D)
       |T1 : D, T2 : STACK|       /* τ1(pop) = D · STACK */
       CASE(P1, T1 := NIL_D, T1 := P1.2.1);             )
       CASE(P1.2.2,                                     |
           P1.1( ),                                     } = ξ(pop)
       T2 := P1.2.2; P1.2(T2.2.1, T2.2.2)); T1.          )
      STACK :: push(P1 : STACK, P2 : D) : D;
                          /* α1(push) = (STACK, STACK · STACK, D) */
        |T1 : STACK|      /* τ1(push) = STACK */
        T1 := NEW.1;                         )
        CASE(P1,                             |
            T1.1( ),                         |
            T1.2(P1.2.1, P1.2.2));           } = ξ(push)
        P1.2(P1, T2);                        |
        P2.                                  )

  end CLASS – SYSTEM
```

Example 5.20 In this example we have two parameters, a class D and a method *fun* belonging to D. The class-system is intended to add two new methods *id* and *double* to D.

```
        GENERIC CLASS – SYSTEM MORE
          parameters
             D     /* Γ0 = ({D}, {fun}, α0) */
             D :: fun(P1 : D) : D;      /* α0(fun) = (D, D, D) */
          classes
                                 /* K1 = ∅ */
          form
                                 /* ι(STACK) = ε */
          methods    /* Σ1 = {id, double} */

             D :: id(P1 : D) : D;       /* α1(id) = (D, D, D) */
                 P1.     /* the identity function for D */

             D :: double(P1 : D) : D;      /* α(double) = (D, D, D) */
                fun(fun(P1)).      /* do fun twice */

        end CLASS – SYSTEM
```

6 Instantiations of Generic Class-Systems

Given the generic class-system for *PSTACK* from Example 5.19, how do we "apply" it to the class-system *NAT-BOOL* given in Examples 3.3 and 3.4 so as to get a new class-system specifying *NAT*, *BOOL* and *STACK-of-NAT*? On an informal, intuitive level the answer is fairly simple: We combine the text of the two examples and simultaneously change every occurrence of D to *NAT* and every occurrence of *STACK* to *STACK-of-NAT*. The changing of *STACK* to *STACK-of-NAT* is not really necessary. However, some such relabeling would be needed were we to "repeat" the operation to extend the class-system to include stacks of *BOOL* in addition to stacks of *NAT*.

Clearly we should also be able to "apply" the generic class-system of Example 5.20 to the class-system of Example 3.3 by, say, "taking" D to *NAT*, and *fun* to *succ*, so as to define an identity operation, *id-NAT*: $NAT \to NAT$, and an operation *double-succ*:$NAT \to NAT$, which takes each $n \in NAT$ to $n+2 = succ(succ(n))$.

These informal ideas are made precise by the definition given below of an instantiation of a generic class-system, $\langle \Gamma_0,\ \Gamma_1,\ \gamma \rangle$, as a **PUB**-morphism from Γ_0 to $\mathcal{U}(\Gamma_2)$ for some appropriate class-system Γ_2. In the above discussion, Γ_2 is the class-system for *NAT-BOOL* from Examples 3.3 and 3.4. The important thing here is that the "application" of the instantiation is carried out by a pushout in **PSM**. The existence of the appropriate pushout is the main result of this section.

Definition 6.21 An *instantiation* of a generic class-system $S = \langle \Gamma_0,\ \Gamma_1,\ \gamma \rangle$, is specified by giving a triple $I = \langle S,\ \Gamma_2, \theta \rangle$ where $\Gamma_2 \in$ **PSM**, and θ is a **PUB**-morphism, $\theta : \Gamma_0 \to \mathcal{U}(\Gamma_2)$ with $\mathcal{U}$ as in Proposition 4.16.

The instantiations of a generic class-system S form a category, $\mathbf{INS}_S$, where a morphism from $I_1 = \langle S,\ \Gamma_{2,1}, \theta_1 \rangle$ to $I_2 = \langle S,\ \Gamma_{2,2},\ \theta_2 \rangle$ is a triple $\langle I_1,\ \rho,\ I_2 \rangle$ where $\rho : \Gamma_{2,1} \to \Gamma_{2,2}$ in **PSM** such that $\mathcal{U}(\rho) \bullet \theta_1 = \theta_2$. □

Example 6.22 The instantiation of *PSTACK* to get *STACK-of-NAT* is the morphism $\theta : \Gamma_0 \to \mathcal{U}(\Gamma_2)$ where $\Gamma_0 = \langle \{D\},\ \emptyset,\ \emptyset \rangle$, $\Gamma_2 = NAT\text{-}BOOL$, and $\theta_K(D) = NAT$.

The instantiation of the generic class-system *MORE* that yields *id-NAT* and *double-succ* is given by the morphism $\theta : \Gamma_0 \to \mathcal{U}(\Gamma_2)$ where $\Gamma_0 = \langle \{D\},\ \{fun\},\ \alpha_0 \rangle$, $\Gamma_2 = NAT\text{-}BOOL$, and $\theta_K(D) = NAT$, and $\theta_\Sigma(fun) = succ$. □

Theorem 6.23 *Let* $S = \langle \Gamma_0,\ \Gamma_1,\ \gamma \rangle$ *be a generic class-system and let* $I = \langle S,\ \Gamma_2,\ \theta \rangle$ *be an instantiation for* S. *Let* $\hat{\gamma} : \mathcal{F}(\Gamma_0) \to \Gamma_1$ *and* $\hat{\theta} : \mathcal{F}(\Gamma_0) \to \Gamma_2$ *be the PSM-morphisms constructed from* γ *and* θ, *respectively, by the adjunction* $\mathcal{F} \dashv \mathcal{U}$ *given in Proposition 4.16. Then* $\langle \hat{\theta},\ \hat{\gamma} \rangle$ *has a pushout* $\langle \theta',\ \gamma' \rangle$ *in* **PSM**. □

The desired class-system, the result of instantiating the parameters of S with I, is the pushout object of the above pushout. While the proof is too long to put in this paper, it, and the proofs of the other results, are available from the author.

7 Subsystems, Extensions and Imports

In the examples of generic class-systems and their instantiations given in Section 6, the resulting class-system, the pushout object, is an "extension" of the class-system *NAT-BOOL*. That is, the new class-system contains all the classes and methods of *NAT-BOOL* and then some additional ones.

The notion that one class-system, Γ_1, an extension of another, Γ_0, is easy to formalize mathematically.

Definition 7.24 Let $\Gamma_0 = \langle K_0, \Sigma_0, \alpha_0, \iota_0, \xi_0\rangle$ and $\Gamma = \langle K, \Sigma, \alpha, \iota, \tau, \xi\rangle$ be partial class-systems and let $\psi = \langle \psi_K, \psi_\Sigma\rangle : \Gamma_0 \to \Gamma$ in **PSM**. We say that Γ *is an extension of* Γ_0 *via* ψ (or that Γ_0 *is a sub-system of* Γ *via* ψ) if both ψ_K and ψ_Σ are injective in **Set**, and ι_0, τ_0, and ξ_0 are preserved, i.e., $\psi_K^{**} \bullet \iota_0 = \iota \bullet \psi_K$, $\psi_K^{*} \bullet \tau_0 = \tau \bullet \psi_\Sigma$, and $\psi_{Expr}^{**} \bullet \xi_0 = \xi \bullet \psi_{Expr}$, as partial functions. □

Example 7.25 Here is a subclass-system of the class-system *NAT-BOOL* given in Example 3.4. Clearly it is just the *BOOL* part of the earlier example, and the morphism ψ is given by the evident inclusions.

CLASS-SYSTEM *CS-BOOL*
classes
BOOL
form
BOOL : ( )( )
methods
BOOL::*true*:BOOL;
NEW.1.

BOOL::*false*:BOOL;
NEW.2.

BOOL::*and*(P1,P2:*BOOL*):*BOOL*;
CASE(P1, CASE(P2, *true*, *false*), *false*).

BOOL::*not*(P1:*BOOL*):*BOOL*;
CASE(P1, *false*, *true*).

end CLASS-SYSTEM □

Example 7.26 Here is a partial class-system that extends the class-system *CS-BOOL* of the previous example. The extension mapping ψ takes the class-name *BOOL* to the class-name *PBOOL* and takes each method-name in *BOOL* to the corresponding method-name in *D-PBOOL* The class-system *D-BOOL* just begs to be made into a generic class-system by taking *D* to be a parameter – more about that later.

CLASS-SYSTEM *D-PBOOL*
classes
D
PBOOL
form
PBOOL : ( )( )
methods

PBOOL::*true*:PBOOL;
NEW.1.

PBOOL::*false*:PBOOL;
NEW.2.

PBOOL::*and*(P1,P2:*PBOOL*):*PBOOL*;
CASE(P1, CASE(P2, *true*, *false*), *false*).

PBOOL::not(P1:*PBOOL*):*PBOOL*;
CASE(P1, *false*, *true*).

PBOOL::ifthnels(P1:*PBOOL*, P2, P3:*D*):*D*;
CASE(P1, P2, P3).

end CLASS-SYSTEM □

If we had started with the class-system *CS-BOOL* and wanted to specify the class-systems *NAT-BOOL* and *D-BOOL* it would save a lot of writing if we didn't have to again write down all the details of *CS-BOOL*. Clearly, what we would want to do is to somehow "import" the specification of *CS-BOOL* into the new specification. That is, informally speaking, it should suffice to write something like the following to specify *D-PBOOL*

Example 7.27 Here is an example of importing the specification one class-system into the specification of another

CLASS-SYSTEM *D-PBOOL*
import
CS-BOOL with class *BOOL* renamed *PBOOL*
classes
D
PBOOL
methods

PBOOL::ifthnels(P1:*PBOOL*, P2, P3:*D*):*D*;
CASE(P1, P2, P3).

end CLASS-SYSTEM □

We now want to show that this informal notion of "importation" can be formalized within our general framework. We start with an observation concerning extensions.

Fact 7.28 *If* Γ *is an extension of* Γ_0 *via* ψ *where* $\Gamma_0 = \langle K_0, \Sigma_0, \alpha_0, \iota_0, \tau_0, \xi_0\rangle$ *and* $\Gamma = \langle K, \Sigma, \alpha, \iota, \tau, \xi\rangle$ *then this allows us to rewrite* Γ *as*

$$\Gamma = \langle K_0 + K_1, \Sigma_0 + \Sigma 1, [\overline{\psi_K} \bullet \alpha_0, \alpha_1], [\psi_K^{**} \bullet \iota_0, \iota_1], [\psi_K^{*} \bullet \tau_0, \tau_1], [\psi_{Expr} \bullet \xi_0, \xi_1]\rangle$$

where the square bracket pairs, $[, \cdots,]$ *are coproduct mediators as defined at the end of Section 2, and*

$K_1 = K - K_0$ *and* $\psi_K : K_0 \rightarrow (K_0 + K_1)$ *is the indicated coproduct injection.*

$\Sigma_1 = \Sigma - \Sigma_0$ *and* $\psi_\Sigma : \Sigma_0 \rightarrow (\Sigma_0 + \Sigma_1)$ *is the indicated coproduct injection*

α_1 *is the restriction of* α *to* Σ_1.

ι_1 *is the restriction of* ι *to* K_1.

τ_1 *is the restriction of* τ *to* Σ_1.

ξ_1 *is the restriction of* ξ *to* Σ_1.

□

Definition 7.29 Let Γ be an extension of Γ_0 via ψ as above. Then, using the above Fact, we define $\Gamma\backslash\Gamma_0$ to be the ill-formed class-system

$$\Gamma\backslash\Gamma_0 = \langle K_0 + K_1,\ \Sigma_0 + \Sigma_1,\ [\overline{\psi_K} \bullet \alpha_0,\ \alpha_1],\ [\bot,\ \iota_1],\ [\bot,\ \tau_1],\ [\bot,\ \xi_1]\rangle.$$

□

A look back at Example 7.27 will show that the informal text there corresponds to what we would get for *D-BOOL*$\backslash$*PBOOL* in a formal treatment. Indeed, it goes a bit further, for the **import** section of the specification specifies the **PUB**-morphism

$$\psi : \mathcal{U}(\textit{CS-BOOL}) \rightarrow \mathcal{U}(\textit{D-PBOOL}\backslash\textit{CS-BOOL}).$$

(that is, it specifies that ψ_K takes *BOOL* to *PBOOL*, and "by default", that ψ_Σ is the identity). The following result shows how we can use this data to reconstruct the full specification of *PBOOL*.

Proposition 7.30 *Let* $\Gamma_0 = \langle K_0,\ \Sigma_0,\ \alpha_0,\ \iota_0,\ \xi_0\rangle$ *and* $\Gamma = \langle K,\ \Sigma,\ \alpha,\ \iota,\ \tau,\ \xi\rangle$ *be partial class-systems and let* Γ *be an extension of* Γ_0 *via* $\psi = \langle\psi_K,\ \psi_\Sigma\rangle : \Gamma_0 \rightarrow \Gamma$. *Then* $S = \langle\mathcal{U}(\Gamma_0),\ \Gamma\backslash\Gamma_0,\ \mathcal{U}(\psi)\rangle$ *is a generic class-system,* $I = \langle S,\ \Gamma_0,\ \mathcal{U}(1_{\Gamma_0})\rangle$ *is an instantiation, and the result of applying* I *to* S *is* Γ. *That is, the pushout for* $\langle\rho,\ \delta\rangle = \langle\widehat{1_{\Gamma_0}}, \widehat{\mathcal{U}(\psi)}\rangle = \langle\langle 1_{K_0},\ 1_{\Sigma_0}\rangle,\ \langle\psi_K,\ \psi_\Sigma\rangle\rangle$ *is* $\langle\rho^!,\ \delta^!\rangle = \langle\langle\psi_K,\ \psi_\Sigma\rangle,\ \langle 1_{K_0+K_1},\ 1_{\Sigma_0+\Sigma_1}\rangle\rangle$ *with pushout object* Γ. □

Remark: We noted, in Example 7.26, that the example just begged to be made into a generic class-system. The same is true of import versions. Let $\Gamma_D = \langle\{D\},\ \emptyset,\ \emptyset\rangle$, then we have obvious **PUB**-morphisms

$$\gamma_{D,1} : \mathcal{U}(\Gamma_D) \rightarrow \textit{D-PBOOL}$$

and

$$\gamma_{D,2} : \mathcal{U}(\Gamma_D) \rightarrow \textit{D-PBOOL}\backslash\textit{CS-BOOL}.$$

corresponding to (possibly ill-formed) generic class-systems,

$$\langle\Gamma_D,\ \textit{D-PBOOL},\ \gamma_{D,1}\rangle,$$

and

$$\langle\Gamma_D,\ \textit{D-PBOOL}\backslash\textit{CS-BOOL},\ \gamma_{D,2}\rangle.$$

respectively.

The idea is that if we apply $\langle\Gamma_D,\ \textit{D-PBOOL}\backslash\textit{CS-BOOL},\ \gamma_{D,2}\rangle$ to, say, *NAT-BOOL* that this will extend *NAT-BOOL* by adding a new method *ifthnels*(P1:*BOOL*, P2,P3:*NAT*):*NAT* to the class *BOOL* in *NAT-BOOL*. How can this be done?

Let Γ_0 denote *CS-BOOL*, let Γ_1 denote *PBOOL*, and let Γ_2 denote *NAT-BOOL*. Let

$$\psi_1 : \Gamma_0 \rightarrow \Gamma_1$$

and

$$\psi_2 : \Gamma_0 \rightarrow \Gamma_2$$

be the indicated extension morphisms. Let $\mu_{D,2} : \mathcal{U}(\Gamma_D) \rightarrow \mathcal{U}(\Gamma_1\backslash\Gamma_0)$ as above, and let

$$I : \mathcal{U}(\Gamma_D) \rightarrow \mathcal{U}(\Gamma_2)$$
$$D \mapsto \textit{NAT}.$$

Then we claim that the desired class-system is the colimit object of the following diagram:

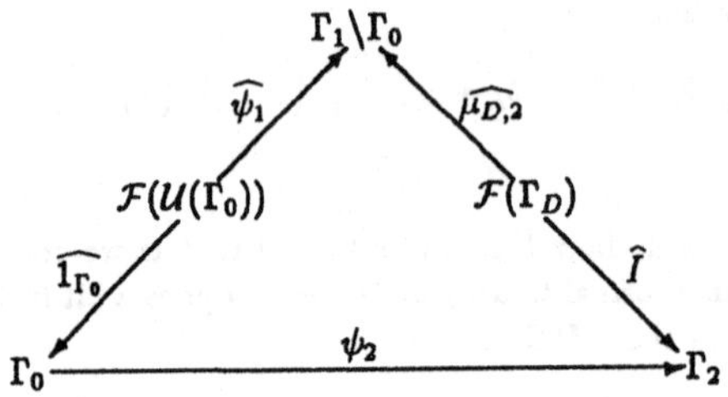

8 Exports, etc.

In this section we will look at a somewhat more elaborate example, and some of the issues that it suggests.

We will define a generic class *LINE* with a single parameter D. The idea is that when D is instantiated with an appropriate class *CHAR* of "characters" that what we get could be informally described as a "line of characters (as on a screen) with the cursor positioned under one of the characters", together with operations such as

- move the cursor right
- move the cursor left
- move the cursor to the left end of the line
- move the cursor to the right end of the line
- insert the character 'X'
- replace the character at the cursor with the character 'X'
- delete the character at the cursor position
- make an empty-line

As we shall see, there are also other interesting instantiations of *LINE*.

Example 8.31 A line is either an empty-line, or it is a non-empty line. A non-empty line is modeled as a triple $\langle L,\ C,\ R\rangle$ where L and R are stacks of D and C is a element of D. The intuition is that the cursor is at C, the left end of the line is in L (backwards), and the right end of the line is in R (forwards). That is, given a line '$d_1 \cdot d_2 \cdots d_i \cdots d_n$' with the cursor at d_i we could picture the triple as follows

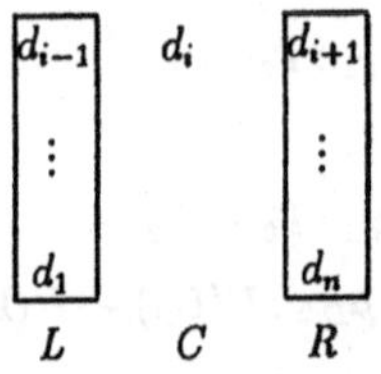

The parameterized stacks that we use here are an extension, *PSTACK2*, of those specificed in the generic class-system *PSTACK* of Example 5.19. These stacks have an additional operation *empty?* which could be semi-formally specified as follows:

```
STACK::empty?(P1:STACK):BOOL
        CASE(P1, true, false).
```

and which, together with the class-system *BOOL*, could be added to *PSTACK* by the methods of the preceeding section.

Then we could write a semi-formal specification for the desired class-system *LINE* as follows:

```
GENERIC CLASS-SYSTEM CS-LINE
 parameters
    D
 import
    the class-system D-PBOOL with
       parameter D of D-PBOOL as BOOL
       (thus giving us a method ifthnels_BOOL : BOOL × BOOL → BOOL),
    the generic class-system PSTACK2 with
       parameter D of PSTACK2 as D of CS-LINE
    classes
       LINE
    form
       LINE : ( )(STACK·D·STACK)
    methods
       LINE::null(P1:STACK):BOOL;
          ifthnels_BOOL(empty?(P1), true, nil_BOOL).

       LINE::moveleft(P1:LINE):D;
          CASE(P1, P1, INST_LINE(null(P1.2.1),
             P1,
             push(P1.2.3, P1.2.2); P1.2<P1.2.1, pop(P1.2.1), P1.2.3>;P1));
          CASE(P1, NIL_D, P1.2.2).

       LINE::moveright( P1:LINE ):D;
          CASE(P1, P1, INST_LINE(null(P1.2.3),
             P1,
             push(P1.2.1, P1.2.2); P1.2<P1.2.1, pop(P1.2.3), P1.2.3>;P1));
          CASE(P1, NIL_D, P1.2.2).

       LINE::leftend( P1:LINE ):D;
          CASE(P1, P1, INST_LINE( null(P1.2.1), P1, moveleft(P1); leftend(P1) ) );
          CASE(P1, NIL_D, P1.2.2).

       LINE::rightend( P1:LINE):D;
          CASE(P1, P1, INST_LINE( null(P1.2.3), P1, moveright(P1); rightend(P1) ) );
          CASE(P1, NIL_D, P1.2.2).

       LINE::insert(P1:D, P2:LINE):D;
          CASE(P2,
             P2.2<makestk, P1, makestk >,
             push(P2.2.1, P2.2.2); P2.2<P2.2.1, P1, P2.2.3>);
          P1.

       LINE::replace(P1:D, P2:LINE):D;
          CASE(P2, P2.2< makestk, P1, makestk>, P2.2<P2.2.1, P1, P2.2.3>);P1.
```

```
LINE::delete(P1:LINE):D;
  CASE(P1,
    P1,
    INST_LINE(
      null(P1.2.3),
      INST_LINE(
        null(P1.2.1),
        P1.1< >,
        P1.2<P1.2.1, pop(P1.2.1), P1.2.3> ),
      P1.2<P1.2.1, pop(P1.2.3), P1.2.3> ) );
  CASE(P1, NIL_D, P1.2.2).

LINE::makelin:LINE;
  NEW.1.
```

end CLASS-SYSTEM

Given the generic class-system *CS-LINE* with parameter D together with a class-system *CHAR* of characters we can instantiate D with *CHAR* to get a new class-system that we might call *LINE-of-CHAR*. That is *LINE-of-CHAR* is the pushout object of the diagram

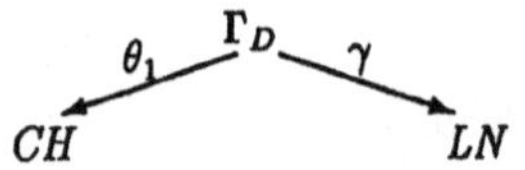

where θ_1 takes D to *CHAR* and $\gamma : \Gamma_D \rightarrow LN$ is is the **PSM** morphism corresponding, as in Theorem 6.23, to the generic specification *CS-LINE*.

But we can do more with *CS-LINE*. For example, in the following diagram let θ_1 be as above and let θ_2 take D to *LINE*:

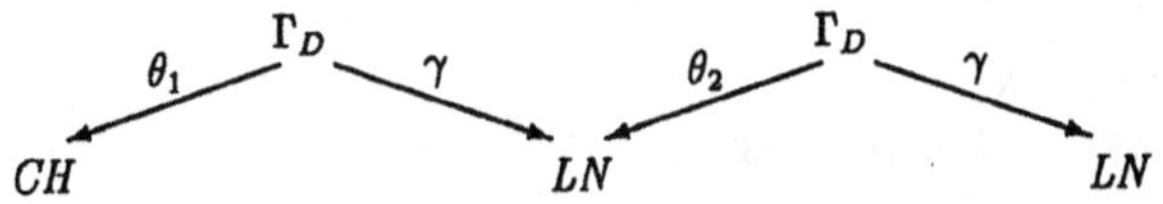

the resulting pushout object will contain *LINES-of-CHAR* and, in addition something we might call *LINES-of-LINES-of-CHAR*, or *TEXT*. Each of the methods of *CS-LINE* will appear twice in the pushout object, once as a method belonging to *LINES-of-CHAR* and once as a method for *TEXT*. Intuitively the *moveleft* method for *LINES-of-CHAR* "moves the cursor to the left" while the *moveleft* method for *TEXT* "moves the cursor to the preceding line". Similarly the *insert* method for *LINES-of-CHAR* "inserts a new character" while the *insert* method for *TEXT* "inserts a new line". Thus we might say that this construction defines an editor. Of course the analogy with your favorite text editor is rather loose.

Pushing even further, consider the colimit of the diagram

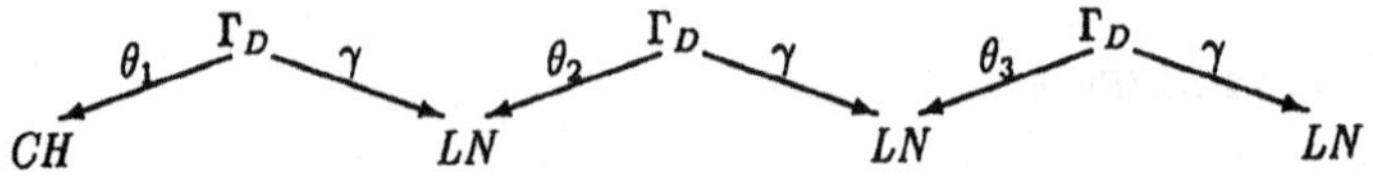

where θ_3 again takes D to *LINE*. This, we claim, gives us what we could well call *LINES-of-LINES-of-LINES-of-CHAR*, *LINES-of-TEXT* or *TEXT-files*. □

We end this section with a look at another issue. One possible complaint about the generic class-system *LINE* is that it openly contains the class *STACK*, and the special method *null*. A user is thus free to exploit *STACK* and *null* when developing further extensions. However, in practice we might want to change the specification *LINE* to a less idiosyncratic implementation, perhaps one using linked-lists, or arrays. How can we modify the above specification of *LINE* so that it does not make *STACK* available. The answer, of course, is to add another section to the specification that states just what classes and methods are *exported*. That is, the export section will specify which classes and methods from the class-system a user is allowed to exploit in further extensions. Here is how we can express this mathematically?

Definition 8.32 Let $\Gamma = \langle K,\ \Sigma,\ \alpha,\ \iota,\ \tau,\ \xi\rangle$ be a class-system, then an *export interface for* Γ is specified by a **PUB**-mono-morphism $m : \Gamma_{exp} \to \mathcal{U}(\Gamma)$. That is, $m = \langle m_K,\ m_\Sigma\rangle$ where m_K and m_Σ are injective.

In effect, if $\Gamma_{exp} = \langle K_{exp},\ \Sigma_{exp},\ \alpha_{exp}\rangle$, then $K_{exp} \subseteq K$ and $\Sigma_{exp} \subseteq \Sigma$.

In general, for a generic type $\langle \Gamma_0,\ \Gamma,\ \gamma\rangle$ to have an export interface $m : \Gamma_{exp} \to \Gamma$ we require that γ factor through m, that is, that there exists $\gamma_{exp} : \Gamma_0 \to \Gamma_{exp}$ such that the diagram

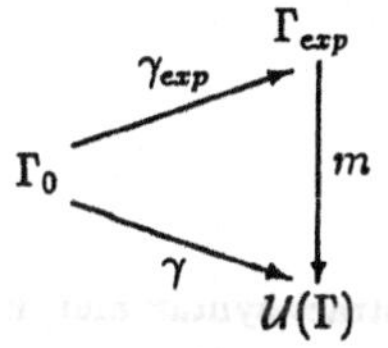

commutes.

Let Γ be a class-system with export interface $m : \Gamma_{exp} \to \mathcal{U}(\Gamma)$, and let $S = \langle \Gamma_0,\ \Gamma_1,\ \gamma\rangle$ be a generic class-system, then a $\langle m,\ \Gamma\rangle$-instantiation of S in an instantiation $\theta : \Gamma_0 \to \mathcal{U}(\Gamma)$ of S in Γ that factors through m. That is, there exists a **PUB**-morphism $\rho : \Gamma_0 \to \Gamma_{exp}$ such that $\theta = m \bullet \rho$. □

The idea is that all instantiating of parameters or importing of classes and methods from Γ must be done through Γ_{exp}. In effect, a user only gets to see, and exploit, those classes and methods from Γ that are in Γ_{exp}.

Example 8.33 For the above example, the desired export interface could be presented by the **PUB**-class-system corresponding to the following

export
  Classes: *CHAR*, *BOOL* and *LINE*
  Methods: *moveleft, moveright, leftend, rightend,*
    insert, replace, delete, and *makelin*

which would, of course, effectively hide all evidence of the fact that the specification was done using stacks of *CHAR*. □

Using such an export, $m : \Gamma_{exp} \to LN$, the specification diagram for *TEXT* = *LINES-of-LINES-of-CHAR* would have the form:

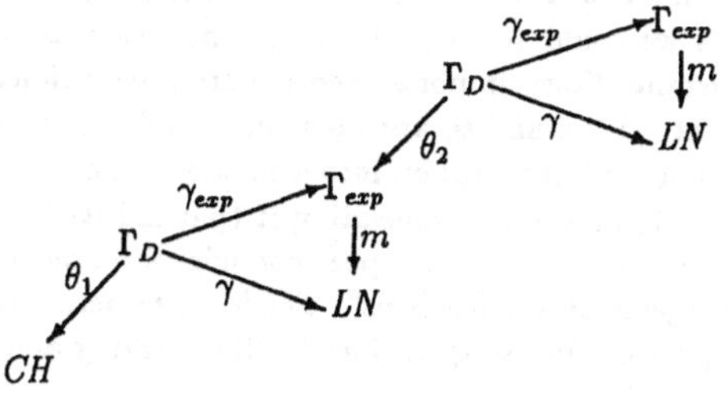

As indicated in the diagram below, taking the colimit of the above diagram gives us the desired class-system L' for $TEXT$ and the colimit E' of the export part of the diagram gives us the desired export-part for $TEXT$, as well as the export morphism $m' : E' \to L'$.

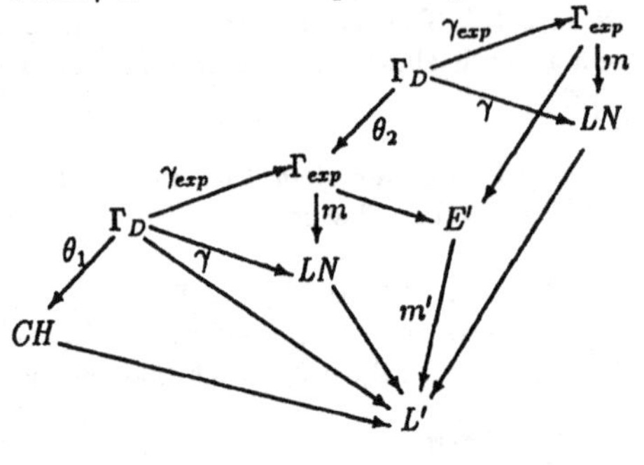

9 Concluding Remarks

What we have done is to present the abstract syntax and informal semantics for the language $\mathbf{LD^3}$ and then to give an equally abstract presentation of a variety of means for specifying and constructing class-systems (programs).

The specifications and constructions are all on the level of syntax. We have not shown, for example, that the generic class-system for $STACK$, given in Example 5.19, has the expected meaning. However, it should be clear that it works on the syntactic level – that is, that instantiating D with NAT does indeed substitute NAT for D on the syntactic level.

We believe that the syntactic emphasis is appropriate in the sense that a large part of the practical motivation behind generic classes is that it is an important means for producing reusable code. Importation is also closely related to code reuse, it provides a for reusing code without recopying it. Exportation fits into this picture as a means for ensuring encapsulation of code. As always, encapsulation is necessary if class-systems are to be such that their implementations can be modified without affecting their behavior as seen by users and reusers.

However, despite the importance of reusable code, it is still desirable to develop results, analogous to those developed for algebraic specifications, showing that the generic constructions have the desired semantics. This is far more complicated here than in the case of algebraic specifications. Not only do "objects have memory" but they have, in effect, two kinds of semantics: a public semantics ("the behavior that the user sees") and a private semantics ("what goes on inside the class"). The semantics given in [9] and [10] is private semantics, i.e., the semantics of class-systems. What we need to duplicate the semantic results of algebraic specifications is a good treatment of the public semantics. That is, we need an abstract semantics, or behavioral semantics. Some first steps towards such a behavioral semantics are given in [8], but much remains to be done.

By using a categorical approach we have been able to give precise definitions of the desired syntactic constructions at a very high level of abstraction. We have given version of a sugared syntax for $\mathbf{LD^3}$ but it is obvious that we could sugar it in many other ways as well. But our definitions of generic class-systems, instantiations, imports, and exports, are defined as abstract categorical constructions on the abstract syntax and so are sugar-independent. In particular, we can introduce generic classes, importation, and exportation into a sugared version of the language in any way we want as long as we provide means for translating it (parsing it) into objects and morphisms in **PUB** and **PSM**. Of course one would not expect compiler for a sugared version of $\mathbf{LD^3}$ to literally "parse programs into objects and morphisms". The idea, rather, is to employ this underlying mathematical structure to provide precise guidelines for the creating and verifying the design.

The language, as described in Section 3, has been implemented in both plain and sugared versions. We are currently investigating how this implementation can be extended to capture the generic constructs given in this paper and the inheritance constructs developed in [10].

References

[1] H. Ehrig, W. Fey, H. Hansen, M. Löwe, and F. Parisi-Presicce. Categories for the development of algebraic module specifications. In H. Ehrig, H. Herrlich, H.-J. Kreowski, and G. Preuss, editors, *Categorical Methods in Computer Science*, pages 157–184. LNCS 393, Springer-Verlag, 1989.

[2] H. Ehrig and B. Mahr. *Fundamentals of Algebraic Specification 1*. Springer-Verlag, Berlin, 1985.

[3] J. A. Goguen, J. W. Thatcher, and E. G. Wagner. An initial algebra approach to the specification, correctness, and implementation of abstract data types. In R. T. Yeh, editor, *Current Trends in Programming Methodology, IV, Data Structuring*, pages 80–149. Prentice-Hall, 1978.

[4] J.A. Goguen and J.J. Tardo. An introduction to obj: A language for writing and testing formal algebraic specifications. In *Proc. IEEE Conf. for Reliable Software*, pages 170–189. IEEE, 1979.

[5] A. Goldberg and D. Robson. *Smalltalk-80: The Language and its Implementation*. Addison-Wesley, Reading, Mass., 1983.

[6] B. Meyer. *Object-Oriented Software Construction*. Prentice-Hall International Series in Computer Science. Prentice-Hall, New York, 1988.

[7] United States Department of Defense, Washington, DC. *Reference Manual for the ADA Programming Language*, 1982.

[8] Eric G. Wagner. Algebraic aspects of data directed design. In *Proceedings of the First Maghrebin Conference on Artificial Intelligence and Software Engineering*. University of Constantine, Constantine, Algeria, 1989.

[9] Eric G Wagner. An algebraically specified language for data directed design. *Theoretical Computer Science*, 77:195–219, 1990.

[10] Eric G. Wagner. Some mathematical thoughts on languages for data directed design. In *Proceedings of the conference 'the Unified Computation Laboratory' at the University of Stirling, Stirling, Scotland*, 1990. *To appear.*

[11] N. Wirth. *Programming in Modula-2*. Springer-Verlag, second edition, 1983.

Design of a Compiler for lazy pattern driven narrowing

Dietmar Wolz

Technische Universität Berlin
Fachbereich Informatik (20)
Institut für Software und Theoretische Informatik
Franklinstraße 28/29, Sekr. FR 6-1
D-1000 Berlin 10
email: dietmar@opal.cs.tu-berlin.de
Tel +49 30 31473510

Abstract

This paper describes the implementation of lazy pattern driven narrowing by extending an abstract machine for lazy rewriting to perform unification and backtracking.

The abstract machine LANAM is based on implementation methods for functional and logic languages like LML and PROLOG.

The approach leads to an efficient unification method for an equational theory and can also be used as a basis for efficient execution of functional logic programs.

We give an abstract definition of the implemented algorithm, describe the architecture of the abstract machine and discuss performance and implementation issues.

1 Introduction

Recently several approaches have been proposed to achieve an efficient implementation for functional logic languages [Red 87]. Most of them are based on Horn clauses with equality and use narrowing as operational semantics. Narrowing subsumes reduction and unification and can be implemented by extending the WAM [War 83], an abstract machine used to implement PROLOG [Bos 89, Bal 89, Han90, Mue 90].

We choose another approach, the extension of an abstract machine for lazy term rewriting LATERM [Wo 89] to handle unification and backtracking. The lazy narrowing machine LANAM uses an environment based architecture like the TIM machine [Fa 87].

For simplicity we restrict ourselves to first order conditional rewrite systems. An extension to arbitrary Horn clauses or higher order functions is straightforward.

We use no flattening of the input program as in [Bal 89, Mor90]. Flattening removes nested patterns and function calls by introducing auxiliary functions and simplifies the implementation. We avoid flattening because the additional functions introduce inefficiencies both at compile time and at run time.

Instead we transform the pattern into decision trees for efficient unification, similar to the technique used for the compilation of LML [Jos 87, Au 87]. There is an optimization of the WAM called full indexing in all arguments [Hi 89] achieving the same goal. Backtracking is restricted to rule selection by conditions, it is avoided for the selection by pattern.

We don't distinct explicitly between constructors and derived operations. If a function is not defined over all constructors it is possible, that the corresponding function symbol cannot be removed from a term by reduction. In this case no backtracking occurs. In a condition goal like $p = true$ the effect is the same as if we would perform backtracking. If p contains a non reducible subterm, p cannot be evaluated to *true* and backtracking will occur because both sides of the goal are narrowed to different normal forms.

The paper is organized as follows. Section 2 gives a short introduction in conditional equations and narrowing, the lazy narrowing strategy is discussed in section 3. Section 4 presents the lazy narrowing algorithm. Section 5 explains the compilation of pattern into decision trees, section 6 contains a description of the LANAM architecture and the LANAM code generation. In section 7 implementation and performance issues are sketched briefly and finally section 8 includes some conclusions and remarks.

2 Conditional Equations

2.1 Notation

A **signature** $SIG = (S, OP)$ consists of a set S of sorts and a S^+-sorted set OP of **operation symbols.** X is a S-sorted set of **variables**, $T_{OP,X}$ denotes the set of well sorted **terms** on OP and X. For $t \in T_{OP,X}$ $V(t)$ denotes the set of variables in t. We say a term t is **ground** if $V(t) = \emptyset$ and T_{OP} denotes the set of **ground terms.**

Substitutions σ are defined as endomorphisms on $T_{OP,X}$ that extend mappings from X to $T_{OP,X}$ with a finite **domain** $D(\sigma)$. A substitution is denoted by $\sigma = [x_1 \leftarrow t_1, \ldots, x_n \leftarrow t_n]$. Applications of substitutions are written in postfix notation $(t\sigma)$.

The **composition** of two substitutions σ and σ' is denoted by $\sigma'' = \sigma\sigma'$. We call σ **a prefix** of σ''.

The **subsumption quasi ordering** $\preceq$ on $T_{OP,X}$ is defined by: $t \preceq t'$ iff $t' = t\sigma$ for a substitution σ. We call this situation a **match** from t to t', t' is an **instance** of t by σ. $\preceq$ can be extended to substitutions in a straightforward manner: $\sigma \preceq \sigma'$ iff σ is a prefix of σ'.

A substitution σ **unifies** two terms t and t' if $t\sigma = t'\sigma$. A unifier σ is called **most general** if σ is a prefix of every unifier of t and t'.

We call a set of equations $P = \{t_1 = t'_1, \ldots, t_n = t'_n\}$ a **goal** and $P \rightarrow l = r$ a **conditional equation** (clause) which can be denoted as $t_1 = t'_1, \ldots, t_n = t'_n \rightarrow l = r$. [1] where $t_i, l, r \in T_{OP,X}$. P and $l = r$ are the **premise** and the **conclusion** of the clause. Empty premises are omitted, we write $l = r$ for $\emptyset \rightarrow l = r$.

The concepts of substitution, variable set, subterm and subterm replacement are extended from terms to equations and goals in an obvious manner.

2.2 The conditional equational calculus

We derive the conditional equational calculus as a special case of the Horn clause calculus described in [Pad 87, Pad 88].

Let C be a set of clauses (conditional equations) and c a single clause. The **conditional equational calculus** consists of the following derivation rules where $C \vdash c$ stands for c is **derivable** from C:

Substitution Rule : For clauses c and substitutions σ,

$$\{c\} \vdash c\sigma$$

Cut Rule : For equations $p = p'$, $q = q'$ and goals G, G',

$$\{G \cup \{q = q'\} \rightarrow p = p',\ G' \rightarrow q = q'\} \ \vdash\ G \cup G' \rightarrow p = p'$$

Composition Rule : $C \vdash c$ and $C' \cup \{c\} \vdash c'$ imply $C \cup C' \vdash c'$.

The set EAX of **equality axioms** consists of all clauses of the form

$$\begin{array}{lcl} & & t = t \\ t = t' & \rightarrow & t' = t \\ t = t', t' = t'' & \rightarrow & t = t'' \\ t_1 = t'_1, \ldots, t_n = t'_n & \rightarrow & op(t_1, \ldots, t_n) = op(t'_1, \ldots, t'_n) \end{array}$$

The **deductive theory of a specification** (SIG, AX) (where AX is a set of clauses), $TH(AX)$ is given by all clauses over SIG which are derivable from $AX \cup EAX$ using the conditional equational calculus. Goals in $TH(AX)$ are called (SIG, AX)**-theorems**. $TH(AX)$ agrees with the congruence relation on $T_{OP,X}$ generated by AX. We call a substitution σ **a solution of a goal** G if $G\sigma \in TH(AX)$.

In general, for all goals g, $g \in TH(AX)$ iff all models (algebras) of the specification (SIG, AX) satisfy g [Pad 88]. [2].

[1] With "equation" we mean an unconditional equation. To achieve a clear distinction we adapt the notation "clause" from predicate logic and call conditional equations clauses.

[2] We assume non-empty carrier sets for each sort

2.3 Narrowing

Narrowing is both a specialization of paramodulation and a generalization of goal reduction.

Only irreducible solutions can be found by narrowing and this is possible only if (SIG, AX) ensures the uniqueness of normal forms rsp. the reduction relation.

Narrowing can be seen as a combination of reduction and substitution. Non-variable prefixes of reduction redices are completed to full redices by substituting into variables.

In the following we assume the set of goal variables GV disjoint from all variables occurring in $AX \cup EAX$. Given a goal-substitution pair (G, σ) with $V(G) \subseteq GV$ and a derivation step from (G, σ) into (G', σ'), we assume that all $x \in V(\sigma) - GV$ are renamed as variables of GV before (G', σ') is subjected to further deduction steps.

Given a partial selection function ST selecting positions in goals and terms. to $POS(SIG)$, let G, H be goals, and σ, γ be a substitution, $G \overset{ST}{\underset{AX}{\vdash}} (H, \sigma)$ is a **narrowing expansion** via ST if the expression $G \overset{ST}{\underset{AX}{\vdash}} (H, \sigma)$ is derivable by the following rules:

Base Rule : If $G\sigma = \{t_1 = t_1, \ldots, t_n = t_n\}$ or $G = \emptyset$ then $G \overset{ST}{\underset{AX}{\vdash}} (\emptyset, \sigma)$.

Narrowing Rule : If $P \rightarrow l = r \in AX$, $ST(G) = K \bullet t$, i.e. $G = K[x_0 \leftarrow t]$,
t is not a variable, and σ is a most general unifier of l and t, i.e. $l\sigma = t\sigma$
and $H = P\sigma \cup K[x_0 \leftarrow r\sigma]$,
then $G \overset{ST}{\underset{AX}{\vdash}} (H, \sigma)$, and $K \bullet t$ is a **narrowing redex** of G.

Composition Rule : $G \overset{ST}{\underset{AX}{\vdash}} (G', \sigma)$ and $G' \overset{ST}{\underset{AX}{\vdash}} (G'', \gamma)$ imply $G \overset{ST}{\underset{AX}{\vdash}} (G'', \sigma\gamma)$.

A selection function ST is a **narrowing strategy** if for each goal G and each term t, either $ST(G)$ rsp. $ST(t)$ is a narrowing redex or undefined. We call a set of substitutions NS **normal** if it contains the identity on X and for all substitutions σ, γ, $\sigma\gamma \in NS$ implies $\sigma, \gamma \in NS$ and for all $\sigma \in NS$, σ is an **irreducible substitution**, i.e. for all $x \in D(\sigma)$, $x\sigma$ is a normal form.

A narrowing strategy is NS**-uniform** if for all goals G and substitutions $\sigma \in NS$ either $ST(G\sigma)$ is undefined or $ST(G)$ is defined and $ST(G)\sigma = ST(G\sigma)$.

Uniformity means that given two instances $G\sigma$ and $G\gamma$ by irreducible substitutions σ and γ, ST must return the same position in G.

NS-uniformity via some NS of the narrowing strategy is a necessary criteria for **completeness** with respect to the deductive theory, i.e. $G\sigma \in TH(AX)$ for an irreducible substitution σ implies $G \overset{ST}{\underset{AX}{\vdash}} (\emptyset, \gamma)$ for a substitution $\gamma \preceq \sigma$. Completeness means, all prefixes of irreducible solutions can be calculated via narrowing [Pad 87].

Unfortunately, computation rules like "lazy " or "leftmost-innermost" do not lead automatically to uniform narrowing strategies.

3 The lazy evaluation strategy

To find an efficient implementation of narrowing not only the narrowing strategy has to be restricted.

Due to the nondeterminism of narrowing there are several strategies to explore the search tree, especially one can choose between a depth first or a breadth first search. To implement a breadth first search all branches of the search tree up to a certain depth have to be stored in memory. This causes an enormous overhead, so we decided to use depth first search [3] which can be implemented by backtracking. Only a single branch of the evaluation tree needs to be stored.

For narrowing, the use of innermost evaluation strategy together with a depth first search in the narrowing tree can lead to nontermination even if the given TRS (Term Rewrite System) is terminating. Consider for example the following equations defining the length of a list:

[3]The RAP system [Huss86] supports a breadth first search, but it runs out of memory even for small examples

```
1)   length(nil)          = 0
2)   length(cons(X,XS)) = succ(length(XS))
```

and the goal to be solved is $length(XS) = 0$. Then the innermost derivation sequence is nonterminating:

```
    length(XS)=0 -i-> length(nil)=0
                 -r-> 0=0 solution XS=0 found
-b-> length(cons(X,XS'))=0
-r-> succ(length(XS'))=0
-i-> succ(length(nil))=0
-r-> succ(0)=0 failure
-b-> succ(length(cons(X',XS'')))=0 -> ...

    where -i-> denotes an instantiation step, -r-> a rewriting step
    and -b-> a backtracking step choosing another instantiation.
```

After finding the first solution, *succ* remains the outermost symbol of the left side of the equation, so there can be no more solution. But the innermost depth first strategy produces a choice before checking failure.

The substitution of XS' has to be deferred until the comparison between the normalized outermost symbols of the equations is done.

One solution is an algorithm called basic reduced narrowing [Hoel88] which alternates between narrowing and rewriting. After each narrowing step the result is rewritten to normal form where logical variables are handled as constants. An implementation of this algorithm is described in [Han90].

A disadvantage of this algorithm is that terms which are not in normal form have to be stored as trees or graphs in the heap instead of being represented virtually by pointers into compiled code. The narrowing redices change after the application of a rewrite rule, so they have to be recomputed at run time.

We choose another solution, the lazy (pattern driven) narrowing algorithm.

Lazy narrowing reduces a term to its **head normal form (HNF)**. A HNF of a term is a term which cannot further be narrowed on the outermost level (even though subterms may be further narrowable). Thus for a term to become completely narrowed, the algorithm has to be applied recursively to all subterms of the solutions. We say, an occurrence in a term is **stabilized** if the subterm at this occurrence is in HNF. **Evaluation** of an expression representing a subterm means stabilizing this subterm.

The lazy evaluation sequence for our example is:

```
    length(X)=0 -i-> length(nil)=0
                -r-> 0=0 solution XS=0 found
-b-> length(cons(X,XS'))=0
-r-> succ(length(XS'))=0 failure
```

The algorithm detects that $succ(length(XS')) = zero$ is unsolvable because both sides of this goal are in HNF and the outermost operation symbols differ. Therefore the concept of head normal form, which is the basis of the lazy strategy, is essential for the early elimination of non solvable goals.

Another advantage is that there is no occur check problem. See for example the following specification of the addition of natural numbers:

```
1)   +(succ(X),Y) = succ(+(X,Y))
2)   +(0,Y)       = Y
```

and the goal to be solved is $+(X,Y) = succ(0), X = succ(X)$. The algorithm detects that there is no solution. By the second equation X is bound to the infinite sequence $s(s(s(\ldots$, but the lazy strategy uses only a finite part of this sequence to prove the unsolvability of the goal.

3.1 Other approaches to implement lazy narrowing

In [JoD 89] an algorithm using the concept of contextual terms and daemons guarding potential redices is introduced. This algorithm is intended to be used for lazy narrowing combined with innermost rewriting.

There are many similarities to our approach, especially if we compare the advantages (reusage of partial unifications, data sharing in the representations for different solutions). But their approach supports only a restricted class of conditions in the axioms, and it is difficult to implement using a compilation technique.

In [Bal 89] an extension of the WAM (Warren Abstract Machine) for lazy narrowing is described. Program clauses were flattened (e.g $f(a(X)) = g(h(X))$ is transformed into $Y = h(X) => f(a(X)) = g(Y)$) and then compiled into extended WAM code. Narrowing is performed by linear resolution. Additionally execution on a parallel machine is supported.

In [Mor90] a lazy implementation of the functional logic language BABEL is described. Similar to our approach a implementation technique for functional languages is used as basis and extended to perform unification and backtracking. But this technique is based on graph reduction [Jos 87]. Flattening is used only for the patterns. Conditional expressions are realized by predefined operations. In BABEL there is a strong distinction between constructors and derived operations. Backtracking occurs, when a derived operation expression cannot be narrowed. In our approach backtracking occurs when a condition goal cannot be fulfilled and all variable bindings computed during condition solving are undone.

4 The lazy narrowing algorithm

This section contains a detailed description of the narrowing algorithm implemented by the abstract machine LANAM.

The algorithm serves as a reference for the explanations in later sections and can be used for correctness considerations.

For the definition of the algorithm we created a special pseudo-code. The symbols l, r, t represent terms where $f(t_1, \ldots, t_n)$ is an application term, f a constant, v a variable. AX is the given set of conditional axioms (regarded as rewrite rules), *rps* represents a set of rulepatterns. We call a triple $(eqs, [p_1, \ldots, p_n], r)$ consisting of a set of unconditional equations *eqs* (condition equations), a list of terms $[p_1, \ldots, p_n]$ (patterns) and a term r (right hand side of a conditional rewrite rule) **rulepatterns**. These are used for the definition of the unification process.

The rulepatterns represent the set of potentially unifying rewrite rules. Initially this set represents all rules derived from the axioms. During unification at a position in the input term the set will be reduced. Finally the set contains all applicable rules at this position.

In our narrowing algorithm terms are not trees but directed acyclic graphs. This means that two different terms t and t' can share subterms. Especially, in a given goal $\{l_1 = r_1, \ldots, l_n = r_n\}$ different equations can share variables.

A current state of execution in the algorithm is represented by the graph of all goals narrowed so far.

We demand that if two variables are equal, then they are shared in all terms. This means that a substitution of a variable v by t, denoted by $v \leftarrow t$ has side effects: all other occurrences of this variable in all terms in the evaluation process are substituted simultaneously. In the same way, the subterm replacement $t[t' \leftarrow t'']$ is defined: all shared occurrences of t' in all terms in the evaluation process (not only in t) are substituted by t''.

The **switch**-command is used for case distinctions over the syntactical structure of its first argument. The **copy** function produces a copy of a rulepattern. The input rulepattern and the result do not share any subterms. All variables in the copy are new and unique. Shared subterms and variables in the original remain shared in the copy. The **select** command selects an element from a set according to the defined conditions. The commands **let**, **if**...**then**...**else** and **return** have their usual meaning.

We use the special commands **choose**...**else_choose**...**exists_no_more** and **fail** to express backtracking. The **choose** command chooses an element from a given set. The execution of **fail** causes a backtrack to the last **choose** or **else_choose** command where all substitutions of variables and subterms are taken back. So the old state of execution is recovered. After a backtrack to a **choose** command another element of the given set is chosen. If there is no more element, execution branches to the corresponding **else_choose** (if there is one). Then the elements from the set given as argument of **else_choose** are chosen, finally execution continues at the corresponding **exists_no_more** command.

4.1 Requirements for the input rules

Any set of rewrite rules with following properties will be suited:

- left-linearity (uniqueness of the variables in the left hand sides of the rules)
- terminating derivation sequences must have unique normal forms,
- left hand sides shall not be single variables,

Extra variables in the conditions and in the right hand sides of the rewrite rules are allowed.

These properties guarantee the correctness of the compiled code. Any result obtained by evaluation using the generated code is a correct solution of the set of input goals.

Left-linearity is not a real restriction because we can substitute non left-linear rules by equivalent left-linear rules by adding additional conditions (e.g $f(X,X) = X$ can be transformed into $X = Y \Rightarrow f(X,Y) = X$.

4.2 The functions of the narrowing algorithm

solve(eqs) gets a goal as input. The procedure solves successively the equations in the goal. An equation is solved by narrowing and comparing simultaneously top down the terms on both sides of the equation using the function *get_HNF*. If an equation cannot be solved, **fail** is executed to cause a backtrack step. This strategy proves to be useful in detecting early unsolvable equations. An equation can often be recognized as unsolvable without complete evaluation.

get_HNF(t) gets a term as input and gives as result the head normal form of this term. First the set *rps* containing all potentially applicable rules is built. These are generated from the conditional axioms where the outermost symbol of the left hand sides coincides with the outermost symbol of *t*. The copy function is used to produce unique instances of the rules. *stabilize_args*$([t_1, \ldots, t_n], rps, t)$ is called to evaluate successively all subterms of *t* to HNF, which are necessary for determination of a set of applicable rules and to perform unification and rewriting.

apply_rule(ts,rps_{app}**,**rps_{papp}**,t)** is used for the application of a rewrite rule. rps_{app} represents the set of applicable rules, rps_{papp} represents the set of potentially applicable, but not already applicable rules. A rule from rps_{app} is chosen and the algorithm tries to solve the corresponding condition equation by a recursive call of *solve(eqs)*. If a solution is found, and no additional binding of a logical variable was produced, this choice is eliminated to fix the application of the rule.

The application of the selected rule is performed by a call of *get_HNF(r)* using the right hand side *r* of the rule. Note that the variables in *r* are already bound to the corresponding terms, because of the variable sharing of both rule sides.

If there was no rule with solvable conditions, the remaining potentially applicable rules are tried using *stabilize_args*(ts, rps_{papp}, t). If there are no remaining rules, the input term is already in HNF and is returned unchanged.

def_at_pos(rps,i) gives the number of nonvariable patterns at position *i* in the set of rules *rps*. This function is used to select the argument to be evaluated next. The aim is to eliminate by this evaluation as much rules as possible. For rules with a variable at the argument position there is no chance of elimination. Unnecessary argument evaluations are possible in the case of overlapping rules. But our approach tries to reduce the amount of such useless computation.

bind_rule_variables(rps,ts) binds the rule variables to subterms of the input terms.

is_applicable(rp) tests whether a rule *rp* is already applicable.

is_variable(t) tests whether a term *t* is a variable.

stabilize_args(ts,rps,t) performs the lazy unification. First a test is made, whether some rules are already applicable. If so, application is performed after binding the arguments to the rule variables, else arguments are evaluated or instantiations of logical variables are performed.

We prefer argument evaluations over condition evaluations, because:

- To avoid backtracking whenever possible.

- To reduce the number of potentially applicable rules.

In this document we represent lists using the SASL notation for lists. [] denotes the empty list and the list constructing operator : associates to the left. ++ denotes list concatenation, $xs!n$ is the n-th element of xs.

Figure 1: The lazy narrowing algorithm:

```
get_HNF(t) :
    switch t
    f(t1,...,tn) :
            let rps = {copy(eqs, [p1,...,pn], r) | eqs → f(p1,...,pn) = r ∈ AX};
            if rps = { } then return t
            else return stabilize_args([t1,...,tn], rps, t)
    f :     let rps = {(eqs, [], r) | eqs → f = r ∈ AX};
            if rps = {} then return t
            else return apply_rule([], rps, { }, t)
    v :     return t

solve(eqs) :
    switch eqs
    { } :   return
    {l = r ∪ eqs'} :
            let l_HNF = get_HNF(l);
            let r_HNF = get_HNF(r);
            switch l_HNF
            f(t1,...,tn) :
                    switch r_HNF
                    f'(t'1,...,t'n) :
                            if f = f' then solve({t1 = t'1,...,tn = t'n} ∪ eqs'); return
                            else fail
                    f' :    fail
                    v :     v ← f(t1,...,tn); solve(eqs'); return
            f :     switch r_HNF
                    f'(t'1,...,t'n) : fail
                    f' :    if f = f' then solve(eqs'); return
                            else fail
                    v :     v ← f; solve(eqs'); return
            v :     v ← r_HNF; solve(eqs'); return

apply_rule(ts, rps_app, rps_papp, t) :
    choose (eqs, [p1,...,pn], r) ∈ rps_app
            solve(eqs)
            if no binding of a logical variable has been performed since the choose above,
                    remove this choice (to fix the application of the selected rule)
            return get_HNF(r)
    exists_no_more
            if rps_papp ≠ { } then return stabilize_args(ts, rps_papp, t)
            else return t

def_at_pos(rps, i) :
    switch rps
    { } :   return 0
    {(eqs, [p1,...,pi,...,pn], r) ∪ rps'} :
            if is_variable(pi) then return def_at_pos(rps', i)
            else return def_at_pos(rps', i) + 1
```

```
is_variable(t) :
    switch t
    f(t_1,...,t_n) : return false
    f :              return false
    v :              return true

is_applicable((eqs, [p_1,...,p_n], r)) :
    return ∀i ∈ {1,...,n} : is_variable(p_i)

bind_rule_variables(rps, [t_1,...,t_n]) :
    switch rps
    {} : return
    {(eqs, [v_1,...,v_n], r) ∪ rps'} :
         v_1 ← t_1; ...; v_n ← t_n; bind_rule_variables(rps', [t_1,...,t_n]);
         return
```

4.3 How to produce solutions for a goal

Now we explain how the algorithm can be applied to produce solutions for a given goal $g = \{l_1 = r_1, \ldots, l_n = r_n\}$ and a set of conditional axioms AX.

The initial state is the graph corresponding to g and the conditional axioms AX. First of all we have to generate a table which relates the variable names in g to their occurrences in the graph so that we can later reproduce the substitutions of the logical variables in g looking at their occurrence in the final state.

After return from *solve*(g), the state graph contains the first solution (if there is one and the algorithm is able to find it).

But this solution can contain unevaluated arguments. To evaluate a solution completely the function *get*_HNF has to be applied top down to all subterms of the solution.

To produce the next solution **fail** has to be executed which causes backtracking. If there is no more choice, we have generated all possible solutions (if this set is finite and can be derived by lazy narrowing).

4.4 Implementation of the narrowing algorithm

The narrowing algorithm can be regarded as an attempt to maximise both power and efficient implementability. The DAG-representation of terms and rules can be used as a basis for the implementation. After a closer look at the definition of the algorithm we can identify some time consuming operations. So we have to optimize the algorithm without changing its operational behavior.

- The copy operation: Copying of rules is not acceptable for an efficient implementation. It is used to store the bindings of the rule variables. For different rule applications of the same rule different variable bindings are possible.

  Therefore we have to think of a better representation of rule variable bindings. Our abstract machine uses environments for this purpose.

- Most of the work in function *stabilize_args* is independent from the input term and can be performed during a preprocessing (compilation) phase. We will produce a set of decision trees, where every node represents a state in the argument evaluation and instantiation process together with the corresponding set of potentially applicable rules. This technique also substitutes backtracking by conditional branching for the rule selection by pattern matching.

- function symbols in the goal to be evaluated should be represented virtually by a corresponding piece of code, which performs the narrowing process for these symbols. Only already stabilized occurrences, which are part of the resulting solution, will be built on the heap by LANAM.

```
stabilize_args([t_1,...,t_n], rps, t) :
  let rps_app = {rp ∈ rps | is_applicable(rp)};
  if rps_app ≠ { } then
    bind_rule_variables([t_1,...,t_n], rps_app);
    return apply_rule([t_1,...,t_n], rps_app, rps − rps_app, t)
  else
    select i ∈ {1,...,n} so that def_at_pos(rps, i) is maximal;
    let t_HNF = get_HNF(t_i);
    switch t_HNF
    f(t'_1,...,t'_k) :
      let rps' = {(eqs, [p_1,...,p_{i-1}, p_{i+1},...,p_n, p'_1,...,p'_k], r) |
                       (eqs, [p_1,...,p_{i-1}, f(p'_1,...,p'_k), p_{i+1},...,p_n], r) ∈ rps} ∪
                 {(eqs, [p_1,...,p_{i-1}, p_{i+1},...,p_n, v_1,...,v_k], r)[v ← f(v_1,...,v_k)] |
                       (eqs, [p_1,...,p_{i-1}, v, p_{i+1},...,p_n], r) ∈ rps};
      if rps' = { } then
        return t[t_i ← t_HNF]
      else
        return stabilize_args([t_1,...,t_{i-1}, t_{i+1},...,t_n, t'_1,...,t'_k], rps', t[t_i ← t_HNF])
    f : let rps' = {(eqs, [p_1,...,p_{i-1}, p_{i+1},...,p_n], r) |
                       (eqs, [p_1,...,p_{i-1}, f, p_{i+1},...,p_n], r) ∈ rps} ∪
                   {(eqs, [p_1,...,p_{i-1}, p_{i+1},...,p_n], r)[v ← f] |
                       (eqs, [p_1,...,p_{i-1}, v, p_{i+1},...,p_n], r) ∈ rps};
      if rps' = { } then
        return t[t_i ← t_HNF]
      else
        return stabilize_args([t_1,...,t_{i-1}, t_{i+1},...,t_n], rps', t[t_i ← t_HNF])
    v : choose (eqs, [p_1,...,p_{i-1}, f, p_{i+1},...,p_n], r) ∈ rps
        let rps' ={(eqs, [p_1,...,p_{i-1}, p_{i+1},...,p_n], r) |
                       (eqs, [p_1,...,p_{i-1}, f, p_{i+1},...,p_n], r) ∈ rps} ∪
                  {(eqs, [p_1,...,p_{i-1}, p_{i+1},...,p_n], r)[v' ← f] |
                       (eqs, [p_1,...,p_{i-1}, v', p_{i+1},...,p_n], r) ∈ rps};
        return stabilize_args([t_1,...,t_{i-1}, t_{i+1},...,t_n], rps', t[v ← f])
      else_choose (eqs, [p_1,...,p_{i-1}, f(t'_1,...,t'_k), p_{i+1},...,p_n], r) ∈ rps
        let rps' = {(eqs, [p_1,...,p_{i-1}, p_{i+1},...,p_n, p'_1,...,p'_k], r) |
                       (eqs, [p_1,...,p_{i-1}, f(p'_1,...,p'_k), p_{i+1},...,p_n], r) ∈ rps} ∪
                   {(eqs, [p_1,...,p_{i-1}, p_{i+1},...,p_n, v_1,...,v_k], r)[v' ← f(v_1,...,v_k)] |
                       (eqs, [p_1,...,p_{i-1}, v', p_{i+1},...,p_n], r)
        return stabilize_args([t_1,...,t_{i-1}, t_{i+1},...,t_n, v_1,...,v_k],
                              rps', t[v ← f(v_1,...,v_k)])
      exists_no_more
        let rps' ={(eqs, [p_1,...,p_{i-1}, p_{i+1},...,p_n], r)[v' ← f] |
                       (eqs, [p_1,...,p_{i-1}, v', p_{i+1},...,p_n], r) ∈ rps}
        return stabilize_args([t_1,...,t_{i-1}, t_{i+1},...,t_n], rps', t[v ← f])
      if rps' = { } then
        fail
      else
        return stabilize_args([t_1,...,t_{i-1}, t_{i+1},...,t_n], rps', t[t_i ← t_HNF])
```

5 Compilation of rewrite rules into decision trees

The algorithm for the compilation of conditional rewrite rules into decision trees can be derived from the *stabilize_arg* function in the definition of the narrowing algorithm.

The selection of potentially applicable rules depending on the symbol in a pattern position can be done during compile time. We have to produce a tree for each function symbol where each node contains a table relating constructors to sets of potentially applicable rules.

Within the decision trees all occurrences of operation symbols are marked whether they construct data or have to be evaluated further. Symbols to be evaluated are prefixed by a '$' sign.

All operation symbols are assumed to be non constructors, unless they have no defining rules.

default clauses handle the case that no rule is applicable. In this case the symbol **$k** is converted in the corresponding constructor symbol *k* to indicate the position as stabilized.

Our example shows the decision trees generated from a simple (and incomplete) *Set* specification:

```
type Set is Boolean
    sorts char, set
    opns a,b           :           -> char
         greaterchar : char char -> bool
         empty         :           -> set
         insert        : char set  -> set

    eqns forall X,Y: char, Xs,Ys: set
         greaterchar(a,a) = true        ;
         greaterchar(a,b) = false       ;
         greaterchar(b,a) = true        ;
         greaterchar(b,b) = true        ;
         X=Y =>
            insert(X,insert(Y,Ys)) = insert(Y,Ys)   ;
         greaterchar(Y,X) = false =>
            insert(X,insert(Y,Ys)) = insert(Y,insert(X,Ys));
```

The corresponding decision tree is:

```
$greaterchar(V1,V2) =
    switch V1
        a(): switch V2
                 b():       false
                 a():       true
                 variable: [inst V2 by b; false,
                            inst V2 by a; true]
                 otherwise: greaterchar(V1,V2)
        b(): switch V2
                 b():       true
                 a():       true
                 variable: [inst V2 by b; true,
                            inst V2 by a; true]
                 otherwise: greaterchar(V1,V2)
        variable: [inst V1 by a; switch V2
                                     b():       false
                                     a():       true
                                     variable: [inst V2 by b; false,
                                                inst V2 by a; true]
                                     otherwise: greaterchar(V1,V2),
                   inst V1 by b; switch V2
                                     b():       true
                                     a():       true
                                     variable: [inst V2 by b; true,
                                                inst V2 by a; true]
                                     otherwise: greaterchar(V1,V2)]
        otherwise: greaterchar(V1,V2)
```

```
$insert(V1,V2) =
    switch V2
        insert(V3,V4): [V1 = V3 => $insert(V3,V4),
                        $greaterchar(V3,V1) = false =>
                                     $insert(V3,$insert(V1,V4))]

        variable:      inst V2 by $insert(V3,V4);
                                [V1 = V3 => $insert(V3,V4),
                                 $greaterchar(V3,V1) = false =>
                                          $insert(V3,$insert(V1,V4))]

        otherwise:     insert(V1,V2)
```

6 LANAM - an abstract machine for lazy narrowing

6.1 Minimizing of the overhead caused by lazy evaluation

As we can learn from PROLOG implementations [Hi 89] to perform backtracking we need the ability to recover intermediate states in our calculation. In the WAM [War 83] the local stack, which stores the environments of procedures is actually implemented as a tree. Heap space needs to be allocated and garbage collection is only possible if a backtrack step to the last choice is performed. [4]

To implement lazy evaluation we have the additional requirement that representations of unevaluated expressions have to be stored in the heap. This facilitates the deferred evaluation of arguments.

In our approach the local stack is used both for backtracking and for lazy evaluation.

So we have no additional overhead caused by lazy evaluation.

We use closures (pairs of code streams and environments containing the corresponding variable bindings) as representations of unevaluated arguments. The environments are part of the local stack and also necessary for backtracking.

6.2 Representation of terms and environments

The goal currently narrowed at a certain evaluation state contains already stabilized term nodes on top and unevaluated subterms in lower positions. The stabilized nodes are represented by pairs (k, e) consisting of a constructor k and environment pointer e representing the argument nodes. In the literature we can find two possibilities of representing environments: as vectors or as linked lists. We prefer the vector representation because of the linear time needed to access an element in the environment. The environment therefore is a frame containing object pointers $a_1, \ldots, a_n$ following one another in the heap.

Unevaluated subterms are represented by closures (I, e), pairs of code to evaluate the subterm together with the corresponding environment pointer.

To prevent the multiple evaluation of arguments, copying of objects for the evaluation of an argument is avoided (sharing).

After the evaluation of an argument the object representing the unevaluated argument has to be overwritten by the root node of the result. So eventually existing other pointers to the evaluated object can profit from the evaluation.

Subterms (especially variables) can be shared, we use a graph representation of the goals as in the definition of the narrowing algorithm.

Logical (free) variables are represented as special objects $\perp$. They are identified only by their position in the heap. When a variable is instantiated by a term t, the corresponding object in the heap is replaced by the top node of t. The resulting term does not contain the variable any more.

If a variable has to be bound to another variable, we use an indirection object (a, nil) containing an argument pointer pointing to one of the variables and replace the other variable by this object.

This is necessary, because both variables could be subterms of different terms in the goal.

---

[4] Garbage collection is also possible in deterministic computations

So we have to bear in mind that a variable can be represented both by $\perp$ or by an indirection object pointing to a $\perp$ object. We defined the LANAM instructions carefully to avoid the construction of long chains of indirection objects.

6.3 The state of the LANAM machine

Because we avoided flattening of the input rules, the machine architecture has to cope with nested patterns and function applications. This causes a relatively complex structure of the lanam evaluation state.

The current state of evaluation is represented by five kinds of objects in the heap:

- constructor object, consists of a constructor and a frame pointer to a frame containing the arguments, represents a stabilized occurrence.
- closure, consists of a code label and a pointer to the corresponding environment containing the local variable bindings, represents an unevaluated occurrence.
- free variable, identified only by its heap address.
- indirection pointer, contains a pointer to another object.

A state in the abstract machine LANAM is a 8-tuple $\langle I, e, l, r, g, cp, T, H\rangle$ where
I, the LANAM-code stream currently being executed.

e, an environment pointer which addresses the current read environment, which represents the variable bindings of the currently executed function.

l = (e_l, f, I_c, e_c), the current local stack, where:
e_l, the environment pointer which addresses the current write environment, the arguments of a function to be called.
f, frame pointer which addresses the current write frame, arguments of a constructor node to be built.
I_c, the continuation LANAM-code stream to be executed after the next return to the caller.
e_c, the continuation environment belonging to I_c. r, the return object pointer (accumulator).

g = (gf, pg), the goal frame pointer which addresses arguments in the current goal to be solved and an index indicating the goal arguments which are currently to be evaluated and compared.

cp, the choice point pointer which addresses the last choice point. Previous choice points can be reached using the choice point pointer stored in the last choice point.

T, the trail stack. In this stack all instantiations of free variables and all lazy evaluations of arguments are recorded. If backtracking needs to be done the trail stack is used to recover the old machine state defined by the last choice point.

H, the heap: a mapping from heap addresses to objects, environments, frames, goal frames and choice points. The objects in the heap represent the term reduced so far.

Environments have the structure $(a_1, \ldots, a_n, e_p, I_c, e_c, cp)$ they contain pointers to arguments, parent environment, continuation and to the corresponding choice point. They have much similarity with task nodes [Mor90]. The difference is, that environments represent the arguments needed for the evaluation of deferred parts of a function body where task nodes in [Mor90] represent arguments of a function call. In other words, environments are related to functions after pattern matching is done, they contain additional arguments generated during pattern matching.

With our approach we avoid LOAD instructions for copying arguments to the local stack. For converting a write environment into a read environment only an environment pointer has to be copied.

But we waste memory, because at allocation time it is not known exactly, how much additional arguments are generated by pattern matching. It depends on the selected rewrite rule.

Frames have a simpler structure $(a_1, \ldots, a_n, f_p)$, they contain the arguments of a constructor and a pointer to a parent frame which is needed for backtracking.

Choicepoints $(I_{fail}, e, l, r, g, cp, T, s)$ contain information needed to recover a stored machine state.

The main differences to the WAM are:

- missing registers. The only register used by LANAM is the return register (accumulator) **r**. Arguments are accessed directly from environments in memory. Our design regards register allocation as an optimization.
- variables are represented in the WAM as self-referential pointers. In LANAM variables are represented only by their memory location. There are no explicit variable nodes.
- support of full indexing in all arguments.
- no read/write mode flag, the different modes are represented by distinct instructions. This enables further optimizations as described in [Roy 90].
- lazy evaluation of the conditions (called clause body for the WAM).

6.4 LANAM instructions

We distinguish four classes of instructions:

Environment and frame instructions

push_arg push accumulator on write environment
push_frame push accumulator on write frame
get_env read accumulator from read environment
update_arg overwrite argument of write environment by the object pointed to by the accumulator
update_env overwrite argument of read environment by the object pointed to by the accumulator
unpack push arguments of the constructor object pointed to by the accumulator on the write environment.
change_env the current write environment becomes the new read environment, the father of this environment becomes the new write environment.
set_inst load accumulator by empty variable binding
set_variables initialize arguments of the write environment by empty variable bindings.
release_env remove current write environment, the father of this environment becomes the new write environment.

Heap allocation instructions

new_environment build new write environment
new_frame build new write frame
new_const build new constant node and load accumulator with a pointer to it
new_node build new constructor node and load accumulator with a pointer to it
get_code build new closure and load accumulator with a pointer to it

Control instructions

call_code jump to instruction, store continuation
call_arg evaluate argument in write environment
call_env evaluate argument in read environment
return return to caller
select perform indexing, branch to code corresponding to a pattern

Backtracking instructions

try_me build choicepoint
retry_me branch to alternative, modify current choicepoint
trust_me remove current choicepoint
test_goal test condition
remove_choice remove current choicepoint if it corresponds to the current read environment

A formal definition of the operational semantics of LANAM can be found in [Wo 91].

6.5 Translating decision trees in LANAM code

LANAM-code of each decision tree consists of four parts:

1. matching code to determine the applicable rewrite rules for given arguments;

2. code for the instantiation of free variables
3. code for the lazy evaluation of the conditions
4. code for the function bodies (corresponding to the right hand sides of the rewrite rules).

The matching code could test each pattern in turn to see whether it matched the argument. In practice it is more efficient to merge these tests into a single matching tree.

All arguments for the function code are expected to be in the current write environment. During the matching process arguments are evaluated and the arguments of the results are appended to the write environment. After a matching rule was found, the read environment becomes this environment, and a new write environment is allocated.

So the read environment then contains a list of all variable bindings needed by the code for the function body.

The code for the instantiation of free variables instantiates variables in the goal to be solved to make a rewrite rule applicable. If there are several alternatives a choice point is stored on the heap. If backtracking has to be performed the old machine state is restored and the evaluation continues with the next alternative.

The code for the lazy evaluation of the conditions determines the applicability of a rewrite rule. Therefore the substitution instances of both sides of the conditions are simultaneously narrowed until normal forms are reached or the stabilized parts of the instances are different.

The code for the function body consists of function calls corresponding to the operation symbols contained in the body.

6.6 LANAM code generation

The code generation is divided into 10 compilation schemes:

G is used to build the global environment δ from the list of decision trees *decs*. δ binds the definitions to the operation symbols of the transformed term rewriting system.

M produces code to perform narrowing of a input goal *eqs*. Execution of this code gives the head normal forms of the first solution if there is one. The other solutions can be calculated via backtracking.

First LANAM is initialized by instruction **init**. The machine starts with an empty heap and trailstack. **new_environment** allocates a new write environment holding the variable bindings of the free variables in the compiled goal. *freenum* is a function to determine the number of free variables in the goal *eqs*. **set_variables** initializes the environment variables. **change_env** moves the write environment to the read environment, and the code from *eqs* by scheme E performs the generation of solutions by narrowing.

F is the scheme producing code for stabilizing a (sub)term which has $\$k$ as its outermost symbol. A local environment γ is built, where every variable is bound to an integer representing the position of the variable binding in the local stack rsp. in an environment of a closure representing a subterm of the function body (right hand side of the compiled rules).

The code given by F expects the arguments [5] in the write environment. These arguments are narrowed to HNF and replaced by the results , if their evaluation is needed to determine an applicable rule.

C gives code that performs the selection of an applicable rewrite rule. **call_arg** stabilizes an argument if it is not already in HNF, **update_arg** overwrites the argument in the write environment by the result and **select** uses the result to select the code for the corresponding path in the decision tree. **unpack** appends the direct subterms of the result to the write environment.

γ is extended to bind the new variables vs_i to these subterms.

A function body t is compiled into a **change_env** instruction which sets the read environment to point to the write environment, and sets the write environment to point to its parent, followed by the code produced by scheme B.

I and CO give code for the instantiation of free variables rsp. the evaluation of conditions.

A list of instantiation alternatives *is* or condition cases *cos* is compiled into a code sequence *try_me*...*retry_me*...*retry_me*...*trust_me*. These instructions implement backtracking similar as in

[5] pointer to subterms under the position of $\$k$ in the term

the WAM [War 83]. **try_me** generates a choicepoint, **retry_me** modifies this choicepoint to point to the next alternative and **trust_me** removes the choicepoint and continues with the last alternative.

An instantiation expression *inst v by t* is compiled into code that builds the term t in the heap (new_const or new_node), overwrites v in the local stack by t (update_arg) and appends the direct subterms of t to the write environment (unpack).

E is used to produce code for the compilation of condition equations and for terms. The code for terms performs lazy evaluation and produces a HNF of the compiled term. E uses an environment α, which gives for every function symbol $\$k$ the maximal environment size needed for the arguments of $\$k$.

A conditional expression $eqs \rightarrow t$ is compiled into the instructions **change_env** to set the read environment, code for the condition equations eqs, **remove_choice** to remove the condition choice point, and finally code for the function body t.

A condition equation $t_l = t_r$ is compiled into a **new_environment 1** instruction to allocate a new write environment of size 1, which is used to store the result of the evaluation of t_l, followed by code for t_l and t_r, a **test_goal** instruction which performs the comparison of the results and finally a **release_env** instruction to release the allocated write environment.

The code produced by scheme E for a term t performs the reduction of t to HNF. A function application $\$k(t_1,\ldots,t_n)$ is compiled into a **call_code** instruction which gets as argument the code for $t_1,\ldots,t_n$ followed by a jump to the code for function $\$k$. **call_code** stores the return address and the current environment.

A constructor application $k(t_1,\ldots,t_n)$ is compiled into code that builds a constructor node in the heap using the instruction **new_node** after the code for $t_1,\ldots,t_n$ was executed (and has put the results of the evaluations of the t_i onto the write frame).

A variable is compiled into the instruction **get_env** to copy its binding to the accumulator.

T produces code for subterms of the body or of the condition equations. The **get_code** instruction is used to build a closure for the deferred evaluation of t.

B gives the code for the function body (the right hand sides of the compiled rules). It calls T for the evaluation of arguments. If the body is an constructor term, a **return** instruction is appended to the code which restores the return address and the current environment of the caller.

D is used to produce code for the default case that means, no rewrite rule is applicable. The function symbol $\$k$ is substituted by the corresponding constructor symbol k, the scheme B is called.

Figure 2: LANAM compilation scheme

1. $\mathsf{M}\,[\![eqs]\!] = [init, new\_environment\ (freenum\ eqs), set\_variables(1, freenum\ eqs), change\_env]$ ++ $(\mathsf{E}\,[\![eqs]\!]\ (\mathsf{G}\,[\![decs_E]\!]\ \delta_{arid})\ \gamma_{arid})$

2. $\mathsf{G}\,[\![[\,]]\!]\ \delta = \delta$

   $\mathsf{G}\,[\![(\$k\ vs = we) : decs]\!]\ \delta = \mathsf{G}\,[\![decs]\!]\ (\delta \oplus \{\$k \mapsto [\![\$k\ vs = we]\!]\})$

3. $\mathsf{F}\,[\![\$k\ vs = we]\!] = \mathsf{C}\,[\![we]\!]\ (\mathsf{G}\,[\![decs_E]\!]\ \delta_{arid}\ \gamma_{arid}\ (1 + \#vs))$

4. $\mathsf{C}\,[\![switch\ v\ [k_1\ vs_1 : we_1, \ldots, k_n\ vs_n : we_n], variable : is, otherwise : we\,]\!]\ \delta\ \gamma\ d$

   $= [call\_arg\ (\gamma\ v), update\_arg\ (\gamma\ v),$
   $select\ (\gamma\ v)$
   $[k_1 : [unpack\ (\gamma\ v)]$ ++
   $\mathsf{C}\,[\![we_1]\!]\ \delta\ (getenv\ vs_1\ d\ \gamma)\ (d + \#vs_1), \ldots,$
   $k_n : [unpack\ (\gamma\ v)]$ ++
   $\mathsf{C}\,[\![we_n]\!]\ \delta\ (getenv\ vs_n\ d\ \gamma)\ (d + \#vs_n)]$
   $(\mathsf{I}\,[\![is\ we]\!]\ \delta\ \gamma\ d)\ (\mathsf{C}\,[\![we]\!]\ \delta\ \gamma\ d)$

   $\mathsf{C}\,[\![t]\!]\ \delta\ \gamma\ d = set\_variables(d, envsize(t)) : change\_env : \mathsf{B}\,[\![t]\!]\ \delta\ \gamma$

   $\mathsf{C}\,[\![cos\ we]\!]\ \delta\ \gamma\ d = set\_variables(d, envsize(co)) : \mathsf{CO}\,[\![cos\ we]\!]\ \delta\ \gamma\ d$

   $\mathsf{C}\,[\![default : t]\!]\ \delta\ \gamma\ d = change\_env : \mathsf{D}\,[\![t]\!]\ \delta\ \gamma$

5. $\mathsf{I}\,[\![[\,]\ we]\!]\ \delta\ \gamma\ d = \mathsf{C}\,[\![we]\!]\ \delta\ \gamma\ d$

   $\mathsf{I}\,[\![[i]\ default : t]\!]\ \delta\ \gamma\ d = \mathsf{I}\,[\![i]\!]\ \delta\ \gamma\ d$

   $\mathsf{I}\,[\![i : is\ we]\!]\ \delta\ \gamma\ d = try\_me\ (\mathsf{I}'\,[\![is\ we]\!]\ \delta\ \gamma\ d) : (\mathsf{I}\,[\![i]\!]\ \delta\ \gamma\ d)$

   $\mathsf{I}'\,[\![[\,]\ we]\!]\ \delta\ \gamma\ d = trust\_me : \mathsf{C}\,[\![we]\!]\ \delta\ \gamma\ d$

   $\mathsf{I}'\,[\![[i]\ default : t]\!]\ \delta\ \gamma\ d = trust\_me : \mathsf{I}\,[\![i]\!]\ \delta\ \gamma\ d$

$$\mathsf{I}' [\![i : is\ we]\!]\ \delta\ \gamma\ d = retry\_me\ (\mathsf{I}' [\![is\ we]\!]\ \delta\ \gamma\ d) : (\mathsf{I} [\![i]\!]\ \delta\ \gamma\ d)$$

$$\mathsf{I} [\![inst\ v\ by\ k;\ we]\!]\ \delta\ \gamma\ d = [new\_const\ k, update\_arg\ (\gamma\ v)] +\!\!+ (\mathsf{C} [\![we]\!]\ \delta\ \gamma\ d)$$

$$\mathsf{I} [\![inst\ v\ by\ k(v_1, \ldots, v_n);\ we]\!]\ \delta\ \gamma\ d = [new\_frame\ n, set\_inst, push\_frame\ 1, \ldots, set\_inst, push\_frame\ n, new\_node\ k\ n, update\_arg\ (\gamma\ v), unpack\ d] +\!\!+ (\mathsf{C} [\![we]\!]\ \delta\ (getenv\ [v_1, \ldots, v_n]\ d\ \gamma)\ (d+n))$$

6. $$\mathsf{CO} [\![[\,]\ we]\!]\ \delta\ \gamma\ d = \mathsf{C} [\![we]\!]\ \delta\ \gamma\ d)$$

$$\mathsf{CO} [\![co : cos\ we]\!]\ \delta\ \gamma\ d = try\_me\ (\mathsf{CO}' [\![cos\ we]\!]\ \delta\ \gamma\ d) : (\mathsf{E} [\![co]\!]\ \delta\ \gamma)$$

$$\mathsf{CO}' [\![[\,]\ we]\!]\ \delta\ \gamma\ d = trust\_me : \mathsf{C} [\![we]\!]\ \delta\ \gamma\ d)$$

$$\mathsf{CO}' [\![co : cos\ we]\!]\ \delta\ \gamma\ d = retry\_me\ (\mathsf{CO}' [\![cos\ we]\!]\ \delta\ \gamma\ d) : (\mathsf{E} [\![co]\!]\ \delta\ \gamma)$$

7. $$\mathsf{E} [\![eqs \rightarrow t]\!]\ \delta\ \gamma = change\_env : (\mathsf{E} [\![eqs]\!]\ \delta\ \gamma) +\!\!+ [remove\_choice] +\!\!+ (\mathsf{B} [\![t]\!]\ \delta\ \gamma)$$

$$\mathsf{E} [\![[\,]]\!]\ \delta\ \gamma = [\,]$$

$$\mathsf{E} [\![eq : eqs]\!]\ \delta\ \gamma = (\mathsf{E} [\![eq]\!]\ \delta\ \gamma) +\!\!+ (\mathsf{E} [\![eqs]\!]\ \delta\ \gamma)$$

$$\mathsf{E} [\![t_l = t_r]\!]\ \delta\ \gamma = [new\_environment\ 1] +\!\!+ (\mathsf{E} [\![t_l]\!]\ \delta\ \gamma) +\!\!+ [push\_arg\ 1] +\!\!+ (\mathsf{E} [\![t_r]\!]\ \delta\ \gamma) +\!\!+ [test\_goal, release\_env]$$

$$\mathsf{E} [\![\$k]\!]\ \delta\ \gamma = [call\_code([new\_environment\ (\alpha\ \$k)] +\!\!+ (\mathsf{F} [\![(\delta\ \$k)]\!]\ \delta))$$

$$\mathsf{E} [\![\$k(t_1, \ldots, t_n)]\!]\ \delta\ \gamma = [call\_code\ ([new\_environment\ (\alpha\ \$k)] +\!\!+ (\mathsf{T} [\![t_1]\!]\ \delta\ \gamma\ (\psi\ \$k)!1) +\!\!+ [push\_arg\ 1] \cdots +\!\!+ (\mathsf{T} [\![t_n]\!]\ \delta\ \gamma\ (\psi\ \$k)!n) +\!\!+ [push\_arg\ n] \cdots +\!\!+ (\mathsf{F} [\![(\delta\ \$k)]\!]\ \delta))$$

$$\mathsf{E} [\![k]\!]\ \delta\ \gamma = [new\_const\ k]$$

$$\mathsf{E} [\![k(t_1, \ldots, t_n)]\!]\ \delta\ \gamma = [new\_frame\ n] +\!\!+ (\mathsf{T} [\![t_1]\!]\ \delta\ \gamma\ (\psi\ k)!1) +\!\!+ [push\_frame\ 1] +\!\!+ \cdots +\!\!+ (\mathsf{T} [\![t_n]\!]\ \delta\ \gamma\ (\psi\ k)!n) +\!\!+ [push\_frame\ n] +\!\!+ [new\_node\ k\ n]$$

$$\mathsf{E} [\![v]\!]\ \delta\ \gamma = [call\_env\ (\gamma\ v), update\_env\ (\gamma\ v)$$

8. $$\mathsf{T} [\![\$k]\!]\ \delta\ \gamma = [get\_code([new\_environment\ (\alpha\ \$k)] +\!\!+ (\mathsf{F} [\![(\delta\ \$k)]\!]\ \delta))$$

$$\mathsf{T} [\![\$k(t_1, \ldots, t_n)]\!]\ \delta\ \gamma = [get\_code\ ([new\_environment\ (\alpha\ \$k)] +\!\!+ (\mathsf{T} [\![t_1]\!]\ \delta\ \gamma\ (\psi\ \$k)!1) +\!\!+ [push\_arg\ 1] \cdots +\!\!+ \cdots +\!\!+ (\mathsf{T} [\![t_n]\!]\ \delta\ \gamma\ (\psi\ \$k)!n) +\!\!+ [push\_arg\ n]s +\!\!+ (\mathsf{F} [\![(\delta\ \$k)]\!]\ \delta))]$$

$$\mathsf{T} [\![k]\!]\ \delta\ \gamma = [new\_const\ k]$$

$$\mathsf{T} [\![k(t_1, \ldots, t_n)]\!]\ \delta\ \gamma = [new\_frame\ n] +\!\!+ (\mathsf{T} [\![t_1]\!]\ \delta\ \gamma\ (\psi\ k)!1) +\!\!+ [push\_frame\ 1] +\!\!+ \cdots +\!\!+ (\mathsf{T} [\![t_n]\!]\ \delta\ \gamma\ (\psi\ k)!n) +\!\!+ [push\_frame\ n] +\!\!+ [new\_node\ k\ n]$$

$$\mathsf{T} [\![v]\!]\ \delta\ \gamma = [get\_env\ (\gamma\ v)]$$

9. $$\mathsf{B} [\![\$k]\!]\ \delta\ \gamma = new\_environment\ (\alpha\ \$k) : (\mathsf{F} [\![(\delta\ \$k)]\!]\ \delta)$$

$$\mathsf{B} [\![\$k(t_1, \ldots, t_n)]\!]\ \delta\ \gamma = [new\_environment\ (\alpha\ \$k)] +\!\!+ \mathsf{T} [\![t_1]\!]\ \delta\ \gamma +\!\!+ [push\_arg\ 1] \cdots +\!\!+ \mathsf{T} [\![t_n]\!]\ \delta\ \gamma +\!\!+ [push\_arg\ n] \cdots +\!\!+ (\mathsf{F} [\![(\delta\ \$k)]\!]\ \delta)$$

$$\mathsf{B} [\![\$k]\!]\ \delta\ \gamma = \mathsf{E} [\![\$k]\!]\ \delta\ \gamma$$

$$\mathsf{B} [\![\$k(t_1, \ldots, t_n)]\!]\ \delta\ \gamma = \mathsf{E} [\![\$k(t_1, \ldots, t_n)]\!]\ \delta\ \gamma$$

$$\mathsf{B} [\![k]\!]\ \delta\ \gamma = [new\_const\ k, return]$$

$$\mathsf{B} [\![k(t_1, \ldots, t_n)]\!]\ \delta\ \gamma = \mathsf{E} [\![k(t_1, \ldots, t_n)]\!]\ \delta\ \gamma +\!\!+ [return]$$

$\mathsf{B} [\![v]\!]\ \delta\ \gamma$ (if v is not free) $= [new\_environment\ 0, call\_env\ (\gamma\ v), update\_env\ (\gamma\ v), release\_env, return]$

$\mathsf{B} [\![v]\!]\ \delta\ \gamma$ (if v is free) $= [get\_env\ (\gamma\ v), return]$

10. $$\mathsf{D} [\![\$k]\!]\ \delta\ \gamma = \mathsf{B} [\![k]\!]\ \delta\ \gamma$$

$$\mathsf{D} [\![\$k(t_1, \ldots, t_n)]\!]\ \delta\ \gamma = \mathsf{B} [\![k(t_1, \ldots, t_n)]\!]\ \delta\ \gamma$$

Figure 3: auxiliary functions

The mapping combining operator $\oplus$ is defined by $\gamma \oplus \{I \mapsto x\} = \lambda I'.((I' = I) \longrightarrow\ x,\ \gamma\ I')$ and by its associativity.

$getenv\ \ (v : vs)\ \ n\ \ \gamma\ \ = getenv\ \ vs\ \ (n+1)\ \ (\gamma \oplus \{v \mapsto n\})$ (builds an environment)

$getenv\ \ [\,]\ \ n\ \ \gamma\ \ = \gamma$

Figure 4: syntax of decision trees

decs	::=	$[dec_1, \ldots, dec_n]$	decision tree list
dec	::=	$\$k\ vs = we$	decision tree
we	::=	*switch v ces variable* : *is otherwise* : *we*	
		| *cos we*| *t*| *default* : *t*	switch expression
ces	::=	$[ce_1, \ldots, ce_n]$	case expression list
ce	::=	*k vs* : *we*	case expression
is	::=	$[i_1, \ldots, i_n]$	instantiation alternative list
i	::=	*inst v by t*; *we*	instantiation alternative
cos	::=	$[co_1, \ldots, co_n]$	condition case list
co	::=	$eqs \rightarrow t$	condition case
eqs	::=	$[eq_1, \ldots, eq_n]$	equation list
eq	::=	$t_l = t_r$	equation
t	::=	$v \mid k \mid \$k$	
		$\mid k(t_1, \ldots, t_n) \mid \$k(t_1, \ldots, t_n)$	term
vs	::=	$[v_1, \ldots, v_n]$	variable list
v	:	variable symbol	
k	:	constructor symbol	
$k	:	function symbol	

7 Implementation and first performance results

LANAM code can both be interpreted or macroexpanded into machine code. A LANAM interpreter written in C is used as part of a LOTOS simulator [Eij 90]. LOTOS is a specification language for the design of protocols and distributed systems and uses algebraic specifications for the formal description of data types.

On a SUN 4/60 the LANAM interpreter performs 15000-25000 narrowing derivations per second.

This is slower than usual WAM-based PROLOG compilers, but it is a good result, if we compare it with other implementations of narrowing. Optimizations similar to WAM optimizations [Hi 89] are possible also for LANAM.

8 Conclusion

We tried to define a narrowing algorithm which maximizes both power and efficiency.

We regard a narrowing algorithm as efficiently implementable, if unification, normalization and comparison of goals can be performed simultaneously by only one tree traversal.

The additional requirement that fruitless narrowing paths have early to be eliminated leads directly to the lazy narrowing algorithm.

Further requirements as shared data representations, reusage of partial unifications, preprocessing of the left hand sides of the rules for unification and virtual representation of unevaluated terms have directed the design of LANAM.

Execution speed can further be increased, if we would combine narrowing and rewriting by usage of LANAM and LATERM [Wo 89]. Therefore the rules have to be subdivided into two groups, one applicable for narrowing, the other only for rewriting.

This division can be done by annotations or automatically by adapting well known data flow analysis techniques from logic and functional programming [Son 89, Roy 90].

Using this technique we get an efficient execution model for algebraic specifications and for logical functional languages.

References

[Au 87] L. Augustsson: Compiling Lazy Functional Languages, Part 2. *PhD thesis, Chalmers Tekniska Högskola, Göteborg, Sweden*, 1987

[Bal 89] G.P.Balboni,P.G.Bosco,C.Cecchi,R.Melen,C.Moiso,G.Sofi: Implementation of a Parallel Logic Plus Functional Language. *P.Treleaven(ed.), Parallel Computers: Object Oriented, Functional and Logic 175-214, Wiley*, 1989

[Bos 89] P.G.Bosco, C.Cecchi, C.Moiso: An extension of WAM for K-LEAF: a WAM-based compilation of conditional narrowing. *Proc. 6. International Conference on Logic Programming(Lisboa), MIT Press*,1989

[Eij 90] Peter van Eijk, Henk Eertink: Design of the LOTOSPHERE Symbolic LOTOS Simulator. *Proceedings of the third symposium on Formal description techniques, (ed) Enrique Vazquez*, 1990

[Fa 87] J. Fairbairn; S. C. Wray: Tim: A Simple, Lazy Abstract Machine to Execute Supercombinators. *Functional Programming Languages and Computer Architecture, Springer, Lecture Notes in Computer Science 274*, 1987

[Han90] M.Hanus: Compiling Logic Programs with Equality. *Springer, LNCS 456*, 1990

[Hi 89] T.Hickey,S.Mudambi: Global Compilation of Prolog. *Journal of Logic Programming 1989:7:192-230*, 1989

[Hoel88] S.Hölldobler: Functional Logic Programming, *Springer, LNCS 353*, 1989

[Huss86] A.Geser,H.Hussmann: Experiences with the RAP system - a specification interpreter combining term rewriting and resolution. *Springer, LNCS 213*, 1986

[JoD 89] A.Josephson,N.Dershowitz: An Implementation of Narrowing. *Journal of Logic Programming 6,1989:57-77*, 1989

[Jos 87] T. Johnsson: Compiling Lazy Functional Languages, Part 1 *PhD thesis, Chalmers Tekniska Högskola, Göteborg, Sweden*, 1987

[Mue 90] A.Mück: Compilation of Narrowing. *Springer, LNCS 456*, August 1990

[Mor90] J.J.Moreno-Navarro,H.Kuchen,R.Loogen: Lazy Narrowing in a Graph Machine. *Springer, LNCS 463*, 1990

[Pad 87] P.Padawitz: Strategy-Controlled Reduction and Narrowing. *Proceedings of the Second Conference on Rewriting Techniques and Applications, Springer LNCS 256, Bordeaux (France)*, 1987

[Pad 88] P.Padawitz: Computing in Horn Clause Theories. *Springer EATCS Monographs on Theor. Com. Sci.*, 1988

[Red 87] U.S.Reddy: Functional Logic Languages. *Workshop on Graph Reduction, Springer LNCS 279*,1987

[Roy 90] P.L van Roy: Can Logic Programming Execute as Fast as Imperative Programming. Report No. UCB/CSD 90/600, University of California Berkeley, December 1990

[Son 89] H.Sondergaard: Semanic-Based Analysis and Transformations of Logic Programs. *Technical Report 89/21, University of Melbourne*,1989

[War 83] D.H.D.Warren: An Abstract Prolog Instruction Set, *SRI International, Technical Note 309*, October 1983

[Wo 89] D. Wolz, P.Boehm: Compilation of LOTOS Data Type Specifications. *Proc. of the IFIP TC6-WG 6.1, 9th International Symposium on Protocol Specification, Testing and Verification (ed. E.brinksma, G.Scollo, C.A. Vissers*, 1989

[Wo 91] D. Wolz: Lazy Evaluation of Functional Logic Languages. *Technical Report, Technical University Berlin, to appear*,1991

Lecture Notes in Computer Science

For information about Vols. 1–454
please contact your bookseller or Springer-Verlag

Vol. 455: C.A. Floudas, P.M. Pardalos, A Collection of Test Problems for Constrained Global Optimization Algorithms. XIV, 180 pages. 1990.

Vol. 456: P. Deransart, J. Maluszyński (Eds.), Programming Language Implementation and Logic Programming. Proceedings, 1990. VIII, 401 pages. 1990.

Vol. 457: H. Burkhart (Ed.), CONPAR '90 – VAPP IV. Proceedings, 1990. XIV, 900 pages. 1990.

Vol. 458: J.C.M. Baeten, J.W. Klop (Eds.), CONCUR '90. Proceedings, 1990. VII, 537 pages. 1990.

Vol. 459: R. Studer (Ed.), Natural Language and Logic. Proceedings, 1989. VII, 252 pages. 1990. (Subseries LNAI).

Vol. 460: J. Uhl, H.A. Schmid, A Systematic Catalogue of Reusable Abstract Data Types. XII, 344 pages. 1990.

Vol. 461: P. Deransart, M. Jourdan (Eds.), Attribute Grammars and their Applications. Proceedings, 1990. VIII, 358 pages. 1990.

Vol. 462: G. Gottlob, W. Nejdl (Eds.), Expert Systems in Engineering. Proceedings, 1990. IX, 260 pages. 1990. (Subseries LNAI).

Vol. 463: H. Kirchner, W. Wechler (Eds.), Algebraic and Logic Programming. Proceedings, 1990. VII, 386 pages. 1990.

Vol. 464: J. Dassow, J. Kelemen (Eds.), Aspects and Prospects of Theoretical Computer Science. Proceedings, 1990. VI, 298 pages. 1990.

Vol. 465: A. Fuhrmann, M. Morreau (Eds.), The Logic of Theory Change. Proceedings, 1989. X, 334 pages. 1991. (Subseries LNAI).

Vol. 466: A. Blaser (Ed.), Database Systems of the 90s. Proceedings, 1990. VIII, 334 pages. 1990.

Vol. 467: F. Long (Ed.), Software Engineering Environments. Proceedings, 1969. VI, 313 pages. 1990.

Vol. 468: S.G. Akl, F. Fiala, W.W. Koczkodaj (Eds.), Advances in Computing and Information – ICCI '90. Proceedings, 1990. VII, 529 pages. 1990.

Vol. 469: I. Guessarian (Ed.), Semantics of Systeme of Concurrent Processes. Proceedings, 1990. V, 456 pages. 1990.

Vol. 470: S. Abiteboul, P.C. Kanellakis (Eds.), ICDT '90. Proceedings, 1990. VII, 528 pages. 1990.

Vol. 471: B.C. Ooi, Efficient Query Processing in Geographic Information Systems. VIII, 208 pages. 1990.

Vol. 472: K.V. Nori, C.E. Veni Madhavan (Eds.), Foundations of Software Technology and Theoretical Computer Science. Proceedings, 1990. X, 420 pages. 1990.

Vol. 473: I.B. Damgård (Ed.), Advances in Cryptology – EUROCRYPT '90. Proceedings, 1990. VIII, 500 pages. 1991.

Vol. 474: D. Karagiannis (Ed.), Information Syetems and Artificial Intelligence: Integration Aspects. Proceedings, 1990. X, 293 pages. 1991. (Subseries LNAI).

Vol. 475: P. Schroeder-Heister (Ed.), Extensions of Logic Programming. Proceedings, 1989. VIII, 364 pages. 1991. (Subseries LNAI).

Vol. 476: M. Filgueiras, L. Damas, N. Moreira, A.P. Tomás (Eds.), Natural Language Processing. Proceedings, 1990. VII, 253 pages. 1991. (Subseries LNAI).

Vol. 477: D. Hammer (Ed.), Compiler Compilers. Proceedings, 1990. VI, 227 pages. 1991.

Vol. 478: J. van Eijck (Ed.), Logics in AI. Proceedings, 1990. IX, 562 pages. 1991. (Subseries in LNAI).

Vol. 480: C. Choffrut, M. Jantzen (Eds.), STACS 91. Proceedings, 1991. X, 549 pages. 1991.

Vol. 481: E. Lang, K.-U. Carstensen, G. Simmons, Modelling Spatial Knowledge on a Linguistic Basis. IX, 138 pages. 1991. (Subseries LNAI).

Vol. 482: Y. Kodratoff (Ed.), Machine Learning – EWSL-91. Proceedings, 1991. XI, 537 pages. 1991. (Subseries LNAI).

Vol. 483: G. Rozenberg (Ed.), Advances In Petri Nets 1990. VI, 515 pages. 1991.

Vol. 484: R. H. Möhring (Ed.), Graph-Theoretic Concepts In Computer Science. Proceedings, 1990. IX, 360 pages. 1991.

Vol. 485: K. Furukawa, H. Tanaka, T. Fullsaki (Eds.), Logic Programming '89. Proceedings, 1989. IX, 183 pages. 1991. (Subseries LNAI).

Vol. 486: J. van Leeuwen, N. Santoro (Eds.), Distributed Algorithms. Proceedings, 1990. VI, 433 pages. 1991.

Vol. 487: A. Bode (Ed.), Distributed Memory Computing. Proceedings, 1991. XI, 506 pages. 1991.

Vol. 488: R. V. Book (Ed.), Rewriting Techniques and Applications. Proceedings, 1991. VII, 458 pages. 1991.

Vol. 489: J. W. de Bakker, W. P. de Roever, G. Rozenberg (Eds.), Foundations of Object-Oriented Languages. Proceedings, 1990. VIII, 442 pages. 1991.

Vol. 490: J. A. Bergstra, L. M. G. Feljs (Eds.), Algebraic Methods 11: Theory, Tools and Applicatlons. VI, 434 pages. 1991.

Vol. 491: A. Yonezawa, T. Ito (Eds.), Concurrency: Theory, Language, and Architecture. Proceedings, 1989. VIII, 339 pages. 1991.

Vol. 492: D. Sriram, R. Logcher, S. Fukuda (Eds.), Computer-Aided Cooperative Product Development. Proceedings, 1989 VII, 630 pages. 1991.

Vol. 493: S. Abramsky, T. S. E. Maibaum (Eds.), TAPSOFT '91. Volume 1. Proceedings, 1991. VIII, 455 pages. 1991.

Vol. 494: S. Abramsky, T. S. E. Maibaum (Eds.), TAPSOFT '91. Volume 2. Proceedings, 1991. VIII, 482 pages. 1991.

Vol. 495: 9. Thalheim, J. Demetrovics, H.-D. Gerhardt (Eds.), MFDBS '91. Proceedings, 1991. VI, 395 pages. 1991.

Vol. 496: H.-P. Schwefel, R. Männer (Eds.), Parallel Problem Solving from Nature. Proceedings, 1991. XI, 485 pages. 1991.

Vol. 497: F. Dehne, F. Fiala. W.W. Koczkodaj (Eds.), Advances in Computing and Intormation - ICCI '91 Proceedings, 1991. VIII, 745 pages. 1991.

Vol. 498: R. Andersen, J. A. Bubenko jr., A. Sølvberg (Eds.), Advanced Information Systems Engineering. Proceedings, 1991. VI, 579 pages. 1991.

Vol. 499: D. Christodoulakis (Ed.), Ada: The Choice for '92. Proceedings, 1991. VI, 411 pages. 1991.

Vol. 500: M. Held, On the Computational Geometry of Pocket Machining. XII, 179 pages. 1991.

Vol. 501: M. Bidoit, H.-J. Kreowski, P. Lescanne, F. Orejas, D. Sannella (Eds.), Algebraic System Specification and Development. VIII, 98 pages. 1991.

Vol. 502: J. Bārzdiņš, D. Bjørner (Eds.), Baltic Computer Science. X, 619 pages. 1991.

Vol. 503: P. America (Ed.), Parallel Database Systems. Proceedings, 1990. VIII, 433 pages. 1991.

Vol. 504: J. W. Schmidt, A. A. Stogny (Eds.), Next Generation Information System Technology. Proceedings, 1990. IX, 450 pages. 1991.

Vol. 505: E. H. L. Aarts, J. van Leeuwen, M. Rem (Eds.), PARLE '91. Parallel Architectures and Languages Europe, Volume I. Proceedings, 1991. XV, 423 pages. 1991.

Vol. 506: E. H. L. Aarts, J. van Leeuwen, M. Rem (Eds.), PARLE '91. Parallel Architectures and Languages Europe, Volume II. Proceedings, 1991. XV, 489 pages. 1991.

Vol. 507: N. A. Sherwani, E. de Doncker, J. A. Kapenga (Eds.), Computing in the 90's. Proceedings, 1989. XIII, 441 pages. 1991.

Vol. 508: S. Sakata (Ed.), Applied Algebra, Algebraic Algorithms and Error-Correcting Codes. Proceedings, 1990. IX, 390 pages. 1991.

Vol. 509: A. Endres, H. Weber (Eds.), Software Development Environments and CASE Technology. Proceedings, 1991. VIII, 286 pages. 1991.

Vol. 510: J. Leach Albert, B. Monien, M. Rodríguez (Eds.), Automata, Languages and Programming. Proceedings, 1991. XII, 763 pages. 1991.

Vol. 511: A. C. F. Colchester, D.J. Hawkes (Eds.), Information Processing in Medical Imaging. Proceedings, 1991. XI, 512 pages. 1991.

Vol. 512: P. America (Ed.), ECOOP '91. European Conference on Object-Oriented Programming. Proceedings, 1991. X, 396 pages. 1991.

Vol. 513: N. M. Mattos, An Approach to Knowledge Base Management. IX, 247 pages. 1991. (Subseries LNAI).

Vol. 514: G. Cohen, P. Charpin (Eds.), EUROCODE '90. Proceedings, 1990. XI, 392 pages. 1991.

Vol. 515: J. P. Martins, M. Reinfrank (Eds.), Truth Maintenance Systems. Proceedings, 1990. VII, 177 pages. 1991. (Subseries LNAI).

Vol. 516: S. Kaplan, M. Okada (Eds.), Conditional and Typed Rewriting Systems. Proceedings, 1990. IX, 461 pages. 1991.

Vol. 517: K. Nökel, Temporally Distributed Symptoms in Technical Diagnosis. IX, 164 pages. 1991. (Subseries LNAI).

Vol. 518: J. G. Williams, Instantiation Theory. VIII, 133 pages. 1991. (Subseries LNAI).

Vol. 519: F. Dehne, J.-R. Sack, N. Santoro (Eds.), Algorithms and Data Structures. Proceedings, 1991. X, 496 pages. 1991.

Vol. 520: A. Tarlecki (Ed.), Mathematical Foundations of Computer Science 1991. Proceedings, 1991. XI, 435 pages. 1991.

Vol. 521: B. Bouchon-Meunier, R. R. Yager, L. A. Zadek (Eds.), Uncertainty in Knowledge-Bases. Proceedings, 1990. X, 609 pages. 1991.

Vol. 522: J. Hertzberg (Ed.), European Workshop on Planning. Proceedings, 1991. VII, 121 pages. 1991. (Subseries LNAI).

Vol. 523: J. Hughes (Ed.), Functional Programming Languages and Computer Architecture. Proceedings, 1991. VIII, 666 pages. 1991.

Vol. 524: G. Rozenberg (Ed.), Advances in Petri Nets 1991. VIII, 572 pages. 1991.

Vol. 525: O. Günther, H.-J. Schek (Eds.), Large Spatial Databases. Proceedings, 1991. XI, 471 pages. 1991.

Vol. 526: T. Ito, A. R. Meyer (Eds.), Theoretical Aspects of Computer Software. Proceedings, 1991. X, 772 pages. 1991.

Vol. 527: J.C.M. Baeten, J. F. Groote (Eds.), CONCUR '91. Proceedings, 1991. VIII, 541 pages. 1991.

Vol. 528: J. Maluszynski, M. Wirsing (Eds.) Programming Language Implementation and Logic Programming. Proceedings, 1991. XI, 433 pages. 1991.

Vol. 529: L. Budach (Ed.) Fundamentals of Computation Theory. Proceedings, 1991. XII, 426 pages. 1991.

Vol. 530: D. H. Pitt, P.-L. Curien, S. Abramsky, A. M. Pitts, A. Poigné, D. E. Rydeheard (Eds.), Category Theory and Computer Science. Proceedings, 1991. VII, 301 pages. 1991.

Vol. 531: E. M. Clarke, R. P. Kurshan (Eds.), Computer-Aided Verification. Proceedings, 1990. XIII, 372 pages. 1991.

Vol. 532: H. Ehrig, H.-J. Kreowski, G. Rozenberg (Eds.), Graph Grammars and Their Application to Computer Science. Proceedings, 1990. X, 703 pages. 1991.

Vol. 533: E. Börger, H. Kleine Büning, M. M. Richter, W. Schönfeld (Eds.), Computer Science Logic. Proceedings, 1990. VIII, 399 pages. 1991.

Vol. 534: H. Ehrig, K. P. Jantke, F. Orejas, H. Reichel (Eds.), Recent Trends in Data Type Specification. Proceedings, 1990. VIII, 379 pages. 1991.